Core Resource

Planning Models for Colleges and Universities

Planning Models for Colleges and Universities

David S. P. Hopkins
William F. Massy

STANFORD UNIVERSITY PRESS
STANFORD, CALIFORNIA
1981

Stanford University Press
Stanford, California

© 1981 by the Board of Trustees of the
Leland Stanford Junior University
Typesetting by Asco Trade Typesetting Limited,
Hong Kong
Printed in the United States of America

ISBN 0-8047-1023-6

LC 78-66176

To Rosemary and June,
our wives,

and to Michelle, Susan, Julie, David,
Willard and June Elizabeth,
our children,

who stood by us through the ups and downs of modeling,
model using, and writing about models

Contents

Tables

Figures

Foreword

Among my favorite bedtime reading are accounts of the financial state of higher education in the 1950's and 1960's. I imagine sitting at a trustee meeting and having discussions on the prudent allocation of the excess of revenues over expenses. How much of it should go into an improvement in the quality of the institution and how much should be added to funds functioning as endowment? How much should go into improvement of faculty salaries? With the number of college-age students increasing explosively, how much should this particular institution expand?

Unfortunately I can only dream about those years, because I took office as President of Dartmouth on March 1, 1970. The 1970's turned into the most financially frustrating years for higher education and the 1980's are likely to be as difficult—and more difficult for some institutions.

A century of expansion for higher education has come to a halt. Endowments of private institutions that once covered a significant portion of expense were seriously weakened by the performance of the stock market in the past decade. High rates of inflation coupled with enormous increases in the cost of energy have added to the woes of colleges. And a decline in the number of eighteen-year-olds coupled with a change in the retirement age has added a new set of problems for the coming decade.

The result has been a raising of consciousness about the necessity for optimizing the use of institutional resources. The question is no longer which of several pleasant alternatives to choose, but how to maintain the quality of the present institution without compromising its future. An era of philosophical discussion on the priorities of a college has been replaced by an era characterized by the necessity of tight management by the central administration and careful long-range planning. Many institutions independently came to the conclusion that the traditional intuitive judgments must be replaced by sophisticated modern management methods.

The appearance of this book may signal the next stage in the management of colleges and universities. It is a comprehensive survey of the state of modeling with an excellent discussion of the philosophical and methodological problems involved. It is illustrated by a wide range of examples and case histories from budgeting to tenure ratios to enrollment models and endowment utilization. I feel certain that the kind of models I came up with will look as primitive compared to the models of the 1980's as did the intuitive methods of the 1960's compared to the early models. Besides the level of mathematical sophistication of the book, I am impressed by the highly sensitive discussion of such issues as: How does one resist the temptation of modeling only that which is numerically measurable and therefore overlook the intangibles that are crucial to the quality of an institution? What criteria distinguish a useful model from one that can actually be harmful? How should a model be designed so that policymakers will both understand its assumptions and make use of it? How does one take into account the fact that all one's predictions are subject to a degree of uncertainty—uncertainty that gets greater as the time horizon grows?

The book will be invaluable for all those who are currently engaged in modeling or are considering entering the modeling age. But by judicious selection (skipping the more complex mathematical sections) anyone interested in planning for universities can gain a great deal from this book. The philosophical discussions, concrete examples, and historical accounts provide lessons about both good and bad models.

We are in a common fight to maintain the quality of the system of higher education. We will not succeed without improving our ability to plan for the future in sophisticated ways. At the same time, we run the danger of achieving the opposite of our goal if we are trapped by *bad* models. Perhaps the greatest danger is that models will be built by those who do not understand our institutions fully, while those who have to make the ultimate decision will accept the output of models without understanding the underlying assumptions. The best way to avoid this trap is through a sharing of experiences among institutions.

JOHN G. KEMENY

Preface

Planning models have been of lively interest at Stanford since the early 1970's. This book is aimed at sharing that experience and the insights gained from it with our colleagues in higher education. Most of the material to be presented was developed here, and much of that has actually been put to use in university planning and problem solving. We believe that it is applicable in a wide variety of other settings.

Models are becoming recognized as very useful aids in planning and decision making. Yet their usefulness is often exaggerated beyond all proportion. This may be done in a context of enthusiasm, with expectations that models will actually produce plans or decisions. Or models may engender fears that they will, without doubt, lead to bad plans or decisions.

Our own view, strongly held, is that models can be powerful tools that permit people to produce better plans or decisions than would be possible otherwise. Our experience in both building and using models tells us that planning and decision making are arts and must remain so. Though there is science in modeling, the essential processes of specifying and interpreting models of the kind to be discussed in this book are not inherently scientific. Subjective judgment prevails.

Models do not "produce" plans or decisions, good or bad. People do. The objective of this book is to help people improve their understanding of relevant phenomena and issues in higher education, so that they can make better judgments.

Naturally a book about mathematical models will involve a good deal of mathematics. We have used mathematical notation freely as a language of expression and, where necessary, have developed solutions or interpretations. However, we have tried also to illustrate the text freely with explanations and numerical examples that are as nontechnical as possible, even though the manuscript has grown as a result and may sometimes bore the mathematically sophisticated. Unusually technical material is relegated to appendixes, or, in a few places, clearly set off in the text.

Our goal in writing has been to make at least most of the book accessible to those whose motivation is high but whose mathematical skills are relatively modest. We suspect that many of our readers will be in this category. Those who wish to apply strong mathematical skills to modeling in the college and university environment will need to apply less effort but should find the book no less satisfying. We should warn in advance, though, that we concentrate on the pragmatics of building and using models rather than on the finer points of theory or elegance. Further mathematical details on most of our models can be found in the various technical articles cited.

The book grew out of a research project sponsored by the Lilly Endowment. The project began in 1973; its history is presented in chapter 2 (chapter 1 describes the advantages and pitfalls of models and model building in general terms). Chapter 2 was a difficult one to write, partly because it had to be presented, for the most part, in the first person, and partly because there can be so many different interpretations of and points of view about the use of planning models at Stanford during that period. We should say that the original manuscript for the book did not include a chapter of this kind, but we were urged by the reviewer and the publisher to write one. We hope it will prove to be interesting and valuable, if only because there are so few treatments of model development and implementation in the management science literature.

Chapter 3 is an excursion into the microeconomic theory of colleges and universities. Although it, too, came together near the end of the writing process, it is in every respect the opposite of chapter 2. What we wanted was a unifying view of our university world as a logical framework for our models. We therefore set out to develop the necessary theoretical apparatus in a working paper that eventually became chapter 3. We believe this apparatus has helped to direct our thinking not only as modelers but as policymakers. Chapters 4 through 9 deal with various classes of models we have found to be interesting and important. As we said earlier, most of these have been applied to Stanford to some degree or another. Chapter 10 focuses upon models and their implementation at other institutions. Part of this final chapter grew out of a series of case studies prepared by Joe B. Wyatt and his colleagues under a subcontract during the second phase of our Lilly Endowment project. In the appendixes we address several questions of interest to the researcher, but which doubtless are beyond the scope of interest of many readers. These questions are considered in order to provide an integrated treatment of our theoretical thinking, to display actual examples of models in action, and in the hope of stimulating further research.

Some of the material in chapters 4 through 10 was prepared for or refined at a workshop on computer-based planning models for university officers and staff that was conducted by the three of us—the two authors and Wyatt—in August 1978, at the Lilly Endowment headquarters in Indianapolis. We should mention also that a major impetus for the writing of this book was our collaboration from 1976 to 1978 in teaching a graduate course at Stanford entitled "Management Science Applied to Higher Education." Much of the material first came together as lectures developed for that course, and the enthusiasm of our students (drawn from the Schools of Business and Education) led us to believe that it was worthy of a wider audience. Then, too, the course had another kind of impact on the book's development as our work became influenced by the ideas of our students, some of whom actively joined forces with us as research assistants after the course was over.

There are a great many people who deserve our thanks for help in connection with this book and the models in it. William F. Miller, Stanford's vice-president and provost from 1971 through 1978, got us started and helped tremendously with concept development no less than implementation. Raymond F. Bacchetti, vice-provost for budget and planning, was an unfailing source of both criticism and encouragement. Stanford president Richard Lyman's support and understanding was much appreciated throughout and indispensable at certain points.

At the Lilly Endowment we had the strong personal support of James Holderman and, later, of Laura Bornholdt and Ralph Lundgren—support that was very important in the funding process and a source of much encouragement and satisfaction. Carol Van Alstyne of the American Council on Education also took an active and helpful interest in our work. WFM is particularly grateful to Gardner Lindzey, former director of the Center for Advanced Study in the Behavioral Sciences, for the opportunity to participate as a visiting scholar at the center during a six-month sabbatical leave from Stanford during 1977, at which time much of his share of this manuscript was written.

We have already mentioned that our close friend and colleague, Joe Wyatt of Harvard, was a consultant and collaborator on the project from its early years onwards. Our other friends who participated in case studies were: Sally Zeckhauser (Harvard); Jon Strauss (University of Pennsylvania); Wendell Lorang and Robert Shirley (State University of New York); and Eric Ottervik (Lehigh). Finally, James Powell (vice-president and provost at Oberlin College) was the first implementer, outside Stanford and Harvard, of one of our "Lilly" models, and he has generously and effectively participated with us in a number of conferences on the subject of modeling.

At Stanford we must recognize a large number of people with whom we worked closely on one aspect of the project or another. We are indebted to Professor Gene Franklin of the Stanford Department of Electrical Engineering, who at the time was associate provost for computing, for solving the set of three nonlinear simultaneous equations that comprised the original long-range financial equilibrium model. Without this boost we might never have taken the model seriously. Graduate students who worked with us were: Nathan Dickmeyer, David Clark, John Curry, and Jay Schoenau (education); Donald Wehrung and Jean-Claude Larreche (business); Delores Conway and Joseph Verducci (statistics); and David Butler, Peter Orkenyi, Philip Heidelberger, Eric Rosenberg, and Alejandro Gerson (operations research).

Faculty members with whom we and our student assistants worked on the project include Bill Sharpe, Jack MacDonald, Chuck Holloway, and Seenu Srinivasan (business); Ingram Olkin (statistics); and Jerry Lieberman (operations research). Richard Grinold of the University of California Business School at Berkeley was a most helpful collaborator in our later work on stochastic modeling. Many of the ideas incorporated in chapter 7 originated with him. Merrill Flood of the University of Michigan visited in the Stanford area and assisted us in the work on value-tradeoff models. Stanford staff with whom we worked closely on model implementation were: Rod Adams, Ken Creighton, Paul Goldstein, Larry Owen, Kent Peterson, Frank Riddle, Janet Sweet, and Bill Witscher. Famah Andrew, Roberta Callaway, and Valerie Veronin typed the original manuscript, while Ginger Radlo prepared the bibliography.

Our acknowledgments and thanks go to all who assisted us in so many ways, including the many who are not mentioned here. We also acknowledge that all the errors and omissions in the final manuscript are our own. Finally, we should say that it was fun to write this book, just as modeling and using models can be a very positive experience when viewed as a process of exploration. We hope our readers share our sense of excitement in the application of planning models to colleges and universities.

Stanford, California
April, 1979

DAVID S. P. HOPKINS
WILLIAM F. MASSY

A Note to the Mathematically Less Sophisticated Reader

Although this book was written primarily for college and university planners and administrators, it is admittedly quite technical in parts. We recognize that not all readers will have the technical background or desire to read through and understand the more mathematical sections of the text, although most readers can get a lot out of these sections even without following the mathematical equations. For those who are not so inclined, we offer the following "roadmap" for steering around the more highly technical sections without losing the main points.

We do not begin using any mathematics until chapter 3, but parts of that chapter are probably the most difficult of all. While the introductory discussion of university economics should be of general interest, the reader may wish to skip most or all of the section on "Value Maximization Subject to Constraints," beginning on p. 86. The following section, "Market Characteristics in the Nonprofit Sector," is less technical mathematically, but it does assume a familiarity with microeconomic theory which some readers may be lacking. This section may also be skipped without much loss in continuity. The next section is primarily nontechnical, and should be read, or at least skimmed, for the main points. The final section, "Applying the Theory to Planning Model Development," is probably worth a quick run through, even if one chooses to ignore the rather complicated mathematical formulations.

For the most part, the level of mathematics employed in chapter 4 is simple and numerical examples are liberally employed to illustrate the meaning of algebraic expressions. With one or two minor exceptions, the same is true of chapters 5 and 6. Some readers may find the detailed algebraic formulations in the first section of chapter 5 ("Disaggregate Production and Cost Models") a bit cumbersome, in which case they can gloss over them with little loss in overall comprehension.

As for chapter 7, our in-depth analysis of random forecast errors does occasionally necessitate the use of somewhat complicated mathematical expressions, particularly in section 3 ("A Model for Stochastic Control"). Our advice for the reader who is less interested in technical details is to skip the first part of this section, and to give only a quick glance at the subsection on "Smoothing Rules" and the beginning of the following subsection on "Determination of the Smoothing Parameters." A fast reading of the remainder of this section and the final one should give the reader a sufficient idea of how smoothing is applied in university budget planning, and to what avail.

The remaining chapters were written so as to require a relatively low level of mathematical understanding for following the entire development. Rather than permitting themselves to get bogged down in any particular mathematical detail, readers can safely pass over such details without losing the sense of our models and discussion. The key point we have tried to make all along is that, while we have made liberal use of mathematical notation throughout the text, our purpose in doing so has been to clarify and make certain points with more precision. We have always used the simplest form of mathematics that would do the job and, in fact, a willingness to follow simple algebra is all that is required of the reader in the sections or chapters not distinguished otherwise in the discussion above.

Abbreviations

We have used these abbreviations in the text, the notes, and the glossary-index.

APO	Academic Planning Office	NCHEMS	National Center for Higher
BAP	Budget Adjustment Program		Education Management Systems
BEP	Budget Equilibrium Program	O & M	Operations and Maintenance
CAMPUS	Comprehensive Analytical Methods	PPV	primary planning variables
	for Planning in University Systems	RMSE	root mean square error
DM	decision makers	RRPM	resource requirements prediction
DSPH	David S. P. Hopkins		model
EMIV	effective marginal intrinsic value	SCH	student credit hours
FTE	full-time equivalent	S & E	supplies and equipment
G & A	general and administrative	SS	student services
GPR	grade progression ratio	TRADES	(*see* Glossary-Index)
LRFE	long-run financial equilibrium	TRANS	transition-to-equilibrium model
LRFF	long-range financial forecast	WCH	weekly student classroom hours
MRFF	medium-range financial forecast	WFM	William F. Massy
M & S	materials and supplies	ZBB	zero-base budgeting

Planning Models for Colleges
and Universities

Part I

Modeling
and the Stanford Experience

Planning models are products of modern decision science. Generally quantitative in nature, they are designed to help managers and policy planners make more-informed decisions about the allocation of resources. Of what use are such cut-and-dried versions of reality to the decision makers who shape and implement the complex goals of universities?

We believe that quantitative planning models, when appropriately designed and applied, can be of great use in aiding us to make decisions of fundamental academic importance. At the same time, we are wholeheartedly opposed to the notion of quantitative modeling as a substitute for the kind of qualitative decision making that is the essence of academic leadership. Planning models can help provide the conditions for academic excellence. But they cannot guarantee it, and would probably be fatal to it if relied on for any such purpose.

A variety of planning models for colleges and universities will be presented in this book. They deal with such inescapable facts of university life as student enrollment, faculty workloads, sponsorship of research, fund raising, and the need for financial tradeoffs. Some of the models are static and others dynamic. All, however, involve subjective judgments and institutional values. It is part of our purpose to show how consideration of such intangibles can—indeed, must—be built into a decision-making process that in any case runs the risk of being dominated by tangibles.

In chapter 1 we explain the nature of modeling and review the current use of planning models in higher education. We maintain that effective modeling in an academic setting requires a clear sense of what is important for the institution. A good model—one that is simple but complete, stable yet adaptable—should make the quantifiable dimension of decision making a far less mysterious place in which to operate, but it will not thereby lessen the burden of choice. The 1970s have seen an end to the boom in higher education from which

American colleges and universities had been benefiting since the end of World War II. As resources for these institutions become scarcer, academic policy makers will have to undertake more planning—effective planning, since the long-range consequences of wrong planning decisions will be serious. Where there is a need for planning there is, we believe, a need for models. But models will not increase scarce resources. What they will do is increase an institution's chances of using those resources wisely. The meaning of "wisely" in such a context is a question that, we are glad to say, lies beyond the scope of this book.

We do have some ideas, however, about the wise use of models, and in chapter 2 we introduce them in the context of the real decision problems experienced at Stanford University in the 1970s. This approach has the extra advantage of introducing some of the planning models to be discussed in detail later. There was a certain unity of purpose in our approach to the various models and this, too, can be seen in our chronological account. Hopefully chapter 2 will provide the reader with both a roadmap for what is to come and the motivation to proceed further.

1

The Case for Planning Models

For the academic process to flourish, a great many decisions must be made by administration, faculty, and students. Many of these decisions are routine, or involve matters of limited consequence or generality. However, planning decisions increasingly stand out as having significant consequences that span many parts of the institution, and they require much analysis and creative thought.

It has been truly stated that a college or university "does its work through creating an environment calculated to bring about desired characteristics in people and to facilitate scholarly endeavor."[1] The creation, nurturance, and, when needed, protection of this environment requires an increasingly refined degree of planning. The problems are getting tougher; the lead times are often longer; the financial constraints grow tighter every day. Of course, the individual choices made by faculty and students in connection with their educational and research pursuits are the ones that really matter. It is the central administration, however, that tries to provide what one of us has called "a stable and predictable financial environment in which the academic process can flourish."[2]

Models can facilitate better planning decisions. Although planning, like other kinds of decision making, must ultimately remain an art, there is much to be gained by applying scientific principles whenever possible. Modeling involves the careful and documented use of deductive and inductive reasoning processes. These processes are designed to bring the resulting plan or decision into as close a conformance as possible with (a) objective, external reality, and (b) the goal structure of those who must commit the institution to one course of action or another. By drawing on our own and others' experience with planning models, we hope to show that they can and should become an integral part of the planning process of colleges and universities. The application of planning models is not limited by type of institution; the kind of thinking that nurtures them and that they inspire can, if they are wisely used, do as much for the complex research university as for the more unified institution with more homogeneous goals and resources.

A central theme of this book is how to design and develop models that will be genuinely useful to decision makers in colleges and universities, that will be perceived as such, and that will actually be used to help solve real and important problems. We must say at the outset that the use of models has not been greeted with universal acclaim in colleges and universities. There is a concern —a legitimate one, we admit—that the focus will be on the wrong things; that the quantifiable will drive out the profound; that the institution will take on too many of the characteristics of a business. These things can happen, but without models as easily as with them. The objective of this chapter, and indeed of the book as a whole, is to demonstrate not only that models can help to solve the immediate problems of university and college administrators but that, in the long run, they can help to conserve academic values.

What Is a Model?

It will be helpful at the outset to consider the fundamental nature of models and model building before addressing the problem of how they can be used in higher education.

Models may be implicit or explicit. Most decisions are taken on the basis of mental models. A mental model usually is implicit unless the decision maker has taken the time to explicate it very carefully. The process of making a model explicit usually means writing it down in some form. The means employed may be words, graphs or geometric representations, physical representations, or symbols of one kind or another. Whether the result is implicit or explicit, the process of modeling is always one of synthesizing known facts, theories, and judgments into a meaningful pattern.[3]

Models are about something; they purport to represent an aspect of something that exists, or might exist, in the world. We call the object of a model the *reference system*. Thus a given reference system can in principle be represented by many different models, each one more-or-less accurate with respect to certain characteristics of the system.

Newly constructed models need to be *verified*, or shown to have been constructed as the design specified. This is not a trivial matter in most cases. Models also must be *validated*; that is, there must be tests to see if the degree of approximation to the reference system is adequate for the purpose at hand. Validation is a continuing process for most models. One's confidence grows each time the model is used and produces credible results.

Models are designed for a purpose. Sometimes this purpose is the improvement of a specific decision. Or it may be to increase one's understanding of some phenomenon in order to advance scientific knowledge; to aid teaching and learning; or perhaps simply to satisfy curiosity. The degree of approximation that will be acceptable in a model depends upon the purpose for which it is being used. The criteria of acceptability are both absolute ("Is the model credible?") and relative ("What are the available alternatives, including mental models?"). Deciding which parts of the reference system to include or not to include in a given modeling effort is very much an art—a matter of good judgment. Putting in either too much or too little may well result in a serious loss of credibility (we will explain why later in this chapter), and too much will also lead to such practical difficulties as mathematical intractability, inordinate demands for data, complexity in computing procedures, endless delay, and excessive cost. All things considered, model building is much more an art than a science, though scientific theories and procedures are much used and extremely valuable.

Although planning models are generally quantitative, this is by no means essential. Symbolic logic, for instance, may be used to describe a qualitative policy statement, or a schematic design may represent information flows or interpersonal interactions. These are explicit models, and indeed they may be processable on a computer, but they do not deal with numbers. Most decision science models, however, do have numerical quantities as central elements, since the problems in question tend to involve allocating amounts of resources to produce certain kinds of values. Even if the values are not inherently quantitative, they can be expressed as ordinal functions in cases where one outcome is more or less to be preferred over others.

Quantitative models form the subject matter of this book. We will be working with costs and revenues, numbers of faculty members and students of different kinds, investment returns, capital budgets and other numerate quantities. In so doing we intend not to lose track of the qualitative dimension, which in higher education cannot be modeled formally with sufficient richness. Our immediate objective is to provide explicit quantitative models to deal with things that implicit mental models often fail to keep track of properly. But we are also intent on learning how to mesh the quantitative models with the decision maker's implicit mental models of the important qualitative factors.

Examples of Models Applied to Higher Education

There is a growing literature about the application of models to higher education. The kit of such modeling tools is powerful and getting more so, and though the adequacy of data is a perennial problem, this too is improving. The many offices of institutional research established during the last decade have done a great deal to search out and process data and make them available in formats that are comparable over time and across academic programs. Some of these offices already utilize modeling; more of them should and will do so.

An ambitious program for collecting and comparing data across institutions, the Information Exchange Program (IEP), has been established at the National Center for Higher Education Management Systems (NCHEMS); other work is going forward at the American Council on Education (ACE), and under the auspices of the Consortium on Financing Higher Education (COFHE). Sessions on higher education models have been conducted in recent years at the national and international meetings of The Institute of Management Science (TIMS), the Operations Research Society of America (ORSA), and the American Institute for Decision Science (AIDS). ORSA and AIDS have established permanent special-interest groups dealing with the subject, and publications are beginning to appear in the journals of all three associations.

A provocative statement supporting the use of models in higher education can be found in a 1972 address by Dartmouth College president John G. Kemeny entitled "What Every College President Should Know About Mathematics." Dr. Kemeny is a mathematician. He writes: "The most serious contribution that the mathematician-president can make is the fact that he knows something about model building . . . . Mathematicians are usually very good at explaining complex mathematical things in fairly simple language to a nonmathematician and that turns out to be a very useful asset to a college president, because you can take a highly complex statement and translate it for the faculty, students, and alumni."[4]

Kemeny cites several examples of simple models that were developed and used during the first several years of his tenure as president of Dartmouth. They represent a good beginning for our survey of modeling in colleges and universities.

1. *Faculty appointment and promotion rates.* The problem was to study the effect of the proportion of assistant professors reappointed and/or promoted to tenure upon the tenure ratio and so on the ability of the institution to bring in new blood. (We will consider models like this in chapter 8.)

2. *Assigning faculty billets to departments.* What factors are or should be used to determine how many faculty are needed in each department of the university? Examples of relevant factors include the numbers of students of various types and the characteristics of the instruction process.

3. *Program options for year-round operation.* Here the issue was how to design a program of year-round operation for Dartmouth. The result was a finding that, in order to maintain a diversity of students and course offerings under year-round operating conditions, the number of courses needed for graduation should be decreased and flexibility permitted as to timing of attendance.

4. *Endowment yield and capital gain to be spent in a given year.* This model dealt with the tradeoff between current spending of endowment yield and capital gain and the need for endowment growth—growth that was needed to finance the effects of inflation and provide for real budget enhancement in the future. (This "spending-saving relationship" is considered in great detail in chapter 6.)

A number of surveys of model building for higher education are available. The most comprehensive one is by Roger G. Schroeder (1973). We shall briefly review his work and that of a few others in order to provide a context in which to discuss the case for planning models in higher education. More detailed references to the literature will be provided as we describe particular types of models.

Schroeder divides the applications of management science to higher education into the following categories: (a) planning, programming, and budgeting systems; (b) management information systems; (c) resource allocation models; (d) models for student planning; (e) faculty staffing models; (f) optimization models. He labels the last three "mathematical models," but that is not very precise because the same term can apply to the third category and some aspects of the first two.

Planning, programming, and budgeting systems (PPBS). This type of work is most easily defined in terms of its name:

> Planning refers to the setting of organizational objectives and goals; programming refers to identifying and evaluating programs or alternatives which meet those objectives; and budgeting refers to providing the resources to support the programs. But PPBS is more than just a new method of budgeting; it includes planning and analysis functions as well. The analysis part of PPBS is usually accomplished by the cost-effectiveness approach, which considers the costs and benefits of alternative programs. Such analysis is an integral part of a PPB system.[5]

PPBS work was performed extensively during the late 1960s, thanks to the example and impetus of federal and state government agencies. In 1973, however, Schroeder reported that there were "no successful ongoing applications of a comprehensive PPBS" in higher education. To our knowledge none have occurred since, although NCHEMS was said to be developing a standard program classification structure "so that institutions can have comparable data on costs of programs and to facilitate statewide, regional, and national planning."[6] Zero-base budgeting (ZBB) is now of great interest; it has some of the same objectives and characteristics as PPBS, especially when applied to academic and institutional support services. In this book we do not address PPBS or ZBB concepts or procedures as such, though some of our models might be useful in that context.

Management information systems (MIS). This refers to the collecting, storing, and retrieving of information for planning and control. Such information includes financial and budget data, student enrollments, course-demand statistics, employment records, and so on. As of 1973 most integrated systems were in the design stage and only a few had been implemented. Schroeder cites a number of references to specific systems and reviews of systems and then points out that in MIS design the question of how to design the data base is itself an issue.

> Advocates of the comprehensive approach argue that we should include a large amount of data in the data base since we cannot hope to predict the data which management will need. This type of approach is advocated by Project INFO [at Stanford University]. The other approach argues that decision making should be analyzed and analytic models constructed where possible to determine what data should be included in the data base.[7]

Having had some personal experience with the problems of Project INFO, we believe strongly that MIS design should be approached in terms of bite-sized pieces. It is simply too expensive to try to anticipate all management needs, and in many cases the problems of maintaining control over the accuracy, consistency, and timeliness of the data elements in a large integrated system are beyond the limits of feasibility. On the other hand, model building can be a very important organizing factor in MIS design; it can even help set priorities. Many of the models we will discuss in this book have significant implications for the design of data bases and MIS reports.

Resource allocation models. These models relate the inputs of the educational process to the resources required. "They translate enrollment projections into demand for courses, faculty, facilities, and support activities. The required resources are then costed and aggregated for various output reports. The purpose of these models is to simulate the effects of changes in enrollment or in technology (student-teacher ratios, class size, etc.) on the resources required." [8]

The best-known resource allocation models are CAMPUS (Comprehensive Analytical Methods for Planning in University Systems), developed at the University of Toronto, and RRPM (Resource Requirements Prediction Model), developed by NCHEMS after an earlier model by George B. Weathersby.[9] In analyzing RRPM, one of us has concluded that "these models are suitable mainly for making cost-per-student calculations under current operating conditions and it is questionable whether the expense of building in a large amount of detail for this purpose can be justified" (Hopkins 1971, p. 476). Further discussion of resource allocation models and the development of alternative formulations based on network flows will be provided in chapter 5.

Models for student planning. The work in this category includes scheduling students to classes, projecting enrollment, and tracking student flows through an institution. Apparently the scheduling problem was attacked first: one-third of ninety-six colleges and universities surveyed in 1969 indicated some use of computers for this purpose. Prediction of enrollment figures for new students involves analyzing and projecting the applicant pool's size, its composition, and its yield rates (the last-named is the proportion of those admitted to the school who actually matriculate). Student-flow analysis deals with the progression of people through the various levels of the school, from freshman to sophomore to junior and so on, taking account of stopouts, dropouts, repeats, and transfers. Projections of enrollment and student flow are important for predicting faculty staffing and other resource needs, tuition income, and in some cases state government appropriations. We will describe a number of different modeling approaches to student planning in chapter 8.

Faculty staffing models. The questions here deal with the age distribution of faculty, their hiring and retirement rates, the proportion of them who have tenure, their work load, and the allocation of faculty billets to academic departments and programs. A variety of interesting approaches exist. They also will be considered in chapter 8.

Optimization models. Optimization means "finding the set of policies, resource mix, etc., that maximizes or minimizes some objective." For instance, business firms may maximize profits or minimize the cost of producing a given amount of output. Colleges and universities generally try to maximize a broader range of values; they also try to minimize the costs of achieving desired outcomes. Optimization models are something of a catchall category. Many different kinds of model, with a variety of reference structure, can be used as bases for optimization.

Schroeder cites models for allocating faculty time to such departmental tasks as teaching and research; for determining admission policies with regard to different types and levels of students; and, in one case, for optimizing the growth trajectories for student enrollments, faculty hires, and construction of needed institutional facilities. We will deal with optimization questions, where appropriate, throughout the book and particularly in chapter 9.

Other surveys of models in higher education are provided by Robert M. Oliver (1972) and Paul Gray (1976). To the categories just described Oliver adds educational planning models developed to aid system-wide administrators or government officials. His general approach, however, is familiar and his categories are not very different from Schroeder's, though some different examples are cited. Gray classifies models in terms of their methodology rather than their application. He gives examples of the use of: (a) linear programming, including goal programming, network flows formulated as linear programs, and integer programming; (b) methods for dealing with uncertainty in terms of probability models, especially Markov chains; (c) computer simulation models; (d) feedback control, or cybernetic, processes. He also describes some of the problems that must be overcome if efforts at modeling are to be successful. We will make use of some of these techniques in our discussion of specific models and applications.

We must conclude this survey with a word of caution. To the best of our knowledge there have been no successful efforts to model comprehensively the two most crucial areas of decision that must be faced by faculties and academic administrators. The first of these is the choice of academic disciplines in which the institution should try to excel: what mix of faculty appointments in particular subdisciplines and specialties will be needed to attain or maintain eminence? The second is the choice of criteria and measures for evaluating individual faculty members for appointment and promotion.

The faculty staffing models that we cited earlier deal either with aggregate factors such as age distributions, tenure ratios, and hiring and promotion rates, or with gross measures of work load such as level of student demand, number of courses to be taught, and size of allocations for organized research. They do not, and in our opinion cannot, aid in assessing the intellectual promise and intrinsic importance of fields and subfields or the qualifications of individual professors. A special quality in these judgments, cumulated over a long period of time, spells the difference between a good institution and one with a credible claim to excellence.

Right decisions about aggregative and quantitative planning factors can provide the necessary conditions for academic excellence—the environment in which teaching and scholarship can flourish. But sufficiency requires, in addition, sensitive and informed judgments of a qualitative kind. Such judgments are the essence of outstanding academic leadership.

Concerns About Modeling

The biggest danger—and the source of most concern—is that applying quantitative decision models to the planning problems of colleges and universities will somehow warp their ability to make the truly fundamental academic and humane judgments. Factors that are crucial for a given decision can all too easily be left out of a model, especially if they are qualitative and intangible. The model may pass a narrow test of validity—for example, by adequately representing the formalistic or numerate parts of the reference system—and yet it may be worse than useless.

A related problem is that the mathematical and computer trappings of many decision models, and the attitudes of some model builders, scare away or exclude the generalist from modeling and model validation. This is extremely dangerous. Professional decision scientists tend, in time, to see the world only in terms that can be modeled. It often takes someone who actually is responsible for conserving and enhancing the value of an institution to help determine where models should or should not be used and where simplifying assumptions may safely be made. Special contributions can be made by the humanist. There are some areas of life where the intellectual or rational processes upon which the valid use of a decision model depends should not be allowed to dominate. Love or loathing, humor or pathos, satisfaction or frustration are but a few of these. Colleges and universities treasure the affective as well as the cognitive dimension of life. Emotion must not be modeled away.

Effective Modeling

"A little knowledge is a dangerous thing. . . ." This is part of the gospel of humility that should be learned by the planners, modelers, university officers, and trustees who are responsible for decision making in colleges and universities. Effective modeling requires some understanding of (a) what is important for the institution, its constituents, etc., and (b) what relations between means and ends—"inputs" and "outputs" in economists' jargon—can achieve these goals. Because the goals of higher education are multifaceted and sometimes controversial, and the processes that transform its inputs into outputs are very complex and subtle, means and ends may be writ large but dimly perceived.

Doubts arise as to the feasibility of planning per se (as well as modeling) in colleges and universities. To quote Howard Bowen:

> In view of the existing monumental ignorance, one must raise the question of whether academic planning [or modeling] is possible—in the sense of measuring the means and the ends. The condition of the industry certainly suggests the need for more knowledge about the relation between the resources and technologies employed and the true

outcomes in human terms. The exploration of these relationships can be seen as the primary task of those who would improve rational planning in higher education. Without adequate knowledge in these areas, which will require decades of research, higher education is in a sense flying blind. It is largely dependent on tradition, intuition, and judgment for guidance in its decision making.[10]

He goes on to say that he is not depreciating tradition, intuition, and judgment, and to point out that we should increase our knowledge about the relationship of decisions and actions to goals.

We agree completely with Bowen's remarks, but the conclusion to be drawn from them is not clear. On the one hand, modeling for academic institutions is fraught with difficulties. On the other, it may be necessary for the efficient use of increasingly scarce resources. It is in any case being mandated as part of the movement for making college and university administration more accountable to governing boards and the political process.

Let us examine the barriers to effective modeling more closely. Here is how one of us viewed them a few years ago in a talk to university planners about models. This was in the midst of our own attempts to develop and implement meaningful decision models at Stanford University.

1. Centralized planning is dangerous because it takes the initiative away from those best able to exercise it—the faculty, department chairmen, and deans of individual schools. There is fear that authority will be exercised by the wrong people. Even if the process is highly participative, the hoops and hurdles of a formal planning process may tend to drive out academic creativity and judgment in a Gresham's Law kind of way.

2. Detailed and scientific modeling schemes that often are associated with centralized planning will make it difficult for profound but qualitative judgments to make themselves felt. A short quotation illustrates the point: "The success which this elegant model has had ... is matched only by its failure to predict correctly the actual course of events—a fine illustration of the ... maxim that a model is never defeated by facts, however damaging, but only by another model." This argument takes force from the fact that the most important judgments an academic institution has to make are value-laden and qualitative. Models used indiscriminately represent unfair and undesirable competition.

3. "Planning doesn't work anyway. We've been planning for five years and look at the mess we're in now!" This view is not necessarily irrational. In a highly uncertain world it may be better to design a control system that relies on prompt response to feedback than to try to preprogram events through detailed planning. In addition, there are real and to some extent justified threats to the credibility of higher education administrators and the planning process they try to lead. An important question is whether imperfect planning leads to more or less stability and predictability of expenditures than periodic reaction to environmental events.

Other, less reasonable, objections also are raised in opposition to the application of planning principles in higher education. These may stem from an inherent mistrust of administration or administrators, a desire to preserve the status quo by "stonewalling" or "do-nothingism," or from simple ignorance or misunderstanding about planning principles or the specific problems facing an institution. Where these are dominant they are hardly a credit to academic values and traditions. However, they should not be confused with the manifestation of differing values and judgments pursued vigorously and in good faith, which make any process of university decision making an intense experience.[11]

Point 1 in this list dramatizes the problem of accountability and the fear that planning will lead to the kind of oversimplification that distorts academic goals and judgments. Point 2 emphasizes the potential power of a model (or a formal plan for that matter) and the dangers associated with its indiscriminate use. Point 3 has to do with a substantive (and researchable) question of control theory; only so much accuracy or predictability, these critics lament, can be expected under the best of circumstances.

A little knowledge *is* a dangerous thing in modeling for colleges and universities because it is possible that people may come to view the objective or quantitative dimensions as the only important ones. This may occur simply because they are easier to plan for and model, or it may be that a disproportionate number of the people attracted to modeling tend to think in objective and quantitative terms. Either way, the objective, quantitative, empirical, and formalistic must not be permitted to squeeze out the qualitative, subjective, and intuitive in university planning and decision making. Among other things, this means careful attention should be paid to the way in which models are constructed and, in some cases, to the choice of areas where model building should be eschewed. These issues will be considered later in this chapter and throughout the book.

In higher education, then, the case for decision models is not self-evident. But despite the caveats we believe it is convincing. Success depends on building models that are properly tailored to the needs and characteristics of colleges and universities. The potential payoffs for such institutions and their constituencies are great, though there are undeniable risks.

From the standpoint of the professional decision scientist, the application of models in colleges and universities is an exciting challenge. One's faith in modeling and one's sense of objectivity are both tested. One senses also, correctly we think, that if planning models can be used effectively in higher education they can be used anywhere!

The case for models is integrally bound up with the growing need for more effective planning and control in colleges and universities.* Planning and control, as we noted earlier, are themselves subjects of considerable interest and controversy, so we must consider their antecedents.

Planning and Control in Colleges and Universities

Planning and control have always been important components of higher education administration. During the expansionary years of the 1950s and 1960s, for instance, administrators and faculty alike were happily involved with planning new academic programs, organizing and developing human resources, and marshaling the financial means needed for growth in size and excellence.

---

*Our use of the word "control" refers to follow-up and evaluation in relation to earlier objectives and plans. "Control" does not in the least suggest the abridging of academic freedom, which we consider to be inviolate.

No one doubted that planning was helpful—indeed necessary—if these objectives were to be achieved.

Control, too, was considered to be desirable and important in a number of contexts. Control of the quality of faculty appointments and promotions is perhaps the most critical variable in the achievement of long-run academic excellence. Carefully designed systems for hierarchical review exist in many institutions to ensure that proper evidence about research and teaching is obtained and that departmental and school decisions flow reasonably from that evidence and are not conditioned by sympathy, favoritism, or other non-academic considerations. These systems are accepted and indeed defended vigorously by most faculty and virtually all administrators.

Other control systems obviously are necessary in addition to these. Fiduciary control of the university's finances and accounting system, of its handling of cash receipts and disbursement and its provisions for meeting donor covenants and following government regulations, is an established part of the academic enterprise. So is management control of the institution's administrative and support systems, construction projects, maintenance of physical plant, and so forth. Many of the management control functions are not visible to faculty, but they are essential for the effective operation of the institution nonetheless.

During the last ten years, however, the words "planning and control" have taken on a more ominous tone in colleges and universities. According to Howard Bowen, this is particularly true when planning problems are couched in quantitative terms, or are associated with approaches developed for use in business firms. Citing the increasing popularity of cost-benefit analysis, accountability, market research, program budgeting, and management by objectives, he cautions against the simplistic assumption that the techniques and points of view of business planning are directly applicable to higher education. As he points out, the idea that sound, hard-headed, rational business management procedures will resolve the financial problems of higher education surely exaggerates the potential returns from any conceivable managerial technique. "Educators," he argues, "should resist the kind of planning, now being thrust on them by a multitude of outside pressures, that reduces everything to a few simple numbers. They should insist on looking squarely at the means and ends in human terms."[12] We agree.

There are several reasons why the new kinds of planning and control, and to a considerable extent the use of decision models, are viewed with alarm. The most obvious and the most valid reason is that some of the techniques that have been highly touted are in fact seriously incomplete with respect to academic and human considerations that are important for making decisions. Usually there is no disagreement in these cases between modeler and academic officer or professor about the fact that the model does not represent the reference system very well in one or more important respects. However, there does tend to be argument over whether the model has achieved the necessary conditions for usefulness, or whether it is so far off the mark that any effort to consider its outputs will distort the decision. The same is true of the more general methods of planning and control reviewed by Bowen: there is legitimate concern that if some of them are adopted, attention will be directed to the wrong variables and criteria.

Planning and control systems and decision models are mistrusted and maligned partly because they are unfamiliar. As we noted earlier, there is cause for concern when the assumptions and methods of the planner or model builder are not accessible to the decision maker, who therefore cannot participate in the process of formulating and evaluating alternatives. However, if the mistrust is only of the unfamiliar, and if there are no efforts to meet the planner or modeler halfway and communicate on important issues, then the situation reflects no credit on an institution that prides itself on its intellectual objectivity.

There are at least two other important reasons why planning and control systems are often mistrusted. First, the growth in their popularity has been correlated with, and to some extent caused by, the end of the academic boom and a constricting of the resources available to higher education. Second, a good many of these systems have been imposed from the outside, in the name of accountability, upon a reluctant or defensive institution. Both points are worthy of a closer examination.

The financial resources available to higher education can no longer meet perceived academic needs: this condition, which dominates the situation today, emerged in the mid-1960s after more than twenty years of continuous expansion. The magnitude of the boom is indicated by William G. Bowen's finding that cost per student (funded by available revenues) at the three institutions he studied grew at the rate of 7.5 percent per year during the 1949–66 period.[13] Of this, 2.2 percent represented inflation and perhaps 2.0 or 2.5 percent was due to real salary growth within the institutions, which leaves growth of quality and specialization to account for the remaining 2.5 percent or so. In other words, any increase in the productivity of academic institutions was more than offset by the cost of a more expensive educational product. To the increase in cost per student must be added the effect of a fairly steady growth in numbers of students due to demographic factors and the increasing accessibility and popularity of higher education. A similar trend existed with respect to government-sponsored research in colleges and universities.

The forces that led to substantial growth in cost per student during the boom years are not difficult to understand. The effect of inflation (which seems small by today's standards) is obvious. Another, less obvious force is increased specialization, a natural consequence of the deepening stock of human knowledge. For instance, twenty years ago Stanford University had neither a computer science nor an operations research department while today it has both. But the importance of the classics department has not diminished, and the department of comparative literature has another two decades of literature to compare. This is not to say that fields and specialties never wane or should never be pruned; nor must all institutions excel at all things. However, there can be no doubt that the stock of intellectual capital is continually deepening, just as the stock of physical capital tends to deepen in an economy as productivity grows. Financial investments are needed to create and exploit stocks of both kinds.

The academic boom lasted long enough for a whole generation of faculty and administrators to reach professional maturity without experiencing any significant long-term scarcity of resources. It was a generation that made every effort to achieve effectiveness without wasting resources but without being overly conscious of their limits either. Quality was a great concern. Some schools were striving to increase quality by broadening the resource base while others worked to maintain quality to the greatest degree possible in the face of rapid expansion in the size of the student body. As so often is the case in boom times and when people are under pressure to achieve results, colleges and universities tended to accumulate organizational slack—less delicately called "fat."

The cumulative effect of these forces was that faculty and administrators learned to expect a favorable response from their institutions to every well-founded request for academic enhancement. Furthermore, programs that continued to meet reasonable standards of quality could be expected to remain on the books. In time, such expectations began to seem not only normal but irrefragable.

Thus the end of the boom represented a greater shock to the academic system than otherwise would have been expected. Possibly, too, the fact that the resources were being tightened just as the Vietnam War plunged universities into crisis made the pill harder to swallow and inflamed attitudes more than otherwise would have been the case. The net result has been a residue of bitterness and a sense of lost opportunity on the part of many faculty and not a few administrators. This mood accounts in part for the cool reception usually given to proposals for employing new planning and control approaches, including decision models, for managing scarce resources. Somehow the feeling persists that, were it not for the new techniques, the degree of scarcity itself would be less severe or the problem not so disruptive.

There were a number of reasons for the decline in resources available to colleges and universities after 1968:

1. The number of students began to grow less rapidly and in some cases declined as the result of demographic factors and changes in attitudes about going to college.

2. Other social priorities such as health, the environment, and the alleviation of poverty through more direct means than higher education, came to the fore.

3. Economic circumstances, including such factors as inflation and dislocation of capital markets, depressed investment returns, private donations, and to some extent the government revenues available for education and welfare programs. These effects have not been all bad in recent years, but there has been considerably more difficulty and uncertainty than was the case during the academic boom.

4. There was—and is—a sense of disenchantment with higher education at many political levels and among many segments of the public at large.

The causes of these phenomena are complex and in any case beyond the scope of this book. Given the situation, however, an argument that places the blame for the higher proportion of negative decisions upon the existence of planning models is badly misplaced.

The truth is that higher education has come of age, with the responsibilities as well as the benefits that this implies. One of the implications is that 5 or 6 percent real growth annually (including a 2 or 3 percent improvement in quality) cannot be sustained over long periods of time given the new conditions and the larger base. Another implication is that society is demanding more effective planning and control systems within colleges and universities—systems that go beyond traditional fiduciary financial control. The issues are fundamental. How is planning to be accomplished? How should resources be allocated? And how can academic institutions demonstrate to third parties that this has been done effectively?

Advantages of Models in a University Setting

An explicit model of a process involving quantitative dimensions is one that lays bare the structure of the reasoning process or calculations. It does the same to the underlying assumptions and the data or judgments used as inputs. In other words, the conclusions obtained from the planning or decision-making process are synthesized from a number—sometimes a large number—of building blocks. This is often a great advantage, since each block can be subjected to scrutiny and if necessary debated, as can the procedures by which the blocks have been linked together.

A model achieves credibility when sufficient support emerges with respect to each area of evaluation. Conversely, models can be disproved or discredited if their foundations can be attacked successfully. In a milieu that aspires to operate according to intellectual criteria, as do colleges and universities, the process of making one's model explicit and then defending it is fundamentally more acceptable than relying upon simple assertion. University planners and decision makers should strive not only to know but to understand why they know. As the result of rational discourse they should be prepared to articulate and if necessary modify their position on important issues. Consultation with faculty, trustees, and students should be viewed as a process of developing and refining judgments and of reaching a collective understanding about the reasons for them.

The use of decision models helps to organize thinking and display it for systematic review. There are enough experts on the faculties of universities so that, with a reasonable amount of effort at communication, the technical aspects of modeling need not prevent it from being evaluated within the university. (Such experts should be sought out by the model builder.) True, the more something is explained, the more easily both it and its author can be misinterpreted or discredited; legal proceedings are a case in point.[14] (This is the converse of the proposition that "only a model can defeat another model"; often one defeats a model by discrediting the model builder.) However, the university is a place where the intellectual model of inquiry, with its reverence for the truth even if it hurts, should be particularly cherished. Self-interest and limits to rationality may sometimes impair the process, but are no excuse for abandoning it.

Our conclusion—not, perhaps, a surprising one—is that wise use of models as an aid to planning is not incompatible with the basic tenets of a university. As we have argued repeatedly, the issues are what kinds of models are developed and how they are used. We do not argue that model building cannot go awry, or think that it has not done so on occasion. However, that need not be the expected result. We shall conclude this chapter with a discussion of how models should be constructed and used so as to minimize the possibility of undesirable side effects.

Some Characteristics of a Good Model

A good explicit model can be defined as one that (a) is used to help develop an important plan or make a decision, and (b) produces a better result than if intuition and judgment—that is to say, implicit models—had been used exclusively. That is the objective to which we aspire. Clearly, the model must pass some test of validity if it is to have any chance of being what we have called a good one. But that is not a sufficient condition, since it is possible that a valid model will not be used or that it may be used badly. Also, it often is not clear just how the test of validity should be applied or interpreted.

When thinking about the characteristics of good models one should consider for a start how decision makers use models in general. In the following dialogue, taken from an article entitled "Models and Managers," an interviewer discusses a model for scheduling production in an oil refinery with the analyst responsible for it.

Interviewer: Do you make regular mathematical programming runs for scheduling the refinery?

Analyst: Oh yes.

Interviewer: Do you implement the results?

Analyst: Oh no!

Interviewer: Well, that seems odd. If you don't implement the results, perhaps you should stop making the runs?

Analyst: No. No. We wouldn't want to do that!

Interviewer: Why not?

Analyst :   Well, what happens is something like this: I make several computer runs and take them to the plant manager. He is responsible for this whole multimillion-dollar plumber's paradise. The plant manager looks at the runs, thinks about them for a while, and then sends me back to make more runs. This process continues until, finally, the plant manager screws up enough courage to make a decision.[15]

The idea being illustrated here is that the manager uses the model as an aid to decision making but does not let it make the decision. The article, which is by John D. C. Little, deals with how to effect a meaningful interchange between model and manager through the process of model design. We will return to this topic presently.

Delegation to Models

The delegation of responsibility by managers to subordinates provides an analogue to the use of models for planning and decision making. There are two polar types of delegation, which for want of better names let us term "line" and "staff" delegation.

1. *Line delegation.* Here the problem—the decision, in this case—is turned over to the subordinate for handling. The delegator expects that the delegatee will be able to handle it successfully but remains available for consultation and is prepared to take back the decision if things appear to be going wrong. (Sometimes elaborate systems for incentive and control are designed to make line delegation work.) Within these limits the delegatee's judgment replaces that of the delegator. The decision is evaluated in terms of its quality (its internal logic, use of data, etc.) and, inevitably, how well things turn out.

2. *Staff delegation.* The decision maker seeks assistance with a problem but does not delegate actual responsibility for making the choice. The staff delegatee may obtain data, do analyses, effect consultations, perform tentative syntheses, recommend alternatives, etc. However, the delegator retains personal responsibility for the decision, so that the delegatee is in a sense an extension of the delegator's person. This is known at the time the assistance is sought.

Obviously the degree of independence enjoyed by the delegatee is in either case a function of the delegator's trust in him or her. There is a qualitative difference, however. In the case of line delegation, the supervisor does not expect to have to come to grips personally with the details of the decision. Here the supervisorial role is one of motivator and monitor rather than problem solver or doer; if the supervisor needs to come to grips with the decision, then the subordinate has failed. This is not the case with staff delegation, where the delegatee's role is to extend the range and effectiveness of the decision maker's own judgment—to stretch his or her mind, so to speak.

The kinds of models discussed in this book are candidates for staff delegation but not line delegation. This applies not only to models in higher education but to policy models generally. The decision maker retains personal responsibility for choice while the role of the model and model builder is to extend the decision maker's judgment.

It should be obvious why policy models cannot be given line delegation. Their degree of validity (measured in the broadest terms vis-à-vis the reference structure of the decision) is insufficient to allow decision makers to relax their hold over policy. It is true that there are cases of line delegation to models, but these are in the area of operations as opposed to policy. A good example is an inventory control model that reorders small items on the basis of current stocks, current or projected demand, and a computerized procedure for determining the optimal ordering policy. The differentiating features of an operations model are that (a) its degree of validity vis-à-vis the reference structure is relatively easy to determine, and (b) it is possible to monitor the results of the model's decisions and to intervene before things get far enough out of control to cost a lot. The latter feature is usually present when the model deals with highly repetitive and routine matters and no particular decision is of major importance. Even under the best of conditions, however, line delegation to models usually meets with a considerable degree of resistance.

We doubt if advances in modeling ever will reach a point where line delegation is feasible for policy issues, since the results of each decision are important, and since low-cost and immediate correction on the basis of feedback is not possible. Policy modeling projects, then, should be chosen with a view to extending, not replacing, the judgment of planners and administrators.

Design Considerations in Modeling

It is possible to specify a number of characteristics of models that enhance their ability to extend people's judgment.[16] The same factors are important for getting acceptance of models from people who have significant decision-making responsibilities but who may not be technically trained.

1. *A model should be simple.* The simpler a model is, the easier it will be to understand. It is essential to understand a model's fundamental characteristics before using it, though of course one need not master its technical details, its mathematical solution, or the techniques for programming it on a computer. Where the details are complex a special effort must be made by the modeler to find a way to accurately characterize in simple terms its fundamental properties, including its inputs, operating characteristics, and outputs. Our experience is that when a model is so complicated that its creator cannot describe these properties in simple terms, there is acute danger that he may be no longer capable of grasping the implications of what it produces. There also is much less chance for acceptance of the model by decision makers, and for good reason.

2. *A model should be complete on important issues.* Although a model should be simple, it should also be comprehensive. Either it should take into account all the main issues of importance to the decision maker or it should be explicit about what has been excluded. In the latter case, it should provide a way for the decision maker to integrate its results with his own thinking regarding the excluded factors. All too often we find the opposite: the model builder has made an allegedly simplifying assumption that emasculates an important aspect of the decision, and there is no way for the decision maker to compensate for this during his use of the model. Models that are judged to be incomplete will tend to be rejected or neglected by decision makers. Failure by the model builder to disclose material elements of incompleteness is of course a failure of trust and responsibility that will have a chilling effect on the use of models by that organization in the long run.

3. *A model should be easy to control.* This means that a model's outputs should be more or less predictable from its inputs, which are known. Also, it should be possible, without an unreasonable amount of effort, to achieve a desired output state by manipulating the inputs. Fear is a major deterrent to the adoption of models. Is the model really complete on important issues? How valid is it? Many other such questions are asked. But there is also fear that the decision maker may lose control of events. We will have more to say about this later. Meanwhile it should be noted that a model easy to control, ideally by the decision maker himself, will not be as threatening as one that often produces major surprises. To be sure, a model's outputs should be surprising, in the sense of producing new insight, but not so surprising as to damage its credibility. "Control," then, implies that the decision maker, perhaps working with the model builder, has achieved intellectual mastery over the model. Obtaining desired output states by adjusting inputs is one way to demonstrate that this degree of mastery has been achieved.

4. *A model should be stable.* Given reasonable inputs, a model should never produce nonsensical answers (well, hardly ever). This is not as easily accomplished as one might think, even with a basically valid model. There may be cases in which the model "blows up," i.e., produces nonsense or simply stops running. A decision maker will not generally be as tolerant of these conditions as will the professional model builder. His or her confidence in the model will be disproportionately shaken by "blowups," especially if they should happen to occur early in the process of gaining experience with the model. Face validity is important and it tends to be undermined if the model is unstable. Achieving a sense of intellectual control over the model is harder if the model is not stable, though of course it may be stable and still not be under control.

5. *A model should be adaptive.* This criterion has much in common with completeness and simplicity. A model should be flexible enough to respond to the changing needs or point of view of the decision maker. "Take-it-or-leave-it" models usually have few takers. The decision maker's thinking must be integrated with results from the model. The more adaptive the model the easier this will be, and the less the model builder will have to anticipate all possible considerations. Also, an adaptive model will seem to be, and probably will be, easier for the decision maker to control; it will be more like a personal tool and hence more credible and usable.

6. *A model should be easy to communicate with.* Models that are awkward to use tend not to get used. This is a fault of the interface between model and decision maker rather than of the model's structure as such, though some structures are inherently easier to deal with than others. Careful attention to ways in which data are input, tested for internal consistency, and saved for future use or modification between runs will help people learn to use the model and make them want to use it again later. The same is true of outputs: appropriate summary results in easy-to-read format (including graphics if possible), as opposed to large stacks of blue-bar paper, may well spell the difference between success and failure. This principle follows from the economic maxim that the lower the cost of something the more of it will be bought. The time and energy of the decision maker and his staff are limited. It makes a difference, then, if communicating with the model is easy or difficult.

Some of the criteria for a good model are clearly incompatible if taken to an extreme. This is particularly true of completeness and stability on the one hand and simplicity and controllability on the other. However, models that effect reasonable compromises among these criteria have been built and are being used. Finding such compromises is a very important part of the modeling art.

In our judgment many of the models proposed for use by colleges and universities and some actually in use are seriously deficient with respect to one or more of the above criteria. The very large models for academic resource allocation such as CAMPUS and RRPM are seriously incomplete when applied to complex research universities, since they consider neither quality-of-education variables nor the joint-product character of graduate education and research (i.e., the fact that they tend to be produced jointly from the same inputs). Also, the fact that these models require thousands of input coefficients makes them very difficult to control, not very adaptive, and hard to communicate with.[17] We do believe, however, that they meet our criterion of simplicity, since despite their technical complexity the concepts on which they are based are easy enough to explain and understand. We will have more to say about the characteristics of these and other models in later chapters.

Our objective in this book is to further not only the development but also the implementation of planning models in colleges and universities. We believe that, for the most part, the models we will be treating are consistent with the six criteria described above. At any rate, the criteria are part of our philosophy and we tried to keep them in mind as we proceeded through conceptualization and development.

We have already said what models are, but what should one expect in trying to develop or use them? Are there any documented cases of success in using models as decision aids in colleges and universities? With such questions in mind we turn in chapter 2 to an account of how many of the models to be described in this book were both developed and implemented, at Stanford.

Summary

Modeling, when done properly, can be of significant benefit to institutions of higher education. Such an activity need not be antithetical to the preservation of academic values if it is conducted with due sensitivity to institutional goals and priorities.

Many models are implicit in the thinking of a decision maker, even though they never appear in explicit form. The application of explicit, quantitative models to college and university planning is the subject matter of this book. This, like most other practical use of models, calls for a certain degree of creativity in deciding how to represent the problem under study, the amount of detail to be included in the analytical framework, and the means to be used for verification and validation of the results.

Among the applications of management science methods to higher education we cite the following: planning, programming and budgeting systems, management information systems, resource allocation models, student enrollment planning, faculty staffing and tenure analysis, and various kinds of optimization models. For a variety of reasons, some applications have been more successful than others; usually, these reasons have to do with the degree to which administrative officers who are attuned to the institution's values have been involved with the application in question.

Effective modeling requires an understanding of both what is important to the institution and what means can be used to achieve the desired ends. Fears about modeling arise concerning oversimplification, indiscriminate use, and an overemphasis on the quantifiable dimensions of a decision situation. Careful attention must therefore be given to choosing areas appropriate for analysis and to constructing models that are properly tailored to the special needs of colleges and universities.

Planning and control systems are not new to higher education. Their character changed, however, as the academic boom of the postwar era came to an end. The ensuing scarcity of resources brought with it a new emphasis on models and other quantitative devices, and these sometimes have been blamed for the problem rather than acknowledged as helping to identify possible remedies. In fact, there are many advantages to using planning models in a university setting: for instance, the model builder must lay bare the reasoning process, assumptions, data, and calculations underlying the decisions that must be made.

The chapter ends by discussing the characteristics of a good model. These include: simplicity; completeness on important issues; ease of control; stability in the face of minor deviations in input assumptions; adaptability to new, yet related, decision situations; and ease of communication with the user. Academic officers should never delegate line authority to models or to their architects, but, rather, must retain personal responsibility for decision making at all times.

Notes to Chapter 1

Works cited here in abbreviated form are more fully described in the bibliography at the end of this book.

1. H. R. Bowen 1977, p. 2.
2. Massy 1974, p. 6.
3. For a highly readable discussion of this material, see Greenberger, Crenson, and Crissey 1976, chap. 3.
4. Kemeny 1972, p. 2.
5. Schroeder 1973, p. 896.
6. Ibid., p. 896.
7. Ibid., pp. 897–98. Project INFO was later discontinued.
8. Ibid., p. 898.
9. For references to CAMPUS, see Judy 1969. An overview of RRPM can be found in Gulko 1971; detailed materials are available from NCHEMS.
10. H. R. Bowen 1977, p. 3.
11. Massy 1975, p. 1.
12. H. R. Bowen 1977, p. 2.
13. W. G. Bowen 1968, pp. 20–21. The three schools are Chicago, Princeton, and Vanderbilt.
14. See Greenberger, Crenson, and Crissey 1976 for a good discussion of these considerations.
15. Little 1970, p. B-468.
16. Most of the terms in the list and many of the basic ideas are due to Little 1970. However, we have freely interspersed our own thoughts with his.
17. See Hopkins 1971, p. 471.

2

The Evolution of Planning Models

at Stanford University

This is an account of how the development and use of planning models evolved at one institution—Stanford University. We shall try to describe what happened, why it happened, and what some of the main effects have been both on further development of the models and on the institution itself.

We believe that this short history will be helpful for three reasons. First, the events are interesting for their own sake as a case study of how models come into being and how they function in important decision situations. Second, the reader will be introduced not only to the kinds of models we will be treating in later chapters but also, we hope, to some of the reasons for using them. Finally, we have described mistakes, false starts, and dead ends that may show the reader what to avoid and in any case will dispel any illusion that modeling is easy.

One of our objectives is to provide as accurate an account as possible of how modeling concepts, specific models, and the use of both actually evolved at Stanford during the period from 1972 to 1978. Although the two of us were principal actors in this process, we want to avoid bias. As safeguards, we shall rely as far as possible upon actual historical materials. At the same time, this is essentially a first-person description of what happened. A definitive account would require a neutral interpreter and systematic interviews with participants, not to mention access to the relevant source materials.[1]

The unusual character of Stanford's position with respect to planning models during this period should not be overemphasized. Nevertheless, Stanford was unique in a number of important and fortunate ways. For instance, beginning in 1971 there was the conjunction in the Stanford central administration of: (a) an analyst with intensive training in operations research and hands-on experience (at the University of California at Berkeley) with the development of university planning models; (b) a business school professor, trained in management science and economics, with extensive experience in the development and application of models for "soft" areas of management such as marketing strategy; (c) a provost, trained in computer science and also experienced in economic and computer performance simulations, who was very interested in man-machine (including man-model) interactions; (d) a vice-provost for planning and budgeting, trained in education and philosophy, who could and did play the role of resident skeptic while providing constructive criticism and personal encouragement. The first two are the authors of this book. In the chronology that follows we shall refer to ourselves as DSPH and WFM; all other persons will be referred to by name and, where necessary, title. The development and adoption of planning models at Stanford was also furthered by the budget stringency it faced during the mid-1970s. It is important to note that Stanford, again for budgetary reasons, had been building needed infrastructure and data for several years before our own modeling work began.

In early 1974 the two of us received a grant from the Lilly Endowment that covered model development expenses through the summer of 1978. Availability of grant funds permitted our work to advance just at the time when its fruits were most useful and conditions for adoption most propitious. The following quotation from our proposal to the Lilly Endowment reflects our objectives as we saw them in the autumn of 1973. This was near the beginning of our work together on planning models and before the serious budget problems referred to earlier had become apparent. However, the objectives continued to serve us well as Stanford's financial situation worsened.

> While the "new depression in higher education" now happily seems to be abating . . . we wonder if the structure of the university planning and administrative process has yet evolved to the point where substantial new surprises are not likely to occur. Do we yet have a fully effective planning discipline at the highest levels of academic management? . . .
>
> Some manifestations of the lack of a sufficient planning discipline at the institutional level include:
>
> **1.** *A tendency to concentrate on incremental income and expense on a year-by-year basis.* It is hard to develop credible multiyear plans. Pent-up needs make pressure for spending all of income increments in good years very hard to control, and the lesson of the late 1960s has taught us that we cannot mortgage future income increments in bad years. This results in a "boom-bust" approach to planning.
>
> **2.** *A tendency to deal with macroparameters one at a time, often setting objectives or constraints on the basis of criteria that are stated in absolute terms rather than by assessing the tradeoffs among desirable (or undesirable) alternatives.* Great pressure is exerted on certain income-generating or expense-reducing parameters which act for a time as safety valves—until a reaction sets in. In recent years tuition increments have served the "safety valve" function in some institutions. Now that this approach to income improvement is under increasing pressure, the soft market for professors suggests that faculty salaries may begin to play this role.
>
> **3.** *The difficulty with which the rationale of macro budget decisions is communicated to faculty, students, and even trustees.* This problem is particularly acute when tuition is being raised or new academic programs are being denied or old ones cut back. It is

1978/79 Operating Budget ($118.7 Million)

1978/79 Consolidated Budget ($386.6 Million)

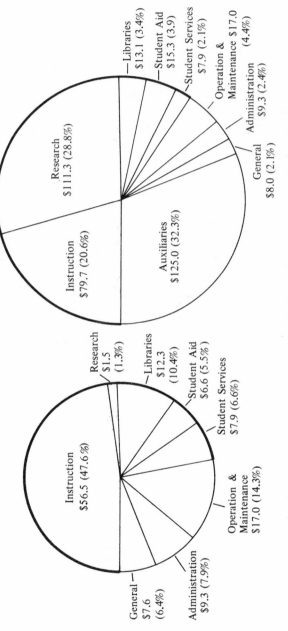

Figure 2.1. Expenditure components of Stanford University budget, 1978/79 ($000)

very difficult to express credibly relations between value tradeoffs and financial factors as these affect the institution over a period of time. Issues of academic and human value are continually confounded with those of financial reality.[2]

Little did we know how soon our ideas on these points, and those of our colleagues, would be put to the test, or how our models would come to play a significant role as decision aids at Stanford. Before going into that, however, it will be helpful to review the situation into which modeling was introduced.

Preconditions and Precursors

Stanford University is a private, single-campus university founded in 1885 and opened in 1891. In the academic year 1977/78 it had about 6,500 undergraduate students and 5,700 graduate and professional students. Admission is selective for all programs; for instance, about 2,500 freshmen were offered admission and 1,560 enrolled from an applicant pool of about 8,500 likely candidates for September of 1977. Tuition for 1978/79 was $5,130 or within the same range as that of Stanford's peer group of Ivy League and similar private institutions. Some 50 to 55 percent of undergraduate students receive financial aid, which is based on need. The faculty numbers about 1,070 professors plus 500 other teaching personnel (in terms of actual people, not full-time equivalents). Federally sponsored research is very important to the faculty and for graduate programs in many fields. Stanford usually ranks between third and fifth among the nation's universities with respect to the dollar amount of federal support provided.

A breakdown of Stanford's consolidated and operating budget expenditures for 1978/79 is presented in figure 2.1. The consolidated budget (right) encompasses all expenditures, including restricted funds for faculty research; dormitories, food services, and the university hospital (under "auxiliaries"); and the Stanford Linear Accelerator Center, a government-owned, contractor-operated facility (under "research"). The operating budget (left) allocates and controls university general funds plus the income from endowed chairs, library acquisition funds, and a few other restricted sources that are closely linked to programs supported by general funds. Most administration and support services are paid for from general funds and are therefore included in the operating budget. It is worth remembering that all the items in the consolidated budget benefit from these services, nearly half of which are paid for by overhead on research grants and contracts (so-called indirect cost recovery). This government funding is in addition to the direct expenditures on research shown under "research" in the consolidated budget.

The style of Stanford's budgeting is basically centralized, as opposed to Harvard's style of "every tub on its own bottom." That is, general-funds budgets are determined centrally on the basis of line-item recommendations from deans and department heads. Little effort is made to attribute sources of general-fund revenue to organizational units. There are two exceptions to these arrangements: the School of Medicine and the Graduate School of

Table 2.1. Selected Data About Stanford University: Alternate Years, 1960–1978 (Operating Budget, Excluding the Schools of Business and Medicine)

	1960	1962	1964	1966	1968	1970	1972	1974	1976	1978
Operating Budget										
Total income applied ($000)	**$14,882**	**$20,776**	**$24,807**	**$29,754**	**$36,029**	**$44,453**	**$52,939**	**$61,297**	**$67,754**	**$85,261**
Total unrestricted	**91.4%**	**91.0%**	**87.2%**	**87.5%**	**88.3%**	**85.6%**	**90.8%**	**86.4%**	**92.4%**	**92.8%**
Tuition and fees	53.0%	52.2%	54.3%	54.2%	52.0%	49.2%	52.0%	51.5%	57.9%	57.9%
Endowment payout	11.9%	12.2%	11.8%	12.8%	12.1%	11.3%	13.6%	10.5%	8.2%	6.9%
Indirect cost recovery	17.0%	16.4%	17.2%	16.9%	22.7%	18.3%	17.9%	17.2%	20.3%	21.3%
Total restricted	**8.6%**	**9.0%**	**12.8%**	**12.5%**	**11.7%**	**14.4%**	**9.2%**	**13.6%**	**7.6%**	**7.2%**
Endowment payout	3.4%	2.6%	3.7%	3.8%	4.8%	5.2%	4.8%	4.5%	5.4%	4.8%
Total endowment payout	15.3%	14.8%	15.5%	16.6%	16.9%	16.5%	18.4%	15.0%	13.6%	11.8%
Income allocated to plant ($000)	$0	$0	$0	$0	$1,599	$674	$2,095	$1,713	$4,672	$5,206
Other Facts										
Autumn enrollment (headcount)	**8,158**	**8,783**	**9,583**	**10,170**	**10,417**	**10,361**	**10,446**	**10,159**	**10,310**	**10,508**
Undergraduate	5,415	5,666	5,648	5,853	5,923	6,221	6,431	6,437	6,499	6,475
Graduate	2,743	3,117	3,935	4,317	4,494	4,140	4,015	3,722	3,811	4,033
Tuition rate	$1,005	$1,260	$1,410	$1,575	$1,770	$2,145	$2,610	$3,135	$3,810	$4,695
Professorial faculty (headcount)	400[a]	480[a]	540[a]	590[a]	650[a]	710[a]	712	724	721	721

[a] Approximate.

Business, both of which receive general funds according to a special formula. There are good reasons for this, but we shall not go into them here. For this book's purposes we will be dealing with Stanford's operating budget excluding the Schools of Medicine and Business. We are left with the Schools of Earth Sciences, Education, Engineering, Humanities and Sciences, and Law, as well as the administrative and support services. These consume the lion's share of the Stanford operating budget.

Growth, "BAP," and the Campaign for Stanford

The period since World War II has seen Stanford grow in size and stature from a very good regional university to one of high excellence and international reputation. Table 2.1 provides some perspective on this growth in size and quality and on the period of stabilizations and retrenchment that followed. The table provides total operating budget income (excluding, for reasons that were described earlier, the Schools of Business and Medicine); the percentage distribution of income by major categories; and a few other selected data series. One measure of perspective is that total income grew at an annual compounded rate of 9.6 percent per year during this nineteen-year period from 1960 through 1978. This represents a real growth rate of more than 5 percent per annum in total and more than 4 percent annually on a per student basis. Of course, Stanford's sponsored research volume (not shown in the table) also grew very rapidly during the 1960s, and indirect cost recovery funded a good deal of the needed growth in administrative and support services that took place during the period. The proportions of the budget supported by tuition and fees, endowment payout, and indirect cost recovery are also shown in the table as is the tuition rate which grew during the period at a compounded rate of 8.5 percent in nominal terms or slightly more than 4 percent in real terms. Student and faculty numbers are provided as well.

Like many other colleges and universities, Stanford's financial picture took a turn for the worse in the late 1960s. This was caused by an end to growth, especially in graduate programs, and the drying up of a number of important sources of funding. Figure 2.2 shows the pattern of surpluses and deficits for the period beginning 1967/68. Before that year there had been consistent surpluses, which had allowed sizable operating reserves to accumulate. The emergence of budget deficits beginning in 1968/69 triggered a Budget Adjustment Program (referred to as BAP) and a five-year, $300-million fund-raising campaign ("The Campaign for Stanford"). Their objective was not only to solve the university's immediate financial problems but also to put its finances on a firm long-term footing.

Planning for BAP began during the budget year 1969/70; the first of five annual phases of adjustment took effect in 1970/71. In 1974/75, when all phases were completed, some $6 million of adjustments had been made on a base operating budget of $68 million in 1972/73 (the middle year of the program). Of this, $3.1 million represented expenditure reductions and $2.9 million was income improvement. The original BAP target was $2.5 million, but this was

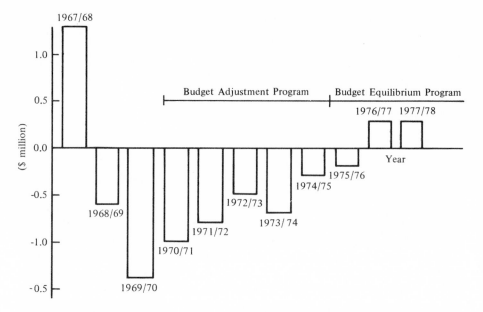

Figure 2.2. Historical budget surpluses and deficits at Stanford University (based on final, year-end accounting figures)

raised quickly to $6 million when the extent of the problem became clearer. The size of the target was a subject of considerable discussion and some controversy within the central administration, and the program itself was a major undertaking with high visibility. It required a great deal of effort from administrators, university officers, and faculty advisors. A second round of adjustments, labeled the "Budget Equilibrium Program" or BEP, was initiated on the heels of BAP, as will be discussed later.

The Campaign for Stanford, with its goal of $300 million over five years, was announced on April 11, 1972. It was an enormous fund-raising task, the largest in higher education up to that time, and it was successful: $132 million was raised for endowment, $57 million for physical plant, and $115 million for other purposes. The campaign raised the annual giving level by about $20 million. The history of the campaign is fascinating in and of itself.[3] For present purposes, however, we need recall only that it was in progress during the years when our models were evolving, that it involved a great many people inside and outside the university who took more than a passing interest in Stanford's financial situation, and that it was successful.

The Infrastructure for Planning and Budgeting

An Academic Planning Office (APO) and an Office of Management and Financial Planning (M & FP) were set up during the BAP years; they played an important role in subsequent events including the development of modeling. APO was (and is) under the direction of Raymond F. Bacchetti, vice-provost for budget and planning and the provost's chief budget officer. The successful functioning of Stanford's budget processes and communications during the period we are studying was largely due to him. The staff of four (later, three) professionals in the APO provided support for the development of academic budgets as well as performing special studies. DSPH joined APO as a staff associate (later senior staff associate) in 1971.

The Management and Financial Planning Office (M & FP), which operated under the auspices of the vice-president for business and finance, was spun off from the Controller's Office (also under the vice-president for business and finance) in the late 1960s. The idea was to separate long-range forecasting and strategy development from accounting and budget control. The two offices shared the task of developing the proximate year's budget parameters throughout the period in question. In 1970 M & FP had five full-time professionals, and the number fluctuated between five and six during the next eight years. Most of the staff of the office had, and have, the MBA degree. The director of M & FP, Kent R. Peterson, and the controller, Kenneth D. Creighton, and their staffs worked very closely with Vice-Provost Bacchetti and the Academic Planning Office on BAP, BEP, and in support of our modeling project. In addition to the staff in M & FP, several people in the Controller's Office devoted substantial time to budget guideline development and special costing studies throughout the period covered in this chapter.

The forecasting and budget process was (and is) coordinated by a Budget Group and a Budget Staff. The Budget Group was chaired by the provost, William F. Miller (he was also a vice-president of the university and was designated in the bylaws of the Board of Trustees as the president's delegate for budget matters). The vice-president for business and finance, or VPB & F (then Robert R. Augsburger), as well as Bacchetti, Creighton, and Peterson and certain of their staff (including DSPH), were members of the Budget Group. The provost asked WFM to join in November 1971, when he was appointed vice-provost for research, because of his background as a professor of business administration and also to have another academic officer involved in the budget process.* Throughout this period President Richard W. Lyman attended meetings of the Budget Group as often as his schedule permitted, and particularly when crucial decisions were to be taken.

It is important to understand that the Stanford Budget Group was not a formally constituted decision-making body. Rather, it was a mechanism for coordinating the budget process and providing a forum for the Provost, the VPB & F, and the president to discuss forecasting and budget matters with members of their staffs. The latter (including DSPH) also met as a joint Budget Staff, under the chairmanship of Bacchetti, to coordinate much of the analytical work underlying the agendas of the Budget Group. During all or most of the period when the models were evolving, the following mechanisms were also

---

*This precedent has been continued: another vice-provost for research (Gerald J. Lieberman, a professor of operations research) became a member of the group after WFM's appointment as vice-president for business and finance in 1977.

present (as indeed they are today). Advice on budget matters was obtained from the faculty, student groups, staff, and others through a variety of formal and informal mechanisms. (The role played by the faculty-staff Budget and Priorities Commission with respect to model adoption will be discussed presently.) A long-range financial forecast was presented to the Board of Trustees in October or November of each year, and budget guidelines for the next year were recommended to the board each March. (The board also kept in touch with developments via an ad hoc Committee on the Budget.)

Two other items of infrastructure need to be mentioned: the *budget protocol* and *long-range financial forecasting* processes. Both were instituted during the period just before we developed our models, which they influenced greatly. As used at Stanford, the term "budget protocol" refers to a written instrument for promulgating general budget and planning information; the protocol also includes questions from the top that require answers from those lower down. The protocol process was introduced in 1972. It is best described by one of its creators, Provost William Miller (the other was vice-provost Raymond Bacchetti).

> Early in the academic year, in September or October, we develop and distribute a set of documents we call budget protocols.
>
> These are sent to schools, administrative offices and support offices, such as the library. The budget protocol documents, and the responses to them constitute, if you like, a transfer function between the institutional level of planning and the program planning that goes on at the departmental and the school levels. The budget protocol documents do two things. First, they set forth the constraints and the criteria that have been developed independently through other processes. Constraints, for example, are criteria of response to affirmative action, enrollment patterns, financial aid, continuing education, faculty-aid distributions—these are part of the constraints and criteria provided to the schools and departments from the central administration.
>
> Secondly, the protocol process solicits data and judgments about program needs and academic directions. The budget protocol sets in motion a process of discussion between the central administration and the deans of schools, between the deans and the chairpersons of their departments, and between various faculty oversight committees.[4]

While on the subject of program needs and academic directions, let us digress a moment to examine the nature of so-called academic priorities as they are viewed at Stanford. Actually, the word "priorities" is a bit misleading, since it might suggest some kind of ordered numbers game. Again, in the words of Provost Miller:

> Rather than priorities, we have some fundamental criteria which become the basis for academic decision making. I consider four general criteria as fundamental in the judgment of programs, whether ongoing or new:
>
> **1.** Is the program academically important?
> **2.** Is there now and will there continue to be a student interest?
> **3.** Can we as an institution be outstanding in this program?
> **4.** Can the program be securely funded?[5]

The question of importance requires peer-group review, by faculty inside or outside the institution. Student interest is basically a marketplace phenomenon;

the interests of both present and potential future students must be assessed and considered. Whether Stanford can be outstanding requires both peer-group and administrative evaluation, since the answer depends both on academic potential and upon the level of resources it is reasonable to assume will be committed to the program. Finally, secure funding requires either that any soft-money sources be regarded as reasonably enduring or that an immediate or eventual commitment of general funds be reasonably possible. These criteria are an important part of planning and budgeting at Stanford, and they have served us well.

Long-range financial forecasting was placed on a firm footing at Stanford beginning in 1973. By a *long-range financial forecast* (LRFF) we mean a five-year forecast of income and expense line items, and the resulting surpluses or deficits. (We think that *medium-range forecast* would be a better term, since five years is not a long time, and we shall use "MRFF" in later chapters. However, "LRFF" is the established term at Stanford and so we shall stick to it in this chapter.) Preparation of the LRFF is the first stage in developing each year's budget. The forecast is presented to the Board of Trustees in November (some years in October) and provides the context in which to evaluate recommendations for the next year's budget. These are presented to the board the following March.

An example of a Stanford LRFF is given in table 2.2. This particular forecast, which was presented to the Board of Trustees on March 12, 1973, was prepared as we approached the final year of BAP. We show it here both to provide an example of a Stanford LRFF of the period and also to establish the data context for the beginnings of our modeling efforts, which we take up in the next section.

It is worth noting from table 2.2 that the *baseline gap* (i.e., actual or potential deficit) in this LRFF was insignificant compared to the budget being proposed for 1974, but that it was projected to grow to more than $5.5 million by 1978. Thirteen management options totaling some $6 million in gap closing were presented along with this LRFF. Of the $6 million, less than half represented expenditure reductions and more than half cuts in proposed incremental faculty and staff positions. It is fair to say that the Stanford administration was confident it could use the signals emanating from the new LRFF and act to ward off the projected deficits without disrupting the institution significantly.

The key to having an effective LRFF is to root each line item in the best data available, supplemented by the judgments of the people in the organization (and outside, where applicable) who are most expert in the particular subject matter. For instance, staff salary growth rates should be a matter for consideration by the Personnel Department; for faculty salaries the provost's staff may be the reservoir of expertise; utility costs should be the province of the energy experts; and so on. It was in 1972/73 that processes were established for getting such data and for instilling in the experts the need for most-likely estimates rather than conservative and safe ones. (Optimistic and pessimistic estimates have also been elicited on occasion.) At the same time, pains were taken to

Table 2.2.   Long-Range Financial Forecast for Stanford University Operating Budget, as Submitted to the Board of Trustees in March 1973 ($000)

	1973 Budget Base	1974 Proposed Budget	Estimated			
			1975	1976	1977	1978
Expenditures						
Faculty salaries	$11,083	$12,055	$12,765	$13,424	$14,089	$14,784
Other teaching salaries	2,828	3,034	3,234	3,412	3,601	3,801
Exempt staff	9,631	10,257	10,881	11,629	12,286	12,959
Non-exempt staff	8,105	8,819	9,440	10,129	10,833	11,464
Teaching assistants	1,095	1,121	1,165	1,212	1,260	1,310
Salary requisitions	614	652	665	716	749	774
TOTAL SALARIES	**$33,356**	**$35,938**	**$38,150**	**$40,522**	**$42,818**	**$45,092**
Staff benefits	$5,359	$6,109	$6,981	$7,821	$8,735	$9,785
Library acquisitions	1,570	1,709	1,941	2,135	2,348	2,584
Undergraduate aid-unrest. portion	2,080	1,910	1,671	1,703	1,850	1,960
Graduate aid-unrest. portion	1,312	1,395	1,729	1,536	1,256	1,387
Student health contract	963	1,003	1,078	1,159	1,246	1,339
Building maintenance	761	824	908	983	1,147	1,215
Utilities	1,452	1,656	1,856	2,021	2,488	2,673
Grounds maintenance	470	478	538	665	741	790
Custodial	1,083	1,158	1,318	1,405	1,628	1,711
All other	7,609	8,365	8,677	9,248	9,824	10,510
TOTAL	**$56,015**	**$60,545**	**$64,847**	**$69,198**	**$74,081**	**$79,046**
Business, Medicine and Hoover Research	$12,242	$13,239	$14,664	$16,132	$17,541	$18,983
TOTAL EXPENDITURES	**$68,257**	**$73,784**	**$79,511**	**$85,330**	**$91,622**	**$98,029**
Source of funds						
Tuition and fees	$33,468	$36,013	$38,093	$40,350	$42,779	$45,158
Unrestricted endowment income	7,529	7,532	7,905	8,331	8,735	9,154
Restricted endowment income	5,073	5,247	5,835	6,568	7,238	7,901
Unrestricted gifts	1,851	1,901	1,958	2,060	2,190	2,295
Restricted gifts and grants	2,425	2,415	3,134	3,485	3,760	4,048
Special funds	1,848	2,223	2,565	2,822	3,078	3,395
Other income	2,217	3,103	3,454	3,469	3,500	3,621
Reimbursed indirect costs	13,396	15,400	15,935	16,975	17,975	19,175
Transfer to plant for renovations	(400)	(600)	(1,000)	(1,500)	(2,000)	(2,500)
TOTAL AVAILABLE FUNDS	**$67,407**	**$73,234**	**$77,879**	**$82,560**	**$87,255**	**$92,247**
Estimated budget savings	$(850)	$(550)	$(1,632)	$(2,770)	$(4,367)	$(5,782)
Estimated income improvement	250	250	250	250	250	250
BASELINE GAP	**$(600)**	**$(300)**	**$(1,382)**	**$(2,520)**	**$(4,117)**	**$(5,532)**

make the LRFF correspond exactly to the central university operating budget, so that it would be easy to compare the two and, later, compare forecast outcomes with actual ones.

From the mid-sixties until 1972 Stanford had relied on a "naive" or simple model that projected a few aggregative factors in the consolidated budget (not the operating budget) for a period of ten years. Growth rates for a given line item (salaries, for example) generally were constant over time, whereas in the new LRFF they have tended to vary from year to year. Estimates were suggested by the analysts in M & FP (in the earlier years, by those in the Controller's Office) and decided upon in the Budget Group. Although this model was successful in helping predict the need for BAP, it suffered from several serious deficiencies: (a) it dealt with the consolidated rather than the operating budget; (b) its parameters were not firmly grounded and were (correctly) regarded as very rough "guestimates"; (c) ten years was too long a period to permit good grounding in data and realistic projection of trends.

The main result was that the naive model was not under very effective intellectual control. It did not generate much commitment from Budget Group members even though its results were presented to the Board of Trustees. Indeed, the members felt free to vary the growth rate guestimates at will within broad limits, something they could not have done if some bona fide expert had generated the parameters. They did so until the resulting string of surpluses or deficits "predicted" by the model more or less fitted their preconceived notions, whether optimistic or pessimistic. The model had some utility, then, but not exactly the sort one has in mind when thinking of a model as a decision aid; in fact, there may have been a certain element of disingenuousness in attributing a prediction "to the model." It was a growing recognition of these problems that led to the development of the new-style LRFF.

The Economics of Endowed Universities

The title of this section refers to a working paper by WFM.[6] Written in June 1973, it was based on a model developed the previous winter. This paper set the stage for our subsequent modeling efforts. The impetus for it was the question, "Will Stanford be financially viable over the long run, that is, after BAP and the Campaign for Stanford and beyond the five-year limit of the LRFF?" The provost asked this question and it was much discussed in the Budget Group. It led to an analysis of long-run price indices and of the economic forces that determine them, particularly the role of the stock market and the economy generally in determining income and capital appreciation from endowment. It also led to the paper, with its somewhat pretentious title.

The context for the analysis included works by Earl F. Cheit (1973) and William W. Jellema (1973) that documented the growing financial difficulties facing colleges and universities, and the argument by William G. Bowen (1968) that higher education was labor-intensive and that costs per student had been rising over the long run and might be expected to continue to do so. True, there were reports that higher education was emerging from its "new depression."[7] But we were still very much concerned about whether new versions of BAP and new fund-raising campaigns would be needed (as we blithely said) "in the next ten years or so." We did not know that a new and bigger BAP was just around the corner.

At a conceptual level WFM's thesis was that it is very difficult for colleges and universities to increase quantitative productivity so as to keep pace with average productivity gains in the economy as a whole. The main reason is that college and university teaching continues to depend on teachers, and that even with new teaching tools and methods it is hard to increase student throughput per faculty member year after year without degrading the character of the institution. No doubt the quality of higher education has improved over the years, and this is a kind of productivity increase. Also, productivity can be expected to increase in administrative and support areas, where the technologies are not much different from those in other kinds of enterprises. However, the thesis that there seems to be great difficulty in making quantitative (as opposed to qualitative) productivity gains in higher education is not affected by these observations nor even by the fact that some progress is being made with respect to computer-aided instruction.

It follows that, in WFM's words, "one of the ironies of higher education is that the better we perform our service to society, the worse off we are likely to be in the long run."

> The basic problem is that a university buys its resources in a market that is dominated by wage and salary rates but sells its services in a market that is—or should be, some would say—limited by increases in the cost of living. Wages and salaries go up faster than the cost of living. And in the long run, the better colleges and universities do their job, *the greater this gap is likely to be! . . .*
>
> The irony [of the situation just described] depends on the relation between a university's outputs and the rate of productivity growth in the economy. We educate students and do research. The more we do, and the better we do it, the greater the benefit to the people involved and to society. But a significant part of this benefit is taken out as increases in productivity—for individuals and for the economy in general. (E.g., better-prepared students are more productive in their jobs, research leads to new technology, etc.) These increases in productivity are translated into higher real wages—increases in which those who work for colleges and universities have a right to share. And this, in turn, exacerbates the financial problems of the educational institution.[8]

Endowment, the paper continued, could mitigate these long-term difficulties because investments could enable the college or university fortunate enough to have an endowment to participate in the growth of total factor productivity in the general economy or in particular investment sectors.

This argument is substantially true in principle, though the economic forces that determine total investment return are more complex than the above might lead one to believe. However, there are distinct limits on the extent to which investment return can overcome the productivity gap caused by the labor-intensive nature of higher education. Moreover, if endowment support for the budget is not managed properly it can exacerbate problems due to imbalance in the growth rates of income and expense. This occurs when the rate of spending from the endowment, which we call the *endowment payout rate*, is too high. Such was the case at Stanford in 1973, although we didn't know it before we began modeling.

The model underlying "The Economics of Endowed Universities" was very simple, not unlike the naive ten-year projection model we described earlier. Its intellectual motivation and mode of use, however, were quite different. Income and expense components that were believed to have roughly similar growth rates were grouped together, and rough long-term estimates of these growth rates were made as functions of economic indices. The model was configured to take effect in 1977/78, at the end of the then-current LRFF period.

Table 2.3. Components of Income and Expense as Percentages of Stanford University Operating Budget for 1978 and as the Basis for Growth Projections

Name of Component	Percentage of Budget	Basis for Projection[a]
Income		
Tuition and fees	48.4%	V
Expendable gifts and grants	7.3	PI
Other income	7.2	I
Indirect costs: W & S[b]	11.8	PI
Indirect costs: other	7.9	I
Endowment income	17.5	V
	100.0%	
Expenditure		
Wages, salaries, and benefits	67.7%	PI
Student aid	3.6	V[c]
Library acquisitions	2.8	D
Transfer to plant	2.6	D
Other: wage and salary	13.2	PI
Other: nonwage	10.1	I
	100.0%	

SOURCE: Massy 1973.
[a] Key: *V* = varies (discussed in text)
   PI = growth rate of personal income
   I = rate of inflation
   D = (discussed in text)
[b] Read: "Indirect cost recovery on contracts and grants: wage and salaries component."
[c] Same as tuition growth rate.

It assumed that the necessary management steps had been taken to close the gaps shown in table 2.2. It therefore started with a balanced budget.

Table 2.3 shows the income-and-expense categories and indices we used. The rate of inflation (*I*) was set at 4 percent (!) and the rate of growth of per capita personal income at 6.75 percent (the difference between these figures can be taken as the productivity gap). Growth in tuition (and financial aid) were viewed as decision variables. Investment return on the endowment ("total return") was set at 9.5 percent nominal or 5.5 percent real (i.e., over and above inflation). Stanford's endowment payout was 6.9 percent at the time, which meant that, in the absence of new gifts, endowment income could be expected to grow by only $9.5 - 6.9 = 2.6$ percent per year unless the payout rate was decreased. Growth in (a) the cost of library acquisitions and (b) the transfer to plant (i.e., the allocation of current funds for capital projects) were subject to special forces that are not within the scope of this summary. Basically, the model did two things: first it projected each item of income and expense according to the indicated growth rate; then it calculated the amount of additional endowment principal that, under the prespecified payout rate, would be needed in each future year in order to balance the budget. A judgment was then made as to whether the needed increments to endowment could be raised through gifts over a period of years.

Crude as this analysis was, it led to some interesting findings. We concluded that:

1. *Tuition would have to grow at near the growth rate of per capita personal income or per capita personal disposable income.* In other words, successive cohorts of people should be asked to pay a constant fraction of their income in order to attend the university. Such a policy would ensure that the price of higher education would steadily increase relative to the prices of most products.

2. *Substantial additions to endowment would be needed from exogenous sources.* Such exogenous additions to endowment, under present conditions, play the role of subsidizing the productivity gap to a greater extent than does the endowment itself.

3. *Extraordinary gifts of endowment should be used to reduce the endowment payout rate rather than to increase endowment income's share of the total budget.* The main reason for this is that funds not paid out can be reinvested and so, hopefully, reduce the pressure on future endowment fund-raising.

4. *In the long run, the rate of inflation does not make much difference to the university's economic structure.* In the short run, of course, the effects of inflation can be devastating, particularly on corporate profits and hence on gift giving and endowment total return. Such effects are not included in our models.

5. *Increases in the rate of productivity in the economy affect the economics of the university in a material and adverse way.* In our model this occurred even when tuition was rising at the same rate as personal disposable income, which itself varies with productivity. Since universities are productivity-enhancing agencies, the above would seem to provide a rationale for increasing public support, should that be desired.

6. *Every run of the model produced substantial increases over time in the amount of endowment needed by the university.* Moreover, the ratio of current endowment to current budget rose in every case. Because of the productivity gap, expenses must of necessity rise faster than current revenues. Thus the private university finds itself in the paradoxical situation that it must become steadily wealthier if it is to break even!*

These findings were discussed extensively by the Budget Group and in March 1973 a presentation was made by WFM to the Board of Trustees in conjunction with the LRFF shown in table 2.2 (the paper itself was not written until the following autumn). We still believe that the conclusions quoted above are substantially true, though of course many of them have been refined and ex-

---

*This finding was important to us because it tended to contradict the arguments attributed to Professors Harold Bierman, Jr., and Thomas Hofstedt of Cornell University to the effect that university administrators were "crying wolf" about budget stringencies while the values of their institutions' investment portfolios were steadily climbing (see "Crying Wolf?" *Newsweek* 7 May 1973, p. 65). WFM's comments at the time are still applicable:

We do not doubt that the value of endowments including the market value of securities is climbing—at least we fervently hope that such is the case. (Stanford was not one of the institutions for which numbers were cited.) Nor do we deny that it is possible to "cry wolf" with no cause. However, it is grossly misleading to argue that an increase in the endowment balance, even in real terms, is a sufficient condition for criticism. So long as the productivity gap exists the real value of endowments *must* rise and continue to rise indefinitely if the institution is to remain private and financially viable. (Massy 1973, pp. 37–39.)

tended. However, we did draw one other overarching conclusion with respect to Stanford's financial future, viz, "We are going to be all right." That one, it turned out, was disproved by the events of 1974.

The Quest for Long-Run Financial Equilibrium

The quest for equilibrium was a central feature of budget planning at Stanford during the period from late 1973 to 1977. It aimed not only at achieving financial stability but at defining and measuring it. The latter objective led to the concept of long-run financial equilibrium (LRFE), the model for transition to equilibrium (TRANS), the Stanford Budget Equilibrium Program (BEP, the successor to BAP), and the planning model, known as TRADES because it facilitates the assessment of tradeoffs among key variables, that is being used at Stanford as we write this book. This period, when modeling concepts evolved and took root, is remembered by us as one characterized by hard choices but also by intense intellectual excitement.

The LRFE Model

The idea behind long-run financial equilibrium is simply that in addition to having the budget in balance in a given year, the aggregate growth rates of income and expense should be equal. When underlying economic forces tend to produce equality in growth rates, and the initial budget is in balance, we describe the institution as being in a state of dynamic equilibrium, or more precisely, of LRFE. Here is the analogy we used in the *1974 Stanford Annual Financial Report*:

> An airplane that is properly balanced and trimmed in flight is in aerodynamic equilibrium: only a minimum amount of intervention by the pilot is needed to keep it flying straight and level. On the other hand, it is a constant struggle to keep an improperly trimmed craft from plunging disastrously. University planners must understand the conditions that lead to financial equilibrium and set their institution's policies so as to minimize start-stop budgeting and the financial crises which tend to undermine academic excellence.[9]

A much more extensive and precise treatment of the LRFE concept and model is provided in chapter 6.

Operationally, the equilibrium model consists of a pair of simultaneous equations that are solved for budget levels (e.g., of income and expense items) and their rates of change. The idea of LRFE arose in 1973, largely out of frustration with the "Economics of Endowed Universities" projection model, which we were running in trial-and-error mode in order to obtain configurations that would be financially feasible over time.

The LRFE concept began to find its way into Budget Group discussions during the early part of the academic year 1973/74 as part of the process of planning for 1974/75.[10] Figure 2.3 displays the LRFE model as we were working with it in late 1973 and early 1974. The model was rather crude, and later refinements and interpretations were not yet available. However, several key concepts were already in place:

B = budgeted expenditures

I = operating income

E = endowment market value

α = fraction of operating income from tuition

β = fraction of budget to student aid

dT = tuition growth rate

f = funded improvement factor

r_0 = cost-rise factor, other than student aid (from LRFF)

i_0 = growth rate of operating income, other than tuition (from LRFF)

g = total return plus gifts rate to endowment

p = endowment payout rate

Conditions for first-order dynamic equilibrium :

(1) $B = I + pE$ (balance)

(2) $rB = iI + (g - p) pE$ (growth-rate equality)

where $i = (1 - \alpha)i_0 + \alpha dT$ (income growth rate)

$r = (1 - \beta)r_0 + \beta dT + f$ (budget growth rate)

Figure 2.3. Long-run financial equilibrium model (as presented in early 1974)

1. The target included not only a balanced budget but an equal rate of growth for both income and expense.

2. Funded improvement, f, was identified as an important primary planning variable (f, in the original LRFE presentation, represents the amount of money available to support new programs, expressed as a fraction of the previous year's budget, over and above (a) cost rise on existing programs and (b) any reallocation of funds from one program to another).

3. The tuition growth rate, dT, was a primary planning variable; it was linked, albeit crudely, to cost rise in financial aid as well as to income growth.

4. The endowment payout rate, p, was a primary planning variable, and its linkage to the growth of endowment was set forth.

From these few concepts a number of useful findings were generated. We shall summarize them here with the help of a working paper we prepared during the summer of 1974.[11]

1. *Tradeoff between tuition growth policy and program improvements.* Our analysis suggested that tuition would have to grow at about the same rate as per capita personal income in order to compensate for cost rise in the operating budget. For each 1 percent of "program improvement" (i.e., of f) added to the operating budget, we estimated that there would have to be an additional 2.7 percent growth in annual tuition. Possibly the tuition growth rate might be slowed down if some of the improvements were financed from current funds, which would have to be reallocated.

2. *Return from the endowment: to spend or save?* In any one year, a larger endowment payout rate permits a larger budget. However, a larger payout rate also implies that endowment income will increase more slowly, since less of the return from investments will be reinvested to provide future income. With these relationships in mind, we suggested that Stanford's endowment payout rate be reduced by a factor of 20 to 50 percent, depending on university policies with respect to tuition growth, funded improvement, and other factors. The reduction, we argued, would have to be accomplished through a larger endowment, one-time budget cuts, or one-time increases in tuition, in the number of students, or both.

3. *Faculty turnover and reallocation of expenditures.* We found that the effect of reallocation upon academic programs could be estimated from the number of faculty positions that would have to be redirected, given a certain rate of reallocation. The number was some 6 to 10 positions annually for each percentage point of reallocation, or between 1 and 2 percent of the faculty. The faculty's expected annual attrition rate at that time was about 7.5 percent a year.

Tradeoffs involving rates. Some tradeoffs between funded improvement and tuition growth are presented in figure 2.4. The solid line was the basis for the 2.7 to 1 tradeoff between tuition growth and funded improvement discussed

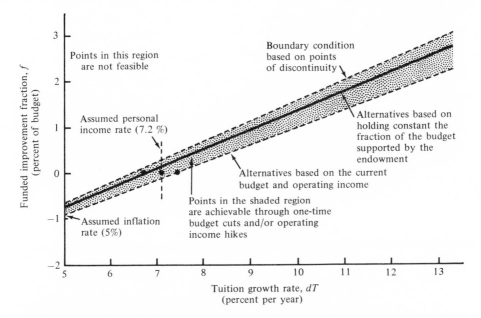

Figure 2.4. Tradeoffs between tuition growth rate and funded improvement fraction

Table 2.4.   Amount of Budget Reduction (in $ Million) and Payout Rate (Percent)

| Tuition Growth Rate (dT) | Funded Improvement (f) | | | |
| | 0.00% | | 0.25% | |
	Amount	Payout	Amount	Payout
7.5%	$0.0	6.5%	$2.3	5.0%
7.1%	$1.3	5.7%	$5.1	3.4%
6.7%	$3.2	4.5%	a	a

[a] Above the boundary condition shown in figure 2.5.

in (1), above. The tradeoff assumes that the endowment payout rate would be reduced to a point at which endowment income was growing at the same rate as the budget. The two dashed lines in figure 2.4 represent: (a) tradeoffs based on Stanford's then-current budget configuration, which incorporated a payout rate of 6.5 percent; (b) a hypothetical situation where the payout rate has been cut to the point characterized by the mathematical discontinuity described below.*

Movement upward and to the left in figure 2.4 is desirable because it makes the tradeoff between tuition growth and funded improvement less binding. However, this strategy requires a reduction in the payout rate that in turn may require cutting the budget and/or increasing operating income at a rate higher than normal. These measures were already being employed in BAP, but additional BAPs would be needed to move off the figure's lower line. Table 2.4 provides some idea of how large a budget reduction the model calculated would be needed for different combinations of tuition growth and funded improvement.

Clearly, budget reductions do not afford much leverage in the payout rate. For instance, shifting the f–dT slope leftward from A to B in figure 2.4 would have required a budget base reduction of $1.3 million, while moving on to point C would have required a reduction of $3.2 million, or nearly 5 percent of the budget. Similar reductions would be needed if funded improvement were increased, i.e., if the curve moved upward. And indeed the calculations showed that there was a theoretical limit to how far we could go towards mitigating the hard choice between tuition growth and funded improvement by means of lowering the payout rate. This limit is the "boundary condition based on points of discontinuity" shown in figure 2.4. It comes about when the root of the quadratic equation used to calculate the payout rate becomes imaginary. (See chapter 6 for further discussion.)

The solid line in figure 2.4 represents what we called a condition of "stationary

---

*The 6.5 percent payout rate does not include the amortization of prepaid land-lease proceeds, which amounted to $900 of unrestricted payout to the budget per year and added 0.4 points to the payout rate. This amortization had been adopted as an income-improvement measure in BAP I. In December 1974 we realized it had to be included in our endowment payout calculations, which led to its being discontinued as of the first year of the Budget Equilibrium Program.

The source of figure 2.4 is William F. Massy and David S. P. Hopkins, *Long-Run Financial Equilibrium Calculations for Stanford's Operating Budget*, Academic Planning Office Report 74-3 (Stanford, Calif.: the University, 1974), figure 2.

equilibrium," i.e., where the endowment and the budget grow at the same rate. We thought that it might be a good idea for the fraction of the budget supported by endowment payout to remain constant over time. Such a requirement provides a strong planning discipline and also has an aura of intergenerational equity, since future students receive the same relative benefits from endowment as current ones. In addition, it simplifies the equilibrium calculations dramatically, since it is obvious that the second equation in figure 2.3 reduces to $r = i$ and $i = g - p$ if the stationary-equilibrium condition is invoked.

The reader should not conclude from this that we consider the stationarity criterion to be a necessary condition of the model. Rather, as we have said before, it represents only "one of a number of possible judgments about what properties would be desirable in an equilibrium solution."[12] Ever since World War II, Stanford's endowment has been supporting less and less of its budget. We recommended a stationary equilibrium because we believed it would arrest this decline. As we shall point out later, the subsequent history of the stationary equilibrium concept contains an interesting twist.

Initial reactions and import. The major direct impact of the LRFE model and its predecessor, the "Economics of Endowed Universities" model, was to concentrate the attention of Budget Group members upon the need to reduce the endowment payout rate and the tuition-funded improvement tradeoff. In addition, it was a necessary precondition of, and set the stage in the Budget Group for, the transition-to-equilibrium model that was invented some months later, in September of 1974. It would be easy to overstate the LRFE model's influence, however, and so a few caveats are in order at this point.

First of all, concern about growth rates at Stanford did not originate with LRFE or the "Endowed Universities" model. Rather, it goes back to the early years of BAP, and was referred to often during the intervening years by Provost Miller and Vice-Provost Bacchetti. Probably they had in turn been influenced by William G. Bowen (1968), whose discussion of the growth in cost per student signaled an end to the boom in higher education. Indeed, the cue that led WFM to begin his modeling efforts was a comment by the provost that endowment could offset the problem of labor intensity cited by Bowen. It should be noted, though, that while growth rates were regarded as important by members of the Budget Group, it was not until the advent of the LRFE model that the quantitative relations among them could be understood.

Second, while the winter and spring of 1974 was a time of deepening financial concern, most of it was inspired by changes in the long-range forecast projections. The LRFE concept not only tended to reinforce the LRFF; it provided a kind of language in which to describe the forces that seemed to underlie the LRFF. But it was confidence in the LRFF and not in the equilibrium model that caused the financial problem to be taken seriously. Third, the whole idea of models was still foreign to many Budget Group members, including the president, the vice-president for business and finance, and the controller. In fact, as one might expect from the experience of other organizations, there was a good deal of resistance to the whole idea of relying on models.

On balance, though, interest in and support of the concepts of LRFE were appearing in Budget Group discussions and the idea that Stanford had a long-term financial problem was sinking in. But while the general nature of the problem was becoming clear, there was as yet insufficient quantification of it or the remedies for it. A major stumbling block was that such quantification as was available from the equilibrium model was not well integrated with the emerging LRFF results or the actions that were being taken. At the December 1973 Board of Trustees meeting the 1974/75 tuition increase had been set at 7.66 percent—much lower than the projected growth of personal income. For this reason the model's message (in the winter and spring of 1974) about the need to raise tuition faster seemed counterintuitive and perhaps threatening. Nevertheless, the LRFE model did provide a useful conceptual backdrop for the events of the next nine months. As time went on, moreover, the basic ideas helped to form public statements by senior officers about the reasons for Stanford's worsening financial picture.

The LRFE model and some related ideas had also been presented by WFM to a Stanford deans' retreat on February 2, 1974. (Deans' retreats are held, off campus, once or twice yearly to provide an opportunity for the school deans and the provost's senior staff to meet with each other and the president and provost to discuss matters of significance to the university, on an informal basis.) The title of this presentation was "Toward an Internally Consistent Overall Planning Discipline." It covered not only the LRFE concept but some principles of multicriteria decision making that had been included in the proposal to the Lilly Endowment (see the discussion of preference optimization, below). The author pointed out that although disequilibrium could be masked for a while by a series of stopgap measures, this would merely postpone and increase the eventual severity of the problem. The meeting was conducted in the fashion of a seminar and a lively discussion ensued for a couple of hours. No real feedback was sought, however, and the presenter came away with the feeling that the subject matter was perceived to be rather abstract.

The LRFE's first real influence on action. The next six months saw more discussion of the LRFE model in the Budget Group. We have already noted that the model tended to direct people's attention to (a) the endowment payout rate and (b) the tradeoff between funded improvement and tuition. The first tangible result that can to some extent be attributed to the model was reduction of the payout rate. This idea had fallen on fertile ground. The payout rate had been in the 4 to 5 percent range until the 1960s, when Stanford like many other institutions embraced the *total return* concept of endowment management, that is, evaluating investment performance on yield plus capital appreciation rather than on yield alone. The change resulted in an increase of payout to a projected 5.5 percent for 1974/75, a rate that, although based on the idea of spending some capital appreciation, remained conservative by many other schools' standards. However, a declining stock market had raised the effective payout rate for 1974/75 to 6.5 percent, and the amount of appreciation available for distribution was dropping rapidly. By April 1974 it was exhausted. The payout rate was immediately reduced to the level of current yield—a necessary but disruptive procedure. Needless to say these events were making all of us rather nervous, so it did not take much to elicit agreement with the LRFE model when it showed that payout should be reduced.

It is worth noting here that although the same course had been proposed by financial experts only two years previously, there had been no support for it whatsoever. Up to 1974/75 the payout rate on the Stanford endowment had been set equal to the yield rate (based on dividends and interest) on the so-called merged or pure endowment pool, which consisted of funds with tight legal strictures against spending appreciation. As a matter of policy the merged pool rate was also applied to the larger and more aggressively managed "yield-and-gain pool." Back in 1972 and 1973 Rodney Adams (director of finance) and Robert Augsburger (then vice-president for business and finance) had proposed decoupling the payout rate for both pools from the merged pool rate. Their purpose, as they explained clearly at the time, was to reduce the amount of payout and increase reinvestment during years when interest rates were high and the bond component of the investment mix heavy. Since this would have permitted a more flexible investment policy, they called the idea "managing endowment earnings." Such, however, was the perceived need for current payout to support the operating budget that the proposal was never seriously considered and the payout formula remained frozen. The thaw did not occur until the case was made in terms of spending rather than investment.

The budget recommendations for 1974/75, which went to the Board of Trustees on March 11, 1974, included a provision for bringing the endowment payout rate down to 5.6 percent. This figure, backed by the same general arguments that Adams and Augsburger had used in favor of managing endowment earnings, was expected to be reduced even further in future years but nobody could say by how much.[14] Although we were beginning to aim for an equilibrium payout rate, no decision had been made at this point about whether to use the figure of 4.25 percent suggested by the model.

The 1974/75 budget did include special adjustments of $679 thousand, but these represented the long-scheduled fifth installment of BAP and were not influenced in any way by the model. It is fair to say that, at the time the main decisions for the 1974/75 budget were being taken, no one (not even the two of us) was prepared to seriously consider significant new cuts on the heels of BAP. Certainly we were not prepared to make such a proposal under the rubric of "shifting the curve in the $f\text{--}dT$ tradeoff upward and to the left," nor yet in the name of reducing the payout rate in and of itself. However, conditions at the time (including the cumulative effect of the BAP reductions) did make it possible to reduce the payout rate a certain amount without a great deal of pain, and that is what was done.

We believe that the LRFE model contributed materially to the decision to reduce the payout rate. The decision was made despite pressure to maintain a higher rate in the interest of academic programs. The nature of the discussions in the Budget Group provides one basis for our belief; another is that WFM was asked to write the lead essay for the *1974 Stanford Annual Financial Report*. The essay, which was entitled "Planning for Long-Run Financial Equilibrium: A Time for Hard Choices," covered LRFE and related matters. It was written during the summer of 1974 and published in the autumn. With circulation to Stanford's external constituencies, including fund-raising volunteers and potential donors, this essay set the stage for the tough budget decisions that were to come. It is doubtful, we feel, that our modeling efforts would have been given this kind of billing if they had not exerted some influence on budget decisions that spring.

By May 1974 flags warning of imminent financial crisis were flying in every office concerned with Stanford's budget. The stock market had collapsed, energy costs were soaring, and the general inflation rate was moving up sharply. We had begun to see these problems even before taking the 1974/75 budget to the board in March, but it was already too late to make changes. In any event, the 1974/75 budget was modified by a hiring freeze and short-run expenditure hold-backs that were begun in May 1974. A new LRFF was prepared the same month (usually this effort does not get under way until September), and the summer was spent in studies and consultations that led in the autumn to decisions about a new round of budget adjustment.

The Budget Equilibrium Program

By the end of summer 1974 Stanford's long-range forecast was showing "gaps" (our euphemism for projected deficits) of $5.7 million in 1975/76 and $9.6 million in 1976/77, increasing to $22.8 million for the year 1979/80. This was on a base operating budget projected to be $76.8 million in 1976/77 and excluding the so-called formula schools, namely, business and medicine. (The actual forecast prepared at that time, and the economic assumptions underlying it, are presented in chapter 4, table 4.3, as part of our discussion of budget projection models.) The gaps now shown for the years 1976/77 and 1977/78 were more than twice those projected in March 1973 (see table 2.2) and they accelerated sharply in 1979 and 1980. There was no doubt now that we had been overtaken by events and that decisive action was needed.

The transition-to-equilibrium model. Action on the modeling front was initiated by DSPH during the middle two weeks of September while WFM was teaching in England. Recognizing that the LRFE model, by itself, was not tightly linked to the LRFF and that this would severely limit its usefulness in the current crisis, he proceeded to combine the two into a new model for calculating the path of transition to equilibrium. We shall call this model TRANS I to distinguish it from a major refinement that came a year later.

The TRANS I model was quickly embraced by WFM on his return, and shortly thereafter presented to and accepted by the Budget Group. It had a significant influence on the design and promulgation of a new program of budget adjustments, which came to be called the Budget Equilibrium Program (BEP).

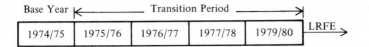

Given :

Actual base-year values for the budget variables *B*, *I*, and *E*.

Estimated growth rates of expenditures and income for the transition period (1974/75 to 1979/80) from the LRFF.

Estimates of endowment total return and new gifts projections from the LRFF.

A funded program improvement policy (*f*).

A 1979/80 tuition rate.

Estimates of long-run factors (*r*, *i*, etc.).

Compute :

Operating budget income and expenditures for 1975/76 to 1979/80.

Schedule of needed budget reductions.

Schedule of endowment payouts.

Equilibrium growth rate of tuition such that : (i) budget is in *balance* in 1979/80; (ii) budget is in *stationary equilibrium* (long-run expected growth rates of budget, operating income, and endowment payout are all equal; (iii) budget reductions follow *specified timing* (e.g., 20% of total reduction in 1975/76, 65% in 1976/77, 15% in 1977/78, and none thereafter).

Figure 2.5. Transition to long-run financial equilibrium model (as presented in October 1974)

The idea behind TRANS is rather simple. It is outlined in figure 2.5, which is an exhibit used by DSPH in one of his early presentations. Starting in the base year (in this case the 1974/75 operating budget, which had taken effect on September 1) the model computes the series of income-and-expense projections and needed budget reductions that would lead to a balanced budget and stationary equilibrium at the end of a five-year transition period. Here, the growth-rate projections during the transition period were from the latest LRFF, while those for the post-transition or LRFE period were based on the equilibrium calculations described earlier. Those calculations, in turn, were based on the kind of long-run growth-rate estimate that came out of the "Economics of Endowed Universities" paper, as illustrated in table 2.3. The 1979/80 tuition rate was set by judgment; as we shall see, it assumed an important and to some extent a misunderstood role. Given these inputs, together with a specification

Table 2.5.   Income, Expenditures, and Deficit During Stanford University Budget Balancing Program, 1974/75–1979/80, Based on Most Likely Assumptions, as Presented in October 1974 ($000)

	1974/75	1975/76	1976/77	1977/78	1978/79	1979/80
Endowment	110,500	116,221	121,610	129,396	140,039	151,902
Payout rate	0.074	0.068	0.062	0.056	0.050	0.046
Operating income	55,755	60,290	65,422	71,417	76,434	82,129
Endowment payout	8,200	7,903	7,540	7,246	7,002	6,987
TOTAL INCOME	63,955	68,193	72,962	78,663	83,436	89,116
Maintenance budget[a]		71,889	76,844	76,725	81,899	88,692
Net new expenditures[b]		652	705	709	759	827
(Less reductions)		(2,042)	(6,638)	(1,532)	(0)	(0)
TOTAL BASE EXPENDITURES	65,235	70,499	70.911	75,902	82,658	89,519
Phase-out expenditures[c]	....	1,021	3,829	2,630	1,047	153
Deficit	1,280	3,327	1,778	(131)	269	153[d]

TOTAL SIX-YEAR DEFICIT = 6,676[e]

[a] From base long-range forecast.
[b] One percent of previous year's base expenditures.
[c] Calculated at 50% in first year, 25% in second year, and 10% in third year.
[d] Excludes $403 thousand of statistical discrepancy.
[e] Total deficit = $5,942 thousand when discounted at 10 percent.

Table 2.6.   Reconciliation of Announced Budget Balancing Target to the Long-Range Forecast ($000)

Long-range forecast gap in 1979/80			$22,823
Less announced budget balancing target		$(10,212)	
Less additional savings due to making budget cuts in the first three years		$(1,891)	
Less differences in assumed net new expenditures			
Per transition calculation	$3,653		
Per long-range forecast	$(13,855)	$(10,202)	
Less difference in 1979/80 tuition income			
Per long-range forecast	$55,038		
Per transition calculation	$(57,475)	$(2,437)	
Less difference in 1979/80 endowment payout			
Per long-range forecast	$9,303		
Per transition calculation	$(7,384)	$1,919	
TOTAL			$22,823

by the user as to the timing of any needed budget reductions (our thinking was that 20 percent of the gap should be closed the first year, 65 percent in the second, and 15 percent in the third), TRANS I solved a set of some twenty simultaneous linear equations to produce its outputs. (The model is described fully in chapter 6.) All data were already in hand; DSPH wrote the program in APL and debugged it in a day or two. The model cost pennies to run.

Some results from the TRANS model, obtained during October of 1974, are presented in tables 2.5 and 2.6 and figure 2.6. The salient features of table 2.5 are: (a) the endowment payout rate drops from the 7.4 percent to which

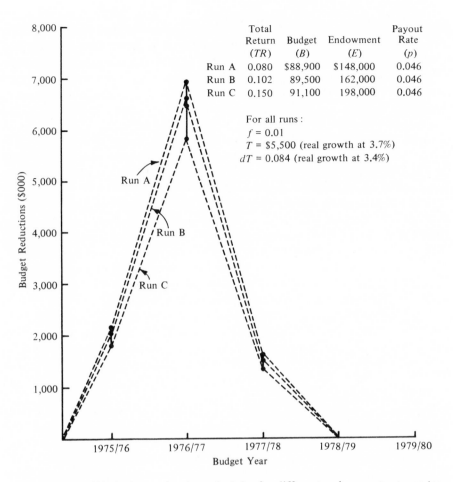

Figure 2.6. Feasible budget reduction schedules for different endowment returns (as presented in October 1974)

it had risen over the summer (the stock market had continued to decline) to a target equilibrium value of 4.6 percent in 1979/80; (b) operating income in 1979/80 is based on an estimated annual tuition rate of $5,500, up from $3,375 in 1974/75 (the increase represents a compounded annual growth rate of 10.3 percent in nominal value and 3.7 percent in real value, i.e., allowing for inflation); (c) funded improvement, f, is assumed to be 1 percent each year, down from 2.7 percent in the LRFF; (d) budget reductions totaling some $10.2 million are called for by the model; (e) deficits totaling some $6.7 million are predicted during the course of the transition period. The deficits, like the phaseout expenditures later added to the model, were assumed to be withdrawn from the endowment, thus reducing the payout predicted to be available in later years. At this point, as the last footnote in table 2.5 indicates, we still had a $403-thousand discrepancy between the deficits calculated by TRANS and those from the LRFF. This was small in relation to the total projected deficit and did not affect the size of the gap materially. The discrepancy was rectified within a few weeks but we have retained it in table 2.5 to emphasize that the model was still work in progress and that we made no bones about its short-comings. This explanation was accepted by our colleagues and by the Board of Trustees.

The fact that the model projected a total 1979/80 gap of $10.2 million in contrast to the LRFF's $22.8 million was, as can be imagined, of considerable interest. Table 2.6 reproduces the reconciliation between the two that was used by the Budget Group, the faculty-staff Budget Priorities Commission (to be discussed later), and the Ad Hoc Budget Committee of the Board of Trustees in their initial evaluation of our proposal for a BEP target of $10.2 million. Here, in outline, are the principal points of the reconciliation: (a) making cuts quickly rather than (as in BAP) spreading them evenly over five years saved $1.89 million of budget base due to reduced deficits being drawn from capital balances; (b) dropping funded improvement from 2.7 percent to 1.0 percent saved another $10.2 million; (c) raising real tuition growth from about 2 percent to 3.7 percent added $2.4 million; (d) reducing the projected endowment payout rate in 1979/80 from about 5.6 percent, as targeted in the LRFF, to 4.6 percent, as needed for stationary equilibrium with 1.0 percent funded improvement, offset the above by $1.9 million. Note that the effects of all these items except (a) could have been computed fairly easily within the context of the LRFF, without TRANS. However, TRANS did serve to pull everything together into a single, internally consistent package.

Figure 2.6 shows an edited version of one of the charts we used in describing the proposed BEP program of $10.2 million to the Ad Hoc Committee and other interested groups. The point illustrated is that a wide swing in the assumed value of investment total return, *TR*, would not have a large effect upon the size of the gap. For instance, if total return were to run at a compounded rate of 15 percent per annum for five straight years, the gap would then have been reduced only to about $8.9 million. Five years of total return at 8 percent would increase the gap to about $10.7 million. (For the post-transition year, that is, the one beyond 1979/80, total return in all these runs was held at its assigned long-run value of 10.5 percent.)

Sensitivity analysis is a method for evaluating the effects of the assumptions that have been fed into a model. Some twenty-six sensitivity analysis runs were made with TRANS I during October of 1974. In addition to varying total return, we explored the effects of changing the policies for tuition growth and funded improvement, *f*, and of a few additional variations in other assumptions. Calculated gaps ranging from a low of $5.4 million to a high of $17.4 million were observed. All of these were presented to the Budget Group. In the end we settled on a particular run, the one shown in table 2.4, as the "official" model result—i.e., as the basis for action. Presentations made to the faculty-staff Budget Priorities Commission and the Ad Hoc Budget Committee included nine variations of model assumptions, the three in figure 2.6 plus two similar charts with *f* = 0 and *f* = 0.02.

Evaluation of the model's initial impact. What effect did the TRANS I model really have on decision making during the critical period in October 1974 when Stanford committed itself to BEP? There is no doubt that the figure of $10.2 million chosen as the BEP target came straight out of the model. We must probe deeper, however, in order to isolate the nature of the factors, whether related to the model or not, that molded the decision.

On October 8, 1974, President Lyman informed the Stanford Board of Trustees of the "overall situation" and presented "a broad sketch of a plan for the necessary corrective action."[14] A series of meetings and consultations followed.* The decision to adopt a BEP target of $10.2 million was announced on November 12, 1974. All of these meetings involved use of the model results described in the previous section, though efforts were made to downplay the model as such and avoid a backlash against the idea of a "mindless computer" deciding Stanford's fate.

An on-campus Budget Priorities Commission had been created by President Lyman and Provost Miller on October 3, 1974. It was chaired by Leon E. Seltzer, LLB, director of the Stanford University Press, and consisted of selected faculty, staff, and students. The idea of the commission was decided upon before the model became a major issue. One of the commission's first actions, however, was to take a look at LRFE, TRANS, and the proposed $10.2-million BEP target. Its general evaluation was that the forecasts and analyses were basically reasonable as far as they could tell, and in particular that TRANS was just what it was intended to be, namely, an aid to understanding the university's financial difficulties and not the cause of them or the administration's perceptions of them. Some commission members expressed concern about the plan to reduce the endowment payout rate but in the end that, too, was accepted.

The model had passed its first important test: its logic had been judged simple and sensible and its results not too surprising. We believe that a sophisticated but arcane model probably would have failed at this stage, if indeed it could have been seriously considered by the commission in the first place.

It can be plausibly argued that the model's greatest impact was as an organizational catalyst. Two years after the event WFM argued that although the reasons why BAP and the Campaign for Stanford were not sufficient to restore Stanford's financial health were fairly clear before the development of the model, it was not at all clear what else should be done.

> The model permitted a sufficiently integrated look at our financial planning parameters, including those representing long-run trends, to allow a consensus to emerge on $10 million rather than $20 million or more. Nevertheless, sensitivity analyses run with different assumptions about endowment total return showed conclusively that no credible assumption about stock-market "bounce-back" would make our financial problems disappear. The power of the equilibrium concept was that it provided a

*These included meetings of: the Budget Group (10/7, 10/28); the Ad Hoc Budget Committee of the Board (11/4); the on-campus Budget Priorities Commission (11/5); the full board (11/12); the deans' retreat (11/16); and the Faculty Senate (11/21). There were also a number of convocations and informal meetings with students and university staff.

rational basis for obtaining the support of people with widely varying views about the seriousness of the situation.[15]

A basis for support was certainly needed. There was also a strong need for a specific BEP target. The model provided one, with an explanation of why it was being recommended. It is probable, also, that key decision makers felt that $10.2 million of budget adjustments could be put in place without undue harm to academic programs, whereas a significantly larger figure would be likely to lead to trouble. A contrary judgment, though it would have had nothing to do with the model itself, might well have elicited a powerful challenge to the model's assumptions and results. In any case, it was found possible to defer to the model as an embodiment of logic and veracity.

If the model had been blamed for the dislocations caused by BEP, our credibility—not to mention BEP's and the model's—would have been seriously undermined. Fortunately, this did not occur. We and our colleagues did our best to forestall it by stressing the underlying causes of Stanford's financial distress in our written and oral communications, and by downplaying the role of the model in our public statements. However, the concept of long-run financial equilibrium was definitely not downplayed, and it continued to receive central billing throughout the BEP period. For instance, our initial article on BEP, headlined "Why Stanford Seeks Long-Run Financial Equilibrium by 1979–80," was published in *Campus Report*, a weekly newssheet distributed free to all staff and faculty; the article treated the LRFE concept at length and summarized the calculations from TRANS—in some detail, although the model itself was not mentioned directly.[16]

It appears in retrospect that the TRANS model, though downplayed publicly, was instrumental in familiarizing both our colleagues and the Stanford community with the LRFE concept. This was to be expected because, after TRANS, equilibrium became an operational concept with tight links to the LRFF whereas earlier it had been an interesting but abstract notion of rather limited use.

Further evidence of the difference made by TRANS is provided by comparison between the charge to the Commission on Budget Priorities, drafted in September before TRANS was unveiled, and the budget protocol sent to deans and administrative department heads on October 21. The commission's principal functions were "to review critically the premises behind the major elements of income and expense in the Operating Budget estimates for 1975–76 and beyond . . . to advise on the causes and severity of present and prospective budget difficulties. . . . [and to] examine and advise on priorities and tradeoffs among primary institutional variables and relationships which extend beyond the general supervision of any single dean or other office of administration."[17] Nothing was said about long-run financial equilibrium or models of any kind.

In contrast, the budget protocol placed long-run financial equilibrium in the the spotlight; it even mentioned "Professor Massy's research" and offered to provide more information about it on request. The LRFF was described as "very much a document perpetually in process" and the concept of long-run financial equilibrium was defined as "a state where reasonable and necessary increases in the cost of *maintaining* the university from year to year are matched by income increases that are recurring and reasonably dependable." The relationship between equilibrium and reallocation of funds was stated with unmistakable clarity: new activities would have to be financed largely by cuts in old ones. For equilibrium to be achieved, the $10-million gap had to be closed. Under conditions of equilibrium, the amount that could be provided for "consolidations and improvements" (i.e., the "new activities" referred to above) amounted to, at most, some 1.0 percent of the operating budget. For the last two years, such consolidations and improvements had been funded at nearly three times this rate.

The protocol also addressed itself to the problem of constructing a schedule. The price of delay, as it pointed out, was high not only in economic terms but in terms of diminishing institutional quality and vitality. The following scenario was proposed:

> *1975/76.* Make the largest gap-closing steps possible in the time allowed; tie many of these to actions planned for the two following years.
>
> *1976/77.* Come close to the full target by making the major effort in this year.
>
> *1977/78.* Reconfirm the overall target, inventory the steps taken, and then make final cuts and adjustments in this year.
>
> (In talking about years, reference is to the year in which actions take effect. For example, 1975/76 will embody actions taken in the next few months, 1976/77 will reflect actions taken prior to or during the autumn of 1975, etc.)[18]

The proportion of the gap to be closed in each year was envisaged as 25 percent in 1975/76, 60 percent in 1976/77, and 15 percent in 1977/78.

To achieve equilibrium, the protocol concluded, three measures were necessary. First, all steps taken to achieve equilibrium would, by definition, be gap-closing alternatives. Second, targets would be set each year for holdbacks of expenditure, a technique already used to some effect in 1973/74. Third, since the first two measures were deemed insufficient, the authors of the protocol were prepared to recommend a deficit budget to the trustees, provided that such a course was "integral to a plan for restoring equilibrium."[21] Clearly, the substance of the protocol and the language used to explicate it followed very closely the conceptual structure of LRFE as well as the numerical results from TRANS.

As a postscript, it is worth noting that the terms "Budget Equilibrium Program" and "BEP" did not come into public use until the autumn of 1975, a year after the program was instituted. Though "equilibrium" was mentioned often, the *Operating Budget Guidelines: 1975–76*, published in March 1974, avoided any catchphrase for "the three-year program of transition to equilibrium." By the following year, however, the idea of seeking equilibrium had caught on across the university to the point at which "Budget Equilibrium Program" was used freely in the *Guidelines*.

In summary, our thesis is that:

1. TRANS confirmed the existence of a real budget problem, in part by demonstrating through sensitivity analysis that the problem would not go away even if a few good things happened;

2. TRANS facilitated the choice of a numerical BEP target by providing an acceptable conceptual structure and an algorithm for computing it;

3. TRANS provided a basis for explaining and rationalizing the choice to various constituencies, even though conscious efforts were made to avoid any kind of "model mystique";

4. TRANS made the concept of long-run financial equilibrium, and the model underlying it, salient for senior officers of the university and, through them, for the broad set of advisory groups and constituencies.

As for the LRFE, it served partly to buttress explanations of the Budget Equilibrium Program but also to highlight the importance of various rates, including the endowment payout rate, and the tradeoffs between them, particularly the one between growth in funded improvement, f, and growth in tuition, dT.

At this point we cannot resist relating an anecdote. Each year in December the university officers present their recommendation for the next year's tuition rate to the Board of Trustees. It is common for student members of the board's committees to argue for an increase lower than the one proposed. In December 1974 the student argument took a significant new twist. A spokesperson told the board that "tuition growth at 3.7 percent real and funded improvement of 1.0 percent is in the wrong place on the f–dT tradeoff line," and that "on balance, a lower level of funded improvement should be set so as to be able to lower the rate of growth of tuition." The tradeoff was recognized, and our day was made! The students' day was made too, but the results did not appear until 1976 when the model assumptions for tuition and funded improvement were indeed reduced as they had suggested. The circumstances of that change will be discussed later.

The middle years of BEP. Let us now trace the life cycle of BEP from the time when it became firmly established, in the autumn of 1974, to a point just before it was officially concluded (so far as forward planning was concerned) with the submission, in March 1977, of the 1977–78 recommended budget guidelines to the Board of Trustees. Naturally we shall focus on the evolving role of models in this cycle.

The history of BEP's achievements (and also those of its predecessor, BAP) is summarized in figure 2.7, which shows annual income and expenditures for the operating budget (excluding the formula schools) in constant dollars. The dashed line traces the pattern of expenditures; the solid one refers to income. For each, two pieces of information are given for a given year:

1. The increase that would have been expected, had no changes been made in program levels or policies, is shown by the slope of the line from one year to the next. This represents the effects of such factors as inflation or

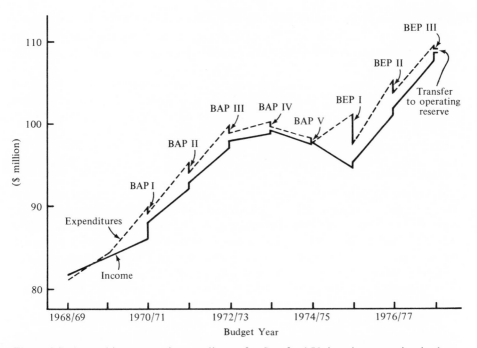

Figure 2.7. Annual income and expenditures for Stanford University operating budget as affected by Budget Adjustment Program (BAP) and Budget Equilibrium Program (BEP), 1968/69–1977/78 (constant dollars, 1977/78 = 100, Consumer Price Index used as deflator)

policies for tuition or salary growth—assuming no change in student, faculty, or staff FTEs, etc.
2. The special adjustments to the income-and-expense bases, due to BAP and BEP, are shown by the vertical line segments at each year. These were accomplished by reducing the number of faculty and staff, finding new sources of income, etc.

The distances between the ends of the vertical line segments for income and expense represent the gap or the deficit for that year, depending on whether one is measuring before or after the special adjustments. For example, the budget was virtually balanced at the end of BAP V (1974/75), but inflation and the drop in the stock market opened up a gap of $101.0 − 94.5 = $6.5 million in 1977/78 dollars the following year. Expenditure reductions totaling $3.5 million and income improvements of $800 thousand closed part of the gap, leaving a deficit of $2.2 million (again in 1977/78 dollars).

The ten-year pattern of growth, gaps, and deficits is shown clearly by figure 2.2. Positive real growth (relative to the consumer price index) persisted through the first four years of BAP. Neither income nor expense could gain in real terms during the very high inflation of the next two years (1974/75 and 1975/76), and of course the gap in 1975/76 was what triggered BEP. Real growth resumed, even while BEP was in progress, as the general inflation rate subsided in 1976/77 and 1977/78. This is somewhat deceptive however, since energy prices were still moving ahead rapidly relative to the CPI during these years and some salary catchup was also undertaken in certain competitive personnel classifications. BEP was completed successfully with the posting of a small surplus (labeled as a "transfer to operating reserve") in 1977/78. After that we hoped that the income-and-expense slopes would coincide, thus indicating that we were in financial equilibrium.

Our ideas and methods evolved steadily during the BEP period. By the autumn of 1975, as we told the Board of Trustees on October 14, we had refined the concept of equilibrium to incorporate the effects of uncertainty. We admitted to the board that future adjustments (i.e., adjustments beyond BEP) might be brought about by unforeseen events. Such events, however, were as likely to be pleasant as unpleasant, and the size of the adjustments was expected to be modest; the concept of equilibrium implied as much. These ideas had also been implicit in our earlier work—for instance, the idea of LRFE under uncertainty was mentioned in the proposal to Lilly—but we had neglected to stress them publicly the previous year and this had caused some questions to be raised.

Another change had to do with the timing of the budget adjustments in BEP. The original assumption had been that 20 percent of the gap should be closed the first year, 65 percent the second year, and 15 percent the third year. By the end of October 1974 Bacchetti was shooting for 25 percent the first year and 60 percent the second year. By October 1975 we knew we had achieved about 40 percent the first year and had decided to shoot for another 45 percent in the second. (The final, three-year tally was 40, 40, 20.) The reason for these changes was our growing awareness that more could be accomplished early, and a conviction that the job should be gotten over with as quickly as possible. The only effect on the model was that its input parameters were adjusted, but the new climate of change, of optimism even, did contribute to the unfreezing of certain numerical targets.

Not only the BEP targets but many other aspects of the model were changed during the two-and-a-half years we are discussing. TRANS II had been developed and debugged during the spring and summer of 1975; it was brought into use in September. Among other advantages, this version was much easier to use, had better report formats, and fitted more closely to the LRFF data categories. Thus it allowed for income improvements as well as budget reductions (TRANS I had been limited to closing the gap by reducing expenditure, even though we knew there would be some improvement in income), and relaxed the TRANS I requirement that the equilibrium achieved at the end of the transition period be a stationary one. In addition, TRANS II incorporated an option for *Monte Carlo simulation* of the transition to equilibrium.

Two points are particularly worth mentioning in connection with the switchover from TRANS I to TRANS II. First, the debugging effort had lagged and we found ourselves in the same position as a year earlier, when

Table 2.7.   Chronology of Transition Model Calculations (Cumulative Gap, 1975/76–1977/78)

Date of Run	Cumulative Gap ($000)	Comments
9/30/74	$10,200	Base case.
11/21/74	$10,600	Cleaned up "statistical discrepancy"; revised phaseout costs.
12/4/74	$12,200	Revised tuition income and indirect cost recovery forecasts; accelerated phasedown of endowment payout rate.
2/7/75	$11,400	Acceleration of gap closing to reflect $4.0 million accomplished in year 1 and $4.0 million target for year 2; some additional data changes.
2/11/75	$10,400	Revised forecast of indirect cost recovery.
3/28/75	$11,900	Revised budget base to conform to final 1975/76 guidelines recommendation; new cost-rise estimates for subsequent years.
10/14/75	$10,200	Revised data, including successful investment results for previous 12 months; TRANS II model.
10/12/76	$9,849	Revised data, including achieved BEP II gap closing of $4.1 million.
3/7/77	$10,319	Final statement of the gap, which was officially announced as closed.

we were striving to gain intellectual control of a model (then TRANS I) at the same time as we were trying to develop policy inferences from it. This is a dangerous situation, and we were lucky both times that nothing really significant went wrong and escaped our attention. Fortunately, the enhancements (i.e., the income improvements, budget reductions, etc.) in the deterministic version of TRANS II were not so great as to produce materially different results than we had been obtaining from TRANS I. Second, we must admit that the effort to start dealing systematically with uncertainty failed. We made a few tentative Monte Carlo runs, from which we concluded that the 90 percent confidence interval for the gap was somewhere around $5 million to $15 million. These figures dismayed our colleagues, who felt (rightly, we're sure) that any such "revelation" would take the heart out of the budget equilibrium program. Moreover, we were not sure either of our data or of the algorithms used in the model to process them. All things considered, it seemed reasonable to wait until BEP was completed and our models were under better control. We did continue to talk about uncertainty, however, even though we could not yet evaluate it quantitatively.

The uncertainty inherent in our estimate of the gap is indicated by the way it varied over time, as input parameters and data were changed. Table 2.7 presents a chronology. These figures are not the product of sensitivity analyses. Each one was our most likely estimate of the gap at the time it was made and was so represented to one or more decision or advisory groups. There are many reasons why the figures changed. For instance, the jump from $10.6 million to $12.2 million during the two weeks between November 21 and December 4, 1974, was caused by: (a) a reestimate of summer session enrollments, the average number of units carried by graduate students, and the returning enrollment ratios for undergraduates; (b) a reestimate, based on new projections of research volume and overhead rate, of indirect cost recovery on contracts and grants; (c) a change in the assumption, used in the model, about the speed with which the endowment payout rate was to be phased down. The first two items came up in the normal course of the forecast and budget development cycle (our estimates of these quantities are updated each year). The third one represented a change in policy dictated, as it happened, by a need to conserve certain restricted endowment funds, which could not form part of the operating budget. Dropping the payout rate has a dollar-for-dollar effect on the operating-budget deficit, and TRANS withdraws deficits from the endowment. Hence this last change did not have much effect on the gap. It did improve the model, however, because it eliminated what otherwise would have been an embarrassing surplus in year 2 of BEP, a surplus that was then being projected as a result of closing the gap at a faster-than-anticipated pace.

Another sharp increment, from $10.4 million on February 11, 1975, to $11.9 million on March 28, 1975, was due largely to adverse information on rising costs for oil, natural gas, and electricity. The increase of the estimated gap by $1 million over three days in February 1975 is also noteworthy. It illustrates the tribulations of model builders and our colleagues' trust and patience (or their desperation and lack of alternatives). The change came about because of an error in the projection of indirect cost recovery. The error was caused by a combination of WFM's effort as vice-provost for research to introduce a new projection submodel for indirect costs (again, at the last minute) and some missed communication about definitions between the Academic Planning Office (APO) and the Controller's Office. The original figure—that is, the lower one—had been discussed by the Budget Group on February 4. The fact that it was too low was discovered and corrected on the eleventh, when we had to improvise our discussion of the new figure with the Ad Hoc Budget Committee. We cite this case to illustrate the applicability of Murphy's Law, "Everything that can go wrong will go wrong," to modeling. We were fortunate: our credibility did not suffer much. But it easily could have if the circumstances had been different. Interestingly enough, another million-dollar error in the projection of indirect cost recovery—an error in the same direction—was made, despite all precautions, in October 1976. It was discovered right after a presentation to the Ad Hoc Budget Committee. WFM was acting vice-president and provost at the time, and so was able to experience anguish both as a modeler and as senior budget officer.

Sensitivity analyses based on the model were performed at a number of stages. We have already described those of October 1974, soon after BEP began. In October 1975 we presented the Board of Trustees with runs having gaps that ranged from $8.7 million to $11.9 million, compared to a most likely value of $10.2 million. In October 1976 the alternatives presented ranged upward to $14.9 million from the most likely value of $9.8 million. The 1976 upper limit of nearly $15 million reflected growing concerns about two policy assumptions upon which previous transition-to-equilibrium calculations had been based: (a) that the growth rate of tuition would remain indefinitely at around 4 percent over the consumer price index; (b) that real salary growth would range from zero to one-half of one percent until 1980, when it would revert to the national wage trend of about two percent. The estimated $15-million gap was based on real tuition growth of only 2 percent per year and growth per year in real salaries and wages of 1.5 percent. We shall return to this matter presently, in the context of the final estimate and closing of the gap. First, however, let us turn to the actions of the Commission on Budget Priorities during 1975 and 1976.

We have already described how the Commission reacted to the model and the BEP target during the autumn of 1974. During the intervening period it had been quite active in reviewing proposed strategies for meeting the target and in evaluating and giving advice with respect to decisions on specific budget items. In February 1975 six task forces had been created to help the Commission with its work. One of these was Task Force V, charged with "monitoring the economics of the transition from fiscal crisis to budgetary equilibrium." The other task forces were assigned to study: "the size and function of the university administration and other support services" (Task Force I); "student support services and activities" (Task Force II); "academic calendar and utilization of academic plant" (Task Force III); "professorial rank and faculty development" (Task Force IV); "professional schools and the operations budget" (Task Force VI). All the task forces with the exception of Task Force V wrote detailed reports that were published in *Campus Report*. Task Force V, the one charged with reviewing our models and assumptions, was chaired by Professor David Starrett of the Department of Economics, and included mostly faculty with experience in management science, operations research, and economics.*

The main point of the president's charge to this "task force on models and assumptions," as we shall call it, was that the university's progress toward financial equilibrium should be evaluated periodically by economic experts. As conditions changed, assumptions that affected the definition of equilibrium —"for example, assumptions about endowment return, utilization, and reinvestment relationships"—would have to be reexamined and updated, as would forecasts of crucial economic parameters. The task force was asked to function as a "critical review panel" that would oversee and, if necessary, correct the work of the university's financial officers.[19]

The task force on models and assumptions met about six times between March and October 1975. These meetings were conducted as seminars and included wide-ranging and spirited discussions of issues relating to modeling in general, the LRFE and TRANS models, their underlying economic and financial assumptions and parameters, and the methods used to obtain them. While the task force never issued a formal report, it is our impression that its

---

*The members, with their departmental affiliations, were Professors David A. Starrett as chairman (economics), Victor R. Fuchs (economics), Gerald J. Lieberman (operations research), William D. Nix (materials science), Alexander A. Robichek (business), and Mr. David G. Clark, a graduate student (education). WFM, DSPH, and Mr. Larry S. Owen of the M & FP Office were included as "administrative consultants and staff support."

members were satisfied with and basically supportive of our work and its fundamental conclusions. Though both we and they were quick to agree on the models' limitations, the task force seemed to accept the fact that the models were doing their job better than any available alternative. If this had not been the conclusion, we are convinced that an appropriate communication would have gone forward to the Budget Priorities Commission, the president, and the provost.

Two themes that colored the interaction between the two of us and Task Force V are particularly worthy of note. One was the matter of incorporating uncertainty in TRANS II. We said earlier that we were not sure of our data or algorithms. Our uncertainty stemmed in part from discussions with the task force during which the stochastic part of TRANS II got a rather cool reception and there was a general skepticism about how much we knew about the parameter values. We have little doubt that the task force was right in its criticism. Though we probably would have backed off the stochastic version of TRANS II sooner or later in any case, the discussion with the task force made that decision easy and avoided what might have been an unfortunate chain of events.

A second theme was the task force's (and especially its chairman's) interest in developing a model formulation that could take account of market phenomena. "What about the *demand functions* for student enrollments and research, and the *supply functions* for faculty and staff?" we were asked. We had come at the question of planning models from the point of view of management science; that is, we had tried to represent a decision problem as it would be seen by the responsible executives. As a highly selective educational institution of great stature, Stanford was not experiencing difficulty in attracting students or faculty members. While demand-and-supply considerations were implicit in our own and our colleagues' thinking, the economist members of the task force, especially, would have preferred to see them represented explicitly in the model. Also, there was concern about the relatively high growth rate for tuition and low growth rate for faculty salaries. The issue was one of what assumptions to use (which of course was also within the task force's purview) rather than of model formulation per se, though a richer model, with demand-and-supply equations, would have invited greater attention to these important subjects.

Our response to the task force's concern about market representations was to design a model that did include demand-and-supply functions, whose parameters would be estimated as best we could in the absence of meaningful data. The formulation was developed in June 1975 and transmitted to the task force in the form of a working paper during the summer.[20] We called this a "decision calculus model" because it resembled the class of marketing models of that name developed by John D. C. Little (1970). Despite our attempts at simplification, the decision calculus model we sent to the task force was formidably complex and would have required a great many interrelated judgments about parameters. It never was discussed seriously, nor was it programmed. We did pursue the development of a condensed version, some two years later, purely as as matter of personal research. The result is presented in chapter 9.

The basic role of the task force on models and assumptions was to provide assurance to the Budget Priorities Commission, and through them to the rest of the campus community, that the model(s) underlying BEP were sound— that policy was not being overprogrammed, so to speak. The role was an important one and it was performed successfully. The task force was also instrumental in avoiding at least one significant error, viz., use of the stochastic version of TRANS. It also stimulated our thinking in ways that were both enjoyable and useful.

The endgame, or hitting a moving target. BEP was concluded, for practical purposes, with the submission of the *Operating Budget Guidelines: 1977–78* to the Board of Trustees on March 7–8, 1977. The box score of adjustments year by year is presented in table 2.8. Adjustments totaled $10.3 million, of which $6.5 million was expenditure reduction and $2.9 million income improvement. In other words, BEP was not a game. Reductions in budget base expenditure included the elimination of 30 faculty and 147 staff positions, the downgrading of many others, and significant curtailment of supplies and expense authorizations. The income improvements included differential tuition rates for certain schools, advanced graduate registration fees (at one-half the regular tuition rate), and reaching agreements with deans to commit more restricted funds (e.g., from expendable gift receipts) to support the operating budget. Thus our efforts as "score keepers" had identified some $9.5 million in actual economies, of which all but $62,000 was placed in the 1977/78 budget.

But what about the $850 thousand labeled in table 2.8 and the *Operating Budget Guidelines: 1977–78* as "Long-run limits on growth"? This figure resulted from two changes in the policy assumptions incorporated in the TRANS model. As early as March 1976, when the 1976/77 budget was recommended to the board, these had been cast as the ultimate gap-closers. They were described on that occasion as involving "changes in two assumptions on which the equilibrium model and resulting gap were predicated." For this

Table 2.8. Summary of Budget Equilibrium Results ($000)

Year	Expenditure Reduction	Income Improvement	Total
BEP I (1975/76)	$3,310	$765	$4,075
BEP II (1976/77)	2,655	725	3,379
BEP III (1977/78)	555	1,460	2,015
TOTAL	$6,519	$2,949	$9,469
"Long-run limits on growth"			850
GRAND TOTAL			$10,319

reason their effects were seen as occurring in the long term—but as no less important for that. The two major effects were described as (a) reducing the funded improvement factor; (b) reducing the long-run expectation regarding the incremental nature of restricted endowment gifts.[21]

The funded improvement factor, described earlier in connection with the long-run financial equilibrium model, represents the amount of net new program growth that would be targeted from general funds each year. The long-run expectation regarding restricted gifts to the endowment refers to the proportion of new endowed chairs that would represent new additions to the faculty. Again the issue is one of program growth: should a gift for a new chair in (e.g.) chemistry be used to add to the size of the chemistry faculty or to pay the salary of an existing professor, thus releasing general funds for use elsewhere? In the end, we invoked both (a) and (b) to the tune of $850 thousand, as calculated by TRANS II.

We have emphasized this point because there were two reasons why these adjustments differed so much from the rest of the BEP economy measures: they were in the nature of assumptions about future decisions rather than commitments incorporated in the budget process; and it was not clear even at this writing that they could actually be implemented. With regard to the latter, the 1978/79 budget included funded improvement at 1.4 percent rather than 0.3 to 0.5 percent, and we had yet to learn how to exercise adequate control over the allocation of new gifts to endowment. On the other hand, the same budget was in surplus by $236 thousand and a surplus of $161 thousand was projected for 1978/79.

We find it interesting not only that the endgame here involved some ex post changes of assumption but that it was desirable—even necessary—to conclude BEP in the same way it had begun, namely, with the TRANS model. As table 2.8 shows, additional reductions in expense had become more and more difficult. We had also exhausted the currently available options for income improvement. It could be that in very private counsels (so private that neither of us was admitted to them) it was decided that, given the uncertainty surrounding the estimate of the income-expenditure gap anyhow, it would not be prudent to take the next, very difficult steps in expenditure reduction, which would probably have meant cutting out a major academic program or department. If such a thing had been done and Stanford's luck had turned out good enough to make the cut unnecessary, the academic program would have been significantly and needlessly damaged. On the other hand, if Stanford's luck had turned out to be bad or if the two proposed policy changes had not been implementable, it would still have been possible to take more drastic measures. This would not have been an irrational position, if indeed anyone had been articulating it.

Whatever the forces that inspired the final $850 thousand, the fact remains that the changes in policy assumption were carefully run through the model and duly vetted as "gap closers." There could be no better evidence of how important it had become to achieve the BEP target, which had become etched on people's minds as ranging from \$10.2 to \$10.5 million. The target actually achieved was \$10.3 million, which clearly symbolized success.

The Introduction of the TRADES Model

Our descriptions of the objectives of BEP underwent a subtle shift from 1974 to 1977, from "achieving" long-run financial equilibrium to "bringing it within reach." There were two reasons for this. First, the more we came to understand about the degree of uncertainty in forecast and equilibrium calculations, the more we realized that we could not guarantee LRFE even with a successful BEP. In addition, we had begun to recognize that we would have some significant unfinished business with respect to policy assumptions and underlying economic trends even after the \$10.2-million BEP target had been achieved. We did feel strongly, however, that BEP would indeed bring equilibrium within reach without another budget adjustment crisis—unless, of course, some exogenous disaster—changes in the tax laws covering charitable giving, for example, or in the government rules about indirect cost recovery on contracts and grants—were to be visited upon us.

Two crucial events in the history of modeling at Stanford were taking place as BEP drew to a close. First, our ideas about tuition and salary growth policies were changing; and second, a new technology (i.e., a model and its infrastructure of data) was being evolved to cope with these new problems. Let us begin with the new technology.

The idea of finding preferred tradeoffs among Stanford's primary planning variables had been a key element in our research ever since our proposal to the Lilly Endowment in 1973. How to define the university's primary planning variables, the importance of tradeoffs between them, and some general principles as to how decision models might aid in the optimization of preferences had been discussed in a seminar with the Budget Group during 1973 and featured in the deans' retreat of February 1–2, 1974. (This was the same deans' retreat at which, as we described earlier, the concept of LRFE had been introduced.) Beginning in 1974 there had been several modeling efforts aimed at quantifying, and then optimizing, administrators' preference functions with respect to alternative planning scenarios. Put another way, the objective was to find a mathematical function that could be used to rank-order administrators' preferences for alternative scenarios, and then to maximize this function subject to appropriate constraints. (See the general review in appendix 1 and the more detailed account in chapter 9.) The results were interesting, but nothing operationally useful was achieved.

The TRADES model, which grew directly out of this earlier research, concentrated on the constraints in the decision problem; it did not attempt to deal overtly with the user's value function. The idea was to model the constraints in enough detail for the model to be complete on important issues, and then provide the user, operating interactively on the computer, with a set of powerful options for searching the space of feasible decision alternatives. The TRADES model was invented and reduced to practice in the autumn of 1976 by Nathan

Dickmeyer, then a doctoral student in the Stanford School of Education and an administrative intern attached to APO.* TRADES is described in some detail in chapter 9.

Naturally, we invoked the conditions for long-run financial equilibrium as constraints in TRADES. That is, the budget was required to be at least in balance, and the growth rate of income had to be at least as great as that for expense starting in 1978/79, the year after the end of the Budget Equilibrium Program. (The TRANS model made projections as far as 1979/80, but the calculations for the last two years were ignored when superseded by TRADES.) Primary planning variables included (naturally) tuition growth, funded improvement, and faculty and staff salary growth, as well as a dozen or so other aggregative measures that were judged to be of importance (the complete set of primary planning variables is given in table 9.2). The endowment payout rate was treated as a dependent variable in these calculations, but within rather narrow bounds that we thought would be acceptable from the standpoint of investment return (not to mention the Board of Trustees).

In short, the TRADES model was set up to explore alternative forms of equilibrium, as it was projected to become at the close of BEP, beginning with the 1978/79 budget year. However, the conditions for equilibrium built into TRADES were more general than those in TRANS: they allowed the use of more options in meeting the constraints on budget balance and the growth rates of income and expense. The TRADES model was also more disaggregative; it permitted, indeed invited, direct manipulation of the primary planning variables by the user.

Development of the TRADES model led to the idea of trading off one primary planning variable against another. This required a set of estimates for the incremental costs and/or revenues associated with each such variable— a very useful by-product. For instance, a change in either the tuition rate or the number of students would change the financial aid requirement, and a change in faculty size would be expected to change such direct-support items as secretarial capacity, travel funds, etc. We had been dealing with these questions for some years; as a result, certain submodels for variable cost-and-revenue determination had been incorporated in TRANS II. With the impetus of TRADES, however, a task force was set up in the autumn of 1976 to examine the matter and come up with an official set of incremental cost-and-revenue

---

*The general idea for the TRADES model was conceived in late spring 1976 after a pivotal meeting that involved DSPH, Don Wehrung, David Clark, Peter Keen, and one or two others. The meeting had been set up to conduct a post mortem of Wehrung's work on interactive preference optimization (which we shall describe later). The group discussed the problems resulting from the experiment and agreed that the model was too tightly structured and too large a chunk to bite off at one time; initial efforts, we concluded, would be better directed towards interactive exploration of the constraints in terms of the primary planning variables. The notion at that time was that an unstructured search algorithm should be developed as a training aid for later use of the automated optimization model. This work was assigned to Nathan Dickmeyer when he became an APO intern in September. He invented the TRADES model soon thereafter, and together we decided to work with it as a free-standing entity rather than try to incorporate it in the preference optimization model. Dickmeyer is now with the American Council on Education in Washington, D.C.

Table 2.9. Changes in Policy Assumptions for Tuition, Salaries, and Funded Improvement over the BEP Period (Annual Percentage Increases, Net of Inflation Where Applicable)

	Tuition Growth		Salary Growth[a]		Funded Improvement	
	Trans.[b]	LRFE[b]	Trans.[b]	LRFE[b]	Trans.[b]	LRFE[b]
LRFF prior to TRANS model (9/74)[c]	3.0	n.a.	0–1.5	n.a.	3.0	n.a.
TRANS runs and LRFF of October 1974	3.7	3.4	2.0	2.0	1.0	1.0
TRANS runs and LRFF of October 1975	4.1	4.1	0.0	2.0	1.0[d]	1.3[d]
TRANS runs and LRFF of October 1976	4.2	4.2	0.0	2.0	1.0[d]	1.3[d]

[a] Faculty and staff salaries.
[b] "Trans." stands for the period through 1979–80 and "LRFE" stands for the post-Trans. or long-run financial equilibrium period.
[c] This long-range forecast showed deficits growing to $23 million annually in 1979–80. No separate estimates for a long-run equilibrium period were made in this forecast.
[d] These are approximate figures due to the impact of operations and maintenance expense on new buildings. Generally, new O & M is not included in the "Trans." figures (it was added into the calculations separately), but it is included in the "LRFE" figures.

figures. The task force was chaired by DSPH and included key personnel from the Controller's Office, the M & FP Office, and APO. A report was presented to the Budget Staff and Budget Group during the spring of 1977, and the results were agreed to and incorporated into TRADES. (Some of the material in this report is included in chapter 4, where we discuss incremental costs and revenues.)

There is an interesting anecdote about the creation of this task force. We had presented an updated version of the tuition-funded improvement tradeoff line, $f–dT$, to the Board of Trustees in October 1975, in connection with the discussion of the long-range forecast. Shortly after the meeting one of the student members of a Board of Trustees committee came to see WFM to point out what he thought was an error in the slope of the line. He was right! The episode occurred shortly after the second of the two errors, described earlier, in the prediction of indirect costs. These events contributed to the decision to form a high-level task force to "get a firm handle" on the incremental cost-and-revenue data to be used in the TRADES model.

The other factor operating during 1975/76 was our growing unease with the assumptions about growth in tuition and in faculty and staff salaries that had formed the basis for LRFF and TRANS since the beginning of BEP two years earlier. Table 2.9 provides a summary of how these parameters, and also the funded improvement factor, f, that is closely linked to them, had evolved. By October 1976 the LRFF and TRANS runs were based on the assumption that tuition would grow at a real rate of 4.2 percent indefinitely, and that faculty and staff salaries could be held at or near the rate of inflation for the next several years.

Table 2.10. Trial Equilibrium Configuration

	Budget Year		
	1978/79	1979/80	1980–
Tuition rate	3.4%	2.9%	2.5%
Faculty salaries	1.0%	1.5%	2.0%
Staff salaries	1.5%	1.5%	2.0%
Utilities	35.0%	15.0%	4.0%
Funded improvement	0.3%	0.3%	0.5%

NOTE: All figures are year-to-year percentage changes, net of inflation.

By the late autumn of 1976 it was becoming apparent that the institutions with which Stanford competes were going to be increasing their tuition rates from 2.0 to 2.5 percent rather than the 4.2 percent we had been using. During BAP and BEP we had moved up in the tuition standings until, in 1975/76, we stood near the top. As a source of market flexibility, tuition had been eliminated. Pressure from students against this "four-plus" tuition policy has already been mentioned. It is also fair to say that President Lyman had never felt comfortable with these projections. Now he was arguing against them with renewed vigor, and so were a number of influential trustees. Indeed, the board expressed great concern about the four-plus policy in December 1976, when the the 1977/78 tuition rate was set. Also a matter of concern were faculty and staff salaries, as effects of the austerity during the BEP years began to show up in comparative salary surveys, attrition, and recruiting difficulties.

Thus the stage was set, during the late fall and winter of 1976/77, for un-freezing the assumptions about tuition and salary growth rates. The problem then, as before, was how to institute a thaw without putting long-run financial equilibrium out of reach. This was the kind of problem for which TRADES had been invented. The highly aggregative TRANS model sufficed to calculate a credible gap figure—useful when we were far from equilibrium—but it was clumsy to use. It was also insufficiently refined to aid us in evaluating alternative forms of equilibrium once that Holy Grail was within reach.

Provost Miller, working directly with the TRADES model, was instrumental in finding a strategy for reducing the growth of tuition, and also for increasing salaries somewhat, within the constraints of LRFE. During February 1977, with the aid of DSPH and (at times) WFM, he explored a series of options for adjusting Stanford's primary planning variables from 1978/79, 1979/80, and beyond. In March 1977 he presented his recommendations to the Board of Trustees (table 2.10). He emphasized that this configuration appeared to be feasible but that it was not necessarily the best available; it was certainly not a "plan." At this point WFM was brought in to show a series of new tradeoff graphs, also obtained from TRADES, that spelled out an agenda for future planning efforts.

Certainly, some such acceptable scenario would have been developed and presented even in the absence of TRADES. There is little doubt, however, that the model made its development faster and easier. We believe that the end result was better as well. The chosen tradeoff involved reducing the funded improvement factor. As a result the gap was also reduced, under the rubric of "long-run limits on growth" (see table 2.8). A new set of estimates was also needed for the rising cost of utilities. All this would have been rather difficult to prepare in a short period of time, during which all the detail of the 1977/78 budget was being finalized, without the aid of a model. We feel confident in saying that TRADES, among other things, permitted an otherwise unobtainable excursion into longer-range planning just as the proximate year's budget was being wrapped up.

In closing this section let us comment upon an event that occurred during the implementation of TRADES, and also describe what happened after March 1977. The event had to do with the concept of stationary equilibrium that we described earlier. Stationary equilibrium requires that the fraction of the budget supported by endowment remain constant over time. Recall that this was suggested by us back in late 1973 or early 1974 as a reasonable kind of policy, and that it was used as a matter of mathematical convenience in the TRANS I model. In developing TRADES Dickmeyer had used equilibrium as a constraint, but not stationary equilibrium. We agreed with this, but had not paid much attention to it. When TRADES was demonstrated to the Budget Group for the first time, a storm of protest arose; stationary equilibrium, with its connotations of intergenerational equity, had been internalized by a number of our colleagues, who now felt they were being betrayed by this new development. We tried to downplay the issue by pointing out that TRADES could accommodate a stationary-equilibrium constraint if anyone wanted one, but that given this "powerful new tool" and the uncertainty surrounding all the estimates there seemed to be no reason for such a tight restriction.* However, the atmosphere of the session was destroyed and little progress was made that day with respect to the introduction of TRADES. Later, however, the concept of stationary equilibrium lost its saliency. The provost's "feasible configuration" in March 1977 was based on a nonstationary-equilibrium solution.

The moral of the story is that, first, judgments about what is or is not salient for the modelers may not turn out to be shared even by their close colleagues. Second, it is possible that a sense of frustration about models may have grown up unawares, and that the combination of yet another model and the potential loss of a familiar concept may have triggered the initial adverse reaction to TRADES.

TRADES has been refined and fully integrated with the LRFF ever since March 1977. Until the autumn of 1978, however, there was no occasion to use it again in such a direct or important way. Probably the reason was that the intervening period was devoted to cleaning up loose ends rather than to

---

*Actually, stationary equilibrium is such a tight constraint that the iterative procedures in TRADES probably would not work very well. However, an inequality constraint, e.g., one specifying that the fraction of the budget supported by endowment could not go down over time, would work perfectly well.

starting new planning initiatives. Hence, basically, we could follow our old trajectory instead of trying to change it by finding new tradeoffs. But a new set of planning challenges was being addressed as this chapter underwent final revision, and TRADES once again had become a key tool for the formulation of alternatives. Indeed, results obtained from TRADES had provided the numerical data for the latest presentation of long-range financial planning options by WFM to the Board of Trustees on November 13, 1978.

This concludes our account of the evolution of these particular planning models at Stanford University; others, related to the search for long-run financial equilibrium but not actually part of it, are described in appendix 1. It should be clear that models have had a significant impact upon policy, but that we have not abdicated our thinking powers in their favor. By "we" in this context we mean of course those of our colleagues with final responsibility for decisions, but also ourselves as both protagonists in behalf of models and participants in the decision-making process. Even when false starts were made, and there were a number of them, the experience so gained contributed in an important way to developments in general. The same holds true—doubly— with respect to our various forays into basic research. Immediate relevance and payoff are of course important considerations for an institution that would like to make a major investment in models, but they should not be the only criteria for every single modeling effort. Another lesson to be drawn from these events is that while in-house staff are essential for implementing models, colleges and universities would do well to listen to faculty in fields related to modeling and should enlist their support and assistance wherever possible. Graduate students in fields concerned with modeling, higher education, or both, can also contribute in important ways, and their involvement provides important educational benefits as well as results that are directly useful to the institution.

Summary

A historical narrative is given of the development and implementation of computer models in the quest for long-run financial equilibrium at Stanford. This includes a discussion of the key actors, management organization, and conditions that led to their use by top administrators there.

The need for a planning discipline encompassing models was recognized in early 1973/74 when Stanford was approaching the end of its so-called Budget Adjustment Program. It was becoming evident at that time that the effects of certain forces on the university's operating budget were not well enough understood. Also, no discipline was in place to ensure that decisions made in the short run would be consistent with longer-run financial goals.

The sequence of model developments recounted here proceeded in stages over a period of about five years' duration. It began in 1973 with a paper, written by one of the authors, exploring certain macroeconomic relationships that characterize the finances of a private university. Next was the discovery of the long-run financial equilibrium concept, which led ultimately to the construction of a model for making the transition to equilibrium. This model played a key role in laying the groundwork for Stanford's Budget Equilibrium Program, announced in fall 1974. The final stage reflected a new emphasis on taking values and preferences firmly into account; as a result, the university ended by adopting an interactive computer model called TRADES for assessing financial tradeoffs among its primary planning variables.

Among the conditions to which are attributed the success of the modeling venture at Stanford are the following: early recognition of the severity and persistence of the institution's financial problems; a tradition for conducting planning in a relatively open and centralized manner; and the gathering together of a management team that included not only persons with a keen sense of academic values but a small group of technical experts as well.

Notes to Chapter 2

Works cited here in abbreviated form are more fully described in the bibliography at the end of this book.

1. One such study was performed in 1975 as a term project in one of our courses by students who also were interns in the Academic Planning Office: David A. Clark, John R. Curry, and Jay D. Schoenau. It begins with the beginning of financial stringency in 1968 and ends with the beginning of the Budget Equilibrium Program in 1974. Our account in this chapter is substantially similar to theirs, and indeed we relied upon their interview results and writeup at certain points.

2. William F. Massy, "Planning models for colleges and universities" (Proposal to the Lilly Endowment, Inc., January 1974), pp. 1–3.

3. See Daryl H. Pearson [Stanford's general secretary], *The Campaign for Stanford: 1972–77* (Stanford University Office of Development, n.d.).

4. Miller 1978, pp. 28–29.

5. Ibid., p. 27.

6. Massy 1973.

7. See, for example, a report about the Carnegie Commission's conclusions in the *Los Angeles Times*, 10 October 1973, to the effect that higher education was "in the process of recovering from a period of depression that followed a time of very high achievement."

8. Massy 1973, pp. 4, 6.

9. Massy 1974, p. 9. Also quoted in Stanford University, *Proposed Operating Budget Guidelines: 1975–76* and *1976–77*.

10. The original idea and Professor Franklin's help occurred during spring 1973. The first rough working paper was written by WFM the following summer, and two formal reports appeared after a long gestation period in September and October 1974. These were: (a) William F. Massy, *A Dynamic Equilibrium Model for University Budgeting*, Academic Planning Office Report 74–2 (Stanford, Calif.: the University, 1974), later published as Massy 1976; and (b) William F. Massy and David S. P. Hopkins, *Long-Run Financial Equilibrium Calculations for Stanford's Operating Budget*, Academic Planning Office Report 74–3 (Stanford, Calif.: the University, 1974). The latter contains most of the information used for budget planning through the summer.

11. Massy and Hopkins 1974; see especially pp. 1–4.

12. Ibid., p. 16.

13. Stanford University, *Proposed Operating Budget Guidelines: 1974–75*, p. 26.

14. The quoted language is from *Campus Report*, 27 November 1974, p. 11, in an article explaining the development of the Budget Equilibrium Program.

15. William F. Massy, "Reflections on the application of a decision model to higher education" (Paper presented at the President's Luncheon of the American Institute for Decision Sciences, San Francisco, November 12, 1976); later published as Massy 1978, pp. 365–66 of which are quoted here.

16. *Campus Report*, 27 November 1974, p. 10.

17. "Charge to the Presidential Commission on University Budget Priorities," drafted by R. F. Bacchetti (Stanford University, October 3, 1974).

18. "1975–76 budget protocol," written by R. F. Bacchetti (Stanford University, October 21, 1974); reproduced in Stanford University, *Operating Budget Guidelines: 1975–76*, pp. 104–5.

19. From "Charge to Task Force V," drafted by R. F. Bacchetti (Stanford University, February 19, 1975); reproduced in Stanford University, *Operating Budget Guidelines: 1975–76*, p. 120.

20. Massy and Hopkins 1975a.

21. Stanford University, *Proposed Operating Budget Guidelines: 1976–77*, p. 21.

Part II

Planning Models in Theory and Practice

We now switch gears entirely and approach the planning and decision problem of colleges and universities in frankly theoretical terms. Our purpose is nothing less than to develop a unifying theory of college and university choice. Readers will doubtless find this harder going than the historical account in chapter 2, but we believe their efforts will be rewarded.

The planning and decision problem is complex. It can be modeled in many different ways—so many, in fact, that no single model can be both comprehensive and implementable. Our theory, by eschewing all claims to direct implementability, represents an effort to build a model that really is comprehensive. This model is the subject of chapter 3. We begin by distinguishing the different types of planning variables, and then proceed to specify the university's value function, that is, the function representing the entire system of values that planning is intended to maximize. Planning, to be effective, must be consistent with financial realities, considerations of demand, and the limitations imposed by technology and human behavior. The university planning problem, then, resolves itself into one of optimizing an institutional value function subject to a set of constraints. The remainder of chapter 3, after comparing the behavior of profit-making and nonprofit institutions, examines these constraints in their static and most general form. Read as a whole, chapter 3 provides not only a backdrop for chapters 4 and 5, which deal with specific planning models, but a unifying structure for the rest of the book.

Chapter 4 deals with budget projection models, particularly the type of budget model that we call a medium-range financial forecast (MRFF). Since this is the point at which many institutions choose to begin the modeling process, construction of an MRFF is explained step by step. The first step is to make a choice of financial submodels that accurately reflects the institution's needs and the financial constraints it is under. A great variety of formats for an

MRFF is possible; we proceed to develop one found useful at Stanford. Having explained the structure of the projection model, we describe and illustrate some of its possible uses. The chapter concludes with an essay on university economics that will be of particular interest to the officers of privately endowed universities.

In chapter 5 we extend the ideas introduced in chapter 4 to obtain some aggregate models for estimating university resource requirements and the variable costs of university programs. The models are of the input-output variety, and therefore involve consideration of university production functions as well as costs and revenues. A major difficulty in specifying such production functions has been the interlocking of research and instruction that is typical of the larger, more complex universities. We demonstrate that earlier work with disaggregate cost-simulation models, which are based chiefly on projections of student enrollment, has failed to overcome this and other difficulties. We then proceed to develop an aggregate production-and-cost model based on two novel features: a flow model of students admitted and degrees earned; and a method of computing instructional costs that relies on estimates of how much time the faculty devotes to instruction and how much to other university functions.

3

A Microeconomic Theory of Colleges

and Universities

The purpose of this chapter is to provide a theoretical foundation, or general conceptual structure, that will not only support the various planning models in a mathematical sense but will make them consistent with the underlying values of colleges and universities. The conceptual structure takes the form of a positive microeconomic theory of university choice. The theory is economic because it focuses on relations among values, capital, productivity, demand, and financial resources, in much the same way as does the economic theory of the business firm. It is positive (as opposed to normative) because it is intended to describe, in abstract terms, how universities really operate rather than provide guidance about how they should operate. Of course, the theory does have normative implications; these will be developed here and in the planning models to be discussed in later chapters.

The theory postulates that colleges and universities exhibit *optimizing be-havior*, a concept with many applications in microeconomics. In economic terms, a university maximizes a multicriterion value function subject to production, demand-and-supply, and financial constraints. Relevant criteria generally include such factors as the quantity and quality of educational and research outcomes, and surrogates for the capacity to produce future outcomes. Thus a university's behavior contrasts with a business firm's, which in theory maximizes a single criterion (profits) subject to production and demand constraints. For present purposes, the value function must be viewed as being implicit, that is, within the minds of the decision makers. (However, in chapter 9 we approach the problem of how to articulate values in an explicit fashion.) Values are beliefs about or attitudes towards the relative importance of situations or outcomes. The values that concern us are held by individuals responsible for making planning and resource-allocation decisions on behalf of the university.

We will speak of the institution's value function, loosely, as the consensus of the values of the key decision makers, although this bypasses the question of whether such a consensus actually exists or, if so, how it is formed. We also intend to bypass questions of organizational structure. We know that a college or university is not monolithic; it has many schools, departments, programs, etc., all with different objectives and different styles of decision making. However, the reality is too complex to deal with in detail at a theoretical level, and so we will content ourselves mostly with considering the university as an entity.

The task of the decision maker in this entity is to maximize his or her institution's value function, subject to various constraints. The constraints can be grouped into three categories:

1. *Physical and behavioral relations.* Teaching, learning, research, and other university "products" result from processes that depend on certain physical and behavioral relations. Following standard economic theory, we shall call these relations "production functions," though we do not mean to imply that either the products or the production processes of a university are like those of a factory.

2. *Market relations.* Equally influential are the physical and behavioral relations that determine how a university interacts with its external environment, that is, with other academic institutions and indeed enterprises of all kinds. At issue are student demand, faculty and staff recruiting, and a host of other important planning variables. These relations will be called "demand-and-supply functions"—"demand functions" if they concern the university's outputs, "supply functions" if they concern its inputs.

3. *Financial relations.* These determine whether the university will be able to make ends meet now and in the future. The factors involved include prices and unit costs as determined by the supply-and-demand functions, and also purely financial factors such as endowment funds. We will speak of: (a) *revenue functions* and *cost functions*; and (b) *financial constraints* that require revenues to cover the cost of university activities.

The task of the university decision maker, let us repeat, is to find a set of activities that (a) maximizes his or her institution's value function and (b) is consistent with the applicable physical, behavioral, demand-and-supply, and financial relations. This, of course, is not the first time that such a formulation has been applied to nonprofit institutions. In fact the idea of maximizing value subject to a break-even constraint and a production function has been used by Mark V. Pauly and Michael Redisch to specify the "value" of the hospital as a physicians' cooperative (1973; see also the several references pertaining to hospitals cited by them). Also, Oliver E. Williamson's "managerial discretion model" (1970) postulates that managers of for-profit firms maximize their own utility functions subject to a profit constraint. He assumes (p. 56) that staff and profit enter the utility function, i.e., that "internal" (e.g., self-serving) and "external" (stockholder-serving) goals are represented. Our formulation for nonprofit institutions is rooted in the idea that their value function represents their governors' perceptions of desirable social goals rather than strictly private ones. In Williamson's terms, then, the value function we have in mind is "externally" oriented.

This chapter will be devoted to analyzing these ideas in more detail and examining some of their implications. Even though abstract, we have found this conceptual structure to be very useful in understanding how various practical models fit together and how specific ones should be interpreted. Indeed, as the theory evolved it began to guide our process of research and development—just as a good theory should. We hope it will help you in the same way.

Building Blocks of the Theory

The main building blocks of our theory, as we have said, are institutional values and the various kinds of constraints. We shall amplify upon them in this section. First, however, we had better pin down the definitions of the variables that enter into the value, production, demand-and-supply, and financial functions.

Planning Variables

Three kinds of planning variables must be distinguished. They are: (a) *activity variables*, (b) *stock variables*, and (c) *price variables*. Examples of each type are given in table 3.1. Activity and stock variables may be "tangible" or "intangible"—a very important distinction given the technology and value orientation of colleges and universities. All the planning variables are assumed to be nonnegative; that is, they are required to be either positive or zero. We shall define and discuss each type of variable and then consider the matter of tangibility.

Activity variables. Almost anything that goes on at the university during a particular period of time may be referred to as an activity variable. For our purposes, activity variables may be *outputs*, such as educational outcomes, research findings, or the cataloguing and placing on the shelves of library acquisitions; or they may be *inputs*, such as faculty FTE-years of a certain type and quality. Some activities are hard to classify as either inputs or outputs— student-years in residence, for example, or course enrollments (perhaps "work in process" would be better here). However, the fine points of the distinction between inputs and outputs need not concern us.

Activities are described in physical or behavioral terms rather than in financial terms. For instance, we will speak of a certain number of faculty FTE-years rather than so many dollars of expenditure on faculty. This distinction is crucial, and often overlooked. The financial factors come in when we "price" faculty time, but what is important now is the activity itself and not how much it costs.

We will use the university's fiscal year as the base unit of time, though some activities would normally be measured in terms of academic years, semesters, or

Table 3.1.   Examples of College and University Planning Variables

Tangible	Intangible
Activities (X)	Activities (X)
Student-years	Quality of students matriculating
Student enrollments in courses	Quality of education obtained
Research articles, citations	Quality of research performed
Library acquisitions	Quality of library materials acquired
Faculty FTE-years	Quality of effort put forth by faculty and
Staff FTE-years	staff
Stocks (S)	Stocks (S)
Buildings and equipment	Quality and style of buildings, etc.
Library holdings	Quality of library holdings
Endowment assets	Quality of human resources
	Good will and reputation
Prices (P)	Prices (P)
Tuition rate	Financial aid judgments[b]
Indirect cost rate on sponsored research[a]	Costing policies and implicit cost sharing
Faculty and staff salaries	Perquisites
Utility rates	

[a]The indirect cost rate is limited by the application of government costing regulations.
[b]Many financial aid policies are explicit and thus enter the "tangible" column.

quarters, and other time periods are possible. (The choice of unit doesn't matter as long as things are defined consistently.) Since activities can be measured in terms of quantity per unit of time, they should be viewed as "flows," a point that will be pursued further in chapter 5. For now it is enough to note that activities occur over time whereas stocks exist *at* a point in time. To summarize: let X be the list of activities of the college or university (activities are measured in terms of physical or behavioral phenomena, not in financial terms; they have the dimension "happenings per unit of time").

Stock variables. Anything that might appear on a university's balance sheet, if a completely exhaustive one could be drawn up, can be classified as a stock variable. Stocks may be physical, behavioral, or financial. Physical stocks include buildings, equipment, land, and library materials. Behavioral stocks include general goodwill and the quality of the university's human resource base (in contrast, the amount and quality of effort actually put forth by the faculty and staff during a given time period are flow variables, i.e., activities). Financial stock variables consist of endowments, expendable fund balances, plant reserves, and the like. Stocks can also be liabilities, as in the case of long- or short-term debt.

Stocks are important because they possess the potential for being turned into flows of activities. For instance, endowment produces investment return that can fund current or future activities, and existing physical and human resources condition the level and quality of activities that can be performed. Likewise, current activities result in changes in stock levels. Activities may produce wear and tear on physical assets, erode behavioral resources, or use up financial balances. Some activities build up stocks: adding to or maintaining physical plant, recruiting faculty, and paying off debt are examples.

A very important issue is how much of existing stocks should be used currently and how much should be retained for the future. Also important are decisions about using current resources to build up stocks. Any planning model worth its salt must deal with these "spending-saving" questions in the course of determining the optimal amount and mix of activities. Let S be the list of the university stocks of assets and liabilities. Stocks may be physical, behavioral, or financial. They are measured as inventories or balances at a point in time.

Price variables. In the present context, price variables are coefficients that attribute monetary value to certain activities vis-à-vis the input or output markets in which the university operates. Prices may be set by the institution (tuition or salary levels, for instance), or they may be fully determined by outside forces (as by the rate structure of an electric utility company). However, the distinction is not as important as it might seem because prices are subject to market forces in either case. In general we will consider the price variables to be determined "outside" the university—that is to say, through market forces over which the university has little if any control—no matter what the institutional procedures may be. The main exception to this is when schools that have some degree of control over the quality and quantity of admissions proceed to set their tuition levels accordingly. This will be dealt with explicitly in the context of student demand.

Let P be the list of prices faced by (or set by) the institution. Prices are largely determined by external forces. They have the dimension "dollars per unit of activity."

We noted earlier that planning variables may be either tangible or intangible. The distinction is important both for obvious practical reasons and in terms of our theory of university choice. We will define a *tangible variable* as one that can be quantified one way or another. Examples are things that can be counted, priced out or costed out, tested reliably, or any of these in combination. The intangible variables are of course not quantifiable, but it is obvious that they are of the utmost importance nevertheless. Examples are the depth or significance of a piece of faculty research, and the quality of a student learning experience. This fact makes the problem of modeling for university planning, and indeed the planning process itself, intellectually difficult and challenging. Any theory of university choice must deal explicitly with the role of the intangible variables.

Planning variables refer to particular periods or points in time. We will assume that each variable has a current level, as well as levels that are predicted or targeted for ensuing planning periods. The predicted values generally will be obtained by applying estimated growth rates to the current levels. The current levels provide the initial conditions for the planning problem. Future levels and/or growth rates play the role of *decision variables*, subject of course to the production, demand-and-supply, and financial constraints that limit the planner's degrees of freedom. The purpose of a planning model is to make more of the constraints specific and help the decision maker identify, evaluate, and choose among alternative configurations of the planning variables that are financially and operationally feasible.

The University's Value Function

The values of the university are central to its choices and indeed to its spirit and reason for being. Important questions pertaining to values are: (a) How are values defined? (b) Whose values should be used? (c) By what means can meaningful, internally consistent preferences for complex combinations of activities be devised and articulated? (d) In what way can a value function be used in an analysis aimed at making realistic planning decisions? We consider questions (a) and (b) now and return to (d) later in this section. Question (c) will be considered in chapter 9. Let us denote $V(X, S)$ as the university's *value function*. By this we mean a mathematical relation that assigns an intrinsic value—designated by a value or utility index—to each combination of the arguments X and S.

Values imply evaluation; they are therefore subjective. The task of estimating a person's value function is to help him understand his preference structure and make evaluations of tradeoffs that are internally consistent and intuitively satisfying. We postulate that activities are the things that are to be valued intrinsically, that is, for their own sake. Stocks are included in the value function because they represent a potential for future activities. While not all elements in the lists of activities and stocks need be (or are) valued intrinsically, we remind ourselves that this is possible by the generality of the notation.

For most purposes it is enough for $V(X, S)$ to be defined only to the point where rankings among alternative planning options are well defined. That is, if there are three options, each involving different magnitudes for X and S, a function that produces value indices $(1, 2, 3)$ would be equivalent to one that produces $(3.4, 19.6, 2001)$ since the ranking of the alternatives is the same in both cases. For some purposes, however, rankings are not sufficient and the value function must be defined with respect to scale as well as rank. In this case the result is called a *utility index* rather than a *value index*. The functions in the above example do not have the same scale; therefore the results cannot be regarded as a utility index. However, the pairs $(1, 2, 3)$ and $(1999, 2000, 2001)$ do have the same scale because the values of the alternatives differ by one in each case. There is an even more stringent criterion that would fix the origin as well as the scale of the function. However, that is not necessary for our purposes. Specifying the scale of a subjectively determined function is much more difficult than helping the decision maker rank-order his alternatives, so we have structured our models around value rather than utility functions wherever possible. When utility rather than value functions are being used, this will be indicated clearly.[1]

"Goals" and "objectives" are terms often used in the planning process. They are related to values, as we have defined them, but are not quite the same thing.[2]

A *goal* is a general statement of criteria, such as, "Old Faithfull University is dedicated to excellence in undergraduate education, with emphasis on _____ and _____ [fields], for students with _____ [characteristics]." On the other hand, an *objective* is a very specific statement of something one seeks to accomplish, such as, "This fall Old Faithfull will enroll 1,000 new undergraduate students, 800 as freshmen and 200 by transfer, with average SAT scores of at least 750 verbal and 700 math."

By our definition, a set of values and the value function that represents it are not as general as a statement of goals nor as specific as a set of objectives. The arguments of the value function may well include numbers of students of various types, average test scores, or other indices of quality and mix, etc., all of which are subsumed in the activity list, X. The value or utility indices assigned as a function of these activities can be regarded as giving concrete reality to a general statement of goals, and of course the value function should be consistent with any such statement. However, the value function does not specify particular outcome targets. They are set at a later stage of the analysis, when the value function is maximized subject to the constraints already mentioned. The results of this optimization effort—i.e., the approved plans—then become the objectives to be implemented during the ensuing period.

Public and private values. Universities and many other nonprofit organizations differ from for-profit enterprises in that their goals are fundamentally public rather than private.[3] This is true whether the nonprofit enterprises are sponsored and controlled by the government or privately. Universities and many other nonprofit organizations produce goods and services that have a strong public as well as a private component. In this context the definition of a public good implies that the benefits derived from it go beyond the specific parties who produce and acquire it. That is, the transactions involve what economists call "positive externalities," and the goods represent benefits to society that cannot be captured by a market price. Consider the benefits of an educated citizenry. Or, what about the long-run benefits of research and scholarship? While some financial rewards for these benefits can be captured by the university in the form of tuition or royalties or whatever, the benefits to society, both financial and otherwise, will be far greater. In contrast, since the for-profit sector produces mostly private goods, the market prices tend to reflect intrinsic value. (Exceptions usually take the form of "negative externalities" such as the effects of environmental pollution; these also can arise in the production of public goods, of course.) Thus, in the case of higher education and similar nonprofit enterprises, the market price of outputs is not an acceptable surrogate for value.

A second difference between universities and for-profit firms is that there are no specific private claimants for the residual value of the enterprise, that is, for its net worth in terms of financial, physical, and human assets, and its goodwill. In theory, the business firm strives to maximize the surplus of revenues over costs for the private benefit of its owners, who claim its residual value for their personal accounts. There is no similar group in the case of the university. In principle, those who determine the university's values do so by interpreting the public good—if not for the general public then for a subset of it. This is obvious for the public or state-sponsored university. For private universities, the clue to the question of how and by whom the values are determined is in the word "trustee," as in "board of trustees" or the equivalent. The question is, "Trustee-ship for whom?" Certainly it is not for the private interests of the trustees them-selves, nor is it for the personal benefit of current faculty, students, and others connected with the university. The answer is that the human, physical, and financial assets of the university are held in trust for public purposes, both short- and long-run (as described in university charters), rather than private ones.

Determination of values. From an operational standpoint, the institution's preferences among alternatives (that is to say, its value function) are determined by one of the following:

1. The governing board (board of trustees, board of regents, or equivalent) working with the administration, after consultation with faculty, students, alumni, and other constituencies.

2. The constituencies, or a subset of them, directly, through a political process whose results are more or less binding on the board and the administration.

In terms of ultimate responsibility and power the first arrangement is almost universal. However, there are well-founded traditions of delegating academic judgments (e.g., on curricula, research, and peer-group evaluations with respect to faculty appointments) to the faculty of the institution and its academic officers. This can amount to a process of the second kind.

Sometimes constituent groups make demands for extending the second kind of value-setting process beyond its traditional academic role. This may be done in the name of "democracy." However, our view is that a large-scale extension of the power to set values, as distinct from the opportunity to influence them through consultation, is inconsistent with the principle of trusteeship. As a practical matter, the institution's long-run public purpose would be diluted in favor of the short-run private objectives of current constituents. Further, the highly political process of determining who gets what benefits would have a chilling effect upon academic values.

For our theory's purposes it is sufficient to assume that in principle the university does have a value function, which it seeks to maximize subject to constraints. The question of how this function is determined is very important for practical modeling purposes and for understanding the complexity of university governance, but it need not trouble us further here.

What activities are the most likely candidates for intrinsic valuation? The most obvious ones are those representing outcomes that bear a close relationship to the university's reason for being: the number of student-years taught, the quality of the educational experience, the amount and quality of faculty research, and so forth. These can be regarded as *primary outputs*. Certain additional outputs serve to facilitate the primary ones. Some of these, such as the ones deriving from a student health service, may also be viewed as having intrinsic value. Others may be purely facilitating, in which case their value is derived from that of the primary outputs and is not intrinsic.

Inputs also may be valued intrinsically, at least in universities. An example would be faculty resources in a discipline that is judged to have importance on an absolute scale but is not producing much in the way of current outputs. Keeping the field alive intellectually may be judged as more important than certain current outputs elsewhere. But the intrinsic valuation of inputs is a tricky business: private benefits so easily get mixed up with public ones. For instance, the view that a hospital is a physicians' cooperative (for which see Pauly and Redisch 1973), or that the university is a faculty cooperative (to which we do not subscribe), emphasizes the private self-interest side of the input valuation. Such an emphasis must be avoided if the public purposes of the university are to be achieved.

Stocks are included in the generalized university value function for two reasons: (a) trustees, administrators, faculty, and others do in fact seem to value them; (b) in theory they represent means by which potentially important but as yet unspecified future courses of action may be set on foot. In other words, stocks can be surrogates for unspecified future activities. Examples of stocks that seem to be valued intrinsically are library holdings, academic buildings, and the level of the endowment balance. Obviously it is impossible to assess the implications of unspecified future actions, which explains in part why such controversy often surrounds the spending-saving decision. The other main reason for disagreement is that individuals' perspectives on the future tend to differ. For example, current students tend to discount the future at a much steeper rate than do trustees, whose eyes are partly on subsequent student generations.

Physical-Behavioral Constraints

The optimization problem faced by university planners is to maximize $V(X, S)$ with respect to the activity and stock variables, subject to the production, demand-and-supply, and financial constraints. The set of production functions can be written as

$$F^k(X, S) = 0 \quad k = 1, \ldots, m. \tag{3.1}$$

There are m separate equations ($k = 1, 2, \ldots, m$), each representing a distinct element of technological or behavioral reality that must be taken into account in planning. The notation $F(X, S) = 0$ means that the elements of the lists of activities and stocks must stand in a particular relation to one another. For example, $X_1 - 3X_2 = 0$ means that three units of X_2 (an input) must be used to produce one unit of output X_1. Following many economic writers (e.g. Allen 1963; Baumol 1961), we define the production function so that increments to output push it in a positive direction while increments to inputs push it in a negative one, as shown in the example.

The production functions involve stocks as well as activities because the availability of facilities (such as buildings and equipment) and library holdings affect the relation between current inputs and outputs. Also, certain production processes lead to changes in the stocks. For example, the activity "acquiring library books," which includes technical processing and cataloguing, will result in an addition to the stock of library holdings. Indeed, the amount of effort required to add a given number of volumes may itself depend on the size of the current holdings and the nature of the library building—in other words, on elements of S. The library acquisitions activity would be one of the m different production functions in equation (3.1). Other activities result in a diminution of stocks; operations that lead to wear and tear on buildings are classic examples.

To extend our ideas, let us examine a simplified version of a particular production function in more detail, taking account of the differences between (a) outputs and inputs and (b) tangible and intangible attributes. Let us denote outputs by Y and inputs by Z, noting that the elements of Y and Z are all members of the master list of activities X. Suppose further that we consider the "instruction production function" for a particular class of students—say, undergraduates in the arts and sciences. Then, at a very simple level of analysis, the output might be the average educational outcome for students enrolled in the program and the input the number of FTE faculty devoted to it. (Other inputs to the educational process and other outputs of the university are ignored in this example.)

Focusing on educational outcome, we see immediately that a quantitative measure like the number of student course enrollments is not comprehensive enough to serve as the basis for analysis.[4] Intangible attributes, which we shall subsume under the rubric "quality of education," are very important. The difficulty or impossibility of measuring them systematically does not make them any less real. Indeed, from the point of view of students already enrolled in the program the quality factors may be the only material variables. Therefore we need to enrich our notation.

Let $\bar{Y}$ = tangible measures of outputs (these are things that can be counted, at least in principle, though we do not preclude test scores and the like if they are judged to be valid measures of important outcomes)

$\tilde{Y}$ = intangible attributes of outputs (these characteristics must be assessed subjectively, and they generally relate to the quality of output)

Clearly a similar dichotomy exists with respect to the input variables, so let us stipulate that the above notation extends to $\bar{Z}$ and $\tilde{Z}$ (and $\bar{X}$ and $\tilde{X}$ for that matter) even though we don't need it in this example.

Now the instruction production function can be written as

$$F(\bar{Y}, \tilde{Y}, Z) = 0.$$

It simply states that there is a necessary relation between the flows of inputs and the tangible and intangible measures of output. If any two variables are specified

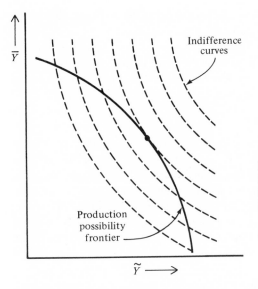

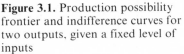

Figure 3.1. Production possibility frontier and indifference curves for two outputs, given a fixed level of inputs

the third can be calculated. For instance, fixing the quantity of output and the amount of input determines the quality of output. If both quantity and quality of output are to be specified, then the needed faculty input is determined automatically. (Faculty quality is ignored in this example, but it obviously is very important too.) If the department has too many faculty some will be underemployed in this simple situation where no faculty research is assumed. Then the department will be inefficient, implying $F < 0$. If there are too few faculty for the specified amount and quality of output the department will be overextended, implying $F > 0$.

Figure 3.1 illustrates how the production function leads to tradeoffs between the quantity and quality of output, given that the amount of input is fixed. The tradoff is along what is called a *production possibility frontier*: each point on this curve represents the most of each output that can be obtained from the specified input level, given the physical and behavioral realities represented by the production function. If the amount of input is increased the production possibility frontier moves upward and to the right, and conversely for a reduction of input. An increase in productivity (by the use of better teaching methods, for instance) would change the production function and thus move the production possibility frontier outward, but without a concomitant change in the amount of input utilized. The figure also presents information, in the form of indifference curves, about the university's value function. All the points along each dashed curve are valued equally. The amount of satisfaction increases as we move outward to successively higher curves—that is, both quantity and quality of educational outcomes are assumed to be perceived as "good."

Suppose that financial factors affect only the amount of input that can be afforded. (An example of such a situation would be a program that is fully endowed or supported from state funds, and for which no tuition revenue exists or is recognized.) This would mean that Z is fixed regardless of the quantity or quality of Y produced. The optimization problem would then amount to finding the furthermost indifference curve that overlaps the production possibility frontier. This occurs at the point M, where the indifference curve is tangent to the production function. In other words, M denotes the point at which value is maximized subject to the physical-behavioral production constraint.

Demand-and-Supply Functions

Colleges and universities, like enterprises of other kinds, are subject to market forces; outputs must be "demanded" from them by users or sponsors. For example, we can think of student demand and the demand for faculty research sponsored by the federal government and private foundations. (Sometimes, too, it is convenient to think of the "supply of sponsored-research dollars." However, "demand" is more appropriate since the sponsor wishes to call forth research activities rather than to "sell" his dollars to the university.) On the input side, the university seeks suppliers of labor, materials, and other factors needed in its production process.

In this sense, then, a college or university faces "demand curves" with respect to the behavior of students, private donors, foundations, government granting agencies, and the like. Such behavior depends upon the current activities of the institution, and quite possibly upon its stocks of assets. For instance, the fund-raising appeal of a university will depend on the quality and quantity of its faculty and students, its fund-raising activities, and the nature of its physical campus. It also will depend on "stocks" of goodwill and on the size of its alumni population, both of which, considered as stocks, are functions of past activities.

We shall denote both the demand and supply functions faced by the university by the symbol D. That is, we postulate a collection of "n" demand-and-supply functions:

$$D^k(X, S, P) = 0 \qquad k = 1, \ldots, n. \tag{3.2}$$

Of course, not all the elements of X, P, and S enter into a given demand or supply function. However, the fact that variables of all three types can and do enter is illustrated by the case of student demand. First, the number of students matriculating, the number of course enrollments, etc., are included in the activity list X. Hence X enters the demand function. Clearly the level of demand depends on the tuition rate, so P enters too. Finally, S enters because demand might well depend on the physical plant, library holdings, and so forth.

University decision makers must understand the demand-and-supply relations as much as possible, and take them into account when making choices.

Financial Constraints

The assumption (used to obtain the optimum in figure 3.1) that outputs and financial results are independent is inappropriate most of the time. In order to examine how the financial function fits into the general optimization problem, let us define the *revenue* and *cost functions* for the university:

$$R(X, S, P) = \text{Revenue}$$

$$C(X, S, P) = \text{Cost}$$

Naturally revenues and costs depend on the activities undertaken, the stocks of assets, and prices. For instance, the number of students and the tuition rate are both determinants of tuition revenue, and the number of faculty and staff, with their salaries and fringe benefits, determines personnel costs. The stocks can enter too. For instance, the market value of the endowment is an important determinant of investment return, and the size and condition of the physical plant may in and of itself affect revenue. However, care must be taken because some revenues or costs that may appear to be associated directly with stocks are really due to activities closely associated with but logically independent of them. Building operation and maintenance (O & M) is a case in point: while the level of O & M activities is strongly influenced by the size of the plant, it is an activity and is therefore subject to a certain amount of freedom of choice on the part of decision makers.

We will come back to the details of the revenue and cost functions presently. For the moment it is sufficient to postulate that the net of revenues and costs must be zero, cumulatively over a series of fiscal periods if not in each period. If costs continually exceed revenues, the institution will run into financial trouble eventually. On the other hand, if revenues continually exceed costs by more than the amounts needed to maintain needed stocks in real terms, the university's nonprofit status will be compromised and questions raised about the nature of its values as an institution.

The University's Optimization Problem

The optimization problem faced by colleges and universities may now be summarized in terms of the building blocks developed in this section. It is

$$\text{maximize } V(X, S, P)$$

$$\text{with respect to } X$$

subject to the constraints

$$F^k(X, S) = 0 \qquad (k = 1, \ldots, m)$$

$$D^k(X, S, P) = 0 \qquad (k = 1, \ldots, n)$$

$$R(X, S, P) - C(X, S, P) = 0 \tag{3.3}$$

$$X \geq 0.$$

This is what we generally will mean, throughout the book, when we speak of the "university's optimization problem" and the concept of "value maximization subject to constraints."

Three important considerations not contained in equation (3.3) must be kept in mind when thinking about the optimization problem faced by colleges and universities. They are:

1. *The list of activities contains intangible as well as tangible elements.* I.e., X can be partitioned into $\bar{X}$ and $\tilde{X}$. Though impossible to quantify, the intangibles are crucial and the decision maker must be alert to see that they are not slighted.

2. *The optimization takes place over time.* Current values must be traded off against future ones, and the effects of current activities upon future stocks must be considered.

3. *Future values of variables and parameters are not known with certainty.* The same applies to the forms of the functions. Hence the decision maker must be aware of his or her limited analytical powers and also take account of risk and uncertainty.

It is worth stressing that the production and demand functions, in particular, are difficult to understand. This is especially true of the intangible variables. We shall present a theory of how college and universities deal with this problem. First, however, let us explore the basic implications of the ideas embodied in value maximization subject to constraints.

Value Maximization Subject to Constraints

In this section we present the basic mathematics and consider some of the ramifications of the idea of maximizing a value function subject to constraints. First we will deal with the simple static case in which the optimization is assumed to take place once and for all, and time is not a consideration. We will also assume that the planner knows everything he or she needs to know, with certainty. We will then extend these ideas in two ways: first by incorporating dynamic considerations; and then by adding uncertainty as to outcome.

Two special kinds of problems will then be considered from the point of view of value maximization. They are: (a) capital budgeting decisions; (b) hierarchical optimization, that is, resource allocation in a hierarchical organization such as a university with a strong central administration. We say "such as" because all the conclusions in this section apply to the broad range of nonprofit organizations, not just to colleges and universities. From time to time we shall make this clear through textual references and examples.

Finally, in this section we shall assume that the nonprofit enterprise in question is small in relation to its input-and-output markets, and that pure competition is a way of life in these markets. This permits us to assume further that all prices are determined by market action, regardless of the choices of our particular enterprise. This, in turn, simplifies the analysis of individual enterprise behavior by allowing us to regard input-and-output prices as fixed numbers and ignore the demand-and-supply functions.

Static Optimization in the Nonprofit Enterprise

When time is not a factor we can consider the institution "as is" and drop explicit reference to the stock variables from the value function. The prices and the demand functions can also be dropped due to the assumption of pure competition, as discussed above. We shall also assume for simplicity that there is only one production constraint (i.e., that $m = 1$ in equation [3.1]) and write the financial constraint as $G(X) = 0$, where $G(X) = R(X) - C(X)$.

Now the optimization problem faced by the enterprise (e.g. a college or university) can be represented as follows:

$$\text{maximize } V(X)$$

$$\text{with respect to } X$$

$$\text{subject to the constraints}$$

$$F(X) = 0$$
$$G(X) = 0. \tag{3.4}$$

We remind the reader that the above is a special case of equation (3.3). The simplifying assumptions will be dropped in later sections, after we have had a chance to understand and examine the implications of the core ideas.

We shall assume that $V(X)$ is strictly concave, $F(X)$ is convex, and $G(X)$ is concave. These assumptions are basically realistic, and they provide the sufficient conditions for achieving a maximum (as opposed to a minimum). For example, they are consistent (to use the language of economics) with a preference function exhibiting decreasing marginal utility, a production function with decreasing returns to scale and decreasing marginal productivity, and a linear financial function.[5]

The nature of the optimization is shown in figure 3.2, beginning in panel A with a diagram of the two constraints. The curved surface encompassed by *OABC* is the production function. Any point on this surface is feasible from the physical-behavioral standpoint. Points inside it represent inefficiency ($F < 0$) and points outside it represent overextension of resources ($F > 0$). The shaded plane depicts the financial function. Points above and to the left of it represent surpluses while those to the right represent deficits. The function as shown rests on the assumption that inputs, Z, are costly and that the output, Y, produces marginal net revenue. The positive intercept RT indicates that, even if output is zero, there is sufficient fixed revenue (e.g. from endowment) both to cover any fixed cost and to support a positive level of inputs.

What makes the financial function move upward and to the right? The answer is: the assumption that outputs produce positive marginal net revenue (before the costs of needed inputs have been substracted). For a university, such an assumption would be consistent with a situation in which the tuition rate exceeds the average financial aid cost per student. It need not do so, however; in many graduate programs, for instance, total aid per student

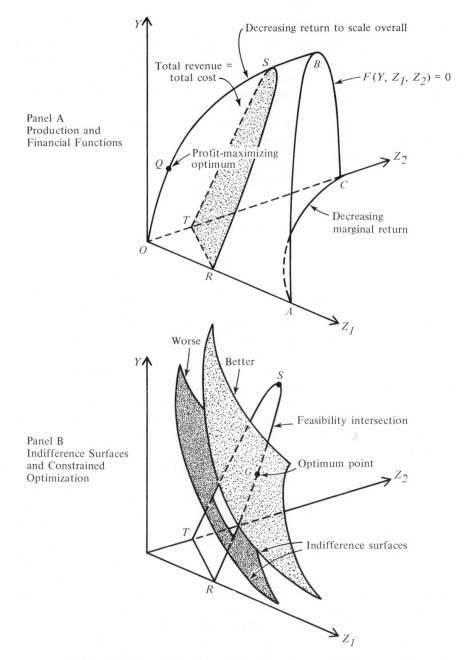

Figure 3.2 The optimization problem in a three-variable system

exceeds tuition, so that the institution loses money at the margin. In such a situation the financial function moves upward and to the left, but this does not introduce any theoretical difficulty so long as there is a sufficient excess of fixed revenue over fixed cost to produce a positive intercept, *RT*.

The locus of points connecting *RST* in panel A of figure 3.2 represents feasibility with respect to both production and financial constraints. It is the intersection of the curvy surface and the plane. The object now is to find the optimum point on *RST*, that is, the point that maximizes the university's value function. This is shown in panel B of the figure, where indifference surfaces (the analogue of the two-dimensional indifference curves in figure 3.1) have been added. To provide an interesting-looking graph, we have assumed that both of the inputs as well as the output are positively valued. The optimum point is shown at *G*, where the indifference surface is tangent to the feasibility intersection *RST*. If the output alone were intrinsically valued, the indifference surfaces would be horizontal planes and the output would be at point *S*—the zenith of the feasibility locus.

We pointed out that the difference between revenues and costs increases as the plane *RST* is shifted to the left, that is, as the same output is obtained with progressively less input. The position of the financial function at *RST* represents the not-for-profit condition. In contrast, the profit-maximizing optimum is at point *Q* in panel A of the figure, where the financial function is tangent to the production function. In other words, the for-profit firm's value function *is* the financial function, whereas the nonprofit enterprise has separate value and financial functions, arrived at independently of one another. Note too that, in the profit-maximizing case, marginal net revenue must be positive and fixed cost must exceed fixed revenue (i.e., the financial function must have a negative intercept and travel upward and to the right).

Of course the maximization problem represented by equation (3.4) can be solved mathematically. We shall use Lagrange's method.

Let λ = the shadow price of the production constraint

   μ = the shadow price of the financial constraint

The objective function is written in terms of the two shadow prices, which, in the present context, are also called Lagrangian multipliers.

$$H = V(X) - \lambda F(X) + \mu G(X) \tag{3.5}$$

The problem now is to maximize H with respect to the X's, λ, and μ, subject to the constraints.

The optimum solution is obtained by setting the partial derivatives of equation (3.5), with respect to each of the n elements of X and the shadow prices, to zero. Let us depict the partial derivatives with respect to X_i as V_i, F_i, and G_i. (Of course these are themselves functions of X.) Then the necessary conditions for the optimum are

$$V_i - \lambda F_i + \mu G_i = 0 \qquad i = 1, \ldots, n$$

$$F(\cdot) = 0 \tag{3.6}$$

$$G(\cdot) = 0.$$

There are $n + 2$ unknowns (the n elements of X, plus λ and μ) and the same number of equations. The sufficient condition for a maximum is that H be strictly concave, which will be the case given the assumptions described earlier for V, F, and G.

The optimum given by equation (3.6) is invariant to monotonic transformations of the value function (see appendix 2). This means, as we shall explain, that the value function can be defined in ordinal terms. The shadow prices λ and μ are determined by the scale of the particular value function utilized. They will be positive so long as H is strictly concave, though their magnitudes are not invariant to changes in the scale of the value function.

An economist can obtain further insight into the optimum for a nonprofit enterprise by returning to equation (3.6), rearranging terms, and taking the ratio of the marginality conditions for any two variables i and j.

$$\frac{V_j + \mu P_j}{V_i + \mu P_i} = \frac{\lambda F_j}{\lambda F_i} = \frac{F_j}{F_i} = MRS_{ji} \tag{3.7}$$

where MRS_{ji} is the *marginal rate of substitution* between variables j and i in the production function and P_i and P_j are the price coefficients (in the financial function, here assumed to be linear) for X_i and X_j. The analogous condition for a profit-maximizing firm is

$$\frac{P_j}{P_i} = MRS_{ji}.$$

This is obtained by maximizing $G(X)$ subject to $F(X) = 0$. For the profit maximizer, any P_k can be viewed as marginal profit, since it is either the value of the marginal product or the cost of the marginal input factor. The same role, as we shall see, is played by V_k and μP_k for the nonprofit organization.

As an example, suppose that i is an input and j is an output, and that only outputs enter the value function. By noting that

$$MRS_{ji} = -\frac{\partial X_i}{\partial X_j}$$

we can write

$$P_i\left(-\frac{dX_i}{dX_j}\right) = P_j + \frac{V_j}{\mu}. \tag{3.8}$$

(Recall that $P_i < 0$ when i is an input.) In other words, the optimality condition is

$$
\begin{bmatrix} \text{Marginal} \\ \text{factor} \\ \text{cost} \\ (MC) \end{bmatrix} = \begin{bmatrix} \text{Dollar} \\ \text{value of} \\ \text{marginal} \\ \text{product} \\ (MR) \end{bmatrix} + \begin{bmatrix} \text{Effective} \\ \text{intrinsic value} \\ \text{of marginal product} \\ \text{(normalized to} \\ \text{dollar terms)} \\ (EMIV) \end{bmatrix}
$$

It follows from the results in appendix 2 that the ratio V_j/μ is invariant to changes in the scale of the value function. Equation (3.8), then, can be used with rank-order preference data.

The above relation is shown graphically in panel A of figure 3.3, where variable j is considered to be an output and variable i an input. In a perfectly competitive market (as assumed throughout this section) marginal revenue equals price, which is independent of X_j. Marginal cost is the product of (a) the amount of X_i needed to produce an incremental unit of X_j and (b) the per unit cost of X_i. The per unit cost, in turn, is $-P_i$ (recall our convention that inputs enter the financial function with a negative sign). The *effective marginal intrinsic value* of X_i is V_j/μ, which is assumed to decline as X_i increases. The vertical axis of the figure represents value measured in dollar terms; intrinsic value is transformed into dollar terms by dividing V by μ.

The optimum point for the profit-maximizing firm is shown at point A in the figure, which is the point at which $MR = MC$. For the nonprofit enterprise, the optimum is at $MR + EMIV = MC$ which is shown at point B. The addition of a positive marginal intrinsic value to the price effect MR increases the amount of X_j produced at the optimum so long as marginal cost is increasing. (If MC is decreasing, X_j still will increase unless the dropoff in MC is faster than that of $EMIV$.) It can also be seen that the extra output for the nonprofit enterprise generates extra value equal to $B - A$ on the vertical axis. According to its own value function, the nonprofit institution prefers the larger output to the smaller, profit-maximizing one.

Panel B of figure 3.3 depicts situations where input, X_i, as well as output, X_j, are valued intrinsically. At point C both are valued, at D the input but not the output, at B the output but not the input, and at A neither (A and B are the same as in panel A). We have argued that, for colleges and universities, some inputs (like faculty) are valued intrinsically while some outputs (like operations, maintenance, and administrative services) are not. Thus all of the above combinations will occur in practice. Intrinsic valuation of inputs tends to produce more output than either the profit-maximizing optimum or the optimum under conditions where only outputs are valued. However, the question is whether the valuation of inputs represents the true preference of the institution or the self-interest of those affected. If the true marginal value of the input for the institution is zero, but it behaves as if it were positive, then the overall value of the decision will be reduced by the distance represented by $B - C$ on the vertical axis.

Panel A. Output Intrinsically Valued

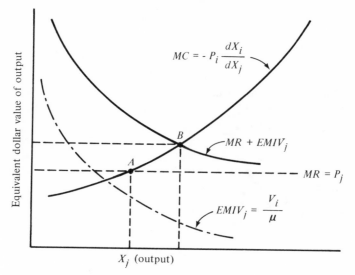

$$MC = -P_i \frac{dX_i}{dX_j}$$

$$MR + EMIV_j$$

$$MR = P_j$$

$$EMIV_j = \frac{V_i}{\mu}$$

X_j (output)

Equivalent dollar value of output

Panel B. Input and/or Output Intrinsically Valued

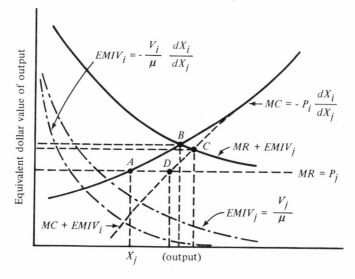

$$EMIV_i = -\frac{V_i}{\mu}\frac{dX_i}{dX_j}$$

$$MC = -P_i \frac{dX_i}{dX_j}$$

$$MR + EMIV_j$$

$$MR = P_j$$

$$EMIV_j = \frac{V_j}{\mu}$$

$$MC + EMIV_i$$

X_j (output)

Equivalent dollar value of output

Figure 3.3. Marginal values, revenues, and costs

Optimization over Time

Up to now we have been ignoring the time dimension and dealing with a static world. The essential new factor in dynamic optimization is that the effects of current activities on stocks, and hence on future activities and future stocks, must be taken into account. We discussed earlier how current activities affect stocks. Library acquisitions, maintenance of buildings or the lack of it, new construction, additions to or withdrawals from the endowment—all are good examples. Changes in stocks may well change future production and financial functions, and hence impact future activity flows and the value that can be obtained from them. Also, as we said earlier, stocks may be given intrinsic value, either immediately or in the future. It is obvious that these interactions between activities and stocks, and among time periods, must be taken into account.

The easiest way to set up the dynamic optimization problem conceptually is to recognize, first, that the current and all future values of the activities act as decision variables. Having done so, one can seek to optimize the discounted intrinsic value of these decisions. Thus the problem is to maximize present discounted intrinsic value over all future years (or enough of them to make the calculation converge) while requiring the production and financial constraints to hold in each year. We also must take cognizance of the "laws of motion" that link the stocks in a given year to the stocks and activities in the preceding year. An elegant approach to the dynamic optimization problem has been proposed by Katherine Schipper (1977). Our approach is much simpler, though not nearly so rich in potential interpretations.

Let the laws of motion be represented by the function $S_{t+1} = M(S_t, X_t)$. Then the dynamic optimization problem facing the nonprofit enterprise can be written as

$$\text{maximize} \sum_{t=1}^{\infty} \delta^t V(X_t, S_t)$$

with respect to $X_t (t = 1, \ldots, \infty)$

subject to the constraints

$$F^k(X_t, S_t) = 0 \quad (k = 1, \ldots, m \text{ and } t = 1, \ldots, \infty)$$

$$G(X_t, S_t) = 0 \quad (t = 1, \ldots, \infty) \tag{3.9}$$

$$S_{t+1} = M(X_t, S_t) \quad (t = 1, \ldots, \infty).$$

The new variable, δ, in the objective function is the institution's *value discount factor*. Its role is very important. If it is near its upper limit of one, what happens in the future is viewed as being nearly as important as what happens now. A smaller value means that δ^t goes to zero faster, so future events are judged to be less relevant. We would not quarrel with the conventional wisdom that students tend to have the smallest value of δ and trustees the largest, with faculty, administrators, and alumni somewhere in between.

The value discount factor must not be confused with the university's *financial discount factor*, which represents the opportunity cost of money. To see the difference, consider the situation where funds are withdrawn from a reserve account and expended for current activities. The expenditure produces value now. However, there will be a reduction in future income from investments because the reserve account balance has been reduced. This, in turn, will reduce future expenditures and hence future value. In this simple example, the financial discount factor would be the rate of return on the reserve balance —e.g., an interest rate—which, of course, determines the amount of the future income to be foregone by spending now. The value discount factor is used to weigh the relative importance of creating value now or in the future. It is an "impatience" or "immediacy" factor, so to speak, and thus it is an integral part of the institution's value system. In contrast, the financial discount factor is objectively determined by analyzing the university's investment alternatives.

In the for-profit sector, the value and financial discount factors usually are combined into a single "internal discount rate," or "target rate of return on capital." For example, a proposed investment in plant or equipment must be expected to produce a certain return (often called a "hurdle rate") before a favorable decision on it will be made. The target return is of course dependent on the amount the stockholders must receive if they are to refrain from withdrawing their capital and putting it to other uses. The confluence of the value and financial discount factors in the for-profit sector is the direct result of the fact that the profit function *is* the value function. As soon as one allows for a divergence between profit and value, the two discount factors become discrete —and quite different—entities. The financial factor can be estimated by analyzing external data; the value discount factor, in contrast, must be determined by introspection.

The formulation in equation (3.9) involves summing up the values calculated for future years, weighted by δ^t. The addition operation requires that the scale of $V(X_t, S_t)$ be well defined: that it be a utility function. Furthermore, the utility functions for the various years must all have the same scale. While such a set of utility functions might be developed, the task would be arduous given the number of variables involved. Also, it would not be easy to find the optimum in the "extensive-form infinite-horizon" problem represented by (3.9), even if the appropriate objective function could be formulated. One way around these difficulties would be to set aside equation (3.9) and try to develop a single value function covering the activities and stocks for all the years taken together: $V(X_1, S_1 ; X_2, S_2 ; \ldots)$. The value information for both the present and future would be weighted implicitly with respect to time preference and represented by a single set of rankings. While this method is correct from a theoretical standpoint, it is hard to see how it could be made to work in practice given the very large number of variables that would have to be valued simultaneously. A more practical alternative is represented by the concept of long-run financial equilibrium, which is analyzed in chapter 6.

Optimization Under Uncertainty

Up to now we have assumed that the planner or decision maker knows, or acts as if he knows, precisely what outcomes would be associated with any given choice of activities. That is, he assumes that once inputs have been selected and instructions consistent with the production function been given, plans will be implemented precisely and on schedule and the anticipated outputs will be obtained. Likewise, financial matters are assumed always to come out as planned. In this situation the planner's main problems (and they are significant) are to ascertain the institution's value, production, and financial functions, and succeed in calculating the optimum either implicitly or explicitly.

Obviously the world is not certain, and things do not work out as planned. Therefore a mechanism is needed for dealing with probabilistic outcomes. Since the basic approach is not unique to our problem and has in any case been dealt with extensively in the literature, we will consider it only briefly here.[8]

Consider that the activity variables in X are plans, and that the eventual outcomes will differ from the plans by a certain amount. Let us call the list of final outcomes X^*. Before the fact, our knowledge about X^* is in the form of a multivariate probability distribution conditional on X and the stocks: $f(X^*|X, S)$. The selection of a set of plans influences the outcome but does not determine it exactly. The influence is strong if the expected value of X^* is near X and its variance is small, and conversely.

The easiest way to think of the optimization problem under uncertainty is to maximize the expected utility of the outcomes, X^*, with respect to the plans, X, again subject to production and financial constraints. In the static case,

$$\text{maximize } E_{X^*} V(X^*, S|X)$$

$$\text{with respect to } X$$

$$\text{subject to the constraints}$$

$$F^k(X, S) = 0 \quad (k = 1, \ldots, m)$$

$$G(X, S) = 0 \tag{3.10}$$

where $E_{X^*} V(X^*, S|X)$ is the statistical expectation of V taken over the final outcomes for a given set of plans, that is,

$$E_{X^*} V(X^*, S|X) = \int_{X^*} V(X^*, S) f(X^*|X, S) dX^*.$$

The above formulation requires that the planned activities be consistent with the production and financial functions; it does not, however, control the probability that the actual outcomes will be consistent. More complex methods are available with which to tackle this problem, but they are beyond our scope here. Also, optimization under uncertainty requires that the scale of the V function be defined—that we deal with utilities, in other words, rather than ordinal values. This is because the equivalent of a weighted average over the V's is being taken in the process of calculating expected utility.

The structure of the university planning problem is such that, in many institutions, many of the tangible items in the activity list are rather tightly controllable. For instance, decisions involving small changes in faculty size, in numbers of students, and other such budget planning variables usually can be implemented if the plans to do so are consistent with financial realities and considerations of demand. Thus, in many situations involving tradeoffs for only a single year, deterministic or "certainty-equivalent" optimization techniques will not be far off the mark. Dynamic optimization raises the additional problem of how to smooth the effects of unanticipated financial contingencies over time. How to do this is the main subject of chapter 7.

Capital Budgeting

How do enterprises decide whether to engage in particular capital investment activities—constructing a new building, for instance, or buying a new piece of equipment? The problem is one of *capital budgeting*, a special case of the problem of optimization over time. Since many aspects of the problem are not unique to colleges and universities, we will often speak in this section of non-profit enterprises generally.

The nonprofit institution, as we have seen, differs from the pure profit-maximizing firm in that its objective function is multidimensional, often involving qualitative as well as quantitative factors. In contrast, the profit-maximizing firm's objective is not only unidimensional but is measured in terms of the ultimate fungible resource—money. This distinction has profound implications for the relation between value and capital and hence, in the nonprofit case, for capital budgeting.

Capital expenditures are made by the profit maximizer if and only if the present value of the time stream of incremental profits exceeds the opportunity loss with respect to the capital in other uses. Furthermore, the financial markets continuously capitalize the stream of the entire enterprise's future profits (adjusted for risk and, if necessary, for liquidation value), thus determining an external benchmark for the firm's cost of capital. This process works because: (a) the residual ownership claims can be expressed in unidimensional terms (which means that less information is needed and interpersonal comparisons of value are simplified); (b) the financial markets make the claims fungible (i.e., liquid) with modest transaction costs.

The residual value of the nonprofit enterprise is complex and the "markets" in which it is "traded" tend to be imperfect and subject to large transaction costs.* "Quality," for example, may well be a value that universities find important, although it is intangible and its benefits are not readily transferable from one recipient to another. However, if a private institution of quality is about to fail financially, it may be transferred to the public sector or receive public

---

*The hospital, viewed as a physicians' cooperative, may be an exception. Here the residual value of the enterprise is transmitted to the "owning" physicians in the form of their individual fees (see Pauly and Redisch 1973).

subsidies. Such an expedient can be viewed as a transaction in a certain kind of "market," though the terms of trade in such a market may be viewed as quite onerous.

From the foregoing it is abundantly clear that there generally is no external standard for the nonprofit institution's "cost of capital." The interest rates on bonds or bank loans do not serve this function any more than they do for the business firm, since these instruments represent fixed rather than residual claims on the value of the enterprise. Thus capital-budgeting decisions must be taken solely in terms of the internal and subjective value function of the institution, regardless of whether the funds are generated internally, borrowed, or received as gifts. To be sure, restricted gifts for specific capital projects (buildings, for example) do provide an external standard of worth, but only in terms of the donor's value function. Even here, however, the receiving institution must weigh the benefits against the remaining costs (including any perquisites that would be due the donor) in terms of its own values.

Single-period model. We are seeking the formal requirements for optimizing capital-expenditure decisions in terms of a multidimensional value function subject to constraints. Such requirements can best be introduced by limiting the analysis to a single fiscal period. To do this we suppose that all costs and benefits accrue during that period.

Let β be a vector of capital items that can be used to affect operations (or provide perquisites) during the fiscal period. Since β also will involve costs, we assume that it enters the parameter set of both $F(X)$ and $G(X)$—and $V(X)$ as well if β is intrinsically valued, as might be the case for a handsome building. Investment in β involves two kinds of costs: those of acquisition and those of operations. A new building, for example, is a project requiring operations and maintenance cost as well as capital outlay. The acquisition process may also bring intrinsic benefits or disbenefits; or it may affect the production function for current outputs (as when construction noise interferes with other work); or it may do both.

Define $dV/d\beta$ as the net change in value associated with operations due to the proposed change in β, taking into account the effects of using $d\beta$ upon all of the functions V, F, and G. Define $dV^*/d\beta$ similarly, except that now the effects of acquiring $d\beta$ are under consideration. (We assume differentiability throughout, even though in practice capital projects may come as discrete alternatives.)

Clearly, the proposed capital expenditure should be undertaken if and only if the value gained in operations exceeds that lost in acquisition. In mathematical terms this condition implies

$$\frac{dV}{d\beta} > -\frac{dV^*}{d\beta} \tag{3.11}$$

where presumably $dV^*/d\beta$ is negative. The form of the two terms is identical, so it is sufficient to evaluate one of them. Now,

$$\frac{dV}{d\beta} = V_\beta + \sum_j V_j \frac{dX_j}{d\beta} \tag{3.12}$$

where the summation in j is over all the activities and the partial derivative V_β is of course not the same thing as the total differential $dV/d\beta$.

The following logic shows that equation (3.12) can be simplified so that $dV/d\beta$ is equal to this simple expression:

$$\frac{dV}{d\beta} = V_\beta + \lambda F_\beta + \mu G_\beta \tag{3.13}$$

where V_β is the marginal intrinsic value, F_β the marginal increase in productivity, and G_β the marginal change in net operating revenue due to the use of the increment β of capital in the operations of the enterprise.

The derivative $dX_j/d\beta$ is the effect on X_j of adding $d\beta$ to capital stocks. This change is a result of interacting forces involving the impact of $d\beta$ on the value, production, and financial functions. An expression for $dX_j/d\beta$ is derived in appendix 2, at equation (2.A.5). If $d\beta$ affects the value function directly, a utility function, not just a value function, is needed. This, too, is discussed in appendix 2. An expression for V_j is easily obtained from the necessary conditions for the optimum, equation (3.6).

Define M as the matrix of cross-partial derivatives of H with respect to X_i and X_j, bordered with $-\lambda F_j$ and μG_j as shown in appendix 2, equation (2.A.4). Let M be the determinant and M_{ij}, M_{jF}, and M_{jG} be cofactors of M. Now we substitute V_j and $dX_j/d\beta$ into (3.12), and note the following identities based on *determinantal expansion* (for which see Allen 1963, p. 401):

$$\lambda \sum_j \mu G_j \frac{M_{jF}}{M} = 0 \qquad \mu \sum_j \lambda F_j \frac{M_{jG}}{M} = 0$$

$$\sum_j \mu G_j \frac{M_{ij}}{M} = 0 \qquad \sum_j \lambda F_j \frac{M_{ij}}{M} = 0$$

which are true by expansion of M by alien cofactors; and

$$\sum_j G_j \frac{M_{jG}}{M} = \mu \qquad \lambda \sum_j F_j \frac{M_{jG}}{M} = \lambda$$

which are true by expansion of M by its own cofactors. Equation (3.13) follows immediately.

Exactly the same result can be obtained for $dV*/d\beta$, which is the change in value (usually a reduction) attributable to building or acquiring the asset.

Thus the criterion for capital asset acquisition, given in equation (3.11), can be rewritten as follows:

$$V_\beta + \lambda F_\beta + \mu G_\beta > -(V_\beta^* + \lambda F_\beta^* + \mu G_\beta^*). \tag{3.14}$$

According to this result, the criterion involves only the direct effects upon values of the proposed project. The optimal mix of inputs and outputs will change when the new asset comes into use, but there is no need to evaluate these changes in detail when making the investment decision.

Multiperiod model. Now suppose that the process of acquiring the capital project takes R periods, that financial payments for acquisition begin in $R + 1$ and are spread over T periods, and that the operational benefits and costs continue for Q periods starting after acquisition is complete. With these assumptions the multiperiod version of equation (3.14) is

$$\sum_{t=R+1}^{R+Q} \delta^t(V_{\beta t} + \lambda F_{\beta t} + \mu G_{\beta t}) > -\sum_{t=1}^{R} \delta^t(V_{\beta t}^* + \lambda F_{\beta t}^*) - \sum_{t=R+1}^{R+T} \delta^t \mu G_{\beta t}^* \tag{3.15}$$

where δ is the factor that discounts future claims to value. Note that the process of taking a weighted average over time requires that $V(X)$ be a utility function rather than a value function.

It is worth emphasizing again that δ is not the same thing as an interest rate or a financial cost of capital; indeed, it may bear little relation to these quantities. Instead, δ expresses the institution's tradeoff of present versus future value. Nonprofit institutions needing to make capital-budgeting decisions would be well advised to think carefully and explicitly about their value for δ.

The financial acquisition cost for period t (i.e. $G_{\beta t}^*$) is the dollar opportunity loss applicable to that period. This depends on the financing scheme selected (i.e., upon the cash payment schedule), and has no relation to the accounting concept of depreciation. However, care must be taken that the dollar opportunity loss is defined in terms of the institution's *current fund*, since the shadow price μ relates only to that fund, which is the one on which the budget constraint bites.

Nonprofit enterprises have three main ways of financing capital expenditures. Each of the three has different implications for current-fund opportunity loss and hence for $G_{\beta t}^*$.

1. *The project is paid for immediately by means of a restricted gift.* (For simplicity, let us assume the gift would not have been forthcoming for any other purpose.) In this case there is absolutely no dollar opportunity loss to acquisition, so $G_{\beta t}^*$ is zero for all periods.

2. *Money is borrowed from external sources to pay for the project, and the loans are repaid over the postulated T periods.* Hence $G_{\beta t}^*$ is the cash outlay (principal and interest) in period t, paid from current funds.

3. *The project is financed internally from reserves.* If the payment is treated as a loan, repayable from the current fund over T periods with interest at market rates, this case is the same as (2). However, an interest subsidy will generate an income loss for the reserve loaning the money, and this in turn is an opportunity loss as represented by $G_{\beta t}^*$, for the current fund. (The timing of the current-fund loss depends on whether the yield on reserve balances is treated as current-fund income or left to accrue.) If the money is never repaid, any interest subsidy will go on forever (i.e., $T \to \infty$).

In closing this section, we note that the transfer of money from the current fund to build up a depreciation reserve amounts to taking an opportunity loss now in order to be able to pay for (perhaps unspecified) future projects. As such, it is no different from any other spending-saving decision. Moreover, once funds have been accumulated, the considerations about income loss discussed in paragraph (3) above apply whether the money is called a depreciation reserve, any other reserve, or even "funds functioning as endowment."

Decentralized Optimization

Colleges and universities often are faced with the problem of allocating resources hierarchically through two or more layers of organization. The judgments needed to do this become more difficult as organizational distance increases. Should the provost make allocations for particular expenditures in specific academic departments, or should the deans have full discretion, as at Harvard? Should a state legislature determine expense line items by field, department, or school, or should discretion (and accountability) be placed in the hands of the university's administration? Such examples could be multiplied, yet one often hears the assertion that all important resource allocations must be made by the central authorities.

The answers people give to these questions depend critically on the degree to which they believe that decision makers at lower organizational levels will make "good" choices, that is, choices consistent with the institution's general well-being. But more specific matters, such as the degree of academic synergy among schools, restricted versus unrestricted endowment, potential for gifts, or the weight of local tradition, are also important. Another critical factor is the consistency of decision makers' value functions at the various levels. Providing incentives for "good" decisions is a problem, just as it is when decentralization is practiced in the for-profit sector.

The business model, of course, ties rewards to economic profit or contribution to profit. Such a model requires that goods and services be transferred among organizational units at prices that either approximate market prices or adjust them in specific ways to take account of externalities with respect to individual departments.[7] For example, the transfer price may be set above the market price if the providing department delivers benefits to the organization that are not captured by the transactions in question. Approaches based on this concept have been proposed for colleges and universities.[8] In this section we shall try to extend the same concept of market-based incentives within the context of our general model for optimization by nonprofit institutions, particularly colleges and universities.

Let s = an index denoting schools or other organizational units, with $s = 1, \ldots, n$

X^s = the activities taking place in schools (X^s is mutually exclusive as to s, i.e., the same unit of activity cannot exist in two or more schools, and exhaustive with respect to the university's activity variables)

P^s = the vector of output prices and unit input costs assigned to school s by the central administration (i.e., P^s is the "transfer price" vector)

$\bar{\bar{P}}^s$ = the vector of output prices and unit input costs as faced by the central administration, with respect to the activities of school s

$V^s(X^s)$ = the value function of school s with respect to its own activity vector

$\bar{V}(X)$ = the value function for the central administration with respect to the activities of all the schools, including school s

It will be convenient to think of X^s as consisting only of tangible elements, although the bar in $\bar{X}$ has been omitted to keep the notation simple. Also for simplicity, we assume that the financial function is linear in the X^s's. The output prices and input costs, which are denoted collectively by P^s, constitute decision variables for the central administration and "givens" for the schools. The market prices, denoted by $\bar{\bar{P}}^s$, are taken as given for the purposes of this analysis. In order for the values denoted by $\bar{V}(X)$ to be compared, we make the strong assumption that the value functions of the schools and the central administration all have the same scale (i.e., that they are all invariant in the same monotonic transformation). The net of fixed revenues and fixed costs for the central administration is denoted by $\bar{P}_0$, which is a given. The financial constraint for each school allows for "subventions," denoted by P_0^s, from the central administration to the school (they may be positive or negative). The subventions P_0^s are included in the transfer prices P^s.

From the standpoint of the central administration the university's optimization problem is

$$\text{maximize } \bar{V}(X^s) \quad (s = 1, \ldots, n)$$

$$\text{with respect to } P^s$$

$$\text{subject to the constraint}$$

$$\sum_s \sum_j \bar{\bar{P}}_j^s X_j^s + \bar{P}_0 - \sum_s \sum_j P_j^s X_j^s - \sum_s P_0^s = 0.$$

That is,

(3.16)

$$\left(\begin{array}{c} \text{net revenue of} \\ \text{central administration} \end{array} \right) - (\text{net outflow to the schools}) = 0.$$

The optimization is with respect to all the elements of P^s, for all the schools.

A word about externalities among schools is necessary at this point. Clearly they exist, since the effectiveness of a program in one area, for example, may depend on faculty and student resources in another. However, there is no need to consider them explicitly once the role of the central administration's value function is understood. Externalities are assumed to enter $\bar{V}(X)$, since the central administration, in its drive for optimization, is viewing the whole enterprise at once. For example, if more faculty in school s are needed to advance a desired program in school s', this will tend to increase the central administration's marginal value of faculty in school s. This, in turn, will lead to a change in the transfer prices or subventions—a process that will continue until the central administration believes a reasonable optimum has been obtained.

In appendix 2 (equation 2.A.13), we show that the necessary conditions for the administration's optimum are

$$\sum_j [(\bar{\bar{V}}_j^s - V_j^s) + \phi(\bar{\bar{P}}_j^s - P_j^s)]\mathcal{S}_{jk}^s = 0 \quad \text{(over } k, s)$$

$$\sum_j [(\bar{\bar{V}}_j^s - V_j^s) + \phi(\bar{\bar{P}}_j^s - P_j^s)]\mathcal{F}_j^s = \phi - \mu^s \quad \text{(over } s) \qquad (3.17)$$

$$\sum_s \sum_j (\bar{\bar{P}}_j^s - P_j^s)X_j^s = \sum_s P_0^s - \bar{P}_0$$

where ϕ is the shadow price on the central administration's financial constraint and the μ^s's are the shadow prices on the financial constraints for the schools. Equation (3.17) shows that various weighted averages of marginal value deviations and price deviations, between the central administration and each school, are set to zero. The weights are $\mathcal{S}_{jk}^s$ and $\mathcal{F}_j^s$, which are, respectively, the schools' *substitution effects* between variables i and j, and their *financial effects* for variable j. These are analogous to the substitution and income effects of consumer demand theory. They are defined in appendix 2 in the list that precedes equation (1.A.6).

The conditions in (3.17) have an easy interpretation when the value functions for the schools and the central administration are identical. In this case the marginal value deviations vanish, leaving

$$\sum_j (\bar{\bar{P}}_j - P_j^s)\mathcal{S}_{jk}^s = 0$$

$$\sum_j (\bar{\bar{P}}_j - P_j^s)\mathcal{F}_j^s = \phi - \mu^s. \qquad (3.18)$$

One solution to the first equation in (3.18) is to set $(\bar{\bar{P}}_j - P_j^s) = 0$ for all j and s, i.e., to set the transfer prices equal to the market prices.* This is the pure

---

*Other solutions to (3.18) appear to be possible if, as is likely, the $\mathcal{S}_{jk}^s$'s do not all have the same sign. However, the simplicity of this solution and the analogy of the profit-maximizing case recommend it strongly.

"market" incentive system discussed earlier; it is also the solution for the profit-maximizing firm in the absence of externalities. If this strategy is adopted the second equation reduces to $\phi = \mu^s$. The subventions are set so that the marginal utility of money is at once equal in all schools and equal to that for the central administration.

Returning now to the general case represented by (3.17), we see that a reasonable decision rule for the central administration is to set the prices and unit costs for each school as follows:

$$P_j^s = \frac{\bar{\bar{V}}_j^s - V_j^s}{\phi} + \bar{\bar{P}}_j^s. \tag{3.19}$$

According to this, the administration would make at least rough estimates of the marginal value differences between it and the dean of each school, and adjust the transfer price accordingly. This adjustment would in turn lead to variations in μ^s across schools when the optimal subventions were determined.

Obviously it is not easy to make the estimates needed to implement equation (3.19). However, it seems likely that the loss of value (to the central administration and trustees) due to errors in transfer price adjustment will be a monotonic function of the weights $\mathscr{S}_{jk}$ and $\mathscr{F}_j$. Therefore attention should be concentrated on variables that are believed to have large substitution (especially own-price substitution) and financial effects.

There may be an issue as to whether the central administration has any right to manipulate the allocation decisions of deans in the first place. We would argue that such a right exists unless it has been given up explicitly—for instance, by the institution's constitution or equivalent, or by a specific agreement with a dean or faculty. There may still be a problem of perceived equity, however, if the transfer prices to one school differ from those to another when ostensibly the same activities are being considered. If the transfer prices equal the market prices, this problem will not generally arise. Judgment is needed as to the degree to which central optimization should be pursued if a school has a decentralized decision structure and highly visible transfer prices.

Even if the market prices are passed through to the schools as transfer prices, there remains an opportunity to optimize the subventions. Judgments need to be made about differences in financial shadow prices among schools, and the subventions should be set so that they are about equal. In contrast, it is often proposed that the subventions should be set on the basis of accounting allocations of fixed costs and revenues. Such a course will generally be suboptimal from the standpoint of both the central administration and the schools, since accounting rules have little if anything to do with an institution's value function. Where flows of benefits are strong and readily identified, it is appropriate to charge out support service costs, thus incorporating them in the transfer price vector. But where flows of benefits are not well defined, it would seem to be better to deal with subvention frankly, in value terms, rather than trying to develop refined allocation rules and public justifications based on them.

Market Characteristics in the Nonprofit Sector

So far we have limited our attention entirely to the internal optimizing behavior of the nonprofit enterprise. We now consider the relations among such enterprises, including colleges and universities, as they interact in the marketplace. Our analysis will examine demand, supply, market power, and entry and exit. In so doing we will relax the assumption of perfect competition in which the previous section was rooted.

Industry Demand-and-Supply Curves

In most cases a nonprofit enterprise will produce external benefits, that is, outputs with value for people outside the organization itself. (An exception would be a private membership organization with no external benefits.) Such benefits may be private or collective. If they are private, the nonprofit firm can capture this external value, as reflected in the demand curve for the output, via the market price. This is not possible in the case of collective or "public" outputs because there will be many "free riders" (i.e., those who benefit from the output but do not pay for it directly). Of course, many outputs of the nonprofit sector are partly private and partly public. Quality education is a case in point, since the individual recipient benefits and so does society in general, beyond the point where the social benefit is reflected by the individual's wages.

We shall define the enterprise's demand curves for outputs bought by individuals and other direct users as representing the private benefits obtained by these users. Demand curves for outputs called forth by the government through grants and contracts represent public benefits, of course. (In theory, government contracts are for "purchases" of goods and services and grants are for sponsorship of the work of the institution. However, the distinction has become blurred in practice.) The industry demand curve for each output is derivable in principle from those of the individual enterprises.

Nonprofit institutions also face "demand curves" with respect to those who supply funds without requiring a specific quid pro quo. Examples are private donors and foundations, and in some cases government granting agencies. "Industry demand curves" exist for philanthropy and for grants as well as for specific outputs of the nonprofit sector, and these are of course related to the demand curves faced by the individual enterprises. All demand curves are treated as given in the analysis that follows.

We now turn to the determination of industry supply. For the profit maximizer, the firm's supply schedule is simply its marginal cost curve. That is, an increase in price elicits an increase in output up to the point where marginal cost has risen to again equal price. The industry supply curve is the sum of the individual firms' marginal cost curves after adjustment for any interfirm reallocations of supply that are elicited by the market price change. Market price is determined by the intersection of the industry demand-and-supply curves.

That the situation is different for nonprofit institutions can be seen from equation (3.8), above, which is restated here in terms of the more expressive notation of marginal cost (*MC*), marginal revenue (*MR*), and *effective marginal intrinsic value* (*EMIV*):

$$MC = MR + EMIV.$$

The supply curve of the enterprise defines the price at which output will have been adjusted so that this equation holds. The marginal revenue of a single enterprise is equal to the price it can obtain, so the supply curve can be written as

$$MR = MC - EMIV.$$

This differs from the supply curve of the profit maximizer by the subtraction of *EMIV* from *MC*.

The supply curve for the nonprofit "industry" is of course the sum of those for the individual enterprises. Market price is determined by the intersection of the industry demand-and-supply curves. The fact that various enterprises may have different value functions does not lead to logical complications, since this is analogous to variations in production functions and hence in marginal cost curves. (Indeed, profit maximizers can exist in the same industry with nonprofit institutions, so far as this analysis is concerned.) Value differences simply lead to supply reallocations as market prices change. These reallocations are predicted in appendix 2, equation (2.A.5), which calculates the differences in an individual institution's output as a function of a change in such an external parameter as a market price.

Industry Price and Output Determination

Figure 3.4 illustrates the supply-and-demand relations for an industry that includes nonprofit institutions, under the assumption *EMIV* > 0 for most if not all firms, for all output levels. For simplicity it may be desirable to imagine that all the firms' marginal cost functions and marginal value functions are equal, thus making the industry curves simply scaled-up versions of those for the individual firms. The upper portion of the figure shows that the industry equilibrium, point *A*, is at a lower price and larger output than would be the case for an industry of profit maximizers. This is just what would be expected on the basis of figure 3.3, which depicted the individual nonprofit firm.

Up to now we have focused only on the marginality conditions without considering explicitly the fact that total costs must be equal to total revenue for each nonprofit enterprise. The effect of this relationship enters via the financial shadow price, μ. Suppose that a shift in donation-market conditions leads to a larger flow of funds to the industry. Other things being equal, we would expect an increase in the flow of gifts to a given institution to decrease its μ-value since the financial constraint will not be as binding. (More formally: value is increased, and by the assumption of concavity we would expect the

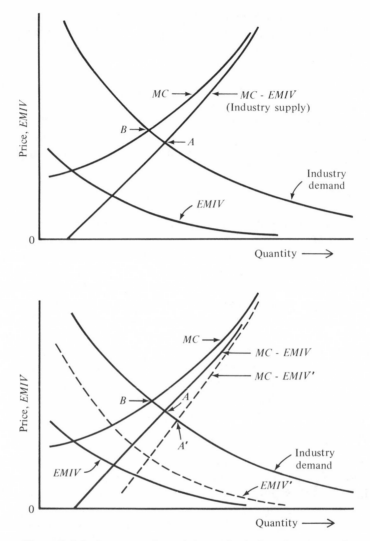

Figure 3.4. Industry supply-and-demand relations for nonprofit enterprises

marginal value of money to decline.) Hence, for any given value of output, *EMIV* probably is increased (recall that $EMIV_j = V_j/\mu$), thus shifting the supply curve to the right. These results are shown by $EMIV'$ and $MC - EMIV'$ in the lower part of figure 3.4. The exact nature of the shifts will of course depend on the number of enterprises receiving the extra gifts, the amounts of the gifts, and any reallocation of supply among firms. Each firm will seek to shift its output to be consistent with its new μ.

The rightward shift in the supply curve leads to a new market equilibrium, signified by point A′ in the lower part of figure 3.4. As we would expect from the assumptions outlined above, the increase in gifts has reduced price and increased output. While this result cannot be proved with generality, it seems likely that it represents the usual situation.

As the level of gifts and other fixed revenues declines, the financial shadow price gets larger and larger. Eventually $\mu \to \infty$ at the point where it becomes unfeasible to meet the financial constraint. (This was the point Q in panel A of figure 3.2.) In this case $EMIV \to 0$ and the supply curve becomes the same as the marginal cost curve—a result that leads to the "profit-maximizing" solution at point B in figure 3.4. It is possible also that fixed revenues will increase to the point where $\mu \to 0$, in which case the marginal cost curve will be essentially irrelevant. (We ignore the possibility that fixed revenue will be so large as to prevent nonprofit status at finite output levels and nonnegative prices.) The above arguments lead to the following proposition: The greater the fixed revenue for a nonprofit institution, the less important will be narrowly economic factors in its decision making and the more important will be the value factors.* Perhaps the converse is less obvious to some of us in colleges and universities, but it is true nevertheless: the lower the unrestricted gifts, investment return from endowment, and the like, the more important must such "crass" economic factors as prices and marginal costs become in making decisions about activity levels.

The Market for Inputs

The market situation for the inputs that nonprofit enterprises use is, with certain exceptions, analogous to the one for the outputs that they produce.

1. Nonprofit enterprises generally use many of the same inputs as other kinds of institutions; for instance, they use ordinary (i.e., profit-oriented) labor, materials, etc. These inputs do not usually have intrinsic value for the enterprise nor can it affect the market price for them. The nonprofit enterprise's demands for these inputs, just like the profit-maximizer's demands for them, are designed to minimize the cost of producing a given output once any intrinsically valued inputs have been determined.

2. Some inputs tend to be used mostly by nonprofit institutions (or particular kinds of them). Hence the value system and donation-demand characteristics of the nonprofit industry, as well as the demand for that industry's output, will affect the inputs' market prices. However, the cost-minimizing behavior of individual enterprises is exactly the same as in (1).

3. Some inputs may be valued intrinsically by the nonprofit enterprise (i.e., $EMIV > 0$ for these inputs). Generally this will occur only when the given type of enterprise is the main source of demand for these inputs, and so intrinsic valuation will tend to bid up their market price. Depending on the nature of this valuation, the phenomenon may amount to the same thing

---

*Compare the statement by Philip R. P. Coelho: "Nonprofit enterprises that do not attract outside funds [gifts] and who do not have an endowment must behave as profit oriented firms or they will not survive" (1976, p. 417).

as providing "above-market" perquisites to certain personnel, even though in this case the market is the governing mechanism. In other words, if a significant number of enterprises in a nonprofit industry decide that certain inputs should be intrinsically valued, the price will be bid up (if supply cannot be expanded readily), and a self-fulfilling and possibly distorting market mechanism will result.

The last point is worthy of further comment. In the for-profit sector, valuation is determined by users of resources and prices are set in arm's-length negotiations in which marginal values and costs play the commanding role. In the nonprofit sector, however, the market process is conditioned by the institution's own value function, which is determined subjectively by its governing board, internal constituencies, and, in the case of public institutions, the political process. If the intrinsic valuation of inputs produces private benefits for those who determine or influence the institution's value function, the process of negotiating in the marketplace loses much of its arm's-length character.

As far as outputs are concerned, there seems no good reason to doubt that, most of the time, the actors in the process of value determination are operating in what would normally be called a "socially responsible" way. That is, they are trying to maximize their perception of the collective benefit rather than working for their own private gain. (Parenthetically, we note that bonus-and-incentive compensation schemes are rarely used in the nonprofit sector.) The same does not necessarily apply to certain inputs, however. Since valuation is subjective, it is easy to confound perceived collective benefit with private gain and justify both in terms of noble goals. Moreover, when inputs are intrinsically valued the information provided by the market does not highlight these "extra payments" and provide the means to control them, but instead serves to reinforce the whole process.

Market Power

For the profit maker, *market power* is a function of the steepness of the slope of the firm's demand curve. For the monopolist the firm's demand curve is the same as that for primary or *industry demand*, and thus has maximum slope. Under pure competition the slope is zero for the individual firm, since any price deviation between the firm and its competitors will result in massive shifts in sales. A downward-sloping demand curve always permits some degree of *monopoly profits* to be obtained.

This definition of market power can also be applied to nonprofit institutions. The implications are not quite the same, however. If the demand curve for the individual enterprise is downward sloping, then that enterprise has an extra degree of freedom in its value maximization. This can be important. Imagine, for instance, an institution selling two outputs, one for which demand is inelastic (the demand curve slopes down sharply) and one with elastic demand. Other things being equal, the price in the inelastic market will be set above that in the elastic one. Let us suppose that the ratio of price to marginal cost would be the same for both outputs if the demand for them were equally elastic (or inelastic). It follows that the existing differences in elasticity will lead to a price increase and reduction of output in the low-elasticity market and usually a (relative) subsidy for outputs in the high-elasticity market. The low-elasticity market's profits are the source of subsidy in question.

The ability to enforce a kind of transfer payment determined by the institution's value function certainly is a kind of market power. This power exists no matter how the enterprise chooses to exercise it; thus a decision (based on the value considerations) to hold the price to below market clearing levels and ration output is still an exercise of market power. The output of selective universities and colleges, for instance, is rationed in this way.

Pure competition among nonprofit enterprises would fix the output prices of each institution and thus eliminate this source of market power. What are the implications for public policy of market power for nonprofit enterprises? They depend upon whether one would prefer decision making in the nonprofit sector to be based on few or many value functions. In developing our argument here we shall assume that institutional value functions tend to be based on collective rather than private criteria. To the extent this is not true, the residual values of the enterprise go to private claimants and the traditional market power implications apply.

We believe that, other things being equal, a single value function is dangerous and plurality is a virtue. (This also provides an argument for the existence of the nonprofit sector itself, as opposed to allowing all collective goods to be supplied by the government.) We do not intend, however, to draw an analogy to the need for eliminating excess profits in the for-profit sector by increasing the number of actual or potential competitors. The argument for enhancing economic efficiency by making price equal marginal cost ceases to be relevant with the introduction of effective marginal intrinsic value. Also, it may be that the welfare of society is best served by a moderate number of nonprofit enterprises, each one with strong traditions of socially responsible value determination, good management, reasonable political and social accountability, and strong sources of fixed revenue. Recall from the last section that fixed revenue tends to increase the weight of the value function—here assumed to be socially responsible—as compared to the production and financial functions. Large numbers of nonprofit competitors locked in strong competition with one another at every turn would not seem to favor social responsibility in any of the ways mentioned.

Entry and Exit of Institutions

The degree and form of competition depends to a great extent upon the nature of the entry-and-exit process for a given industry. Let us assume homogeneity of demand and equal access to factors of production. Then entry into a nonprofit industry will occur when a potential firm's value of $MC - EMIV$ is smaller than that of existing firms at the margin, that is, where the potential entrant is not in equilibrium at zero output given the industry conditions at point A in figure 3.4, above. This condition may occur due to any or all of the following factors, assuming all other things are equal and there are no barriers to entry.

1. The entrant's production process is more efficient than that of the current marginal firm; this pushes its MC down.

2. The entrant places a greater marginal intrinsic value on the output in question; this means a larger V_j and hence—other things being equal—a larger $EMIV$.

3. The entrant is better endowed with fixed revenues. This leads to a smaller μ and a larger $EMIV$.

The first condition is of course the same as for profit maximizers, but the last two are unique to the not-for-profit sector. For (2), entrance can occur simply because a new group comes into existence and *decides* to value the jth output more heavily than do existing enterprises. For (3), the enabling factor is the reduction of the financial shadow price to the point where the value function (assumed common across the industry unless specified otherwise) can be more freely exercised. Numerous examples of both types of entrance readily come to mind.

The process of exit is of course the mirror image of the one for entry. However, we believe that this is yet another case in which the nonprofit sector's value-determination process results in a contrast with the for-profit sector. Suppose things are going badly for a nonprofit firm. "Going badly" could take the form of more price competition, thus lowering MR. Or a falloff in fixed revenue might have increased μ, or the firm might be less efficient than its competitors and therefore more vulnerable if the industry as a whole curtailed its output.

The classical method of adjustment would be to reduce output—which would tend to increase MR, probably decrease MC, and increase $EMIV$—until the equality of the $MR = MC - EMIV$ relation is restored. Exit would occur if equality could not be restored at positive output. But such a program of adjustment will undoubtedly produce strains within the organization. Advocates for the output in question, and for the inputs that go into it, will be heard. Since the value function is subjective in the first place, these voices have a chance of changing the value function so as to reduce the needed adjustment. (In contrast, the MR and MC functions, which are all that enter into the decision process of the pure profit maximizer, cannot be changed just because one wants to do so.) Clearly some adjustments will have to be made, since the financial and production constraints must be met in the end. However, the tendency will be to spread the problem widely through numerous subtle changes in the value function. This behavior is characteristic of colleges and universities, where administrators often must defend the very concept of hard choices (in addition, they may be the target of loud exhortations to "raise more money"). In some cases, too, institutions have gone public when in financial trouble, thus changing a part of their value system to avoid the need for major changes in output and input levels.

In one sense, modification of values is desirable because it gives the nonprofit enterprise more flexibility in dealing with its problems. The profit maximizer has no such option; his criterion of value is fixed and quantitative. In theory, at least, investors are quick to react to variations in the fortunes of his firm. Thus the flexibility of the nonprofit enterprise means that, other things being equal, it has more staying power than its for-profit counterpart.

On the other hand, there is a danger that the changes in the value function will be ad hoc and responsive chiefly to internal private interests. In that case, the enterprise may be diverted from its original long-run objectives, perhaps to the point where it ceases to truly serve the public good. The gradual but steady deterioration of the enterprise will alienate those who provide fixed revenue through philanthropy. Since, however, there are no organized "markets" for the assessment of institutional values, the exit process will be much slower and more uncertain in many nonprofit industries—including, we suspect, higher education.

This completes our excursion into a general theory of choice and market behavior for nonprofit enterprises, with particular emphasis on colleges and universities. We now shall return to our main subject, higher education.

Functional Constraints on Colleges and Universities

In this section we shall develop the idea of value maximization subject to constraints by looking in more detail at the structural and behavioral characteristics of colleges and universities. We shall begin with a general discussion of their production functions and then move on to consider demand, revenue, and cost functions, as well as alternative measures of costs.

Production Functions

Determining a college's or university's production function may be more vexing than determining its value function, which in itself is very difficult. Production functions certainly are more difficult to define and quantify than financial functions. There are two reasons for this, neither of which is likely to be alleviated in the foreseeable future.

1. The qualitative or intangible characteristics of an academic institution's inputs and outputs are absolutely central to its functioning. The quantity of its teaching and research cannot be estimated in any meaningful way unless their quality is also considered. The problem is that few systematic measures, much less quantitative ones, are available for comparing quality across programs or over time.

2. Little is known about the process by which education and research inputs are transformed into outputs other than that (a) the process is labor intensive; (b) it depends a great deal on the motivation and attitudes of both teachers and students; (c) the tradeoffs between quality and quantity can be substantial. The last point is the critical one for present purposes. It is indeed dangerous to use quantity of output as a surrogate for hard-to-measure qualitative attributes, or to assume that the qualitative attributes tend to be invariant to changes in quantity.

We believe that the concern felt by many faculty and students about "doing things by the numbers" in university planning is rooted in the difficulty of evaluating academic production functions. They are right to be concerned; this is a case where a little knowledge is indeed a dangerous thing. While some valid analyses can be performed (we will discuss some of them in chapter 5), great care must be taken not to overreach and oversimplify, and thus fall prey to some of the problems we cited in chapter 1.

There is a way to solve the production-function problem while remaining within the conceptual structure of value maximization subject to constraints; in fact, this is what seems to be going on in practice. We will return to this point in a moment. First let us examine some distinctions among outputs and inputs, and the relations between them, that ought to be taken into account by university planners.

Classes of outputs and inputs. Colleges and universities produce three major categories of primary outputs: education, research and scholarship, and public service. Roughly speaking, these can be described as: (a) transmitting knowledge; (b) creating new knowledge; (c) performing public service tasks— originating radio and television programs, for instance, or running extension services. In addition, there are many kinds of secondary outputs, among which academic support services and student services are prominent. This is perhaps the best place to add a third category: *tertiary outputs*, such as institutional support (including administration and governance) and operation and maintenance of plant.

The primary, secondary, and tertiary outputs represent our breakdown of the activities of the university into what are called *functional categories.*[9] It should be clear that secondary and tertiary outputs serve as inputs to the production of primary outputs. However, some secondary functions have a strong claim to be considered final (and strongly valued) outputs in their own right. Examples are certain activities of libraries, museums, and galleries; university presses; demonstration schools; and counseling and career guidance; and cultural events.

The basic inputs or factors of production for a university are faculty and staff services, inputs from the students themselves, supplies and similar expense items, and usage of plant and equipment stocks, including library holdings. Inputs from the students themselves are considered basic because of the importance of self-motivation and effort, and also because the process of becoming educated contributes to the education of others and sometimes to research and public service. Categorization of basic inputs in this way corresponds to what has been called classification by object of expenditure in the university's accounting system.[10] Sometimes we will speak of classification of expenditures by *line item*. Table 3.2 presents the relationships of inputs

Table 3.2. Classification of Inputs and Outputs for Colleges and Universities

Output Category (Function)	Output	Input by Function	Input (Object) Faculty	Staff	Students	$S \& E$[a]	$P \& E$[b]
Instruction(I)	Y^I	Z^I	$= \{F^I$	S^I	Q^I	$S \& E^I$	$P \& E^I$ }
Research (R)	Y^R	Z^R	$= \{F^R$	S^R	Q^R	$S \& E^R$	$P \& E^R$ }
Public service (PS)	Y^{PS}	Z^{PS}	$= \{F^{PS}$	S^{PS}	Q^{PS}	$S \& E^{PS}$	$P \& E^{PS}$}
Academic support and student services (AS)	Y^{AS}	Z^{AS}	$= \{F^{AS}$	S^{AS}	Q^{AS}	$S \& E^{AS}$	$P \& E^{AS}$}
Institutional support and operation and maintenance of plant (IS)	Y^{IS}	Z^{IS}	$= \{F^{IS}$	S^{IS}	Q^{IS}	$S \& E^{IS}$	$P \& E^{IS}$}
Joint production: Instruction and Research	...	Z^{IR}	$= \{F^{IR}$	S^{IR}	Q^{IR}	$S \& E^{IR}$	$P \& E^{IR}$}
Total by object	...	...	$F^{\cdot}$	$S^{\cdot}$	$Q^{\cdot}$	$S \& E^{\cdot}$	$P \& E^{\cdot}$

[a] Supplies and expenses.
[b] Plant and equipment.

to each other by object and by function, and lists the major categories of outputs. Consider the first row of the table: the notation $Z^I = \{F^I, S^I, \dots\}$ means that the list of inputs to instruction (Z^I) consists of faculty time (F^I), staff time (S^I), etc. These result in the "production" of Y^I units of output. The sum down each object column is the total of that input used by the university: for example, F is total faculty time used in the fiscal period. (There is no total for inputs by function, for outputs, or across rows, since these are not measured in commensurate units.) The lists of inputs and outputs should be thought of as including separate entities for each of a number of types and/or quality levels.

The next-to-last row of table 3.2 articulates a very important characteristic of universities: in certain situations instruction and research are *joint products*, for instance, when a professor doing his or her own research involves a graduate student in the work. The student is being educated and research is being conducted simultaneously, with the same set of inputs. Thus it is impossible to separate the inputs (faculty time for instance) according to output category except on the basis of some externally determined allocation rule, such as an accounting convention. Therefore a separate output category is required in the table. It probably is true that small amounts of joint production exist with respect to many other combinations of output categories. These amounts would become more important if the functional categories—instruction for instance—were broken down by subcategory (in this case, by academic program). Instruction and research have been singled out because, for them, the joint production process is absolutely central to the workings of the research university.

A convenient way of thinking about the various production functions of a university is to classify them according to the output categories in table 3.2. There is a kind of hierarchy or recursion in the system, in that the production function for each primary output (I, R, PS) depends on the secondary and tertiary outputs. In turn, the secondary production function (AS) depends on the tertiary output (IS).

The production functions for instruction and research are linked together by the joint inputs (Z^{IR}), which are mostly faculty time. Also, there may be other linkages in that the outputs of one process may serve as inputs to another. The distinction between the latter kind of linkage and joint production is that, when an output becomes an input to a higher-level process, there is a simultaneous-equation system but no ambiguity as to the functional assignment of inputs. This should be clear from table 3.2: thus F^{AS} is still assigned to the "academic support" function, even though Y^{AS} is an input to the instruction process. We will have occasion to use these concepts in chapter 5, where we develop and discuss network flow models.

Dealing with the intangible attributes. Despite the intrinsic difficulties of understanding academic departments' production functions, university officers and faculty continue to allocate resources among them. At one level of analysis, it can be said that the allocators come to know the situation well enough to understand productivity relations (including such intangibles as quality and motivation) and to integrate them with financial and value considerations—all implicitly. This certainly is the way things work, and much can be learned by provosts, deans, and heads of departments when they focus on particular fields or programs. Indeed, next to the ability to judge individual faculty qualifications this ability is the most important intellectual attribute of the successful academic officer.

How, then, can we modify our theory of university choice to take account of the implicit way in which academic officers evaluate the production function? The answer lies in the distinction, discussed earlier, between tangible and intangible variables. The tangible variables are usually sufficient to specify the university's financial function. They also enter the production function, but here the intangible variables also play a key role. Both the tangible and intangible variables are important for determining the value function. Thus there is an asymmetry between the financial function, on the one hand, and the production and value functions on the other. We believe that academic resource allocators tend to think in terms of: (a) the financial relationship among the tangible variables; (b) a combined productivity-value function involving both the tangible and intangible variables. Such "two-equation behavior" can, however, be reconciled with our three-equation theory in a reasonable and instructive way. Recall how we partitioned the list of activities into sublists of tangibles and intangibles. As before, let $\bar{X}$ be the tangible activities and $\tilde{X}$ be the intangible ones. Note that if all the items in the list $\bar{X}$ are chosen, the available options with respect to $\tilde{X}$ are circumscribed considerably by the production function. For example, setting $\bar{X}$ determines the ratio of students to faculty and this conditions the type and quality of teaching that can be offered. Then we postulate that the academic planner believes that, for any choice of the tangible factors, $\bar{X}$, the intangible factors, $\tilde{X}$, will be optimized within the limits of feasibility determined by $\bar{X}$ and by physical-behavioral realities. For instance, choices maximizing the quality of education (an element in the list $\tilde{X}$) can be made by deans or department heads once tangibles like the numbers of students and faculty have been determined. These choices and the outcomes associated with them depend on the given level of $\bar{X}$; in principle there is only one "best" $\tilde{X}$ for each $\bar{X}$. Hence the value associated with the "best" available $\tilde{X}$ can be attributed to each $\bar{X}$.

Senior academic officers usually don't know exactly what changes in $\tilde{X}$ would be induced by a proposed change in $\bar{X}$, but it is part of their job to have a pretty good idea. Naturally the prediction process is intuitive: it is based on knowledge of teaching and learning, of the academic disciplines and often the particular individuals involved. Moreover, the value determination process is itself subjective. Adding the need to make predictions about what will happen to the intangibles to the requirement that all the variables be valued imposes an intellectual burden but does not change the process qualitatively. To repeat our earlier point: experience tells us that the above is precisely what successful academic officers do. At Stanford, for instance, when the number of undergraduate applicants who are to be admitted is changed by policy, it is assumed that the mix will be optimized by the dean of admissions. Nobody else knows exactly what changes will ensue, but a general idea usually is available and can be taken into account. The same is true of changes in the quality of education as the numbers of students or faculty are varied: rough judgments can be made (and debated if necessary) even though the production process as such cannot be modeled.

Formally, we postulate the following two-stage optimization procedure. Define $V(\tilde{X}|\bar{X}, S)$ as the value of the intangibles, given the stocks and a certain set of fixed magnitudes for the tangible variables. If we assume that revenues and costs do not depend materially on the intangible factors—a restriction that will be relaxed later, in the context of the university's demand functions—we have this problem in conditional optimization:

$$\text{maximize } V(\tilde{X}|\bar{X}, S)$$

$$\text{with respect to } \tilde{X}$$

$$\text{subject to the constraint}$$

$$F(\tilde{X}, \bar{X}, S) = 0. \tag{3.20}$$

We have stressed that this optimization is performed subjectively. It depends on an intuitive understanding of "what will work" (i.e., of the production function) as well as of "what is important" (i.e., of the value function).

Equation (3.20) serves to associate a value with each realization of $\bar{X}$, because we assume that given $\bar{X}$ there is only one optimal $\tilde{X}$. Denote the value associated with this optimum by $V(\bar{X}, S)$. It is important to note that the information in the production function is used (implicitly) in the determination of $V(\bar{X}, S)$ so $F(\bar{X}, \tilde{X}, S)$ need not appear again in the analysis.

The final stage of optimization, then, is

$$\text{maximize } V(\bar{X}, S)$$

$$\text{with respect to } \bar{X}$$

$$\text{subject to the constraint}$$

$$R(\bar{X}, S, P) - C(\bar{X}, S, P) = 0. \tag{3.21}$$

That is, the optimal solution for the tangible factors is determined subject to the financial constraint. Since the latter can be estimated objectively, the process often amounts to finding the set of tangible planning variables, $\bar{X}$, that, among the set of financially feasible configurations, has the most intuitive appeal. The Stanford TRADES model, which will be described in chapter 9, facilitates just this process.

If desired, constraints which represent subjectively determined bounds on the $\bar{X}$'s, based on judgments about the acceptable ranges of the $\tilde{X}$'s, can be added to (3.21). These act as a supplement to the intuitive process described in equation (3.20). For example, individual elements of $\bar{X}$ can be bounded, as in

$$a_j \le \bar{X}_j \le b_j \quad \text{(for any or all } j).$$

Alternatively, bounds can be defined in terms of functions of the X's. Consider, for example, $a \le Y \div Z \le b$, where Y is the number of students and Z is the number of faculty. Here the lower bound on the student-faculty ratio might depend on politics or on the credibility of the institution's appeals to potential donors and the upper bound upon minimum quality-of-education goals.

We will call the above *operational constraints* to distinguish them from constraints based on financial considerations. The operational constraints may be determined subjectively; they reflect the decision maker's value system and his or her assessment of the relation between the tangible and intangible activity variables. In some cases there will be enough facts available about the relations between inputs and outputs to develop constraints based on partial models of the production function. The network flow models of the instruction process to be discussed in chapter 5 can be helpful for this purpose.

Outside the academic sector it will sometimes be possible to construct reasonable production-function models. This is true, particularly, for those institutional support services that are not much different from the support services of a manufacturing firm. For other support services where mathematical modeling is difficult or impossible, process-oriented techniques for evaluating tasks and productivity may prove to be useful. Zero-base budgeting (ZBB) is one example of such a technique that has been used successfully at Stanford. While the problem of predicting and evaluating the impact of quantitative changes upon the intangible variables does sometimes arise in connection with support services, the thrust of our main comments in this section apply to the direct academic functions of teaching and research.

Demand, Revenue, and Cost Functions

Colleges and universities participate in markets with respect to inputs and outputs, and also with respect to financial factors. A university buys its inputs, including labor, in the appropriate markets just like any other nonprofit or profit-maximizing enterprise. Indeed, most of its input markets are the same as those for other kinds of enterprises: the markets for administrative and technical staff, utilities, supplies, and travel, for instance. The main exception is faculty: for many (though not all) disciplines higher education represents the only market for the services and talents in question. Thus universities collectively exert a strong impact on the market wage rate for faculty, whereas they do not have much influence with respect to the prices of other inputs.

For most inputs, including faculty, there will be a reasonably well-defined market price that serves as a guide to purchasing and salary setting. This price enters into the cost function as a parameter. Examples are wage and salary rates, fringe benefits, utility rates, and costs of books and supplies. Differences in the quality of inputs sought (intangibles again) may affect both the market price and the availability of faculty, but these variations are reasonably predictable for a given institution. Failure to meet market-determined wage rates for faculty will impair the institution's ability to attract and hold faculty of high quality.

A university operates in three major output markets: (a) student demand; (b) demand for sponsored research and similar projects; (c) demand for donations. There may be some confusion as to the definition of these as "output markets," since students who decide to apply to a university (and actually come if admitted), as well as the funds and ideas supplied by sponsors and donors, are in a sense raw materials and may properly be thought of as inputs. We do not dispute this and accept the semantic ambiguity. However, there is an analogy here between a university and a service business, where "demand" consists of someone entrusting the enterprise with the processing of his or her "inputs." The output of the firm consists of this processing, and demand for it depends on the price charged, the firm's reputation, and other factors seen as important by customers. This analogy given above is rather precise in the case of students, and needs no further comment. For research sponsors, it is money and time that is being entrusted to the university. For donors the situation is less clearcut. On balance, however, it seems reasonable to think of potential donors as generating a market demand for entrusting the university with their dollars. The alternative would be to view the transaction as one where the university "buys" the resources as an input, "paying" for them with psychic satisfaction or perquisites. In either case, a university's tangible and intangible characteristics will enter into its benefactors' psychological equation though the mechanism seems more direct if donation demand is viewed as being for university outputs. Happily, the fine points of the distinction are not crucial for present purposes.

Demand functions and prices. Prices are associated with and enter into the demand function of each output market. Thus tuition rates and financial aid policies affect student demand; the institution's internal cost structure (including its indirect cost rates on grants and contracts) affects the amount of funding for sponsored programs; and the terms and conditions for accepting gifts (including financial terms, such as the size of gift needed to name a building or endow a faculty chair) affect the willingness of private donors to give. In addition, the activities and stocks of the university will affect all three types of demand, for reasons that should be obvious.

The output markets in all three areas are reasonably well defined, which implies a substantial amount of competition among institutions. However, the evidence seems to indicate that while price differences can be important, nonprice competition predominates.

Let us formalize the output-demand system in the following way:

$$D^j(\bar{X}, \tilde{X}, S, P_j) = 0 \qquad j = 1, \ldots, n. \tag{3.22}$$

Here there are n different demand functions, each depending in principle on all the activities and stocks and on the price of the particular output in question.

The output-demand systems of colleges and universities, like their production functions, has been little studied. It is less difficult, however, to build models of demand than models of production, since the issues are not as complex and few model builders are tempted to overquantify the demand relations. The demand equations can be incorporated into our theory of college and university choice behavior in one of two ways, depending on the circumstances.

1. Price can be viewed as market-determined, in which case the price coefficient in the revenue function is made to depend on the decision variables via the demand functions. By market-determined we mean that once X is specified the resulting price is the one that clears the market. In other words, we solve (3.22) to get the price

$$P_j = d^j(\bar{X}, \tilde{X}, S),$$

which is substituted for the P_j term in the revenue function. In this situation price is not a true decision variable, i.e., it is one only in the short run, as the institution tries to match itself to market forces.

2. Price can be viewed as a decision variable in its own right (i.e., in the long run). This can be done only if there is excess demand, in which case the institution is exercising market power by rationing its supply of outputs or use of inputs.

The second situation, where price is a true decision variable, describes student demand in selective institutions. The number and quality of students matriculated will be independent of the tuition rate so long as students of the desired quality are being turned away—that is, so long as there is excess student demand. In this case price is a free variable (free, at any rate, up to the point where excess demand vanishes) and therefore can be included in the choice set. For the nonselective institution, however, price is tightly linked with the number and quality of students enrolling. Therefore, as soon as one of these variables is specified the others are determined. Price cannot be in the choice set if the quantitative and qualitative variables are there already.

As in the case of production functions, the existence of important intangible attributes—student mix and quality, for instance—softens the impact of the demand functions on the tangible factors by shifting the area of concern to the value function. Consider student demand for the nonselective institution. It might be possible to alleviate the demand problem by abandoning the school's objectives as to student mix and quality and taking anyone who is willing to pay an arbitrarily determined tuition rate. (We do not advocate this, but it does further illuminate the role of values and their interaction with output demand.)* Thus even a nonselective institution can use price as a choice variable if its intangible objectives are modified to meet the demand constraint. However, if the school is committed to a particular student mix and quality the relation between the number of enrollees and price must be taken into account explicitly. In practice, we suppose, planning behavior in nonselective schools must fall somewhere between these extremes, so that perhaps they should be labeled "quasi-selective."

For the truly selective institution there is no problem with the price-quality aspect of the demand relationship, since the excess demand tends to be dominant. However, there still may be problems with respect to a particular group that is strongly sought after—e.g., top scholars, highly qualified minorities, or blue-chip athletes. Since these groups may well be sensitive to price, a careful analysis of the school's values and its financial aid policy is called for. Problems of competitive dynamics must also be considered. For instance, a policy of financial aid based on academic merit might well touch off a "price discount war" that would leave no institution better off in terms of student mix and quality but that would reduce net revenues and lead to what many would consider an element of inequity in pricing. The alternative is financial aid based on need, which is the policy of most truly selective institutions.

We argued earlier that decision makers engage in a two-stage optimization process. In so doing, they eliminate the intangible variables and the production function from the second stage of the process, which concerns the tangible variables and is subject to the financial constraint. The same theorem applies to the demand functions, whether or not price is a decision variable: we assume

---

*Note, too, that the mix and quality of students is an input variable to the education process in that students help "teach" other students. This effect is subsumed in the above since we already have merged the production functions into the value function.

that the decision maker adjusts the tangible variables—price too, if the institution is selective—while taking account of their probable effects on the intangible variables via the value function. Hence equation (3.21) is extended to read

$$\text{maximize } V(\bar{X}, S, P)$$

$$\text{with respect to } \bar{X}$$

$$\text{subject to the constraint}$$

$$R(\bar{X}, S, P) - C(\bar{X}, S, P) = 0. \tag{3.23}$$

The only change is that now P is included in the value function in order to reflect the effects of changes in $\bar{X}$ (and in P itself if it is a decision variable) upon the intangibles. These effects are due to the demand functions, which have now been eliminated by the first-stage optimization.

Revenues and costs. Consider now the revenue and cost functions of the college or university. We begin with the revenue function, which is built up, with appropriate allowances for prices and/or demand effects, from the complete list of institutional activities. Output demand and/or price enter the revenue function in one of four ways.

1. Where specific outputs are "priced," revenue is determined by price times quantity. For instance, tuition (gross of financial aid) is charged on a per-student-term or per-academic-unit basis. In some states appropriations to public universities are tied to similar measures, a legislative formula that looks like "price times quantity" so far as the institution's revenue function is concerned. Since an output factor must be measurable if it is going to be priced, only tangible variables (i.e., $\bar{Y}$) can enter the revenue function this way.

2. When outputs are intangible but inputs can be identified with specific transactions, revenue may be determined by a cost-reimbursement formula. That is, the output is specified only in general terms but the resources used in producing it are costed out and a negotiated portion of this cost is reimbursed by the sponsor. (Procedures for allocating fixed costs or the costs of joint inputs must be included in the agreement with the sponsor.) Sponsored research and instruction contracts and grants from the federal government or foundations are examples of cost-reimbursement transactions. These transactions enter the revenue function in terms of "cost times an allocation fraction," and there is a tight link between the cost and the revenue function that ought to be taken into account in planning. Strictly speaking, only those agreements that allow for carryforward or renegotiation of overhead costs are of the pure cost-reimbursement type. A strictly predetermined overhead rate amounts to a "price," even though it must be justified at the outset in terms of anticipated cost allocations. If it must, the result is a mixed, "price-and-cost-reimbursed" arrangement.

3. Another class of revenues is not tied very closely to specific outputs or inputs but does depend upon them indirectly and in the long run. Such is the case with gifts and lump-sum appropriations where the amount is fixed in advance rather than varying with specific outputs or inputs. (If a gift is tightly restricted it may have the flavor of a cost-reimbursement agreement but is really more flexible, since it is not subject to detailed cost-allowability rules and renegotiations.) Linkage of revenues with inputs and outputs may vary all the way from relatively tight (as with highly restricted gifts or government appropriations) to relatively loose (as with unrestricted giving). We call revenues in this category "indirectly attributable" to activities. In the short run they are in the constant term of the revenue function, but in the long run they should be associated with outputs, inputs, or both.

4. Revenues from investment and similar business activities do not stem from university operations as such and so do not depend even indirectly on inputs or outputs. They do depend on stocks of assets (which form the basis for investment), but the returns are determined by external markets in which the characteristics of the university are not a factor. These revenues contribute to the fixed or constant term in the revenue function in the short run, and comprise all the fixed revenue in the long run.

In summary, the revenue function depends on the tangible and intangible variables, on the stocks, and on the prices. Thus the revenue function is made up of four kinds of terms, as follows:

$$
\begin{array}{lll}
R(\bar{X}, \tilde{X}, S, P) & \text{total revenue} & \\
= P\bar{Y} & \text{priced output} & \\
+ a(\bar{Z})C(\bar{Z}) & \text{cost reimbursement} & (3.24) \\
+ R^I(\bar{X}, \tilde{X}, S, P) & \text{indirectly attributable revenue} & \\
+ R^0 & \text{fixed revenue} &
\end{array}
$$

where
$a(\bar{Z}) =$ a cost-allocation function, used in cost-reimbursement agreements. (It is based on measurable input factors, which are taken as surrogates for flows of benefits.)*

$R^I(\bar{X}, \tilde{X}, S, P) =$ the effect of all the university's activities, stocks, and prices upon indirectly attributable revenues. (This was described in paragraph [3] above.)

Where outputs or inputs are specified we have used Y and Z, as has been our custom; otherwise the master activity list X is used. R^0 is of course fixed revenue, and $C(\bar{Z})$ is the cost of inputs subject to reimbursement under sponsored projects agreements. Strictly speaking, stocks should have been included as

---

*For example, the costs of building operations and maintenance may be allocated according to square footage used, while G & A costs may be allocated on the basis of relative directly attributable salaries or total direct cost. For a directly attributable expense, $a(\bar{Z}) = 1$, unless a reduction is needed due to cost sharing. Allocation functions rarely if ever are based on outputs or output prices or on intangible attributes.

arguments in the cost function to allow for use charges and depreciation on buildings and equipment. However, this would have complicated the ensuing discussion to no useful purpose, and so is ignored for now. Likewise, we shall continue, in later sections, to use P to stand for all kinds of prices and cost-reimbursement parameters. That is, P's may be either specific numbers like the tuition rate, or sets of factors like cost coefficients and overhead rates for sponsored research.

The cost function can of course be decomposed into variable and fixed terms. If we assume that $C(\bar{Z})$ is linear, we may write

$$C(\bar{Z}) = \sum_i c_i Z_i + c^0 \tag{3.25}$$

where c_i = average variable costs of inputs

c^0 = fixed cost attributable to the time frame being analyzed

Types of Cost Measures

Because the question of costing causes so much confusion, we shall take this opportunity to discuss types of cost measures even though the main point is redundant with respect to equations (3.24) and (3.25). All needed cost information can and (ideally) should be built up from variable and fixed components, with allocations of cost coming in only as needed for the negotiation of cost-reimbursement agreements. Still, the world is never as simple as any theory, and the concept "full average cost" (which sometimes is called "fully allocated cost" or simply "average cost") does tend to dominate decision making in some situations.

Costs may be measured in terms of either inputs or outputs. For inputs the situation is relatively clear: we can think of adding one unit of the resource after another, and of each increment as costing a particular amount. There may be practical problems such as lack of homogeneity of the resources (e.g., successive additions to faculty may involve persons of different seniority levels or in different fields), but in principle they are not too difficult to solve. Thus we can speak unambiguously about the *average variable costs of inputs*— i.e., the c_i in equation (3.25).

For outputs the determination of incremental cost is complicated by the fact that different scales and mixes of production may require different mixes of inputs (including different capital intensities) in order to be efficient or even feasible. Thus we must distinguish between long-run and short-run incremental costs, the difference being whether any needed adjustments in the input mix have or have not been accomplished. For instance, it may be possible to add undergraduate students with very little incremental costs other than for financial aid (but with much incremental revenue) in the short run, whereas the extra costs necessary to maintain needed levels of quality, student demand, donation demand, etc., in the long run may be substantial. Perhaps one can ask the faculty to work extra hours or the students to get along with suboptimal housing for a time, but after a while the effects will show and word will get around.

Often these long-run increments in output cost are not known very precisely because they involve the institution's intangible attributes, its production and demand functions, or both. In this case one should model the costs that can be seen clearly (usually the ones immediately associated with the decision) and make sure to take the others into account subjectively in the value-determination phase of the analysis.

The problem of determining *average* or *fully allocated cost* is even more vexing. There simply is no single logically determinable way to attribute either fixed or joint costs to outputs. In other words, fixed is fixed and joint is joint; nothing more can be said in logical or empirical terms. The attribution method to be used must result from a negotiation or mandate, which will depend on the reasons for the attribution and the points of view of the principals. For instance, government negotiators often take the point of view that most or all joint costs should be allocated to the instruction function, "since the university existed before the government began to sponsor research." University negotiators, on the other hand, argue for a more even allocation between functions. It is important to note that the issue here is not so much a matter of economic principle as of bargaining over price. In contrast, incremental costs are always objectively determinable in principle because they refer to the variable costs of inputs and/or to the cost of the optimum mix of extra resources that will be needed to produce an extra output.

The concept of *flow of benefit* is used as the basis for allocating indirect costs for purposes of reimbursement. Where the flows cannot be observed directly (which is nearly always the case for overhead items), use is made of surrogates such as square footage, total direct cost, or direct salaries and wages. This procedure suggests that, contrary to the preceding paragraph, there exists in principle an objectively determinable way of attributing indirect costs to outputs. The classic example, usually presented with the dictum that "there can only be one president," is the division of the president's time among such functions as instruction and sponsored research. The argument is that in principle a fixed cost is herewith being allocated "objectively," and that the only problem is how to make a reasonable estimate of how the president divides his or her time.

There are two major flaws in this argument. First, while the president does indeed spend time on things that are strictly instruction, I, or research, R, he also spends time on the joint function, IR. An example is when he reviews faculty appointment papers, clearly an IR task. Separate flows of benefit to instruction and research cannot be determined for IR, even in principle. Second, many costs that appear to be fixed are really variable. It is true that there can only be one president, but what about the population of the president's office? Surely the quantity of people and costs will (or should) expand and contract with material changes in the volume of instruction and sponsored research activity. Joint costs aside, flows of benefits can in principle be ascertained

Table 3.3.   Types of Cost Measures

A.	Inputs:	Costs associated with input flows: for example, the cost per faculty FTE-year.
	Outputs:	Costs associated with output flows: for example, the cost per under-graduate degree or course.
B.	Direct incremental (variable cost):	The direct cost of adding one more unit of the designated input or producing one more unit of output: for example, the salary, benefits, travel, etc., of a professor, or the variable cost of the teaching function for a course or degree.
	Full incremental (variable cost):	To the direct incremental cost add the variable overhead cost as determined by a flow of benefit analysis: for example, when counseling and other student services are added to the direct costs of various degrees.
	Full average cost:	The sum of the specific (not joint) direct and attributed variable indirect costs, plus an allocation of joint and fixed costs according to an agreed-upon formula: e.g., the "full average cost" of a degree or course, including an allocation of joint teaching and research costs.
C.	Short-run:	Costs are calculated under the assumption that stocks of capital goods and the methods of teaching, research, and providing support services are fixed.
	Long-run:	Costs are calculated under the assumption that all production processes are optimized given (a) the new value for the variable under study, (b) output prices, (c) variable input costs, and (d) the institution's value function.

with respect to these variable (though indirect) costs. The flow-of-benefit concept is very useful in sorting out time allocations to I, R, and IR, and also in getting at indirect variable costs. However, it does not solve the problem of joint and fixed costs. Our earlier assertions that, objectively speaking, "joint is joint" and "fixed is fixed" cannot be contradicted.

Although we have been talking about the average or full cost of an output, the same points apply to inputs. Consider the full average cost of a faculty member. All this means is that indirect costs (including perhaps an agreed-upon allocation of joint and fixed overhead) have been attributed to the faculty member, as have the direct costs of his or her salary, benefits, supplies, and travel. Naturally, the caveats, discussed above, about the non-uniqueness of fixed and joint cost allocations apply to inputs as well as to outputs.

The full array of cost measures that may be of interest in university budget planning is summarized in table 3.3. Section A deals with the attribution of costs to inputs or outputs. Section B shows that, for each, it is possible to define *direct incremental* variable *cost, full incremental cost* (including variable overhead), or *full average cost*. Finally, section C states that each of the above may be calculated for the short run, where everything except the items to be varied is fixed, or for the long run, where everything is optimized according to the change in the variable under study. Thus there are $2 \times 3 \times 2 = 12$ different types of costs, or more if it is recognized that the long and short run are poles on a continuous time scale.

For most purposes in this book we will be using short-run direct incremental costs, where "short-run" means about one fiscal year. (This will be the meaning of the term "variable cost" unless otherwise noted.) It is difficult to use long-run costs in the absence of substantial knowledge about production functions and intangible attributes; instead, one must deal with future prospects subjectively via the value function. The calculation of full incremental cost requires more knowledge about the necessary relations between support services and academic program than one normally possesses, although there are important exceptions —the operation and maintenance of new buildings, for example. Full incremental cost is used whenever a change in overhead activity is mandated by a change in direct activity. Mostly, however, the linkages between the two are so imprecise that the scale and quality of support services are best viewed as decision variables in their own right.

Applying the Theory to Planning Model Development

We shall conclude this chapter by showing how the salient features of our theory apply to the set of practical models dealt with in the remainder of the book. In so doing, we hope to clarify the relation between our theory and our practice.

Up to now we have avoided writing down in full the optimization problem facing a college or university. Here it is.

$$\text{Maximize} \sum_{t=1}^{\infty} \delta^t E\{V(\bar{X}_t^*, \tilde{X}_t^*, S_t^*, P_t | \bar{X}_t, \tilde{X}_t, S_t)\}$$

(discounted expected value)

with respect to $\bar{X}_t$, $\tilde{X}_t$

subject to the constraints

$$F^k(\bar{X}_t, \tilde{X}_t, S_t) = 0 \quad (k = 1, \ldots, m): \text{production functions}$$

$$D^k(\bar{X}_t, \tilde{X}_t, S_t, P_t) = 0 \quad (k = 1, \ldots, n): \text{demand functions}$$

$$R(\bar{X}_t, S_t, P_t) - C(\bar{X}_t, S_t, P_t) = 0: \text{financial function} \tag{3.26}$$

$$S_{t+1} = M(\bar{X}_t, \tilde{X}_t, S_t): \text{laws of motion}$$

$$\bar{X}_t, \tilde{X}_t \geq 0 \quad (\text{for all } t)$$

where $X_t =$ planned values of the activities

$X_t^* =$ "final outcomes" (See the discussion at equation [3.10].)

$\bar{X}_t =$ the set of tangible activity variables

$\tilde{X}_t =$ the set of intangible activity variables.

The dynamics of the process are as described in connection with equation (3.9).

Let us deal with this in stages. At each stage we will show how the models in the remaining chapters fit in.

1. *Dealing with the intangible variables.* These are very important but may be impossible to quantify. In any case, they are very difficult to deal with centrally in a systematic way. Likewise, the production and demand functions are difficult to quantify and deal with objectively. The solution to this is the two-stage optimization process. In the second stage, decision makers' judgments about intangibles and the production and demand functions are incorporated into the central administration's value function, which as a result is defined only over the tangible set $\bar{X}$. The theory of this process was presented at equations (3.20), (3.21), and (3.23). Hence the optimization problem can be reduced to

$$\text{maximize} \sum_{t=1}^{\infty} \delta^t E\{V(X_t^*, \bar{S}_t^*, P_t | \bar{X}_t, \bar{S}_t)\}$$

$$\text{with respect to } \bar{X}_t$$

$$\text{subject to the constraints}$$

$$R(\bar{X}_t, \bar{S}_t, P_t) - C(\bar{X}_t, \bar{S}_t, P_t) = 0$$

$$\bar{S}_{t=1} = M(\bar{X}_t, \bar{S}_t) \tag{3.27}$$

$$\bar{X}_t \geq 0 \quad \text{(for all } t\text{)}.$$

This notation reflects the fact that the stocks themselves may be tangible or intangible ("good will" is an example of an intangible stock). The intangible stocks are subsumed under the value function just like the intangible activities.

A number of techniques for eliciting information about decision makers' values and for estimating and using value functions are given in chapter 9. All the work we have done on this subject at Stanford assumes explicitly that demand and physical-behavioral relationships are incorporated in the value function. (Instructions given to the subjects demonstrate this assumption.) Some statistical work on undergraduate yield models is presented in chapter 8; this, too, has a certain relevance for understanding the demand function.

2. *Dealing with uncertainty.* This is another difficult task, both in theory and in practice. We postulate that, for most purposes, certainty-equivalent models will suffice for the purposes of long-range forecasting, tradeoff analysis, and strategy determination. Hence the objective function in equation (3.27) can be further simplified to

$$\text{maximize} \sum_{t=1}^{\infty} \delta^t V(\bar{X}_t, \bar{S}_t, P_t) \tag{3.28}$$

$$\text{with respect to } \bar{X}.$$

The certainty-equivalent formulation is the one dealt with in chapter 9 and throughout most of the book.

There is a set of planning problems, however, for which the simplification to certainty equivalence is not appropriate. These problems fall under the heading of *smoothing models*, which are designed explicitly to moderate the effects of uncertainty. Smoothing models that deal with such uncertainty-absorbing devices as variations in the endowment payout rate, the maintenance of an operating reserve, and so-called conditional or tentative expenditure authorizations are considered in chapter 7.

3. *Dealing with the problem of optimizing over time.* The process of determining a utility function (as opposed to a value function) and maximizing its present value still is a very difficult undertaking even when the uncertainty has been taken care of. We have developed a practical approach, based on the concept of *long-run financial equilibrium*, which is described in chapter 6. This concept is based on two empirical considerations:

a. If the financial constraint is satisfied for T successive years, it will be nearly satisfied for many more years into the future as long as conditions do not change. For instance, it appears that a good approximation to satisfying the financial constraint for years 3, 4, or more can be obtained with as few as two successive years (i.e., years 1 and 2) of budget balance or, equivalently, one year of balance followed by a year in which the aggregate growth rates of income and expense are equal. We have called this *first-order equilibrium*.

b. It is natural to include the growth rates of key decision variables in the value function. Examples are the growth rate of tuition and the rate by which the proportion of the budget supported by endowment income is changing over time. Indeed, these growth rates become important decision variables in their own right.

These two considerations permit the dynamic optimization problem to be rewritten as

$$\text{maximize } V(\bar{X}_0, \bar{S}_0, P_0, g)$$

$$\text{with respect to } \bar{X}_0, g$$

$$\text{subject to the constraints}$$

$$R(\bar{X}_0, \bar{S}_0, P_0) - C(\bar{X}_0, \bar{S}_0, P_0) = 0$$
$$R(\bar{X}_1, S_1, P_1 | g) - C(\bar{X}_1, \bar{S}_1, P_1 | g) = 0 \qquad (3.29)$$
$$\bar{X}_0 \geq 0$$

where $\quad \bar{X}_0, \bar{S}_0, P_0 = $ conditions at $t = 0$

$\quad \bar{X}_1, \bar{X}_1, P_1 | g = $ conditions at $t = 1$

$\quad g = $ a list of growth rates of activities and stocks.

Note that the growth rates of stocks are derived from $\bar{S}_{t=1} = M(\bar{X}_t, \bar{S}_t)$, and that revenues and costs in period 1 depend on these growth rates and also (though this is not shown in the notation) on the conditions at $t = 0$. Therefore it was not necessary to include explicitly the laws of motion presented by the M function in equation (3.29). All this will be described in more detail in chapter 6.

4. *Dealing with other modeling problems.* The process of model construction is itself a complex one. Growth rates must be forecast for externally determined variables; expressions must be formulated for the growth rates of decision variables. Also, changes in one variable (an element of X, S, P, or g) often induce changes in other variables—changes that must be predicted as part of the planning and optimizing process. Finally, accounting data need to be analyzed and judgments made about fixed, variable, and joint costs. Chapter 4 deals with these important subjects.

Earlier in chapter 3 we argued that information on production functions is very difficult to come by. For this very reason the production function was eliminated from the optimization process by incorporating the intangible variables into the definition of the value function (see item 1, above). However, some progress has been made in modeling physical-behavioral linkages among certain tangible variables. To the extent that these are known and accepted they can be incorporated as operational constraints (see the discussion that follows equation 3.21). Chapter 5 deals with models of this type.

It is not necessary to master the details of the theory presented in this chapter in order to understand, and even utilize, the specific operational models that form the subject matter of the rest of the book. We believe, however, that the theory and the argument accompanying it provide a useful background to the operational models and that, in the long run, many users of the models will come to ask the same fundamental questions about planning as we did. We hope that the theoretical framework presented here will help to clarity, and answer, such questions.

Summary

This chapter presents a microeconomic theory of college and university optimizing behavior. In the introduction we state our belief that a comprehensive theory can be an important guide to practical analysis and model building. Our theory postulates that a university seeks to maximize a multicriterion value function subject to production, demand-and-supply, and financial constraints.

We begin by describing the building blocks, or components, of the theory. Planning (or decision) variables are of three types: activity variables (like faculty FTE's), stock variables (like library holdings), and price variables (like the tuition charged to students). A second distinction is made between variables that are tangible or intangible. The value function represents the "value" derived from selecting a particular combination of decision variables. Such a function is capable of ranking alternatives according to their relative desirability.

Production functions relate output activities to input activities and stocks. To do justice to the institution, outputs must be dealt with in both quantitative and qualitative terms. Demand-and-supply functions for university outputs and inputs must be recognized as well. Finally, there are the institution's own revenue and cost functions, which are used to describe feasibility in financial terms.

This value maximization problem is complicated by a number of factors—the intangible nature of many university planning variables, the added dimension of time, and uncertainty about the future, to name a few. The basic mathematics is worked out initially for the simplified case of a static decision problem (i.e., one dealing with a "once-and-for-all" type of decision) with no uncertainty; later in the chapter, this is embellished to include considerations of both timing and uncertainty. Additionally, two special kinds of value-maximization problems are analyzed, namely, those arising in connection with capital budgeting decisions, and optimization in multilayered administrative structures. To complete the theory, we discuss the economic behavior of nonprofit enterprises as they compete in the marketplace for their inputs and outputs.

Most of the results in the first two-thirds of this chapter are general, applying equally to colleges, universities, and other nonprofit organizations.

In the next-to-final main section, we specialize these results to the case of educational institutions. This part begins with a discussion of production functions, and then takes up the special nature of university demand, revenue, and cost functions. It concludes by differentiating among the alternative measures of costs so often mentioned in discussions of university finances.

The chapter concludes by showing how salient features of the microeconomic theory apply to the set of practical models dealt with in the remainder of the book. In particular, the notions of long-run financial equilibrium and smoothing are introduced as mechanisms for dealing with intertemporal considerations and uncertainty in operational models for college and university planning.

Notes to Chapter 3

Works cited here in abbreviated form are more fully described in the bibliography at the end of this book.

1. The most comprehensive resource on estimating values and utilities is Keeney and Raiffa 1976. Though the book is generally mathematical, we strongly recommend chaps. 1 and 2 to anyone who is interested in getting a perspective on the subject.

2. See Keeney and Raiffa 1976, chap. 2, for a further discussion.

3. See the two undated papers by Weisbrod in the bibliography.

4. For a very readable discussion of comprehensiveness and other aspects of the problem of structuring objectives see chap. 2 of Keeney and Raiffa 1976.

5. See any good microeconomics text (e.g., Baumol 1961, chap. 9) for definitions and discussion.

6. Cf. Raiffa 1968.

7. The transfer-pricing problem for business firms is analyzed in Baumol and Fabian 1964.

8. A direct approach to a "market" system of incentives for decentralization is presented in Rogers and Van Horn 1976. Systems based on "full cost allocations" and "revenue attribution" have many of the same characteristics; see, for example, Strauss 1976.

9. A list of the commonly accepted functional categories is given in National Association of College and University Business Officers 1974, p. 212.

10. Ibid., p. 215.

4

Budget Projection Models

Our focus in this chapter will be on deepening the reader's understanding of the components that make up a typical college or university operating budget. We will emphasize especially the interrelationships that exist among many of these components. By combining a structural model of such a budget with a description of the economic forces that bear on it, we will be able to study its evolution over time.

The framework for this discussion will be a typical financial projection model that takes the current operating budget, in whatever form and amount of detail it is described, and determines the dollar growth in each item to be expected over the short-to-medium run—say, for the next three to five years. Such models are quite commonplace in higher education, although they often lack sufficient completeness to be dependable. We refer to the output of such a model as a *medium-range financial forecast*, or MRFF for short.

It may seem initially as though financial projections of budget line items could just as easily be done by hand as with the aid of a computer model. We have found through our experience at Stanford, however, that there are distinct advantages to a formal modeling approach. In the first place, it is apparent that significant financial dependencies exist between one revenue or expense item and another, or even between a revenue and an expense item. To cite an obvious example, tuition income and the financial aid provided to students by the institution obviously are linked together, both through the size of the student body and through the price that is set for tuition. Unless these dependencies are properly quantified, calculations of revenue from tuition and expenditures for financial aid are quite likely to be mutually inconsistent.

It is not sufficient merely to work out the details of such dependencies on paper, however, if one intends to produce—as we do routinely at Stanford—many sets of financial projections at various stages of the budget planning process. Then it becomes important to assure consistency between one set of projections and the next. The best way of doing so is to build the relationships that characterize the dependencies and the data that go along with them into a computer program that is always used for making the projections. In our experience, considerable benefits are to be derived from seeking the agreement of the budget planning group to a set of financial submodels and then demonstrating to them that the submodels have been properly incorporated in the projection routines. Not only does this procedure lessen the chances for inconsistency between one set of financial calculations and another but, equally important, it ensures that as organizational learning occurs, the results are noted and incorporated in the model then and there. Having once gone through the task of defining each structural interrelationship, the planning group will then be free to move on to other matters until and unless an overt decision is made to reevaluate and possibly change them.

We will discuss several financial submodels in some detail. In essence, our aim will be to develop a more detailed formulation of the cost, revenue, and demand functions defined in chapter 3. We will adhere, whenever it seems appropriate, to our representation of an income or expense item as the product of a physical (i.e., a flow or stock) variable and a unit price or rate. The actual selection of submodels to be presented here was guided mainly by our understanding of Stanford's operating budget, an understanding gained after several years of analytical effort. We would venture to say, however, that many, if not all, of these relationships are both valid and significant for most other private universities as well. Even a small college would probably find some of the submodels applicable, although presumably it would require a less elaborate structure for its budget model. Finally, we do not imagine these financial submodels would be particularly useful to a public institution whose budget is rigidly controlled by an outside funding authority. In the extreme case of public control, appropriations are made line item by line item through the political process, so that whatever financial dependencies do exist within the system are hard to characterize and always subject to change. Of course, if the process includes the use of formulas it would make good sense to incorporate both them and their constituent variables into the budget model.

Having developed a formulation for the college's or university's budget, we turn next to the issues involved in preparing an MRFF. Additional data are required for making projections, and they are of a particular kind. Fundamentally, the task is one of estimating the growth rates, year by year, of each dollar quantity in the budget model. Who is to make these estimates, and by what means? We will propose some answers to these important questions. In so doing, we will draw on the experience Stanford has had with preparing such forecasts for its Board of Trustees since the early 1970s.

In the course of considering the appropriate choice of growth rates for forecasting purposes, we will draw attention to the fact that, at least over any extended period of time, a university budget is subject to many of the same macroeconomic forces that affect other kinds of institutions. After recognizing what these forces are and do, we will identify various constraints on the growth-rate variables. Although some of these constraints apply chiefly in the long run, they need to be taken into account when one is specifying growth-rate estimates for the MRFF.

Before concluding this introduction, we must be careful to distinguish conceptually between a forecast and a plan. A *forecast* is a set of results that are expected to occur under a particular realization of the salient growth rates and other variables. To the extent that some of these growth rates fall under institutional control, only one of many possible policies will be represented by a single forecast. *Plans* are built by experimenting with many different forecast scenarios: having determined which plans are feasible, the planner chooses the one that best suits the institution's objectives. Often, the forecasting model by itself is insufficient for planning purposes. This is because, while it certainly can project future expected budget surpluses or deficits, it cannot by itself identify strategies for dealing with them. Sometimes a feasible solution can be found by trial and error. It is far preferable, however, to embed the projection in a model that explores the entire space of feasible configurations. (TRADES, which is such a model, will be described in detail in chapter 9.)

When (as was actually the case at Stanford in the fall of 1974) the future budget deficits revealed by the MRFF are very large, a different sort of model may be needed to show how the budget can be balanced during the planning period. Such a "transition-to-equilibrium model" will be described in chapter 6.

Format of the Medium-Range Financial Forecast

A university's budget can be disaggregated in many different ways; obviously, one's choice depends on the purpose being served. Typical issues to be considered in establishing a structure for the MRFF are:

1. Should the entire consolidated budget be projected, or simply that portion represented by the operating budget?*
2. Is it more desirable to have the budget represented by *function* (i.e., purpose) or by *object class* (i.e., in this case, line items), or both?
3. Is it necessary to forecast income and expenditures separately by organizational unit, or will a university-wide forecast be adequate? (The answer to this question will depend on the degree of central control, and on the formal allotment of responsibility.)
4. What level of detail is appropriate in representing both the expense and income sides of the budget?

To illustrate the variety of possible formats, we show the example of two institutions that have taken different tacks in preparing an MRFF. The first

---

*In most private universities, it is the operating budget that controls the expenditure of unrestricted funds for mainstream academic and institutional support activities. The consolidated budget contains in addition monies spent on sponsored research and training and on restricted student financial aid. These items obviously interrelate with the operating budget. The consolidated budget also contains budgets for auxiliary enterprises (e.g., dormitories or the university hospital) that operate as independent cost centers and may have little influence on the operating budget.

Table 4.1.   Expenditure Forecast Summary by Object of Expenditure, 1976/77 (Baseline)
Through 1981/82

Object of Expenditure	1976/77 (in $000) Base Year	Average Annual Price Increase	Projected Expenditures (in $000)				
			1977/78	1978/79	1979/80	1980/81	1981/82
Salaries and wages							
Instructional	15,632	6.0%	16,570	17,564	18,618	19,735	20,919
Noninstructional	17,729	6.0%	18,793	19,922	21,115	22,382	23,725
Temporary service	1,366	2.0%	1,393	1,420	1,448	1,480	1,508
Supplies and expense	4,470	5.7%	4,721	4,989	5,271	5,570	5,884
Utilities	2,502	15.0%	2,878	3,306	3,805	4,376	5,032
Equipment	706	5.5%	744	786	829	875	922
Library acquisitions	903	15.0%	1,038	1,194	1,373	1,579	1,816
Student aid	364	6.0%	386	409	434	460	487
GRAND TOTAL	43,672	6.5%	46,523	49,593	52,893	56,457	60,293

SOURCE: Shirley and Lorang 1979, p. 184. Reproduced by permission of the publisher, EDUCOM, Inc., Princeton, NJ.
NOTE: This table summarizes the expenditure levels in future years that are necessary to maintain 1976/77 levels of programmatic activity.

is the State University of New York at Albany (SUNY Albany), a medium-sized state university campus. Tables 4.1 and 4.2 display some budget projections made at this campus in the mid-1970s. This particular institution found it convenient for projection purposes to model its *consolidated* budget, broken down by function and object of expenditure in accordance with the standard classification scheme established by the state funding agency. Growth rates were estimated separately for each object class within each function type, and these were applied to the corresponding array of base-year dollar values. The results then were aggregated by objects of expenditure (table 4.1) and by function (table 4.2) to form two different displays. (Further details on this model are given in Shirley and Lorang 1979.)

The SUNY Albany model is a good example of how one might get started effectively in using the computer to help make budget projections. (It is also noteworthy in that it applies to a public university, whereas most of our other examples apply to the private sector.) The model utilizes judgments about average growth rates over a five-year period. These are easier to obtain than year-by-year estimates, though of course the latter bring more information to bear. The object categories of expense are relatively aggregative but still are rich enough to capture important differences in growth rates. The model is ambitious in that expenditures are categorized by function as well as object. The projections for the two are required to be consistent, as can be seen by comparing the footings of tables 4.1 and 4.2. In some cases the growth rates of certain object categories will differ by function, which lends an important element of richness to the model.

By way of contrast, Stanford has chosen to prepare forecasts of its operating budget in the format shown in tables 4.3 and 4.4, below. Expenditures are tracked by object class only, but the line items are considered in greater detail than was the case in table 4.1. This choice was guided by the following several

Table 4.2. Expenditure Forecast Summary by Function, 1976/77 (Baseline) Through 1981/82

Function	1976/77 (in $000) Base Year	Average Annual Price Increase	Projected Expenditures (in $000)				
			1977/78	1978/79	1979/80	1980/81	1981/82
Instruction & departmental research	21,682	5.9%	22,958	24,314	25,749	27,271	28,883
Organized research	563	5.9%	595	632	669	708	749
Extension & public service	122	5.8%	129	137	144	153	162
Organized activities	1,414	5.7%	1,493	1,576	1,663	1,757	1,854
Library	2,843	9.0%	3,087	3,359	3,660	3,996	4,372
Student services & aid	2,362	5.8%	2,499	2,643	2,796	2,960	3,130
Maintenance & operations	5,584	8.3%	6,034	6,528	7,073	7,674	8,337
General administration	1,931	5.8%	2,043	2,161	2,287	2,420	2,561
General institutional services	3,699	5.5%	3,901	4,115	4,339	4,577	4,820
Housing	3,472	9.3%	3,784	4,128	4,513	4,941	5,419
GRAND TOTAL	43,672	6.5%	46,523	49,593	52,893	56,457	60,293

SOURCE: Shirley and Lorang 1979, p. 183. Reproduced by permission of the publisher, EDUCOM, Inc., Princeton, NJ.

NOTE: This table summarizes the expenditure levels in future years that are necessary to maintain 1976/77 levels of programmatic activity.

Table 4.3. Five-Year Forecast of Operating Budget Expense, Stanford University ($000)

	1974/75 Base (Est.)	Increase[a] %	Increase[a] Amount	1975/76 Base	Increase[a] %	Increase[a] Amount	1976/77 Base
Faculty salaries	$15,138	7.0%	$1,060	$16,198	7.0%	$1,134	$17,332
Other teaching	831	7.0	58	889	7.0	62	951
Other personnel	21,949	10.1	2,214	24,163	8.9	2,159	26,322
Teaching assistants	1,166	8.0	93	1,259	6.0	76	1,335
Salary requisitions	785	8.0	63	848	6.0	51	899
TOTAL SALARIES	$39,869	8.7%	$3,488	$43,357	8.0%	$3,482	$46,839
Staff benefits	$6,778	15.1%	$1,026	$7,804	14.0%	$1,095	$8,899
TOTAL SALARIES AND STAFF BENEFITS	$46,647	9.7%	$4,514	$51,161	8.9%	$4,577	$55,738
Library acquisitions	$1,945	13.0%	$253	$2,198	13.0%	$286	$2,484
Undergraduate aid (unrestricted)	1,941	30.5	592	2,533	24.8	627	3,160
Graduate aid (unrestricted)	1,535	10.4	160	1,695	9.7	164	1,859
Student health	1,138	10.0	114	1,252	10.0	125	1,377
Building maintenance	877	8.4	74	951	9.1	87	1,038
Utilities	1,863	10.6	197	2,060	7.4	153	2,213
Grounds	526	8.4	44	570	9.1	52	622
Custodial	1,353	8.4	114	1,467	9.1	133	1,600
Equipment	399	8.0	32	431	7.0	30	461
Travel	907	7.0	63	970	7.0	68	1,038
Materials and supplies	6,668	6.0	400	7,068	5.0	353	7,421
Other[b]	3,423	6.0	205	3,628	4.0	145	3,773
Chargeouts[c]	(4,987)	10.8	(537)	(5,524)	8.1	(445)	(5,969)
TOTAL MAINTENANCE	$64,235	9.7%	$6,225	$70,460	9.0%	$6,355	$76,815
Improvements and consolidations	—		$1,734	$1,734		$2,111	$3,845
Operations and maintenance on new buildings	—		200	200		118	318
TOTAL NEW EXPENDITURES	—	3.0%	$1,934	$1,934	3.1%	$2,229	$4,163
TOTAL EXPENDITURES	**$64,235**	12.7%	$8,159	**$72,394**	11.9%	$8,584	**$80,978**
TOTAL INCOME (see table 4.4.)	**$64,235**	3.8%	$2,437	**$66,672**	7.1%	$4,720	**$71,392**
GAP	**$0**			**$5,722**			**$9,586**

SOURCE: Stanford University 1974.

NOTE: This table excludes the Graduate School of Business, the School of Medicine, and Hoover Institution research.

[a] Economic assumptions:

Consumer price increase	9.0%	7.0%
Gross national product deflator increase	7.5%	6.0%
Personal income increase	10.5%	8.5%
Bay area consumer price increase	8.0%	6.0%

[b] "Other" includes charges for insurance, legal and audit fees, computer charges, taxes, and similar expenses.

[c] "Charge-outs" refers to expenses that are transferred to units outside the operating budget—for example, the charging of Fire Department expense to the residence halls.

| Increase[a] | | 1977/78 | Increase[a] | | 1978/79 | Increase[a] | | 1979/80 |
%	Amount	Base	%	Amount	Base	%	Amount	Base
7.0%	$1,213	$18,545	7.0%	$1,298	$19,843	6.5%	$1,290	$21,133
7.0	67	1,018	7.0	71	1,089	6.5	71	1,160
6.9	1,826	28,148	6.4	1,813	29,961	6.4	1,929	31,890
5.5	73	1,408	5.5	78	1,486	4.0	59	1,545
5.5	48	948	5.5	52	1,000	4.0	40	1,040
6.9%	$3,228	$50,067	6.6%	$3,312	$53,379	6.3%	$3,389	$56,768
12.5%	$1,114	$10,013	12.0%	$1,197	$11,210	11.4%	$1,279	$12,489
7.8%	$4,342	$60,080	7.5%	$4,509	$64,589	7.2%	$4,668	$69,257
13.0%	$322	$2,806	13.0%	$365	$3,171	13.0%	$412	$3,583
26.0	823	3,983	22.1	881	4,864	13.8	673	5,537
9.1	169	2,028	8.6	174	2,202	8.0	176	2,378
9.5	131	1,508	9.5	143	1,651	8.5	140	1,791
7.3	76	1,114	6.7	75	1,189	6.8	81	1,270
6.1	134	2,347	5.1	119	2,466	5.0	124	2,590
7.3	45	667	6.7	45	712	6.8	48	760
7.3	117	1,717	6.7	115	1,832	6.8	125	1,957
5.0	23	484	4.0	19	503	3.0	15	518
6.0	62	1,100	6.0	66	1,166	6.0	70	1,236
4.0	297	7,718	4.0	309	8,027	3.5	281	8,308
4.0	151	3,924	4.0	157	4,081	3.5	143	4,224
7.0	(417)	(6,386)	6.6	(424)	(6,810)	6.3	(429)	(7,239)
8.2%	$6,275	$83,090	7.9%	$6,553	$89,643	7.3%	$6,527	$96,170
	$2,499	$6,344		$2,941	$9,285		$3,379	$12,664
	633	951		164	1,115		76	1,191
3.9%	$3,132	$7,295	3.4%	$3,105	$10,400	3.5%	$3,455	$13,855
11.6%	$9,407	**$90,385**	10.7%	$9,658	**$100,043**	10.0%	$9,982	**$110,025**
7.1%	$5,027	**$76,419**	7.1%	$5,415	**$81,834**	6.6%	$5,368	**$87,202**
		$13,966			**$18,209**			**$22,823**

6.0%			6.0%			5.0%		
5.5%			5.5%			4.5%		
7.5%			7.5%			6.5%		
5.5%			5.5%			4.5%		

Table 4.4. Five-Year Forecast of Operating Budget Income, Stanford University ($000)

	1974/75 Base (Est.)	Increase %	Increase Amount	1975/76 Base	Increase %	Increase Amount	1976/77 Base
Tuition and fees[a]	$35,489	9.5%	$3,362	$38,851	10.1%	$3,924	$42,775
Unrestricted endowment:							
Pool[b]	$5,549	(9.5%)	($529)	$5,020	1.2%	$62	$5,082
Specific investment	929	1.6	15	944	....	....	944
Amortization of leases	900	....	....	900	....	....	900
Net annual rentals	(50)	160.0	80	30	(33.3%)	(10)	20
TOTAL	$7,328	(5.9%)	($434)	$6,894	0.8%	$52	$6,946
Restricted endowment:							
Pool[b]	$2,781	(11.2%)	($310)	$2,471	7.4%	$183	$2,654
Designated	11	(9.1%)	(1)	10	....	....	10
TOTAL	$2,792	(11.1%)	($311)	$2,481	7.4%	$183	$2,664
Unrestricted gifts:							
Unrestricted	$1,800	(7.8%)	($140)	$1,660	6.0%	$100	$1,760
Ford engineering	28	(100.0%)	($28)	....	....	....	....
Overhead on nongovt. grants	173	5.8	10	183	5.5	10	193
TOTAL	$2,001	(7.9%)	($158)	$1,843	6.0%	$110	$1,953
Restricted gifts[c]	$1,014	7.0%	$71	$1,085	7.0%	$76	$1,161
Special funds	$346	9.5%	$33	$379	10.1%	$38	$417
Other income:							
Expendable funds pool	$1,466	(12.3%)	($180)	$1,286	(1.6%)	($20)	$1,266
SRI[d]	609	12.5	76	685	4.5	31	716
Security loans	110	....	....	110	....	....	110
Other[e]	939	(5.4%)	($51)	888	2.9	26	914
TOTAL	$3,124	(5.0%)	($155)	$2,969	1.3%	$37	$3,006
Reimbursed indirect costs	$12,801	3.4%	$429	$13,230	3.3%	$440	$13,670
Transfer to plant	($1,000)	40.0%	($400)	($1,400)	10.0%	($140)	($1,540)
Allocation by formula schools	90	....	....	90	....	....	90
UNIMPROVED TOTAL	$63,985	....	$2,437	$66,422	....	$4,720	$71,142
Income improvement	$250	....	....	$250	....	....	$250
TOTAL INCOME	**$64,235**	3.8%	**$2,437**	**$66,672**	7.1%	**$4,720**	**$71,392**

SOURCE: Stanford University 1974.

NOTE: This table excludes the Graduate School of Business, the School of Medicine, and Hoover Institution research.
[a] Tuition rate $3,375   10.0% $345 $3,720   10.0% $375 $4,095
[b] New endowment added:
     Unrestricted (net after $900k) $1,030 $1,015
     Restricted $2,000 $2,850
[c] Additional restricted gifts may be part of the reallocation.
     Total gifts received as follows: $53,100 $50,500
[d] Income from SRI International. Per an arrangement in effect since the year 1970, this figure represents a fixed percentage of SRI's adjusted gross revenue.
[e] "Other" includes income from sources such as fines, royalties, and allowances.
[f] Sponsored research volume $63,500 $67,000
     Reimbursed indirect cost rate   48%   48%

| Increase | | 1977/78 | Increase | | 1978/79 | Increase | | 1979/80 |
%	Amount	Base	%	Amount	Base	%	Amount	Base
9.2%	$3,935	$46,710	9.1%	$4,251	$50,961	8.0%	$4,077	$55,038
1.2%	$60	$5,142	1.1%	$57	$5,199	1.1%	$57	$5,256
....	....	944	....	....	944	....	....	944
....	....	900	....	....	900	....	....	900
(150.0%)	($30)	(10)	(200.0%)	(20)	(30)	(66.7%)	(20)	(50)
....	$30	$6,976	0.5%	$37	$7,013	0.5%	$37	$7,050
6.5%	$173	$2,827	5.6%	$159	$2,986	5.6%	$167	$3,153
10.0	1	11	....	....	11	9.1	1	12
6.5%	$174	$2,838	5.6%	$159	$2,997	5.6%	$168	$3,165
5.7%	$100	$1,860	5.9%	$110	$1,970	5.6%	$110	$2,080
....	....	....	....	....	....	....	....	....
5.2	10	203	4.9	10	213	4.7	10	223
5.6%	$110	$2,063	5.8%	$120	$2,183	5.5%	$120	$2,303
7.0%	$81	$1,242	7.0%	$86	$1,328	6.5%	$86	$1,414
9.2%	$38	$455	9.1%	$41	$496	8.0%	$40	$536
(1.6%)	($20)	$1,246	(1.6%)	($20)	$1,226	(1.6%)	($20)	$1,206
4.5	32	748	4.6	34	782	4.5	35	817
....	....	110	....	....	110	....	....	110
2.8	$26	940	2.8	26	966	2.7	26	992
1.3%	$38	$3,044	1.3%	$40	$3,084	1.3%	$41	$3,125
5.7%	$775	$14,445	5.9%	$850	$15,295	6.4%	$985	$16,280
10.0%	($154)	($1,694)	10.0%	($169)	($1,863)	10.0%	($186)	($2,049)
....	....	90	....	....	90	....	....	90
....	$5,027	$76,169	....	$5,415	$81,584	....	$5,368	$86,952
....	....	$250	....	....	$250	....	....	$250
7.1%	**$5,027**	**$76,419**	7.1%	**$5,415**	**$81,834**	6.6%	**$5,368**	**$87,202**
9.0%	$375	$4,470	9.0%	$405	$4,875	8.0%	$390	$5,265
		$1,010			$1,010			$1,070
		$2,790			$2,650			$2,880
		$49,100			$47,000			$49,300
		$70,700			$74,600			$78,700
		49%			50%			51%

considerations. First, the operating budget was the main instrument of control over academic expenditures, and a good deal of authority in setting parameters for the operating budget resided in the central administration. Second, objects of expenditure seemed to be highly relevant for distinguishing between items with fundamentally different growth rates, while functions did not. For example, staff salaries (i.e., those for "other personnel" in table 4.3), library acquisitions, and materials and supplies were expected, for reasons that could be explained in simple economic terms, to behave quite differently over the forecast period. A forecast for the "library" function, on the other hand, would only have been obtained by aggregating over these and the other relevant categories of expense in the library budget, and we did not need to do this in order to compare the bottom-line expense and income figures for the operating budget as a whole.

The level of detail selected for Stanford's MRFF was determined mainly by two factors: the degree to which we understood the primary importance of certain budget components; and our ability to project the growth rates of each item in a systematic way. Major items with an intrinsic relationship to separate policy decisions (e.g., the growth rate of faculty salaries as opposed to staff salaries) were kept separate from one another. So also were items that were characterized by peculiarly high growth rates in the short-to-medium run— library acquisitions, the student health contract, and utilities costs, for example. We also separated the line items when it seemed sensible to link one item explicitly to another through an appropriate submodel. We have already cited the example of undergraduate financial aid and tuition income both being linked with the tuition price. A different set of principles was used to determine the aid budget for graduate students, and hence a different submodel needed to be applied. Further details on these and other financial submodels will be covered in the next section.

If one adds up all the items listed above the "total maintenance" line for any year shown in table 4.3, one obtains the so-called maintenance budget for that year. This is the amount of money that would be required in that year to fund the same set of activities that were in effect in the base year (i.e., 1974/75). We call the growth rate of the maintenance budget the ordinary rate of cost rise, or *internal inflation rate*, for it represents the additional amount the university would have to pay in order to purchase the same market basket of resource inputs as it did last year. Obviously, the cost-rise rates in table 4.3 are in nominal terms, which is to say that they include the projected rates of inflation for the economy as a whole as represented by the figures given in note 1.

Two categories of incremental new expenditures are added to the maintenance figures in Stanford's MRFF to obtain the total operating budget. These are identified by the labels "improvements and consolidation" and "operations and maintenance on new buildings" in table 4.3. The former category aggregates the net incremental growth in the budget that exceeds ordinary cost rise. It includes all provisions for new programs and activities (but not for new buildings) on a net basis, that is, above and beyond the level that can be funded by reallocating money already in the previous year's budget. (This line was later split into two parts in order to differentiate between items that are more or less mandatory—e.g., another auditor, to keep up with federal monitoring requirements—and those that are truly discretionary.) The second category of incremental new expenditures is separated from other types of improvement to emphasize the impact on the operating budget of capital improvement programs that already have been approved. We refer to the sum of these two categories, expressed as a fraction of the prior year's total operating budget, as the *budget enrichment factor* and we denote it by the symbol f. This factor has come to be viewed as a major policy variable in Stanford's budget planning process; its critical role will become more evident in later chapters. In preparing the 1974 MRFF shown in tables 4.3 and 4.4, a value of 2.7 percent was assigned to f, which corresponds to its average actual value at Stanford during the preceding three years.

The same set of principles that was applied to expenditures is here used to decide upon the appropriate level of detail for projections of income (table 4.4). While further detail actually is given—often for rather idiosyncratic reasons—the university's income falls into five major categories. Listed in order of decreasing magnitude, these are: tuition and fees (55 percent of total base-year income); indirect cost recovery on grants and contracts (20 percent); income from endowment (16 percent); expendable gifts (5 percent); and income from all other sources (4 percent).

Two items that appear near the bottom of table 4.4 deserve special mention. "Transfer to plant" refers to a regular flow of general funds from the operating budget into a plant depreciation reserve. This money is used to fund a portion of the renovation projects that are continually being undertaken on the campus to maintain academic facilities in a reasonable state of repair. Other sources not shown here of funds for these projects include gifts for capital improvements, allocations not part of the regular budget but made at year end (see the discussion of the "conditional budget" concept in chapter 7), and possibly some debt, financed by the selling of Stanford bonds under the California Educational Facilities Act (CEFA). The payments on such bonds, however, are part of the budgeted "transfer to plant" item. The second income item requiring a special explanation is the one labeled "income improvement." This represents nothing more than an expectation that something like $250,000 will turn up in extra income or reduced expenditures by the end of any particular budget year. While the exact source (or sources) of such income cannot be identified ahead of time, the figure has turned out to be a fairly dependable one in recent years. In chapter 7 it will be recommended that this item be dropped in favor of making accurate and unbiased estimates of all regular income quantities.

The note below tables 4.3 and 4.4 draws attention to the fact that Stanford's MRFF excludes two schools (business and medicine) and a part of the Hoover Institution. Each of these entities operates on a more or less free-standing basis and therefore is responsible for doing its own financial planning. On the other hand, all other schools are budgeted centrally at Stanford, and so it is meaningful to aggregate their income and expenditures in the MRFF. Many institutions now employ a form of *responsibility center budgeting*; that is, they attribute income to each of their major academic units and generally expect that expenses will be covered by the income that is generated. Sometimes disparities between units are made up for by means of centrally allocated subventions. Where such a budgeting system is in effect, the financial forecast must take explicit account of the formulas used for determining each unit's revenue base; probably all results will need to be displayed on a unit-by-unit basis. In Stanford's case, the net flow of funds from the so-called formula schools to the general operating budget is lumped together in a single item at the bottom of the income table.

Modeling the Budget

At this point, we postpone further discussion of the multiyear forecast, and turn instead to a deeper analysis of how the operating budget can be modeled in any given year. There are three principles we shall want to employ in constructing a model of the budget for planning purposes:

1. Whenever possible, a dollar item in the budget should be separated into (a) the associated physical variable (i.e., a stock or an activity variable) and (b) the associated unit price.
2. The model should incorporate in explicit form the full incremental cost and revenue associated with each physical primary planning variable.
3. Important linkages that are known to exist between components of the budget should be built in as explicit submodels.

We now give examples of the application of each of these principles in formulating a model of Stanford's operating budget.

Representation in Physical Variable Terms

In table 4.5 we have listed the items in tables 4.3 and 4.4 with which we can readily associate the appropriate physical and price variables. These are essentially the same quantities that appeared in the "tangible" column of table 3.1. If X represent a physical variable and P is its unit price, then the dollar amount shown in the corresponding line of the budget is simply P times X. Building P and X into the budget model as separate variables really facilitates planning, since it enables one to focus on either when making projections into the future. It also draws attention more directly to the primary variables that are (at least somewhat) under institutional control, so that they can get proper consideration in the planning process.

On the expense side most if not all the prices are set by outside markets. The salaries and fringe benefits paid to faculty and staff may be exceptions, although it can be argued that, in setting the prices it is willing to pay for its

Table 4.5. Physical Variables Associated with Budget Line Items

Item	Associated Physical Variable (X)	Associated Unit Price (P)
EXPENSE ITEMS:		
Faculty salaries	Regular faculty FTE (X_1)	Average faculty salary (P_1)
Other teaching salaries	Auxiliary faculty FTE (X_2)	Average auxiliary faculty salary (P_2)
Other personnel salaries	Staff FTE (X_3 and X_4)	Average staff salary (P_3 and P_4)
Teaching assistant salaries	Teaching assistant FTE (X_5)	Average TA salary (P_5)
Staff benefits	Total FTE $(X_6 = X_1 + X_2 + X_3 + X_4)$	Average benefit cost per employee (P_6)
Library acquisitions	Volumes acquired per year (X_7)	Price per volume (P_7)
Undergraduate aid	Undergraduate enrollment (X_8)	Average aid per undergraduate (P_8)
Graduate aid	Graduate student enrollment (X_9)	Average aid per graduate student (P_9)
Student health contract	Total enrollment ($X_{10} = X_8 + X_9$)	Health contract cost per student (P_{10})
Building maintenance	Total square footage (X_{11})	Maintenance cost per square foot (P_{11})
Utilities	BTU, therms, KWH, etc. consumed (X_{12})	Price per energy unit (P_{12})
INCOME ITEMS:		
Tuition and fees	Student enrollment ($X_{13} = X_{10}$)	Tuition price (P_{13})
Endowment income	Endowment market value (X_{14})	Payout rate (P_{14})
Interest earned on expendable funds pool	Expendable funds pool average balance (X_{15})	Interest rate earned on expendable funds (P_{15})
Indirect cost recovery	Direct cost of research (X_{16})	Indirect cost rate (P_{16})

personnel, the institution really is establishing a level of quality in accordance with the relevant labor markets. It should be apparent from a quick scan of the list of underlying physical quantities in table 4.5 that the institution has considerable discretionary control over its expenses. On the income side, both the associated physical variables and the unit prices (which here are set by the institution) can also be manipulated within certain limits.

A simple example may illustrate the advantages of the format shown in table 4.5. Suppose utilities costs are projected to increase by 10 percent next year over this year. One might have derived this figure from data showing a past trend of 5 percent increases in energy consumption coupled with 5 percent increases in unit cost, the latter being an "uncontrollable" input price. Alternatively, one might have estimated that the unit cost would go up by 15 percent and that conservation measures would be employed to reduce consumption by 5 percent. It is essential to know which of these assumptions is being built into the forecast—and impossible to tell which unless the volume of consumption and the unit price are projected and reported separately.

We do not mean to suggest that every line item in the budget be split up into price and volume variables. Many items are either so small or so hard to describe in terms of physical units that this sort of treatment is not justified. For instance, it would make little sense to separate the aggregate amount of wages paid to casual ("hourly") employees (this is the item labeled "salary requisitions" in table 4.3) into an FTE and a unit wage figure. Items such as these should be represented as straight dollar quantities in the budget model.

Incorporating Incremental Cost and Revenue Coefficients

If the budget model is to be expressed in physical variable terms, then care should be taken to estimate the *full incremental cost* and revenue coefficients associated with each primary planning variable.* Once estimated, these coefficients should be built into the model separately from fixed costs and revenue. Otherwise, the results given by running the model with different variable settings are likely to be misleading.

Our approach to full incremental costing is best described with an example. Let us consider the various costs associated with the primary planning variable X_1 (regular faculty). If the average salary (i.e., unit cost) for regular faculty is P_1, the *direct cost* of faculty salaries is given by $P_1 X_1$. This product is the quantity that appears on the first line of table 4.3. In addition to direct faculty salaries, several other categories of expense tend to vary with regular faculty FTE. These *ancillary costs* would include salaries for academic support staff (e.g., secretaries and administrative assistants in the departments); fringe benefits for the faculty and their associated staff; travel; materials and supplies consumed in academic departments; and perhaps some other expenses too. Since incremental faculty can be expected to add to these costs as well, an appropriate amount of each item must be included in the cost coefficient for X_1.

Illustrative numerical calculations of the direct and ancillary costs associated with the faculty at Stanford are shown in table 4.6. To prepare such a table, it is necessary first to make assumptions about which line items will tend to vary with the given primary planning variable, or PPV, and then to decide what portion of each relevant item is to be characterized as a variable expense associated with that, as opposed to some other, PPV. Sometimes a particular line item, or at least a portion of it, will be assumed not to vary with any PPV, in which case we would refer to that portion as a *fixed expense*. In the example at hand, only expenses that occurred directly in the schools were assumed to vary with the regular faculty PPV.

Before we get into a fuller explanation of the origin of the figures in table 4.6, it will be helpful to have an algebraic formulation of the budget model with variable costs and revenues. Let $X_j (j = 1, 2, \ldots, n)$ be the set of PPVs, of which we assume there are n in all, and let P_j be the unit cost or price of X_j. There are m line items of expense (or income), which we shall label $i = 1, 2, \ldots, m$. The *direct* cost of (or revenue from) X_j is given by the product $P_j X_j$, and we may reasonably assume that this full amount is included in the total for some particular line item (see table 4.5). In addition to its direct cost, each PPV has associated with it certain "induced," or ancillary, costs that may affect several

---

*In this section, and indeed in the rest of this chapter, we shall use the terms "incremental cost," "full incremental cost," and "variable cost" interchangeably.

Table 4.6. Example of Full Variable Costing of Regular Faculty (Thousands of 1974/75 Dollars)

Line Item (No.)	Amount	Amount per Faculty (c_{il})[a]
Faculty salaries (1)	$15,138	$23.289
DIRECT COST OF FACULTY	$15,138	$23.289
Academic support staff salaries (3)	$4,500	$6.923
Staff benefits (6)	3,340	5.138
Travel (16)	200	0.308
Materials and supplies (17)	1,500	2.308
Other (18)	300	0.462
ANCILLARY COST OF FACULTY	$9,840	$15.138
TOTAL VARIABLE COST OF FACULTY	$24,978	$38.427

SOURCE: Stanford University, Task Group on Incremental Costs and Revenues, 1976 (based on university operating budget, 1974/75).
[a] Figures in this column were obtained by dividing the corresponding value in column 2 by the number of regular faculty FTE, which was 650.

of the other line items. We let c_{ij} = the unit contribution of X_j to expenditure item i. The c_{ij}'s are the incremental cost coefficients about which we have been speaking. Once derived, they can be employed in the budget model to compute either the total cost associated with each PPV or the total budget for each expense item.

It is convenient to think in terms of a two-dimensional array, or table, whose rows (labeled i) represent the line items of the budget and whose columns (labeled j) refer to the PPVs. The numerical entries in the array denoted C_{ij} (or R_{ij} in the case of a revenue table) represent the portion of a given dollar item that is judged to be variable with a given PPV. For any particular X_j (say, regular faculty), there will usually be some particular item i (say, faculty salaries) for which

$$C_{ij} = P_j X_j.$$

For all other items i, we would have

$$C_{ij} = c_{ij} X_j.$$

The full amount of variable expense associated with X_j, which we denote by $C_{.j}$, is obtained merely by summing the entries in the jth column of the array. Algebraically, this operation can be written as

$$C_{.j} = P_j X_j + \sum_{i=1}^{m} c_{ij} X_j \qquad (4.1)$$

where we have employed the notation $\sum_{i=1}^{m} c_{ij} X_j$ as shorthand for the algebraic sum $c_{1j} X_j + c_{2j} X_j + \ldots + c_{mj} X_j$.

The relation expressed in equation (4.1) can be simplified by factoring out X_j from both terms, so that we can write

$$C_{.j} = \left(P_j + \sum_{i=1}^{m} c_{ij} \right) X_j. \tag{4.2}$$

This gives us a simple, compact way of looking at things, for the quantity in parentheses on the right side of equation (4.2) is the total variable cost per unit of X_j. It is multiplied in our model by a particular value of X_j to yield $C_{.j}$, the total variable expense in the budget due to X_j. A similar relation, in which the unit cost coefficients, c_{ij}, would be replaced by unit revenue coefficients, r_{ij}, holds for the total variable revenue associated with X_j.

Deriving numerical values for the c_{ij}'s can be rather tricky because estimates of fixed, variable, and joint costs are by nature equivocal. The basic notion is that some portions of certain line items can be attributed to a given PPV, X_j. Usually one starts with aggregate budget data and, by following certain rules, proceeds to allocate the line items across the set of PPVs to obtain a table of C_{ij}'s. (The same process yields a table of R_{ij}'s on the income side.) Once the C_{ij} table has been filled in, it is an easy matter to compute the unit cost coefficients, c_{ij}: one simply divides each C_{ij} by the actual value of the corresponding X_j to obtain c_{ij}.

Returning to the numerical example worked out in table 4.6, we note that the quantities in the first column are the allocated budget figures, C_{ij}. These figures make up the first column in the budget array, since they are the ones associated with variable number one, regular faculty FTE. The first item, which happens to correspond to line-item number one in the operating budget, is the full amount of direct salaries paid to regular faculty. Dividing this by the FTE, we get the unit direct cost, P_1, of faculty. This quantity is shown in the first line, second column, of table 4.6. Lines 3 to 7 itemize the ancillary costs that we chose to associate with the same variable X_1. These include total salaries for academic support staff (which were for staff personnel located in the schools and thus comprised a rather small portion of the total salary budget for "other personnel"), and a portion of the school budgets for "travel," "materials and supplies," and "other expenses." The three last-named entries were derived by allocating the total amount budgeted for each item between regular faculty, X_1, auxiliary faculty, X_2, and support staff, X_3, in proportion to their relative FTE numbers. This allocation rule assumed, in effect, that each new employee, whether a member of the regular faculty, auxiliary faculty, or support staff, would "consume" the same quantity of these items on the average as any other employee, and that these quantities would be the same as the average amounts "consumed" by all current employees.

The following example will show how the allocations were made. A total of \$1,725,000 was budgeted for materials and supplies (M & S) in the various schools. The aggregate FTE numbers were 650 for X_1, 150 for X_2, and 350 for X_3. Since X_3 was itself considered to vary in full with X_1, the amount of M & S expense allocated to X_1 was computed by the above-mentioned rule to be

$$C_{17,1} = [(650 + 350)/(650 + 150 + 350)] \times \$1,725,000 = \$1,500,000.$$

This figure is shown on line 6 of table 4.6. Note that the remaining $225,000 of M & S expense (that is, $1,725,000 − $1,500,000), which by assumption is attributable to auxiliary faculty (X_2), would occupy the cell in row 17 (line-item number), column 2 (PPV number), of the budget array. Dividing each quantity in column one of table 4.6 by the faculty FTE yielded the unit cost coefficients c_{i1}, for $i = 3, 6, 16, 17$, and 18. All other c_{i1} were, by assumption, considered to be zero. Finally, adding the sum of these quantities to the average direct salary gave us the total variable cost per faculty, as shown on the bottom line, second column, of the table.

How does one arrive at assumptions of the kind used in estimating the variable cost of faculty of Stanford? Lacking any firm and unequivocal data or hard-and-fast allocation rules, one must apply reasonable judgment to whatever data are available. In this instance, the data on travel, materials, and other expenditures came aggregated across all schools; all that was desired was a simple rule for approximating the portion of these costs attributable to faculty.

Assumptions like these, made centrally on the basis of broadly aggregated data, will always have a somewhat ad hoc character. An alternative would be to do a detailed accounting of financial data related to the activities of individual faculty members in each department. Since, however, we do not believe that fine precision is needed for making aggregate financial projections, we do not recommend undertaking such a costly and time-consuming task. Most of the time it is better to approximate the data and then use the model results with appropriate caution rather than depend on the model for precise answers that it cannot give anyway.

The key to approximations of this sort is to recognize that one is trying to predict ancillary decisions that would be made if it were decided to change a given PPV (X_1 in our example). Obviously there is no prior commitment to make such decisions, but if one thinks that, on average and in the aggregate, they probably would occur, their effects should be included in the calculation of variable cost. In making such predictions one will need to have in mind some relevant range over which the PPV is likely to vary in the planning exercises that will be performed. Our assumption, for instance, was that the faculty size at Stanford probably would not vary more than 15 percent from its base value of 650. In our judgment, this meant that we could ignore any expenditures made outside of academic departments (e.g., for libraries or central administration) in computing the incremental cost of faculty. Having built these assumptions into our model, however, we certainly would be ill-advised to project, say, the consequences of a 30 percent change in faculty size. More generally, there is an obvious yet important caveat to be borne in mind whenever one is using a model to make incremental cost or revenue calculations: the coefficients will be valid only for some particular range in the associated variable, and so the model must not be relied upon for projecting consequences when the variable is moved beyond the limits of that range. Actually, there is a still more general point to be made here about modeling per se. Both the structure and the data incorporated in any mathematical model are valid only within certain limits. While this range of validity usually cannot be specified with much precision, the model user must be aware that the limits exist and must try to avoid pushing the variables too far.

An alternative approach is to specify the components of a variable cost or revenue coefficient directly (i.e., without reference to the historical budget data), through a process of simple reasoning. For instance, had we had more confidence in our ability to infer the figures directly, we might have arrived at an estimate for the variable cost per faculty by reasoning as follows.

1. On average, an incremental faculty member costs $27,000 in direct salary plus benefits.

2. That same faculty member requires (also on average) 0.5 FTE support staff (with salary and benefits that cost $6,000), plus a travel budget of $500, plus $2,000 in materials and supplies, plus $500 in miscellaneous other expenses.

3. Thus the full incremental cost per faculty member is $36,000.

This approach certainly is preferable whenever one has a sound basis for coming up with the figures. The trouble is, of course, that in practice one usually lacks direct knowledge about the ancillary effects of changes in the PPVs, and this forces one to rely upon the aggregate budget data as a proxy.

Calculations like the ones described above yield the costs and revenues associated with each PPV. Total cost and revenue can be obtained by summing up these variable costs and revenues over the set of PPVs, and then adding in the appropriate fixed amounts. To set the budget model up for forecasting, however, a different "slice" is taken through the array of costs. Since the focus when one is making financial projections is on line items rather than on PPVs, it must be possible to express the total cost of line item i in terms of the components generated by each PPV. To do this, one can work with the same unit cost coefficients, c_{ij}, as before, but this time one adds together all the terms involving line item i regardless of which PPVs contributed to them. In other words, the budget array should be summed across rows rather than down columns. Algebraically, the total budget for line item i is given by

$$C_{i\cdot} = C_{i0} + P_{j(i)}X_{j(i)} + \sum_{j=1}^{n} c_{ij}X_j \qquad (4.3)$$

where C_{i0} is the fixed (i.e., nonvariable) portion of line item i, and $j(i)$ identifies the PPV that is directly associated with line item i, if any.

To take a specific example of the calculations specified by equation (4.3), consider the figures given in table 4.8. Here the Materials and Supplies (M & S) expense, which is line item number 17 in Stanford's budget, is juxtaposed with each of the PPVs. The first column gives the entries for row 17 of the budget array. These figures were derived from the data shown in table 4.7. To get the original data, the M & S expense falling in each budget entity was analyzed to

Table 4.7.   Illustrative Allocation of Materials and Supplies Expense to Primary Planning Variables (in Thousands of 1974/75 Dollars)

M & S expense in school budgets[a]		= $1,725
Allocated to regular faculty (X_1)	$983	
Allocated to auxiliary faculty (X_2)	$225	
Allocated to academic support staff (X_3)	$517	
M & S expense in student services budgets[b]		= $954
Fixed portion	$428	
Allocated to undergraduates (X_8)	$321	
Allocated to graduate students (X_9)	$205	
Other M & S expense[c]		= $3,989
Fixed portion	$1,995	
Allocated to nonacademic staff (X_4)	$1,994	

[a] Allocated according to FTE breakdown:
      Regular faculty FTE   =   650 (57%)
      Auxiliary faculty FTE   =   150 (13%)
      Academic support staff FTE =   350 (30%)
                                         1,150
[b] Assumes 45% of total M & S expense in these budgets is fixed. Variable portion allocated according to chief recipient of the services, or, if services are joint, allocated in proportion to enrollments.
[c] Breakdown into fixed and variable parts assumes one-half of these costs are fixed.

Table 4.8.   Illustrative Breakdown for the Materials and Supplies Expense Item (in Thousands of 1974/75 dollars)

PPV	Amount Associated with the PPV	PPV Value	Amount per Unit of PPV
Regular faculty (X_1)	$1,500[a]	650	$2.308
Auxiliary faculty (X_2)	$225	150	$1.500
Nonacademic staff (X_4)	$1,994	1,350	$1.477
Undergraduates (X_7)	$321	6,500	$0.049
Graduate students (X_8)	$205	4,500	$0.046
FIXED PORTION	$2,423		
TOTAL	$6,668		

[a] This figure includes the allocation to academic support staff (X_3), which by assumption varies with regular faculty FTE.

see what portion might reasonably be assigned to the relevant PPVs. As the top portion of table 4.7 shows, the M & S expense that appeared in the "school" instruction budgets was assumed to vary with the number of regular faculty, auxiliary faculty, or academic support staff, and further, the expense per person was judged to be the same for each of these three categories of personnel. Thus the total amount was allocated to each category in proportion to its FTEs. Scrutiny of the "student services" budget for M & S indicated a large fixed component. The rest of this budget varied with the number of undergraduates or graduate students, depending on which class a particular office served. Finally, the remainder of M & S expense was judged either to be fixed or to vary with the number of nonacademic staff personnel (X_4). Note that the allocation of M & S expense between PPVs and fixed cost, represented in table 4.8, is both mutually exclusive and exhaustive of the total budget for that item in table 4.3.

Our purpose for including these details is to indicate what sort of process needs to be followed in generating data for the coefficients of the budget model. Again, it should be clear from the type of reasoning employed that the values obtained are estimates based on informed judgments about relationships in the aggregate. They are not the same as the precise figures that might have resulted from a painstaking effort to work out the associations of individual cost entries with PPVs in minute detail for particular departments or programs.

In our example, it will be seen from table 4.8 that the total cost (in thousands of dollars) for M & S is given in terms of the PPVs by

$$C_{17.} = 2,423 + 2.308 X_1 + 1.500 X_2 + 1.477 X_4 + .049 X_7 + .046 X_8.$$

Similar equations may be obtained for most of the other line items. The interested reader will find a more detailed discussion of incremental cost and revenue analysis as applied to universities in the excellent paper by D. Robinson and his colleagues (1977).

In some areas of the budget there are definite quantitative relationships between two or more line items. Where these are significant, they should be identified and additional structure built into the budget model. We next turn our attention to formulating certain submodels that can be used to represent some of the important relations among items in a typical university's operating budget.

Formulation of Financial Submodels

As the result of several years of experience with a variety of budget planning models, we have come to single out five areas in Stanford's operating budget for which special structures needed to be developed.

1. *Fringe benefits for personnel.* These depend on faculty and staff FTEs, salaries, and tuition price.
2. *Tuition income.* This depends on full-time equivalency factors, tuition price, and demand for enrollment.
3. *Student financial aid.* This depends on FTE enrollments, cost of attending the institution, and the institution's financial aid policy.
4. *Indirect cost recovery on research grants and contracts.* This depends on costs incurred, demand for research, and allocation of indirect costs to the research objective.
5. *Endowment total return and payout.* These depend on the investment mix of the endowment portfolio, expected rates of return from the various investment markets, amount of new gifts added to endowment, and growth rate of the operating budget.

Note that only the first two items on our list belong on the expense side of the budget. This should not be surprising, for it has already been shown that line items of expense in the university's operating budget are modeled quite well by taking the products of institutional activity variables times their unit costs. In most cases, the unit cost is determined or strongly influenced by an outside market. The two items we have singled out are exceptions, however, for the unit cost of benefits, or the *staff benefits rate*, will depend heavily upon institutional goals and philosophy. This is true also for the unit cost of financial aid. Our object in this subsection will be to examine the nature of these relationships in greater detail.

The remaining three items on our list probably represent the major categories of income in any private university's operating budget (in Stanford's case, they add up to a whopping 91 percent of all income). For obvious reasons, we feel it is important to recognize the dependence of these items on outside demand as well as institutional variables. In view of their very substantial size, they need to be modeled in a form that will enable us to study how they vary with changes in policy or *internal prices* (i.e., those prices that are set by the university).

Clearly, identification of the budget areas that need to be modeled in depth is an important task and one that should be taken on early in the process of forecast development. The list of items obviously will vary by institution, although we suspect the relative emphasis given to the different items would vary more than the list itself. In particular, we would expect that the items identified above for Stanford would be just about as important to other private research universities. A small private college, on the other hand, would show most interest in predicting tuition income, financial aid expense, and the staff benefits cost, with little or no interest in indirect cost recovery or endowment return. If that institution is concerned about maintaining its enrollment, it would probably want to develop more sophisticated models of student demand.

Public institutions, the bulk of whose income is provided in the form of a state appropriation, are in an entirely different situation. While expenditure submodels may still be valuable here, more emphasis should be given to modeling the appropriation as a function of institutional factors and state resources. In some cases, the funding level is largely determined by a formula that depends on student enrollments and faculty FTEs, and this is easily built into a budget projection model. In other cases, where it is determined by a loosely structured negotiation, more effort should be devoted to seeing how well the outcome can be predicted by models that involve whatever quantifiable variables are known to have major impact. With these caveats in mind, we will now describe the five budget submodels.

Submodel 1: Fringe benefits. The fringe benefits provided by a university to its faculty and staff employees typically fall into four categories: (a) ones that vary directly with FTEs (e.g., medical and life insurance plans); (b) ones that vary directly with salaries (e.g., contributions to retirement plans); (c) ones that vary with FTEs and the tuition price (e.g., tuition scholarships for faculty and staff children); (d) ones that do not vary with FTE or salaries and that, for our purposes, may be considered as fixed.

The first step in constructing a benefits model is to sort the various programs offered by the institution into these four categories. Let B_i denote the dollar cost of programs in category i. Next, convert these dollar totals to coefficients, b_i, that represent the *unit* cost of programs in each category:

$$b_1 = B_1/(X_1 + X_2 + X_3 + X_4)$$
$$b_2 = B_2/(P_1X_1 + P_2X_2 + P_3X_3 + P_4X_4)$$
$$b_3 = B_3/[P_{13}(X_1 + X_2 + X_3 + X_4)].$$

(We have assumed that teaching assistants, X_5, are not eligible for the benefits programs.)

Earlier, we expressed the benefits expense (line 6 in the expense table) as the simple product of total FTE (X_6) and the average (unit) benefits cost per employee (P_6). It will now be seen that the unit cost P_6 actually depends on some of the other prices. Our more refined benefits model takes the form

$$C_6. = B_4 + \sum_{i=1}^{4} (b_1 + b_2P_i + b_3P_{13})X_i. \tag{4.4}$$

Stanford budget data for fringe benefits programs in the year 1974/75 are shown in table 4.9; here, they have been grouped into the four categories defined above. Summing the items within each category leads to the aggregate dollar figures, B_i, as indicated. Dividing these sums by the appropriate units shown in the next-to-last column yields the unit coefficients, b_i. Finally, we can use the model in equation (4.4) to reconcile the results to the total "staff benefits" figure for 1974/75 (see table 4.3, line 7, column 1):

$$\$6,778 = \$1,158 + (\$3.163)(650) + (\$1.158)(150) + (\$1.991)(350)$$
$$+ (\$1.991)(1,350).$$

Of course, if changes were made in any of the FTE, average-salary, or tuition variables the benefits model would compute some other figure for the total fringe benefits cost—which is exactly why we have chosen to build it into our budget planning model.

We should note that some institutions associate the costs of different benefits programs with different classes of employees; for example, there may be one fringe benefit rate for faculty and another for staff. In such cases one would probably want to develop a separate benefits submodel like equation (4.4) for each.

Submodel 2: Tuition income. Accurate predictions of tuition income are so much needed by most private institutions that it is well worth developing a good model.

Table 4.9. Fringe Benefits Submodel Applied to Stanford Data (in Thousands of 1974/75 Dollars)

Category	Variable with:	Program	1974/75 Budget	Units Applied	Unit Expense
A	FTE	Medical insurance	$652		
		Compensation insurance	87		
		Unemployment insurance	201		
		Misc. retirement	61		
		SUBTOTAL	$B_1 = \$1,001$	2,500[a]	$0.400($b_1$)$
B	Salaries	University retirement	$2,070		
		Social Security	1,850		
		Group life insurance	142		
		Long-term disability insurance	232		
		SUBTOTAL	$B_2 = \$4,294$	$37,918[b]	$0.113($b_2$)$
C	Tuition × FTE	Tuition waiver programs	$B_3 = \$325$	$8,438[c]	$0.039($b_3$)$
D	"Fixed"	Research/teaching assistant tuition	$1,001		
		Miscellaneous benefits & programs	157		
		SUBTOTAL	$B_4 = \$1,158$		
		TOTAL BUDGET	$= \$6,778$		

NOTE: Figures shown are for the operating budget (net of the schools of business and medicine) share of benefits expense only.
[a] Total operating budget FTE.
[b] Total operating budget salaries for faculty "other teaching," and "other personnel" (see table 4.3).
[c] Tuition rate × operating budget FTE.

Let X = fall quarter (or semester) head-count enrollment level

γ_i = returning enrollment ratio between quarters (or semesters) i and $i + 1$

ϕ = fraction of students who are part-time

α = average fraction of full-time tuition paid by part-time students

P = full-time tuition rate per academic year

TI = tuition income of the university (R_1 in Stanford's budget array).

(For simplicity, we have dropped the subscripts on X and P in the present discussion.)

We start with head-count enrollments and use the factors γ_i, ϕ, and α to convert these to FTEs. The returning enrollment ratio, γ_i, refers to the ratio of a new quarter's (or semester's) head-count enrollment to the enrollment in the quarter (or semester) just preceding it. Thus, it is a measure of the net attrition of students between quarters (or semesters). For the time being, we will assume that these and the other behavioral factors just defined are stable parameters. If necessary, more refined models for predicting enrollments by quarter can be constructed; these will be described in chapter 8.

Suppose, first, that the institution has no difficulty in finding qualified students to fill its freshman class up to the capacity that it has set as optimal. This means that the total head-count enrollment, X, at the beginning of the year is determined by the institution and not by exogenous demand factors. Since P is the tuition rate for a full academic year, we must first adjust X for attrition between quarters. Now according to the definition of γ_i the number of students remaining in the winter quarter is $\gamma_1 X$, and the number remaining in the spring is $\gamma_2(\gamma_1 X)$. Thus the average number of tuition-paying students for the academic year is

$$X' = (1 + \gamma_1 + \gamma_1\gamma_2)X/3. \tag{4.5}$$

Of these a fraction, $1 - \phi$, pays tuition at the full rate, P, while the fraction ϕ pays at the average part-time rate, αP. So the average tuition paid per student is $(1 - \phi)P + \alpha\phi P$. Combining these results leads to the tuition submodel:

$$TI = P[(1 - \phi) + \alpha\phi]X'. \tag{4.6}$$

As equations (4.5) and (4.6) reveal, tuition revenue is a complicated function of a number of different factors, some of which are primarily behavioral in nature while some, like ϕ and α, depend more on institutional policies. The advantage of keeping these factors separate in the tuition model should be evident: it permits one easily to assess the effects of changes in any of them, whether taken singly or in combination with changes in some of the others. We also note that equation (4.6), just like the fringe benefits model, is non-specific as to the type of student generating the tuition revenue. Presumably one would want at least to have separate equations for undergraduate and graduate student tuition, although the functional form would be the same for each.

To illustrate, we give data on the relevant enrollment and tuition factors for the year 1974–75 at Stanford in table 4.10. Applying the formulas to these data yields the following results:

	FTE Enrollment (X)	Tuition Revenue ($000) ($R_{tuition}$)
Undergraduates	6,230	$21,026
Graduate students	3,327	11,228
Other students	140	472
TOTAL	9,697	$32,726

Note that this total tuition figure, when added to a summer quarter tuition income of $2,106 thousand and fee income of $657 thousand, agrees with the figure labeled "tuition and fees" that is shown in line 1, column 1, of table 4.4.

What about the institution that is constrained by lack of student demand? Presumably, further tuition increases in any particular year would tend to reduce demand. It clearly would be advantageous for such a school to make some form of demand function an element in its tuition model. However,

Table 4.10.   Approximate Stanford Data on Enrollment and Tuition Factors, 1974/75

	Student Type		
	Undergraduate	Graduate	Other
Fall head count, X	6,475	4,500	280
Returning enrollment ratios, γ_i	0.98/0.925	0.96/0.92	. . . .
Fraction part-time, ϕ	0	0.4	1.0
Part-time tuition fraction, α	. . . .	0.45	0.5
Full-time tuition rate, P ($000)	\$3.375	\$3.375	\$3.375

there may be no easy way to identify the proper demand function, let alone to specify values for its parameters. If so, the best course is to use a reasonably good approximation that has only one or two unknown parameters. A good first choice might be a *constant-elasticity demand function* with parameter η:

$$X(P) = X(P_0)\left(\frac{P}{P_0}\right)^{\eta}. \tag{4.7}$$

In this expression P_0 represents the current price, and $X(P_0)$ the current enrollment. Note that $X(P)$ here means "X as a function of P," not "the product of variables X and P." The exponent, or "elasticity coefficient," η, represents the *percentage* change in demand (i.e., X) for every 1 percent change in price. (In this context, "price" might be either the tuition rate or tuition plus room and board.) If $\eta = 0$, demand is constant, whereas any negative value signifies that demand goes down as price goes up.

To be sure, estimating the proper value of η will be a difficult task. Even in the absence of hard data, however, a formulation incorporating equation (4.7) will enable the institution to perform sensitivity analyses that vary η within limits that are judged to be realistic. A rough estimate of η based on judgment is better than an implicit assumption that $\eta = 0$, which is what results from ignoring demand effects altogether.

Submodel 3: Financial aid. In table 4.5 we noted that the financial aid budget is the product of (a) the FTE enrollment and (b) the amount of aid provided per FTE student. The first of these two factors is given by equation (4.5), but we still need to develop an expression for the second in terms of known quantities and planning variables. In so doing we shall recognize two fundamentally different types of financial aid policy, either one of which, it turns out, can be accommodated by the same aid model.

Under a *need-based* financial aid policy, the institution is committed to meeting the demonstrated need of each student from its own resources. This policy is characteristic of aid programs for undergraduates at most of the nation's larger colleges and universities. Demonstrated need is calculated, for each individual, by subtracting from the total cost of attendance (i.e., tuition, room and board, and incidental expenses) an expected contribution from the student and his or her parents plus the amount of aid that will be

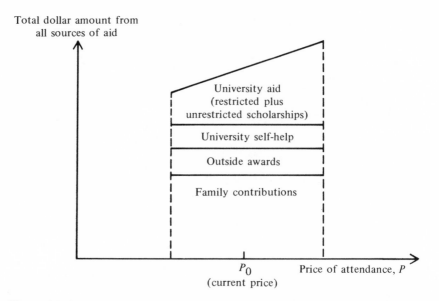

Figure 4.1. Sources of funds for a constant population of financial aid recipients

provided from sources outside the university (e.g., a state scholarship program). The parents' expected contribution is calculated by means of a formula, established nationally by the College Scholarship Service, that takes account of the parents' income and liquid assets and the student's accumulated savings, if any.

Once a student's need has been determined, a financial aid package is put together. It consists of: (a) a required amount of self-help (i.e., earnings from summer and term-time jobs plus a certain amount of loan money); (b) a combination of scholarship money awarded from restricted university aid funds and scholarship money from unrestricted university funds (i.e., general funds), or either of these by itself. The reason for distinguishing between the two types of university scholarship is that at many schools (Stanford is an example) only the unrestricted scholarships show up under "aid expense" in the operating budget. In such cases the income from and expenses charged to restricted aid are accounted for outside the operating budget. Since restricted aid money normally would be used up before unrestricted funds are made available, it must be recognized that, for financial aid recipients, price increases on the margin will have to be met entirely from unrestricted funds unless the school has been underspending its restricted aid resources. For the same reason, restricted aid must be incorporated in the financial-aid budget model.

With this information in hand we can now outline an explicit representation of the average amount of unrestricted aid required per student in the operating budget of a university with a need-based aid program. To begin with, consider the illustration shown in figure 4.1 of total student aid, from all sources for all aid recipients, regarded as a function of the price of attendance. For a preliminary aid model we shall assume a constant population of aid recipients; that is, as the price of attendance goes up we shall assume that few, if any, additional students will come to need scholarship aid.

Figure 4.1 shows that, for the given population of students, all outside sources of contribution are relatively fixed, as is the self-help component set by the university. The figure assumes, then, that the ceilings typically imposed on outside scholarships and self-help have already been reached for nearly all students. Under these conditions, university aid will be required to fill the gap between (a) the total cost of attendance and (b) a relatively fixed amount of contributions from outside scholarships plus self-help. In other words,

$$
\begin{array}{l}
\text{Total university} \\
\text{scholarship aid}
\end{array}
= \left(
\begin{array}{l}
\text{Price of} \\
\text{attendance}
\end{array}
\times
\begin{array}{c}
\text{Number of students} \\
\text{on aid}
\end{array}
\right)
-
\begin{array}{l}
\text{Family} \\
\text{contributions}
\end{array}
$$

$$
-\;
\begin{array}{l}
\text{Outside} \\
\text{scholarships}
\end{array}
- \text{Self-help}.
$$

This expression can be stated more formally, as follows.

Let X' = FTE student enrollment

β_1 = fraction of students on university scholarship aid

P = average price of attendance (here, average per-student tuition plus room and board plus other incidental expenses)

FC = total family contributions for aid recipients

OS = total outside scholarships for aid recipients

SH = total self-help for aid recipients

RA = funds available for restricted university scholarships

$A(P)$ = total unrestricted aid budget (C_8 in Stanford's budget array) expressed as a mathematical function of the price of attendance.

Thus the sum $FC + OS + SH$ = the total contribution for students on financial aid from sources other than scholarships controlled by the university. Now write

$$A(P) = \beta_1 PX' - FC - OS - SH - RA. \tag{4.8}$$

Finally, since the totals for outside contributions and self-help are all associated with the given population of students, it makes sense to express them as average amounts per aid recipient. (Note that the same reasoning certainly does not apply to the contribution from restricted aid.) This logic leads us to a simple formula for expressing the unrestricted aid budget in terms of the price, P, and the aid recipient fraction, β_1 :

Total dollar amount from
all sources of aid

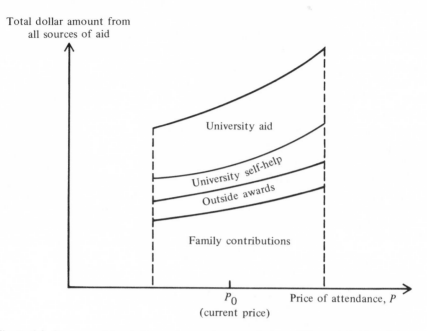

Figure 4.2. Sources of funds for an increasing population of financial aid recipients

$$A(P) = (-\beta_0 + P)\beta_1 X' - RA. \tag{4.9}$$

The coefficient β_0 measures the average contribution per FTE aid recipient. To derive its value from data on FC, OS, SH, and X', one would take the total contribution for aid recipients divided by their total FTE; that is,

$$\beta_0 = (FC + OS + SH)/\beta_1 X'.$$

The data for undergraduate aid at Stanford in 1974/75, expressed in thousands of dollars, were (approximately) $\beta_1 = 0.5$, $P = \$5.510$, $X' = 6,230$, $FC = \$7,323$, $OS = \$3,000$, $SH = \$2,400$, $RA = \$2,500$, and $A = \$1,941$. Thus, our model for that year becomes

$$A(P) = (-4.084 + P)0.5X' - 2,500.$$

It will be remembered that we just made two assumptions: the population of aid recipients remains constant, and the outside scholarship recipients all receive the maximum amount available from the sources enumerated. But these assumptions are good only as first approximations. In reality, whenever the price shifts by a significant amount in the given year we would expect to observe some change in the fraction of students on aid (i.e., in β_1) and some change in outside scholarships (which would affect β_0). This is the situation depicted in figure 4.2. A good "second-order" model should recognize these dependencies, although it would still logically have the form

$$A(P) = [-\beta_0(P) + P]\beta_1(P)X' - RA \qquad (4.10)$$

where now $\beta_0(P)$ and $\beta_1(P)$ are functions of the price of attendance.

In contrast to the first-order approximation represented by equation (4.9), the notation in (4.10) signifies that the average aid per student is actually a (somewhat) nonlinear function of the price of attendance. The development of proper expressions for the functions $\beta_0(P)$ and $\beta_1(P)$ involves taking integrals over the frequency distributions of family contributions and outside scholarships—a complicated procedure. For the technically oriented we have included the second-order financial aid model as appendix 3. We would not recommend this model to a new user, and indeed we have stopped short of adopting it at Stanford, feeling that the first-order approximation is good enough for present purposes.

The second type of aid policy that operates in many institutions is one that is *based on merit*. Only certain students are designated to receive aid, and the amount of aid awarded may not bear much relationship to the student's need. Such policies are commonly applied to graduate students at many universities. Students enrolled in graduate programs may receive financial aid from many different sources. These would include aid from federal and other agencies outside the university that provide fellowships for graduate study, as well as institution-based support in the form of a teaching or research assistantship or an outright fellowship. In addition there will probably be some students— perhaps a relatively small proportion of the total graduate population—who receive no aid at all (professional graduate programs such as those in law, medicine, and business often have many of these, however).

Typically, it is only the university fellowship budget that is included in the operating budget—and then only the part of it financed by unrestricted funds. Each individual student on a university fellowship receives a stipend, the amount of which is set by policy, plus a payment for the tuition charges actually incurred. A model for this type of aid program is easily developed. We adapt our previous notation as follows.

Let X = head-count enrollment

μ = the FTE factor, derived from equations (4.5) and (4.6)

α = the fraction of students on university fellowships

P = full-time tuition rate

S = stipend level (i.e., amount of fellowship, on average, provided in addition to the tuition payment).

Now we can write

$$A(P) = (S + \mu P)\alpha X - RA. \qquad (4.11)$$

This equation easily rearranges to the same form as (4.9), where now $\beta_0 = -S/\mu$ and $\beta_1 = \alpha$.

Before leaving the topic of financial aid submodels we wish to introduce one further refinement. Its significance will become apparent later when we discuss how the restricted portion of university financial aid is itself derived from two sources, both of them, in effect, gifts donated to the university by alumni and others. Some of these gifts—typically the ones that are relatively small in amount—are designated as "expendable" and are in fact spent nearly as soon as they are received. Others (and this usually forms the major source for restricted aid) are added to the endowment, so that only a small fraction (usually some 4 to 5 percent) of the amount of the gift is available for spending in any given year. Moreover, as we saw in chapter 2, the endowment payout rate is a financial policy variable that, for any institution with a sizable total endowment, is of major importance in assuring budget stability over the long run. At Stanford the amount of endowment used in support of the operating budget in table 4.3 was around $110 million in 1974/75 (the base year in the MRFF). In addition, about $40 million of endowment was restricted to financial aid, and there was an annual expendable-gift flow for aid of around $2 million.

New definitions are needed to take proper account of the manner in which the endowment payout rate affects the unrestricted financial aid budget.

Let EGA = annual amount of expendable gifts for financial aid

   ENA = market value of restricted financial aid endowment

   p = endowment payout rate (expressed as a fraction of endowment market value).

Now we rewrite equation (4.9), replacing RA by its expression in terms of the quantities just defined:

$$A(P,p) = (-\beta_0 + P)\beta_1 X' - EGA - (p)ENA. \qquad (4.12)$$

The aid formula now explicitly recognizes the feedback effect of changes in the endowment payout rate on the unrestricted financial aid budget.

Submodel 4: Indirect cost recovery. The next budget submodel to be discussed is one for estimating income from recovering the indirect, or overhead, costs of sponsored research grants and contracts. To understand the estimation procedure we are about to recommend, it is necessary first to become familiar with the whole notion of indirect cost—what components it is typically made up of, and how some of it comes to be recaptured as general-funds revenue from sources outside the university.

Stated very simply, *indirect costs* are costs borne by the institution that are not directly attributable to any single primary institutional objective. Fundamentally, they are shared costs, so that allocating the proper portion to each primary objective requires the use of special accounting procedures.

At Stanford, there are three final cost objectives: instruction (which includes so-called departmental research); sponsored research; and sponsored instruction (i.e., training grants and the like). (Some institutions would add a fourth, viz, "public service.") Of the three, only expenditures in the first category appear in Stanford's operating budget; all sponsored projects, whether for research or instruction, are accounted for elsewhere.

Indirect costs are incurred in support of the final cost objectives, to which they are eventually allocated. They fall into the following six categories:

1. *Depreciation* (*DEP*). Use charges for buildings, equipment, and plant improvements.

2. *Operations and maintenance* (*O & M*). Utilities, custodial care for buildings and grounds, insurance, etc.

3. *General and administrative* (*G & A*). This includes the expenses of most central administrative offices—the president's and vice-president's staff, the business office, etc.

4. *Departmental administration* (*IDA*). Expenses incurred at the school or department level for all kinds of administration, including faculty and staff time spent in connection with administrative tasks.

5. *Student services* (*SS*). All such services except financial aid.

6. *Libraries* (*LIB*).

Notice the special nature of category (1): only depreciation is not a cash-flow item. Indeed a charge for depreciation is rarely, if ever, included in a university's operating budget, although it is becoming less unusual for the budget to show a "transfer to plant" item (see table 4.4), which is money specifically allocated to meet capital needs. The full costs falling in any of the remaining five categories are funded from the operating budget. Since a portion of these costs is attributable to sponsored-research and sponsored-instruction activities, money must be recovered from the sponsoring agencies as reimbursement to the operating budget. The aggregate sum of reimbursements is designated as the income item labeled "reimbursed indirect costs."

Intricate and detailed accounting procedures have been developed by the U.S. Office of Management and Budget (1979) for distributing each type of indirect cost to the various final cost objectives. For example, the depreciation and O & M pools are distributed on the basis of the square footage occupied by activities in each type of function (i.e., final cost objective), while library expenses are distributed according to the relative usage of libraries by different population groups—faculty, staff, and students—and the sources of pay for these same groups.

To observe the results of applying these procedures to an actual year's set of cost figures, look at table 4.11. This is a so-called step-down schedule for the year 1974/75 at Stanford; it is a convenient way to view the process of indirect cost allocation. The six indirect cost pools are displayed in the first six rows of the table and the three final cost objectives (plus one "other" category) are shown in the rows beneath them. Entries in the first column (i.e., the one headed "preallocation totals") are the total allowable amounts of each indirect cost and the net total direct cost (i.e., net after exclusions required by

Table 4.11. Step-Down Schedule of Indirect Costs at Stanford, 1974/75 ($000)

	Preallocation Totals	Depreciation	O & M	G & A	IDA	Student Services	Library	Post-allocation Totals
Depreciation & use charge	$4,664	($4,664)	....	....	....	....	....	....
Operations & maintenance	$8,377	$152	($8,530)	....	....	....	....	....
General & administrative	$9,809	$288	$648	($10,745)	....	....	....	....
Department administration (IDA)	$15,517	$1,241	$2,233	$1,400	($20,391)	....	....	....
Student services	$5,025	$129	$204	$453	....	($5,811)	....	....
Library	$8,513	$685	$1,623	$551	....	....	($11,373)	....
	$51,906							
Instructional & departmental research	$31,971	$555	$921	$2,885	$9,650	$4,961	$7,773	$26,744
Sponsored research	$42,065	$1,439	$2,591	$3,796	$9,316	$759	$2,883	$20,783
Sponsored instruction	$6,539	$143	$237	$590	$1,426	$80	$359	$2,835
Other	....	$33	$73	$1,070	....	$10	$358	$1,544
								$51,906

NOTE: Totals may not agree perfectly with individual entries due to rounding. Figures in parentheses indicate negative entries, i.e., totals to be allocated.

the federal government) associated with each cost objective. The columns to the right show the results of applying the allocation rules that distribute each indirect cost to the other cost categories. As can be seen from the table, the indirect costs are distributed not only to the cost objective rows, but also to other indirect cost pools. For example, depreciation costs are distributed to O & M, G & A, etc., as well as to the cost objectives of instruction, sponsored research, etc.

This process of allocating costs from one indirect cost pool to another is called *cross-allocation*. The preallocation costs of the pool and the cross-allocations of indirect costs from other pools are collected, and the total then distributed to final cost objectives and to other indirect cost pools where appropriate. For example, let us follow the allocation of library costs in table 4.11. The original preallocation total expense for the library pool is $8.513 million. Proceeding across row 6 of the step-down schedule, we see that each of the other indirect cost pools, except for departmental administration (IDA) and student services, makes a cross-allocation to the library pool. To the pre-allocation costs of the library pool, then, has been added an allocation of $0.685 million for depreciation, $1.623 million for operations and maintenance (O&M), and $0.551 million for general and administrative (G&A) costs. These figures bring the total library cost to $11.373 million, which is the figure shown in column 7 of row 6, and this total is then distributed down the same column to the final cost objectives.

After all the indirect costs have been distributed to the cost objectives by the "step-down" method just described, they are accumulated across the lower rows to yield the postallocation totals shown in column 8. For example, "sponsored research" accumulates allocations of depreciation, O & M, etc., that total $20.783 million. Observe that the sum of the postallocation totals of indirect costs equals the sum of the preallocation totals, thus indicating that all of the indirect costs have been distributed to the final cost objectives.

The indirect costs referred to in line 21 of Stanford's operating budget (table 4.4) are recovered chiefly from sponsored research. The figure of $12.801 million in column 1 was arrived at by taking an early estimate of the total allocations to sponsored research (which afterwards turned out to be the figure of $20.783 million in the last column of table 4.11), and proceeding through several additional steps. First, we applied an *effective recovery factor* that relates the theoretical recovery amount (as computed in the step-down table) to what is actually recovered (the difference has to do with waivers of overhead collection on particular projects, research conducted off campus, and the like). Next, we apportioned the effective recovery amount between the formula and nonformula schools according to their respective research volumes (recall that the income-and-expense figures in table 4.4 are for the nonformula schools only). Finally, we added a fixed sum for recovery from sponsored instruction (fixed because of restrictions that prevent certain training grants from paying their full share of indirect costs), and also added or subtracted several other miscellaneous fixed items. One of the last-named was a portion of the roughly

Table 4.12.   Sample Calculation of Operating Budget Indirect Cost Recovery,
Stanford University, 1974/75 (Approximate)

Estimated indirect costs allocated to sponsored research	$21,600
Times effective recovery factor	× 0.93
Effective recovery to the university	$20,076
Less formula school portion	($8,432)
Net effective recovery on sponsored research	$11,644
Plus estimated recovery on sponsored instruction	$647
Plus miscellanous fixed items	$1,010
Less transfer to plant (depreciation reserve)	($500)
NET OPERATING BUDGET INDIRECT COST RECOVERY	**$12,801**

NOTE: This table excludes the schools of business and medicine.

$1 million expected in recovery of depreciation costs; this was scheduled to
be transferred to plant funds for capital improvements. (It may help the reader
to refer to the data in table 4.12 in following the steps just described.)

Our construction of a budget submodel for indirect cost recovery proceeds
in three stages: first, we identify the cost functions and demand functions associated with the recovery calculations; second, we consider simple models of
how the various indirect cost pools are allocated to research; and, third, we
express net recovery in terms of these allocations. We will then discuss some
refinements of this basic model. In particular, we will consider the effects, in
determining the indirect cost rate, of a carryforward of recovery from a prior
year, and the effects of that rate on the demand for research.

Let ICP_i = preallocation total of indirect cost pool i

DCI = (net) total direct cost of instruction

$DCSR$ = (net) total direct cost of sponsored research

$DCSI$ = (net) total direct cost of sponsored instruction

α_i = the fraction of indirect cost pool i that is (ultimately) allocated
to sponsored research

ϕ = the fraction of costs allocated to sponsored research that actually
is recovered (i.e., the effective recovery factor)

R_0 = the fixed component of indirect cost recovery due to sponsored
instruction and special lump-sum agreements, net of allocation
to plant, and other adjustments

ICR = the operating budget income derived from the recovery of indirect
costs.

To begin with, we need to recognize that the first two variables in this list
belong in the operating budget and are functions of the planning variables, X,
and prices, P, at the institution in question. If desired, internal cost functions

for the ICP_i and DCI can be constructed in much the same manner as the budget models covered in the previous section, that is, by (a) breaking each indirect cost pool or the direct cost of instruction down into its component line items, and (b) expressing each line item in terms of the activity and price variables, just as we did in equation (4.3). For example the operations and maintenance pool is a function of energy consumption and utility rates, while DCI depends on faculty and staff FTEs and other departmental expenses.

$DCSR$ and $DCSI$, on the other hand, do not appear in the operating budget: they represent the demand by outside sponsors for research and training programs at the university. For these variables we may need to develop *demand functions* that show their dependence on institutional activity and price variables. A critical price variable in the demand function for sponsored research is the indirect cost rate (yet to be defined), which in a real sense represents a major component of the price of doing research at the given institution.

Suppose now that the proper functional equations for ICP_i, DCI, $DCSR$, and $DCSI$ have been developed, so that these quantities are known. Our next task is to develop a model for the allocation coefficients, α_i. Of course it would be possible, in theory, to program the actual set of allocation procedures into the model and obtain a very accurate representation of the α_i, but far more detail would be required than is warranted for an aggregate budget model. The simplest option would be to take the coefficients actually calculated from the most recent year's step-down schedule (appendix 4 shows how these calculations easily can be made), and assume they will remain fixed at these values in the future. The result, though, would surely be too crude a model, for it would not be able to adjust for even the first-order effects that occur, for example, when the mix of direct costs shifts away from research and towards instruction. When the mix changes in this way, we naturally expect that a somewhat smaller proportion of indirect costs will be allocated to research. The model should be able to react accordingly.

Our Stanford experience has led us to conclude that a reasonably good first-order approximation to these allocation coefficients can be obtained. It is given by a function that involves both a fixed term and a term that varies with the direct cost mix of sponsored research, instruction, and sponsored instruction. Specifically, we would propose using the formula

$$\alpha_i = \alpha_{i0} + \alpha_{i1} [DCSR/(DCI + DCSR + DCSI)] \qquad (4.13)$$

$$i = 1, 2, \ldots, 6,$$

in which the expression in brackets is the fraction of total direct costs represented by sponsored research. Notice that, with $\alpha_{i1} > 0$, this model will have the desired property mentioned above. Also, if a more aggregate model is desired, the ICP_i can be combined in a single pool with a single, aggregate allocation fraction, α, being expressed as in equation (4.13).

Total indirect cost recovery for the budget is obtained by: (a) applying each allocation coefficient in (4.13) to the corresponding indirect cost pool; (b) summing these dollar allocations over the six pools; (c) multiplying the result by the effective recovery factor; (d) adding in the fixed recovery. All of these steps are summarized by the equation

$$ICR = \phi \sum_{i=1}^{6} \alpha_i ICP_i + R_0.$$ (4.14)

Prediction of indirect cost recovery in the short run is complicated by the fact that most institutions have arrangements with their federal sponsors that permit them to carry forward the amounts under- or overrecovered during a prior year. How are these amounts generated? What happens in actuality is that, well before a new fiscal year begins, an *indirect cost rate* is agreed upon by the university and a designated sponsoring agency. The rate is determined by plugging estimates of all the relevant factors (including ICP_i, $DCSR$, DCI, and $DCSI$) into the detailed allocation formulas to obtain an estimate of the amount to be recovered (including carryforward from a prior year, if any) and then dividing by an estimated $DCSR$. This rate (let us call it u) is then applied to money that actually is expended on direct research throughout the year. That is, each \$1 of direct research expense "earns" an extra \$$u$ of unrestricted income for the university. If $\overline{DCSR}$ is the actual year-end value of $DCSR$, then an amount equal to $u \times \overline{DCSR}$ (actually $\phi \times u \times \overline{DCSR}$) will have been collected. After the books have been closed on the year in question, indirect cost recovery is recomputed with the *actual* values of ICP_i, $DCSR$, DCI, $DCSI$, etc. Inevitably, this process leads to a figure that differs from actual collections, and the dollar amount of the difference is then carried forward to the next year for which the indirect cost rate is to be negotiated.

At Stanford we do not include these carryforwards in the operating budget, since they represent unanticipated "overs" and "unders" from previous years. Instead we attempt as much as possible to budget only income that is regular and sustainable over the reasonably long run. Under the carryforward agreement, and as long as the rules of the game are not changed, we know that eventually we will recover the allocated portions of the indirect cost pools. Thus, we feel safe in budgeting the allocated amounts of the pools (adjusted, of course, for effective recovery) for the year in question. Any amount carried forward to that year is viewed as a one-time adjustment to income (hence, an item of "conditional" income) and therefore is not permitted to influence the operating-budget base.

As a possible refinement of the indirect cost recovery model presented above, it would be worth taking explicit account of the demand relationship between the direct cost of sponsored research, $DCSR$, and the indirect cost rate, u. The price of doing one dollar's worth of research at the university is \$1 + \$$u$. Presumably, there is a demand function that relates this price to $DCSR$. Unfortunately, just as we found with the demand function for student enrollment, little is known about the proper form for the function, let alone the values of its parameters. Since we also know little about the effect of an institution's indirect cost rate on the demand by outside research sponsors, we would once more recommend the use of a constant-elasticity demand function, this time of the form

$$DCSR = DCSR(u_0)\left(\frac{1 + u}{1 + u_0}\right)^\eta, \tag{4.15}$$

where u_0 is a recently observed value of the rate and $DCSR\,(u_0)$ the corresponding observed value of $DCSR$. The relevant range for the parameter η, which represents the price elasticity of demand for sponsored research, is $-1 \le \eta \le 0$. If $\eta = 0$, changes in the indirect cost rate have no effect on direct research volume, since all extra overhead is paid by the sponsor. At the other extreme, with $\eta = -1$, changes in the rate lead to no changes in *total* research volume (i.e., in direct plus indirect costs), which means that the extra indirect costs are paid for in reduced direct expenditures. The true value of η obviously lies somewhere in between; we suspect that, for high-quality research universities, it tends to be closer to 0 than to -1.

Recall that the indirect cost rate was obtained by means of the calculation

$$u = \frac{\text{Indirect costs allocated to sponsored research}}{\text{Direct cost of sponsored research}}$$

$$= \frac{\displaystyle\sum_{i=1}^{6} \alpha_i ICP_i}{DCSR} \tag{4.16}$$

when the effects of carryforward on the rate are ignored. If we are to incorporate the demand function into the model, the system of equations represented by (4.13), (4.14), (4.15), and (4.16) must be solved simultaneously. Given the nonlinearities involved, this is a difficult mathematical task. We have had good success, however, from separating the calculations into two parts and then iterating between them to get values that are consistent with both. In the first part, we fix $DCSR$ and calculate the rate using (4.13), (4.14), and (4.16). Plugging the resulting value for u into (4.15) then leads to a new estimate for $DCSR$ that can be used to recompute the rate. This sequence of calculations is continued until the necessary change in $DCSR$ is small enough to be ignored, a result that usually occurs after a very few iterations.[1]

Submodel 5: Endowment total return and payout rate. Spending and investing a university's endowment, if it is substantial, involves critical decisions for trustees and budget planners. Before the introduction of the *total return* concept in the 1960s, it was commonplace for universities to invest a major portion of their endowment in fixed-income or high-yield securities and to pay out to the budget whatever income was earned in dividends and interest. Such policies were consistent with the view that a university should seek only relatively safe investments for its endowment. Such investments assured a flow of income that, while it did not grow very fast (except when sizable new gifts were added to the endowment), at least was steady and dependable. Then, in the late 1960s, many institutions succumbed to the promise of superior performance by the equities market and began to invest more heavily in growth stocks and less heavily in bonds. When they did so, they often adopted spending rules that were still tied to the amount of cash actually earned on the endowment but that would permit drawing upon capital gains, if necessary, to make up for the income lost by preferring growth to yield. Many of these payout rules remain in effect today, as do others that merely set payout at a fixed percentage of endowment market value (or, more usually, at a moving average of recent market values). In the latter case, the value chosen for the fixed-percentage payout rate often results from tradition and may be hard to justify on strictly financial grounds.

Logically speaking, investment policy and spending policy involve separate decisions based on quite different considerations. Provided the endowment portfolio is buffered by sufficient realized capital appreciation or cash reserves (which can be drawn on, if necessary, in case earned income should fall short of the planned payout), it is advisable to deal with investment and spending separately. Choosing an investment mix is fundamentally a matter of deciding where on the spectrum of risk/return possibilities the institution should aim to be. Whatever investment policy is pursued, one must then choose a payout rate that strikes a proper balance between spending and saving.

We shall now elaborate further on each of these points, using some rough numerical calculations for illustration. According to the tenets of modern investment theory, an investor in the capital asset marketplaces is faced with a full spectrum of risk/return possibilities (see, for instance, Sharpe 1978). In the case of university endowments, we are talking about three classes of instrument for investment: stocks, bonds, and short-term cash equivalents. Each has associated with it a pair of statistics that designate where it falls on the risk/return spectrum. The first member of the pair is the mean, or expected, value of the total return for that class of investments; the second member, which measures risk, is the standard deviation of total return. Both of these quantities are normally measured after the rate of inflation has been subtracted out, so they are expressed in terms of real percentage increases.

The spectrum of possibilities, roughly quantified, is shown in figure 4.3. On the horizontal axis we have plotted actual observed values for the standard deviation of total return, and on the vertical axis the corresponding mean value for the three classes of university investment. The data series used in these calculations covered annual returns for the period 1926 through 1973 (Ibbotson and Sinquefield 1976). As figure 4.3 clearly shows, cash-equivalent investments such as US Treasury bills, which offer low risk and low expected return, are at one end of the spectrum, and the stock market is at the other; the bond market falls somewhere in between. By drawing a smooth curve through the three points one can get some idea of the range of possibilities facing a university administration that must decide on the proper mix of assets

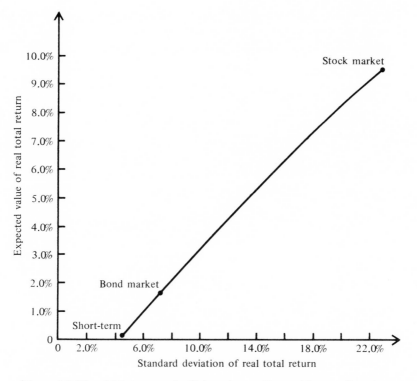

Figure 4.3. The risk/return tradeoff, based on a 47-year history of market performances

for the endowment portfolio. Although it is barely discernible from these data, the shape of the risk/return curve is definitely concave, which indicates that successive increases in expected return can be obtained only at the cost of increasing incremental risk.

The magnitude of the uncertainties involved in estimating investment return often surprises persons encountering it for the first time. We can hardly disagree with them. For example, if we take the historically based statistics on market returns to represent the parameters of a normal probability distribution, we find that, with a probability of roughly two-thirds, annual *real* returns for the three classes of instruments fall somewhere within the following ranges:

	Real Return (% Per Annum)
Cash equivalents	−4.5% to +4.7%
Long-term bonds	−5.6% to +8.8%
Stocks	−13.3% to +32.3%

There is still a probability of one in three that returns on any of these markets as a whole would be outside the given range. One must recognize, moreover,

```
PROP  IN  SHORT,  BONDS,  AND  STOCKS?.1,.3,.6
BETA  FOR  THE  STANFORD  PORTFOLIO?1
DESIRED  YIELD  DIFFERENTIAL  ON  STOCKS?0

5      YEAR  TOTAL  RETURN  (GEOMETRIC  MEAN)
MEAN,  STD.  DEV=          13.0623          6.82312

    -3.00    -2.01      3    :===
    -2.00    -1.01      1    :=
    -1.00    -0.01      1    :=
     0.00     0.99      1    :=
     1.00     1.99      2    :==
     2.00     2.99      6    :======
     3.00     3.99     10    :==========
     4.00     4.99      2    :==
     5.00     5.99      6    :======
     6.00     6.99     16    :================
     7.00     7.99     11    :===========
     8.00     8.99      8    :========
     9.00     9.99     18    :==================
    10.00    10.99     22    :======================
    11.00    11.99     23    :=======================
    12.00    12.99     22    :======================
    13.00    13.99     19    :===================
    14.00    14.99     21    :=====================
    15.00    15.99     16    :================
    16.00    16.99     11    :===========
    17.00    17.99     13    :=============
    18.00    18.99     12    :============
    19.00    19.99     10    :==========
    20.00    20.99      8    :========
    21.00    21.99      6    :======
    22.00    22.99      3    :===
    23.00    23.99      2    :==
    24.00    24.99      7    :=======
    25.00    25.99      2    :==
    26.00    26.99      8    :========
    27.00    27.99      2    :==
    28.00    28.99      2    :==
    29.00    29.99      1    :=
    30.00    30.99      1    :=
    31.00    31.99      1    :=
    32.00    32.99      0    :
    33.00    33.99      1    :=
    34.00    34.99      1    :=
    35.00    35.99      0    :
    36.00    36.99      0    :
    37.00    37.99      1    :=

ANOTHER  YEAR?0
```

Figure 4.4. Sample frequency distribution of mean total return from Stanford Investment Simulator

that further risk ("nonsystematic risk," in the language of investment theory) is introduced whenever an investment portfolio selects only a portion of the assets available in the market as a whole. That is, additional variance is added to the total return through less-than-complete diversification. Estimating total return on endowment is a risky business indeed.

It was in the hope of bettering our understanding of these risks that the Stanford Investment Simulator, a computer model that shows how total return varies with changes in investment policy assumptions, was developed at Stanford under the direction of William Sharpe and John McDonald. The model performs Monte Carlo simulations of the return processes and displays a frequency distribution of likely portfolio returns.[2] A sample output from this model is shown in figure 4.4.

The operation of the Stanford Investment Simulator program may be sketched briefly as follows. Each class of investment market (i.e., short-term, bond, and stock) is modeled separately. Wherever possible, account is taken of historically based relationships between predictable parameters and the return on the market. For example, simulations of bond-market return incorporate a so-called liquidity premium in the calculation of forward interest rates. These rates are used to determine the one-year change in present worth of a bond with fixed maturity date. These individual models are given sufficient information to characterize the probability distribution of returns on each of the markets (the distributions are adjusted for the nonsystematic risk that is typical of Stanford's endowment portfolio). To estimate the total return on a portfolio of investments, the individual distributions are "mixed" according to the following investment policy variables.

Let α_C = the fraction of the portfolio invested in short-term cash equivalents

α_B = the fraction of the portfolio invested in bonds

α_S = the fraction of the portfolio invested in stocks

where, presumably, $\alpha_C + \alpha_B + \alpha_S = 1$.

For a given set of alphas, the program will draw a large sample of random numbers from the appropriate probability distribution, and will then proceed to calculate and display the simulated portfolio returns. Figure 4.4 shows, for example, the frequency distribution of 200 simulated returns on a portfolio that is 10 percent short-term cash equivalents, 30 percent bonds, and 60 percent stocks. Each range shown in the first two columns of the table corresponds to the geometric mean annual return based on a five-year simulation of the portfolio's performance. These returns are expressed in nominal terms, that is, including the effects of inflation. (The simulator program also contains a statistical submodel of the inflation process.) With this mix of investments, the simulated geometric mean annual return ranges from -3.0 percent to $+38.0$ percent (-10.0 percent to $+31.0$ percent on a real basis, that is, after subtracting out about 7 percent per year for inflation), with the mean value equal to 13.1 percent (approximately 6.1 percent in real terms) and the standard deviation equal to 6.8 percent. Further details on the mathematical specification of the investment simulation model are given in appendix 5.

Simulations of the type just described can be very useful as a means of getting decision makers to think about tradeoffs between risks and expected returns when they select investments. Simulations also help to show what various investment strategies might do to the endowment. Institutions anxious to find the mix of investments that is best for them should certainly find simulations useful in this regard. The investments in question should be determined by maximizing the expected total return subject to an acceptable limit on risk, and possibly to other constraints felt necessary by the institution's decision makers. Let us assume that the investment mix has been chosen, giving a particular value for the expected total return, and turn next to the issue of endowment payout.

Before we can discuss rules for endowment payout, we must be clear what we mean by a payout and how it differs from an operating surplus or deficit. The concept of payout, as we shall use it here, refers to the regularly sustainable flow of money from endowment into the operating budget. It is the product of management decisions that are made well before the budget year actually begins, so that the income to be made available from this source can be determined ahead of time. The operating deficit or surplus also usually involves the transfer of money between an operating reserve or funds functioning as endowment and the budget, but such a transfer occurs only at the end of the year, after the books have been closed on actual receipts and expenditures. Thus, it is the amount actually needed to balance the budget in the given year, and should be close to zero over any sufficiently long sequence of years. Otherwise, the institution has a problem of perennial imbalance that should be corrected.

The proper endowment payout rate cannot be determined from just a single year's budget. Otherwise, the institution would choose to spend in that year the maximum amount allowable by law. The difficulty, obviously, is that every dollar spent in one year is one less dollar (probably more than one, actually, since it could have been invested) available for spending in future years. Thus, the issue of intergenerational equity—of meeting the needs of current students, faculty, etc., and the needs of future generations as well—enters unavoidably into the discussion of how much the institution can afford to pay out of its endowment into the current operating budget. In fact, rather than asking directly how much should be spent, it is more pertinent to turn the question around and ask how much should be saved. A very simple model will help us here to get a grasp on possible answers, and thereby to indicate an appropriate payout rate for any particular institution. It is clear by now that the endowment payout rate establishes a very important link between one year's budget and the next. Our model should take this into account and it does so, by considering the rate of growth of expenses in the operating budget along with the rate of total return on the endowment. The result is a simple version of long-run financial equilibrium, more complex versions of which will be considered in chapter 6.

Let E_t = market value of endowment at the beginning of year t

P_t = dollar payout from the endowment during year t

G_t = dollar amount of new gifts added to the endowment during year t

ρ = rate of total return on the endowment

r = the overall rate of growth of expenses in the operating budget

We assume a constant payout rate policy, that is,

$$P_t = pE_t, \text{ for all years } t, \tag{4.17}$$

where p is the payout rate.

Suppose, first of all, that the institution desires to have the payout from endowment cover a constant share of total expenses in every future year. (We have dubbed this a *stationary equilibrium policy*, and we believe it deserves serious consideration whenever an institution has reached a mature state in its evolution.) This means that P_t must grow at the rate r and, in view of equation (4.17), so also must E_t. Now consider the money conservation equation that relates the market value of endowment in year $t + 1$ to its value in year t. The result is obtained by taking the original value at t, adding in the total return and new gifts, and subtracting the payout. Assuming for convenience that return is earned on the payout but not on the new gifts, we would write this equation as

$$E_{t+1} = E_t + \rho E_t + G_t - pE_t. \tag{4.18}$$

This immediately factors into

$$E_{t+1} = (1 + \rho + \zeta - p)E_t \tag{4.19}$$

where we have let ζ stand for the fraction G_t/E_t, that is, for new gifts expressed as a fraction of endowment market value. Equation (4.19) helps us to identify the net growth rate of the endowment as $\rho + \zeta - p$. Setting this equal to r and solving for p leads to the result

$$p = \rho + \zeta - r. \tag{4.20}$$

What this equation says is that the rate of spending is the growth rate of endowment from investment return and gifts combined, less the growth rate of the operating budget. For example, if $\rho = 10$ percent, $\zeta = 2$ percent, and $r = 7.5$ percent, we would need to save 7.5 percent out of a total growth rate of 12.0 percent and so could afford to pay out only 12 percent $-$ 7.5 percent $= 4.5$ percent of the beginning market value. It should also be apparent from this simple analysis that whenever p is greater than the quantity $\rho + \zeta - r$, the share of the operating budget covered by endowment is shrinking, and whenever the reverse inequality holds, the opposite is true.

Models like equation (4.20) are useful for setting target values for the endowment payout rate. Given the extreme volatility of the endowment total return process, however, we would not recommend a strict adherence to the payout formula given by (4.17) in every year. Most institutions attempt to dampen this volatility by replacing the current market value, E_t, in (4.17) by an average taken over several prior time periods. Since most financial experts believe that immediately past investment performance has little, if any, predictive value in estimating short-run future performance, it would appear that this practice has the disadvantage of introducing extraneous information into the payout calculation. It also is likely to leave too much volatility still in the result. We shall have some alternative smoothing formulas to propose in chapter 7.

This completes our discussion of submodels for the operating budget. In the next section we return to the multiyear financial projection model, and show how it is constructed by combining the budget model with a structure that incorporates information about the rate of growth of income-and-expense items.

Medium-Range Budget Projections

We began this chapter with a definition of the Medium-Range Financial Forecast, or MRFF. Before we specify the projection model on which it is based, we should take a minute to consider what purposes we want it to meet and how it fits into the overall budget process. Its primary purpose is obvious: we need a flexible instrument that is capable of simulating a large number of possible scenarios for future budget growth. Such an instrument can be used to advantage at all stages of the budget process. At the beginning of a new budget cycle, one prepares an initial series of MRFFs to set the stage for further analysis. These early runs identify the areas of the budget where problems are likely to arise in the next and subsequent years. They therefore establish a context for discussions aimed at refining information about these critical items, and, ultimately, gaining control of them. Later on, as the process of setting parameters for the new year's budget continues, the MRFF becomes less of an early warning device and more of a check on the dynamic feasibility of the proposed parameters. Here it is used to project the consequences over several future years of adopting these parameters, so that one can readily see whether they are consistent with maintaining a stable relationship between operating expense and income.

A second type of use for an MRFF is to generate estimates for the aggregate future rate of expense-and-income rise in the university's operating budget. These growth rates should be calculated on an unmonitored basis, that is, under the assumption that no special actions will be taken to bring them under control if they should diverge. Also, they must be based on unbiased estimates, so that the results can safely be taken to be "most likely" or "expected" forecast values of the aggregate rates. Such unmonitored indices of university expense and income provide direct information about imbalances between the growth rates on one side of the budget and those on the other. The indices, as we shall see in later chapters, are also used as basic data in more advanced models for budget control.

Next, we should say a few words about the *planning horizon* for the MRFF; that is, for how many future years should the projections be made? Here, ideally, one should strike a sensible balance between a horizon that is too short because it does not take advantage of all the financial information that is at hand, and one that is too long because it extends beyond the forecaster's (or anyone else's) capacity to judge.

To help determine the appropriate horizon, it may be useful to keep in mind certain basic macroeconomic relationships that are bound to hold over the long run. For example, assuming the quality of university personnel is not to decline, average salaries and wages per individual will have to increase at the rates established by the relevant outside labor markets. As long as national productivity is increasing, these rates will generally be higher (by perhaps as much as two or three percentage points) than the rate of inflation.

In the short run, a university may want to deviate from these long-run assumptions either because it feels there is some slack in the current budget—say, in the case of salaries—or because of extraneous economic pressures. One test to employ, then, is to examine how far into the future our current knowledge would lead us to forecast growth rates that differ from those expected in the long run. In our experience, a forecast planning horizon somewhere in the range of three to five years is about right.

Given our structural model of the operating budget, specifying the financial projection model is fairly straightforward. Ancillary costs aside, we can express each major budget line item as the product of physical variable, X, and its associated unit price or cost, P, while introducing a time subscript.

Let C_{it} = amount of budgeted expense for line item i in year t

$\quad\quad l_t$ = rate of general inflation between years t and $t + 1$ (according to, say, the Consumer Price Index)

$\quad dP_{it}$ = the real rate of growth in the unit price of X_i between years t and $t + 1$

$\quad\quad f_t$ = the budget enrichment factor for year $t + 1$ (expressed as a fraction of the year t budget)

This enables us to write

$$P_{i,t+1} = (1 + l_t + dP_{it}) P_{it} \quad\quad\quad (4.21)$$

$$X_{i,t+1} = (1 + f_t) X_t \quad\quad\quad (4.22)$$

$$C_{i,t+1} = P_{i,t+1} X_{i,t+1}. \qu\quad\quad\quad (4.23)$$

The budget enrichment factor, f_t, used in equation (4.22) above, deserves special mention. It represents all net incremental growth in the expense budget that exceeds ordinary cost rise on the prior year's activities. Although we were slow to reach this conclusion in our work at Stanford, we would say now that its importance as a central planning-and-control variable cannot be over-emphasized. In support of this conclusion we offer two considerations: f_t is probably the most discretionary item in the forecast (discretionary in the sense that everything else is subject to more prior constraints); and its leverage with regard to operating-budget growth is very large. This leverage will become more apparent in chapter 6, where we work with dynamic equilibrium models of the budget.

Note that in writing the system of equations (4.21) to (4.23), we have made two implicit assumptions about the manner in which f_t operates. First, we have assumed that budget enrichment occurs only through changes in the underlying physical variables, and not through increases in the price paid per unit; and, second, we have assumed that the enrichments will be spread evenly throughout the budget or, in other words, that f_t will apply to all items. Obviously these assumptions are only approximately true, though probably good enough for forecasting purposes. If not, however, one can amend the model formulation accordingly.

Note also that we have chosen to separate the growth rates of the unit prices into two parts: a general inflation rate, and a real growth rate specific to the item being priced. Aside from the fact that this separation makes good economic sense, we have found it helpful in communicating not only with persons involved in providing the growth-rate estimates but also with any members of the university community who are interested in the premises behind the MRFF. The advantage of using a reference point such as the general inflation rate is especially clear when the subject of communication is the university's planned growth in wages for its own faculty and staff.

Finally, note that the forecasting model projects revenue items in a manner completely analogous to the projection of expense items. Simply replace the variable $C_{i,t+1}$ by $R_{i,t+1}$, which stands for the dollar amount of revenue item i in year $t + 1$, in equation (4.23), and use the X_i and P_i variables appropriate to that revenue item. (Of course, f_t generally would not apply to the income side.)

As a sample application of the basic projection model, consider the line item corresponding to faculty salaries expense (line 1 in Stanford's expense budget), which is the product of average salary and FTE. If dP_{1t} is the real growth rate of faculty salaries, then the average salary will increase at the rate $(\iota_t + dP_{1t})$, while the FTE will increase at the rate f_t. The new year's projected faculty salary budget therefore becomes

$$P_{1,t+1}X_{1,t+1} = (1 + \iota_t + dP_{1t})(1 + f_t)P_{1t}X_{1t}.$$

Some items, such as the travel budget ($C_{16,t}$), are represented as lump sums, in which case we would simply write

$$C_{16,t+1} = (1 + \iota_t + dP_{16,t})(1 + f_t)C_{16,t}.$$

To conclude, we will take an example on the income side: tuition revenue, $R_{1,t+1}$, is projected on the basis of price increases alone, unless a change in enrollment is specifically planned. That is, if $X_{1,t+1} = X_{1t}$, then

$$R_{1,t+1} = (1 + \iota_t + dP_{13,t})X_{1t}.$$

Estimating the Forecast Parameters

How does one obtain the growth-rate estimates, dP_{it}, that are needed for the forecast? In going about this task, it is useful to bear in mind the distinction between growth rates that are primary planning variables (PPVs) and those that are exogenous to the university. Any growth rate whose impact on the operating budget is substantial (either because the base dollar level or the growth rate itself is large in comparison with the others) and that is subject, at least in the short run, to some central university control is a good candidate for PPV status. For example, at Stanford we have singled out growth rates in the following as PPVs:

1. Faculty salaries
2. Staff salaries
3. Staff benefits costs
4. Utility costs
5. Library acquisition costs
6. Tuition price

(In addition, of course, we include the budget enrichment factor, f, as a PPV.) These growth rates are given a prominent role in our forecasting and tradeoff assessment models to permit easy experimentation with alternative values.

Growth rates for other items are more properly viewed as exogenously specified, even for short-run planning purposes. These include such items as student health insurance, custodial expenses, materials and supplies expense, gift income, and income from special funds. Estimates of these growth rates are best obtained through so-called bottom-up analysis performed by those who are most familiar with the area in question. For instance, growth in the cost of student health insurance should be estimated by the insurance manager in consultation with the relevant providers, while projections of gift income would depend heavily on estimates made by the fund-raising office. Central planners can often help line managers exercise their judgment by making sure that they are in touch with available experts. Planners can also provide them with estimates of basic economic parameters, such as inflation and wage rates, so that each line manager's response pertaining to items under his or her jurisdiction will be based on the same underlying economic assumptions as the others. Very often, economists outside the university administration (faculty members, for example, or local bankers and businessmen) can be called upon for assistance in preparing a forecast of the necessary external economic parameters.

Constructing a Cost or Income Index

We pause here to consider the mechanics of constructing a cost or income index for the university's operating budget. Such an index is of central importance in financial planning models. The steps to be followed are these:

1. List the items of expenditure or revenue in whatever order and amount of detail is desired, along with their dollar amounts for year t.

2. In a column next to the dollar amounts, put a weight for each item that represents its fractional share of the year t budget. If C_{it} is the amount budgeted for item i in year t, the weight for line item i is given by

$$w_{it} = C_{it} / \sum_k C_{kt}.$$

3. In a third column, list the one-year growth rate of each item. For a pure cost-rise index, do not include budget enrichment in the growth-rate figures.

4. Multiply each growth rate by its associated fractional weight and form the sum over all items to obtain the overall cost (or income) index. If r_{it} is the growth rate of item i between years t and $t + 1$ and w_{it} is its weight, the cost index, r_t, is given by

$$r_t = \sum_i w_{it} r_{it}.$$

To illustrate: using the 1974/75 budget data from table 4.3 in more aggregate form, we obtain the anticipated cost-rise index at Stanford for 1974/75 to 1975/76 from

	1974/75 Budget Base	Weight	One-Year Growth Rate
Faculty salaries & benefits	$18,684	0.291	7.9%
Staff salaries & benefits	$25,680	0.400	11.0%
Student financial aid	$3,476	0.054	21.6%
Library acquisitions	$1,945	0.030	13.0%
Other	$14,450	0.225	6.3%
	$64,235	1.000	9.7%*

*Cost index for 1974/75 to 1975/76

Notice that the calculations just described work equally well whether the growth rates one uses are nominal or real. The cost index in our example was expressed in nominal terms; to convert to real cost rise we can either subtract the rate of inflation from each nominal growth rate before forming the weighted sum or, equivalently, since the weights add to one, subtract it from the final result. In our example, the expected inflation rate, ι_t, for the year in question was 9.0 percent, and so the cost index in real terms would have been 9.7 percent − 9.0 percent = 0.7 percent. (This value was unusually low due to unexpectedly high inflation in the year in question. As we will explain below, normally we expect the rate of university cost rise to exceed inflation by two or more percentage points.) Also, the methodology is the same no matter whether one is working with short- or long-run growth rates. In the remainder of this book we shall use the notation r_t for the (real) rate of cost rise specific to year t, and r for the long-run (real) rate.

The above description of cost index computations is cursory at best. For a complete treatment of this methodology applied to the entire higher education sector, the reader should consult the interesting pamphlet by D. Kent Halstead (1975). That author's analysis of historical price increases for higher education inputs over the period 1961 to 1974 deserves to be read by any serious student of university finance (see also Halstead 1977).

Making Financial Projections

Once the requisite growth-rate data have been obtained and inserted in the financial projection model, one can proceed to simulate the impact of alternative PPV configurations on future budgets. If budget growth is reasonably well balanced during the forecast period, feasible solutions (i.e., configurations that lead to the budget being balanced and staying balanced) can often be found by trial and error. If, however, there is a very substantial imbalance in growth rates—the kind of imbalance that is evident from Stanford's 1974 MRFF projections in tables 4.3 and 4.4—it is necessary first to identify the size of the budget gap, and then to begin making decisions about how it will be closed. It is the first task that requires the more powerful models, since they have to be capable of dealing simultaneously with imbalances in the budget base and in budget growth rates.

To illustrate the importance of distinguishing between base-level gaps and growth-rate gaps, we present the following simple hypothetical examples. Suppose, in the first case, that current income and current expense are both equal to $50 million, but that the expense growth rate during the next five years is projected to be 7 percent per year while income is projected to grow at only 5 percent. The consequence of this gap are shown by expense curve A in figure 4.5: the budget that started out in balance is in deficit by about $6.3 million five years later.

In the second case, we assume that the initial expenses are 2 percent higher than initial income, so that the budget starts out with a $1-million deficit, but that the growth rates of income and expense are each 5 percent per year. Here, as can be seen from comparison of the income curve with expense curve *B* in figure 4.5, the fifth-year deficit is only about $1.3 million—about one-fifth of the deficit in the first case. Rate gaps, then, tend to be more insidious than level gaps when they are sustained for even a few years. Moreover, the remedies for the two types of problems are different, for there is absolutely no one-time adjustment in income-and-expense levels that can compensate for a chronic imbalance between growth rates.

In 1974, we had reason to believe that the Stanford operating budget was subject to imbalances of both kinds. On the surface, tables 4.3 and 4.4 seem to show that there was no income-expense gap in the 1974/75 budget base; after

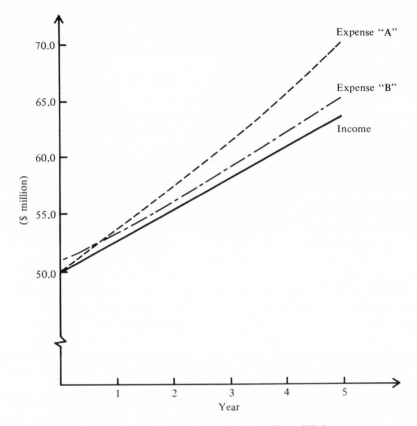

Figure 4.5. An illustration of budget disequilibrium

all, the budgeted levels of income and expense are perfectly balanced on the bottom line. This balance was achieved, however, by budgeting a payout from the endowment of $8.3 million (line 2 plus line 7 in table 4.4), which represented a hefty 7.5 percent of the then-current endowment market value. We had to question whether this level of spending could be increased to keep up with the rate of cost rise in the expense budget. If not, it was clear that some reduction in the payout rate would be necessary, and that this would of necessity require a downward adjustment in total expense.

The models that were developed to analyze this situation will be described in chapter 6. Before going further into the subject of dynamic budget models, however, we will want to explore static (i.e., single-year) models of production and cost. Such models are the topic of chapter 5.

Some General Observations About University Economics

Given the emphasis of this chapter on financial projections, it seems appropriate to conclude it with a few basic observations about the economics of an endowed university.[3] The observations in question have been gleaned from a quick analysis of long-run growth-rate relationships. We are not concerned here with the growth-rate patterns peculiar to any short-run period. Rather, we wish to infer certain generalities from the long-run dependence of growth in the university's budget on fundamental macroeconomic forces, such as inflation and wage rates.

The first observation is that a very large part of a university's expense budget consists of the salaries of its faculty and administrators, the wages of its employees, and contracts for items like custodial services that are essentially wage-driven. At Stanford in 1974/75, for example, such wage-related items amounted to some $49.4 million out of $69.2 million, or approximately 70 percent of the university's total expenses before chargeouts (see table 4.3). Now, speaking in general terms, nominal wages and salaries tend to rise at a rate that is the sum of the rate of inflation and the rate of productivity increase in the economy (real wages, however, tend to rise at about the same rate as productivity). Of course, there is likely to be a lag in this relationship in periods of high or rising inflation, but things must average out over time and across industries if labor's share of the economy's output is to remain roughly constant.

Some historical perspective on these economic growth rates is provided by the figures shown in table 4.13. The entries in the first column, under "per capita personal income," are roughly equivalent to the money wage rate for the US economy as a whole. "Personal disposable income" (column 2) refers to personal income minus taxes and nontax payments to the government. The change in the consumer price index (column 3) is often taken as the rate of inflation (though perhaps a better case could be made for the GNP implicit price deflator). As the last column of table 4.13 shows, during the twenty-six-year period from 1950 to 1976 the real wage (or productivity) rate generally tended to fall somewhere in the 2 to 3 percent range.

Wages are not the only source of pressure on the university's budget: necessary provisions for budget enrichment can easily add another full percentage point to the rate of regular cost rise, even when allowance is made for a reasonable amount of reallocation. (Recall that Stanford's f value was 2.7 percent as recently as 1974/75.)* Thus, in the absence of substantial productivity increases inside the university, we might expect the expenditure side of the budget to increase at something like $1 + (0.7 \times 2.5) = 2.75$ percentage points above the inflation (as measured by the CPI).

Turning now to the income side of the budget (table 4.4), we observe that tuition and fees amount to no less than 63 percent (i.e., $35.5 million divided by $56.0 million) of all operating income, which is income other than regular endowment payout. Indirect cost recovery, which may possibly increase at the same rate as the overall budget (unless, of course, the price elasticity of demand for sponsored research is significant), accounts for only 23 percent of the operating income. Other sources of income make up the remaining 14 percent;

---

*A minimum of 1 percent annual budget enrichment (they called it "self-renewal") was recommended by the Carnegie Commission on Higher Education (1972, p. 105).

Table 4.13. Annual Growth Rates of Key Economic Quantities, 1950/1976

	Per Capita Personal Income (1)	Per Capita Personal Disposable Income (2)	Consumer Price Index (3)	Real Wage Rate (1) Minus (3)
1950/60	4.00%	3.57%	2.09%	1.91%
1960/70	5.92%	5.71%	2.76%	3.16%
1970/76	8.54%	8.60%	6.34%	2.20%

these are predominantly tied more to the rate of inflation than to the wage rate.

It follows that the private university is faced with a very grave dilemma. Because its expenses appear likely to grow faster than its income, it is faced with the following options:

1. Achieving internal productivity increases on a continual basis, that is, year after year.

2. Holding the growth rate of the wages it pays to its faculty and staff below the growth rate of wages in the economy.

3. Increasing tuition faster than the wage rate in the economy.

4. Continually finding new sources of income to subsidize the costs of academic programs.

Of course, these options can be—and surely will need to be—taken in combination. None of them, however, is particularly favorable to the institution or its intended mission. Quantitative productivity increases, for example, require at least one of the following:

1. Increasing the ratio of students to faculty members.

2. Decreasing the ratio of administrative and clerical staff to faculty members.

3. Increasing the ratio of auxiliary faculty to regular faculty members.

The first two of these measures would tend to increase the number of units of output (for which a fee like tuition is charged) per unit of input; the third would substitute cheaper inputs in the production mix.

Most academics would agree that taking any of the three would have a negative effect on the quality of the institution's educational program. Certainly, some temporary increases in productivity would result from a short, sharp treatment of this sort. However, unless student/faculty ratios or other determinants of quantitative productivity are to be allowed to grow year by year at a compounded rate and without any bounds, the first option would not be a viable long-run solution. (Qualitative productivity increases still are possible, of course, and are always occurring in universities where new generations of students are being trained at successively higher levels of intellectual sophistication than earlier ones.) The second option, namely, holding salary growth below the national norm, is also problematic. The university competes for many, it not most, of its staff employees in labor markets that are dominated by business firms. The wage paid to a staff person of given quality is therefore likely to rise at an exogenously determined rate that includes an increment for productivity. It follows that if the wages paid to staff employees by the university are held down, the quality of the staff must eventually suffer. Usually, however, very good faculty expect a very high standard of performance from the staff as well, and would not tolerate a lowering of staff quality.

It might still be argued that, since universities compete only with other universities for faculty members, the growth rate of faculty salaries ought to be less than that of other kinds of wages. Since the market for faculty members was characterized, at least in the late 1970s, by an oversupply of highly qualified job applicants, one could be sure that faculty salaries would increase at a reduced rate for the foreseeable future. Nevertheless, as we have already argued, faculty members at good research universities certainly do contribute, through their teaching as well as their research, to increases in the nation's productivity. Their failure to participate, just like other wage earners, in added wage growth due to productivity raises serious ethical problems. In any case, such an imbalance in wage rates will lead in time to shortages of good faculty members in many fields.

The third option listed above—raising tuition to cover the excess of expenses over other income—is also possible and may be necessary in the short run. (Some amount of tuition increase can after all be justified on the basis of improvement in quality.) But it is doubtful whether the price of higher education can increase faster than wages indefinitely, even when significant sums are plowed back into financial aid. The situation of private universities is particularly difficult, given the existence of low-cost, high-quality public institutions.

The last option, seeking new sources of outside support or accelerating the growth of current ones, reduces to seeking new donors, either public or private, and keeping the pressure on for increased contributions. Along with many, especially in the private sector, we believe that some institutions ought to remain independent. Hence relying on the government for general-fund support has distinct disadvantages. Even so, a more liberal attitude by federal authorities towards the funding of university research (its indirect costs no less than its direct ones) as well as sponsored instruction projects would provide much-needed support without undue sacrifice of independence. Similarly, direct federal or state aid to students—aid that, to be effective, should be related to tuition levels—would be an attractive solution to the long-run problem.

Alternatively, an increasing level of support can be sought from philanthropic organizations and private individuals. There is no doubt that nearly all private institutions will rely in part on this strategy. However, there are limits to the amount of funding that can be obtained from private sources, especially with no strings attached.

Finally, there are strategies aimed at keeping the university's endowment growing fast enough to finance a progressively larger share of the budget. This might be done by: (a) increasing the total yield-plus-gain from the endowment portfolio; (b) spending a smaller fraction of the total yield-plus-gain (this might have to be coupled with cost-cutting or revenue-enhancing tactics in the short term); (c) designating annual budget savings as endowment rather than as expendable reserves; (d) seeking substantial gifts to endowment; (e) any of these in combination.

In summary, then, there are severe and unabating economic pressures that are acting to drive private university budgets out of balance. These pressures are due to the combination of the labor-intensive nature of the operation, the difficulty of achieving productivity gains in quantitative terms (and, indeed, a persuasive case can be made for budget enrichment to provide for productivity gains in *qualitative* terms), and the inherently low growth rate of many income items. Confronting these pressures and developing strategies to overcome them are likely to occupy the attention of university administrators for some time to come. We have proposed certain types of strategies for consideration; it is hoped that the models developed in this and later chapters will prove useful in gauging their quantitative effects. The information from such models, while by no means sufficient in and of itself, should make easier the task of selecting the best policy for achieving financial stability at a particular institution. What is "best," of course, will have to be judged in terms of the institution's own value function. In other words, the proper way in which to view this decision problem is in terms of constrained value maximization, the procedure we introduced in chapter 3 and will take up in more detail in chapter 9.

Summary

This chapter deals with constructing models of the operating budget in terms of underlying variables, parameters, and relationships. Both single-year representations and multiyear forecasts of the budget are considered. Initially, certain questions are presented concerning the form of the financial forecast desired by the institution in question, with examples of different kinds of responses. This presentation is followed by a detailed discussion of how to model the budget in a single year.

Certain principles must be adhered to in order to ensure that the model will give a true enough representation of reality for planning purposes. Invoking these principles requires budget planners to dissect the financial relationships underlying their universities' budgets, so that the major driving forces can be recognized and properly represented. Examples are given of how these principles were applied at Stanford. In particular, we show how Stanford has gone about applying full incremental costing to its primary planning variables, and constructing financial submodels of its important items of income and expense. These methodologies are applicable, in varying degrees, to other kinds of institutions as well.

The process of constructing a medium-range budget projection model is then discussed in more detail. Questions answered include, Who should provide information concerning future trends in underlying variables and parameters? and, How far out should we go in making these projections? It is also shown how one can easily use such a model to obtain an index of cost- or income-rise for an institution in either the medium or the long run.

The chapter concludes with some general observations about the economic conditions and trends that must be reckoned with when one is planning future budgets, particularly when this is taking place at a private college or university. These observations point out a serious dilemma for the private sector in post-secondary education, one that does not yield to easy solutions.

Notes to Chapter 4

Works cited here in abbreviated form are more fully described in the bibliography at the end of this book.

1. Complete details of the full-blown indirect-cost recovery model can be found in Massy, Hopkins, and Curry 1976.

2. Actual analyses performed by this model at Stanford are written up in Adams 1977.

3. Much of the material in this section originally appeared in Massy 1973.

5

Production and Cost Models

In this chapter we discuss input-output models of the university and how these can be used to represent production, cost, and revenue functions for the primary objectives of instruction and research. In chapter 3 we introduced the functions $F^k(X, S)$, $C(X, P, S)$, and $R(X, P, S)$ in general form, and in chapter 4 we related them to direct measures of instructional activity, such as enrollment levels and faculty and staff FTEs. Our next task will be to develop expressions for these functions directly, in terms of measurable outputs of the educational system such as students earning degrees or dropping out before completing an academic program. (Although we would like to include outputs that are not directly measurable, unfortunately we are limited by knowing little about them.) As we shall see, a proper understanding of the relationship between faculty staffing levels and student enrollments is central to this task.

We begin with a general description of the disaggregate production and cost models that have been widely proposed (under the rubric of "cost-simulation models"), and in some instances tried, as college and university planning tools. While these models have been used with some success at smaller colleges with rather rigidly defined curricula and faculty who do little but teach, we find them largely inapplicable to more complex institutions. The main reason is that research and instruction at such institutions are closely interlocked, so that the production and cost functions for instruction (which the cost-simulation model is intended to represent) can be specified only after one has developed a reasonable procedure for separating the inputs, and hence the costs, of doing research from those of instruction. Nearly all reported efforts in the past aimed at developing university production functions have failed to confront this problem.

Having pointed out the deficiencies of cost-simulation models, we proceed to derive a production function specific to instruction (after taking account of research) at a complex university. A university planning model is formulated that permits one readily to examine the consequences of changes in a variety of factors—including technological constraints (as incorporated in the production function) and behavioral parameters, such as student dropout rates—on the unit costs associated with instructional outputs. This model was conceived for use as a tool for *strategic* planning at the central university level (or perhaps at the level of an individual school or college within the university). It therefore contains far less detail than the cost-simulation model, which generally distinguishes between individual academic programs. A numerical example is used to demonstrate the capabilities of the alternate approach.

Disaggregate Production and Cost Models

In recent years, a variety of efforts have been undertaken to develop models for costing and resource allocation at the level of an academic department or a small group of departments representing a discipline. These models, probably the most widely known among the various quantitative tools so far developed to assist in college and university planning, have often been referred to as *cost-simulation models*. Examples include the Resource Requirements Prediction Model (RRPM), developed by the National Center on Higher Education Management Systems at Boulder, Colorado; and Comprehensive Analytical Methods for Planning in University Systems (CAMPUS), developed by the Systems Research Group of Toronto, Canada.[1]

In terms of the theoretical framework we developed in chapter 3, the cost-simulation model represents a type of disaggregate production function and focuses on an academic department or other small unit within the university. The only output considered is instruction, and its measure is in terms of the enrollment of student majors in the department's various degree programs. (Some would argue that this is an indirect measure indeed, and one that is more reflective of the relative popularity of majors than anything else!) Inputs are measured in terms of faculty FTEs, staff FTEs, and assorted categories of nonpersonnel resources. The model produces figures, for each department, on the levels of resource inputs, and the resulting total dollar cost, that are supposedly needed to service a given set of enrollments. In so doing, it tries to take into account the multiple student-faculty interactions caused by students majoring in one department and taking courses from another.

Formulation

Before proceeding any further, we need to develop an algebraic formulation of models in this class. The relationships postulated among the variables are really quite simple. Regrettably, to differentiate properly between categories of resources and the departments in which they are consumed requires the use of notation that makes the model look more complicated than it really is. In the hope of making a long list of definitions easier to assimilate, we divide it into output variables, input variables, and parameters of the model.

Output variables:

Let y_j = FTE enrollment of students in major-level combination j (e.g., upper-division undergraduates majoring in history), where $j = 1, 2, \ldots, J$.

Input variables:

Let z_i^F = number of FTE faculty assigned to department/rank combination i (e.g., associate professors of English), where $i = 1, 2, \ldots, I$

z_k^S = number of FTE staff of type k (may be classified by location and/or rank), where $k = 1, 2, \ldots, K$

z^O = an aggregate variable representing the dollar cost of all other resources.

Model parameters:

Let a_{ij} = ratio of faculty of type i to students of type j

b_{1kj}^S = incremental FTE staff of type k per student of type j

b_{2ki}^S = incremental FTE staff of type k per faculty of type i

b_{1j}^O = incremental other expense per student of type j

b_{2i}^O = incremental other expense per faculty of type i

s_i^F = salary plus benefits per FTE faculty of type i

s_k^S = salary plus benefits per FTE staff of type k.

Obviously, the first step in formulating the model is to list the academic units—that is, the departments—for which separate resource projections are desired. This step, together with the decisions about how many levels or ranks of students, faculty, and staff are to be included, defines the model's level of disaggregation. Our notation, by the way, uses superscripts to distinguish among the types of resources (here designated as "faculty," "staff," and "other"), and subscripts to distinguish among the various location/rank combinations for each resource type.

At the heart of the cost-simulation model is the postulated relationship between faculty inputs and student outputs. In particular, it assumes the existence of a set of faculty/student ratios, a_{ij}, such that one can write

$$z_1^F = a_{11}y_1 + a_{12}y_2 + \ldots + a_{1J}y_J$$
$$z_2^F = a_{21}y_1 + a_{22}y_2 + \ldots + a_{2J}y_J$$
$$\vdots \qquad \vdots \qquad \vdots \qquad \vdots$$
$$z_i^F = a_{i1}y_1 + a_{i2}y_2 + \ldots + a_{iJ}y_J \qquad (5.1)$$
$$\vdots \qquad \vdots \qquad \vdots \qquad \vdots$$
$$z_I^F = a_{I1}y_1 + a_{I2}y_2 + \ldots + a_{IJ}y_J.$$

(Henceforth, we shall use the shorthand notation $\Sigma_{j=1}^J a_{ij}y_j$ to refer to sums such as the one appearing on the right-hand side of the ith equation above.) The manner in which the ratios a_{ij} typically are derived from data in university records will be described below.

Incremental staff FTE and other expenses are assumed to vary in proportion to students and faculty. Thus, we write

$$z_k^S = z_{k0}^S + \sum_{j=1}^{J} b_{1kj}^S y_j + \sum_{i=1}^{I} b_{2ki}^S z_i^F \quad (k = 1, 2, \ldots, K) \tag{5.2}$$

$$z^O = z_0^O + \sum_{j=1}^{J} b_{1j}^O y_j + \sum_{i=1}^{I} b_{2i}^O z_i^F. \tag{5.3}$$

The coefficients b_{1kj}^S and b_{2ki}^S in equation (5.2) represent estimates of the incremental staff FTE required per student and per faculty FTE, respectively, and similarly for b_{1j}^O and b_{2i}^O in the equation for other expenses. The numbers z_{k0}^S and z_0^O, then, refer to the fixed components of staff FTE and other expenses, respectively.

PROCEDURE 5.1. When taken together, equations (5.1), (5.2), and (5.3) describe a production function, $F(\mathbf{y}, \mathbf{z}^F, \mathbf{z}^S, z^O)$, that relates the inputs of university resources to student enrollments. Given additional financial parameters for the institution being modeled, it is straightforward to construct the cost function, $C(\mathbf{y})$, that is supposed to represent the cost of educating y_j students of each type j.

The first step is to write total cost as the sum of the costs of each separate type, i.e., of faculty costs, staff costs, and all other costs:

$$C = \sum_{i=1}^{I} s_i^F z_i^F + \sum_{k=1}^{K} s_k^S z_k^S + z^O. \tag{5.4}$$

Substituting in this equation the expressions for z_i^F, z_k^S, and z^O that make up the production function enables us to write costs as a function of students alone:

$$C(\mathbf{y}) = c_0 + \sum_{j=1}^{J} c_j y_j$$

where $\tag{5.5}$

$$c_0 = z_0^O + \sum_{k=1}^{K} s_k^S z_{k0}^S$$

and the c_j are complicated functions of the a_{ij} and other model parameters. (The interested reader will find the detailed representation of these functions in appendix 6, where we have provided a compact matrix formulation of these production and cost functions.)

With reference to equation (5.5), observe that we have derived a cost function that is linear with respect to the numbers of students enrolled. Observe too that c_0 represents fixed costs, and that it includes terms corresponding to staff, z^S, and nonpersonnel expense, z^O, but *not* to faculty, z^F. This is because the number of faculty FTE was assumed to vary in direct proportion to students, with no fixed component.

The coefficient c_j that appears in this cost function has the interpretation of being the incremental cost of educating a student of type j. Of course, the existence of the fixed term, c_0, makes this different from the *average* cost per student. In fact, we are not able to calculate average costs without first agreeing upon a reasonable rule for allocating this fixed cost among the different types of students.

Data Estimation

Having worked through the basic formulation of the cost-simulation model, we now address the practicalities of implementing it with real data. In the first place, the reader must be wondering where one is to obtain the ratios a_{ij} that are the crucial parameters in equation (5.1). After all, university records do not contain numbers representing, for example, the number of FTE associate professors of English needed to instruct an upper-division history major. Obviously, these figures must be derived from recorded data—course enroll-ments, for instance, and faculty teaching loads—that pertain to the interaction of faculty with students.

PROCEDURE 5.2. The standard sequence for generating these ratios from historical records can be described as follows. One starts with data on student credit-hours, by major and level of student, in courses which are differentiated by level and by the department in which they are taught (the so-called *induced course-load matrix*). From these, one can determine ℓ_{kj}, which is defined as the average number of credit-hours in courses of type k "induced" by a student of type j. To convert to units of classroom time, these ratios must be multiplied by the ratios of *weekly student classroom hours*, WCH, to *student credit-hours*, SCH, for course types k. Next, we divide by the average class size in courses of type k, u_k, to obtain the number of *faculty classroom hours*, FCH. These are apportioned among the categories of faculty according to fractions p_{ik}, which represent the proportion of courses of type k assigned to faculty of type i. Finally, one divides by the *average teaching load* (i.e., weekly classroom hours per FTE faculty) for faculty of type i, b_i, to obtain the ratio of faculty type i to students type j, a_{ij}.

The computational sequence just described is represented by the following formula:

$$a_{ij} = \sum_k \ell_{kj} \times r_k \times \frac{1}{u_k} \times p_{ik} \times \frac{1}{b_i} \tag{5.6}$$

where a_{ij} = faculty/students

ℓ_{kj} = SCH/students

r_k = WCH/SCH

$\dfrac{1}{u_k}$ = FCH/WCH

$\dfrac{1}{b_i}$ = faculty FTE/FCH.

Note that the summation in equation (5.6) is over all course types (i.e., department-level combinations) being accounted for.

As to the origin of the model's remaining coefficients, namely, the fixed and variable costs of staff and other resources, these are typically obtained from a time-series analysis of historical data. Such an analysis usually involves the application of ordinary least-squares regression to estimate the coefficients in equations (5.2) and (5.3), given actual data for several past years on the y_j, z_i^F, z_k^S, and z^O.

Difficulties with This Approach

At this point, we must remark on the sheer size of the model just described.[2] For application at the level of academic departments, we must consider probably at least thirty student majors and locations for faculty and staff, even for a medium-sized institution. If one wants further to differentiate between, say, four levels of students (e.g., lower-division undergraduates, upper-division undergraduates, candidates for master's and first professional degrees, and advanced doctoral candidates) and five ranks of faculty (e.g., lecturer, instructor, assistant professor, associate professor, and professor), this will expand the number of categories of students, J, to 120 and of faculty, I, to 150. Thus, the number of faculty/student ratios, a_{ij}, is of the order of 20,000, and of course computing them according to equation (5.6) requires the processing of many times this number of actual data items. Even if the raw data are available in computerized form, this task will surely involve a considerable investment of time and expense. (When these models were first released, most institutions found that they did not in fact maintain computer files with the data in the exact form in which they were needed. It was not uncommon for the setup cost to reach $50,000 and for the setup task to consume one or more man-years of effort.)

There are other implications for a model of this size that go beyond the simple cost of implementation. In order to generate such a multitude of parameters, one has little option but to rely upon data that represent what has gone on in the past. And once they have been generated, there simply is no opportunity to apply judgment in deciding what the proper values for them should be, as opposed to what they actually have been. For instance, if one is concerned with planning for the future, the incremental staff and other costs associated with students and faculty might better be obtained by applying judgment and careful reasoning, as we illustrated in chapter 4. This approach is not practical, however, when there are more than a small number (say, ten to twenty) of such parameters to be estimated.

A further problem posed by this reliance on historical data files is that one is at the mercy of the form in which the data happen to have been recorded. The problem may be particularly serious in the case of the data on faculty FTEs used in calculating the ratios a_{ij}. Typically, what is recorded is the percentage of a faculty member's time that is charged to a university general account rather than to outside sponsors. This account is usually associated with a function labeled something like "instruction and departmental research." The trouble with using these accounting data to generate the ratios of faculty classroom hours to faculty FTEs (i.e., the teaching loads, b_i) is that it builds into the model the assumption that all the faculty time paid for by the university is associated strictly with instruction, and, furthermore, that all instruction takes place in the classroom. While there are many institutions for which this is a reasonably accurate description, it does present a major obstacle to the employment of the cost-simulation model at any institution that supports research leading to the creation of new knowledge as an objective in its own right. We shall propose a means for dealing with the joint outputs and joint costs of instruction and research later in this chapter.

Still other problems are created by the level of disaggregation used in constructing the model. The first of these is the statistical instability of behavioral parameters, such as the induced course-load factors, ℓ_{kj}, when they are viewed at such a microscopic level of detail. After all, many institutions pride themselves on allowing students considerable freedom in selecting courses outside their major department, and it is no wonder if the students' selections vary unpredictably from year to year.

Secondly, the very structure of the model relating faculty by department and rank to students by major and level is unrealistic. Let us examine this part of the production function in more detail to see where the difficulties lie. Consider the set of unit faculty inputs, $a_{1m}, a_{2m}, \ldots, a_{I,m}$, that is associated with a particular category of students (which we have designated by the label m)—say, upper-division history majors. Two of these numbers might represent, for example, inputs of assistant professors of English and full professors of economics per upper-division history major. Suppose these values happen at the present time to be 0.05 and 0.005, respectively. By building such numbers into the model we are ensuring that this ratio of ten assistant professors of English to one full professor of economics will always be applied to this particular category of students. Such calculations fail to recognize the extent to which faculty of one department/rank combination substitute for faculty of another when it comes to satisfying the demand for courses. In addition, the formulation

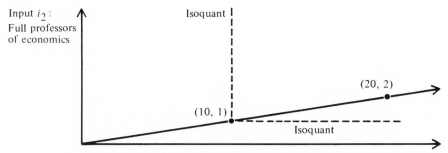

Figure 5.1. An illustration of the production function of a cost-simulation model

assumes constant returns to scale in the production process so that, for example, a doubling of the number of upper-division history majors will result in a doubling of the faculty supposedly required to teach them. Some of the model's proponents claim that the a_{ij} coefficients are not fixed, and that one can affect their values by changing any of the parameters involved in equation (5.6). We have already argued, however, that the size of the model makes it impractical to judge how to make such changes.

These points are perhaps best illustrated by the simple graph shown in figure 5.1, where the broken lines represent the implicit set of feasible input combinations corresponding to a given number of students (an *isoquant*, in the language of economists), and the solid ray emanating from the origin is the path of inputs for a growing enrollment of students. Why must the isoquants for this form of production function have the shape drawn in figure 5.1? They must because one has implicitly assumed that there is only one optimal input mix corresponding to each level of enrollment, namely the one obtained from our historically based ratio values. (In economists' terms, we have represented the faculty input process as a "single-efficient-point technology.")

In any production process there are normally many efficient input combinations capable of yielding the same quantity of output. We have no reason to believe that the instruction process being modeled here is any exception. The usual form of isoquant, therefore, is a smooth curve that faces outward from the origin, as shown in figure 5.2. Now, this smooth curve could be approximated reasonably well by a sequence of line segments, as we show in the lowest curve in the figure, which would correspond to a linear model incorporating several alternative input mixes for each type of student. In theory, then, we could alleviate this particular problem by building into the model several different *sets* of possible input coefficients, a_{im}, for each type of student. The problem when we try to put this theory into practice, of course, is that we really have no way of knowing what these alternative input mixes might be. Even if we did, it would

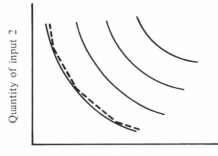

Figure 5.2. Inputs for a typical production process

be hard to characterize the objective function needed to select the best of all possible alternatives.

To summarize, then, we have worked through the formulation of a typical cost-simulation model in some detail and have found that as a university planning tool it is unsatisfactory in a number of ways. In the first place, it fails to take proper account of the multiple objectives of most universities and, in particular, to separate the costs of research from the costs of instruction. Second, there is too much detail in such models to make them very useful for planning at the central levels of an administration, even though they were originally conceived for that very purpose. The disaggregation leads to an unbelievable formulation and makes it difficult, if not impossible, to identify and hence to manipulate variables that are in some sense subject to central control. Finally, a policy planner cannot be expected to go through twenty or thirty pages of computer output every time he or she makes a model run, particularly since it is not obvious that doing so would increase understanding of the process actually being studied.

We conclude that these efforts to characterize and model the instructional production function at a disaggregate level have been largely unsuccessful. The concepts probably do apply reasonably well in an institution whose faculty are engaged almost solely in classroom teaching and where rather rigid control is maintained over the ability of students to select and of faculty to teach alternative courses. While certain classes of institutions engaged in postsecondary education may fit this description reasonably well, there are a large number that clearly don't. Whether adequate models of the production processes taking place in an academic department of a more complex institution ever can be developed for practical use is seriously open to question. We think it makes better sense, in the short run at least, to settle for more aggregate representations of university inputs, outputs, and costs, and to concentrate instead on developing tools that are especially suited to strategic planning at a fairly central level.

An Aggregate Production and Cost Model for University Planning

Our purpose in this section will be to formulate an input-output model that represents the production and cost functions of a complex university.[3] We will do so by developing a prototype model for instruction and research that can easily be generalized to include other forms of inputs, outputs, and institutional constraints if desired. In contrast to the disaggregate modeling approach discussed in the previous section, the planning model described below is quite aggregate; that is, the number of categories of students and faculty is very small. Students are differentiated according to broad categories of degree programs, such as bachelor's, master's, and Ph.D, while faculty are viewed as belonging to three groups that play fundamentally different roles in the instruction process: regular faculty, auxiliary faculty, and graduate teaching assistants. Since the model is intended to be used for strategic planning at a central university level (or possibly at the level of a large school or college within a university), we do not propose to distinguish among students or faculty according to where in the university (or school) they are located. By keeping such details to a minimum, we will be able to concentrate more fully on the task of developing a model that is reasonably true to university life.

Our objective, like that of the cost-simulation models, is to develop a model for the production and cost functions of instruction. Unlike those models, however, ours will use as primary measures the input and output *flows* of students rather than enrollment levels. Examples of such flows are the numbers of new students added to the campus and of old students leaving the campus, either as degree winners or dropouts, in a single annual cycle. The units of measurement are students per year. (Contrast this with enrollments, which merely represent the stocks of students carried over from one period into the next.)

While it obviously introduces time as an added dimension, and hence as an added complication, to the model, working explicitly with these flow variables does offer several advantages. In the first place, colleges and universities often are subjected to constraints, whether internally or externally generated, that operate directly on these flows. Perhaps the most obvious example is the flow of new students into a college that admits all qualified applicants. In this case, the exogenous demand of potential students for attendance at the designated institution determines the input flow of new students, which, in turn, determines the number of students enrolled. As strategic planners we would like to be able to examine the effects of changes in these constraints on such dependent variables as enrollments, degrees, and the cost of instruction.

A second advantage to a model formulated in terms of student flows is that it can calculate the costs associated with the entire degree program rather than simply the costs of attendance for a single year. Since the student earning a degree is a more direct measure of instructional output than is a year of attendance, the flow model comes closer to fitting the classical economic concept of a production function. Finally, since it differentiates between degree winners and dropouts from degree programs, this model can calculate costs separately for these two different outputs, whereas a model based on enrollments alone cannot.

This section is organized as follows. In the next subsection we develop the basic static-equilibrium model of student flows; its constraints lead to a solution for flow rates and enrollment levels in terms of a small number of behavioral and technological parameters and exogenous variables. This is followed by a faculty staffing model that expresses the requirements for faculty in terms of the enrollment levels of students, and is closely akin to the models described at the beginning of this chapter, although, of course, it operates on a much more aggregate level. We then develop the production and cost functions for instructional outputs (i.e., flows of degree winners and dropouts). A simple, yet reasonably rich, numerical example is used to illustrate the concepts throughout the development of the model.

Network Representation of Student Flows

At this point, we need to introduce the notion of a *cohort flow* of students, this being the primary type of variable we will be working with in the remainder of this chapter. We have already explained what we mean by a flow. By a *cohort* of students we mean a group of them who enter the university at the same time, at the same level, and who follow the same pattern of enrollment in degree programs once they are at the university. For example, one cohort might be students who enter as freshmen and pursue a bachelor's degree, while another might be undergraduate transfers pursuing a bachelor's degree.

As we have already indicated, we shall want to differentiate in our flow model between degree winners and dropouts. Accordingly, rather than having only a single cohort to represent the input flow of freshmen, we shall need two, the first corresponding to those who eventually succeed in obtaining a bachelor's degree and the second representing those who do not. Of course, the identity of which students belong in each of these two cohorts cannot be known at the time a group of new freshmen first arrives at the university. This turns out not to matter, however, in determining the aggregate rates of flow.

A model with eight cohorts. For the purposes of illustration, we shall work with a model involving the eight cohorts defined in table 5.1. In looking at these definitions, the reader should immediately note that the eight cohorts really correspond to four degree-winner/dropout pairs. In this example, we view the degree programs of the institution to be three: (a) bachelor's programs; (b) graduate programs—master's, first professional, and Ph.D—without a teaching experience (i.e., as a teaching assistant); (c) graduate programs (presumably Ph.D) with a teaching experience. We are not interested in differentiating between graduate students who enter a program after receiving a bachelor's degree from the same institution and those who come from outside. If they were judged important, such distinctions could of course be incorporated in the flow model, but this would require a significant expansion of the number of cohorts. In our example, we would need to define new pairs of cohorts

Table 5.1. Degree Winners and Dropouts, by Entry Status and Enrollment Pattern (Illustrative Example)

Cohort Number	Description		
	Entry Status	Enrollment Pattern	Terminal Status
(1)	Freshman	Undergraduate	Received bachelor's degree
(2)	Freshman	Undergraduate	Dropout
(3)	Upper-class transfer	Undergraduate	Received bachelor's degree
(4)	Upper-class transfer	Undergraduate	Dropout
(5)	Graduate	Graduate	Received graduate degree
(6)	Graduate	Graduate	Dropout
(7)	Graduate	From graduate to teaching assistant	Received Ph.D degree
(8)	Graduate	From graduate to teaching assistant	Dropout

corresponding to students who enter as freshmen, earn a bachelor's degree, enroll in a graduate program, and then either earn a graduate degree (with or without a teaching experience) or drop out—and similarly for undergraduate transfers. As this example illustrates, adding links between programs quickly inflates the number of flow variables and hence the size of the model. It is advisable, therefore, to include only those flow patterns that need to be considered separately for policy planning purposes. It will further suit our purpose of constructing a simple example to assume that different costs of instruction (the values of which are yet to be determined) must be allowed for with respect to just three categories of enrolled students: undergraduates, graduate students not serving as teaching assistants (TAs), and teaching assistants.

The pattern of cohort flows defined in table 5.1 is represented in compact form by the network flow diagram of figure 5.3. The circles, often called the *nodes* of the network, represent the status of enrolled students and are collection points for flows into and out of the system. The arrows represent cohorts that flow through the system; each cohort follows its designated pattern. We denote the primary unknowns of this model by a set of rate variables.

Let h_k = flow rate (in students per year) for cohort k.

A fundamental assumption of the model is that the flow system is in *static equilibrium*. This means that the flow rates of students, h_k, all behavioral and technological parameters, and all institutional constraints are the same in one year as in the next. This being the case, the output flow rate of each cohort will equal its input flow rate. Since these rates are the same in every year, there is no need to add a time subscript to them or, for that matter, to any of the other variables.

How realistic is this assumption of static equilibrium? The answer, of course, depends on the exact nature of the institution being considered, especially on the level of maturity of its academic programs (that is, whether these have reached a stable size or still are destined for substantial growth in the future).

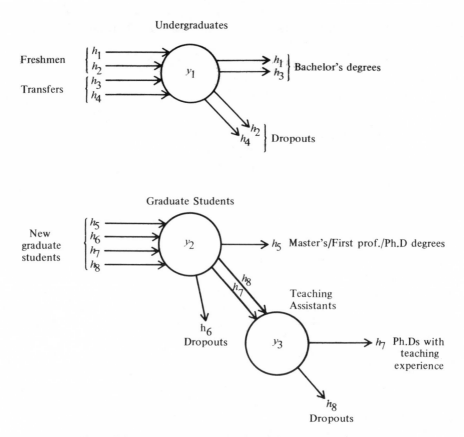

Figure 5.3. Network representation of the eight-cohort model

Our research, using data from several major university campuses, revealed the existence in most cases of a long-established and essentially steady-state pattern of student flows, and also of relatively stable enrollment levels.

To illustrate, table 5.2 gives historical data on admissions rates, degree output rates, and enrollment levels at Stanford University for the five-year period beginning with 1972/73. One can see that most of these figures have remained surprisingly constant over the period. The only exceptions, perhaps, are undergraduate admissions, where the mix in the past two years has been shifted somewhat towards a higher ratio of freshmen to transfers; and graduate degrees, for which the statistics reveal a recent trend (but not a very dramatic one) towards substituting master's for doctoral students.

The point to bear in mind here is that, as long as the system under study is reasonably mature, the model should indicate roughly how large the responses to major changes are going to be. And this is all that should be expected of a policy planning model. Once new policies of merit have been identified, they can be examined more closely by other means.

Returning now to the network of cohort flows shown in figure 5.3, we see

Table 5.2.   Historical Admissions, Degrees, and Enrollments at Stanford University, 1972/73–1976/77

	Academic Year				
	1972/73	1973/74	1974/75	1975/76	1976/77
New students					
Freshmen	1,485	1,504	1,540	1,502	1,515
Upperclass transfers	462	402	430	291	259
TOTAL UNDERGRADUATES	1,947	1,906	1,970	1,793	1,774
Graduate students	1,546	1,542	1,637	1,618	1,619
Degrees conferred					
BA/BS	1,691	1,699	1,589	1,779	1,645
MA/MS	1,258	1,236	1,276	1,327	1,283
First professional	224	208	198	193	188
Ph.D	517	474	474	456	420
TOTAL GRADUATE DEGREES	1,999	1,918	1,948	1,976	1,891
Fall-quarter enrollments					
Undergraduates	6,361	6,399	6,500	6,499	6,412
Graduates[a]	4,613	4,528	4,512	4,601	4,757

SOURCES: *Stanford University Registrar's Reports*, 1972/73–1976/77 (new students [freshmen and upper-class transfers]); *Stanford University Operating Budget Guidelines 1978/79* (new students [graduate students] and degrees conferred); *Stanford Student Directory*, 1972/73–1976/77 (fall-quarter enrollments).

NOTE: All figures in this table exclude students from the schools of business and medicine.

[a] Includes "terminal graduate students." Enrollment figures are not recorded separately for teaching assistants and other graduate students. (In 1976/77 there were the equivalent of approximately 500 half-time teaching assistants.)

that it is a simple matter to express either input rates of new students or output rates of degree winners in terms of the flow variables, h_k: one need only sum these variables over the appropriate cohorts. The number of new freshmen matriculating per year, for example, is given by the sum $h_1 + h_2$, while the number of bachelor's degrees earned in a year is $h_1 + h_3$.

Associated with each pair of cohorts, k and $k + 1$, is a dropout parameter, γ_k, defined as follows:

Let γ_k = fraction of students in the pair of cohorts who eventually drop out before earning a degree.

For example, the freshman dropout fraction, γ_1, is defined as the ratio $h_2/(h_1 + h_2)$, while the dropout fraction for transfers, γ_2, is $h_4/(h_3 + h_4)$. We view the γ_k to be predominantly behavioral parameters that cannot normally by manipulated by the institution. Studies of student persistence in degree programs at Stanford and other schools indicate that aggregate dropout fractions calculated in this way exhibit remarkably stable behavior. This justifies their use in a model of equilibrium flows such as is being considered here. Later on, in chapter 9, we will show how a time-dependent version of the cohort-flow model can be used to produce student enrollment projections year by year.

Lifetimes and enrollments. Also associated with each cohort of students, k, is a set of *lifetime parameters*, v_{jk}, which have the following definition:

Let j = enrollment status, that is, a level of study in which students from a given cohort spend some time

v_{jk} = average length of time spent by students from cohort k in enrollment status j.

For instance, v_{11} represents the number of years a student who enters as a freshman attends in undergraduate status before he earns the bachelor's degree. Its value is generally about four years, although some freshmen enter with advanced placement and graduate in less than four. The parameters v_{21}, v_{31}, and v_{41} represent undergraduate lifetimes for, respectively, freshmen dropouts, transfers earning bachelor's degrees, and transfers dropping out. These numbers are quite likely to differ from one another, which explains why we have chosen to model these cohorts separately.

The reader may be wondering how lifetimes are computed for those students who "stop out," or take time off from their studies, sometime in the middle of their courses. The answer is that only time spent enrolled at the campus is counted in the v_{jk}. This works because, in equilibrium, a student who enrolls for two years, stops out for one year, and then returns to enroll for two more years has the same effect on the system as one who is enrolled for four years straight.

The reason for introducing the lifetime parameters, v_{jk}, is to make it easy to calculate equilibrium enrollment levels once the cohort flows, h_k, are known. Enrollments can be obtained simply by taking the product of a flow rate and its corresponding lifetime. To see this, consider the simplest case in which undergraduates are admitted only as freshmen, there are no dropouts, and every student graduates in exactly four years (i.e., $v = 4$). If freshmen arrive at the rate of 1,000 students every year (i.e., if $h = 1,000$), there will be 1,000 students in each of four classes, or a total of $4 \times 1,000 = 4,000$ undergraduates. Statisticians have shown that this same relationship holds between group *average* lifetime, flows, and stocks (i.e., in this case, enrollments), even when individuals differ according to how long they spend in the system. (A proof is given in Little 1961.)

When there is more than one cohort passing through a given enrollment node, one obtains the total enrollment at that node by summing up the enrollments contributed by each cohort, calculated as above. On the basis of this information, we can write total undergraduate enrollment (node 1) as

$$y_1 = v_{11}h_1 + v_{21}h_2 + v_{31}h_3 + v_{41}h_4,$$

total graduate enrollment (node 2) as

$$y_2 = v_{52}h_5 + v_{62}h_6 + v_{72}h_7 + v_{82}h_8,$$

and total teaching assistant enrollment (node 3) as

$$y_3 = v_{73}h_7 + v_{83}h_8.$$

NUMERICAL EXAMPLE 5.1. We now pursue the formulation of a cohort flow model for a hypothetical institution, with student dropout and lifetime parameters as given in table 5.3. (Actually, these figures represent our rough

Table 5.3. Student Dropout and Lifetime Parameters (Illustrative Example)

Lifetimes, v_{ij}, in enrollment status i	Cohort number							
	1	2	3	4	5	6	7	8
Undergraduate ($i = 1$)	3.75	2.8	2.5	1.5	0	0	0	0
Graduate ($i = 2$)	0	0	0	0	2.5	1.5	3.5	2.5
TA ($i = 3$)	0	0	0	0	0	0	1.0	1.0
Dropout fractions (γ_j)	0.13		0.10		0.25		0.45	

estimates for Stanford University.) First, we write four equations expressing the flows of dropouts in terms of the dropout fractions defined above and enumerated in table 5.3:

$$h_2 = 0.13(h_1 + h_2) \tag{5.7}$$

$$h_4 = 0.10(h_3 + h_4) \tag{5.8}$$

$$h_6 = 0.25(h_5 + h_6) \tag{5.9}$$

$$h_8 = 0.45(h_7 + h_8) \tag{5.10}$$

Four additional constraints involving either student flows or enrollment levels operate at the institution in question. These are:

1. The flow rate of new transfers is limited by the quality of applicants to 400 per year.
2. The effective ceiling on total undergraduate enrollment is 6,500.
3. The financial aid budget for graduate students who are not TAs is limited to $4 million. Assume that 20 percent of the students are on university aid and each receives a total of $5,000 as payment for tuition and stipend.
4. TAs are needed for undergraduate instruction in the ratio of one for every thirteen undergraduates.

Using the data from table 5.3, we can easily express these constraints as linear equations in the h_k:

$$h_3 + h_4 = 400 \tag{5.11}$$

$$3.75h_1 + 2.8h_2 + 2.5h_3 + 1.5h_4 = 6,500 \tag{5.12}$$

$$(.20)(5,000)(2.5h_5 + 1.5h_6 + 3.5h_7 + 2.5h_8) = 4,000,000 \qquad (5.13)$$

$$1.0h_7 + 1.0h_8 = (3.75h_1 + 2.8h_2 + 2.5h_3 + 1.5h_4)/13. \qquad (5.14)$$

Now rewrite equations (5.7) to (5.14) to show that we have a system of eight linear equations in eight unknowns, which is of full rank:

$$\begin{cases}
-.13h_1 + .87h_2 & = 0 \\
\quad\ -.10h_3 + .90h_4 & = 0 \\
\qquad\quad -.25h_5 + .75h_6 & = 0 \\
\qquad\qquad\quad -.45h_7 + .55h_8 = 0 \\
h_3 + h_4 & = 400 \\
3.75h_1 + 2.8h_2 + 2.5h_3 + 1.5h_4 & = 6,500 \\
2.5h_5 + 1.5h_6 + 3.5h_7 + 2.5h_8 = 4,000 \\
-.288h_1 - .215h_2 - .192h_3 - .115h_4 \qquad + h_7 + h_8 = 0
\end{cases} \qquad (5.15)$$

This system can be solved uniquely for the h_k, and from these values we can obtain the enrollment levels, y_j. The solution is given in figure 5.4.

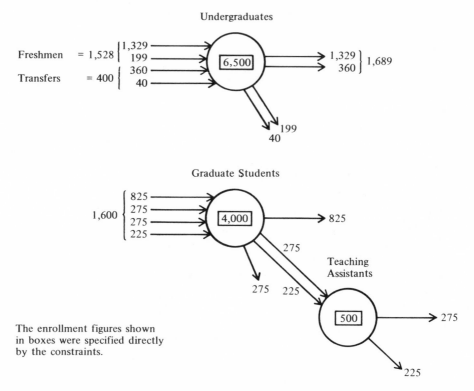

Freshmen   = 1,528
Transfers   = 400

The enrollment figures shown in boxes were specified directly by the constraints.

Figure 5.4. Numerical solution to the eight-cohort model

The reader may be curious to discover how well this solution fits the Stanford data shown in table 5.2. Let us review how the parameters in our equations were obtained. The lifetimes and dropout fractions in table 5.3 above represent our own (chiefly subjective) estimates of the values for these parameters at Stanford; they were chosen independently of the other quantities used in the equations. The choice of right-hand-side values in equations (5.11) to (5.13) effectively fixed the transfer admissions, undergraduate enrollment, and graduate enrollment figures at roughly their average Stanford values. Every other quantity shown in figure 5.4 was derived by the model from these data. In particular, the flows of new students, degree winners, and dropouts were calculated, not specified a priori. The fact that the results match these data quite well indicates that the model corresponds quite well to reality, at least at Stanford.

Formulation as a problem of value optimization. We have now completed development of the cohort flow model. Before moving on, however, it would be worthwhile to consider the entire problem of student flows and enrollment levels in the more general context of university decision making, as discussed in chapter 3. Although we have chosen in our example to specify a full set of constraints on the cohort flows, h_k, and thus to remove all degrees of freedom in determining them, we could have limited the formulation to constraints that are truly technological in nature.

We must suppose that a value function, $V(\mathbf{h}, \mathbf{y}, \mathbf{z})$, has been specified, in which the vector $\mathbf{h}$ stands for cohort flows, $\mathbf{y}$ stands for enrollment levels of students, and $\mathbf{z}$ stands for faculty staffing levels. Suppose, in addition, we are given: (a) a *partial* set of m (inequality) constraints on the n flows, h_k, $m < n$, where we shall denote the coefficient of h_k and the right-hand side in the ith constraint by m_{ik} and b_i, respectively; (b) the complete set of student lifetimes, $\{v_{jk}\}$; (c) a set of faculty/student ratios, $\{a_{ij}\}$, representing the technology of instruction at the given institution. This information would be sufficient to formulate the selection of cohort flows, enrollments, and faculty FTEs as a problem of constrained value maximization of the form described in chapter 3, namely:

Find $\mathbf{h}$, $\mathbf{y}$, and $\mathbf{z}$

to maximize $V(\mathbf{h}, \mathbf{y}, \mathbf{z})$

subject to the constraints

$$1. \quad \sum_{j=1}^{n} m_{ij}h_j \leq b_i \qquad (i = 1, 2, \ldots, m)$$

$$2. \quad y_j = \sum_{k=1}^{n} v_{jk}h_k \quad (j = 1, 2, \ldots, J)$$

$$3. \quad z_i = \sum_{j=1}^{J} a_{ij}y_j \quad (i = 1, 2, \ldots, I)$$

$$4. \quad h_k \geq 0.$$

In practice, we probably lack sufficient information to specify the value function, V. Thus, we are forced to work with a full set of constraints, recognizing that these result in many cases from the implicit optimization of values at an earlier stage. In our example, the exogenous-demand constraint of transfer admissions obviously reflects judgments about the quality of admissible students. Likewise, the specification of an enrollment ceiling for undergraduates, as in equation (5.12), results in large part from value judgments about the effects of scale on the institution's "quality of life" and, one supposes, also on how this attribute is perceived by the institution's clientele. So also with the constraint that limits graduate financial aid: the size of the financial aid budget was determined (at least implicitly) by maximizing the value of institutional outputs, subject to overall financial constraints. Of the four constraints we added to the behavioral equations for dropouts, then, only the one relating teaching assistants to undergraduate enrollments was primarily technological in nature.

Of course, one of the model's more valuable uses is in testing out the numerical consequences of altering such value-laden parameters as admissions quotas and enrollment ceilings. By performing sensitivity analyses of this kind, university decision makers can acquire quantitative information upon which to exercise their judgment.

Computation of Faculty Staffing Levels

To proceed in our development of a prototype cost model, let us assume that the enrollment levels of students already have been calculated by the method just described.

Let y_1 = undergraduate enrollment

y_2 = graduate enrollment

y_3 = teaching assistant enrollment.

In this section, we determine the staffing levels (expressed in FTE terms) of faculty that are needed to instruct these students. Three types of faculty are considered in our example.

Let z_1 = number of FTE regular faculty (RF)

z_2 = number of FTE auxiliary faculty (AF)

z_3 = number of FTE teaching assistants (TAs).

By working with FTEs we mean to distinguish in the model between faculty members who work full-time for the university and those who work less than full-time, regardless of the source of their funding. That is, two faculty members each of whom is employed on a half-time basis equal one FTE, even though they may both be supported in part by outside research grants. It is not our intention at this stage to calculate FTEs on the basis of any particular set of accounts. Later on we shall see how an analysis of faculty effort can be used to split them into teaching, research, and joint teaching/research FTEs.

Notice that teaching assistants are included in the model both as faculty and as students. This is appropriate since these graduate students do in fact play both roles in the university; it should pose no particular problem provided the FTEs are calculated on a consistent basis. Although it was not evident from our flow diagram in figure 5.3, the role played by TAs as instructors of undergraduates is an important one that did enter the flow model as a techno-logical constraint. Its importance might have been demonstrated more dramat-ically in our example had we taken the graduate financial aid budget to be only $1 million, instead of $4 million. Had this limitation been in effect, and had all other constraints and parameters remained the same, we would have found no feasible solution for the flows in the network and consequently no solution for enrollments. The reason is a compelling one: the 500 TAs required as instructors of undergraduates would themselves consume more than the amount allotted to the aid budget during the time they would have to be enrolled as regular graduate students.

In order to calculate the staffing levels of faculty, z, needed to teach the students represented by the vector y, we follow essentially the same logic as was used in the disaggregate models of the last section. For the current purpose, as before, it will suffice to consider these values as depending simply on student-induced demand for classroom teaching. The need to take the multiple activities of faculty explicitly into account will not arise until later, when we derive production and cost models for the instruction function alone.

The following quantities are used to calculate faculty staffing levels:

d_j = average number of (classroom) courses taken in a year by a student of type j

u_j = average number of students enrolled per class (i.e., the average class size)

p_{ij} = fraction of classes taken by students of type j that is taught by faculty of type i (note that $\sum_i p_{ij} = 1$)

b_i = average number of classes taught per year by an FTE faculty member of type i (i.e., average class load per full-time faculty member).

Of these parameters, d_j, u_j, and p_{ij} may be viewed as essentially being specified by the technology of instruction at the institution concerned. To be sure, value judgments are a factor here and are obviously reflected in, for example, the average class size, u_j. For the most part, however, these numbers will tend to follow established norms for the given category of institution. Technology probably also is the chief determinant of the course loads, b_2, for auxiliary faculty (AF), and b_3, for TAs. In the case of AF, the value of b_2 employed by the institution will be based on its assessment of what, according to generally accepted norms, should constitute a full-time teaching load, while for TAs it

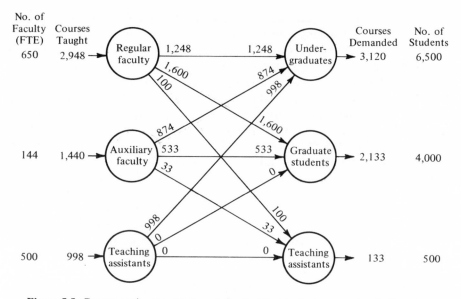

Figure 5.5. Course-assignment network for faculty/student course-load allocations

will be based more on an assessment of what is educationally sound for a graduate student who is learning how to teach.

In contrast, we view the average course load for regular faculty, b_1, as being fundamentally different from the other two course-load parameters, for this one is determined chiefly by value judgments relating to the level of effort expected of a professor in classroom teaching as opposed to the other important functions he or she performs. The current value of b_1 can of course be computed from real data, but there obviously is much disagreement among university experts as to what its value *should* be. Since b_1, then, must be determined judgmentally, we treat it in our model as a decision variable that must be specified at *run time*, i.e., the time at which the computer program is asked to make its calculations. To observe how this works, see the sample run included as appendix 7.

The raw figures for the distribution of classes taught by the various types of faculty to the various types of students can be represented compactly in network form. Figure 5.5 displays the data obtained from course enrollment reports at Stanford. Here we visualize classes as being "shipped" along arcs that originate with a particular type of teacher and terminate at a particular type of student. The value of p_{ij} is obtained by dividing the number of classes taught by teachers i to students j by the total number of classes taken by students j. (In this context, a "class" means any course or section of a course in which a teacher or instructor meets with one or more students on a regularly scheduled basis throughout an academic term.) This explains how the values

Table 5.4. Course Distribution Matrix

Fraction of Courses Taught by:	Taught to:		
	Undergraduates	Graduates	TAs
Regular faculty (z_1)[a]	0.40	0.75	0.75
Auxiliary faculty (z_2)[b]	0.28	0.25	0.25
Teaching assistants (z_3)[c]	0.32	0.00	0.00
	1.00	1.00	1.00

[a] Regular faculty course load $(b_1) = 4.53$ courses per year.
[b] Auxiliary faculty course load $(b_2) = 10.3$ courses per year.
[c] Teaching assistant course load $(b_3) = 2.0$ courses per year.

Table 5.5. Enrollments, Student Course Load, and Average Class Size, by Type of Student

	Undergraduate	Graduate	TA
Enrollments (y_j)	6,500	4,000	500
Student course load (d_j)	12	8	4
Average class size (u_j)	25	15	15
TOTAL COURSES $(= d_j y_j / u_j)$	3,120	2,133	133

of p_{ij} are derived initially. Of course, we may want to experiment with different values for these as well as for some of the model's other parameters, so it is important that the computer program have the facility for permitting such changes to be made very easily.

The p_{ij} derived from the data in figure 5.5 are shown in table 5.4, which is labelled as the "course distribution matrix." The figures in table 5.5 give approximate Stanford data for the other course-related parameters of the model. Notice that the total numbers of courses taken by each type of student appearing in table 5.5 are the same as the quantities that are shown coming out on the right side of the network in figure 5.5.

Having defined the parameters of the faculty staffing model, we can write

$$z_i = \frac{1}{b_i} \sum_{j=1}^{3} p_{ij}(d_j y_j / u_j) \quad (i = 1, 2, 3). \tag{5.16}$$

That is, one computes the number of FTE teachers of type i by adding up the classes demanded by each category of student and dividing by the full-time faculty class load. Note that the product, $d_j y_j$, which represents class enrollments, must be divided by the class size, u_j, in order to obtain the number of classes needing to be taught.

Returning for a moment to equation (5.6), which was used in developing the cost-simulation model, we find a basic similarity between it and the formula just derived. Since the units being tracked here are classes rather than credit-hours, we have used the single parameter d_j in place of the product $\ell_{kj} r_k$, but the remaining parameters are exactly the same in both formulas. At the outset, it would seem as though our formulation, like the models discussed earlier, suffers from the problems associated with the assumption that factor proportions are fixed. Because the current formula is intended for use in a model of much smaller dimensions, however, we can vary the technological parameters in a meaningful way, thereby changing the input mix as desired. To get a firmer grasp of this point, observe that our current example involves just three types of teachers ($i = 1, 2, 3$) and three types of students ($j = 1, 2, 3$), which means that the total number of parameters incorporated in equation (5.16) is only eighteen. As a consequence, these parameters can be manipulated far more easily in experimental sensitivity runs of this model than of a model with parameters numbering in the tens of thousands.

As the reader can now see, the formula expressed in (5.16) is sufficient to calculate the numbers of faculty needed to teach all the courses, and thus to calculate total faculty size. We must not forget, however, that this formula was constructed purely on the basis of what goes on between faculty and students in the classroom. In particular, it ignores demands on faculty time that are made by students in other settings. Also, the faculty time needed for research, both sponsored and unsponsored, has not been filtered out.

Obviously, these other demands are significant in many institutions. This is not the proper model, then, with which to allocate costs to the instruction function, since more information would be required than has been given here. Here we have the major failing of many past efforts at developing cost models: usually, they have not distinguished at all between resource determination and cost allocation. For resource determination, it is sufficient to match the number of faculty to the number of students through regularly tabulated data on classroom teaching; the other activities of the faculty are allowed for in the particular choice of values assigned to the classload parameters, b_i. For cost allocation, however, we must know what fraction of his or her time, on the average, a faculty member spends on activities other than classroom teaching. A procedure for identifying and allocating the costs of instruction is presented next.

The Instructional Production, Cost, and Revenue Functions

How can we best formulate the production, cost, and revenue functions for instruction as distinct from other major institutional activities? In the case of the production function we will derive a set of relationships between student cohort flows—which we take to represent the instructional outputs of the system—and the faculty and staff FTEs and other inputs of instructional resources that are "consumed" in the process of educating these students. The cost function is one that adds up the costs of the various resource inputs to obtain the dollar cost per unit of instructional output (i.e., per dropout or student earning a degree), while the revenue function uses price information in a similar way to determine the dollar revenue per unit of output. Initially, we will express the cost and revenue functions in terms of enrollments, faculty FTE, and staff FTE; then we will make use of the relationships derived earlier in this section to express the enrollments and FTEs, in turn, in terms of the cohort flows.

We will assume, as we did earlier in equations (5.2) and (5.3), that the inputs of staff FTEs and other resources associated with instructional outputs can be expressed as linear functions of student enrollments, on the one hand, and the faculty FTEs associated with instruction, on the other. The central task, then, reduces to determining the FTE faculty of each type that is used in instructing each type of student. This determination is straightforward in the case of auxiliary faculty and TAs since, by assumption, they are entirely associated with the instructional objective. By referring back to equation (5.16) we can readily see that the unit inputs of auxiliary faculty and teaching assistants used in instructing a student of type j are given, respectively, by the quantities

$$a_{2j} = \frac{p_{2j}d_j}{b_2 u_j}$$

$$a_{3j} = \frac{p_{3j}d_j}{b_3 u_j}.$$

The values of these ratios for the numerical example are shown in the last two rows of table 5.6.

The same formula *cannot* be applied directly to the regular faculty, however, since this group's total FTE, which is already known from (5.16), is associated with several university outputs, only one of which is instruction. To do the job of apportioning these FTEs to the proper outputs, we must first decide on the relative amounts of faculty effort associated with each type of output and then, having identified the FTE associated with instruction, decide upon a reasonable procedure for apportioning this total to the various types of students. Actually, the apportionment procedure will vary according to the type of faculty activity being considered.

Suppose that we have identified the following five areas or *activity classes* as encompassing the major set of activities in which regular faculty members are engaged:

1. Classroom teaching (including preparation)
2. Teaching outside the classroom
3. Joint teaching and research
4. Pure research
5. Administration

Category 2 refers primarily to directed-reading courses and informal discussions with students that take place outside the classroom (or laboratory). It also includes any time spent by a professor in the coaching of teaching assistants. Category 3 encompasses on-the-job teaching of research assistants, supervision of Ph.D dissertation projects, and whatever portion of the faculty member's own research provides material for the courses he or she teaches. Category 4 represents the remainder of the faculty member's research effort. Finally,

Table 5.6.   Ratios of Instructional Faculty FTE to Students

	Student Type (j)		
	Undergraduate	Graduate	Teaching Assistant
Regular faculty (z_1)			
Classroom teaching (z_1^1)	0.0148	0.0309	0.0155
Out-of-class teaching (z_1^2)	0.0041	0.0081	0.0122
Joint allocation to teaching (qz_1^3)	0.0000	0.0153	0.0076
TOTAL	0.0189	0.0543	0.0353
Total regular faculty (z_1)	0.0189	0.0543	0.0353
Auxiliary faculty (z_2)	0.0134	0.0133	0.0067
Teaching assistants (z_3)	0.0769	0.0000	0.0000

FACULTY INPUT COEFFICIENTS (a_{ij})

category 5 refers to committee work, faculty meetings, research proposal writing, and other administrative tasks that support indirectly the university's main objectives of instruction and research.

Note that this list was composed for an institution that has only two primary objectives, instruction and research. If there were a third major objective, such as public service, this would obviously add to the list of categories needing to be considered. However, the same methodology advanced in this section for allocating costs would also apply to this more complicated situation.

Note too that the extent of a faculty member's research effort is not necessarily equivalent to the proportion of his or her salary that is charged to an outside grant. In the first place, many grants do not pay for the full amount of a person's time associated with that research. Secondly, he or she may be doing other unsponsored research as well. Finally, for our present purposes we mean to use the word "research" broadly, so that it covers all activities directed towards adding to and broadening the base of knowledge in whatever field the faculty member happens to be working. In particular, this will include the time spent by a history or English professor in writing a new book, which probably would not be paid for by any outside agency.

Fundamental to our treatment of faculty costs is the assumption that there exist fractions, λ_k, that represent the proportion of faculty effort, averaged over an entire academic year and across the whole university, going into activity class k. This information rarely, if ever, is captured by accounting data on the sources of funds used to pay faculty salaries. Many institutions have considered schemes to report faculty effort on a systematic and all-encompassing basis; some have even tried them. They usually involve requiring each member of the faculty to keep a time budget (i.e., a careful account of how one's time is spent) and to submit it periodically to a central office which then compiles summary statistics. The costs of such an undertaking can be great, both in terms of personnel and computer processing time and in terms of the perceived threat to faculty autonomy. Also, we doubt whether the extra precision to be gained has much significant value when good results can be obtained simply by asking knowledgeable persons (including faculty members themselves) how the faculty spend their time. Certainly, this is good enough for our purpose, namely, assessing relative costs of instruction for different degree programs by order of magnitude. In fact, we believe it is good strategic planning to leave the values of the λ_k unspecified until the computer program is to be used rather than build them into the program from historical data.

Assume, then, that the faculty effort proportions, λ_k, have been specified by the model's user. To simplify the calculations, let us also assume that the time a faculty member spends in category 5 activities (i.e., administration) is attributable to the other four categories in proportion to the amount of effort devoted to each. For example, if classroom teaching consumes twice as much of the average person's time as teaching outside the classroom, the assumption would be that twice as much of the person's administrative time should be apportioned to category 1 as is apportioned to category 2. In other words, the total effort represented by λ_5 can be apportioned to the other effort categories in proportion to their λ_k values. It follows that, in apportioning the total faculty FTE, we can drop consideration of category 5 entirely and deal only with the "direct" efforts associated with λ_k, where $k = 1, 2, 3, 4$.

Before proceeding further, it will be useful to develop some notation for the FTEs associated with each primary activity class and, within a class, with each type of student.

Let z_{1j}^k = FTE regular faculty associated with activity class k and student type j

$\quad\ a_{1j}^k$ = FTE regular faculty associated with activity class k per student of type j (equals z_{1j}^k/y_j).

Note that, in the notation we will use, k is a superscript denoting the activity class, not an exponent.

PROCEDURE 5.3. Now, we take up the task of outlining a procedure for determining the allocation coefficients separately for each activity class, k.

1. *Classroom teaching FTE* (z_{1j}^1). This should be determined on the basis of the relative work load imposed by students through the formal classroom courses that they take. Since $p_{ij}d_j/u_j$ in equation (5.16) represents the courses taught by regular faculty per student of type j, b_1 is the course load per faculty member, and λ_1 is the proportion of faculty time associated with classroom teaching, the appropriate calculation is given by

$$a_{1j}^1 = \lambda_1 p_{1j}d_j/b_1 u_j \quad (j = 1, 2, 3). \tag{5.17}$$

2. *Out-of-class teaching FTE* (z_{1j}^2). The FTE associated with this activity is given by $\lambda_2 z_1$. Before we can apportion this FTE we need to know, on a per student basis, the relative weights associated with students of each type. By "relative weight" we mean a number that indicates the relative amount of out-of-class teaching time taken up by a given student type.

Let w_j^2 = the relative weight, for student type j, for faculty effort spent in out-of-class teaching.

These weights, just like the λ_k's, are viewed as judgmental parameters to be supplied by the model's user while the program is being run. They are obtained by asking a question phrased somewhat as follows: "If we assign a weight of one to the time you spend with one undergraduate in teaching outside the classroom, what numbers would you give to represent the amount of time you spend in this activity with a regular graduate student or a teaching assistant?" A faculty member who answered "Two and three," for example, would be indicating that the amount of his or her time taken up in this activity by a regular graduate student or a teaching assistant averaged twice or three times as much, respectively, as the time taken up by an undergraduate.

To do the apportioning, we make use of an identity which states that the total out-of-class teaching FTE must also equal student enrollments, weighted appropriately by the w_j^2, times the out-of-class teaching FTE per weighted student:

$$z_1^2 = \lambda_2 z_1 = k_2(w_1^2 y_1 + w_2^2 y_2 + w_3^2 y_3), \tag{5.18}$$

where $\lambda_2 z_1$ = total out-of-class teaching FTE

$\quad\quad k_2$ = out-of-class teaching FTE per weighted student.

By substituting the known values for λ_2, z_1, w_j^2, and y_j, we can solve the above equation for the value of k_2. This calculation is made at run time, since we are relying on the user's judgment to supply values of the parameters b_1, λ_k, and w_j that are all mutually consistent. Also, we remark that, if the expression (5.18) for z_1^2 is used to represent faculty inputs while student enrollments are varying, one must be assuming that the production function relating enrollments to out-of-class teaching FTE is linear homogeneous (i.e., is exactly proportional to the enrollment levels). Such an assumption probably is reasonable, within a considerable range either above or below the current actual enrollment values. Finally, the coefficients associating regular faculty out-of-class teaching with students of type j are given by:

$$a_{1j}^2 = w_j^2 k_2. \tag{5.19}$$

3. *Joint teaching/research FTE* (z_{1j}^3). Since our focus is on obtaining *instructional* costs per student, we again must apply judgment, this time to separate these joint costs into teaching (i.e., instruction) and research costs. Let q denote the fraction allocated to teaching. Following the procedure used in apportioning out-of-class teaching FTE, we must inquire about relative weights for the teaching component of joint teaching/research FTE associated with each type of student.

Let w_j^3 = a weight representing faculty effort associated with the teaching component of the joint teaching/research activity that is expended on students of type j, as opposed to teaching other categories of students.

As before, we write

$$q\lambda_3 z_1 = k_3(w_1^3 y_1 + w_2^3 y_2 + w_3^3 y_3). \tag{5.20}$$

By inserting current data into this formula, we can calculate the constant k_3, which is the joint teaching/research FTE for instruction per weighted student. Finally, the coefficients associating these FTEs with the various student types are obtained as

$$a_{1j}^3 = w_j^3 k_3 \quad (j = 1, 2, 3). \tag{5.21}$$

The process just described for allocating and apportioning the joint teaching/research component of the faculty is portrayed graphically in the *allocation tree* shown in figure 5.6.

We must be careful to distinguish the nature of the subjective parameter q from any of the other elements of our model. In a real sense, the value of q is arbitrary, for there is no objective truth about how a faculty member's joint efforts should be split between teaching and research. The value assigned to q, therefore, will depend on the context in which the question is raised and on the user's own objectives in making the allocation. In contrast, the parameters λ_k and weights w_j^3 are, at least in theory, behavioral quantities that can be estimated by objective means. We note further that, while both teaching and research may be carried out by the same faculty member at the same time, this rarely occurs in the presence of more than one level of student at a time. Once the teaching portion of the joint FTE has been extracted, then it is meaningful to ask independently for the relative weights, w_j^3, that distinguish the amount of teaching effort being given to students by their various levels.

4. *Pure research FTE* (z_1^4). By definition, this category has no association with students, so we have

$$a_{1j}^4 = 0 \quad (j = 1, 2, 3). \tag{5.22}$$

This completes the apportioning of regular faculty FTE to types of student by kind of instruction. A diagram of the scheme just presented, with illustrative values for the allocation and apportionment parameters, course-related data from tables 5.4 and 5.5 and the total regular faculty FTE from figure 5.5, is shown in figure 5.7. When the instructional FTE figures for the various kinds of teaching are divided by the enrollments in tables 5.4 and 5.5, we get the unit coefficients that appear in the top three rows of table 5.6 above. The reader should note that neither the FTE associated with the pure research category nor that associated with the joint teaching/research activity and allocated to research has been included in the calculations of instructional FTE. As a consequence the

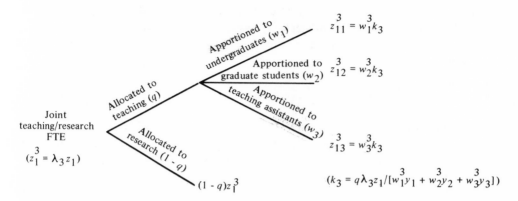

Figure 5.6. An illustration of the allocation and appointment of joint teaching/research faculty FTE

total instructional FTE will always be less than the total FTE—in fact, much less in the case of our numerical example—and, to the extent that costs vary in proportion to faculty FTEs, so will instructional costs be less than total costs.

We now are in a position to write down an expression for the production function for instruction. Faculty inputs are given as the sum of products of the unit instructional FTE coefficients just derived and the appropriate enrollment variables:

$$z_i^{FI} = \sum_{j=1}^{3} a_{ij} y_j \quad (i = 1, 2, 3) \tag{5.23}$$

where the regular faculty input coefficients are obtained from

$$a_{1j} = \sum_{k=1}^{4} a_{1j}^{k} \quad (j = 1, 2, 3), \tag{5.24}$$

as shown numerically in table 5.6. Note that we have introduced a superscript *FI* in the notation to signify inputs of *faculty* that are associated with the *instruction* function. Inputs of staff, z^{SI}, and of other resources, z^{OI}, for instruction are obtained from equations (5.2) and (5.3), except that, in place of z_i^F, we should use z_i^{FI}.

Since we prefer to view student flows, rather than student enrollments, as the outputs of instruction, the final step in constructing the production function is to use the relationships defined in the previous subsection to write

$$z_i^{FI} = \sum_{k=1}^{8} \left(\sum_{j=1}^{3} a_{ij} v_{kj} \right) h_k \quad (i = 1, 2, 3) \tag{5.25}$$

and similarly for z^{SI} and z^{OI}. Note that the summation occurring inside the parentheses in (5.24) is over student types, while the outside summation is over cohorts. This rather formidable-looking equation simply says that the input of

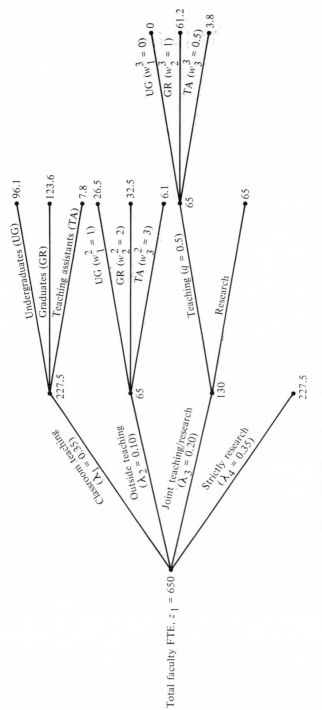

Figure 5.7. Illustration of the apportionment of regular faculty FTE

faculty per unit cohort flow can be found by summing the annual input of faculty, a_{ij}, per student enrolled in each enrollment status times the number of years a student from that cohort spends in that status, v_{kj}. (In standard economics notation, our production function would be written in implicit form with inputs having a negative sense; that is,

$$\sum_k \left(\sum_j a_{ij} v_{kj} \right) h_k - z_i^{FI} = 0.)$$

Finally, we need to know the unit cost and revenue coefficients associated with the input variables z_i^{FI}, z^{SI}, z^{OI}, and with the enrollments. A method for finding these coefficients was given in chapter 4. The coefficient c_j^y below accounts for all direct student costs, such as student services (counseling, registration, etc.), except for financial aid, which is accounted for in a separate term. The expression for the cost of financial aid in terms of tuition rates, t_j, enrollment levels, y_j, and student FTE factors, α_j, also was derived in chapter 4. Accordingly, we can express instructional costs and revenues in terms of the enrollments and faculty FTEs by

$$C^I = c_0^I + \sum_{j=1}^{3} c_j^y y_j + \sum_{j=1}^{3} (\beta_{0j} + \beta_{1j} t_j) \alpha_j y_j + \sum_{i=1}^{3} c_i^z z_i^{FI}$$

$$
\begin{array}{c}
\text{Total} \\
\text{instructional} \\
\text{costs}
\end{array}
=
\begin{array}{c}
\text{Fixed} \\
\text{component}
\end{array}
+
\begin{array}{c}
\text{Costs of staff} \\
\text{and other resources} \\
\text{associated directly} \\
\text{with students}
\end{array}
+
\begin{array}{c}
\text{Cost of} \\
\text{financial} \\
\text{aid}
\end{array}
$$

$$
+
\begin{array}{c}
\text{Direct cost of instructional} \\
\text{faculty plus cost of staff} \\
\text{and other resources associated} \\
\text{with faculty}
\end{array}
$$

and

$$R^I = r_0^I + \sum_{j=1}^{3} r_j^y y_j + \sum_{j=1}^{3} \alpha_j t_j y_j + \sum_{i=1}^{3} r_i^z z_i^{FI}$$

$$
\begin{array}{c}
\text{Total} \\
\text{revenue from} \\
\text{instruction}
\end{array}
=
\begin{array}{c}
\text{Fixed} \\
\text{component}
\end{array}
+
\begin{array}{c}
\text{Revenue from} \\
\text{overhead recovery} \\
\text{associated directly} \\
\text{with students (e.g.,} \\
\text{student services)}
\end{array}
+
\begin{array}{c}
\text{Tuition} \\
\text{revenue}
\end{array}
$$

$$
+
\begin{array}{c}
\text{Revenue from overhead} \\
\text{recovery associated} \\
\text{directly with faculty (e.g.,} \\
\text{indirect departmental} \\
\text{administration).}
\end{array}
$$

Table 5.7.   Illustrative Data on Variable Costs and Revenue per Student and Faculty
Member (in 1975/76 Dollars)

	Per Student Costs		Per Student Revenue	
	Financial Aid	Other	Tuition	Other
Student type				
Undergraduates	$0.20t_1$	$260	$0.97t_1$	$35
Graduates	$0.25t_2$	$400	$0.86t_2$	$65
Teaching assistants	0	$400	$0.43t_3$	$65
	Per Faculty Costs		Per Faculty Revenue	
Faculty type				
Regular faculty	$40,600		$6,050	
Auxiliary faculty	$22,500		$620	
Teaching assistants	$3,450		$0	

Substituting the linear relations (5.23) for faculty in terms of students enables
us to rewrite these expressions more compactly as

$$C^I(\mathbf{y}) = c_0 + \sum_{j=1}^{3} c_j(t_j) \cdot y_j$$

$$R^I(\mathbf{y}) = r_0 + \sum_{j=1}^{3} r_j(t_j) \cdot y_j. \tag{5.26}$$

In writing the cost and revenue functions in this form, we have collapsed the sum
of coefficients that represent the unit incremental cost and revenue associated
with student type j into the single terms $c_j(t_j)$ and $r_j(t_j)$, respectively, both of
which depend directly on the tuition rates, t_j. As the last step, we substitute for
enrollments in (5.26) to obtain the cost and revenue functions expressed in terms
of tuition rates and cohort flows:

$$C^I(\mathbf{h}) = c_0 + \sum_{k=1}^{8} \left(\sum_{j=1}^{3} c_j(t_j) \cdot v_{kj} \right) h_k$$

$$R^I(\mathbf{h}) = r_0 + \sum_{k=1}^{8} \left(\sum_{j=1}^{3} r_j(t_j) \cdot v_{kj} \right) h_k. \tag{5.27}$$

The quantities in parentheses in (5.27) give the desired values of variable costs
and revenue per unit of instructional output, h_k.

The rather abstract formulas just developed will appear more relevant if we
work through a numerical example. Suppose that the unit cost and revenue
figures associated with students and faculty are those displayed in table 5.7.
These figures were estimated from Stanford data by means of the procedures
described in chapter 4. For example, the unit costs were obtained by (a) estimating the portions of various budgets that tend to vary directly with students
and faculty, and (b) dividing these dollar sums by the appropriate enrollment

and FTE figures. In particular, the $40,600 unit cost for regular faculty is the same as the $38,427 derived in table 4.6 plus an increase of 5.7 percent due to one year's inflation. Revenue associated with faculty and "other revenue" associated with students consist of money recovered by the university through partial reimbursement of indirect costs, whether of departmental administration or of student services, by government grants and contracts. To take a specific example, we estimated that indirect departmental administration would be 35 percent of the unit cost for regular faculty and that, of this amount, 42.6 percent would be recovered. Thus, the unit revenue coefficient for regular faculty became $0.35 \times (0.426 \times \$40,600) = \$6,050$.

PROCEDURE 5.4. Let us now go through the steps of building the unit cost and revenue coefficients for (a) undergraduate enrollments and (b) the output flow of bachelor's degree recipients.

First, we take the ratio of instructional faculty FTEs to undergraduate students from column 1 of table 5.6, apply them to the per faculty costs in column 1 of table 5.7, and add the results:

$$(0.0189)(\$40,600) + (0.0134)(\$22,500) + (0.0769)(\$3,450)$$
$$= \$1,334 \text{ per undergraduate.}$$

Then we do the same for the per faculty revenue in column 2 of table 5.7:

$$(0.0189)(\$6,050) + (0.0134)(\$620) + (0.0768)(0)$$
$$= \$123 \text{ per undergraduate.}$$

To these costs and revenues directly associated with faculty who instruct undergraduates must be added the costs and revenues directly associated with the students themselves. Again referring to table 5.7, we obtain, for a tuition rate of $4,000,

$$\text{Direct cost per undergraduate} = (0.20)(\$4,000) + \$260 = \$1,060$$

$$\text{Direct revenue per undergraduate} = (0.97)(\$4,000) + \$35 = \$3,915.$$

Combining these two sets of numbers leads to the results that

$$\text{Variable cost per undergraduate} = \$1,334 + \$1,060 = \$2,394$$

$$\text{Variable revenue per undergraduate} = \$123 + \$3,915 = \$4,038.$$

To translate these figures into terms relating to cohort flows, we need only multiply by the appropriate student lifetime parameters from table 5.3. Thus the variable cost and revenue values associated with recipients of bachelor's degrees who enter as freshmen are

$$\text{Cost} = (\$2,394)(3.75) = \$8,978$$

$$\text{Revenue} = (\$4,038)(3.75) = \$15,142$$

while for recipients of bachelor's degrees who enter as transfers they are

$$\text{Cost} = (\$2,394)(2.5) = \$5,985$$

$$\text{Revenue} = (\$4,038)(2.5) = \$10,095.$$

Finally, to get the variable cost and revenue per recipient of a bachelor's degree, one would average the cohort values according to the relative rates of flow given in figure 5.4. This procedure yields:

$$\text{Average variable cost per bachelor's degree} = \frac{1329}{1329 + 360}(\$8,978) + \frac{360}{1329 + 360}(\$5,985)$$

$$= \$8,340$$

$$\text{Average variable revenue per bachelor's degree} = \frac{1329}{1329 + 360}(\$15,142) + \frac{360}{1329 + 360}(\$10,095)$$

$$= \$14,066.$$

A complete set of figures calculated in this manner for our numerical example appears in table 5.8. It is interesting to note that the university seems to generate considerable amounts of incremental net revenue on all undergraduate cohorts, even after we have allowed for the costs of financial aid, and that it loses very little on any of the graduate cohorts. Although the data we have used in these calculations are purely illustrative, they are reasonably representative of a private research university.

That these results seemingly fly in the face of conventional wisdom about private universities having to subsidize their students is easily explained. In the first place, such statements usually are based on calculations of *average total* costs rather than *variable* costs. If we had chosen to allocate a portion of the fixed instructional cost, c_0^I, to students—and note that we would have had to invent rules both for splitting this quantity out from total fixed costs and for allocating it to student types—we would have added substantially to the unit costs. (It would not be surprising to find fixed costs amounting to nearly half of total expense.) Second, most previous efforts at unit costing have failed to remove the direct and joint costs of research prior to deriving the costs per student attributable to instruction. This observation also helps to explain why the ratio of graduate student costs to undergraduate costs is quite a bit less than expected, for if the costs of research are not split out beforehand, they are more likely to be attributed to graduate students than to undergraduates.

The calculations relating to the instructional production and cost functions derived in this chapter are easily automated in the form of an interactive computer program, i.e., one that is conversational with the user at run time. A sample output from Stanford's program, derived from the data in tables 5.3, 5.4, and 5.5, and in figure 5.7, is shown in appendix 7. Note that we have provided the user with easy access to the model's parameters, which are relatively small in number. This setup makes it much easier to perform sensitivity

Table 5.8.   Variable Unit Cost and Revenue Values (Numerical Example)

	Variable Cost (*VC*)	Variable Revenue (*VR*)	*VR* − *VC*
Per student:			
Undergraduate	$2,394	$4,038	$1,644
Graduate	$3,904	$3,842	($62)
Teaching assistant	$1,984	$2,003	$19
Per cohort:			
Freshman earning BA/BS	$8,978	$15,142	$6,164
Freshman dropping out	$6,703	$11,306	$4,603
Transfer earning BA/BS	$5,985	$10,095	$4,110
Transfer dropping out	$3,591	$6,057	$2,466
Graduate student earning degree without teaching assistantship	$9,760	$9,605	($155)
Graduate student dropping out without teaching assistantship	$5,856	$5,763	($93)
Graduate student earning degree with teaching assistantship	$15,648	$15,450	($198)
Graduate student dropping out with teaching assistantship	$11,744	$11,608	($136)

analyses in which one or more of the input parameters are varied and changes in the model's outputs are observed. Contrast this with the large-model cost simulations, discussed earlier, where the control parameters are difficult to distinguish and each run consumes a much larger amount of setup and processing time.

A Sample Application of the Planning Model

We conclude with an example of the sort of analysis that can easily be performed with the costing model just described. Various proposals for shortening the bachelor's degree program have been quite widely discussed by educators in recent years. The arguments usually given have to do with the fact that a freshman entering college today supposedly is far better prepared academically than was his or her counterpart many years ago when the concept of a four-year bachelor's program was developed. The proposal for a three-year bachelor's program was given further legitimacy when it was advanced in the early 1970s by the Carnegie Commission on Higher Education (1971, pp. 15–16).

Our purpose here is not to debate the educational merits of the proposal but rather to examine its cost and revenue implications. Let us take, in particular, the case of the institution for which we have given all of the requisite data in tables 5.3, 5.4, and 5.5 and in figure 5.7. First, we must consider the potential impact of the proposal on the constraints that operate on student flows. To make the example more interesting, let us suppose the university administration to have determined that the following constraints would operate if the proposal were implemented:

1. The size of the freshman class would be limited to 1,700. This is because the quality of the freshman applicant pool would permit only 3,000 new freshmen to be accepted, and of these only 1,700 could be expected to come.

2. Due to the small number of applicants, new transfer students would continue to be limited to 400 per year.

3. To compensate for a loss of undergraduates, graduate enrollment could be increased by up to 200 students. All of these additional students would require financial aid, however, and so $200 \times \$5,000 = \$1$ million would need to be added to the graduate financial aid budget. (We assume that $\$5,000$ is the amount of aid currently being awarded to each aid recipient.) As a result, the proportion of regular graduate students on aid would become $(800 + 200)/(4000 + 200) = 0.24$.

4. The undergraduate/TA ratio would remain at $13:1$.

Also, let us assume that the new lifetimes for the undergraduate cohorts would be: $v_{11} = 3$ years, $v_{12} = 2$ years, $v_{13} = 2$ years, and $v_{14} = 1.5$ years. Finally, due to the shorter degree lifetime, the dropout rate for undergraduates entering as freshmen would be reduced from 0.13 to 0.10. All other data for the model (i.e., the course-related parameters for students and faculty, the regular faculty allocation factors, and the variable coefficients for instructional costs and revenue) would remain the same except for the financial aid cost per graduate student, which would have to increase from $\$4$ million$/4,000 = \$1,000$ to $\$5$ million$/4,200 = \$1,190$ (see constraint [3] above).*

With these changes in the constraints, the solution for cohort flows obviously would change; so, too, would the enrollments. New enrollment values in the faculty staffing formulas lead to new FTE values and, consequently, to new instructional costs and revenues. Finally, by taking $\$30$ million as the amount of expense and income that is fixed, i.e., judged not to vary with students or faculty, we can compare the total budgeted expense and income for the campus before and after implementation of the three-year bachelor's program. These comparative results are given in table 5.9.

As one can readily see, the new constraints and parameters would lead to changes in practically every calculated quantity. Moreover, since the changes are of different relative magnitudes and, in many cases, even of opposite sign, they probably could not have been estimated very well without the aid of a model. Looking more closely at the comparison in table 5.8, we see that implementing the new plan would have these effects, not all of which would be salutary from the single institution's point of view:

1. There would be more new students each year at both the undergraduate and graduate levels.

2. Because of the reduced dropout rate for freshman cohorts, the percentage increase in the output of bachelor's degrees (11.9 percent) would be somewhat higher than the percentage increase in undergraduate admissions (8.9 percent).

3. Ninety-five more graduate degrees would be produced per year and the

---

*These changes in constraints and parameters may seem rather ad hoc. We believe, however, that they are illustrative of the kinds of changes that might actually be anticipated by a school like Stanford if it were to consider adopting the three-year bachelor's proposal.

Table 5.9. Analysis of Proposal for Three-Year Bachelor's Degree

	Status Quo	With Three-Year Bachelor's Program	
New Students			
Freshmen	1,528	1,700	(+11.3%)
Transfer	400	400	(....)
Graduate students	1,600	1,711	(+6.9%)
Degrees			
Bachelor's	1,689	1,890	(+11.9%)
Graduate without teaching assistantship	825	954	(+15.6%)
Graduate with teaching assistantship	275	241	(−12.4%)
Enrollments			
Undergraduates	6,500	5,710	(−12.2%)
Graduate students	4,000	4,200	(+5.0%)
Teaching assistants	500	439	(−12.2%)
Faculty			
Regular	650	639	(−1.7%)
Auxiliary	144	135	(−6.2%)
Teaching assistants	500	439	(−12.2%)
Costs			
Instructional (variable)	$32.2 mil.	$31.7 mil.	(−1.6%)
Research cost for regular faculty	11.9	11.7	(−1.7%)
Other	30.0	30.0	(....)
TOTAL	$74.1 mil.	$73.4 mil.	(−0.9%)
Revenue			
Instructional (variable)	$42.6 mil.	$40.1 mil.	(−5.9%)
Research revenue for regular faculty	1.8	1.7	(−5.6%)
Other	30.0	30.0	(....)
TOTAL	$74.4 mil.	$71.8 mil.	(−3.5%)
DEFICIT	($0.3 mil.)	$1.6 mil.	
VARIABLE COST/REVENUE PER DEGREE			
Bachelor's			
Variable cost	$8,340	$6,726	(−19.3%)
Variable revenue	$14,066	$11,344	(−19.4%)
Graduate without teaching assistantship			
Variable cost	$9,760	$9,650	(−1.1%)
Variable revenue	$9,605	$9,605	(....)
Graduate with teaching assistantship			
Variable cost	$15,648	$16,315	(+4.3%)
Variable revenue	$15,450	$15,450	(....)

proportion earning graduate degrees with a teaching experience would decline from 25 percent to 20 percent, due to the reduced demand for TAs.

4. Total enrollment would be reduced from 11,000 to 10,349, and the mix of students would change from 59 percent undergraduate to 55 percent undergraduate.

5. There would be some reductions in faculty FTE but, except in the case of TAs, these would not be proportional to the declines in enrollment.

6. Total costs would go down but total revenue would go down considerably more. According to the model's calculations, the new policy would create a budget deficit of $1.6 million where there was a $300,000 surplus before.

This is due, according to the model, to the loss of tuition revenue from undergraduates who, on the margin, contribute much more than they cost.

7. The cost per bachelor's degree would be considerably less than before, although the decline would be nowhere near the 33 percent some persons might have expected. The effect would be diminished both by transfers (who we assumed would graduate only half a year sooner), and by the significant number of freshmen who already graduated early, even before the changes were made. Because of these students, the degree lifetime was 3.75 years to begin with, instead of a full four years.

While it certainly should not be taken too seriously, this analysis should serve to illustrate the utility of the kind of model we have described. Once it has been implemented in a flexible on-line computer program, the model will enable one to experiment with a variety of basic parameters directly while stationed at the computer terminal. Because the number of variables and parameters is relatively small, and the computer output restricted to a single page of numbers, it is well suited to strategic planning by top-level college or university administrators.

Summary

In this chapter we derive expressions for the production, cost, and revenue functions that we introduced in chapter 3. These are derived with specific reference to instructional programs, whose outputs are taken to be flows of students earning degrees or dropping out, rather than just levels of enrollment in a single year.

First, we review earlier work in the field with cost-simulation models. These are enrollment-driven models that yield estimates of the university resources required to instruct given numbers of students. Usually, the enrollments and resources are described in terms of discrete departmental programs, and hence the models include a rather large amount of detail. A typical formulation is described, and then we discuss the difficulties inherent in this sort of approach when it is applied at a university.

The remainder of the chapter describes the formulation and application of an aggregate production-and-cost model for strategic university planning. A prototype model is developed to help answer such questions as, What will be the effect on instructional costs of changing the mode of instruction (i.e., class sizes, faculty work loads, etc.), or of shortening the time required for a bachelor's degree? Student admission and degree flows are represented in network form, and program lifetimes are used to relate these to levels of enrollment. Faculty staffing levels are computed from enrollments by means of faculty and student work-load factors. The instructional component is then derived through subjective estimates of the relative amounts of faculty effort being devoted to each primary university function.

Finally, cost and revenue functions are constructed from the calculated enrollments and instructional FTE and from their respective unit cost and revenue coefficients. To illustrate both the concept and the utility of the model, liberal use is made of a numerical example.

Notes to Chapter 5

Works cited here in abbreviated form are more fully described in the bibliography at the end of this book.

1. For the RRPM, see Gulko and Hussain 1971; for CAMPUS, see Systems Research Group 1969.

2. Most of the difficulties mentioned in this section are discussed in Alper 1968 and Hopkins 1971.

3. The initial development of the model described in this section is reported in Oliver, Hopkins, and Armacost 1972. A subsequent formulation, which was applied both to Stanford and to the University of California at Berkeley, will be found in Oliver and Hopkins 1976. The model was also applied to data from the University of Colorado by a group of students enrolled in a graduate engineering program there.

Part III

Modeling
for Financial Equilibrium

In part III we explore in depth the problems associated with budget planning for two or more consecutive years. Consideration of the dynamic budgeting problem leads us at last to confront the quicksand in which so many good plans have foundered: that treacherous area known as uncertainty. There is only one outcome of which planners can be completely certain, namely, that nothing will turn out exactly as planned. In the short run, perhaps, the deviations from what was expected may not be very great. But to make only short-run plans is to store up disaster.

Our modeling strategy in the face of uncertainty is to establish two distinct levels of analysis. On the first level, which is explored in chapter 6, we operate in terms of "certainty equivalents," that is, particular forecast values that are assumed to represent future states of the world exactly. These certainty equivalents are central to our method of constructing models applicable to more than one planning period. To call them "central" is not to confess a taste for wishful thinking, since they do in fact represent the most likely future outcomes of actual probability distributions. Planning models based on certainty equivalents are meant to embody feasible plans that permit acceptable tradeoffs between present certainties and future eventualities. Such models tell a university what it can afford to have now in order to be able to afford what it will need for an acceptable future.

The concept of certainty equivalence plays an important part in our model for attaining long-range financial equilibrium (LRFE)—our term for the conditions under which the university budget is likely to stay more or less balanced. Since this is a dynamic model, the notion of what constitutes balanced growth receives as much attention as the problems of balancing the budget at any particular stage of growth. Finally in chapter 6, we analyze our experience with TRANS, a model that was used to plan for the transition to LRFE at Stanford.

The second level of analysis, which deals explicitly with uncertainty, can be applied only after a certainty-equivalent model has been set up. It is recognized, on this second level, that since things won't work out exactly as forecast, modifications in the plans will need to be made year by year. In chapter 7, decision rules are specified for "smoothing" the effects of unexpected events. Attempts are also made to optimize the behavior of operating reserves and similar mechanisms for absorbing financial impacts while this smoothing is taking place. The general concept employed is that of feedback control: the model regulates itself by reacting to externally generated financial impacts. The concept of long-run financial equilibrium is now extended to include particular sources of uncertainty such as the stock market, the cost of living, and fund raising. Here the problem is to find ways to deal with short-term fluctuation in investment return and other financial variables without losing the planning discipline afforded by the equilibrium concept.

With our strategies for absorbing uncertainty and controlling the effects of unexpected events, we show how our dynamic planning system can be installed permanently; it is not just an emergency measure for determining a "budget gap" during a period of crisis. To this end, we develop a control model and use it to establish guidelines for a particular area of budgetary policy, namely, dollar payout from endowment. The model is put through its paces and the results evaluated. Here, too, we use data drawn from our experience at Stanford. We then attempt a more general and theoretical development of feedback control in a series of increasingly elaborate dynamic models with smoothing rules that allow for ever more comprehensive representations of uncertainty.

6

Long-Run Financial Equilibrium

Detailed budget planning is for a limited fiscal period only, but it must be done with a much longer period in mind if it is not to fall short. Unfortunately, the options and values of one period may be hard to reconcile with those of another. We shall refer to this as the *multiperiod problem* and to models that deal with more than one period as *dynamic*.

The multiperiod problem will be dealt with here in terms of *certainty equivalents*, or particular forecast values that are assumed to represent future states of the world exactly. It is further assumed that the relations between decision variables and outcomes in the present or future have been modeled precisely. A certainty equivalent is not just an assumption, however; in fact it can be viewed as a proxy for the future value of the variable in question: we know the situation probably won't come out quite that way but we feel comfortable making plans based on the proxy. Summary measures that can be used as certainty equivalents in studies of probabilistic outcomes include the expected value of the probability distribution and also its most likely (i.e., modal) value.

The medium-range financial forecast (MRFF) discussed in chapter 4 is a prime source of certainty-equivalent proxies. Generally speaking, forecasters are asked to indicate minimum, most likely, and maximum values for the planning variables; the consensus on the most likely values is used in the analysis. The TRADES model that is described in chapter 9 provides a good example of how certainty-equivalent information about the future may be used in planning. There as here, we have been guided by the following general principle.

A necessary objective in certainty-equivalent dynamic modeling is to quantify the tradeoffs between present and future values of the university's tangible planning variables. Since there are many planning variables and a potentially infinite number of future planning periods, some method for reducing the dimensionality of the problem is needed. Such a mechanism is provided by the concepts of *long-run financial equilibrium* and *transition to equilibrium*, which are the subject of this chapter. Quantification of the tradeoffs between present and future activities and values permits more reasoned judgments about the timing of resource commitments, and invites the application of an effective planning discipline or even formal optimization procedures.

Deterministic Dynamic Planning

Generally the problem of dynamic optimization under certainty amounts to finding configurations of current activities, including activities that result in changes in the stocks, that will result in *preferred trajectories* for the future values of both activities and stocks.[1] The spending-saving problem is a good example: for colleges and universities it takes the form of having to set the endowment payout rate and/or decide whether to accumulate or reduce fund balances. Such decisions affect not only current activities but also future stocks of endowments and fund balances, which in turn means they affect future options. The problem in dynamic optimization, then, is to find the time streams of activities, and hence the trajectories of financial balances and other stocks, that are preferred, given the university's value structure.

We open with a general discussion of dynamic planning concepts applicable to colleges and universities. Then the long-run financial equilibrium construct is defined and its characteristics examined. The chapter closes with a model for the transition to equilibrium and a method for linking the new machinery with that of the TRADES model.

The Dynamic Planning Paradigm in Extensive Form

The formulation of the general dynamic optimization problem for colleges and universities (under certainty) was given in chapter 3, where it formed part of our general theory of university choice. We reproduce it here in the two-construct version, where value is maximized over the tangible variables only, subject to a financial constraint. (Production-function and demand information is subsumed in the value and financial functions because the intangible variables are treated subjectively, as described in chapter 3). The model is:

$$\text{Maximize} \sum_{t=1}^{H} d^{t-1} V(X_t, P_t, S_t)$$

with respect to X_t and P_t

subject to the constraints   (6.1)

$$R(X_t, P_t, S_t) = C(X_t, P_t, S_t)$$

$$S_{t+1} = M(X_t, P_t, S_t) \quad (t = 1, \ldots, H)$$

where X_t = the list of activities (i.e., inputs and outputs) at time t

P_t = the list of prices (e.g., the tuition rate)

S_t = the list of stock (e.g., the endowment balance, library holdings, or buildings and equipment)

d = the value discount factor.

We discussed all these variables in chapter 3; the revenue and cost functions were also treated in chapters 4 and 5. As will be seen presently, a specific long-term planning horizon, H, has been introduced purely for convenience.

Equation (6.1) states that present discounted value is to be maximized with respect to the activities and prices for each year up to the planning horizon, H; that the budget must be in balance each year; and that the laws of motion that determine stocks as a function of the previous year's planning variables must not be violated.

A schematic representation of *extensive-form* dynamic optimization is given in figure 6.1. The time horizon is taken as ten years, which is about the minimum for truly long-range planning. There are fifteen decision variables, the same number used in the Stanford TRADES model. (These are the fourteen variables defined in table 9.2, plus the endowment payout rate.) The rightward-facing arrows in figure 6.1 represent the laws of motion that precondition the options in year t as functions of the state of the system in year $t - 1$. The optimization would have to be performed over 150 variables. However, due to value discounting, the decisions for future years would become successively less important, as indicated in the figure.

Despite the existence of powerful mathematical techniques, large-scale dynamic systems like the one just mentioned are very difficult to optimize. For colleges and universities, they present three major difficulties.

1. *Value must be optimized for each future year, subject to the financial constraint for that year.* Since the laws of motion link the decision options in each year to the decisions in previous years, either the optimization must be performed simultaneously for all years or some kind of sophisticated (and difficult) mathematical procedure must be utilized. If the list X has n elements and the list P m elements, then the dimensionality of the problem is $(n + m)H$, which can easily be staggering.

2. *Knowledge about the laws of motion is likely to become increasingly vague as one moves into the future.* For example, it may be possible to predict utility rate hikes or local labor market conditions for next year and maybe the year after, but what about a period of nine or ten years? There appears to be a qualitative difference between approaches to making short- or medium- and long-run predictions that should be taken into account by planners.

3. *Because we are taking a weighted average over the yearly evaluations, the value function* $V(X_t, P_t, S_t)$ *must be defined in terms of numerical scale as well as rankings.* That is, $V(\cdot)$ must be a *utility* rather than a *value function.* (The distinction was discussed in chapter 3.) While the information needed to assess utilities can in principle be elicited from decision makers, the process requires another step in what already is a difficult process.

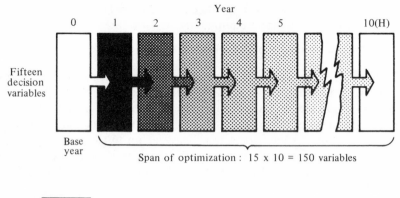

Figure 6.1. Paradigm for extensive-form dynamic planning

The extensive form of the dynamic optimization problem does not provide a very practical handle by which to grasp the multiyear planning problem. A more promising method, as we shall see, is to partition the problem into medium- and long-run components, and deal with the latter in terms of aggregated proxy variables.

Two-Stage Dynamic Planning

Figure 6.2 illustrates how the dynamic planning problem can be spread over a transition period and an equilibrium period. This is the strategy that has been used at Stanford since 1974. It makes the multiyear planning problem intellectually and operationally tractable.

For the transition-to-equilibrium period it is best to think in terms of the medium-range financial forecast (MRFF). The MRFF, as we explained in chapter 4, is highly detailed and is developed from the bottom up, that is, by having many different responsible experts provide information on its subcomponents. For purposes of illustration we have chosen four years as the MRFF time horizon. (In general, somewhere between three and five years seems to us about right.) The MRFF provides the data for the transition period's laws of motion. Since any decision variable may be altered during years 1 to 4, there are fifteen free variables in all for each year of transition to equilibrium.

Beyond the MRFF time horizon both the model and the decision problem are simplified dramatically. First, the set of activity variables is reduced by aggregation. Thus one variable is used for total expenditures, instead of a series of disaggregated variables such as faculty size, staff size, etc. Second, constant growth rates are assumed to apply to the period beyond the MRFF horizon. For example, tuition is assumed to grow by the same percentage in year 5, year 6, and on out to year 10 or beyond. From the material in the next section we have concluded that at least eleven decision variables are needed to

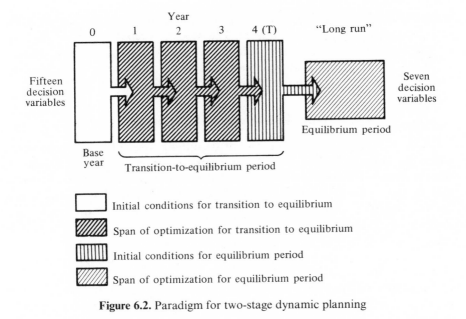

Figure 6.2. Paradigm for two-stage dynamic planning

adequately describe the university over the long run. Of these, four are initial conditions that are determined from the MRFF for the last year of transition to equilibrium. Thus the dimensionality of the problem beyond the MRFF horizon is relatively small.

The power of the two-stage dynamic optimization approach stems from these considerations:

1. The MRFF horizon can be limited to the point where analysts feel comfortable making detailed year-to-year estimates based on relatively specific knowledge or projections. Beyond this point, broad generalities based more on economic reasoning than on specific predictions are used to represent an indefinite future period called the "long run."

2. The simple eleven-variable formulation of long-run financial equilibrium (LRFE) permits the planner to get an intuitive feel for his or her options over the long run. The LRFE model can also be used to perform "back-of-the-envelope" calculations to balance the growth rates of income and expense. These would be difficult to perform with the MRFF by itself. If substantial problems appear to be in the offing, the aggregative transition-to-equilibrium model described at the end of this chapter can be used to provide a year-by-year schedule of modifications to the income-and-expense totals of the MRFF.

3. Finally, either TRADES or some multicriterion optimization model is used to find a preferred solution, consistent with the terminal constraints represented by LRFE, for each year of the transition period.

A wide choice of procedures may be used to implement the two-stage approach. In any case, though, the final output is a series of annual plans for the transition-to-equilibrium period—plans that culminate (at the MRFF horizon) in a satisfactory LRFE configuration. The process is repeated iteratively until all the annual plans and the resulting LRFE can be thought of as jointly preferred, in terms of ranking, to any reasonable alternative. Experience at Stanford suggests this can be done with reasonable time, effort, and training.

Long-Run Financial Equilibrium

LRFE is simply a shorthand way of describing a set of conditions under which the university's budget will stay balanced, or approximately balanced, over a period of years. In other words LRFE represents feasibility over time with respect to the financial constraints discussed in chapter 3 and summarized in equation (6.1). We shall see that there are many ways in which such *dynamic feasibility* can be achieved. Therefore, selection of a particular LRFE configuration is itself a matter of value maximization.

We will begin by specifying aggregate laws of motion and solving them for financial feasibility defined with varying degrees of rigor. Then the properties of the solutions will be examined, after which important tradeoffs and structural questions related to the choice of alternative LRFE configurations will be discussed.

Laws of Motion

A simple but useful representation of a university's cost and revenue functions is in terms of: (a) total expenditure; (b) income from academic operations; (c) income from investments; (d) gifts to the endowment. For present purposes it is convenient to include expendable gifts in revenues from academic operations. To specify the laws of motion we need to define the following variables. (Sample numerical values are attributed to each to illustrate their magnitudes and provide a convenient reference for later examples.)

Activity and stock variables. We begin with variables related to the X and S of our theory of university choice.

Let B_t = total expenditures during year t, regardless of the source of funds ($100 million might be the operating budget of a good-sized private university)

I_t = income from academic operations during year t, including tuition revenue, expendable gifts, indirect cost recovery, and miscellaneous income (we will use $91 million in our examples)

E_t = market value of the endowment at the beginning of year t, where "endowment" is defined to include all funds held for investment, regardless of legal form ($200 million is a good-sized but not incredible amount)

G_t = gifts to the endowment received during year t, where the gifts are added to the endowment at the end of year t and thus increment the endowment market value at the beginning of year $t + 1$ (assume $5 million per year, mostly from major donors and bequests).

We will refer to the activity and stock variables as "levels" to distinguish them from the rate variables, in the strict sense, that will be introduced later. Here, B_t and I_t are aggregative proxies for the activity variables discussed in earlier chapters, while E_t is of course a stock variable. We speak of proxies because the activities themselves are physical or behavioral "happenings," whereas B_t and I_t are built up from components that have been reduced to dollar terms through the application of price coefficients. The level of gifts to endowment, G_t, is of course a proxy for certain fund-raising efforts and outcomes.

Growth rates of expenditures, revenues, and stocks. The level variables will evolve through time as determined by the laws of motion. Therefore, we need to specify a set of rate parameters to describe their growth.

Let r = cost rise on total expenditures, that is, the extra cost needed to fund last year's activity levels at this year's prices (the value of 0.021, net of inflation, that will be used in our examples is a reasonable one to assume over the long-run for an institution of constant size)

i = rate of change of income from academic operations (the value of 0.023 that will be used in our examples, again for an institution of constant size, may be a bit high, given recent trends towards resisting tuition increases)

ρ = total investment return, including interest, dividends, and capital gains (results from the investment simulator described in chapter 4 suggest that a value of 0.055 might be about right)

g = rate of change of gifts to endowment (this is very hard to judge; we will use a value of 0.030, which is a little higher than the probable long-run average growth rate of per capita personal income).

The coefficient r can be computed by taking a weighted average of the cost-escalation factors for the activities in B; that is, r is the university's *internal price* (or *cost-rise*) *index*. Similarly, the coefficient i can be computed by taking a weighted average of the tuition growth rate, the expendable-gifts growth rate, and so on.

It is convenient to think of all these growth rates as being in real terms, i.e., net of inflation. The university's internal price index will generally rise faster than such indices of the whole economy as the CPI or the GNP deflator because of the labor-intensive character of university operations; hence r will be positive even though it is expressed in real terms. For now we will consider all the rates of change to be market determined, and thus not under the control of the university. The tuition rate, however, will be made a decision variable in an extension of the model that we plan to introduce later.

Policy variables. To complete our model we need a few additional variables that describe policies within the institution.

Let f = net budget enrichment factor, that is, the amount of funding for new activities in a given year, less funds transferred from other uses, expressed as a fraction of the previous year's budget

p = the endowment payout rate, that is, the fraction of the previous year's endowment market value that is made available to fund current activities

h = the fraction of new gifts to endowment that is used to provide budget enrichment over and above f.

It is clear that the budget enrichment factor, f, should be nonnegative if at all possible. Historically, values of 3 percent or so have been considered reasonable, but in today's environment, as we shall see, universities may have to live with much less. As for the endowment payout rate, p, for practical (and often legal) reasons it should be less than or equal to total return. There is no economic reason, however, why it should be limited to interest plus dividends; accordingly, it should not be confused with so-called investment yield. Values of p within the 0.04 to 0.05 range are consistent with current attitudes among investment managers and potential donors, though rates of 0.055 or even 0.060 were not uncommon in the late 1960s and early 1970s. Finally, we should point out that new endowment generally provides extra budget enrichment, as represented by h, when it carries tight restrictions that lead to extra and continuing commitments of expenditure by the university. We will assume that the university exercises tight control over these commitments and will therefore assign a value of 0.05 to h. However, the need to provide incentives may well lead the university to make incremental expenditure commitments for one-third, one-half, or an even higher fraction of the payout on new restricted endowment gifts, instead of the 5 percent reflected by our assumption about h. These three policy variables, plus the four growth-rate variables described in the previous subsection, make up the set of seven decision variables assigned to the equilibrium period in figure 6.2 above. Finally, the four activity and stock variables (that is, B_t, I_t, E_t, and G_t) are the four initial conditions we referred to, in our discussion of the two-stage optimization schema, as being outputs of the MRFF.

Basic laws. Now we are in a position to write the law of motion for each of the four activity and stock variables:

$$B_t = (1 + r + f)B_{t-1} + hpG_{t-1}$$
$$I_t = (1 + i)I_{t-1}$$
$$E_t = (1 + \rho - p)E_{t-1} + G_{t-1}$$ (6.2)
$$G_t = (1 + g)G_{t-1}.$$

These laws are straightforward except perhaps for the budget equation (i.e., the one for B_t), which includes new expenditures because of incremental restricted gifts to the endowment. (Recall that gifts received in year $t - 1$ are added to the endowment at the beginning of year t, and thus their payout becomes available to the budget in year t.) The endowment growth is of course equal to total return on investment minus endowment payout (both expressed as fractions of the previous year's market value) plus new gifts.

Alternative Equilibria

Long-run financial equilibrium is defined as budget balance that continues over time. Conditions of varying degrees of stringency (and practicality) can be determined, as we shall now demonstrate.

The least stringent condition is *zero-order* or *static equilibrium*. It requires only that the budget be balanced in the initial year. By "initial year" we mean the last year of the transition-to-equilibrium period shown in figure 6.2. This is the initial condition for the equilibrium period.

$$B_0 = I_0 + pE_0 \tag{6.3}$$

An easy solution is to set the payout rate, p, so as to balance the budget with whatever values of B_0, I_0, and E_0 are desired and/or predicted. If we use the numerical values suggested earlier,

$$p = \frac{B - I}{E} = \frac{100 - 91}{200} = 0.045.$$

Happily, this is within the range of values for p that most informed persons would consider reasonable.

What would happen, though, if the initial budget had been (say) $102 million instead of $100 million? In that case,

$$p = \frac{102 - 91}{200} = 0.055$$

which is a bit on the high side but perhaps not out of the question.

How could one decide whether the higher budget level and payout rate are fiscally prudent? To answer this question we must take account of the growth rates of the planning variables as well as their levels, and consider how the effects of a given policy will unfold over time. Table 6.1 provides some representative results based on our illustrative data. If budget enrichment is at zero, a payout rate of 0.055 is not only prudent but will also generate substantial surpluses. If $f = 0.003$, however, the prognosis for $p = 0.055$ is that there will be deficits. Changing p back to 0.045 almost eliminates the deficits for $f = 0.003$, but no acceptable value of p will balance the budget over time if enrichment is to be as large as 0.6 percent.

The table shows clearly that: (a) there are strong interactions among the

Table 6.1.   Effects of the Enrichment Factor, the Payout Rate, and the Initial Budget on the Evolution of Surpluses or Deficits (in Millions of Constant Dollars)

Budget Enrichment[a] (f)	Payout Rate[a] (p)	Initial Budget[a] (B_0)	Surplus or Deficit After:[b]			Budget in 10 Years
			1 Year	2 Years	10 Years	
0.000	0.045	100.0	0.297	0.607	3.627	123.2
	0.050	101.0	0.259	0.531	3.186	124.5
	0.055	102.0	0.212	0.435	2.653	125.7
	0.060	103.0	0.155	0.320	2.034	127.0
0.003	0.040	99.0	0.027	0.055	0.339	125.6
	0.045	100.0	−0.003	−0.007	−0.040	126.9
	0.050	101.0	−0.044	−0.089	−0.518	128.2
	0.055	102.0	−0.094	−0.191	−1.088	129.5
0.006	0.035	98.0	−0.247	−0.506	−3.077	128.0
	0.040	99.0	−0.270	−0.554	−3.388	129.4
	0.045	100.0	−0.303	−0.622	−3.805	130.7
	0.505	101.0	−0.347	−0.710	−4.321	132.0

NOTE: All dollar figures are net of inflation.
   [a] Other parameters are as described in the text: $I_0 = 91$, $E_0 = 200$, $G_0 = 5$, $r = 0.021$, $i = 0.023$, $p = 0.055$, $g = 0.030$, $h = 0.05$.
   [b] The surplus or deficit is zero in the base year.

various planning variables, interactions that have a very important effect on the financial health of the institution; (b) the growth rates as well as the levels of the variables play a key role. Therefore, any static or *zero-order policy* oriented toward balancing the budget in a single year is bound to fail.

For another example of the interaction between the variables, consider the following scenario. First, the policy for program enrichment is $f = 0.003$, but the current budget is \$102 million and people are reluctant to reduce it. Also, there is a policy that endowment payout must be limited to current yield, that is, to interest and dividends. In order to achieve the desired value of $p = 0.055$, the investment managers shift the portfolio into securities with more current yield but with a total return such that $\rho = 0.040$ (real) instead of, as formerly, the higher value 0.055. A balanced budget is achieved this year, but there will be the following deficits in the future.

1 Year	2 Years	10 Years
0.259	0.522	2.825

(Remember, these figures are in millions of constant dollars.) Now that total return has been reduced by 1.5 percentage points, the deficit shown for $f = 0.003$ and $p = 0.055$ in table 6.1 has nearly tripled.

It is apparent from table 6.1 that there is a combination of planning variables and parameters that produces a balanced budget which is sustainable over time. The rest of this chapter deals with how to find this combination, with the properties of the solution, and with how to make the transition to such a state of dynamic equilibrium. First, though, we need to consider two additional points.

There is considerable evidence to indicate that for private institutions, budget enrichment per FTE student has been at a rate closer to 2.5 or 3 percent per year than to the approximately 0.3 percent needed to balance the budget over time in table 6.1.* For instance, D. Kent Halstead (1975, table II.2) reports data that imply budget enrichment rates of 2.5 percent per year compounded over the period 1961 to 1969, after deflation by the Higher Education Price Index. (The rates dropped dramatically thereafter, averaging only 1.7 percent for the 1969–74 period and only 0.1 percent for 1974 compared with 1973.) William G. Bowen (1968) reported data, drawn from three private institutions, that suggest an f in the range of 3 percent over periods of many years ending in the mid-to-late 1960s. That seems to have been our experience at Stanford as well, as best we can reconstruct it.

While we have not argued the validity of the growth rates in our illustrative example, we believe them to be in the right ball park. Returning to Halstead (ibid., table 1), we find the following compounded annual figures for real cost rise in higher education (recall that we are using the consumer price index as a benchmark for inflation):

	1961–69	1961–74
Higher Education Price Index	4.8%	5.3%
Consumer Price Index	2.3%	3.5%
REAL COST RISE	2.5%	1.8%

These figures are not far from our estimate of 2.1 percent per year. Indeed our estimate may be somewhat conservative, since the decline in the growth of the index in the 1970s may reflect postponement, due to inflation, of certain expenditure increases—higher salaries, for instance—that will have to be made up at a later date. On the income side, our estimate of 2.3 percent growth may be rather high, since it includes growth of tuition at a rate greater than the growth rate of per capita personal income.

Taken together, the evidence implies that, unless new revenue sources can be tapped, the feasible rate of budget enrichment for private universities will be much more like the rates we will be calculating here than the historical ones.

Table 6.1 also shows that while deficits due to growth-rate imbalances cumulate to large numbers, they tend to start quite modestly. Given a history of annual budget enrichment at a high rate to meet "imperative academic needs," it would not be suprising if an emerging growth-rate problem were to be ignored as long as possible—as long, in fact, as the disparity seemed like nothing out of the ordinary and so-called special adjustments and the like

---

*The f in our notation is equal to enrichment per FTE student if the size of the student body is constant.

could be made in various accounts. (Many institutions have various odd sums of money set aside that can be drawn upon to fund what appear to be temporary financial problems.) However, if the basic economic trends have changed, temporizing methods are bound to falter eventually. An institution's failure to look hard at growth rates as well as budget levels can easily mean that it has strayed far from financial equilibrium. It may be some time before the nature, extent, and probable persistence of the problem are diagnosed.

A balanced budget, then, does not necessarily lead to financial equilibrium. Let us propose a second financial desideratum, that of *first-order dynamic equilibrium*. The conditions are

$$B_0 = I_0 + pE_0$$
$$(B_1 - B_0) = (I_1 - I_0) + p(E_1 - E_0).$$

(6.4)

That is, in addition to balancing the budget the institution must insure that the change in expenditure from year 0 to year 1 equals the change in revenue. The reader can easily verify that if the above conditions are met the budget will be in balance for both years.

We will come back to the solution for first-order equilibrium presently. First, though, we might as well define financial equilibria of higher orders. For instance, the addition of

$$(B_2 - B_0) = (I_2 - I_0) + p(E_2 - E_0) \tag{6.5}$$

to (6.4) yields the conditions for *second-order dynamic equilibrium*. The equality of changes in expenditure and revenues up to

$$(B_n - B_0) = (I_n - I_0) + p(E_n - E_0) \tag{6.6}$$

implies n^{th}-*order dynamic equilibrium*. Zero-order equilibrium implies balance of the level variables, while higher-order equilibrium deals with the time derivatives up to the nth order. In other words, we are approximating the trajectories of B, I, E, and G by the first n terms of their respective Taylor's series expansions (see appendix 8 for the mathematical details). Thus the higher the order of the equilibrium, the more stringent the constraints on the policy variables and parameters. The most stringent constraints occur for $n \to \infty$, which is the condition of *perfectly balanced growth* and *infinite-order equilibrium*.

In general, an equilibrium solution of order n does not imply that the budget will be balanced in year $n + 1$. The degree of approximation to balance in year $n + 1$ and subsequent years gets better as n increases, but at a decreasing rate. It turns out that the improvement is very substantial as n goes from zero to one, but then declines rapidly. In other words, use of first-order equilibrium gets us most of the way along the road to perfect long-run financial equilibrium, even though the first-order model is relatively crude compared with the higher-order ones. This is consistent with our experience of other first-order models, as discussed in earlier chapters.

First-Order Equilibrium

Though the conditions for first-order equilibrium are conceptually simple, they are rich in implications for financial planning. We will introduce these implications briefly here, and then go on to comparisons with higher-order equilibria and other issues.

Begin by substituting the laws of motion given in equation (6.2) for B_1, etc., in (6.4), and collecting terms. Then we have the simultaneous equation system

$$B_0 - I_0 - pE_0 = 0$$

$$E_0 p^2 - [\rho E_0 + (1 - h)G_0]p + [(r + f)B_0 - iI_0] = 0.$$

(6.7)

Suppose the initial conditions are fixed. Then the free variables are f, p, and h, since r, i, and ρ are assumed to be market determined. But h is more a function of donor demand than university policy (though it may be influenced by policy), which leaves p and f as the primary policy variables.

Solution for p *and* f. Given the above assumptions, there are two equations and two dependent variables. The solution is obtained by finding p from the first equation in (6.7) and substituting the result into the second. This avoids having to solve a quadratic, and yields

$$p = \frac{B_0 - I_0}{E_0}$$

$$f = \left[\frac{iI_0}{B_0} - r\right] + \left[\frac{\rho E_0 + (1 - h)G_0}{B_0}\right]p - \frac{E_0 p^2}{B_0}.$$

(6.8)

It will be helpful to return to our numerical example at this point. Using the values described earlier for everything except p and f, we have

$$p = \frac{100 - 91}{200} = 0.045$$

$$f = \left[\frac{0.023 \times 91}{100} - 0.021\right] + \left[\frac{0.055 \times 200 + (1 - 0.05) \times 5}{100}\right] \times 0.045$$

$$- \frac{200 \times 0.045^2}{100} = -0.00007 + 0.00709 - 0.00405 = 0.00297.$$

The value $p = 0.045$ is also the zero-order equilibrium solution, and $f = 0.00297$ is very close to the 0.003 that almost balanced the budget over time in table 6.1.

Examples of other solutions. Any pair of variables may be taken as dependent, and their solution (conditional on the other variables) computed from (6.8). For instance, suppose our hypothetical university decided that a 4.5 percent payout rate is too high and a 0.3 percent budget enrichment too low. Analysis of (6.7) suggests that, other things being equal, an increase in the endowment would bring down the payout rate and increase the budget enrichment factor. Suppose that $p = 0.04$ is judged to be about right, and that a capital campaign is to be mounted to increase E_0. How big must the campaign be to get the payout rate down, and how much will the budget enrichment factor go up as a result?

The solution now is for E_0 in terms of p:

$$E_0 = \frac{B_0 - I_0}{p} = \frac{100 - 91}{0.04} = 225.$$

In other words, the campaign must net $25 million. Now f can be obtained from the second part of (6.8):

$$f = \left[\frac{0.023 \times 91}{100} - 0.021 \right] + \left[\frac{0.055 \times 225 + (1 - 0.05) \times 5}{100} \right] \times 0.04$$

$$- \frac{225 \times 0.04^2}{100} = -0.00007 + 0.00685 - 0.00360 = 0.00318.$$

The additional endowment has increased f by only about 0.02 percentage points, though it has reduced the payout rate. Suppose that the campaign also is assumed to double the base level of future gifts, so that G_0 moves from $5 million to $10 million. Then the revised value of f is increased by more than 0.2 percentage points to 0.00508, which might be considered satisfactory. Incidentally, the reason for the bigger effect here is that the extra $5 million of annual gifts to endowment is equivalent to $5/$225 million $= 0.022$ of extra investment return. In other words, this use of the $5 million incremental annual flow has the same effect as moving p from 0.055 to 0.077.

Finally, suppose that a capital campaign is not feasible but a budget enrichment factor larger than 0.00297 is viewed as being imperative anyway. The president of the university might say: "After all, the world of knowledge is broadening and we must be prepared to seize new academic opportunities. Let us reduce the budget now by cutting out the fat, so that we can reach the very modest goal of half a percent of budget enrichment from here on, in perpetuity." How far must the budget be reduced and what will the payout have to be in order to reach the target of $f = 0.005$?

The method of solution for (6.7) is harder, but it is still manageable. First eliminate B_0 from the second equation of (6.7) by substituting in the first equation. Then collect terms. The result is:

$$p^2 E_0 - [(p - r - f)E_0 + (1 - h)G_0]p + [r + f - i]I_0 = 0$$

or

$$200p^2 - [(0.055 - 0.021 - 0.005) \times 200 + (1 - 0.05) \times 5]p$$
$$+ [0.021 + 0.005 - 0.023] \times 91 = 0. \tag{6.9}$$

That is,

$$200p^2 - 10.55p + 0.273 = 0$$

or, more generally, $ap^2 + bp + c = 0$. The "quadratic formula" was invented for situations of this kind. Let us try to apply it.

$$p = \frac{-b \pm \sqrt{b^2 - 4ac}}{2a} = \frac{10.55 \pm \sqrt{111.3 - 218.46}}{2 \times 200}$$

$$= \frac{10.55 \pm \sqrt{-107.1}}{400} \ldots$$

The calculation has come to a screeching halt because the quantity under the square root is negative. If $f = 0.005$, the payout rate is imaginary. Unfortunately, though, imaginary endowment payout won't buy much, so we must conclude that a budget enrichment factor of 0.5 percent is infeasible given the values of the other parameters.

What would be feasible? We can find out by repeating the calculation with different values of f. For our old value of $f = 0.00297$ we have

$$p = \frac{10.95 + \sqrt{120.0 - 70.4}}{2 \times 200} = 0.045$$

which, of course, is consistent with equation (6.8). Once p is determined we calculate the budget by $B = I + pE$, which of course is $100 million. (The larger root of the quadratic is used because more budget is preferred to less; the smaller root produces a payout rate of 0.0064 and a budget of only $92.3 million.) At $f = 0.00333$ we have $p = 0.0388$ and $B = \$98.8$ million. Pushing on toward higher values of f, we come to the point where $b^2 - 4ac = 0$. This occurs at $f = 0.00361$, which implies that $p = 0.0271$ and $B = \$96.4$ million. We can go no farther mathematically; however, the very low value of p suggests we have outrun the limits of practicality before reaching the mathematical barrier.

Among other things, this example is meant to point out the futility of trying to solve growth-rate problems by means of adjustments to levels. Take the improvement of f from 0.00297 to 0.00333, for instance. This amounts to an extra $0.00333 \times 98.8 - 0.00297 \times 100 = 0.032$ or $32 thousand (in constant dollars) of budget enrichment each year, in perpetuity. The "cost" of this is $100 - \$98.8 = \$1.2$ million of base annual expenditure. A rough calculation indicates that it will take $1.2 \div 0.032 = 37.5$ years to "pay back" the effects of budget cutting now. If the $1.2 million is really fat there is nothing but net gain, so the plan should be undertaken. However, the terms of trade for excision of somewhat valuable programs to provide future enrichment opportunities are not very favorable. Of course a payback period of thirty-seven years is specific to our illustrative numbers, but the conclusion is quite general.

Since there are severe restrictions on what can be accomplished through changes in budget, endowment, and other level variables, we ought to turn our attention to changes in the growth rates themselves. For example, consider the effect on f of changing cost rise, operating-income growth, and/or investment return by a factor of 0.005. We assume the level variables are constant and $p = 0.045$ throughout. The following results are computed from equation (6.8).

	Change	f	Change in f
Base case	....	0.00297	....
r	$-.005$	0.00797	0.00500
i	$+.005$	0.00752	0.00455
ρ	$+.005$	0.00342	0.00045
All	$+.005$	0.01297	0.01000

As is obvious from a glance at (6.8), changes in cost rise carry straight through to budget enrichment. However, changes in operating-income growth have only 80 percent as much effect (because operating income is 80 percent of the budget), and changes in investment return, for a similar reason, have only a 20 percent effect. In other words, the effect of the growth rates on each other are proportional to their bases when we are using first-order equilibrium with fixed initial conditions.

Perhaps the most interesting aspect of the above is that adding a constant to all the growth rates has no effect. This can be seen from (6.7) if we look hard: the constant can be factored out as a product of $(B_0 - I_0 - pE_0)$, which of course is zero if the equilibrium conditions are satisfied. We have just shown that the conditions for first-order dynamic equilibrium do not depend on the long-run rate of inflation.

Higher-Order Equilibria

Higher-order equilibrium solutions require n successive years of budget balance beyond the initial conditions, where $n \geq 2$. In this section we shall deal with second-order solutions (for which $n = 2$) and perfectly balanced growth (for which, in effect, $n = \infty$).

Second-order equilibrium. The solution for second-order equilibrium requires the zero- and first-order conditions in equation (6.7), and also the following:

$$(r + f)^2 B_0 - i^2 I_0 - p(\rho - p)^2 E_0$$
$$+ p[h(r + f + g) \tag{6.10}$$
$$- (\rho - p + g)]G_0 = 0$$

This is obtained by setting up an equation for budget balance in year 2 and successively substituting the laws of motion to eliminate all the level variables except the initial conditions. Since there are now three equations, three variables must be taken as dependent.

To explore the characteristics of (6.10), we return to the numerical example of the previous section. The first-order solution for (p, f) was $(0.045, 0.00297)$. Plugging these values and the other assumptions about the coefficients into

(6.10), we obtain an expression for the error in period 2 due to using a solution for $n = 1$. It is

$$\text{Error}_2 = -0.00057B + 0.000053I + 4.50 \times 10^{-6}E_0 + 0.00168G_0.$$

Inserting the initial conditions into the above and completing the calculation, we obtain

$$\text{Error}_2 = 1.22 \times 10^{-5}.$$

This is very small (about \$12.20 to be exact), so the first-order solution fits quite well. Such an outcome, however, should come as no surprise after table 6.1.

Lest we leave the impression that the second- and higher-order equilibrium conditions are completely irrelevant, let us rerun the calculations with $g = -0.10$, that is, with gifts to endowment falling short of the economy-wide rate of inflation by 10 percent. (This would be unfortunate but it is not out of the question given the economic and legislative possibilities.) The first-order equilibrium solution is not affected by changes in g, but (6.10) becomes

$$\text{Error}_2 = -0.000574B_0 + 0.000529I_0 + 5.0 \times 10^{-6}E_0 - 0.0039G_0$$

$$= -0.028.$$

The error is only \$28 thousand but in ten years it will have grown to \$1.086 million, or 0.9 percent of the budget, and in twenty years to \$4.1 million, or 2.5 percent. While it is true that any diverging patterns of exponential growth can produce frightening results if carried far enough, it is also true that small but real variations in growth rates can add up to big differences over the periods considered by planners.

To finish the example we ask what change in the initial conditions would produce second-order equilibrium with the first-order values of p and f. (For this exercise we return to our original assumption that $g = 0.03$.) The results are presented below, along with the first-order data for comparison (the solution procedure is described in appendix 6).

	First-Order Equilibrium	Alternative Second-Order Equilibrium Solutions			
		1	2	3	4
B	100	100.00*	100.17	98.36	99.09
I	91	90.85	91.00*	89.36	90.03
E	200	203.34	203.68	200.00*	201.50
G	5	5.05	5.05	4.96	5.00*

*Indicates that the variable is predetermined.

As shown in the table, second-order equilibrium with $p = 0.045$ and $f = 0.00297$ requires relatively minor adjustments. Since there are three constraints (one each for $t = 0$, $t = 1$, and $t = 2$), there must be three unknowns; hence one variable in each column is predetermined. Adoption of any of the alternatives reduces Error$_2$ to zero. Though Error$_n$ will be nonzero for $n > 2$, after ten years there will be a deficit of only about $500.

In this case the solutions for second-order equilibrium are quite tractable, and though the amount of improvement is small, a purist might be tempted to use the second-order conditions as a practical criterion for a university's financial health. This would be a mistake. The second-order equilibrium solution is quite unstable, as is illustrated by the following array of solutions (for E predetermined), which are based on different values of the growth rate for gifts to endowment.

g	0.025	0.0275	0.03	0.03007
B	12.0	44.6	98.4	100.0
I	3.0	35.6	89.4	91.0
G	3.0	3.8	5.0	5.0
E	200.0*	200.0*	200.0*	200.0*

*Indicates that the variable is predetermined.

Tiny changes in g produce big changes in the initial conditions needed for second-order equilibrium. (Similar results would be obtained if any other variable were predetermined.) Second-order solutions with positive values for B, I, and G cannot be obtained for any value of g much below 0.025.

The foregoing demonstrates that whereas first-order equilibrium is very important, the results of applying the second-order conditions are not operationally meaningful. We now turn to the conditions for infinite-order equilibrium—conditions that, while even more rigorous than the ones for second-order equilibrium, are easier to understand and therefore easier to simplify.

Perfectly balanced growth. By perfectly balanced growth we mean that all four components of the budget are growing at the same rate. The conditions for such growth involve both the growth rates and the initial conditions. This is not true of first- and second-order equilibrium, where solutions can often be obtained for any combination of growth rates, initial conditions, or both—in the requisite numbers, of course. Perfectly balanced growth requires the following constraints.

On growth rates alone:

$$i = g$$
$$i > \rho - p$$
$$i > r + f \text{ if } h > 0$$
$$i = r + f \text{ if } h = 0.$$

On initial conditions and growth rates:

$$(r + f - i)B + hpG = 0$$
$$(\rho - p - i)E + G = 0 \qquad (6.11)$$
$$B - I - pE = 0 \quad (I > 0).$$

The derivation is provided in appendix 8. However, the interested reader should be able to infer the necessity for $i = g$ and $i = r + f$ if $h = 0$ by inspection of the laws of motion (equation [6.2]). The inequality constraints on the growth rates are necessary if the level variables are to be positive.

The data of our numerical example do not meet the conditions for perfectly balanced growth. For one thing, $i \neq g$. Also, $r + f = 0.021 + 0.00297 = 0.02397$, which is greater than $i = 0.023$. Suppose, however, that i were increased to 0.030—as it could be if, for instance, a greater long-term rate of tuition growth were selected. Since the conditions on the growth rates are now satisfied, we can proceed to solve equation (6.11). Suppose E is predetermined at $200 million, as in some of our earlier examples of second-order solutions. Now we can solve for G, then B, and finally I. Unfortunately, the results are:

$$G = 4.0 \quad B = 1.5 \quad I = -7.5$$

which of course is absurd.

Let us make another try. Suppose the fraction of endowment gifts that leads to commitments for new programs, h, is set at zero rather than 0.05. This is a small change. Now the constraint on the growth rate requires that $i = r + f$, which permits the budget enrichment to be determined as follows:

$$f = i - r = 0.030 - 0.021 = 0.009.$$

(Recall that i was increased to 3 percent so that it is equal to g.)

Since the left-hand side of equation (6.11) is zero for all B and G, we are free to set I at its original value of $91 million and compute G and B from the last two equations. The result is:

$$B = 100 \quad I = 91 \quad G = 4 \quad E = 200 \quad \text{(predetermined)}$$

or

$$B = 102.25 \quad I = 91 \quad G = 5 \quad E = 250 \quad \text{(predetermined)}.$$

Other combinations are possible, of course.

Alternatively, suppose g is set at 0.023, the original value of i. Since g probably is not known with much precision, this may not do violence to anyone's convictions. Then (again for $h = 0$) we have $f = 0.023 - 0.021 = 0.002$, and

$$B = 100 \quad I = 91 \quad G = 2.6 \quad E = 200 \quad \text{(predetermined)}$$

or

$$B = 108.3 \quad I = 91 \quad G = 5 \quad E = 384.6 \quad \text{(predetermined)}.$$

While the above numbers are not pathological, anyone could be pardoned for doubting whether it really is worthwhile to reduce gifts from $5 million to $2.6 million (assuming endowment cannot be increased) in order to achieve perfectly balanced growth! However, these and similar results in this section are in the "back-of-the-envelope" category. If they are pursued from time to time, the result will be a growing understanding of how rates and levels interact in university finances.

Let us give just one example of the kind of insight that can be important. Suppose $g = i$, so that the basic condition for perfectly balanced growth is satisfied. Now divide the second equation in (6.11) by E and rearrange. The result is:

$$\rho - p + \frac{G}{E} = i.$$

The quantity G/E is important enough to have its own symbol.

Let $\zeta = G/E$, that is, new gifts to endowment expressed as a fraction of the current endowment market value.

It is obvious that ζ has the effect of adding to "effective investment return."

Now substitute $G = \zeta E$ in the first equation and divide through by B. Then the constraints can be written as

$$r + f + (hp\zeta)\frac{E}{B} = i = \rho + \zeta - p = g. \tag{6.12}$$

It can be seen that B, I, E, and G all grow at the same rate, as is required for perfectly balanced growth. Furthermore, since G and E grow at the same rate, ζ is constant over time—just as we have shown it.

Equation (6.12) is very convenient for analysis, because once p is determined such that the initial budget is balanced, all the other rates can be obtained without reference to the initial conditions other than the ratio B/E. (Even that vanishes if $h = 0$.) We will use this property in the transition-to-equilibrium model, which will be discussed later in this chapter.

Perfectly balanced growth may have some intrinsic merit as well as being a technical-mathematical convenience. The fraction of the budget supported by endowment remains constant over time. This means the university retains the same reliance on investment income, as opposed to revenues from current operations and gifts. Considerations of intergenerational equity also rate here, because the university's financial assets will pay for the same fraction of costs in the future as they do now. Furthermore, if the growth rate of tuition is equal to i, which is another reasonable condition for perfectly balanced growth, the idea of intergenerational equity also applies to students' and parents' tuition payments.

On the other hand, these arguments can be overdone. The growth rates of the components of B and I, it may be objected, will not be equal over long periods; hence there will be needs and opportunities that will at times dominate the criterion of perfectly balanced growth. Indeed, the constraints needed for perfectly balanced growth may have little to do with financial reality.

This objection applies with particular force to the assumption that ζ is time-invariant. A perfect correlation between G and E implies, among other things, that success in fund raising varies inversely with the level of p that is set by policy. But the relation should if anything be positive, since with a high payout rate a given amount of endowment buys more program, which implies a lower effective price to the donor and hence is likely to lead to greater demand. Likewise, there would appear to be no compelling reason for allowing policy on tuition growth to be determined mechanically by (for example) government tax treatment of charitable donations of appreciated property—treatment that will exert a strong effect on g.

Finally, this is a good context in which to note that while gifts to endowment may look like extra return on investment so far as unrestricted funds (or the programs that draw on them) are concerned, their effects may be materially different. Consider an endowed faculty chair in an institution where the endowment payout is supposed to cover all the expenses associated with the faculty member, with no aid from general funds. From equation (6.12) we can see that, other things being equal, a high level of gift flow means a larger payout rate. Suppose that faculty chairs are priced with this level of p in mind. Because new gifts are continually being added to the endowment, it will grow at the same rate as the budget. But a given endowment fund, once received, will grow only at the rate $\rho - p$, while the expenses associated with it may grow at about the rate r. Empirical data suggest that $\rho - p$ is less than r by perhaps 0.5 to 1.5 percentage points, as it is in our example. Therefore, the chairholder may expect to get caught in a cost squeeze of 0.5 to 1.5 percent a year (or perhaps a total of 25 percent during a faculty member's tenure) unless corrective action is taken.

One obvious action would be to require $\rho - p = r$. However, for our illustrative data this would mean that $p = 0.055 - 0.021 = 0.035$, which undoubtedly is too low for a variety of practical and policy reasons. Another approach might be to try to funnel a share of new gifts to endowment into old endowment funds. This would a good idea if, and only if, the strategy had donor appeal. (We understand one prestigious private university is giving it a try.) Otherwise the only answer is to supplement payout from existing restricted endowment funds with general funds when the need becomes material.

Tradeoffs Involving Rates

Deterministic dynamic equilibrium models are particularly helpful in defining tradeoffs among growth rates and other rate variables such as f and p. Recall the two-stage characterization of the dynamic optimization problem that we discussed in connection with figure 6.2. Here, the second-stage optimization problem is to maximize value with respect to the characteristics of the equilibrium period (defined in terms of growth rates) and the initial conditions (which result from choices made during the transition-to-equilibrium period), all of which are subject to the constraint of long-run financial equilibrium.

Since both p and f are policy variables, which can be used to compensate for the effects of external forces, they are involved in some very important tradeoffs. The value of h can also be used as a policy variable, though its effect is less than that of p or f. Finally, the growth rate of tuition cannot be overlooked as an important policy variable, especially for selective institutions. We have not yet had occasion to focus on tuition apart from noting that it is a component of operating income, but it is not difficult to extend the model to deal with it explicitly.

Let T_t = tuition revenue in year t, which is equal to the number of students or FTE enrollment times the tuition rate (suppose here that tuition accounts for $50 million out of $80 million of operating income)

τ = growth rate of tuition (for the moment assume a value of 0.025, net of inflation)

F_t = student financial aid expenditures in year t (assume this is $15 million, or 15 percent of total expenditures).

For simplicity we assume that the growth rate of student aid is the same as the growth rate of tuition, though more realistic aid models were discussed in chapter 4. Here, I_t and B_t are redefined as other operating income and other expenditures, respectively, and r and i as their growth rates. (Formerly τ was included in both i and r.) Budget enrichment f is assumed to operate only on nonfinancial aid expenditures.

The equations for first-order equilibrium are readily generalized from the simultaneous equation system (6.7):

$$B_0 + F_0 = T_0 + I_0 + pE_0$$
$$p^2E_0 - [pE_0 + (1 - h)G_0]p + [(r + f)B_0 + \rho F_0 - \rho T_0 - iI_0] = 0. \tag{6.13}$$

Any two variables from the expanded set may be taken as dependent, and a first-order equilibrium solution obtained for them in terms of the remaining variables. Perfectly balanced growth (with $G_t/E_t = \zeta$ and $h = 0$) now requires

$$r + f = \tau = i = \rho + \zeta - p = g. \tag{6.14}$$

In other words, everything must grow at the same rate, and the proportion of tuition revenue to total revenue and of aid to total expense must remain constant over time.

Perfectly balanced growth in this expanded model suffers from a major drawback: the tuition growth rate, τ, must be equal to the growth rate of other operating income, i, which is determined mostly by external factors not related to student demand. Hence equation (6.14) is too restrictive to be of much use in practice.

Types of tradeoffs. Tradeoffs in equation (6.13) can be separated into four types, depicted in figure 6.3. A tradeoff of type 1 involves only rates other than p, one of type 2 involves only level variables, one of type 3 involves p and other variables, and one of type 4 involves both rates (other than p) and levels. Let us consider each type separately.

1. Tradeoffs of type 1 are linear, and occur in pairs. For instance, the tradeoff of f versus τ, with everything else the same, is

$$f = \text{constant} + \left[\frac{T_0 - F_0}{B_0} \right] \tau$$

where the constant is easily determined from the second part of (6.13). An example of this type of tradeoff, based on numerical values from the example used previously, is given in the upper left-hand corner of figure 6.3. (Another example, based on actual Stanford data, was presented in figure 2.3).

2. Tradeoffs of type 2 are linear and occur in groups of three (this type of tradeoff, as we have said, does not involve rates, but we include it here for completeness and continuity). Consider B_0, E_0, and G_0, for instance. Collecting terms in (6.13) for these three variables yields

$$B = k_{10} + k_{11}E$$
$$B = k_{20} + k_{21}E + k_{22}G$$

where the coefficients are obtainable by inspection. Specifying any two variables determines the third. Thus, if someone proposed a capital campaign to increase the endowment, E, and the annual rate of giving, G, we would also have to consider a budget adjustment, B, in order to obtain equilibrium. This tradeoff is illustrated in the upper right-hand corner of figure 6.3, where the solution is seen to sweep upward along the budget balance line as G_0 increases from \$5 million to \$15 million.

3. Tradeoffs of type 3 must allow change in variables in addition to p, and at least one of them must be a level variable. This can be seen by following the effect of a change in p through (6.13). Initially, there must be a change in a level variable in order to restore equality to the first part of the system. This, in turn, requires a change in a growth rate, or G_0, to rebalance the second part. The resulting equations are quadratic, so not all tradeoffs involving p have real solutions. (We have already reviewed an example of an imaginary solution for p.)

A tradeoff of type 3 is illustrated in the two middle panels of figure 6.3, where p, f, and B are assumed to vary (I is held constant in this example, as indicated in the lower panel). Increases in f are seen to decrease p and B at an accelerating rate until, finally, the discriminant of the quadratic form for p becomes negative and p becomes imaginary. This is the point at which the curves for p and B turn under: larger values of f are impossible unless other data are changed. Note too that since, other things being equal, more expenditures are preferred to less, the positive root of the quadratic in p is chosen.

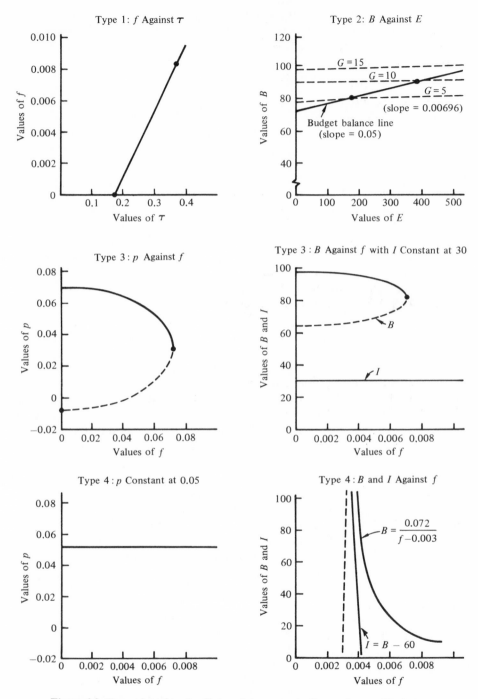

Figure 6.3. Examples of tradeoffs involving rates in first-order equilibrium

4. Tradeoffs of type 4 also occur in groups of three, since both parts of (6.13) are involved. The equations may be linear or nonlinear, depending on the choice of variables. The bottom panel of figure 6.3 gives an example. The right-hand portion shows how B and I vary with f, while the left-hand portion emphasizes that p is held constant. Note that B and I go to infinity as f goes to 0.003, and I goes to zero as f goes to 0.0042. An important lesson that we have considered before is being demonstrated here. The lesson is that it is very difficult to solve growth-rate problems by manipulating only level variables, as we are trying to do when variations in f are permitted only to affect B and I. Since the growth rates are fixed, only the mix of expense and income items can be changed. This is not much leverage, and the level variables must be shifted a great deal in order to have major impact.

The payout rate's critical role. By now it should be clear that the endowment payout rate is a central planning variable for those institutions lucky enough to have sizable endowments. This is because it provides the only direct link between levels and rates. By this we mean that p not only plays a major role in balancing the budget; it is also a major determinant of the endowment growth rate and therefore of endowment payout. We have just seen that the degree of leverage offered by type 4 tradeoffs is modest. Tradeoffs among growth rates with p fixed do not affect levels at all.

We are led to conclude that p is a very important dynamic control variable. It should be set not only to sustain the future purchasing power of the endowment but also to moderate the effects of changes in the external world upon the internal world of the university. This "smoothing," in turn, will permit a more preferred point on the university's value function to be reached and avoid some of the adjustment costs that otherwise would be associated with a changing external environment. The value of p that satisfies (6.13), for LRFE, provides a benchmark to which payout should return after smoothing has been completed. As such, it provides the discipline needed to avoid undue spending from endowment resources.

Table 6.2 dramatizes the point that p is an important control variable. The first pair of columns portrays the effect on B of changes in data when p is allowed to take up some of the slack. The second pair of columns holds p fixed and forces any adjustment between rates and levels to be made indirectly through changes in the revenue mix. The figures shown are *elasticities*; thus, they are the amount of change in the column variable needed to compensate for a 1 percent change in the row variable while maintaining first-order equilibrium. For instance, a 1 percent change in $r + f$ (i.e., 0.00062) requires a -1.77 percent change in B (to \$95.6 million) and a -11.54 percent change in p (to 0.0416). (Note that this table, because of its origin, does not separate out tuition revenue and uses different data than the examples used earlier.)

In all cases the amount of budget adjustment needed to compensate for a change in data is far less when p is allowed to vary than when it is not; the factors of difference are in the range of fifteen to fifty. While it is true that more complicated tradeoffs involving (say) two rates (other than p) and two level

Table 6.2.   Elasticities of Selected Equilibrium Solutions with Respect to Parameters and Initial Conditions

	Two-variable solutions with:			
	$I = 82.4$		$p = .055$	
	B	*p*	*B*	*I*
Base solution	97.3	0.047	40.8	23.2
Elasticity with respect to:[a]				
$r + f$	−1.77	−11.54	−30.07	−52.84
i	1.41	9.22	17.60	30.93
ρ	0.41	2.67	20.47	35.97
h	−0.01	−0.04	−0.28	−0.49
p	n.a.	n.a.	−10.86	−19.85
B	n.a.	n.a.	n.a.	n.a.
I	0.80	−0.31	n.a.	n.a.
E	0.10	−0.31	−4.31	−8.33
G	0.11	0.69	5.31	9.33

SOURCE: Massy 1976, table 1, p. 252. Reprinted with the permission of *Management Science*.
NOTE: Dollar figures are in millions (see text).
[a] $r = 0.062, i = 0.060, \rho = 0.095, h = 0.05, f = 0.0, E = 320, G = 8.3.$

variables can sometimes stabilize the system with *p* fixed, we cannot avoid the fact that *p* is likely to be the single most important variable for this purpose.

Many remember the days when prudent university administrators were bound to peg the payout rate at the level of endowment yield as determined by dividends and interest. Of course, that policy abdicates the use of *p* as a dynamic control variable. Then came the freewheeling days of the so-called total-return philosophy, under which most or all capital appreciation was viewed as a candidate for expenditure on the grounds that "money is money, regardless of the source." Many institutions including Stanford lost money when the stock market went down in 1974; however, there would have been a real problem even in the absence of market risk.

The problem with the original total-return philosophy of making payment independent of yield was that no corresponding discipline was placed on the spending-saving relation. The link between rates and levels was ignored, and so there was no assurance that the purchasing power of the endowment would be sustained. The results of this chapter provide the needed discipline, but without regard to any distinction between yield and gain. Therefore, it is possible to make payout independent of yield, which seems eminently desirable and justifiable, while avoiding the problem of excess payout.

An alternative discipline, based on a simplified view of equilibrium, is to set the payout rate equal to the difference between total return and the university's rate of internal cost rise. (A simpler version of the same thing is to use the difference between real total return and the CPI.) The approximation is fairly good if budget enrichment, *f*, is set equal to the annual payout on new gifts to endowment, and becomes perfect if operating income also grows at the rate $r + f$. (These are just the conditions of equation [6.12], with $f = \zeta$.) However, there ought to be a better reason for requiring these conditions than to provide a prima facie discipline for setting the payout rate. This alternative, then, is not as general, or as useful, as is LRFE itself.

Certainly a strong discipline is needed on the endowment payout rate, since it determines the university's spending-saving position. Short-run expenditure should not be the deciding factor here. However, the discipline of even first-order financial equilibrium is adequate in most cases. Ad hoc restrictions on p, like tying it to yield or to a simple cost-rise formula, are unnecessary. To the extent that the first-order conditions need to be buttressed, the proper approach is to work through the characteristics of alternative equilibria and smoothing procedures, not to peg p at an arbitrary value.

Characteristics of the equilibria. Aside from the values of the parameters and initial conditions themselves, the following are potentially important characteristics of any given LRFE solution: (a) the effective *order* of the equilibrium, as measured by the expected surplus or deficit some years in the future; (b) the *fractions of the budget* supported by endowment, tuition, and the rate of change of these fractions over time. We already have explored (a) at length, so let us turn our attention to (b).

Universities with different values of pE/B and T/B will rely to different degrees on the capital market (i.e., investment) as opposed to the market represented by student demand. The capital market is probably the more reliable generator of income over the long run; at any rate, it permits more diversification than can be had in terms of student demand alone, and the return does not depend on what happens on campus (except, naturally, for the university's decisions about investment policy). On the other hand, the capital markets are far more volatile on a year-to-year basis than is student demand, especially in the case of selective institutions. Certainly most institutions would prefer to rely on endowment than tuition revenue, and additions to endowment do of course tend to ease the pressure on the tuition growth rate. Arguments of a similar type can be made with respect to the ratio of expendable gifts to total revenue, and (for a disaggregative model) with respect to reliance on direct charges and indirect cost recovery on grants and contracts and the like. If the mix of income items is an important characteristic of an equilibrium, then the relative growth rates of the various items must also be important. If one is satisfied with the current mix, then balanced growth should be the ideal even though it may have to be sacrificed in order to achieve more important objectives.

The university's value function should include certain important fractional breakdowns for income, with their rates of change. The TRADES model displays the fraction of operating income accounted for by tuition revenue and endowment payout. Other possibilities are the fractions of revenue represented by indirect cost recovery and expendable gifts, respectively. These are not in themselves decision variables, but they can be computed as functions of the decision variables.

The same line of argument can be applied to the mix of expenditure components. For instance, what fraction of the budget is accounted for by support services? What fraction by faculty salaries? How are these fractions changing over time? Here, though, the focus is less on volatility or exposure to adverse market trends, as is the case for income, and more on the direct implications of budget decisions. (There are exceptions, as with energy costs, for example.) The basic point is that planners ought to concern themselves with the fine structure of an equilibrium solution—that is, with the mix of income-and-expense items and how it is expected to change over time—as well as with such basic policy parameters as budget enrichment and tuition growth.

Transition to Equilibrium

Chronologically, the transition to equilibrium is the first part of our two-stage representation of university choice (see figure 6.2). Starting from a given base year, we propose to effect an optimal series of choices covering the years up to the medium-range planning horizon. These choices will produce the initial conditions for a preferred equilibrium configuration that can be applied to later years. We have defined the transition-to-equilibrium period as coinciding with the medium-range financial forecast (MRFF). The MRFF is based on detailed and disaggregative inputs. The growth rates of expenditure and revenue components, and of policy variables like f, p, and h, may therefore be expected to vary year by year. In contrast, we assume that *all* the growth rates and policy variables are constant during the post-MRFF period.

An Aggregative Transition-to-Equilibrium Model

TRANS, the model to be described in this section, determines the size of the special adjustments in expenses, income, or both, that will be needed during the transition period in order for an equilibrium with certain specified characteristics to be achieved at the end of the period. The TRANS model, as we have recounted in chapter 2, was created and used at Stanford in 1974.[2] This was after we had worked out the equilibrium concepts but before we had developed the TRADES model, with its capacity for making disaggregative expense and income adjustments year by year. A method for using TRADES and TRANS together will be presented later.

Transition period. The main part of the TRANS model is a system of equations describing cash flows during the transition period. In addition, there needs to be a constraint requiring a balanced budget at the end of the transition period (i.e., as the initial condition for equilibrium), and a decision rule for moving the endowment payout rate from its initial value in the base year to the chosen equilibrium value.

The cash-flow equations are simple extensions of the laws of motion, modified to deal with the MRFF data and to allow for budget adjustments and deficits.

Let A_t = the "gap" to be filled in year t by means of a special expenditure and/or income adjustment, where $t = 1, \ldots, T$ denotes the years of the MRFF period (the A_t's are the key dependent variables of the system)

ϕ = the proportion of gap closing that represents reduction in expenditures rather than additions to income (the value of ϕ is estimated judgmentally and entered in the model)

c_1 = the proportion of expenditure reductions in a given year that, though removed from the operating budget, will still cost money in that year (the values of the c's are also judgmental inputs)

S_t = the "bottom line" for the budget (positive values are surpluses and negative ones deficits).

It is assumed that measures taken to close the gap will be enduring, i.e., that they will be carried over into future periods as part of the continuing budget base. The variable defined as c_1, in contrast, is essentially a phaseout cost. The coefficients c_2 and c_3 are defined in the same way, except that c_2 refers to the previous year's gap closers and c_3 to the year's before that. In this model, surpluses are assumed to be added to and deficits subtracted from endowment.

Other variables are defined as in the section on long-run financial equilibrium, except that the growth rates and policy variables are permitted to vary from year to year during the MRFF period. The MRFF, as we showed in chapter 4, contains projections for a great many object categories of income and expense. These data permit calculation of the year-to-year growth rates of total expenditures, r_t, and total operating income, i_t. (The values r_t and i_t include the effects of planned tuition increases and any enrollment changes, both of which are dealt with explicitly in the MRFF.) Estimates for gifts to endowment in each year are also contained in the MRFF; they will be denoted by G_t. If there is any reason to believe that ρ_t will deviate from its long-run value, this, too, can be included in the MRFF and hence in the TRANS model.

Assume a specific equilibrium value for the endowment payout rate (the method by which it has been specified will be discussed later). It will take effect at time T, and be denoted by p_T. However, p_T may not be the same as the base-year value p_0. Hence a decision rule governing the transition from p_0 to p_T must be specified. One such rule is linear change:

$$p_t = p_0 + \frac{p_T - p_0}{T}.$$

(Other perhaps more realistic rules are possible, of course.) Changes in p_t affect the deficit, which in turn produces a dollar-for-dollar adjustment of the endowment. Hence the decision rule for p_t does not affect the values of A_t, which are the model's main results. The rule's importance, then, is purely cosmetic.

Now we are ready to write the cash-flow equations based on the laws of motion, and by so doing complete the model.

$$B_t = (1 + r_t + f_t)B_{t-1} - \phi A_t \quad (t = 1, \ldots, T)$$

$$I_t = (1 + i_t)I_{t-1} + (1 - \phi)A_t \quad (t = 1, \ldots, T)$$

$$E_t = (1 + \rho_t - p_t)E_{t-1} + G_{t-1} + S_{t-1} \quad (t = 2, \ldots, T) \tag{6.15}$$

$$S_t = I_t + p_t E_t - B_t - \phi(c_1 A_t + c_2 A_{t-1} + c_3 A_{t-2}) \quad (t = 1, \ldots, T)$$

$$B_T = I_T + p E_T.$$

Several points should be noted.

1. The gap is allocated between expenditure reduction and income improvement, but no distinction is made between tuition revenue and aid expense, on the one hand, and other expenditures and other operating income on the other. These breakdowns do not affect cash flow, and they may be tracked outside the model.

2. The surplus or deficit in each year includes the effect of phaseout costs even though these expenditures have been eliminated from the ongoing budget base. Though the differences are irrelevant to the determination of cash flows, it may be desirable to report the two components of the deficit separately.

3. There is no endowment equation for year $t = 1$. This is because E_1, the endowment value at the beginning of year 1, is given by the MRFF.

4. The last equation specifies that the budget must be balanced at year T, the end of the transition period (that is, S_T must equal zero). This is a required initial condition for long-run financial equilibrium.

The dependent variables in (6.15) are B_t, I_t, S_t, and A_t, where $t = 1, 2, \ldots, T$; and E_t, where $t = 2, \ldots, T$. This adds up to twenty-four variables. However, there are only twenty equations. If a solution is to be obtained, either four additional constraints must be specified, or a value function introduced and maximized. For simplicity we choose the first approach. (Of course, it should be understood that the following equations do represent a series of value judgments about when to try closing the gap.) The additional equations are

$$A_1 = \delta_1(A_1 + A_2 + A_3 + A_4 + A_5)$$

$$A_2 = \delta_2(A_1 + A_2 + A_3 + A_4 + A_5)$$

$$A_3 = \delta_3(A_1 + A_2 + A_3 + A_4 + A_5) \tag{6.16}$$

$$A_4 = \delta_4(A_1 + A_2 + A_3 + A_4 + A_5)$$

In words: the amount of gap assigned to year 1 is to be a fraction, δ_1, of the total gap, and so forth. (An equation for year 5 would be redundant, since the deltas sum to one.) The values of δ must be based on judgments as to the speed with which the university should proceed with budget adjustments. When applying the model at Stanford in 1974, we started with $\delta_1 = 0.20$, $\delta_2 = 0.65$, $\delta_3 = 0.15$, and $\delta_4 = 0$ (see chapter 2). Our objective was to get the job of gap closing over with as soon as possible, but there was a great deal of concern about how much could be accomplished during the first year. Hence δ_1 was set at a rather small value, whereas δ_2 was large. In the light of experience we later modified this to $\delta_1 = \delta_2 = 0.40$, $\delta_3 = 0.20$, and $\delta_4 = 0$.

With (6.16) there are now twenty-four equations and twenty-four unknowns. The system is linear, so it is easy to obtain a solution. Indeed, the original version was programmed in APL and debugged in less than a day; moreover, it cost only pennies to run. Sample results from that application will be presented shortly.

Equilibrium period. The transition-period equations provide gap-closing targets, etc., that are conditional upon a prespecified rate of endowment payout, namely, the equilibrium value that we have called p_T. The critical role of p_T should come as no surprise given our previous findings. How should it be determined? Clearly the value chosen must depend upon the long-run growth rates and policy variables f, τ, etc. The general relation was given by equation (6.7), which is written here with the appropriate time subscript of the transition-to-equilibrium model:

$$E_T^2 p_T - \left[\rho E_T + (1 - h) G_T \right] p_T + (r + f) B_T - i I_T = 0. \qquad (6.17)$$

Note that the value of p_T holds for the equilibrium period generally, so we could have just written p instead.

Suppose that the long-run budget enrichment factor, f, is determined by policy and input to the model. Then a solution for p_T could be obtained from (6.17). The solution, however, depends on E_T, B_T, and I_T, which are obtained from (6.15). Furthermore, the dependence in nonlinear, so we cannot simply add (6.17) to the system in (6.15) and (6.16) and solve by means of simultaneous linear equations.

A practical way out is to proceed iteratively. A starting value for p_T is assumed, the transition-period solution is calculated, the results are plugged into (6.17) to obtained a new value of p_T, and the process is repeated until convergence is obtained. Usually only one or two iterations are needed, since p_T is sensitive only to the relative magnitudes of B_T, I_T, and E_T.

In some cases it will be acceptable to specify that the equilibrium is to exhibit perfectly balanced growth; that is, equal rates of growth for expenditures, operating income, the endowment, and gifts to endowment. The resulting conditions on the growth rates and long-run policy variables are given by equation (6.12), above. If $h = 0$ we can compute p_T from

$$\rho + \zeta - p_T = i = r = f \qquad (6.18)$$

which, of course, does not depend on B_T, I_T, or E_T. The transition and equilibrium solutions are separable in this case, since we can solve (6.18) for p_T once and for all.

In closing, we should note that the model can be respecified so that income improvements and expenditure reductions affect tuition revenue and student

Table 6.3. Planning Estimates for the Transition to Equilibrium (All Dollar Figures in Thousands)

	0[a] 1974/75	1 1975/76	2 1976/77	3 1977/78	4 1978/79	5 1979/80	Equilibrium 1980/81
Inflation (INF)	....	0.075	0.060	0.055	0.055	0.050	0.050	INF = 0.050
Cost rise (r_t)	....	0.102	0.090	0.082	0.079	0.073	0.073	$r = 0.0456 + 0.243\tau$
Funded improvement (f_t)	....	0.010	0.010	0.010	0.010	0.010	0.010	$f = 0.010$
Income growth (i_t)	....	0.005	0.034	0.073	0.025	0.054	0.054	$i = 0.0176 + 0.700\tau$
Endowment total return (ρ_t)	....	0.102	0.102	0.102	0.102	0.102	0.105	$\rho = 0.105$
Gifts to endowment (G_t)	....	$4,765	$4,700	$4,560	$4,850	....[b]		$\zeta = 0.017$
Tuition (T_t)	$3,375	$3,800	$4,225	$4,650	$5,075	$5,500	$5,964[c]
Endowment (E_t)	....	$116,221	$121,645	$129,067	$140,565	$152,863	$164,186
Payout rate (p_t)	0.0740	0.0685	0.0627	0.0572	0.0513	0.0455	0.0455
Endowment payout ($p_t E_t$)	....	$7,958	$7,633	$7,390	$7,208	$6,963	$7,471
Operating income (I_t)	$55,755	$60,290	$65,422	$71,416	$76,435	$82,129	$88,426
TOTAL INCOME ($I_t + p_t E_t$)	....	$68,248	$73,055	$78,806	$83,643	$89,092	$95,897
Preliminary budget ($[1 + r_t]B_{t-1}$)	....	$71,889	$76,768	$76,398	$81,486	$88,245	$95,006
Funded improvement ($f_t B_{t-1}$)	....	$652	$704	$706	$755	$822	$891
Budget reductions (A_t)	....	($2,112)	($6,864)	($1,584)	$0	$0	$0
PLANNED BUDGET (B_t)	$65,235	$70,429	$70,608	$75,520	$82,241	$89,067	$95,897
Phaseout expenditures	....	$1,056	$3,960	$2,719	$1,082	$158	$0
SURPLUS/DEFICIT (S_t)	....	$3,237	$1,513	($567)	($320)	$133	$0

SOURCE: Hopkins and Massy 1977, table 1, p. 1166. Reprinted with permission of *Management Science*.

[a] Only data actually needed as input to the model are shown.

[b] The equilibrium rate of gifts to endowment is assumed to hold in year 5, since the Campaign for Stanford will have ended.

[c] In equilibrium, $\tau = 0.0844$.

financial aid costs disproportionately. We have followed this strategy in our later work and believe it to be a good idea generally. In this case an iterative solution will be required whether or not there is perfectly balanced growth with respect to endowment and operating income.* The reason is that i and r will depend on the amount of gap closing computed during the transition period. Again the effects are of the second order, so the iteration converges rapidly.

A sample application. We described in chapter 2 how the transition-to-equilibrium model was used in 1974 to determine Stanford's Budget Equilibrium Program target, hereafter called "the gap." We are now in a position to review the assumptions and results of the model run in more detail.

Table 6.3 presents the MRFF data and long-run assumptions, with the results of the central model run. All figures below and to the right of the dividing line were calculated by the model, the others being input data. Growth rates are given in nominal terms, with the assumed rate of inflation shown in line 1. More for convenience than for anything else, perfectly balanced growth was chosen as a condition of long-run financial equilibrium. In this early application, all adjustments were assumed to take place on the expenditure side (i.e., $\phi = 1$). The annual gap-closing assignments were set at $\delta_1 = 0.20$, $\delta_2 = 0.65$, and $\delta_3 = 0.15$; the phaseout coefficients were $c_1 = 0.50$, $c_2 = 0.25$, and $c_3 = 0.10$.

The program was written so that different values of the long-run budget enrichment factor, f, and the tuition rate at the end of the transition period were entered on line. The long-run growth rate of tuition could then be determined from equation (6.18), and the values for r and i calculated from the formulas shown in table 6.3. In these formulas the coefficients for τ—0.243 and 0.700—represent the fractions of expenditures and operating income that are accounted for by student aid and tuition, respectively. The MRFF growth rate, i_t, to the left in the table, excludes tuition revenue, which is calculated separately. Once τ, r, and i are determined it is a simple matter to obtain p from (6.18).

The base year's payout rate was 0.0740 because of the sharp drop in the market value of the endowment that had occurred during spring and summer 1974. (The payout rate originally planned for that year was 5.9 percent.) This was adjusted linearly to the computed equilibrium value of 0.0455, as shown in the table. A target tuition rate of $5,500 for 1979/1980 was selected judgmentally, and the starting tuition adjusted to it in equal arithmetic increments. Values for B_0 and I_0 were obtained directly from the current year's budget (1974/75), while that for E_1 was calculated by projecting forward the September 1974 market value of the endowment to the beginning of fiscal 1975/76 with $\rho = 0.102$.

The model predicted that about $10.6 million of budget reductions (in

---

*This was the method used in TRANS II, discussed in chapter 2. The original and simpler TRANS I model, also discussed there, assumed perfectly balanced growth, with $h = 0$ and no disproportionate effects.

current dollars) would be needed in order to achieve equilibrium in 1980/81.*
Substantial deficits were forecast during the first two years even if the targeted
budget reductions were achieved. The last two years represented relatively
minor adjustments, mostly to compensate for phaseout costs.

This run assumed a total return on the endowment of 10.2 percent during
the transition period and 10.5 percent thereafter. The equilibrium total return
was set at a real rate of 5.5 percent, while that for the transition period aggregated to a real rate of 4.3 percent compounded over five years. These critical
assumptions were made after discussions with the cognizant university officers
and with professional contacts in the field of finance. The funded improvement
factor, f, was set at the lowest value we felt could be achieved consistently.
(In recent years total funded improvements have been in the neighborhood of
2 to 3 percent of the previous year's budget.) The resulting value of τ was a
real rate of about 3.4 percent. The value of $5,500 that was entered for tuition
in 1979/80 represented a real rate of about 4.4 percent compounded growth
during the transition period.

Table 6.4 presents some sensitivity analyses that were useful in assessing the
conclusions to be reached from the model. Run A is the one given in table 6.3.
Run set B was presented to members of the Board of Trustees and various
faculty advisory groups in October 1974, about the time that a gap of $10
million or more was announced. It showed that the size of the target was *not*
particularly sensitive to the assumed variations in endowment total return—an
important finding for the skeptics who believed our problem would go away
"when" (not "if") the stock market rebounded. (The calculated gap was
somewhat more sensitive to the budget enrichment factor. Even so, the main
problem with a larger value of f was the bigger tuition growth rate associated
with it.)

Run C calculates the transition path for a "stretched-out" budget reduction
program; the values of c in equation (6.16) were revised so that 20 percent of
the total reductions would be made each year. The dollar value of the total
gap increases, but since the model is couched in nominal rather than real
terms this could be misleading. However, the value of the budget in year 5
is a valid basis for comparison, so we can see that stretching out the gap-closing
process "costs" about half a million dollars of program in that year. This is
because the deficits total nearly $14 million, compared to about $4 million in
run A, which leads to a lower terminal endowment value.

Set D investigates the effect of substituting an arbitrary value for p in place
of the equilibrium value. Our purpose here was to address the criticism that
we, the model builders, might be "creating" a huge hardship in the name of
an abstract concept—equilibrium. Legal factors and general prudence would
have prevented Stanford from sustaining a payout rate greater than about 6
percent, and there were strong arguments in favor of a 5 percent limit. There-

---

*Actually, the original model runs predicted $10.2 million, as described in chapter 2. The run
being discussed here is the one that was listed for 11/21/74 in the second line of table 2.6.

Table 6.4.   Sensitivity Analyses of Transition Model Results (All Dollar Figures in Thousands)

Run Set	f	ρ_t	τ	p	Budget Reductions	Budget in Year 5	Endowment at Start of Year 5
A	0.01	0.102	0.084	0.046	$10,600	$89,100	$153,000
		0.102		0.046	$10,200	$89,500	$162,000
B	0.01	0.080	0.084	0.046	$10,700	$88,900	$148,000
		0.150		0.046	$8,900	$91,100	$198,000
		0.102		0.031	$11,200	$92,500	$169,000
B	0.02	0.080	0.104	0.031	$11,500	$92,100	$154,000
		0.150		0.031	$9,900	$93,700	$206,000
		0.102		0.061	$9,300	$86,400	$156,000
B	0.00	0.080	0.062	0.061	$10,000	$85,000	$142,000
		0.150		0.061	$7,700	$88,400	$189,000
C	0.01	0.102	0.084	0.046	$11,900	$88,600	$145,000
				0.046	$10,200	$89,500	$162,000
D	0.01	0.102	0.084	0.050	$9,700	$90,200	$160,000
				0.055	$9,200	$90,800	$158,000
				0.060	$8,700	$91,500	$157,000

SOURCE: Hopkins and Massy 1977, table 2, p. 1167. Reprinted with the permission of *Management Science*.
NOTE: All runs made October-November 1974.
Run A: final planning estimates, with phaseout expenditures (from table 6.3).
Run B: variations of *f* and ρ; no phaseout costs.
Run C: effect of stretching the budget reductions equally over five years; phaseout costs calculated as in A.
Run D: effect of setting endowment payout in 1979/80 and beyond at arbitrary values as shown. Except for $p = 0.046$, these do not represent terminal equilibrium solutions. Phaseout costs are not included.

fore, run D made it clear that bringing down the endowment payout rate to obtain equality of the income-and-expense growth rates for 1980–81 was not by itself a major cause of Stanford's problems.

Completing the Transition

We are now in a position to understand the conditions for long-run financial equilibrium and the adjustments needed to get there. The necessary calculations, as we have seen, can be performed in terms of aggregate variables and policies. The results must now be linked to a detailed representation of the university such as that provided by the TRADES model. First, however, let us pause for a moment to look back over the road we have just traveled.

Summary of deterministic dynamics. This chapter began with an analysis of deterministic optimization over time—an analysis in terms of value maximization subject to constraints. However, the dynamic model in its extensive form was deemed too complex for ordinary use. Therefore we developed separate representations of the medium- and long-term future under the rubric of, respectively, the "transition-to-equilibrium" and "equilibrium" periods. The former was the province of the medium-range financial forecast (MRFF), later supplemented by the TRANS model, while the latter was founded on long-run growth rates and analyzed by means of the long-run financial equilibrium model.

We proceeded to base our formulation of the LRFE model on a set of aggregate variables and laws of motion. The conditions for dynamic equilibrium were explicated and their properties studied. An understanding of the relations between rates and levels, of tradeoffs involving rates, and of the endowment payout rate's critical role as a control variable were among the fruits of this analysis. As a general rule, first-order equilibrium was found to produce an adequate set of conditions for a proper spending-saving discipline and long-term financial helath. First-order equilibrium requires budget balance in two successive years and hence consideration of rates as well as levels. Zero-order equilibrium, or budget balance in a single year, is not an adequate condition for financial health. Higher-order equilibria up to perfectly balanced growth can be specified, but the increasingly stringent conditions they involve will not usually be acceptable for policy planning. The rate of change in tuition revenue for instance, or in the fraction of the budget supported by endowment payout, is itself an indicator of balanced growth (or the lack of it), and concern should focus on such rates rather than on the order of the equilibrium as such.

Finally—to determine "how to get there from here," so to speak—we married the conditions for long-run equilibrium to the data from the MRFF. We accomplished this with the TRANS model. Though operating in terms of aggregate laws of motion, the disaggregative MRFF data can be added up to produce aggregative quantities for input to TRANS. What TRANS can offer is a practical understanding of how to get past short-run transient conditions to achieve an acceptable long-run condition of budget equilibrium. In other words, the long-run equilibrium conditions place a "terminal constraint" on choices in the transition period, thus reducing a problem with a potentially infinite horizon to one involving only three to five years.

An iterative procedure for "sizing the gap." In 1974 the transition-to-equilibrium model produced a "gap" of about $10 million for Stanford. As we explained in chapter 2, an implicit judgment was made that this target could be achieved mostly by improvements in efficiency and marginal changes in operations. We committed ourselves to closing this gap without forming any very clear idea about what the consequences would be for academic programs. Certain aggregative policy variables such as budget enrichment, tuition growth, and the size of the gap itself were considered, but no quantitative judgments were made about number of faculty, degree of staff support, tenure ratios, or specific departments or programs.

While such a plunge was necessary given Stanford's situation and the state of our modeling in 1974, we do not recommend it as a general approach. There are many alternative equilibrium configurations and these will produce gaps of different sizes. Tradeoffs among these alternatives should not be divorced from consideration of what measures will be needed to close any gap once it has been targeted. Coming to grips with these measures may well require further tradeoffs among disaggregative expenditure and income variables. The entire issue can be explored by means of the TRADES model, which will be described in chapter 9. We shall outline the approach now, though the reader may wish to study the materials on TRADES in chapter 9 as he or she moves forward.

PROCEDURE 6.1. The following steps provide a procedure for developing a plan for transition to equilibrium, taking account of disaggregative expenditure and income variables. The approach is to alternate the use of TRADES and TRANS, in iterative fashion, until one is satisfied with the results from both models.

1. *Execute TRADES in forecast mode, projecting to the end of the MRFF period.* This is equivalent to running the MRFF program, which we assume has been incorporated into TRADES (see chapter 9). A starting set of initial conditions for long-run equilibrium will be generated by this step.

2. *Experiment with alternative equilibrium configurations.* Use the aggregative equations presented earlier in this chapter; or the TRADES model, which should be running in tradeoff mode based on long-run growth rates; or both. The output of this step is a set of long-run policies for f, τ, and p. They must be consistent with the long-term growth rates and with either the starting initial conditions from step 1 or a tentative modification of them.

3. *Enter f, τ, p, etc., into TRANS and solve for the gap and the other dependent variables.* Note that the value of ϕ needed for TRANS can be set judgmentally; it may also be calculated from the tentative adjustments obtained in step 2. The output of the present step is a set of figures on aggregative expenditure and revenue that covers each year of the transition-to-equilibrium period, including year T (the planning horizon). The figures will be consistent with first-order equilibrium.

4. *Cycle back to step 2 and use TRADES to find a new equilibrium solution.* This step, of course, is optional. The new solution is based on B_T, I_T, and E_T from step 3, and on the disaggregative growth rates and policies. Note that B_T, I_T, and E_T can be incorporated directly into TRADES by the specification of these three new constraints:

$$B_T \leq \bar{B} \quad I_t \geq \bar{I} \quad E_{t+1} \geq (1 + \rho + \zeta - p)\bar{E} \qquad (6.19)$$

where $\bar{B}$, etc., are the TRANS results, for $t = 1, \ldots, T$.

It may be desirable to run the new values of p, f, and τ through TRANS to see whether B_T, I_T, and E_T have changed significantly. If they have, step 4 should be repeated. In any case, the output of this step is an equilibrium position that is preferred in terms of *both* level *and* rate variables.

5. *Return TRADES to the base year and move forward to develop more detailed plans.* In other words, make tradeoffs for each year of the transition period. For each incorporate constraints of the form (6.19), using the TRANS value of B_t for $\bar{B}$, etc. If there is little or no slack in each year's preferred solution, the overall result will be consistent with the final run of TRANS. The result will be a series of adjustments to the primary planning variables that will result in a preferred LFRE configuration at the end of the MRFF period.

This five-step procedure, while apparently complicated, works out quite naturally once the user has gained a basic mastery of TRADES and TRANS and of the equilibrium concepts in general. Step 3, which involves TRANS, can be left out if the overall degree of budget adjustment is modest and/or the equilibrium policies are firmly in place. However, it is easy to lose intellectual control of a succession of tradeoffs for different years, especially when significant deficits or surpluses affect future options and the long-run target values are not firmly in mind. The role of the TRANS model is to force consistency between cash flows and fund balances during the transition period, and between rate and level variables during the equilibrium period. It then provides a series of annual milestones, B_t, I_t, and E_t, to guide the development of more detailed strategies by means of TRADES.

Summary

The chief purpose of this chapter is to determine financial conditions for stable budget growth. These conditions are developed as though future values of all the relevant variables and parameters were known with certainty. Models constructed on the basis of such "certainty equivalents" are useful in quantifying the tradeoffs between present and future values of university planning variables. It follows that they are also useful in mapping out a viable financial future for the institution in question. Where information about the nature and extent of uncertainties in future budgets is needed, the more advanced models described in chapter 7 can be applied.

Central to the development of feasible plans for budget growth is the concept of long-run financial equilibrium (LRFE), which refers to a set of conditions under which the budget is likely to stay balanced, or approximately balanced, over a period of several years. First to be introduced are the structural equations that describe, in aggregate terms, budget growth between consecutive time periods. Conditions for financial equilibrium are then established—conditions that can be solved for feasible configurations of the important budget planning variables. Alternative solutions are examined, and important tradeoffs and structural questions related to the choice of alternative configurations are discussed with reference to representative numerical data from Stanford University.

At this point, we return to the problem of multiyear budget planning. Operational solutions are obtained from the conditions for LRFE only after these conditions are imbedded in a more elaborate model for planning the transition to equilibrium over a sequence of years. The TRANS model determines the size of the special adjustments in expenses and income that are needed during a transition period (generally, the period of time covered by the university's medium-range financial forecast) in order for an equilibrium with certain specified characteristics to be achieved by the end. The basic formulation is given, as are the details on how it was used to set the numerical target for Stanford's Budget Equilibrium Program in 1974.

The chapter concludes by tying together the aggregate LRFE and transition-to-equilibrium models with the TRADES model for conducting tradeoff analyses and budget planning in less aggregate terms. A procedure is outlined for working one's way back and forth between the models to obtain an optimal plan for the short-to-medium run in terms of the institution's primary planning variables.

Notes to Chapter 6

Works cited here in abbreviated form are more fully described in the bibliography at the end of this book.

1. The theory and practice of dynamic control in most contexts requires considerable mathematical effort. The interested reader may wish to consult Bellman and Dreyfus 1962 for a general treatment. Our models are based on more restrictive assumptions and thus are more tractable.

2. A version of the model was reported in Hopkins and Massy 1977. An account of how and why the model was successful in aiding Stanford's financial planning during the budget crisis of 1974/75 can be found in Massy 1978.

7

Financial Planning Under Uncertainty

Nothing is more certain than that forecasts and plans will not come out exactly as anticipated. In this chapter we address the problem of taking into account the probable discrepancy between anticipation and outcome. Strategies must be found for predicting the nature of this discrepancy and coping with it when it occurs. Of course, forecasts and plans based on new outcomes are no less uncertain than their predecessors, and this fact must be recognized.

Our discussion of financial planning under uncertainty will proceed in four phases: (a) a brief review of the theory of uncertainty and the principles of dynamic control; (b) a discussion of the annual budgeting cycle and how it can take account of the need for coping with uncertainty; (c) development of a first-order model for control under uncertainty and application of this model to the issue of Stanford's endowment payout; (d) generalization of the model to higher-order and more powerful control systems. In addition to providing normative guidance about how to smooth budgetary fluctuations affecting income and expense items, the model will tell us which results fall within tolerable limits. Although a degree of variation between forecast and outcome is always to be expected, variations beyond a certain size should inspire both surprise and remedial action. Our models for financial planning under uncertainty show when to be surprised.

Basic Principles of Probability and Control

In this section we will outline briefly some basic ideas about how to characterize uncertainty or risk, and how to deal with it through dynamic control models that we will characterize as "stochastic." According to the 1963 Funk and Wagnalls *Standard College Dictionary*, the word "stochastic" means "denoting the process of selecting from among a group of theoretically possible alternatives those elements or factors whose combination will most closely approximate the desired result." One objective in this chapter is to present models that attempt to do just that.

An Example Based on Investment Risk

Consider as a motivating example the total return on investment for endowment funds, which (our research indicates) is the most volatile of all the financial variables. Up to now we have assumed that total return is always the same, year after year—impossible, of course. A better way is to view total annual return, expressed as a percentage of the fund's market value, as having a probability distribution with a mean or expected value and a variance or measure of dispersion.

Expected value. For a representative portfolio of stocks and bonds the expected value might be calculated as follows. (The actual magnitude of these figures is subject to much discussion and controversy, and there is no real consensus on the matter.)[1]

	Real Rate of Return		Expected Inflation		Risk Premium (Stocks) or Liquidity Premium (Bonds)		
Expected return for common stocks	0–1%	+	$X\%$	+	6.5%	=	Total return
Expected return for bonds	0–1%	+	$X\%$	+	0–1.5%	=	Total return

The *real rate of return* is the amount investors need in order to compensate them for postponing other potential uses of their money; in other words it is a time discount or "impatience" factor. When the rate of inflation anticipated by investors is added in we have the expected return on a *risk-free asset*. To this must be added an amount that compensates the investor for the assumption of risk. Such an amount is called a *risk premium* in the case of stocks and a *liquidity premium* in the case of bonds. Note that if a bond could be turned in for par value at any time, there would be no loss of liquidity and no risk either, other than that of default. Since bonds, when default is not a factor, can be sold at market (as opposed to par) value, the liquidity premium is really a compensation for assuming risk.

Figures for expected total return are usually based on long-term geometric averages of actual total returns. That is, the figures are weighted geometric averages of possible total returns, with the long-run frequency of occurrence of each return figure taken as the weight. The figures given above are "guesstimates" based on long-term averages of Standard and Poor's index of 500 common stocks and the Salomon high-grade bond index. Obviously, the expected total return for particular stocks and bonds will differ from the market aggregates. Also, the total return of an endowment portfolio consisting of both stocks and bonds (and of risk-free assets such as US Treasury bills, for that matter) will be an arithmetically weighted average of its component total returns. (See chapter 4 for discussion.)

We would be amazed if the total return on our portfolio were precisely at its expected value in any given year. A host of economic, political, and psychological factors affect the capital markets and lead to deviations from long-

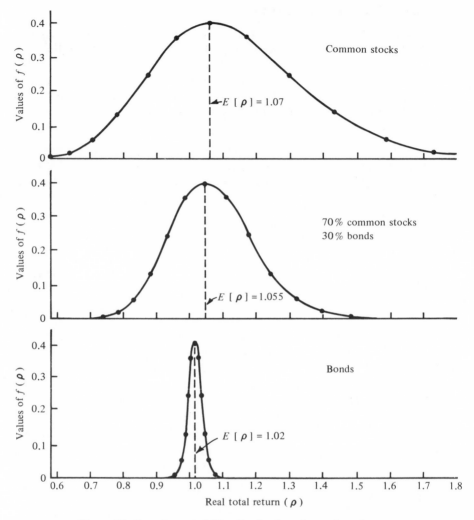

Figure 7.1. Sample probability distributions for real total return
for common stocks and bonds

term averages. These effects cannot be predicted, but their overall impact can
be represented by the probability distribution of total return. Figure 7.1 shows
the approximate distribution of real total return (actually, $1 + \rho$ where ρ is
total return net of inflation) for common stocks, bonds, and a 70/30 percent
mix of the two. The shape of these distributions is what is called "log-normal"
(note the long right-hand tail). The expected values are the ones given earlier.
The *standard deviation* (or σ) is a measure of dispersion: we have estimated
it to be 21.5 percentage points for common stocks, 2.0 percentage points for
bonds, and 12.0 percentage points for the mixed portfolio.

The Stanford Investment Simulator output shown in figure 4.4 differs from the foregoing because: (a) inflation is included, and the run assumes high inflation; (b) the portfolio mix is 60 percent common stocks, 30 percent bonds, and 10 percent treasury bills; (c) some of the underlying data assumptions are slightly different. We want to emphasize that the distributions shown in figure 7.1, as well as all the data in this example, are for demonstration purposes only and should not be used for decision making.

The total return parameter, ρ, in the certainty-equivalent models of chapter 6 can be thought of as the expected total return of the endowment portfolio. Suppose the portfolio were 100 percent in common stocks. Then ρ would equal 0.07. But in any given year the actual value of ρ might easily be as low as -0.12 or as high as $+0.30$. (This is the range of plus or minus one standard deviation, a range that encompasses about two-thirds of a normal distribution.) Neither would be consistent with our calculations of long-run financial equilibrium. Of course the range of probable variation could be reduced dramatically by going to a portfolio consisting entirely of bonds, or it could be reduced to zero by investing fully in Treasury bills. Unfortunately the increase in precision would be achieved only at a substantial cost in expected total return, which would go down to perhaps 2 percent in real terms for bonds or from 0 to 1 percent in real terms for T-bills. What a difference *that* would make in the LRFE calculations! Clearly a mechanism is needed to cope with investment risk and, if possible, to optimize the tradeoff between expected total return and risk that was discussed in chapter 4.

The problem of stochastic control can be more clearly defined in terms of the first-order conditions for long-run financial equilibrium. Suppose that there is a (naive) policy of holding the payout rate constant, and of always adjusting the budget and operating income so as to restore equilibrium the year after any deviation from expected investment return is observed. Also, suppose for the present that investment return is the only source of uncertainty; everything else comes out exactly as anticipated. Even the amount of endowment payout used to support current expenditures is fixed at the beginning of the academic year, and is adhered to regardless of how the portfolio fares during the year.

The process is illustrated in figure 7.2. Since it goes on year after year we can break in at any point we find convenient after the plans for year t are set. Plans are denoted by putting a caret, "^", over the variables, as shown in the first box in the figure. After the year is over we discover the actual as opposed to the planned values of the variables. In our simple example we assume that there is no uncertainty except with respect to total return. Accordingly, the second box shows actual values as equal to planned ones except for the market value of the endowment, which is displaced by a random disturbance, $u(t)$. We assume that $E(t)$ is the endowment balance at the end of year t.* Prior

---

*Specification of an ending balance is a change from the notation in chapter 6, where $E(t)$ referred to the *beginning* value of stocks. It turns out that the beginning value was convenient there but that the ending value is more convenient here. In this chapter, then, $E(t)$ refers to the ending market value of the endowment, after gifts have been added and payout deducted.

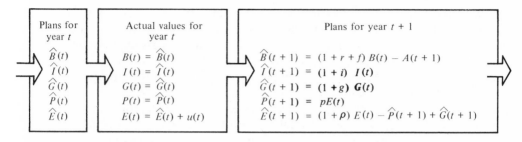

Figure 7.2. A rudimentary stochastic control model

to the start of that year we had expected it to be $\hat{E}(t)$, but the vagaries of investment performance over the year have produced $E(t)$ instead. However, the payout (in dollars) was planned to be $\hat{P}(t)$, and since spending commitments have already been made this is not changed over the year (i.e., $P(t) = \hat{P}(t)$). The risk inherent in year t's total return will show up as an effect on the payout in year $t + 1$.

How can the disturbance term $u(t)$ be related to the probability distributions for total return that we discussed above? To anticipate development later in this chapter we write

$$u(t) = E(t)\varepsilon(t)$$

where

$$\varepsilon(t) = \rho(t) - \rho$$

is the deviation of total return in year t from its long-run expectation ρ. This formulation is consistent with the fact that $\varepsilon(t)$ has a log-normal probability distribution with a large standard deviation.

The final step in this rudimentary model is to prepare plans for year $t + 1$, as shown in the third box in figure 7.2. These are based on the now-known value of $E(t)$. Chronologically the steps are:

1. Set dollar payout equal to $pE(t)$, i.e., at the equilibrium payout rate times the endowment market value as of the end of the previous year (or the beginning of this year), which has just been observed.
2. Project "normal" cost rise, budget enrichment, and operating income growth, based on the parameters r, f, and i, which must be consistent with p in the first-order LRFE equations.
3. If total return deviated from its expectation last year (which was to be anticipated), this year's projected budget will not balance even though the expected growth rates of income and expense are equal, as required by LRFE. The gap is closed by a budget adjustment equal to $A(t + 1)$, which restores LRFE until a new deviation in total return occurs.
4. The endowment market value at the end of year $t + 1$ is projected by calculating expected growth due to investment return, minus payout, plus

new gifts. This step is not necessary in order to compute the budget adjustment for year $t + 1$, but it is necessary in order to complete the picture and prepare to repeat the cycle for time $t + 1$.

Table 7.1 shows some hypothetical results from applying the above process. The parameters used to generate tables 7.1, 7.2, and 7.3 are as follows (all growth rates are in real terms):

$$r = 0.021 \quad i = 0.025 \quad \rho = 0.055$$

$$f = 0.005 \quad h = 0.000 \quad G/E = 0.025$$

This produces first-order equilibrium with $p = 0.05$, as can be verified from equation (6.7). The probability distribution of total return is assumed to be log normal with $\rho - \sigma = -0.057$ and $\rho + \sigma = +0.181$. About two-thirds of the probability is encompassed within this range. (The asymmetry is due to the skewness of the log-normal distribution.) All monetary values are in millions of constant dollars.

The left-hand column of table 7.1 gives the initial conditions; they are assumed to have been the actual values for year t. The rest of the table gives alternative sets of plans for year $t + 1$, depending upon how return on investment turned out during the previous year. For instance, if there has been no deviation of actual from expected total return the market value of the endowment at the beginning of year $t + 1$ will be $412 million, dollar payout will be $20.6 million, and no base adjustment will be needed to balance the budget. However, if total return has been off by one standard deviation (i.e., if $\rho(t)$ has been at -5.7 percent in real terms instead of $+5.5$ percent) the endowment market value will be $412.0 - $44.8 = $367.2 million. Then dollar

Table 7.1. Effect of Investment Risk on Budget Adjustments: Payout Rate Fixed and No Smoothing (Hypothetical Data)

		Deviation from Plan		
		$\rho(t) = \rho$	$\rho(t) = \rho - \sigma$	$\rho(t) = \rho + \sigma$
	Planned at End of Year t			
E	$412	$0	$-$44.8	$+$50.4
	Actual for Year t		Planned for Year $t + 1$	
p	0.050	0.050	0.050	0.050
P	$20.0	$20.6	$18.4	$23.1
I	$80.0	$82.0	$82.0	$82.0
B	$100.0	$102.6	$100.4	$105.1
			Needed Budget Adjustment	
A	n.a.	$0	$-$2.2	$+$2.5

NOTE: Money values are in millions of constant dollars. For parameter values, see the text.

payout will be only \$18.4 million and a base adjustment (i.e., a budget reduction) of \$2.2 million will be needed to balance the budget. If, on the other hand, total return has been up by one standard deviation, a favorable adjustment of \$2.5 million will be possible.

It is as well to remind ourselves that the "normal" budget increment over and above cost rise (f , the budget enrichment factor) is only 0.005, or \$500 thousand in this example. Yet in one year out of three, on the average, an additional change that *exceeds* the range of $-\$2.2$ to $+\$2.5$ million will be needed to compensate for unplanned fluctuations of investment return. Clearly the unplanned budget adjustments dominate the planned rate of budget enrichment! Indeed, the probability that the net budget enrichment will be negative (i.e., that a negative adjustment will exceed normal enrichment) is a whopping 47 percent in this example. (This calculation is based on the fact that the loss of \$500 thousand of payout is equivalent to losing 0.17σ of endowment market value.) Thus there will be net budget reductions 47 percent of the time even though net enrichment is targeted at an annual rate of $+\$500$ thousand.

A number of approaches are available for stabilizing the situation. The most natural one, based on the discussion in chapter 6, is to free up the payout rate and obtain a first-order equilibrium solution for B and p based on the quadratic form in equation (6.9).* Table 7.2 shows what happens if this is done. The new equilibrium solutions for p are 0.052 and 0.047, which would seem to be acceptable. However, the needed budget adjustments are still $-\$1.4$ million and $+\$1.1$ million. This is still too large a range when one considers we are encompassing only two years out of three.

An alternative approach is to spread out the period of adjustment over a number of years. The rationale for this is that a bad result one year may be offset by a good one in the future, so that the need for drastic action may be avoided. Indeed, spreading out the adjustment can be an effective strategy whether or not one expects bad years to be followed by good years more often than not. The general idea is to refrain from leaping forward after good deviations in order to avoid having to slam on the brakes whenever a bad one occurs.

This process of spreading out the adjustment over a period of years is called *smoothing*. A popular method of smoothing endowment payout is to apply the desired payout rate to a moving average of endowment market values (i.e., to an average taken over the most recent n years). The result is that some of the year-to-year fluctuation is eliminated while a link to market values is maintained over the long run. Although we do not like this method—it weights all n years in the calculation equally—we see it as a step in the right direction.

---

*Recall from chapter 6 that first-order equilibrium solutions require two free variables, which here are B and p. In the earlier solutions with p fixed (as in table 7.1), B was allowed to vary but a second free variable was needed as well. This could easily have been f. However, if f had been designated as the second free variable the resulting changes in it would have been small and completely dominated by the variance in investment return. Hence we ignored it to simplify the discussion.

Table 7.2. Effect of Investment Risk on Budget Adjustments: Payout Rate Varies
According to First-Order Equilibrium Conditions (Hypothetical Data)

	Actual for Year t	Planned for Year $t + 1$		
		$p(t) = p$	$p(t) = p - \sigma$	$p(t) = p + \sigma$
E	$412	$0	$-$44.8	$+$50.4
p	0.050	0.050	0.052	0.047
P	$20.0	$20.6	$19.1	$21.7
I	$80.0	$82.0	$82.0	$82.0
B	$100.0	$102.6	$101.1	$103.7
		Needed Budget Adjustment		
A	n.a.	$0	$-$1.4	$+$1.1

NOTE: Money values are in millions of constant dollars. For parameter values, see text.

Later we will have an alternative to suggest; meanwhile let us see how far we
can get with the moving-average approach.

Using an *n*-period moving average reduces the standard deviation of total
return by a factor of about $1/\sqrt{n}$. Table 7.1 appears to support a reduction of
σ from 0.12 to perhaps 0.024—a reduction for which the probable adjustments
would be in the mid-hundreds of thousands rather than in millions of dollars.
But to go from 0.12 to 0.024 (that is, to achieve an improvement factor of 5)
would require an *n* of 25, which flies in the face of common sense. The maximum
practical value of *n* would seem to be about 5 years, which yields an improvement factor of about 2.24 (e.g., from 0.12 to about 0.054). Such a policy would
leave the range of annual budget adjustments—a range that, it will be recalled,
is $\pm 1\sigma$—in the vicinity of ± 1 million, and the probability of a negative net
budget adjustment at about 0.43.

The results of combining the variable payout rate policy with a five-year
moving average are shown in table 7.3. It will be seen that there is a further
improvement but that considerable downside risk remains with respect to the
budget. (The fact that the upside potential disappears more rapidly than the
downside risk is a result of the nonlinearity of the calculation. This relation
would be modified if some other conditions of the example, such as the rate
of gifts to endowment, were changed materially.) Our conclusion is that while
this particular combination of smoothing arrangements might just be adequate,
there is need for a more thorough examination of the smoothing question.

By now it should be apparent that we need an integrated approach to stochastic control rather than ad hoc rules based on conventional wisdom. There
are a great many sources of uncertainty besides investment risk. These may or
may not be correlated with each other or over time and the ways they interact
may affect things for better or for worse. Also, there are many uncertainty-
absorbing methods and smoothing strategies, and these too interact with one
another. Tradeoffs are necessary in the stochastic realm: for example, tighter

Table 7.3.   Effect of Investment Risk on Budget Adjustments: Payout Rate Varies According to First-Order Equilibrium Condition and Endowment Market Value Is Smoothed with a Five-Year Moving Average (Hypothetical Data)

	Actual for Year t	Planned for Year $t + 1$		
		$\rho(t) = \rho$	$\rho(t) = \rho - \sigma$	$\rho(t) = \rho + \sigma$
E	$412	$-$44.8	$-$20.7	$+$21.8
ρ	0.0500	0.0500	0.0504	0.0481
P	$20.0	$20.6	$19.7	$20.9
I	$80.0	$82.0	$82.0	$82.0
B	$100.0	$102.6	$101.1	$102.9
		Needed Budget Adjustment		
A	n.a.	$0	$-$1.5	$+$0.3

NOTE: Money values are in millions of constant dollars. For parameter values, see text.

control over the endowment payout rate will mean looser control somewhere else (e.g., it may result in start-stop budgeting). We present a model capable of assessing such tradeoffs in this chapter. First, however, it will be useful to discuss some of the general principles of dynamic control under uncertainty, and to illustrate an annual planning cycle in which a typical college or university can apply them.

Approaches to Stochastic Control

The general principles of decision making under conditions of uncertainty are to observe current conditions, predict the future as well as possible, and take actions that are optimal in a priori terms while recognizing that unpleasant surprises and second thoughts can and will occur after the event. The model underlying the principles of dynamic control is that the whole system is moving continuously through time and that decisions in one period condition those in later periods. These two sets of principles combined supply the method we have called *dynamic control under uncertainty* or, more simply, *stochastic control*.

The considerable literature on stochastic control identifies three approaches of increasing complexity, all of which are relevant to our models.[2] They are: (a) *feedback control*; (b) *optimal control*; (c) *adaptive control*. We will review each briefly. First, however, let us postulate the following simple system to which the three approaches can be applied for purposes of illustration.

Let $x(t) =$ state of the system at time t (e.g., actual level of expenditures)

   $\bar{x}(t) =$ desired state of the system at time t (e.g., desired level of expenditures)

   $v(t) =$ the "control" to be applied to the system at time t (e.g., the budget adjustment)

$u(t)$ = a random shock that will hit the system at time t, after the control has been decided on (e.g., unexpected inflationary cost increases).

The law of motion is defined first in terms of the planned x and then in terms of the actual outcome:

$$\hat{x}(t + 1) - x(t) = ax(t) + v(t + 1)$$

or $\qquad\qquad\qquad\qquad\qquad\qquad\qquad\qquad\qquad\qquad\qquad\qquad$ (7.1)

$$x(t + 1) = \hat{x}(t + 1) + u(t + 1)$$

where quantities denoted by "$\hat{}$" are anticipatory and others are actual outcomes, just as in figure 7.1. In words: the planned change in the system from t to $t + 1$ is equal to "normal" growth at rate a plus the control $v(t + 1)$. (The control depends on the desired state of the system, as we shall see.) The final outcome is of course the plan plus a random deviation. The above law of motion can also be written as

$$x(t + 1) = (1 + a)x(t) + v(t + 1) + u(t + 1) \qquad (7.2)$$

The analogy of these equations to tables 7.1 and 7.2 should be obvious. The random deviation of investment return is of course $u(t + 1)$ and the budget adjustment A represents the control. The task now is to find an expression for $v(t + 1)$.

Feedback control. This is the easiest kind of control to understand and implement. For example, a simple feedback control mechanism would be

$$v(t + 1) = \ell[\bar{x}(t) - x(t)]$$

where ℓ is a constant between 0 and 1. In words: next period's control is set equal to a fraction of the gap between the desired state of the system and the outcome that has just been observed. The system is smoothed if only a portion of the gap is closed in the immediately ensuing period, i.e., if ℓ is less than one. Feedback occurs in the sense that the output of the system is compared to a standard and a portion of the discrepancy is fed back to the input of the process for the next period.

A slightly more sophisticated feedback control system would be to calculate a discrepancy based on the gap that would be *anticipated* for next period in the absence of special action. That is,

$$v(t + 1) = \ell[\bar{x}(t + 1) - (1 + a)x(t)]. \qquad (7.3)$$

This model "looks ahead" one period before computing the control. In our simple example this might seem to make little difference. But it can be important in practice, especially if the next period's value of a is judged to be different from its long-run value. (We ignore for the moment how $\bar{x}(t + 1)$ is determined.) Such *look-ahead* of more than one period may be incorporated in the model if desired. The transition-to-equilibrium model of chapter 6 can be viewed as a feedback control model with a look-ahead of T periods. We will return to this point later.

In the foregoing example the control is proportional to the size of the discrepancy. Other possibilities that may occur singly or in combination are: (a) making the amount of control depend on the rate at which the aforementioned discrepancy of the state variable x is changing (this is called *derivative* or *differential control*); (b) making the amount of control depend on the cumulative sum of past discrepancies (this is called *integral control*). The three types of feedback control have very different characteristics, and it may be hard to predict the results for alternative systems. For instance, perfectly innocuous feedback control systems often produce violent oscillations (so-called hunting behavior).[3]

We will be using various combinations of proportional and integral feedback control in this chapter. Tradeoffs among long-run growth rates that are made as part of the process of seeking long-run financial equilibrium can be viewed as a kind of differential control.

Optimal control. To use this type of control one must introduce a criterion function by which to define optimality. Let us denote this by the value function $V(x,v)$, which indicates that in general we want to know how much effort will be needed to effect control (this depends, of course, on the amount of control, v) as well as what the resulting outcomes, x, are likely to be. Suppose $x(t)$ is the size of the budget and $v(t)$ is the adjustment A of tables 7.1 through 7.3. (The target enrichment factor f is included in the a of equations 7.1 and 7.2.) Then one criterion for effective control will be the variance of $v(t)$ over time, with a large variance implying start-stop budgeting and its attendant institutional costs. Another possible criterion, since it is painful to cut the budget in absolute terms, will be the fraction of the time that $v(t) - fx(t)$ is expected to be negative, i.e., that $\Pr[v(t) - fx(t)] < 0$.

Having defined a criterion function we can think of optimizing the parameters of any given feedback control system. For instance, the value of ℓ that minimizes the variance of the adjustments or the probability of budget reductions can be determined once certain system characteristics—the variance, for example, or the correlation of random shocks from period to period—have been specified. While the simple system consisting of equations (7.1) and (7.2) offers relatively little latitude for optimizing the control parameters, this is not true of the richer systems to be discussed later.

One quite general approach to optimal feedback control is called *dynamic programming*. Suppose the only structural requirement for the determination of controls is that they be linear functions of the state variables, where the targets $\bar{x}(t)$, like the current values of the activity and stock variables, are defined as being states of the system. Let $x_j^*(t)$ be a particular state variable, given this expanded definition, and $v_i(t)$ a particular control. Then the foregoing assumption states that

$$v_i(t + 1) = \sum_j \ell_{ij} x_j^*(t) \tag{7.4}$$

which holds for each control i. The reader can verify that the equation $v(t + 1)$ $= \ell[\bar{x}(t) - (1 + a)x(t)]$ is a special case of the above. Since there is great freedom in choosing the components of $x_j^*(t)$, equation (7.4) can encompass proportional, differential, or integral control. However, there is a difference between this approach and what is usually thought of as feedback control. The latter imposes considerable structure on the values of ℓ_{ij}; that is, ℓ_{ij} in feedback control is assumed to be zero unless there is some explicit linkage between state variable j and control i. In contrast, dynamic programming does not put any a priori constraints on the values of ℓ_{ij}.

The dynamic programming problem is to find the values of ℓ_{ij} that minimize the expected value of

$$\sum_{t=1}^{\infty} \delta^t V[x^*(t), v(t)]$$

where $V =$ an appropriate value function

$\delta < 1 =$ an appropriate discount factor.

The laws of motion and any side conditions on the values of $v(t)$ are used as constraints in the minimization. Taking the expected value of the present discounted value of the value function reduces the problem to certainty-equivalent form, though the stochastic information is not lost because the expected value of V depends on the variances and covariances of the random disturbances. Provided the value function is convex and of a suitably simple form (usually quadratic), the dynamic-programming algorithm provides a practical computational procedure for what otherwise would be an intractable problem.[4]

We will continue to differentiate between smoothing and dynamic programming as approaches, although both make $v(t + 1)$ a function of $x^*(t)$ and hence represent a feedback or closed-loop system.[5] With present technology one can optimize smoothing rules involving only a few parameters for a wide variety of criterion functions, but only if the system is in a steady state. (This is done by numerical search procedures.) Or one can use dynamic programming to optimize stationary or nonstationary systems with respect to the full array of ℓ_{ij}'s in equation (7.4), but only for a quadratic criterion function. We shall discuss some practical consequences of the difference between optimal smoothing rules and dynamic programming later in this chapter.

Adaptive control. Up to now we have implicitly assumed that an optimal feedback control system would be determined, implemented, and then left to run. That is, the optimal values of the appropriate ℓ_{ij} would be computed once and for all and then applied to each period's values of $x(t)$ in order to obtain the controls for period $t + 1$. While predetermined smoothing rules can be thought of as providing a planning discipline, this view is needlessly restrictive.

Suppose that each year produces an update of the medium-range forecast and the estimates of long-run growth rates. Also, the parameters of the probability distributions of the deviations from these forecasts (which will be discussed later) are updated each year. If dynamic programming is the system of choice, then it makes sense to rerun the dynamic programming algorithm each year, with the new data base. In other words, it makes sense for a whole set of ℓ_{ij}'s to be computed each year, used once, and then discarded. (Fortunately the cost of doing this is quite reasonable.) This is an example of an adaptive control system.

We will apply the above principles in developing some specific stochastic control models for aggregate budget quantities in colleges and universities. In so doing we shall have more to say about how these models relate to the long-run financial equilibrium and transition-to-equilibrium models of chapter 6. Our objective is both to present a specific control model with practical implications and also to complete a unifying conceptual structure for dynamic control of a university budget. First, however, let us digress for a moment to consider some strategies by which a college or university may absorb some of the uncertainty inherent in the budgeting process. An understanding of such strategies is essential for studying the problem of stochastic control in a practical way.

Strategies for Absorbing Uncertainty

By "absorbing" uncertainty we mean mitigating its effects, not ignoring or doing away with it. We assume that the amount of uncertainty has already been reduced to a practical minimum by the use of effective techniques for medium-range financial forecasting. The problem now is to learn to live with the uncertainty that remains as the result of forecast errors and, it may be, the unavoidable miscarriage of certain plans. We shall consider first the annual planning and budgeting cycle and then—more closely—two particularly useful uncertainty-absorbing constructs: the operating reserve and the conditional budget.

The Annual Planning and Budgeting Cycle

The application of stochastic control principles does not take place in an organization without conscious effort by a significant number of people. Many if not most of these people will be neither model builders nor management scientists. The organization of tasks into an annual planning cycle is important if the necessary activities are to be motivated and coordinated.

Figure 7.3 illustrates a planning cycle much like the one that has evolved at Stanford (and probably at many other private colleges and universities too). The university's fiscal year is assumed to start on September 1. However, not a great deal would be changed if July 1 were used instead. The lead times and relations with the governing authorities will be more complex for public institutions because of the interface with state budget offices and legislatures; however, many of the basic features will carry over. The main point of concern for present purposes is how the process proceeds sequentially through the various stages of estimating, planning, and determination of control variables;

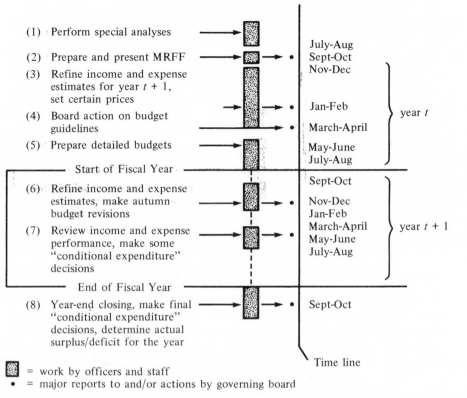

(1) Perform special analyses

(2) Prepare and present MRFF

(3) Refine income and expense estimates for year $t + 1$, set certain prices

(4) Board action on budget guidelines

(5) Prepare detailed budgets

— Start of Fiscal Year —

(6) Refine income and expense estimates, make autumn budget revisions

(7) Review income and expense performance, make some "conditional expenditure" decisions

— End of Fiscal Year —

(8) Year-end closing, make final "conditional expenditure" decisions, determine actual surplus/deficit for the year

July-Aug
Sept-Oct
Nov-Dec

Jan-Feb

March-April

May-June
July-Aug

Sept-Oct
Nov-Dec
Jan-Feb
March-April
May-June
July-Aug

Sept-Oct

year t

year $t + 1$

Time line

▨ = work by officers and staff
• = major reports to and/or actions by governing board

Figure 7.3. An illustrative planning and budgeting cycle for year $t + 1$

refining estimates and assessing results; and coping with unanticipated outcomes.

The planning and budgeting cycle in figure 7.3 consists of eight steps, which start more than a year before the beginning of the period for which planning is to take place. The following is a brief description of the steps involved in preparing and carrying through the budget for an arbitrary year, $t + 1$.

1. Special analyses of cost-rise and income-growth factors, demand characteristics, and, if necessary, the effects of policy changes are performed, often during the summer months. Such analyses provide background for and often merge into the preparation of the medium-range financial forecast (MRFF).

2. The MRFF is prepared and presented to the governing board. The MRFF provides a context for planning during the ensuing months, and the MRFF elements for year $t + 1$ provide the starting point for the more detailed projections of step 3. If necessary, transition-to-equilibrium calculations are also started in step 2.

3. During the November-January period of year t, through a series of iterations, estimates of income and expense by object category are refined, and decisions about budget enrichment, reallocations, etc., are made. To provide adequate lead time for implementation, certain prices such as the tuition rate and the indirect cost rates for research may need to be set during this period.

4. Budget guidelines are prepared and acted upon by the governing board. The guidelines list aggregate income and expense items by object and perhaps by function. When approved, they represent the authorization under which the detailed budget documents for line items and organizational units are prepared. This step is the critical point in financial planning so far as policy tradeoffs are concerned.

5. Detailed budget documents are prepared and disseminated to schools, departments, and other organizational units. These documents put meat on the bones of the budget guidelines by providing detailed authorizations for expenditure and listing sources of funds at a micro level.

6. At this stage a good many factors that were uncertain at the time of budget guideline preparation come more sharply into focus. Estimates are refined and budget revisions made where necessary. While the fiscal year has begun, it still is early enough to effect significant changes in particular line items and hence the planned surplus or deficit by means of the autumn revisions.

7. By March or April a great deal more uncertainty has been removed. Of course there are fewer degrees of freedom too, since most actions and commitments are already in place. Step 7 is a time for stock taking before the summer months. Certain expenditures that had been considered only tentatively are authorized or else cancelled. (This is part of the *conditional budgeting process* to be discussed in more detail under the rubric of uncertainty-absorbing constructs.) While a major review, followed by a report to the governing board, is shown in figure 7.3 as part of step 7, it is important to understand that reviewing and reporting go on continuously throughout the year. This is depicted by the dashed lines connecting steps 5, 6, 7, and 8.

8. The final step in the annual cycle is closing the books at year end. By this time all uncertainty about year $t + 1$ is gone and nearly all the degrees of freedom have been used up. The last decisions, then, are to authorize or cancel the remaining conditional budget items, and to determine the final surplus or deficit for the year. (The conditional budget expenditures authorized at year end actually are made in year $t + 2$ or later, but are grouped with the previous year's decisions for purposes of financial planning.)

The cycle just described is for a single year's budget, but it actually takes place over a period of some twenty-eight months spanning four fiscal years. Of course, activities for different fiscal years go on at the same time and are mutually reinforcing. For example, the year-end closing results for year $t + 1$ affect the autumn revisions for year $t + 2$ and the MRFF for year $t + 3$. Needless to say, the processes for separate years should be kept separate.

The entire sequence of planning steps can be viewed as, first, efforts to bring the financial picture into focus through successively more refined estimates and plans; which then lead to commitments to transform plans into actions; which finally require actions to cope with deviations from estimates and plans as each deviation becomes apparent. The process starts with a medium-range financial forecast. A maximum in degrees of freedom is available at this stage, but there is also maximum uncertainty since the year for which plans are being made will not begin for another ten months. The final step is that of closing the books at year end some twenty-four months later, by which point all uncertainty and nearly all degrees of freedom for action have been removed.

The process of optimal stochastic control begins with decision rules for setting budget guidelines (step 4), which are based on the MRFF and on the detailed income-expenditure estimates (steps 2 and 3). Control continues as the institution fine tunes the budget during the fiscal year (steps 6 and 7), since these actions must be consistent with the long-term strategy. The final step is deciding how to absorb the residual deviations of anticipation from outcome. The choice is between adjustments to conditional authorizations of expenditure and changes in the operating reserve through the surplus/deficit account.

In the stochastic control model that follows we have made some simplifying assumptions with respect to the budgeting cycle depicted in figure 7.3. The thrust of these assumptions is that the year-end closing results for year t are known before the budget for year $t + 1$ is decided upon. That is, we will assume that the decisions about control actions to be applied to year $t + 1$ are based on information about fiscal results for year t, the market value of the endowment at the end of year t, etc. The true situation is that the budget guidelines are approved and final decisions for some key quantities like the tuition rate are made some seven months before year end. These decisions must be based on estimates of year-end results, which of course are subject to error. Some of the error is corrected in the budget revision process that autumn. We will consider the remainder to be characterized by the same uncertainty as the relation between anticipations and outcomes for year $t + 1$.*

By simplifying the process for modeling purposes we can avoid having to use two representations of uncertainty, viz, from March of year t to October of year $t + 1$ (with respect to year t's closing values), and then from October to August of year $t + 1$. We can also live with a two-stage rather than a three-stage control process: since the autumn revisions can be ignored, control occurs only through budget guidelines and year-end closing. Because the revisions made in autumn interact with other decisions, our simplifying assumptions reduce the complexity of the model by more than half. We doubt very much whether the validity of the model is much affected by the simplification so long as the autumn revisions are relatively minor and basically consistent with long-run strategy.

Uncertainty-Absorbing Constructs

Two important constructs for absorbing uncertainty in the short term have been developed at Stanford, within the context of the annual budget cycle described above. (They are commonly employed at other schools too, though

---

*Nothing would be lost by stipulating that the endowment payout rate should apply to the endowment market value as of (say) January 1 of the previous year. This would shift the phase of the stocks and flows slightly but would not change either the dynamic or the stochastic characteristics of the system. The situation is more complicated for the flow variable, however, because events during the latter part of year t will generally affect both that year and the base for year $t + 1$.

not always in as formal a way.) The constructs are the *operating reserve* and the *conditional budget*. In addition, the transition-to-equilibrium approach of spreading adjustments over a period of years, discussed at the end of chapter 6, could be classed as an uncertainty-absorbing mechanism or control procedure for use in the longer term. We shall return to it presently.

The operating reserve. There is nothing mysterious about the operating reserve; it is simply a special fund balance that is earmarked for handling budget surpluses or deficits. Sometimes a surplus or deficit is planned at the beginning of the year in order to smooth out anticipated income or expense. In addition, unanticipated changes in expense or income can produce changes during the year. Whatever the original plan, the operating reserve is incremented or decremented at year-end closing by the actual amount of surplus or deficit. In addition, the fund balance in the operating reserve earns investment return during the year. At Stanford the operating reserve is part of the so-called expendable funds investment pool, which earns a lower total return but is more liquid and less risky than the endowment portfolio.

The existence of an operating reserve balance permits a deficit to be run without causing the alarms and repercussions that would occur if, say, it were necessary to dip into funds functioning as endowment. However, a drawdown of the operating reserve in order to balance the books will (or should) initiate a desire to restore it to some optimal value. This desire introduces an integral control requirement into the system.

The conditional budget. Another uncertainty-absorbing construct is the conditional budget. An ordinary or "unconditional" budget consists of a set of authorizations for expenditure together with a listing of anticipated sources of income. The authorizations are not irrevocable but they are not regarded as tentative or conditional either; people expect to be able to act upon them throughout the year. In contrast, the conditional budget is a set of tentative or conditional authorizations. People may anticipate being able to use the money, but commitments to spend it must not be made until the line item is transferred from the "conditional" to the "regular" category.

The conditional budget construct is illustrated in figure 7.4. As the bell-shaped probability curve indicates, there is uncertainty as to the amount of total revenue that will be produced during the year. (There may also be uncertainty as to actual expenditures; for example, there may be unanticipated cost increases or savings. These can easily be incorporated in the conditional budget schema, but they are ignored in figure 7.4.) The unconditional budget is represented by the distance B and the expected conditional budget by the distance C. For present purposes it is assumed that a deficit will be allowed only if the degree of freedom afforded by the conditional budget is used up, that is, only if income falls so far short of expectations that the conditional budget is reduced to zero. The probability distribution of the amount of conditional budget money that will actually be spent is shown by the unshaded portion of the bell-shaped curve. The shaded area represents the probability that expen-

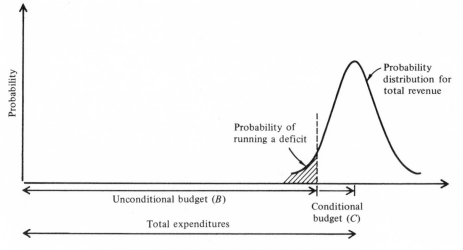

Figure 7.4. Illustration of conditional budget concept

diture holdbacks will be needed with respect to the unconditional budget—i.e., that the shortfall in revenue will exceed the uncertainty-absorbing capacity of the conditional budget.

Notice that while the budget is divided into unconditional and conditional components, there is no need to divide up the income line items in this way. The probability distribution in figure 7.4 represents the net of overs and unders for specific income items; there is no advantage in spending much time on efforts to segregate these items in advance. From an accounting standpoint, it may be desirable to designate certain income items as conditional when developing detailed budgets in step 5 of the annual cycle. These items will not then be shown as sources of funds for the regular budget. At Stanford, portions of both indirect cost recovery and security lending income are used in this way (both are subject to more than the usual amount of fluctuation from year to year). However, this choice has no effect on expenditure authorizations and its effects are obliterated at year-end closing.

The conditional budget construct will work well if people really are willing to live with conditional authorizations that will not be realized some of the time. If they are not willing, the money may be implicitly committed before the actual level of income is known, in which case it will be hard for administrators to avoid authorizing it in the end. Then the uncertainty-absorbing properties of the conditional budget will be lost.

At Stanford we have evolved a hierarchy of conditional budget items, depending on how difficult it is to cancel or defer them. As the year progresses, the income scene becomes clearer and any unanticipated variations in the regular budget gradually become visible. Conditional budget line items are authorized part way through the year if that is justified; some items are unequivocally canceled. Final decisions on the conditional budget are made during the closing process at year end. Another device used at Stanford is to classify part of the transfer to the physical plant account, which is used to build up a depreciation reserve, as a conditional budget item. (At Stanford, a transfer to physical plant is also included in the regular operating budget.) There is flexibility in the timing of these transfers from year to year, though it is important that sufficient planning discipline be exerted for a target level of transfers to be achieved over a period of years. However, inclusion of the transfer makes the conditional budget more truly conditional on a year-to-year basis.

We are sure that conditional budgeting is performed at many schools, under the rubric of "holding back" income from the regular budgetary process. Income estimates may also be deliberately slanted toward the conservative side, so that a certain amount of slack will be available to handle contingencies. However, at Stanford we have found that it is better to prepare and publish unbiased income estimates and then withhold the authorization of certain important but postponable expense items until later in the year. Among other things, we feel it is desirable to begin to bring these conditional budget items into focus well before year-end closing. It is also good to avoid the problem of credibility that arises if one consistently "finds" unexpected income at the end of the year. Of course this strategy implies that, as often as not, we will fail to reach our most-likely income estimates. But recognition of this fact is probably a healthy thing in and of itself, provided of course that effective actions are being taken to absorb the uncertainty that really does exist.

A Model for Stochastic Control

Let us now particularize the stochastic control process by proposing a specific model that can provide guidance to decision makers at various stages in the budgeting cycle. Our strategy will be to lay out laws of motion in probabilistic terms (i.e., in a way that represents uncertainty), and then propose a set of smoothing rules that deal with the uncertainty. The laws of motion are extensions of those proposed in chapter 6; the smoothing rules are of the kind we have labeled "first-order feedback control." Feedback control is used because it is the simplest of the available alternatives. We limit ourselves to the first order for the same reason that we used first-order equilibrium, viz, simplicity. While our models are aggregative and relatively simple compared to the general class of stochastic control models, the reader will find that they are surprisingly rich in structure and have interesting implications. We will comment on some other stochastic control models for colleges and universities in the last section of this chapter.

Probabilistic Laws of Motion

For the purposes of stochastic control, the aggregate laws of motion for a university's expenditures and incomes, given in chapter 6, have to be modified in three ways:

1. Uncertainty-absorbing mechanisms such as a conditional budget must be added.

2. Differences between plans and outcomes must be represented in terms of probability distributions whose parameters can be estimated or determined by judgment.

3. Smoothing rules (or other approaches to applying stochastic control) must be provided for, and then integrated with the laws of motion.

First we shall define the new variables that will be needed to accommodate these three constructs. Except where noted, all other names of variables mean the same as they did in chapter 6. (One important difference, noted above, is that endowment market value, $E(t)$, and other stock variables refer here to balances at the end of period t rather than the beginning.)

Let $R(t)$ = fund balance of operating reserve at end of year t, after books are closed

$S(t)$ = surplus or deficit in year t (positive values indicate a surplus)

$C(t)$ = conditional budget in year t.

These are actual or ex post values; planned or a priori values will be denoted with a caret "$^\wedge$" as before. Here are the target values of the above three variables.

Let $\bar{R}(t) = \Pi B(t)$

$\bar{S}(t) = 0$

$\bar{C}(t) = \Omega B(t)$,

where Π and Ω are new policy parameters. Thus the operating reserve balance and the conditional budget targets are indexed to $B(t)$, while the target value of the surplus/deficit is of course zero, because we would like the budget to be balanced.

Finally, we need a law of motion for the operating reserve.

Let γ = annual total return on the operating reserve balance.

This is analogous to total return on the endowment, ρ, but its value tends to be smaller because the operating reserve, like the university's other expendable funds balances, is generally invested in lower-risk, lower-return securities. In certainty-equivalent terms the law of motion for the operating reserve balance is

$$R(t + 1) = (1 + \gamma)R(t) + S(t + 1) \tag{7.5}$$

where it is assumed that the surplus or deficit is added at year end, just before the new balance is computed.

In order to track LRFE precisely, it is necessary to allow for an additional (and automatic) transfer to the operating reserve equal to $\lambda \Pi B(t)$, where λ is a new parameter. The purpose of the automatic transfer is to compensate for any difference between γ and $r + f$. However, the difference is quite small (less that 0.1 percent of the budget for Stanford), and so the automatic transfer is omitted from (7.5) in order to simplify the notation. The full mathematical treatment of the model includes both this adjustment and the expenditure adjustments, mentioned in connection with the definitions of $\hat{A}(t)$.[6]

The next step is to specify the variables that will be used as controls in the system. The choice obviously depends on the college's or university's planning process and objectives, but we believe the following is a fairly general representation of what might be reasonable to use in many situations. The controls are defined in terms of the following planned or ex ante variables.

Let $\hat{A}(t)$ = the amount of special budget adjustment to be applied in planning the budget for period t

$\hat{P}(t)$ = the planned dollar payout from endowment to be used to fund expenditures in year t

$\hat{S}(t)$ = the planned surplus or deficit in year t, as defined earlier.

The variable $A(t)$ consists of adjustments in expenditure that subtract from or add to normal budget enrichment. The target value of $A(t)$ is zero; positive values denote reductions to conform with the usage of chapter 6. (Adjustments in operating income could have been added here, as they were to TRANS, but we have ignored them.) The planned dollar payout, $\hat{P}(t)$, is declared in terms of cents per pooled fund share at the beginning of the year; this "contract" is adhered to no matter what the eventual yield and/or capital gain. The target value of $P(t)$ is $pE(t-1)$, that is, the equilibrium payout rate times the beginning market value. In order to stabilize the budget system, however, the dollar value of payout has to be smoothed. Finally, the target value of $S(t)$ is of course zero.

Once the rest of the system is specified, the magnitude of the planned conditional budget, $\hat{C}(t)$, can be determined from the following identity for planned sources and uses of funds. Thus

$$\hat{B}(t) + \hat{C}(t) + \hat{S}(t) = \hat{I}(t) + \hat{P}(t) \qquad (7.6)$$

where $\hat{B}(t)$ is of course the expected value of the budget after any special adjustments. Hence $\hat{C}(t)$ can also be viewed as a control variable, though in this model it is determined indirectly, from the other three controls. We will specify the equations for $\hat{A}(t)$, $\hat{P}(t)$, and $\hat{S}(t)$ later, under the heading of "smoothing rules."

In the next section, which deals with the representation of uncertainty, we shall describe the growth rates used in the laws of motion as *random variables*. They will be denoted by $\tilde{r}(t)$, etc., to emphasize this fact. Inflation must also be considered; this will be denoted as $\tilde{\imath}(t)$, since i denotes operating income. Anticipating this discussion, but using the above notation, we can write the following probabilistic laws of motion for the actual outcomes of the system. (They are based on the results of chapter 6, augmented by [7.5].)

$$B(t + 1) = [1 + \tilde{\imath}(t + 1) + \tilde{r}(t + 1) + f_{t+1}]B(t) - A(t + 1)$$

$$I(t + 1) = [1 + \tilde{\imath}(t + 1) + \tilde{\imath}(t + 1)]I(t)$$

$$E(t + 1) = [1 + \tilde{\imath}(t + 1) + \tilde{p}(t + 1)]E(t) + G(t + 1) - P(t + 1) \qquad (7.7)$$

$$R(t + 1) = [1 + \tilde{\imath}(t + 1) + \tilde{y}(t + 1)]R(t) + S(t + 1)$$

$$G(t + 1) = [1 + \tilde{\imath}(t + 1) + \tilde{g}(t + 1)]G(t)$$

The planned values for these five quantities—$\hat{B}(t + 1)$, $\hat{I}(t + 1)$, etc.—are given by equations that are identical to (7.5) except that the expected values of the growth rates are used instead of the rates actually realized during the year.

There are five equations numbered (7.7), but since there are eight variables (B, I, E, R, G, plus A, P, and S) we need three more to close the system. Two of them are obtained by assuming that the plans for budget adjustment and endowment payout are adhered to exactly. That is,

$$A(t + 1) = \hat{A}(t + 1)$$

$$P(t + 1) = \hat{P}(t + 1).$$

The situation for the surplus or deficit needs to be more complicated if the system is to be realistic, however. Let

$$S(t + 1) = \hat{S}(t + 1) \qquad (7.8)$$

$$+ \omega[I(t + 1) - \hat{I}(t + 1) - B(t + 1) + \hat{B}(t + 1)].$$

In words: we are assuming that the ex post surplus is equal to the ex ante surplus plus a fraction, ω, of any unplanned gap between income and expense during the year. Since the dollar value of endowment payout is pegged at its planned value, the only relevant "surprises" that can occur during the year involve the operating income and expenditure variables; the quantity in the brackets is the net of these surprises.

Once the ex post value of the surplus or deficit has been determined, it is of course a simple matter to calculate from the ex post cash flow identity the amount of money available for the conditional budget. The ex post identity has the same form as the ex ante version, equation (7.6), except that of course outcomes are used instead of plans. It is worth noticing at this point that the effect of (7.8) is to split the "surprises" between the surplus/deficit account and the conditional budget. This is a decision that can be made at year-end closing, which is when Stanford does make it. However, it is reasonable to assume for purposes of analysis that, on average over the years, the fractional split will be equal to a certain value, which will be determined by the optimization routine.

Representation of Uncertainty

The development of a stochastic control model requires an explicit representation in probability terms of one's beliefs about uncertainty. It is convenient to think of the growth rates of our various financial variables during each year as the elements in the model that are uncertain. This means that $B(t + 1), I(t + 1)$, $E(t + 1), G(t + 1)$, and $R(t + 1)$ are uncertain even though their values are known at time t.

Each variable is subject to two distinct kinds of influence: one kind, which we shall call the variable's *own-effect*, is due to its own particular driving forces, and one is due to economy-wide inflation. The resulting growth rate is the sum of the two. Changes in the general inflation rate will introduce correlation among the variables even if their own-effects are statistically independent of one another. (Independence of the own-effects is not required by the model, and indeed we have reason to believe there may be correlations among certain real growth rates.) It is possible for the own-effect of a variable to be positively or negatively correlated with general inflation, with obvious results. Naturally the range of uncertainty expressed in dollar terms will increase as $B(t)$, etc., increase, even though the variances of the growth rates themselves remain constant over time. Finally, it is important to allow for the possibility that the random disturbance affecting a growth rate in a given year may depend in some way on the previous year's disturbance. This is called *serial correlation*. A positive serial correlation indicates that a deviation in a given direction is likely to persist into the future, whereas a negative serial correlation implies an alternating pattern of deviations.

Let us now specify the above mathematically. The following terms apply to any particular item from the set of random growth rates ($r, i, \rho, g,$ and γ).

Let $\tilde{\jmath}(t)$ = *numerical value* for growth rate j at time t, as determined ex post facto

j_t = *expected growth rate* for variable j at time t, written simply as j if it does not vary over time (this is the set of growth rates from the MRFF, as used in chapter 6)

$j(t)$ = deviation of the actual from the expected growth rate for variable j at time t, again measured ex post facto

$\varepsilon_j(t)$ = the "basic" probabilistic variable or element of uncertainty for variable j at time t

$\imath$ = general rate of inflation, with $\imath(t)$, etc., following the same conventions as j.

The following identity holds for each j and for $\imath$:

$$\tilde{\jmath}(t) = j_t + j(t). \tag{7.9}$$

To introduce the possibility of serial correlation, we postulate that the deviations follow the autoregressive structure:

$$j(t) = \alpha_{jt} j(t - 1) + \varepsilon_j(t). \tag{7.10}$$

The coefficient α_{jt} is what is called a *carryover parameter*.

Let s_j = the serial correlation coefficient between $j(t)$ and $j(t-1)$.

Then it can be shown that

$$\alpha_{jt} = s_j \frac{\sigma[j(t)]}{\sigma[j(t-1)]}$$

where $\sigma[j(\cdot)]$ is the standard deviation of j at the time indicated. It can be shown that $\sigma[j(t)] \cong (1 + j_t)\sigma[j(t-1)]$, and so $\alpha_{jt} \cong (1 + j_t)s_j$. Thus α_{jt} is the serial correlation coefficient adjusted for the difference in expected dollar values between $t-1$ and t. A carryover parameter, then, represents the amount of the previous period's deviation that is "carried over" to the current period; it usually has a value between $+1$ and -1. The new random disturbance, $\varepsilon_j(t)$, is added to the carryover effect.

Recall from equation (7.1) that the outcome for any variable $x_j(t+1)$ is written as the sum of its planned value and a random disturbance expressed in dollar terms. That is,

$$x_j(t+1) = \hat{x}(t+1) + u_j(t+1).$$

Now we are in a position to define $u_j(t+1)$:

$$u_j(t+1) = [j(t+1) + \iota(t+1)]x_j(t).$$

After substituting equation (7.9) we have:

$$u_j(t+1) = [\alpha_{jt}j(t) + \alpha_{\iota t}\iota(t)]x_j(t)$$
$$+ [\varepsilon_j(t+1) + \varepsilon_\iota(t+1)]x_j(t). \tag{7.11}$$

In this formulation we have $u_j(t+1)$ in terms of the *previous* period's deviations, $j(t)$ and $\iota(t)$, and state variables, $x_j(t)$. Only the new disturbances, $\varepsilon_j(t+1)$, are contemporaneous with $u_j(t+1)$.

We shall assume that the $\varepsilon_j(t+1)$ are random variables with mean zero; that they are serially independent, i.e., that $\varepsilon_j(t+1)$ does not depend on $\varepsilon_j(t)$; and that they are statistically independent of all previous states of the system, i.e., that $\varepsilon_j(t+1)$ does not depend on any $x(t)$ or $j(t)$. Hence we can write the expectation of the products in the second term of (7.11) as, for example,

$$\mathscr{E}[\varepsilon_j(t+1)x_j(t)] = \mathscr{E}[\varepsilon_j(t+1)]\mathscr{E}[x_j(t)] = 0\mathscr{E}[x_j(t)] = 0. \tag{7.12}$$

Notice that $x_j(t)$ is itself a random variable any time after $t = 0$; the initial conditions, $x_j(0)$, are assumed to be known. The expectation of the carryover effect (i.e., the first term of [7.10]) also vanishes, as can be seen by repeated substitution of equation (7.9) and application of (7.11). Hence we know that $\mathscr{E}[u_j(t)] = 0$ for all j.

What about the form of the probability distribution of the disturbances, ε_j? The "purist" assumption is that growth rates are distributed log-normally.

Accordingly, $ln\ (1 + \varepsilon_j)$ would be multivariate normally distributed with parameters that can be computed from (a) the vector of means and (b) the variance-covariance matrix of the raw variables. The advantage of this assumption is shown by the following argument. Suppose

$$x(t + 1) = (1 + \varepsilon_x)x(t)$$

which implies

$$ln\ x(t + 1) = ln\ (1 + \varepsilon_x) + ln\ x(t).$$

If $ln\ (1 + \varepsilon_x)$ is normal, it can easily be shown by iteration that $ln\ x(t)$ and $ln\ x(t + 1)$ will be normal as well, since the sum of normal variates is normal. Hence the logarithms remain normally distributed over time, and the raw variables are log-normal.

However, our model is not as neat as the one above. We have equations like

$$R(t + 1) = (1 + \gamma)R(t) + S(t)$$

which for $t > 0$ involve sums of random variables. Now, sums of log-normal variables are not in general log-normal, so we are stuck if we try to be precise in our representation of the probability distributions. To get out of this mess we use the approximation described below, which allows us among other things to assume ε_j to be multivariate normal. We do not believe this misrepresents the situation significantly, because: (a) it is the distribution of $1 + \varepsilon_j$ that is at issue; (b) the variance of ε_j is usually small relative to 1; (c) there is a large element of approximation in all the data anyhow.

The argument for $(1 + \varepsilon)$ being log-normal appears to stem from the elegance and power of the log-normal probability process (see Tintner and Sengupta 1972, p. 66). The process depends in turn on the log transform given above and the usual requirement that $1 + \varepsilon_j$ be strictly positive. However, these points lose some of their force if $var(\varepsilon_j)$ is small, as will be the case in our models for everything except investment return. Fortunately, much of what we are doing here does not depend on the form of the probability distribution once the approximation has been invoked.

The representation of uncertainty as described so far is sufficient for doing Monte Carlo simulations, in which the process is calculated recursively, year by year, on the basis of pseudorandom numbers generated in the computer. The simulation begins with $t = 0$, and known initial conditions. Values of $\varepsilon_j(1)$ are then generated randomly and equation (7.9) is used to calculate the $u_j(1)$. These, plus the controls that will be specified later, are sufficient to calculate the $x_j(1)$. When the process is repeated for $t = 1$, the $x_j(1)$ are of course known from the previous iteration. However, the analytical solution needed for optimal smoothing requires that the variances and covariances of the state variables, $x_j(t)$, be available. The means of the state variables are easy to calculate, since $\mathscr{E}[u_j(t)] = 0$ for all j and t. Calculation of the variances and covariances of the $x_j(t)$ from those of the underlying random variables, $\varepsilon_j(t)$, requires an approximation, which is justified and described as follows.

SOLUTION PROCEDURE 7.1. The leading implication of products like $\iota(t + 1)x(t)$ is that the effect of a random deviation in the rate ι is "scaled" by the size of the current base. The problem is that once the system has moved off the initial condition, future "bases" are random variables. Thus we have products of random variables that, because of additive terms elsewhere in the system, cannot be linearized by taking logarithms.

Suppose, however, that in place of $x(t)$ we substitute its expected value, which is $(1 + j + \iota)^t x(0)$ if the system has constant growth rates. While the expression is more complicated if the system has variable growth rates, it is still relatively easy to compute. Notice that the expected trajectory of $x(t)$ involves no random deviations and hence no application of the controls provided that the system was in equilibrium at $t = 0$. The approximation changes the expression for $u_j(t + 1)$ to the form

$$u_j(t + 1) = [j(t + 1) + \iota(t + 1)](1 + j + \iota)^t x(0)$$

which is linear in the deviations. We have found that this degree of simplification is sufficient for calculating the needed variances and covariances.[7]

The approximation introduces a small error in the scaling of the random variables, both in absolute terms and relative to one another. (The error is of the order of the squares and cross-products of the deviations.) However, it is hard to believe this will be important given the degree of approximation already involved in specifying the variances and covariances for the ε_j, as well as other parameters. The fact that an adaptive control formulation can be achieved by updating the parameters by means of each new year's data is another redeeming factor. Accordingly, we assume with a clear conscience that, for analytical purposes, the random deviations can be scaled by expectations rather than outcomes. Also, the fact that the system now is completely linear makes the assumption of multivariate normal random variables quite attractive.

Let us turn now to the kinds of data that are needed to inform our representation of uncertainty with respect to the aggregates of expenditures and income for colleges and universities. Table 7.4 presents the needed data array and also a set of sample values. These data are used in the computer runs presented later in this chapter. They are based mostly upon judgments we have formed by looking at Stanford's financial data, though external data obviously influenced our choice of figures for investment return and general inflation. We emphasize that, so far, there is very little experience upon which to base estimates for most of the entries, which can therefore quite properly be classed as "guesstimates." Still, a guesstimate is better than assuming a value of zero and ignoring the phenomenon entirely. Given the small number of entries in table 7.4, it seems entirely possible to develop the experience necessary to make reasoned estimates of important quantities; we have, after all, learned to do as much for the expected values of the variables through the mechanism of the medium-range financial forecast.

Here is the reasoning behind the entries in table 7.4. We present it to indicate

Table 7.4. Illustrative Dispersions, Correlations, and Serial Correlations for Growth-Rate Deviations

	Variables					
	ι	r	i	ρ	g	γ
Standard deviations	0.008	0.003	0.010	0.120	0.100	0.001
Correlations						
ι	1.00					
r	0	1.00				
i	−0.20	0.25	1.00			
ρ	−0.10	0	0.10	1.00		
g	−0.25	0	0.10	0.50	1.00	
γ	0	0	0.10	−0.10	0	1.00
Serial correlations α	0.25	0.20	0.10	0.00	−0.50	0.00

NOTE: This table is based on financial data for Stanford University and (for ι and ρ) relevant external data.

the kinds of things that should be considered rather than to justify the specific numbers in the table.

1. *Standard deviations.* The largest standard deviation, 0.120, is for total return on endowment portfolio, ρ, which is assumed to consist about 70 percent of common stocks. The smallest is for total return on operating reserve, γ, which is invested in the expendable funds pool and consists for the most part of short-term fixed-income securities. Gifts to endowment, g, is volatile because the state of the securities markets affects gifts from living individuals, and bequests are unpredictable and sometimes large. Operating income, i, is less predictable than total expenditures because it includes expendable gifts, income on specific investments and on much of the expendable funds pool, and tuition revenue, which may fluctuate due to changes in student FTE registrations.

2. *Correlations between inflation and other growth rates.* The value (ιi) is set at −0.20 because higher inflation tends to depress temporarily both the real amount of expendable gifts received and the real earnings from some specific investments. That for ($\iota \rho$) reflects investor psychology (empirical analysis suggests that this correlation is slightly negative). The value of (ιg) is set at −0.250 to reflect the negative impact of inflation on donor psychology.

3. *Correlations among growth-rate variables.* There is a relatively large correlation between r and i due to indirect cost recovery on research contracts and grants. It is assumed that a rightful share of cost deviations will be recovered through a carryforward agreement or by some other means, though the possibility of a lag in recovery is ignored. Since the biggest cost deviations are likely to be in the overhead areas—due to changes in utility rates, for example, or in insurance or legal costs—the amount of potential recovery can be substantial.

Operating income, i, is correlated with both ρ and g due to a commonality of factors that affect expendable gifts, and with γ due to earnings on the expenable funds pool that are used to support the operating budget. The negative value of ($\gamma \rho$) is intended to reflect the effect of short-term fluctuations in interest rates upon the return on equities. The big value of ($g \rho$), 0.50, serves the same purpose for donor psychology in relation to the stock market.

4. *Serial correlations.* The serial correlations for total return on the endowment, ρ, and the operating reserve, γ, are strictly zero, as the tenets of modern capital market theory require them to be. Those for inflation, ι, cost rise, r, and operating income, i, are positive and reflect different degrees of persistence of deviations of these quantities from their trend values. The value of α_r has been made greater than that of α_i in order to allow for the tendency to spread out problems of underbudgeting; this is consistent with the smaller standard deviation of r.

Finally, the large negative value of α_g is an artifact of our serial correlation structure. Big bequests are statistically independent of one another and of everything else the university does in the short run. When one comes in, the base of giving to endowment is temporarily increased to a point from which future growth probably cannot be sustained. This effect can be represented by a negative α_g. The further implication of a negative serial correlation is an alternation of effects in subsequent years: this is counterintuitive but the effects doubtless will be small.

Smoothing Rules

The decision rules that must be applied to the laws of motion are of two kinds: (a) long-term strategic plans; (b) short-term adjustments, or controls. In chapter 6 we dealt extensively with the problem of strategic dynamic planning in terms of certainty-equivalent models. Let us stipulate that the long-run values of r, i, f, p, etc., must be consistent with long-run financial equilibrium. Another condition is that $R(t)$ grow at the same rate as $B(t)$. This, as we have noted, can be ensured by a small automatic budget transfer. If we ignore any higher-order effects caused by departures from perfectly balanced growth, we can expect that once any short-lived initial effects have worn off the following relationships will hold good:

$$\mathscr{E}[A(t)] = 0 \qquad\qquad \mathscr{E}[C(t)] = \Omega B(t)$$
$$\mathscr{E}[P(t)] = pE(t-1) \qquad \mathscr{E}[R(t)] = \Pi B(t).$$
$$\mathscr{E}[S(t)] = 0$$

We are now in position to develop a set of first-order smoothing rules that will set the controls so as to correct deviations from the equilibrium growth trajectory.

The definition of "first-order" is the same as it was in the equilibrium context: in getting the result, the initial conditions and the projection for one year ahead are both considered. Zero-order smoothing is of course possible—it was illustrated earlier, in fact—but no competent institution would consider looking only at the year just ending and ignoring projections for the ensuing year. First-order smoothing can be effective when the expected growth rates are not likely to change very much from year to year.

To get a reasonable smoothing rule for the budget adjustments we have only to define a measure of short-term disequilibrium (which we shall denote by Q), and then decide to close a portion of this gap during the forthcoming year. It is instructive to illustrate Q in zero-order terms, and then to extend the idea to first-order expression. The zero-order measure is:

$$Q_0(t + 1) = [1 + \Omega B(t) - I(t) - pE(t - 1)].$$

This utilizes the newly known values for last year's B, I, and E. Application of the target conditional budget and payout parameters produces a gap based on the data of the year just ended. The first-order gap projects last year's data forward one year, according to the expected growth rates obtained from the MRFF. The result is:

$$Q_1(t + 1) = [1 + \Omega][1 + \iota_{t+1} + r_{t+1} + f_{t+1}]B(t) \\ - [1 + \iota_{t+1} + i_{t+1}]I(t) - pE(t). \tag{7.13}$$

Note that the first-order gap Q_1, depends on the expected growth rates for next year only. If the expectations for later years are different, closing the one-year gap will not be sufficient to restore LRFE. That would involve identifying and closing a "T-order" gap, which requires a multiperiod model such as will be described in the next section.

Once a gap has been detected the obvious thing to do is to close a certain fraction of this gap next year. Therefore the decision rule for budget adjustment is

$$\hat{A}(t + 1) = \ell \frac{Q_1(t + 1)}{1 + \Omega} \tag{7.14}$$

where ℓ is the fraction in question (ℓ is analogous to the constant in equation [7.3]). The quantity $1 + \Omega$ in the denominator takes care of the fact that a change in the operating budget also is assumed to change the conditional budget target proportionately.

The smoothing rule for endowment payout is similar in spirit but differs somewhat in detail. Suppose we define the needed adjustment to the endowment payout as

$$pE(t) - [1 + \iota_{t+1} + r_{t+1} + f_{t+1}]P(t).$$

This adjustment is the difference between (a) the equilibrium payout rate, as applied to the latest endowment balance, and (b) last year's dollar payout, as accelerated (without account being taken of the budget adjustments) to keep pace in terms of budgetary purchasing power.[8] Suppose now that we decide to set $\hat{P}(t + 1)$ so as to close a fraction, κ, of the disequilibrium in dollar payout. Then a little algebra yields

$$\hat{P}(t + 1) = \kappa pE(t) + [1 - \kappa][1 + \iota_{t+1} + r_{t+1} + f_{t+1}]P(t). \tag{7.15}$$

This amounts to setting dollar payout equal to an exponentially weighted moving average of the equilibrium payout values, with expected budget growth taken into account. We have found this rule intuitively appealing and relatively easy to explain to colleagues; it also possesses the mathematical desiderata of having the control be linear in the current values of the state variables.

The smoothing rule for the third control variable, $\hat{S}(t + 1)$, is based on the difference between the desired and projected operating reserve (provided there is no new surplus or deficit) at the end of next year. If we close a fraction, χ, of this difference, the control equation is

$$\hat{S}(t + 1) = \chi\{\Pi[1 + \iota_{t+1} + r_{t+1} + f_{t+1}]B(t) - \Pi\hat{A}(t + 1)$$
$$- [1 + \iota_{t+1} + \gamma_{t+1}]R(t)\}. \tag{7.16}$$

Taken together, the two terms multiplying Π represent the expected expenditure level next year. The last term is the expected growth of the operating reserve due to investment return (any automatic transfer to the operating reserve would have to be included here too). We can include the planned budget adjustment in (7.16) without destroying the linearity of the system because $\hat{A}(t + 1)$ is itself a linear function of the state variables. It is desirable to do so because the current year's adjustments will have a very important effect on any surplus or deficit.

Should anyone be wondering why the planned budget adjustment was not included along with f_t in equation (7.15), the answer is that this would have involved the term $[\hat{A}(t + 1)/B(t)]P(t)$, which is not linear in the state variables. Happily, though, the relative effect of the budget adjustments is far less on the payout than on the surplus or deficit.

Notice that $\hat{A}(t + 1)$ and $\hat{P}(t + 1)$ depend only on the state variables in period t. The value of $\hat{A}(t + 1)$ is used to calculate $\hat{S}(t + 1)$, which in turn allows the computation of $\hat{C}(t + 1)$ from the planned cash flow identity, equation (7.6). Systems in which the variables can be solved for one at a time rather than in terms of a set of simultaneous equations are called *recursive*. This is a desirable property because the calculations can be done by hand and are easier to explain. (On the other hand, when one is using a computer the cost difference is trivial for systems as small as the ones we are dealing with here.) The present model presents a simple, recursive, and—we think—intuitively appealing method for determining the control variables.

It will be instructive to "walk through" the operation of these decision rules to see what is involved. Figure 7.5 provides a roadmap; it starts at the top, with the box for last year's outcomes. The process begins in step I, with calculation of the unmonitored expectations of the budget quantities, where "unmonitored" means "before application of the controls." The controls are calculated in steps II through V. Notice that the determination of $\hat{A}(t + 1)$ in step II proceeds independently of the determination of $\hat{P}(t + 1)$ in step III, and also that while $\hat{P}(t + 1)$ does depend on the expected growth rate of expense it does *not* depend on $\hat{x}(t + 1)$ in general or on the projected budget gap in particular. Once the smoothing parameter, κ, has been determined, this formulation permits the decision rule for endowment payout to be calculated prior to the rest of the

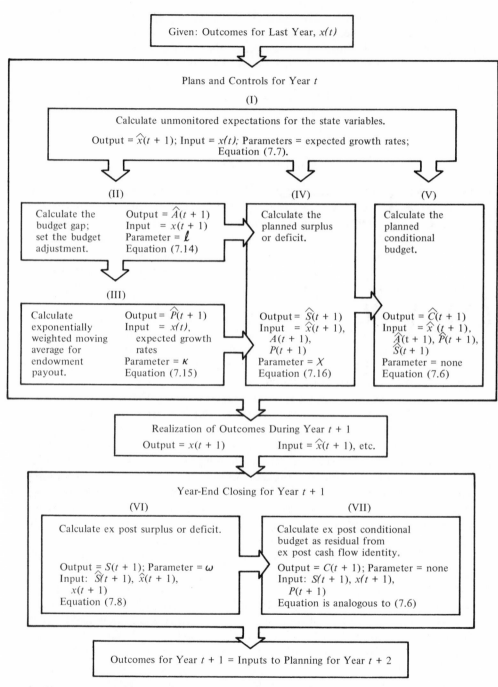

Given: Outcomes for Last Year, $x(t)$

Plans and Controls for Year t

(I)

Calculate unmonitored expectations for the state variables.

Output = $\widehat{x}(t + 1)$; Input = $x(t)$; Parameters = expected growth rates;
Equation (7.7).

(II)

		(IV)	**(V)**
Calculate the budget gap; set the budget adjustment.	Output = $\widehat{A}(t + 1)$ Input = $x(t + 1)$ Parameter = ℓ Equation (7.14)	Calculate the planned surplus or deficit.	Calculate the planned conditional budget.

(III)

Calculate exponentially weighted moving average for endowment payout.	Output = $\widehat{P}(t + 1)$ Input = $x(t)$, expected growth rates Parameter = κ Equation (7.15)	Output = $\widehat{S}(t + 1)$ Input = $\widehat{x}(t + 1)$, $A(t + 1)$, $P(t + 1)$ Parameter = X Equation (7.16)	Output = $\widehat{C}(t + 1)$ Input = $\widehat{x}(t + 1)$, $\widehat{A}(t + 1)$, $\widehat{P}(t + 1)$, $\widehat{S}(t + 1)$ Parameter = none Equation (7.6)

Realization of Outcomes During Year $t + 1$

Output = $x(t + 1)$ Input = $\widehat{x}(t + 1)$, etc.

Year-End Closing for Year $t + 1$

(VI)	**(VII)**
Calculate ex post surplus or deficit.	Calculate ex post conditional budget as residual from ex post cash flow identity.
Output = $S(t + 1)$; Parameter = ω Input: $\widehat{S}(t + 1)$, $\widehat{x}(t + 1)$, $x(t + 1)$ Equation (7.8)	Output = $C(t + 1)$; Parameter = none Input: $S(t + 1)$, $x(t + 1)$, $P(t + 1)$ Equation is analogous to (7.6)

Outcomes for Year $t + 1$ = Inputs to Planning for Year $t + 2$

Note: $x(t) = [B(t), I(t), E(t), R(t), G(t)]$

Figure 7.5. Flowchart for first-order smoothing process

budget process. Thus it can exert a very strong planning discipline with respect to the spending-saving decision, which is likely to please those responsible for the institution's investments.

Planning for year $t + 1$ continues with the determination of the ex ante or planned surplus or deficit (step IV). The object here is to balance the impact of deviations of the conditional budget from its target, on the one hand, with the desire to move the operating reserve back on target, on the other. The planned conditional budget is determined in step V, which completes the planning cycle for year $t + 1$.

Time passes, and at the end of the year the final or ex post outcomes for the budget variables are known. The final surplus or deficit, calculated at year-end closing, is the sum of the planned surplus or deficit plus a specified fraction of the net deviations that occurred over the year. Once again, the object in determining the fraction ω is to balance the effects of this decision on the operating reserve and the final conditional budget. The latter is determined as a residual from the ex post cash flow identity (step VII). This completes all the activities for year $t + 1$, and provides the inputs necessary to plan for year $t + 2$.

We have a few concluding comments to make before going on to consider how optimal values of the smoothing parameters ℓ, κ, χ, and ω can be determined. First, the decision rule for $\hat{S}(t + 1)$ puts a very strong element of integral control into the system because it depends on a target for the operating reserve *balance*, which in turn is a function of past surpluses and deficits. "The greater the emphasis on reaching the operating reserve target, the greater will be the strain on the conditional budget, which is also affected by the endowment payout smoothing rule." Our experience has shown that the strength of one's desire to make adjustments in the operating reserve may well depend on the projected size of the conditional budget for the year in question. For example, imagine a situation in which not only is the reserve well below target (which it normally would be if a planned surplus were called for) but dollar payout from the endowment happens to be below the equilibrium rate. Together these factors would put a double squeeze on the planned conditional budget, so that it might seem desirable to postpone any buildup of the operating reserve. The possibility that the planned surplus or deficit might depend on the projected conditional budget is not included in our model, though it could be added by inserting a new term (and a new parameter) in equation (7.16). Such a term could also be added to equation (7.8), for the ex post surplus.

Another possible approach to control, which we do not consider in our model, is that the budget adjustments, $\hat{A}(t + 1)$, might be made to depend not only on the projected budget gap but also on the difference between the operating reserve balance and its target. In other words, when the reserve balance is down one might be tempted to reduce the unconditional (i.e., regular) budget by an extra amount in order to generate more surplus. Once again, this procedure could be added to the model by introducing a new term (and a new parameter) in equation (7.14). We should say, though, that in principle this idea seems to have some disadvantages. It would amount to changing the operating-budget base (which, we have argued, should be viewed as a flow of funds) in order to compensate for a problem in the level of the operating reserve. While there may be circumstances where this would be an appropriate strategy, it also could be quite destabilizing.

Finally, we should point out that while the smoothing rules for budget adjustment and endowment payout (equations [7.14] and [7.15]) are based on a fixed target payout rate, they do not have to be. (We showed earlier how p can be a stabilizing force.) The payout rate that is consistent with LRFE—a rate based on the latest market value for the endowment—can be calculated from basic LRFE theory (see equation [6.9]). Then the new value of p can be used in the smoothing equations (7.14) and (7.15). Since the change in p is in the direction of greater stability, the result should be to increase the amount of smoothing for given values of ℓ and κ. However, the LRFF solution for p involves a quadratic, and so the linearity of the system is destroyed. This would pose no problem in practice or for analysis (for instance, by means of Monte Carlo simulation). It would, however, preclude us from optimizing the parameters of the system based on the linear theory discussed later in this chapter.

Determination of the Smoothing Parameters

Our model is now complete except for the question of how to determine good values for the smoothing parameters. For this we must ask ourselves in more specific terms about the model's objectives. Common sense suggests a number of objectives, among them the following.

1. *To avoid "start-stop" budgeting.* Among the harmful consequences of start-stop budgeting are loss of predictability in the institution's programs, decline in faculty and staff morale, and erosion of the administration's credibility. The more erratic the budget adjustments, $A(t)$, the more such "adjustment costs" will be incurred. Negative values of $A(t)$ are of course the most troublesome ones, but unfortunately any control model that leads to positive deviations is also going to produce some negative ones.

2. *To avoid large surpluses and deficits.* Large surpluses tend to represent forgone academic program opportunities, while large deficits draw down reserves and raise questions about financial viability.

3. *To avoid large fluctuations in the conditional budget.* Even though $C(t)$ is expressly "conditional," it is nice to be able to predict final allocations to the conditional budget at year end with some degree of confidence. Also, it is a very serious matter if the conditional budget "goes negative," since then there will either have to be an unexpectedly large deficit or holdbacks on previously authorized expenditures.

4. *To avoid drift in the effective endowment payout rate.* The "effective endowment payout rate" is the chosen dollar value of payout divided by the beginning endowment market value: i.e., $P(t + 1)/E(t)$. It should not be confused with the "equilibrium" or "target payout rate," which is simply p. An effective payout rate that is too high may violate policy or legal restrictions on spending capital appreciation; in any case, it is bound to raise serious and legitimate questions about the university's financial discipline. A rate that is too low may also be very difficult to explain, since many people tend to confuse the payout rate with investment yield; for instance, it may discourage potential donors of gifts to the endowment.

These are all worthwhile objectives. The problem is that they are mutually contradictory. What is needed is a method for trading off one against the other, as when the values of the smoothing parameters are varied. For instance, if $\ell = 0$ there are never any budget adjustments, so objective 1 is maximized. However, objectives 2 and 3 are hit hard. Or, setting $\kappa = 1$ pegs the effective payout rate at the equilibrium payout rate, which maximizes objective 4 at the expense of the other three. We already have noted how setting χ and ω allocates the bottom line of the operating budget between the surplus or deficit and the conditional budget.

How can the effect of a given set of parameter values on the objectives be evaluated? The most direct way, which will have some appeal, no doubt, as a first step into the arena of stochastic control models, is to use Monte Carlo simulation. This technique is well known to management scientists and will be described here in outline only (see chapter 4 for a discussion). First, random numbers are generated in the computer according to the probability distributions that have been specified for the uncertain parameters in the laws of motion. All the relevant quantities in the model are then computed in accordance with each such realization of the random process. The computation proceeds sequentially, one year at a time; a long sequence of years constitutes a *run* of the model. Each run thus represents a set of outcomes that are chosen at random and based upon the prespecified set of initial conditions. A group of runs, or *replications*, may be needed before one can get some idea of the variables' mean values and ranges. Obviously, if two groups of runs differ only with respect to the values chosen for the smoothing parameters, the effects of this difference can be evaluated by examining the simulation outputs. Successive trials can be undertaken until the results appear to the decision maker to be reasonable.

Though the process of Monte Carlo simulation is straightforward it is also somewhat cumbersome and can be expensive in terms of computer time. Another approach is to define an *objective function* that quantifies the considerations represented by the four general objectives given above, and then seek to derive a mathematical expression for approximating its expected value.* If this can be done, the value of the objective function is calculable quickly and inexpensively for each of a large number of combinations of ℓ, κ, χ, and ω. This, in turn, permits at least a rough optimization of the parameter values.

We believe that the following objective function comes close enough to

---

*The expected value of the objective function can also be calculated from the output of a group of Monte Carlo simulation runs, and it may represent a useful summary measure for these runs.

meeting the mathematical criteria described earlier. Moreover, a good approximation to its expected value can be computed without a great deal of difficulty provided that: (a) the laws of motion, stochastic elements, and controls are linear in the system variables; (b) the serial correlations are zero.[9] Our system conforms to (a), given the method for representing uncertainty that we described in solution procedure 7.1. Zeroing out the serial correlation is not a great sacrifice, and the degree of distortion so introduced can be checked later by comparing the analytical results with those from Monte Carlo simulations.

PROCEDURE 7.1. Let $y_k(t)$ be a list of components of the objective function evaluated at time t. Then we write the objective, U, as a weighted sum of squares of the y_k, discounted over time:

$$U = \sum_t \delta^t \sum_k \beta_k y_k^2(t) \tag{7.17}$$

where δ is an appropriate discount factor. The reason for discounting over time is that the salience of forthcoming events will decline as they recede into the future. For example, the prospect of a large deficit ten years from now is not as frightening as the prospect of one next year.

We define the elements y_k as follows:

Let $y_1 = \mathscr{E}[A(t)^2]^{\frac{1}{2}}$, the mean square deviation of $A(t)$ about its target value, which is zero (a large value denotes a climate of "start-stop" budgeting)*

$y_2 = \sigma[P(t)]$, the standard deviation of endowment payout (large values impose a potential hardship on programs that depend on restricted endowment)

$y_3 = \mathscr{E}[S(t)^2]^{\frac{1}{2}}$, again a mean square deviation, this time of the surplus or deficit (large values signal instability in financial conditions)

$y_4 = \mathscr{E}[\{C(t) - \Omega B(t)\}^2]^{\frac{1}{2}}$, the mean-square error of the conditional budget around its target (large values mean less predictability for expenditures in the conditional budget)

$y_5 = \mathscr{E}[\{R(t) - \Pi B(t)\}^2]^{\frac{1}{2}}$, the mean-square error of the operating reserve balance (large values signal even more financial instability than do variations in $S(t)$ by themselves)

$y_6 = Pr[C(t) < 0]$, the probability that the conditional budget is negative

---

*The root mean square error (RMSE) is a measure of dispersion or, more precisely, the square root of a sum of squares. It is analogous to the standard deviation, except that the sum of squares is taken around the origin (the natural zero-point for the variable) rather than the mean. Here, the RMSE is used for most variables because their means are intended to be zero, and we want any deviation to be penalized. The target value for P is pE, but we were not concerned about the slight deviations generated by limiting ourselves to first-order equilibrium (see chapter 6). Hence the standard deviation was used for P.

(a negative value for the conditional budget implies cancellation of previously authorized expenditures, which is a very disruptive event)

$y_7 = Pr[R(t) < \Pi_L B(t)]$ (an operating reserve below some lower limit, Π_L, may not be able to handle unexpected events due to transient effects, misspecifications built into the model, or both)

$y_8 = Pr[P(t) < p_L E(t - 1)]$ (an endowment payout rate below some lower limit p_L will raise questions internally and also turn away potential donors of gifts to endowment)

$y_9 = Pr[P(t) > p_U E(t - 1)]$ (an endowment payout rate above its upper limit P_U will worry financial advisors and perhaps violate legal constraints on the expenditure of capital appreciation).

Obviously variations on these definitions suggest themselves, and we would not argue strenuously for any particular detail. We do believe, however, that this list includes many factors of relevance to the handling of uncertainty in college and university budgets.

Table 7.5 gives examples of the kinds of judgments needed to determine the weighting parameters, β_k, in the objective function. We found it convenient to focus upon variation in the surplus or deficit as a *numeraire*. Imagine that the RMSE for the surplus or deficit is $1 million. Since the expected value of $S(t)$ is zero, this means that in roughly two years out of three the surplus or deficit will be in the range of $\pm$\$1 million. Now we ask ourselves: What value of dispersion for the budget adjustments, $A(t)$, would make us indifferent to a value of $1 million for the dispersion in the surplus or deficit? Suppose the answer is $500 thousand. This pegs the *indifference value* for y_1 in the table at 0.500 which in turn permits us to calculate the value of β_1 as 4.0. (The β value is the reciprocal of the square of the indifference value: "reciprocal" because tighter bounds should imply a greater weight; and "squared" because y_k is squared in the objective function.) In other words, we want to control budget

Table 7.5. Example of Objective-Function Weights

Name	Variable	Definition	Indifference Value[a]	Beta Weight[b]
$SM(A)$	y_1	$\mathscr{E}\,[A(t)^2]^{\frac{1}{2}}$	0.500	4.0
$SD(P)$	y_2	$\sigma[P(t)]$	0.707	2.0
$SM(S)$	y_3	$\mathscr{E}\,[S(t)^2]^{\frac{1}{2}}$	1.000[c]	1.0
$SM(C)$	y_4	$\mathscr{E}\,[\{C(t) - \omega B(t)\}^2]^{\frac{1}{2}}$	1.414	0.5
$SM(R)$	y_5	$\mathscr{E}\,[\{R(t) - \pi B(t)\}^2]^{\frac{1}{2}}$	0.250	16.0
Pr(C low)	y_6	$Pr[C(t) < 0]$	0.025	1,600.0
Pr(R low)	y_7	$Pr[R(t) < \pi_L B(t)]$	0.100	100.0
Pr(p low)	y_8	$Pr[P(t) < p_L E(t - 1)]$	0.200	25.0
Pr(p high)	y_9	$Pr[P(t) > p_u E(t - 1)]$	0.200	25.0

[a] In millions of dollars for y_1 through y_5; probability points for y_6 through y_9.
[b] $\beta_\kappa = $ (indifference value $_\kappa$)$^{-2}$.
[c] y_3 is taken to be the numeraire.

adjustments twice as tightly as the surplus or deficit in this example, and this implies that their weights should differ by a factor of four. The weights for the other variables were determined in a similar manner.

The results given in the next section are intended to provide some insight into the model's behavior; they are based on the objective function just presented. Later, we shall present additional results that represent work in process on applying the model to the decision problem of Stanford's endowment payout.

Sample Results

A first step in evaluating any model is to exercise it to the point at which its operating characteristics are understood. The data for these runs need to be representative, but it is not necessary that they refer to a specific decision problem. The results described in this section are based on the objective-function weights in table 7.5, the data pertaining to uncertainty given in table 7.4, and the following values for the expected growth rates and other parameters.*

Growth-rate expectations and rate parameters:

$\iota = 0.050$	$\rho = 0.055$	$\Omega = 0.030$
$r = 0.021$	$\gamma = 0.025$	$\Pi = 0.020$
$f = 0.003$	$p = 0.045$	$\Pi_L = 0.015$
$i = 0.023$		$P_L = 0.040$
$g = 0.000$	$\delta = 0.707$	$P_U = 0.055$

Initial conditions (in millions of dollars):

$B(0) = 100$	$E(0) = 217$	$A(0) = 0$
$I(0) = 94$	$R(0) = 2$	$P(0) = 9$
$G(0) = 5$	$C(0) = 3$	$S(0) = 0$

The first step in the analysis is to determine the values of the smoothing parameters that maximize the objective function. In the present case this was done heuristically, which means that we sat at the computer terminal and searched through various combinations until we were reasonably sure the optimum had been approximated. This was surprisingly easy, since the characteristics of the parameter space and objective function turned out to be rather simple. The optimal values are as follows:

---

*The model formulation upon which these results are based allowed for a fraction, ϕ, of the adjustments to be allocated to expense and $1 - \phi$ to operating income, as in the transition-to-equilibrium model in chapter 6. (For laws of motion, analogous to the ones used here, that incorporate ϕ see equation [6.15]; for extension of the smoothing model to include ϕ, see Massy et al. 1979). The results given here use $\phi = 0.900$.

Smoothing Rule	Parameter	Value
Budget adjustment	ℓ	0.30
Endowment payout	κ	0.25
Planned surplus/deficit	χ	1.00
Ex post surplus/deficit	ω	0.00
Value of the objective function	U	4.12

Before discussing the implications of these values, it will be worthwhile to observe how the system evolves when the optimal smoothing parameters are utilized. This information is presented in table 7.6. The upper portion of the table gives the means expressed in constant dollars, based on the expected value of $B(t)$. The means are calculated from the same mathematical approximation used to get the variances and covariances as part of calculating the expectation of the objective function. The array of means simply shows that the system is indeed fairly close to dynamic equilibrium, since the average adjustments are very small and the operating reserve and conditional budget remain near their target values. The conditional budget drifts downwards because the system is not quite in equilibrium, and income shortfalls are taken out of $C(t)$. However, this drift is not consequential.

The evolution of system variability or, in other words, the cumulative effect of uncertainty is shown by the standard deviations in the lower part of the table. The most striking features are: (a) the dominant role played by the variance of investment return, a role that shows up in the standard deviation of the endowment balance; (b) the great stability of the surplus/deficit account and the operating reserve. We will return to these points in a moment. The other point of interest is that the degree of variation increases rapidly from year to year when t is small, after which the rate of increase slows but never stops. The initial rapid increase results from two factors: the initial conditions are assumed to be known (i.e., not subject to the uncertainty to which the system was subject in prior years); and it takes some time to approximate the ongoing uncertainty of a going concern. The ongoing rate of increase, which is smaller, should be seen as a normal attribute of an evolving random process. The longer one looks ahead, the more time there is for the process to "wander" and hence the more distance off the equilibrium trajectory it is likely to be.

Implications of the optimal parameters. Let us now return to the optimal values of the smoothing parameters. Here we meet with a real surprise with respect to χ and ω, the two that determine the surplus or deficit, the operating reserve, and the conditional budget. With $\chi = 1$ we will plan to bring the operating reserve all the way back to its target value every year. (Recall from equation [7.16] that χ is the fraction of the operating reserve gap that we try to close by planning a surplus or deficit.) Moreover, with $\omega = 0$ we will never change our plan for the surplus or deficit, and any change in the bottom line during the year will be taken up by the conditional budget. The implication of these results is that, if the operating reserve starts at its target value, i.e., if

Table 7.6. Means and Standard Deviations of State Variables and Controls from the Analytical Model, in Constant Dollars Based on the Expected Values of $B(t)$, Using the Optimal Smoothing Parameters

	Year					
	1	2	4	6	10	18
Means:						
$B(t)$	$100.00	$100.00	$99.99	$99.97	$99.88	$99.52
$I(t)$	93.91	93.81	93.62	93.44	93.07	92.37
$E(t)$	219.11	221.14	224.88	228.17	233.35	238.45
$R(t)$	2.00	2.00	2.00	2.00	2.00	1.99
$G(t)$	4.89	4.78	4.57	4.36	3.99	3.32
$A(t)$	0.00	0.00	0.01	0.01	0.03	0.07
$P(t)$	9.02	9.06	9.17	9.30	9.55	9.89
$S(t)$	−0.00	−0.00	−0.00	−0.00	−0.00	−0.00
$C(t)$	$2.93	$2.88	$2.81	$2.77	$2.74	$2.74
Standard deviations:						
$B(t)$	$0.79	$1.13	$1.79	$2.44	$3.63	$4.54
$I(t)$	1.00	1.41	1.97	2.39	3.05	4.04
$E(t)$	24.40	35.21	51.59	64.90	86.86	120.01
$R(t)$	0·02	0.03	0.04	0.05	0.07	0.11
$G(t)$	0.46	0.63	0.86	1.02	1.22	1.43
$A(t)$	0.00	0.41	0.55	0.58	0.59	0.60
$P(t)$	0.00	0.26	0.83	1.43	2.55	4.29
$S(t)$	0.00	0.02	0.02	0.02	0.02	0.02
$C(t)$	$0.86	$1.05	$1.17	$1.20	$1.22	$1.22

$R(0) = \Pi B(0)$, the only way in which an operating reserve gap can originate is from unplanned variations in its own investment return. But the reserve is assumed to be invested conservatively (e.g., in the university's expendable funds pool), so that the variance of its investment return is small. Hence the closing of 100 percent of any operating reserve gap each year does not introduce much variability into the rest of the system.

The effect of the optimal solution for χ and ω is, for all practical purposes, to preclude use of the operating reserve as an uncertainty-absorbing mechanism. The only reason for having a surplus or deficit is to adjust for unplanned deviations in the reserve's return on investment. It seems, however, that if there were no reserve there would not be any such deviations to be compensated for. Obviously this conclusion needs to be scrutinized with care. We shall find that, while not fully general, it does stem in an intuitively understandable way from the basic characteristics of a structure that has both an operating reserve and a conditional budget.

Table 7.7 presents a sensitivity analysis for χ and ω. The columns of the table show computed values for the relevant components of the objective function (the weights for these components are given in the column headings, for easy reference). The rows represent different combinations of values for χ and ω, for three selected time periods: 1, 2, and 6. Results for three different values of χ (with ω at its optimum value) are given in the upper portion of the table, while ω is varied in the bottom portion.

Notice first that reductions in χ from its optimal value shift the burden toward criteria relating to the surplus or deficit and operating reserve and away from criteria relating to the conditional budget. This is to be expected, of course. What is important, however, is that the terms of trade, as we might call them, are quite onerous. That is, as χ is reduced we lose a great deal of stability in $RMSE(S)$ and $RMSE(R)$ but gain only a little in $RMSE(C)$. The same is true with respect to the probability criteria $P_r(C$ low) and $Pr(R$ low). It would be possible to change the objective function weights in order to penalize variations in the conditional budget to a greater extent, but any such change would have to be rather large in order to counteract the above effect. Our conclusion is that, to the extent the basic assumptions of the model are realistic, it is best to close an operating reserve gap as soon as it appears. If this is not done, the reserve and the surplus/deficit accounts will diverge from their targets with increasing rapidity.

The situation with respect to ω is even more interesting. Notice that, after year 1, the variation in both the conditional budget and the surplus/deficit and operating reserve increase as ω is increased (year 1 is an anomaly due to the influence of the initial conditions). There is no tradeoff here at all: the optimum for ω is unequivocally zero no matter what weights we choose for the objective function.

The reason for this unexpected finding is not hard to determine. Recall that the model contains no backlog of unmet conditional budget needs. We assumed

Table 7.7. Sensitivity Analysis for χ and ω, Based on the Analytical Model (with the Other Parameters at Their Optimum Values)

Time Period	Parameter Value	$SM(S)$ (1.000)	$SM(C)$ (0.707)	$SM(R)$	$Pr(C$ Low) (40.0)	$Pr(R$ Low) (10.0)[a]
For χ (optimum is 1.0):						
1	0.0	0.067	0.867	0.072	0.000	0.000
	0.5	0.035	0.867	0.040	0.000	0.000
	1.0	0.000	0.869	0.019	0.000	0.000
2	0.0	0.616	0.864	0.612	0.000	0.305
	0.5	0.306	0.921	0.311	0.000	0.081
	1.0	0.021	1.062	0.019	0.003	0.000
6	0.0	0.870	0.864	1.050	0.000	0.570
	0.5	0.324	1.114	0.700	0.005	0.330
	1.0	0.022	1.226	0.194	0.011	0.000
For ω (optimum is 0.0):						
1	0.0	0.000	0.869	0.019	0.000	0.000
	0.5	0.430	0.442	0.433	0.000	0.123
	1.0	0.860	0.074	0.862	0.000	0.281
2	0.0	0.021	1.062	0.194	0.000	0.000
	0.5	0.607	1.126	0.432	0.005	0.123
	1.0	1.214	1.465	0.862	0.024	0.281
6	0.0	0.022	1.226	0.194	0.011	0.000
	0.5	0.607	1.281	0.433	0.014	0.123
	1.0	1.215	1.588	0.862	0.039	0.281

[a] Effective weight $\beta^{\frac{1}{2}}$ (from table 7.5); weights are not comparable between SM and Pr, due to difference in scale.

implicitly that, on average over time, the overs and unders would balance out, but we did not keep book on the backlog. (Our omission was consistent with the way in which the conditional budget concept evolved at Stanford.) Contrast our attitude toward the operating reserve, where the balance is monitored and compared with a target. When a surplus or deficit causes a variation in the balance, as would often be the case where $\omega > 0$, we are not only penalized because of RMSE(S), but—as long as $\chi > 0$—are also forced to plan countervailing surpluses or deficits in the future in order to restore the reserve to its target value. (We are also penalized through RMSE(R), and possibly $Pr[R$ low], for every year that the reserve deviates from its target.) Restoring the operating balance induces variation in the conditional budget, other things being equal, because a surplus or deficit that would not otherwise have been necessary must now be planned.

The conclusion is very strong: deviations that affect the operating reserve will just have to be compensated for later if the target is to be maintained. Thus they will incur penalties in the conditional budget sooner or later. They will also incur a string of penalties in terms of the surplus or deficit (one penalty in going into the reserve and another in coming out) and the operating reserve balance. It is better to absorb the ex post surprises in the conditional budget right away, and avoid having to "pay the middleman" (i.e., by "storing" them temporarily in the operating reserve).

These conclusions should not be construed to mean that surpluses and deficits are meaningless or that an operating reserve is unnecessary. To conclude anything of the sort would be to place too much faith in the model. Certainly, surpluses and deficits will occur. Sometimes they fulfill a need to send a signal to one constituency or another—a deficit, for instance, indicates financial stringency and helps to justify budget adjustments. Or, the budget requests in a given year may be so much more (or less) compelling than usual that the decision rules in the model should be set aside. Finally, changes in external conditions may give rise to problems that are too large to be handled with the conditional budget. We saw an example of this phenomenon in our discussion of the transition-to-equilibrium model, in chapter 6.

Let us now turn to the other two smoothing parameters: ℓ and κ. We should say that $\ell = 0.30$ strikes us as perhaps about right. In retrospect, however, $\kappa = 0.25$ seems too low to provide a sufficient discipline on the effective endowment payout rate. For that value of κ, here are the payout rate probabilities:

Year	$Pr(p$ Low)	$Pr(p$ High)	$Pr(p$ Low or High)
1	0.08	0.01	0.09
2	0.14	0.04	0.18
4	0.17	0.08	0.25
6	0.18	0.10	0.28
10	0.17	0.11	0.28
18	0.15	0.14	0.29

These data show that in one year out of four or slightly more often, the payout rate will be less than 4 percent or higher than 5.5 percent, a prospect that strikes us as not being very satisfactory; probably, the objective-function weights we assigned to these variables in table 7.5 were too small. It is true that, even with a relatively loose control on the payout rate, the degree of variation in dollar payout is quite large and increases rapidly over time (see table 7.6). However, this merely underscores the fact that the very large variance associated with investment return (which, it should be remembered, is based on empirical studies) requires some hard choices between smoothing dollar payout and smoothing the payout rate.

To examine these choices further we redefine the budget adjustment term in the objective function (which depends heavily on payout), to be somewhat more interpretable than the root mean square that we used originally. Instead, we use the probability that the adjustments would reduce the budget by $250 thousand or more, which experience has led us to think is a reasonable "threshold of pain." (Notice that this measure is asymmetric, in that upward adjustments are not penalized.) Hence y_1 in objective function becomes, for this analysis only:

$$y_1(t) = Pr[A(t) > 0.25].$$

The new value of β_1 is set to $(0.10)^{-2} = 100$, which makes this term of the same importance as $Pr[R(t) < \Pi_L B(t)]$.

Figure 7.6 shows the value of $Pr[A(6) > 0.25]$ as a function of ℓ, with κ equal to its old value of 0.25. The probability rises steeply at first but then become less sensitive above $\ell = 0.2$ and considerably less above $\ell = 0.3$. The new optimum is at $\ell = 0.4$, compared to $\ell = 0.3$ with the old objective function. The optimal values for the other parameters, including κ, are unchanged. We conclude that despite the relatively loose control on the payout rate it will be very hard to avoid downward budget adjustments exceeding $250 thousand, since they will occur with an average frequency of about one year in three.

Values of l smaller than 0.2 or so are possible. However, they would dangerously lengthen the time taken by the system in responding to unanticipated changes in the expected values of income and expenditures (see below, subsection headed "Nonstationary expected growth rates"). If κ is increased to generate more control on the payout, as seems to be necessary, the problem will be even worse. We will return to these questions later, when we come to discuss the setting of Stanford's endowment payout rate.

Monte Carlo simulations. Experience has shown that, whenever possible, important problems should be explored by a variety of methods. We therefore constructed a Monte Carlo simulation to process the stochastic laws of motion and evaluate the effect of the smoothing rules. The equations and data of the simulation model were as presented earlier, while the random shocks were assumed to be multivariate normally distributed (this requirement was eventually relaxed, since there was no need to assume that the shocks were serially independent). The simulation was executed for a period of eighteen years, the

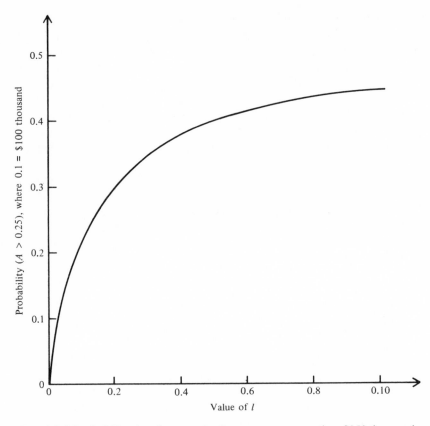

Figure 7.6. Probability that downward adjustments are more than $250 thousand, as a function of ℓ

same period needed for convergence of the optimization program. Each group of runs consisted of 100 replications of the eighteen-year sequence, starting from the same initial conditions. The simulation was coded in APL and the cost of each group of runs was about $15.00 at Stanford's campus computer facility.

Runs with the serial correlations set to zero were intended to track the results of the analytical calculations. They did so quite well, as demonstrated in table 7.8.[10] The z-values, given in the upper part of the table, reflect the statistical significance of differences between the means. They were obtained by subtracting the means in table 7.6 from the analogous quantities obtained from the simulation, and then dividing through by the appropriate standard deviation in table 7.6. A z-value outside the range ± 1.96 would be statistically significant, as indicated by the "critical values" given at the bottom of table 7.8. The lower part of the table presents information on the degree to which the standard deviations from the two models differed from one another. The test of statistical significance for this difference is based upon χ^2, critical values for

Table 7.8. Test of Significance of the Differences Between the Means and Standard Deviations from the Monte Carlo Simulation and the Analytical Model (Based on the Optimal Smoothing Parameters)

	Year					
	1	2	4	6	10	18
z = values:						
$B(t)$	$-$\$0.09	$-$\$0.11	$-$\$0.18	$-$\$0.23	$-$\$0.12	$-$\$0.04
$I(t)$	-0.10	-0.10	-0.12	-0.14	-0.11	-0.05
$E(t)$	-0.01	-0.01	-0.06	-0.04	-0.06	-0.07
$R(t)$	-0.05	-0.08	-0.18	-0.20	-0.06	-0.05
$G(t)$	0.06	0.07	0.26	0.25	0.21	0.68
$A(t)$	0.00	0.03	0.08	0.14	-0.05	0.16
$P(t)$	0.00	-0.01	-0.06	-0.09	0.00	-0.03
$S(t)$	0.00	-0.02	0.01	-0.06	0.10	-0.03
$C(t)$	$-$\$0.03	$-$\$0.03	\$0.03	\$0.09	\$0.10	\$0.09
χ^2 = values:						
$B(t)$	\$105.28	\$106.69	\$119.22	\$100.15	\$105.10	\$96.77
$I(t)$	102.48	110.29	123.56	112.51	109.59	117.64
$E(t)$	90.97	104.49	106.56	100.72	102.77	80.14
$R(t)$	75.95	111.66	127.65	101.06	104.12	89.53
$G(t)$	90.87	112.54	132.51*	119.85	111.65	84.00
$A(t)$	90.00	111.79	109.02	121.28	134.47*	98.34
$P(t)$	90.00	88.20	95.03	90.35	90.33	73.14*
$S(t)$	90.00	95.20	111.08	85.47	134.07*	114.07
$C(t)$	\$116.76	\$93.56	\$104.88	\$117.00	\$97.76	\$95.86

Critical values: $z(0.975) = 1.96$; $z(0.025) = -1.96$; $\chi^2(0.975, 99) = 73.36$; $\chi^2(0.025,99) = 128.50$.

which are also given at the bottom of table 7.8. A standard deviation obtained from the Monte Carlo simulation is significantly different from its counterpart in table 7.6 if the relevant χ^2 is outside the range of 73.36 to 128.50, and values meeting this criterion are indicated with an asterisk in table 7.8.

The null hypothesis that the means are equal was not rejected for any variable or year. For the variances, the null hypothesis (of equality) was rejected in only four out of fifty-four variable-year combinations, and no two of these were for the same variable. The value of the objective function, based on the optimal parameter values, was 3.74 for the simulation compared to 4.12 for the analytical result given earlier. The reason for this difference is not clear, but an examination of the components of the objective function did not disclose any material or interesting differences. All in all, the two models tracked each other very well considering their internal complexity. This added to our confidence in both of them.

The next step was to relax the requirement that the serial correlations be zero, and substitute the values of α in table 7.5. A comparison was made by rerunning the simulation with the same random number sequence used in the group of runs for which the serial correlations had been zero. The object of this strategy was to eliminate the random or Monte Carlo variance from between the two groups of runs, and so to sharpen our ability to compare their outputs.

The results are presented in table 7.9. Changing the serial correlations within

Table 7.9. Means and Standard Deviations of State Variables and Controls from the Monte Carlo Simulation, with and Without Serial Correlation, in Constant Dollars Based on the Expected Value of $B(t)$, Using the Optimal Smoothing Parameters

	Year					
	2		6		10	
	$\alpha = 0$	$\alpha \neq 0$	$\alpha = 0$	$\alpha \neq 0$	$\alpha = 0$	$\alpha \neq 0$
Means:						
$B(t)$	$99.88	$99.86	$99.39	$99.30	$99.43	$99.32
$I(t)$	93.67	93.65	93.10	93.01	92.01	92.65
$E(t)$	220.72	220.66	225.36	224.90	239.06	238.14
$R(t)$	2.00	2.00	2.00	2.00	1.99	1.99
$G(t)$	4.82	4.81	4.62	4.55	4.24	4.16
$A(t)$	0.01	0.01	0.09	0.10	0.00	0.00
$P(t)$	9.06	9.06	9.17	9.16	9.55	9.53
$S(t)$	-0.00	-0.00	-0.00	-0.00	0.00	0.00
$C(t)$	$2.85	$2.85	$2.88	$2.88	$2.86	$2.86
Standard deviations:						
$B(t)$	$1.17	$1.30	$2.46	$2.84	$3.74	$4.22
$I(t)$	1.49	1.60	2.55	2.93	3.21	3.77
$E(t)$	36.17	36.05	65.46	65.25	88.50	87.52
$R(t)$	0.03	0.01	0.05	0.06	0.08	0.09
$G(t)$	0.68	0.55	1.12	0.77	1.30	0.89
$A(t)$	0.44	0.44	0.65	0.66	0.69	0.70
$P(t)$	0.24	0.24	1.37	1.37	2.44	2.43
$S(t)$	0.02	0.02	0.02	0.02	0.03	0.03
$C(t)$	$1.02	$1.07	$1.31	$1.41	$1.21	$1.30

the range considered does not have a material effect on either the means or the standard deviations. The only exception is for gifts to endowment, $G(t)$, where the standard deviation is reduced by about one-third when $\alpha \neq 0$. However, this effect does not carry over into the other variables to any great extent. The value of the objective function (not shown in table 7.9) increased from 3.74 to 3.95, a difference of about six percent, when $\alpha \neq 0$. This implies that the existence of nonzero serial correlations destabilizes the system by a small amount. On balance, though, our conclusion is that the effects of the serial correlations can safely be ignored.

It is possible that the optimal values of ℓ and κ would change slightly if these effects were not ignored, but on a priori grounds it seems unlikely that there would be changes in χ and ω. And any change in ℓ or κ almost surely would be very small compared to the change that would be introduced by different weights for the objective function. Hence we feel comfortable in ignoring the serial correlations unless new information suggests that they are quite large relative to our current assumptions.

Nonstationary expected growth rates. Up to now we have been examining the operation of the smoothing rules under the assumption that the budget quantities' growth rates will remain constant. Clearly this is not likely to be so. Indeed, the paradigm for two-stage dynamic planning that we presented in chapter 6 expressly provided for a transition period followed by a period of long-run equilibrium. The transition period, it will be recalled, is characterized by the medium-range financial forecast, in which the expected growth rates of income and expense normally will vary from year to year. Only in the long run, which lies beyond the influence of specific factors that can be known currently, is it reasonable to assume a constancy of growth rates—and even here the assumption stems from lack of knowledge rather than conviction.

The justification for optimizing a dynamic control model on the basis of constant expected growth rates is that they provide the most general benchmark for performance that is possible. One need only consider the converse to see why this is true. Suppose we were to incorporate a particular nonstationary pattern of growth rates, as might be obtained from a given year's MRFF, into our model and optimize the smoothing parameters accordingly. The result would be a system that would be oriented toward the pattern in question and perform well on it, but that would not perform nearly as well on the opposite kind of pattern. We conclude that if one wants a general as opposed to an adaptive control model, and if one does not have strong a priori notions about what kinds of nonstationary patterns will be encountered, it is best to optimize on stationary data that are representative of the midpoint of what is likely to occur. We will return to the idea of adaptive control in the last section of this chapter.

Despite the powerful reasons for optimizing smoothing rules with stationary data, such questions as "What happens if the model was not specified correctly?" are quite relevant. We would like our models to be robust with respect to at least the most likely kinds of misspecification. In other words, a model that would lead one to disaster if its assumptions are not quite correct is not a very good one.

To test how our model would perform under specified nonstationary conditions we used the setting faced by Stanford at the beginning of the Budget Equilibrium Program in the autumn of 1974. For expected growth rates we used the MRFF of that period. (The data were presented in table 6.3 in connection with the transition-to-equilibrium model.) This forecast started very far from equilibrium and the expected growth rates varied a great deal from year to year until the end of the MRFF period, in year 5, when long-run assumptions were used. The initial operating reserve was set at \$1.605 million (the actual value at the time) and the original conditional budget was set at $\Omega B(0)$. While the conditional budget concept had not yet been invented in 1974/75, a certain amount of income was being held back from $I(0)$ to deal with contingencies. To take care of this we added $\Omega B(0)$ back into $I(0)$. The other initial conditions were the same as in table 6.3. Finally, the stochastic parameters (including the nonzero values for the serial correlations) were taken to represent deviations from the expectations generated by the MRFF.

Figure 7.7 compares the means from the Monte Carlo simulation with the results from the transition-to-equilibrium model (which were also given in table 6.3). The variables chosen for comparison are the budget adjustments $A(t)$,

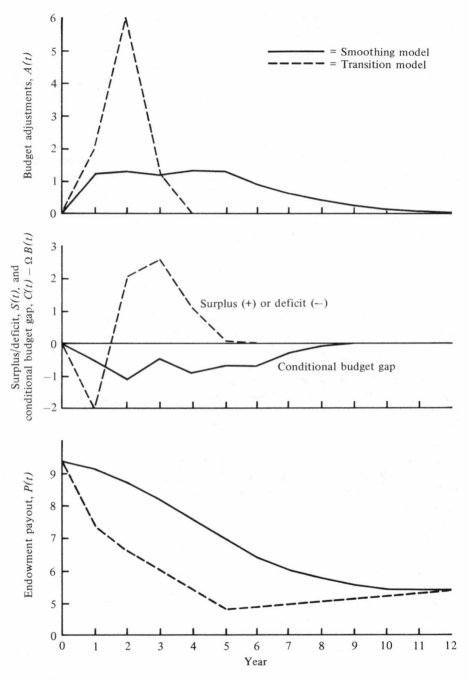

Figure 7.7. Comparison of smoothing and transition-to-equilibrium models for Stanford's 1975–78 data

the endowment payout $P(t)$, and two measures of short-term dislocation—the conditional budget gap, $C(t) - \Omega B(t)$, for the simulation, and the surplus/deficit, for the transition model. (Because $\chi = 1$ and $\omega = 0$, deviations of the operating reserve from its target are roughly equivalent to deficits in the transition model. Phaseout costs have been removed from the TRANS deficits to improve the comparability.) All figures are expressed in constant dollars.

The most obvious finding is that the smoothing model takes nearly a decade to close the budget gap, whereas the transition model was constrained to get the budget adjustments over with in three years. However, the total amounts of the adjustments (i.e., the areas under the curves) are not much different. A similar pattern holds for the conditional budget gap which, while never exceeding about $1 million per year, are spread out over six or seven years. The dollar value of endowment payout also declines rather slowly in the smoothing model, whereas in TRANS it was required to drop rapidly for five years, after which it assumed its equilibrium growth trajectory. (The mean payout in the smoothing model would also begin to grow, but not until after year 12.) All in all, the smoothing model does indeed close the gap, even though the growth rates are nonstationary and there are continuous random shocks built into the model, but it does so much more slowly than the transition-to-equilibrium model.

It seems to us that ten years is too long to hold an institution's feet to the fire, and that on this ground alone one would have done well to have set the smoothing model aside and accelerated the pace toward financial equilibrium had the circumstances represented by figure 7.7 actually come to pass. (Notice that the simulation assumes only the data available to us in October 1974, so the length of the response period would have been predictable.) In addition, there is always the possibility that things will get even worse than shown in any given MRFF. When one is very far from equilibrium it is good to try to recover fairly fast so as to be able to parry any new blows.

One other factor would have argued for speeding up the adjustment process, had we been looking at the smoothing model results during the autumn of 1974. It is evident from the following data for the mean and standard deviation of the conditional budget during the transition period.

Year	Conditional Budget ($ Million)	
	Mean	Standard Deviation
1	1.54	0.56
2	0.86	0.73
4	1.10	0.87
6	1.30	0.87
10	1.99	0.78

Notice that in year 2 the mean has declined to the point at which it is not much bigger than the standard deviation. $C(t)$ is approximately normally distributed, so a ratio (actually a t value) of $0.86 \div 0.73 = 1.18$ implies that there is about a 12 percent chance that the conditional budget will be negative. That would require expenditure holdbacks or unplanned deficits, and though 12 percent is not a terribly large risk we would be skating on thin ice. The risk declines over the next few years, but at a rather slow rate. Traveling faster along the road to equilibrium would significantly reduce the level of vulnerability in the conditional budget.

The analysis just completed has had the dual purpose of demonstrating how a given smoothing model can be evaluated by simulation and of improving our insight into the model itself. Our conclusion is that the model with $\ell = 0.30$ and $\kappa = 0.25$ performed adequately, in the sense that no disasters occurred. (An example of a "disaster" would be a consistently negative conditional budget, or a failure of the model to converge in any reasonable period of time.) Certainly this basically reasonable result, given a MRFF that was badly out of equilibrium, plus the fact that one can always choose to set the model aside temporarily and accelerate progress toward equilibrium, add an element of comfort.

An Application to Endowment Payout Policy

How to determine endowment payout is among the more vexing questions of policy that face university officers and trustees. Not only are spending and saving needs at odds but the large variations in endowment market values make it very difficult to know what would be prudent and what overly frugal. In the hope of obtaining a reasonable and understandable discipline for setting the dollar value of endowment payout, we have undertaken to apply the smoothing rule concept to the budgeting process at Stanford. The following subsection describes work in process with respect to that project.

The version of the model used in our work, for reasons made clear earlier, has excluded the operating reserve mechanism. (We simply started the reserve balance at its target value and set $\omega = 0$, $\chi = 1$, and the variance of investment return at zero.) Growth rates are based on Stanford's current assumptions for long-run equilibrium; the uncertainty parameters are as described earlier. The analytical version of the model is used to perform the calculations. The problem of judgmental or implicit optimization is, of course, to find satisfactory values of the smoothing parameters ℓ and κ. The criterion variables are the amounts of variation in the payout rate, p, net budget enrichment, f, and the conditional budget, c. These have replaced the objective function of equation (7.17).

We have not attempted to set up a formal objective function for this analysis, but have chosen instead to deal with the three variables directly. All variables are evaluated at year 6, which, as noted earlier, approximates the steady-state operation of the system. The conditional budget is expressed as a ratio to the operating budget, i.e., $c = C(6)/B(6)$. Hence all three criterion variables are expressed as fractions. Mean square errors about the target or equilibrium variables are used as measures of variation unless otherwise noted.

It is clear, of course, that the primary tradeoff is in terms of how much investment risk should be borne by the budget and how much by the endowment itself. The payout smoothing rule is

$$P(t + 1) = \kappa \bar{p} E(t) + (1 - \kappa)[1 + \imath + r + f]P(t)$$

where $\bar{p}$ is the equilibrium payout rate. If $\kappa = 0$, dollar payout increases at the expected growth rate of the budget, in which case the endowment bears all the risk. Thus changes in $E(t)$ lead to variations in the effective payout rate, p, and hence to departures from equilibrium. On the other hand, if $\kappa = 1$ the effective payout rate is pegged at $\bar{p}$ and the budget bears all the risk.

A primary question, then, is, "How much variation in the payout rate is permissible?" Figure 7.8 gives some important tradeoff information. The curve for $Pr[p > 0.055]$ tracks the (allowable) likelihood (allowable by us, that is) of exceeding the maximum payout rate. The Employee Retirement Income Security Act of 1974 provides for a "corridor" of plus or minus 20 percent for the valuation of pension fund assets. The provision recognizes the effect of investment risk and offers a certain degree of latitude before adjustments need to be made—which amounts to a kind of smoothing. An analogous criterion might be helpful in the case of endowment. In the above calculations the equilibrium payout rate is 0.475, so the corridor is from 0.038 to 0.057. For the upper bound, this is about halfway between the two curves dealing with the payout rate in figure 7.8. In any case, the value 0.040 is the smallest payout rate we would like to see. However, because the probability distribution is approximately symmetrical the curve for this lower bound nearly coincides with that for the upper bound, at $p = 0.055$, so it is not shown. The curve for $Pr[p > 0.060]$ represents an even more extreme limit—one we would not like to see under any circumstances. Together, the two curves indicate how much investment risk is being borne by the endowment for each value of κ.

The other two curves in the figure provide a rough measure of how much investment risk is being transmitted to the budget. The one for $Pr[P$ declines$]$ tracks the probability that the dollar value of payout declines in nominal terms from one year to the next. The one labeled $Pr[$real P declines$]$ does the same thing for real dollar payout. Obviously other measures are possible but these two give a reasonably clear picture of the tradeoff.

Analysis of figure 7.8 inclines us towards the conclusion that a κ value of between 0.33 and 0.40 might be about right. A value of 0.40 implies that the payout rate will tend to fall within the range of 4.0 to 5.5 percent about two-thirds of the time. Nominal dollar payout will decline about one-sixth of the time and real payout about one-third of the time. A value of 0.33 provides a little more smoothing, but increases the variance of the endowment payout rate slightly. On balance, we have decided to use a value of 0.40 at Stanford, at least for the time being. Of course a more refined analysis might produce different results. Also, we are considering the desirability of using a different set of decision rules when the payout boundaries are reached. For instance, it may be desirable to use the smoothing formula as long as $0.040 \leq p \leq 0.055$, but set it aside when the limits are exceeded and simply set p at the given boundary. This would truncate the probability distributions and very likely have the effect of

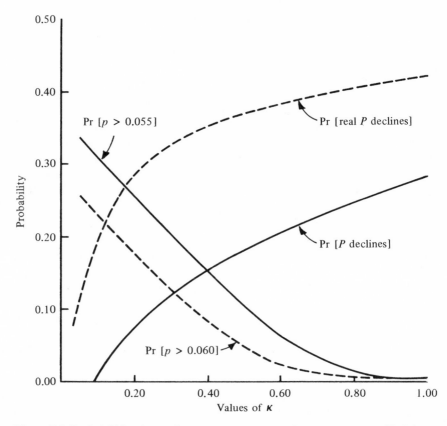

Figure 7.8. Probabilities that endowment payout, P, and payout rate, p, will violate specified constraints, as functions of the smoothing parameter, κ

slightly lowering the probabilities for the payout rate being out of bounds while increasing those for a decline in dollar payout. Obviously, more sophisticated combinations of rules are also possible.

The next problem is to determine a reasonable value for ℓ, the variable that splits the variations in payout between the regular and the conditional budgets. Relevant data are presented in figure 7.9, which shows the tradeoffs between the mean squares for f and c for different values of ℓ when $\kappa = 0.4$. One way to analyze these data is to draw a set of indifference lines between f and c, as has been done in the figure. If one has equal preference (or rather aversion) for the two quantities, the slope of the indifference line is 1 : 1. In this case the optimal value of ℓ is about 0.35, where the indifference line is tangent to the tradeoff curve. If the preference ratio is 1 : 2, ℓ should be about 0.40; if it is 2 : 1, the value goes to about 0.25. The sharp knee in the curve more or less pegs the value of ℓ within the range of 0.25 to 0.5 which may well be precise enough, since this decision rule is used more to indicate a general objective than to compute a

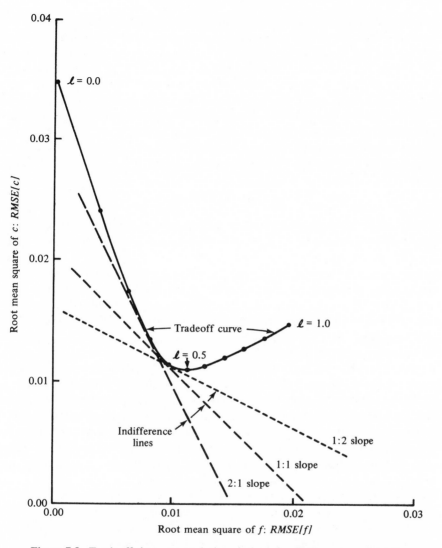

Figure 7.9. Tradeoffs between variations in base funded improvement (f) and conditional budget (C), for $\kappa = 0.40$, and for variations in δ in 0.1 increments from 0.0 to 1.0.

particular budget quantity. Our own preference, colored by a rather hearty aversion for budget base adjustments, runs toward an ℓ value of perhaps 0.25 to 0.30.

The outcome we are considering at Stanford is to use the endowment payout rule as a policy statement for determining the dollar value of endowment payout each year. That is, we would actually calculate dollar payout according to the formula and seek authorization from the trustees to spend this amount. (The final formula may incorporate some limiting concept, as indicated earlier.) A rigorous policy of this kind seems to us to be appropriate for endowment payout because the spending-saving decision is so controversial and so much uncertainty is involved. Both of these conditions make it hard to bring independent judgment to bear on a year-by-year basis, and thus suggest the need for a systemic solution Once dollar payout had been determined we would propose to use the smoothing equation (the one involving ℓ) to set a target for the year's net funded improvement. However, this target would be "soft" in the sense that the particulars of the annual budget process would and should lead to deviations from it as the final budget for the year is put together.

Generalizations

The road we have traveled has taken us from a general description of dynamic control processes to a specific model that, we have found, has some useful implications for the planning of college and university budgets. It has not been an easy road; both conceptually and mathematically, models incorporating uncertainty are among the most complex in this book. We shall now proceed even further down the same road and describe some models that are more general, more powerful, and more complex. By traveling with us to the end, the hardy reader will not only get to see these models but also gain better insight into the ones previously introduced.

Let us begin by looking at the basic idea of feedback control as expressed in graphic form in figure 7.10. Suppose that expense and total income are in equilibrium prior to time t_P. That is to say, income was equal to expense at t_0 and their growth rates were equal as well, so that the two trajectories coincided. A perturbation, such as might be caused by an unanticipated dose of inflation for example, is assumed to occur at time t_P. Though both growth rates are assumed to be increased, that for expense is driven up more sharply, thus throwing the system out of equilibrium and opening a budget gap.

We hypothesize that the control system begins to respond at time t_C. Control is applied to the expense side of the budget, beginning at point C. The growth of expenditures is turned down to the point where, for a while, it is less than that for income. This may be done by a series of budget base reductions, though something will also have to be done to bring the growth rates back together before equilibrium can be restored. The solid line for expenses assumes that past gaps do not need to be made up, an assumption that permits the expense curve to settle back to the income curve from above. This is the situation with the conditional budget as we described it in the previous section. (The gap is the shaded area in the figure.)

Suppose, however, that the gap represents a series of deficits, and that it is necessary to restore the operating reserve to its target value. Then much stronger control must be applied. The effect of such control is shown in figure 7.10 by the broken curve for expenditures, which diverges from the solid one at point D. This expenditure path eventually drops below the income curve (thus generating

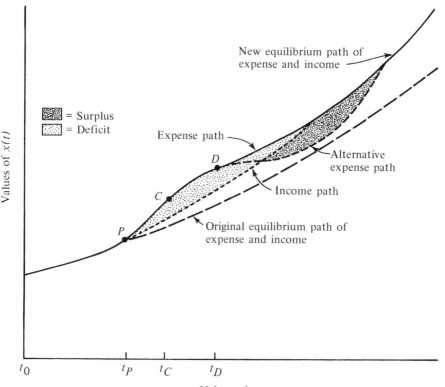

Figure 7.10. Example of a dynamic control process

surplus, as shown by the dotted line in the figure), and then approaches the new equilibrium path from below. Needless to say, the solid curve will be better because there are significant costs due to the application of control. (Budget base reductions or expenditure holdbacks are harmful to academic programs.) This is why we found that the conditional budget was a better device for absorbing uncertainty than the operating reserve.

Figure 7.11 depicts the stochastic element in dynamic control under uncertainty. The two heavy curves represent the expected trajectory of any variable, $x(t)$, starting from t_0 or t_Q, respectively. The dashed curves delimiting the shaded areas represent one standard deviation (σ) above and below the expected trajectories. Notice that the variance is zero at t_0, since the initial conditions are assumed to be known. Then the variance grows steadily through time, as was shown empirically in the last section. This is the *random walk* phenomenon we alluded to earlier: the more time the process has been running the more it may have wandered from its expected path. Suppose that the random walk has brought the system to point Q at time t_Q. This would not have been very probable as viewed from time t_0, but it could happen. Once we have observed point Q, however, it is no longer uncertain and, in fact, forms a new initial

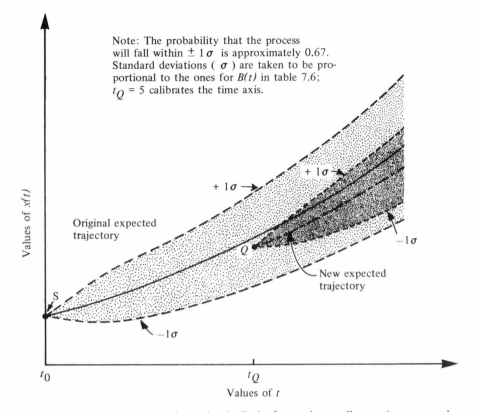

Figure 7.11. Expected trajectories and $\pm 1\sigma$ limits for random walks starting at t_0 and t_Q

condition. Looking forward from t_Q, we see a new expected trajectory and a new set of variances that start small and grow over time. These are shown by the broken curves emanating from point Q in figure 7.11.

Consider a set of smoothing rules of the kind we discussed in the previous section. That kind of system is based on parameters that have been determined once and for all. In other words, we find a good set of smoothing parameters (by optimization or judgment) and then use it for a period of years until we revise our estimates or decide to set the model aside. Suppose we desire to evaluate the performance of the model by predicting what will happen if we were to use the decision rules to make future decisions. To do this it is appropriate to start the system at some point S (the initial conditions) and then let it evolve, with expanding variances as shown in figure 7.11. The evaluation is done for each year from t_1 onward. If an objective function is used, the time discount factor must go to zero more rapidly than the variances expand; otherwise the sum of discounted annual variances will not converge. In nontechnical language: we evaluate the system by imagining we stand at a fixed point and are looking forward into the future.

When the smoothing rules are actually used to make a decision, however, every year is a whole new ball game. There is a new set of initial conditions and a new financial forecast, both of which certainly should be used instead of the ones from the previous year. When the model is in use, only the values of the smoothing parameters will remain invariant from year to year. Hence each year we will have updated ourselves and started a new trajectory, just as shown at point Q in figure 7.11. We will be looking forward to small-but-expanding variances and we may well be on a new trajectory.

The model in evaluation and model in use can be reconciled in terms of the theory of conditional probability. Since the formal proof of this is hard to state briefly, we will not pursue the matter further. However, it will be important to keep these two aspects of modeling in mind as we proceed to discuss more complex (and more powerful) stochastic control models. These models are of two types: (a) multiperiod (or higher-order) smoothing rules; (b) dynamic programming.

Multiperiod Smoothing Rules

The smoothing rules presented earlier in this chapter were first-order, that is, they looked ahead only one period. For instance, the gap, on which the budget adjustment calculation was based, used the values of the variables at $t - 1$ and their expected growth rates from $t - 1$ to t (see equation [7.13]). A zero-order rule would have defined the gap in terms of the observed values at $t - 1$, without using the growth rates, while rules of orders higher than first would have used expected growth rates for years $t + 1$, etc., as we shall see.

The effect of look-ahead in dynamic control is described graphically in figure 7.12. The vertical axis depicts the logarithm of income and expense; logs are used so that constant growth rates can, as a matter of convenience, be depicted as straight lines. We have assumed in all three panels of the figure that income and expense are in equilibrium prior to t_0, at which point income takes a favorable turn. The trend is short-lived, however, for income is back at its old level at time t_2 and then declines even further until it reaches a new stable trajectory at t_4. Control is assumed to be exerted entirely on the expenditure side, with one-half of the current gap being closed each period (i.e., $\ell = 0.5$). Gaps are denoted by $\Delta_n(t)$, where n is the order of the process being considered.

Zero-order smoothing. The top panel of the figure depicts zero-order smoothing. The model senses no gap at t_0, so no budget adjustment is planned for t_1. Of course, this turns out to be a mistake, since a large gap emerges at t_1. (The fact that the gap is positive is immaterial for present purposes.) The zero-order rule takes account of the gap that has just emerged at t_1 and sets out to close the desired 50 percent of it under the assumption that the new relation between income and expense will persist. Hence the budget base is increased at time $t + 2$, just soon enough to be caught by the income dropoff that occurs then. The budget adjustments track the decline of income during subsequent periods, and the system has returned to equilibrium by about period 7—assuming there are no more perturbations, of course.

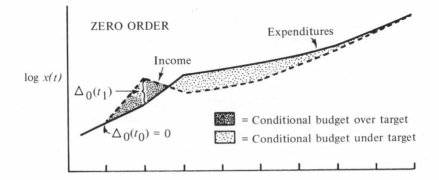

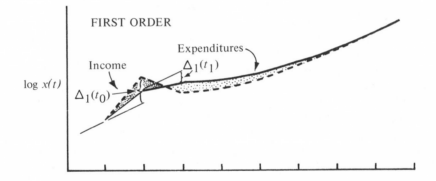

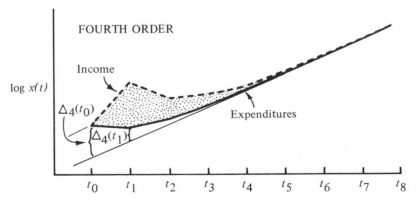

Figure 7.12. The effect of look-ahead in dynamic control

First-order systems. The second panel of figure 7.12 shows a first-order system that depends upon the availability of reasonably accurate one-year forecasts. (The graph assumes 100 percent accuracy.) Now the potential gap at t_1 is sensed at t_0, and the appropriate adjustment can be planned before the fact. The system also "sees" the turndown at t_2 and makes an adjustment equal to one-half of the gap that is projected to result. (Note that this does not return expenditures to their original trajectory.) The first-order system converges more rapidly than the zero-order one, and the overs and unders in the conditional budget are much smaller. There is no doubt about the efficacy of even one year's worth of forecast information.

An operational first-order system will represent a combination of the top two panels of figure 7.12. The middle panel, just discussed, represents the variations in the growth rates that can be forecast, i.e., the expected growth rates. Deviations from the forecasts—what we earlier called "surprises"—are of course apparent only after the fact; these are represented in the top panel. Within this context, improvements in the accuracy of forecasts can be viewed as moving one toward a more effective first-order (or higher-order) system.

Higher-order systems. Now we are ready to look at a multiperiod smoothing rule. A fourth-order system is depicted in the lower panel of figure 7.12. In this example the full gap represented by the original and final income trajectories is sensed immediately at t_0. Half of it is closed during the first period; the other half is the gap at t_1. ($\Delta_4(t_1)$ compares the projected budget to projected income at t_5.) The adjustment process continues until equilibrium is restored at t_4. There was no unjustified increase in the budget base at t_1 here, because the fourth-order smoothing rule was sensitive enough to detect that the growth in income was temporary. (Actually, a second-order system would have sufficed for that.) In this example, considerable funds were saved for the conditional budget. Under the right circumstances a higher-order system can provide more effective smoothing and reduce start-stop budgeting.

How can higher-order systems be constructed? The easiest way is suggested by the example just concluded. To get an nth order system base all gap calculations on the projections for year n of the medium-range financial forecast, ignoring the data for all the intermediate years. In other words, if $n = 3$, and if the MRFF projections for total budget growth (inflation, cost rise, and funded improvement) were 9.5 percent, 10.7 percent, and 8.9 percent, the expected overall growth rate in equation (7.13), for the budget adjustment, would be changed to

$$i + r + f = 1.095 \times 1.107 \times 1.089 - 1 = 0.320.$$

Of course this would be the compounded rate of growth for three years instead of one, but that is immaterial so far as the smoothing rules are concerned.* The

*However, all the variance and covariance estimates would have to be increased to account for the new time interval. Also, there would be two years of overlap in the data for successive planning periods, so the serial correlations could not be ignored.

system could be simulated in the usual way, and appropriate values for the parameters determined. To the extent that significant nonstationary patterns in the growth rates exist and are accurately predicted by the MRFF, we would expect this model to outperform the first-order one to some extent.

The transition-to-equilibrium model. There is something unsatisfying about ignoring the time pattern of changes for years 1, ..., n, as in the above model. For example, it makes no difference in calculating the three-year growth rate whether the order of changes for individual years is 9.5 percent, 10.7 percent, 8.9 percent, or 8.9 percent, 9.5 percent, 10.7 percent—or any other combination of numbers that compound to 0.320. So let us explore some richer multiperiod models.

The transition-to-equilibrium model presented in chapter 6 is one such model. It needs to be augmented to take account of the conditional budget and the operating reserve, but this is not difficult. The terminal conditions of the expanded TRANS model are simply

$$[1 + \Omega]B(n) = I(n) + P(n)$$

$$P(n) = pE(n - 1)$$

$$R(n) = \Pi B(n).$$

These must be met at period n, the end of the look-ahead period. In addition, we have the laws of motion for the five state variables B, I, E, R, and the cash flow identity, for each year from 1 to n. The unknowns are the above five variables plus the four controls (A, P, S, C), again for each year. The laws of motion and cash-flow identity provide $6n$ equations and the terminal conditions 3 more. We need $3(n - 1)$ more equations to reach the $9n$ needed to close the system. These are provided by specifying the time pattern of A, P, and S over the transition period, as we did in the TRANS model (see equation [6.16]).

The parameters of the timing equations are really no more than smoothing parameters, now expanded to include the time dimension. We have ℓ_τ, κ_τ, and χ_τ, for $\tau = 1, 2, \ldots, n - 1$. (The nth parameter is redundant, since each series must sum to one.) For example, the solution of the simultaneous linear equation system in the model will generate a figure for the overall budget gap. A fraction, ℓ_1, will be closed the first year, ℓ_2 the next year, etc. Notice that this model always projects that 100 percent of any gap will be closed by the nth period. All our other control models are designed in such a way that the new equilibrium is approached asymptotically; that is, the system gets closer and closer to equilibrium but never quite reaches it.

There is no problem in using the TRANS model; indeed, we have used it extensively. However, there seems to be no practical, inexpensive way to optimize its parameters, not even by a Monte Carlo simulation, since a simultaneous equation system would have to be solved at each step. However, such a simulation would be easy enough to construct and could be undertaken if the need arose.

All things considered, we do not recommend either a model of the TRANS type or a simple one-step multiperiod model for routine use in the stochastic setting. There are two reasons for our opinion. First, the advantages of a multiperiod look-ahead model depend strongly on the availability of accurate MRFF data. It is likely, however, that the accuracy of most forecasts for most variables declines markedly as one gets more than a year into the future. Both the models of this section weight the forecasts for the years 1 to n equally. The use of inaccurate forecast data means either that real transients will not be sensed and eliminated (a failure that negates the advantage of extending the look-ahead period) or that extraneous ones will be introduced and acted upon.

The second drawback is that, for purposes of routine use, both TRANS and one-step models are to a considerable extent dominated by other models. In contrast, the TRADES model to be described in chapter 9 can be used to get most of the benefits of a multiperiod smoothing model under certainty-equivalent conditions. Such a model should suffice under most circumstances and is much more flexible and explainable. If a more sophisticated approach is desired, the dynamic programming model is far more powerful and does not require equal weighting of future forecasts.

We suggest that a simple first-order smoothing model be used to generate policies for dealing with uncertainty, or at least to obtain some insight into them. For routine planning, TRADES should be used—with any such policies taken into account, of course. If a very large budget gap appears to be opening up in the near future, TRANS can be run in conjunction with TRADES as described in chapter 6.

A Dynamic Programming Model

Dynamic programming deals directly with the combinatorial problem that a set of decisions in year t affects the options, and hence the decisions, in year $t + 1$, etc. This mathematical and computational procedure is the most general and powerful of any of the approaches for feedback control under uncertainty that we have discussed.[11]

One can think of the unfolding of successive rounds of decisions as a branching process. Suppose there are 100 options in year t and that each of these generates 100 more options at $t + 1$, and so forth. In five years there will be $100^5 = 10^{10}$ possibilities. The number of alternatives in any practical problem is far too large to evaluate by enumeration, so some kind of special procedure is called for. Dynamic programming provides one such procedure, the LRFE concept another.

We will not go into the solution algorithm for dynamic programming, since it is complex and well represented in the literature.[12] However, it will be helpful to examine some other aspects of the approach and compare them with our smoothing models. Dynamic programming can be used when the controls are linear functions of the state variables and there are no restrictions on the coefficients of these functions. The solution algorithm finds the best values for these coefficients, where "best" is defined in terms of the expected present value of a quadratic objective function. (The objective function can be developed with the desiderata given earlier, though for dynamic programming we must restrict ourselves to a quadratic form.) Two other key points should be remembered: (a) there can be no restrictions on the coefficients; (b) optimization of the present discounted value of an objective function is used in place of a set of terminal constraints.

The coefficients are of course the ℓ_{ij} of equation (7.4). They are analogous to ℓ, κ, and χ of our first-order smoothing model. But where there is a comprehensible structure embedded in the smoothing rules, with parameters that mean something like "the fraction of the gap to be closed next year," the ℓ_{ij} are simply elements in a table of numbers. Some will be positive and some negative, quite possibly with no coherent pattern. It is impossible to require any of the ℓ_{ij} to be zero or to fall within any prespecified range. Thus the dynamic programming procedure has a kind of "black-box" character to it.

The algorithm for dynamic programming can accommodate both the time-varying nature of the MRFF growth rates and the fact that the future is uncertain. The computed values of the controls for next year (year $t + 1$, or $\tau = 1$) will reflect a transition *towards* equilibrium. Unlike the TRANS model, however, the dynamic programming solution does not contract to reach equilibrium by period T in the absence of further shocks, but only to approach it. On the other hand, the TRANS model's terminal conditions are based on the convenient fiction that there will be no further random shocks.

The dynamic programming model does resemble the first-order smoothing model in that both approach equilibrium asymptotically rather than getting there within a particular planning horizon. However, dynamic programming takes account not only of our expectations about future growth rates, but of the probable deviations from them as well. By using the dynamic programming solution algorithm to recompute the ℓ_{ij} each year as new MRFF and other data become available, and applying them to the current period's state variables, a very powerful adaptive feedback control system is obtained.

Richard C. Grinold and the two of us have developed a dynamic programming formulation for university budget planning.[13] It is based on quite a different representation of the university's planning problem and objective function than the one provided here, but it does provide an example of how dynamic programming can be used for financial planning under uncertainty. It also offers a preliminary quantitative analysis of how changes in the investment mix for the endowment affect funded improvement and tuition policy.

We have already noted that the dynamic programming approach produces results that are difficult to explain to those who are not expert in operations research. Therefore, it would have to offer very significant advantages in order to be a serious candidate for adoption. Though our work in this area is not yet complete, we do not believe that any such clear-cut advantage over the smoothing-rule model is likely to be discovered. We see dynamic programming as a way to gain insight that may be useful in developing practical rules of thumb for dynamic control under uncertainty, but we do not advocate it for direct application. However, for reasons we described earlier in this chapter, direct application of smoothing models does seem to us to be appropriate for arriving at a formula for endowment payout.

Summary

We are concerned in this chapter with the control of a college or university budget in the face of imperfect knowledge about the future. Major areas of uncertainty to be reckoned with include inflation rates, stock- and bond-market returns, and fund-raising. The overall objective is to develop a set of "smoothing rules" that will help to cushion the impact of unanticipated swings in any of these variables on budgets in the short run. Such rules should be worked out within a logically consistent framework that takes subjective preferences of the relevant decision makers directly into account.

We begin with a brief review of some basic principles of probability and control. Using a specific example based on investment risk, we trace through how uncertainty or risk can best be characterized for modeling purposes, and how various types of dynamic control models can be used in dealing with it.

This is followed by a section on strategies for absorbing uncertainty. As a preliminary, we discuss a typical annual budget cycle and how the need for coping with uncertainty can be recognized and taken into account. Then we consider two important constructs for absorbing uncertainty in the short run: the operating reserve and the conditional budget.

A first-order model is developed for control of uncertainty; it is used to establish guidelines for setting the dollar payout from endowment. Control variables and random variables are combined in a set of probabilistic laws of motion for budgetary evolution. A set of smoothing rules is proposed that can be incorporated in the same framework, thus enabling us to study their effects as a function of certain key parameters. In particular, data approximating the situation at Stanford are used to study the rules and to optimize the smoothing parameters. The resulting rules, along with the relevant data, are incorporated in a stochastic simulation model to test how the rules would perform in an uncertain environment. Several interesting implications for university budgetary policy are drawn from these analyses.

In the concluding section, the model is generalized to include higher-order (i.e., multiperiod) and more powerful control systems. The use of multiperiod smoothing rules allows for more elaborate "look-ahead" features than the one-period rules discussed in the main section of the chapter. One example of such a multiperiod formulation is the transition-to-equilibrium (TRANS) model of chapter 6. A still more powerful (and general) technique for optimizing feedback control under uncertainty is dynamic programming, although certain of its features render it of more theoretical than practical interest.

Notes to Chapter 7

Works cited here in abbreviated form are more fully described in the bibliography at the end of this book.

1. For a nontechnical review of many published studies see Malkiel and Firstenberg 1976. The figures used in the present example happen to be more conservative than those used in chapter 4.

2. Useful but rather mathematical treatments of control theory are given in Tintner and Sengupta 1972; Tou 1964; and Bellman and Dreyfus 1962. The threefold categorization can be found in the first-named work.

3. Forrester 1961 provides a number of good examples, taken from inventory control and similar phenomena, of "runaway" feedback systems.

4. Cf. Bellman and Dreyfus 1962.

5. See Tintner and Sengupta 1972, section 3.1.1, for a discussion of open- and closed-loop systems and other issues of classification.

6. See Massy et al. 1979.

7. Ibid.; and Grinold, Hopkins, and Massy 1978.

8. This approach to defining "payout gap" is consistent with Malkiel and Firstenberg 1976 and a number of other recent treatments.

9. The derivation is provided in Massy et al., 1979; it is long and involves complex mathematics. Since we plan to have it published in a more widely available form, we have not included it here.

10. Further comment about Stanford's policies, together with some later results from the model, can be found in Massy et al. 1979. There, as here, we conclude that $\kappa = 0.40$ is optimum. However, the optimal value of ℓ is raised to 0.35. All other conclusions are consistent with those of the subsection just concluded.

11. We are indebted to Richard C. Grinold for the dynamic programming formulation of our planning problem, and for great assistance in working out the laws of motion and other relations.

12. Cf. Bellman and Dreyfus 1962.

13. See Grinold, Hopkins, and Massy 1978.

Part IV

Further Applications of University Planning Models

In part IV we broaden university planning models' field of application, both to other kinds of decision problems and to other kinds of institutions. Chapter 8 is about the quantitative side of planning as it applies to the major categories of human resources, namely, faculty, students, and staff. We consider various models, from simple to relatively complex, of faculty appointment, promotion, and retirement; of student enrollment and the "yield" from the admissions process (i.e., what proportion actually matriculate, earn degrees, drop out, etc.); and for affirmative action planning, including evaluation of progress toward affirmative action goals. Examples are given of the types of policy analyses that administrators can undertake with these models. Although some of the models use actual data from Stanford, we show that modeling, if approached in the right way, can help any academic institution in its human resources planning.

In chapter 9 we approach the frontiers of management science. We have already defined the university planning and decision problem as one of optimizing an institutional value function subject to a static set of financial constraints. Chapter 9 deals at some length with the problem of quantifying the relative desirability of many different but interrelated alternatives, the consequences of which are often difficult to predict. Not surprisingly, we conclude that the problem has no direct solution; our efforts at finding an optimization algorithm remain chiefly of theoretical interest. There is, however, an indirect solution that has already demonstrated its practical worth. TRADES, the history of which was given in chapter 2, is a model that has become Stanford University's principal means of making financial forecasts and of analyzing financial trade-offs. The model supplies decision makers with a detailed picture of the financial and other constraints that any policy must adhere to; the decision makers supply the values that underlie the policy.

With TRADES, the decision makers' task becomes one of searching for feasible configurations of planning variables—configurations that would not necessarily occur to them if the computer were not available to perform the "bookkeeping." At the same time, the computer does not overwhelm the user with data, since it can present the results in terms of as few variables as may be necessary. Nor is the search a passive one: the user, even one who is a novice in computer science, may order TRADES to show the results of changes in one or more variables and state if the resulting configuration is feasible. With practice, a user will learn to consider a number of variables in combination. Examples of such interaction between computer and decision maker are considered throughout the main portion of chapter 9, which concludes with an account of a pilot experiment in value optimization that we conducted with a group of Stanford administrators.

Finally, in chapter 10, we discuss the problem of how to apply TRADES and the other planning models at colleges and universities other than Stanford. We also review the feasibility of models for academic subunits such as schools and departments. We conclude that the transferability of individual planning concepts is likely to be less of a problem than the general prospect of inviting computers into the decision-making process. We therefore recommend a number of ways in which modelers and decision makers can make their often difficult relationship more fruitful. In our opinion, success will often depend on how favorably models are perceived during the early stages of their introduction. But there is also a danger that they may arouse expectations that cannot be met. Decision makers should be cautious not only in how they use models but in what they say about the results they get or hope to get from them. Nevertheless, we hope the reader will come to share our opinion that "getting started in modeling" is not nearly as difficult as it sounds.

We conclude with an agenda for research into three main areas: financial projection and tradeoff models (where we would particularly like to see the stochastic control methods of chapter 7 applied to TRADES); value optimization (the entire state of the art needs to be advanced); and personnel planning. Here, as elsewhere, our purpose is not to increase the control of human beings by machines, but rather to broaden the scope of human choice in a world that threatens to become too complex for human values.

8

Human Resources Planning

A university is, above all, a collection of people; its faculty, students, and staff are essential to the fulfillment of its most basic purposes. In a very real sense these people *are* the university's primary resource. We make no apology, then, for including a chapter on modeling university personnel systems. Such a chapter provides an important supplement to our in-depth treatment of purely financial models of the university.

Let us consider, for a moment, some of the reasons why human resources planning is so important here. First, the expense side of the university budget is so completely dominated by salary costs for faculty and staff that planners can scarcely avoid having to work with the employment levels of university personnel as primary planning variables. At the same time, employment levels should be manipulated only after due consideration of their impact on academic vitality. For example, cutbacks in faculty size might be an easy measure for achieving rapid budgetary retrenchment, were it not for the restrictions imposed by a tenure system and the importance of maintaining an adequate flow of new faculty into the institution's academic programs. As we shall see, simple models can be constructed to inform us about how changes in faculty or staff size will affect the annual number of openings for new hires.

Just as costs directly associated with faculty and staff tend to dominate expenses, so also does tuition revenue tend to dominate income. (Some 63 percent of Stanford's operating budget is supported by tuition, and the percentage for a less research-oriented college or university would be much greater.) This dependence on income from tuition creates a need for accurate projections of student enrollments. At an institution like Stanford, the need is chiefly for predicting the enrollment behavior of old returning students, since once the size of the freshman class has been stipulated there have always been enough good students to fill it. At other institutions, where student demand is the driving force, models are also needed to predict the size of the freshman class given certain characteristics of the applicant pool and of the institution relative to its competitive market. Actually, we at Stanford are also interested in modeling its freshman yield (i.e., the ratio of those coming to those admitted), but more because we want to check on the success of our financial aid policy in removing economic barriers than because we need to calculate the number of new freshmen.

A third force behind the interest of universities in human resource planning is the recent concern over the representation of women and members of ethnic minority groups on the faculty and staff. The emphasis on so-called affirmative action in hiring and promotion is relatively new and immediately raises questions about how much reasonably can be accomplished and by when. With the aid of an analytical model, one can begin to test the effects of staff size and hiring mix on the future numbers of minority group members employed. The results enable one to set goals that lie within the limits of feasibility rather than being merely the products of wishful thinking.

These, then, are some of the issues we shall examine analytically in this chapter. Our basic task will be to develop models that relate staffing or enrollment levels to attrition patterns and hiring or admission rates. With these data we aim to predict the future evolution of whatever personnel system is being studied as a function of a small set of primary controls. The models in question will all involve aggregate representations of personnel status; we are not concerned with the problem of faculty or student enrollment planning at the departmental level. In the case of faculty- and staff-flow models our chief purpose will be to develop a sense of which central planning variables are most significant, and how much influence they can exert on important measures such as turnover rates and salary costs. In modeling student enrollments we will want, for budget planning, to develop accurate projections of the overall numbers of new and returning students.

We shall discuss several different methods for modeling personnel flows; the choice of model will depend on the purpose being served. In general, we shall want to exploit whatever special structure can be found in the personnel system being studied. For example, models of the faculty obviously must take account of the important links between nontenure and tenure ranks.

Although we shall be working with a variety of models in this chapter, all of them will have certain basic features in common. These include:

1. The designation of a discrete set of categories, called *states* and denoted by a subscript j, into which members of the personnel system can be arranged;

2. *Stock* variables, $N_j(t)$, referring to the number of personnel in state j at time t;

3. *Flow* variables, $f_j(t)$, referring to the input rate of new personnel (e.g., the hiring rate of faculty or staff, or the matriculation rate of new students) in state j during the time period ranging from $t - 1$ to t (typically, one year).

In certain cases we shall be performing static-equilibrium analyses for which the time references on N_j and f_j can be dropped. These variables will then denote, respectively, average stock level and average input flow rate. Both will be averages over time for a stable system in which not only policy variables but also behavioral parameters take on fixed values year after year. Such analyses are useful for gauging the eventual effects of permanent changes in these quantities.

The first main section of this chapter deals with faculty planning models. We present these first because of the primary importance of faculty to the university, and also because the special structure imposed by a faculty tenure system lends itself particularly well to simple forms of analysis. This section is followed by one on enrollment projection models. There, we focus on the problem of estimating the size of the returning student population, given a known size for the freshman class. As we shall see, there are several ways of doing this, a freedom of choice that makes enrollment planning a useful application for studying the various types of flow models that can be used. The third section deals briefly with models of freshman yield, which differ fundamentally from other models discussed in the chapter in that they attempt to explain the enrollment behavior of individual students in terms of a set of salient background characteristics such as academic achievement and family income. The fourth and final section presents a cohort model of nonacademic staff with specific application to goal-setting for affirmative action. It also includes a Markov chain model for statistically evaluating an institution's progress in achieving such goals.

Before proceeding, we should add that the chapter is written in such a way that these major sections can be read in any order. That is, to understand the material in one section the reader does not need to have mastered the material from the sections that preceded it. A reader whose primary interest is in affirmative action planning, for instance, should feel free to proceed directly to the fourth section without first having to deal with the other topics in between.*

Analysis of Faculty Appointment, Promotion, and Retirement Policies

In the 1950s and 1960s, when higher education was in truth a growth industry, universities could afford substantial increases in faculty size. During that period, there was little concern (too little, some would say) over the faculty's distribution by rank and age. After all, as long as one could create a significant number of new faculty positions each year, there was always plenty of flexibility to meet most, if not all, of the pressing academic needs. With the far more stringent financial conditions under which nearly all institutions are operating now, universities no longer can afford major increases in the number of faculty. Openings for the new faculty needed to expand or revitalize academic programs must now be created for the most part through attrition. For this reason there has been much concern over the proportion of older, tenured faculty and the

---

* Readers who desire a more detailed coverage of the models we discuss should consult Grinold and Marshall 1977, which provides the most comprehensive treatment of the field to date.

uneven age distributions that are evident within many institutions. Since the change in retirement laws this concern has deepened. By putting an end to mandatory retirement, the new legislation threatens to do away with an important source of regular attrition.

With a faculty personnel system that is tightly constrained, it surely pays to study its properties and, in particular, its responses to changes in identifiable policy variables. The main thing we need to know is what, given reasonable limits on institutional control, is feasible under these conditions, which might almost be called "steady-state." Among the questions to be answered are:

1. How many vacancies are likely to occur through attrition in a typical annual cycle?

2. What will be the age and rank composition of a constant-size faculty in five or ten years?

3. What measures can be employed by the institution to increase the rate of turnover of its faculty positions, if necessary, and how effective they are likely to be?

As it happens, rather simple models can be exploited to shed light on these and similar issues.

Equilibrium Analysis

To begin with, consider the simple flow diagram of a faculty tenure system shown in figure 8.1. Faculty are assigned to one of two states, nontenure or tenure, and six distinct flow variables are recognized. The first two flows, f_1 and f_2, represent direct inputs of new faculty members from outside the university into the nontenure and tenure states, respectively. (While many institutions hire faculty only at the nontenure level, a research-oriented university often needs to bring in a certain number of established scholars as well; hence the inclusion of the second flow variable, f_2. We shall see that the relative rates of appointment to tenure and nontenure are important controls in the evolution of a faculty personnel system.) Three variables designate flows leaving the system: f_{13}, for resignations, deaths, and nonpromotions from nontenure; f_{23}, for resignations and deaths from tenure; and f_{24}, for retirements from tenure. The two last-named flows are kept separate because, while the retirement rate can be influenced through institutional policy (e.g., by changing the mandatory retirement age, if any, or by implementing a voluntary early retirement program), presumably the resignation and death rates cannot. The final flow variable, f_{12}, represents the single link between the two states of the system, namely, promotions to tenure.

For current purposes, we shall assume that the system is in a state of equilibrium, with a fixed faculty size $(N_1 + N_2)$ and flows that do not vary from one time period to another. We wish to study the properties of such a system under varying institutional policies. Note that of the six flow variables defined above, all but one, f_{23}, is chiefly determined by the appointment, promotion, and retirement policies of the institution in question. Accordingly, we should

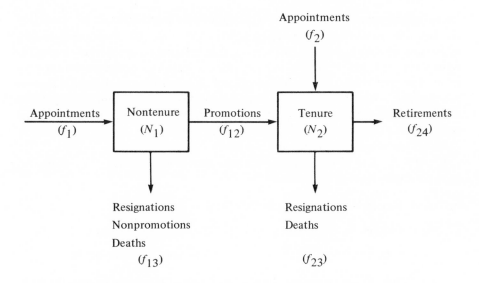

Note: $N_1 + N_2$ is fixed.

Figure 8.1. Two-state flow diagram of a faculty tenure system

be able to construct a fairly rich model for policy analysis using only this small set of variables. In so doing, we shall place particular emphasis on two key ratios that represent the primary controls, as follows.*

Let r = the tenure appointment fraction (i.e., the fraction of all appointments made directly to tenure)

q = the promotion fraction (i.e., the fraction of nontenure faculty eventually promoted to tenure).

Before proceeding to develop a model, let us pause to consider what should be the primary goals of a university in controlling the faculty personnel system as it evolves. First, a university needs to preserve a reasonable amount of flexibility, for the repatterning of academic programs. In terms of our model, this would imply seeking to keep the ratio of nontenure to tenure faculty, N_1/N_2, representing the degree of flexibility, from dropping below some critical threshold value. Second, it needs to maintain a substantial flow of new blood into the faculty each year, that is, to keep the appointment rate, $f_1 + f_2$, high. Third, it would like, if at all possible, to keep the junior faculty well-motivated by maintaining a high rate of promotion, f_{12}.

Unfortunately, these goals conflict. For example, one can hold down the

---

*In speaking of "controls," we do not mean to be advocating the use of quotas of any kind. Rather, we are referring to the aggregate numerical effects of whatever standards and guidelines the institution chooses to set for appointments and promotions to tenure.

tenure ratio by some combination of measures that might include: (a) restricting the rate of promotion to tenure, f_{12}; (b) increasing the proportion of new appointments made to nontenure, i.e., of f_1 relative to f_2; (c) increasing the retirement rate; (d) stretching out the average length of a nontenure appointment. The first three of these measures will also help to maintain the flow of new faculty, which is goal 2; the fourth, however, will have just the opposite effect. And, of course, keeping up a high promotion rate (goal 3) is in direct conflict with the other two. The purpose in developing a model, then, is to express these tradeoffs in quantitative terms.

We still need to define parameters referring to the service lives of faculty members appointed or promoted.

Let w_1 = average service life (number of years) in nontenure

w_2' = average service life in tenure for those promoted from nontenure

w_2'' = average service life in tenure for those appointed to tenure.

These parameters are related to the staffing levels of faculty in exactly the same way as the student lifetime parameters were related to enrollments in chapter 5. If, for example, the service life in nontenure is five years, hiring 50 nontenure faculty per year will result in $5 \times 50 = 250$ persons serving as nontenure faculty at any one time. We have chosen to define two tenure lifetimes because we expect w_2' to be greater than w_2'', perhaps by as much as five to ten years, for faculty hired to tenure from outside are generally older than those promoted from within.

We seek expressions for the input rate of faculty, $f_1 + f_2$, and the tenure ratio, $N_2/(N_1 + N_2)$, in terms of the controls q and r. Since the system is in equilibrium, the inflow of new faculty exactly balances the outflow of those leaving the system. We shall refer to the magnitude of these flows, when it is expressed in terms of faculty members per year, as the *turnover rate*. Also, the number of faculty in each state is equal to the product of the input rate with the average service life. This gives us the two queueing equations

$$N_1 = w_1 f_1 \tag{8.1}$$

and

$$N_2 = w_2' f_{12} + w_2'' f_2. \tag{8.2}$$

Notice that the number of tenured faculty is obtained by adding together those who were promoted and those who were hired to tenure, and that each of these terms is the product of a service lifetime with the corresponding input flow rate.

Next, we state definitional equations for the policy fractions q and r:

$$q = f_{12}/f_1 \tag{8.3}$$

and

$$r = f_2/(f_1 + f_2). \tag{8.4}$$

Finally, we stipulate that the total faculty size is a fixed number, N:

$$N_1 + N_2 = N. \tag{8.5}$$

These five equations are sufficient to yield the results we are after. Substituting (8.1) and (8.2) in (8.5), using (8.3) and (8.4) to eliminate f_{12}, f_1, and f_2, and rearranging terms, we obtain for the total appointment rate

$$f_1 + f_2 = \frac{N}{[(1-r)(w_1 + qw_2') + rw_2'']} \tag{8.6}$$

and for the tenure ratio

$$\frac{N_2}{N} = \frac{[(1-r)qw_2' + rw_2'']}{[(1-r)(w_1 + qw_2') + rw_2'']}. \tag{8.7}$$

(We note in passing that the tenure ratio is a good proxy for the relative cost of an institution's faculty, for salaries paid to tenured faculty tend to average much more than salaries paid to nontenured faculty.)

There is a simple interpretation for equation (8.6). The total flow of faculty into the system, as the equation shows, is equal to the number in the system divided by an expression involving the service lifetimes and policy fractions. Since we recognize this to be in the form of a standard queueing equation, we know that the expression in the denominator must be the average lifetime in the system for a random faculty member. That this is in fact so is not too difficult to see. A fraction $(1 - r)$ of the faculty enters the system, spends w_1 years in nontenure, and then separates into two parts: a fraction q who are promoted and then spend an additional w_2' years in the system; and a fraction $(1 - q)$ who leave. Finally, the fraction of faculty r enters the system at the tenure level and stays there for an average of w_2'' years. The overall average lifetime is obtained as the properly weighted sum of these individual averages.

The direction of change in either of the measures of interest with respect to policy variables can be found by inspection of the equations we have just derived. For example, increasing the promotion fraction, q, will always lead to a lower appointment rate and a higher tenure ratio. Extending the nontenure lifetime will decrease the tenure ratio but it will also decrease the appointment rate. The effect of the other policy variable, r, is not so obvious. Ordinary intuition might have led us to expect that it is always better in terms of these measures to hire at the nontenure rather than the tenure level. If w_2'' should be less than the quantity $w_1 + qw_2'$, however, the reverse would be true. Let us assume that $w_1 =$ five years, $w_2' =$ twenty years, and $w_2'' =$ fifteen years. This condition would then be met whenever $q > (15 - 5)/20 = 0.5$. This leads to the rather surprising result that, for these data, whenever the policy is to promote more than half the faculty who are appointed to nontenure ranks, hiring faculty at the nontenure level will actually cause a *lower* overall appointment rate than hiring directly into tenure!

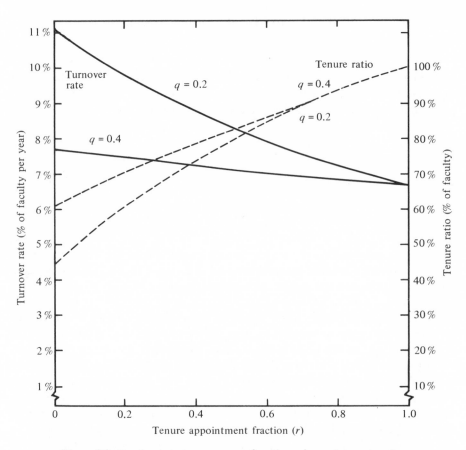

Figure 8.2. Steady-state turnover as a function of appointment policy

By graphing the relationships given in (8.6) and (8.7) we can gain more insight into the relative importance of the two policy variables, r and q. In figure 8.2 we examine the dependence of the turnover (or appointment) rate (here expressed as a percent of the faculty size, N) and the tenure ratio on the tenure appointment fraction, r, assuming the values for service lifetimes given in the paragraph above. The two solid lines refer to the turnover rate (measured on the left vertical axis) under two different promotion policies, namely, $q = 0.2$ and $q = 0.4$. It is readily observed that decreasing the fraction r has a small effect on the turnover rate if $q = 0.4$, that is, if the promotion rate is high. The reason is that under these circumstances the expected service lifetime for a junior faculty member is comparable to that of one appointed to tenure. Decreasing the promotion fraction, q, to 0.2 leads, however, to a stronger dependence on the tenure appointment fraction, r.

The broken curves in figure 8.2 show the equilibrium tenure ratio (measured on the right vertical axis) as a function of the tenure appointment fraction, for the same two promotion policies. The tenure ratio rises quite rapidly as the

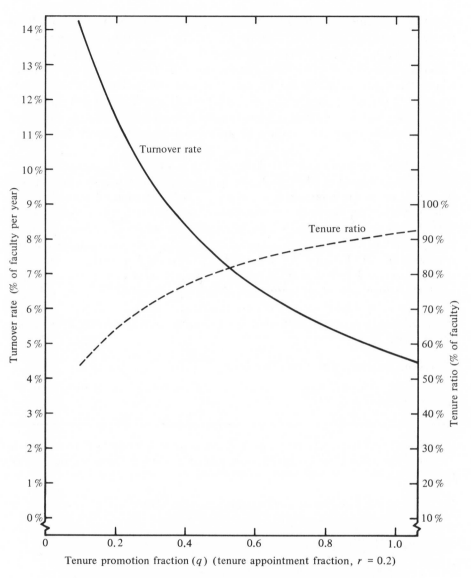

Figure 8.3. Steady-state turnover as a function of promotion policy

fraction of tenure appointments increases and varies, for instance, between 60 and 75 percent in the quite reasonable range of $r = 0.2$ to 0.4, when $q = 0.2$. This large sensitivity of the tenure ratio to small changes in the tenure appointment fraction, r, indicates that r should be monitored frequently by administrators even though it does not, on this evidence, seem to have a large apparent effect on the turnover rate.

The dependence of the turnover rate and the tenure ratio on the fraction of junior faculty promoted to tenure, q, is shown in figure 8.3. In drawing these curves, we assumed a value of 0.2 for the tenure appointment fraction. By a comparison of the solid curve with the one in figure 8.2 we can see readily that the turnover rate is a much steeper function of q than it is of r. The result is that, under a reasonable appointment policy, once the fraction of junior faculty who get promoted reaches 0.3 the turnover rate will be less than 10 percent per year; at this point the average service life of a faculty member will exceed ten years. The turnover rate declines less rapidly beyond this point to a minimum of 4.6 percent which corresponds to an average service time of twenty-two years.

The above discussion should illustrate the advantages to be gained from working with a basic, and, in fact, very simple flow model. It involves only a small number of variables and parameters, is easy to understand, and yet is rich in terms of the insights it can provide. But we must be aware of its limitations as well. Although the model highlights informative relationships among primary policy variables and behavioral parameters, it really does not say what options are available for changing the distribution and flow of faculty over the short to medium run. Faculty administrators are plainly more concerned with projections of turnover rates, tenure ratios, and age distributions over the next five to ten years, say, than with the eventual steady state. For this purpose, we must develop time-dependent models capable of tracing faculty flows from year to year.

Short-Run Analysis: The Two-State Case

We begin by formulating the time-dependent analog of our two-state equilibrium flow model.

FORMULATION 8.1. Here, we add notation indicating time to the stock and flow variables, and we introduce so-called transition fractions, defined as follows:

Let p_{ij} = the fraction of faculty who move from state i (e.g., nontenure or tenure) to state j in a single time period

where p_{ii} = the fraction who stay in the same state

$1 - \sum_j p_{ij}$ = the fraction who leave the system

Note that for our purposes it is sufficient to treat the p_{ij}'s as deterministic quantities representing fractional flow rates of faculty per unit time. If we were concerned with the statistical properties of the system, these quantities would have to be interpreted as *expected* rates of transition, with the understanding that, of course, the actual rates will be different in any particular year. (For a full treatment of Markov chain and cohort flow formulations as stochastic models, see chapter 4 in Grinold and Marshall 1977.)

Now, in place of (8.1) and (8.2), we write, for $t = 0, 1, 2, \ldots,$

$$N_1(t + 1) = p_{11}N_1(t) \qquad\qquad + f_1(t + 1) \tag{8.8}$$

and

$$N_2(t + 1) = p_{12}N_1(t) + p_{22}N_2(t) + f_2(t + 1). \tag{8.9}$$

These equations merely state that the number of faculty occupying state j at time $t + 1$ is the number remaining in that state from time t, plus (in the case of tenure only) the number being promoted, plus the number of new hires. The equation involving the policy variable r becomes

$$f_2(t + 1) = r[f_1(t + 1) + f_2(t + 1)] \tag{8.10}$$

and, finally, we express the restriction on total faculty size in time period t by means of

$$N_1(t) + N_2(t) = (1 + \theta)^t N(0). \tag{8.11}$$

This form of the faculty-size constraint allows for growth (or decline) of the faculty at the constant rate θ.

The flow equations (8.8) and (8.9) are those of a *Markov chain model*, which means that the number of people occupying a state in time period $t + 1$ depends only on the numbers occupying the various states in the just-preceding period and on the number of new hires. We shall examine alternatives to this type of flow model later in the chapter, when we take up enrollment and staff affirmative-action planning. *Transient models* such as this are solved iteratively; that is, one starts with known values for the numbers of faculty initially occupying each state $N_i(0)$, as well as for the parameters p_{ij} and policy variables r and θ.

SOLUTION PROCEDURE 8.1. In general, given values for $N_1(t)$ and $N_2(t)$, we solve for $N_1(t + 1)$, $N_2(t + 1)$, $f_1(t)$, and $f_2(t)$ by going through the following sequence of operations:

1. The total number of persons remaining on the faculty in the subsequent year is determined by: (a) applying the appropriate transition fractions to the given year's faculty numbers; (b) summing the results.
2. The total number of new hires is calculated by subtracting the number continuing on the faculty from the total faculty size as given by (8.11).
3. These new hires are apportioned between the nontenure and tenure states by means of (8.10).
4. The values for $f_1(t)$ and $f_2(t)$ just obtained are used to solve for the new faculty numbers, $N_1(t + 1)$ and $N_2(t + 1)$, via equations (8.8) and (8.9).

Notice that it is possible for the subtraction performed in step 2 above to result in a negative number of new hires. This will occur whenever one uses a rate of decline in overall faculty size that is faster than the rate of natural attrition. In that case, the implication is that the university would have to either accept a lower rate of decline in faculty size, or else consider modifying one or more of the transition fractions, p_{ij}, to increase attrition. One of the benefits to be gained from using a model is that it shows when conditions like these are likely to hold.

The reader may be wondering what has become of the important policy variable q in the transient version of the flow model. The answer must be that it has somehow been incorporated in the values of the transition fractions p_{11} and p_{12}, where p_{11} = the fraction of nontenured faculty continuing in non-tenure and p_{12} = the fraction of nontenured faculty being promoted, both in a single time period. To find the exact correspondence, assume the system (8.8)–(8.11) is in equilibrium, with $\theta = 0$, in which case we can drop the time variable and express the equilibrium flows f_1 and f_{12} in terms of N_1 as follows:

$$f_1 = (1 - p_{11})N_1$$

and

$$f_{12} = qf_1 = p_{12}N_1.$$

The first equation is simply the steady state version of (8.8). The second equates the two expressions for the promotion flow variable f_{12}, one being the product of the cohort (i.e., lifetime) fraction q with the flow rate f_1, and the other being the product of the cross-sectional (i.e., one-year) transition rate, p_{12}, with the employment level, N_1.

Comparing these equations for f_1 with (8.1), we see that

$$(1 - p_{11}) = \frac{p_{12}}{q} = \frac{1}{w_1}$$

which leads to the results

$$p_{12} = \frac{q}{w_1} \tag{8.12}$$

and

$$1 - p_{11} = \frac{1}{w_1}. \tag{8.13}$$

In words: equation (8.12) says that the one-year transition rate from nontenure to tenure is the same, in the steady state, as the cohort promotion fraction, q, divided by the average stay in nontenure. The second result is that the fraction leaving nontenure in any year is the reciprocal of the nontenure lifetime, so that, in w_1 years, everyone has moved up or out.

Now obviously, a similar relationship to that shown in (8.13) exists between the tenure attrition fraction, $1 - p_{22}$, and the tenure lifetimes, w_2' and w_2''. But here we are dealing with much longer service lifetimes, and ones that are significantly affected by transient changes in the faculty age distribution. After all, in any particular year, one would expect the fraction leaving tenure to depend a great deal on the actual ages of the tenured faculty. This is because resignation and death rates vary by age and, otherwise, attrition occurs only through retirement at the high end of the age scale. A model that uses a single parameter, p_{22}, to represent the fractional attrition rate averaged over all age groups and for all future years fails to anticipate changes in the age distribution, even though they are likely to occur. Thus one would be ill advised to rely on this model for making projections of faculty year by year. Rather, a more elaborate version is called for that takes age directly into account, at least for the tenured faculty.

As further motivation for refining the model in this direction, we remark that, during the past several years, many institutions have been attempting to influence the retirement rate of older members of their tenured faculties by offering financially attractive early retirement plans. (The details and analysis of one such plan are given in Hopkins 1974*a*.) More recent interest in this topic has been stirred up by legislation aimed at putting an end to mandatory retirement altogether. A properly formulated flow model can be a valuable aid in predicting what can be accomplished by various institutional responses to this changing situation.

Given the inaccuracy mentioned above and the heightened interest in faculty retirement, we are led to consider another version of the Markov chain model that is better adapted to performing the desired kinds of short-run analyses. Here, the trick is to expand the number and definition of states so that differential rates of promotion and attrition can be taken properly into account.

Short-Run Analysis: A Model with Fifteen States

We must take care to define the states in a way that is both useful for analyzing changes of policy and meaningful as a description of group behavior. We know that the promotion and resignation rates of nontenured faculty tend to vary closely with length of service, while the resignation, death, and retirement rates of tenured faculty depend chiefly on age. This suggests that we should work with a fifteen-state model that classifies faculty into the groups listed below.[1]

State	Description	State	Description
1	Nontenure—first year	8	Tenure—age 30 to 34
2	Nontenure—second year	9	Tenure—age 35 to 39
3	Nontenure—third year	10	Tenure—age 40 to 44
4	Nontenure—fourth year	11	Tenure—age 45 to 49
5	Nontenure—fifth year	12	Tenure—age 50 to 54
6	Nontenure—sixth year	13	Tenure—age 55 to 59
7	Nontenure—seventh year	14	Tenure—age 60 to 64
		15	Retirement

The institution, we assume, adheres strictly to a seven-year "up-or-out" policy for nontenured faculty, which means that service for more than seven years in nontenure is impossible. Tenured faculty are placed in five-year age groups, both to keep the model from getting too large and to have a statistically mean-ingful number of individuals in each state. We assume further that retirement occurs at or before age 65. As before, the parameter p_{ij} represents the one-year fractional flow rate from state i to state j. The general law of motion is given by

$$N_j(t + 1) = \sum_{i=1}^{14} p_{ij}N_i(t) + f_j(t + 1) \qquad j = 1, 2, \ldots, 14. \qquad (8.14)$$

This expanded system of flow equations is shown schematically in figures 8.4 and 8.5, the former for nontenured faculty, the latter for tenured. As a model it has several interesting features. In the first place, most of the transition fractions, p_{ij}, in equation (8.14) are zero. This is so because from each state i there are only a few states j that can be reached in a single time period. For example, the nontenure states were defined in such a way that a transition must occur either to the next-higher nontenure state, to tenure state 8 or 9 (we assume promotion takes place before a person's fortieth birthday), or to out-side the system (see figure 8.4). It follows that if i is a nontenure state, $p_{i,i+1}$, p_{i8}, and p_{i9} may be positive and all other p_{ij} are zero. Similarly, if i is a tenure state (in which one may remain for as long as five years), only p_{ii} and $p_{i,i+1}$ are different from zero.

It is important to bear in mind that certain of the p_{ij} are the very policy variables that we might wish to change. At institutions like Stanford, where the initial appointment for nontenured faculty normally is for three years, it would seem reasonable to think of the nontenure reappointment fraction, p_{34}, the tenure promotion fractions, p_{i8} and p_{i9}, and (perhaps) the retirement fractions $p_{13,15}$ and $p_{14,15}$, as being chiefly determined by administrative policy. The remainder are behavioral parameters supplied to the model as data obtained from a study of historical faculty flows.

The transition fractions shown in table 8.1 were in fact obtained from actual data on the movements of faculty in Stanford's School of Humanities and Sciences during the six-year period September 1, 1966, through September 1, 1972. These statistics were compiled by tabulating the movements of each faculty member who served in the school at any time during that period. As an example, each time some individual was observed to move between two consecutive years from the fifth year in nontenure to tenure at an age below thirty-five, the count in the cell located in row 5, column 8 was incremented by one. As it happened, there was a total of sixty-eight movements *out of* state 5 during the period studied, and seven of these were *into* state 8. This explains the entry of $7/68 = 0.10$ in the corresponding place in table 8.1.[2]

The data in table 8.1 reveal very clearly the degree to which termination rates in nontenure do indeed depend on length of service, and those in tenure depend on age. One further comment on these data: given the five-year age groupings of tenured faculty, in the absence of external arrivals to or departures from the tenure states one would expect the ratio of advancers to those remain-

Table 8.1. Fractional Flows of Faculty, 1966–72, School of Humanities and Sciences, Stanford University

From State	\<- To State: Nontenure							Tenure							Retire- ment	Resigna- tion	Death	Faculty Levels as of 9/1/72
	1	2	3	4	5	6	7	8	9	10	11	12	13	14				
1		.95														.05		22
2			.91													.06		29
3				.76				.02	.01	.01		.01				.18		22
4					.79			.04	.02		.02	.01				.15		26
5						.65		.02	.03	.05	.03	.02				.19		15
6							.36	.10	.21	.14						.19		13
7								.12	.29			.14		.02		.43		8
8								.69	.29							.02		12
9									.74	.22						.04		44
10										.78	.19					.03		58
11											.79	.18				.03		49
12												.80	.18			.02		51
13													.77	.22		.005	.005	31
14														.80	.18	.01	.01	35
Actual age distribution of promotions to tenure								.43	.34	.08	.06	.07	0	.02				
Actual distribution of appointments to tenure								.17	.33	.17	.19	.05	.07	.02				

SOURCE: Hopkins 1974a, table 1, p. 406.

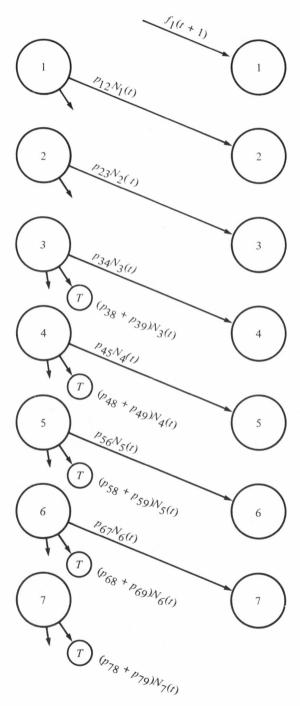

Figure 8.4. Flow diagram for nontenured faculty in 15-state model

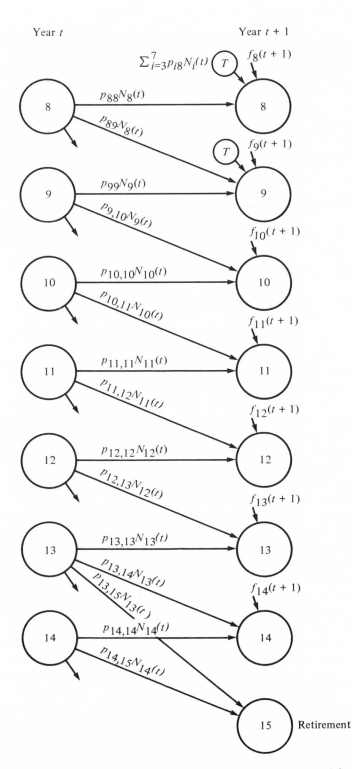

Figure 8.5. Flow diagram for tenured faculty in 15-state model

ing in the state to be about 1 : 4 (i.e., 1/5 = 20 percent move up and 80 percent stay in any given year). Yet we observe significant deviations from this theoretical ratio in the historical figures. These deviations arise primarily because appointments, promotions, and terminations do occur in these states; generally they affect persons who are in between the age limits that define the states.

We can make faculty projections with a fixed set of policy and behavioral assumptions if we follow the same sequence of steps as before. With the more refined model, however, the appointment policy is represented by a fourteen-element vector that contains the fractions of appointments made to each state. Of course, new faculty can enter only in nontenure state 1 or in one of the tenure states. To accommodate this, the vector combines an overall tenure appointment fraction, r, representing the policy variable, with a distribution of tenure appointments by age. The distribution is primarily actuarial in nature and is provided by an analysis of historical flows. Appointment data for Stanford are given at the bottom of table 8.1.

Typical applications. We now give two examples of the sort of analysis this model is designed to perform.[3] In the first, we project Stanford's Humanities and Sciences faculty ahead ten years under alternate assumptions about the natural attrition rate from tenure. In making these projections, we fix the tenure appointment fraction at 0.33 and the promotion fraction at 0.40—their actual average values from the 1960s. Also, we assume that the school will cut back 10 percent on its faculty by eliminating 42 out of its initial 425 positions during the first three years. (Faculty cuts of this magnitude were seen as a very real possibility at Stanford when we first performed this analysis.) In making the runs for figure 8.6 we used the historical resignation rates for tenured faculty given in table 8.1. For the Stanford faculty this corresponded to overall attrition from tenure of about 2.4 percent per year.

What figure 8.6 shows is that the 10 percent reduction target could be met if the school were willing to appoint only about 40 percent as many new faculty during the first three years as it would appoint if it were to maintain the appointment rate at its level in the recent past. (The average rate during the ten-year period from 1964 to 1974 was 37.5 appointments per year.) If the reduction were achieved, the appointment rate would increase again and average 22.8, or 61 percent of the historical average over the subsequent seven years. (The large appointment rates in future years 4 and 5 are related to the unusually large number of assistant professors who were in their second year of service at the start of the period.)

Because a large proportion of the attrition must come from junior faculty who are terminated, and because we assume high tenure appointment and promotion fractions, the tenure ratio rises markedly over the first six years, from 67 percent to 81 percent, and then declines slowly to an equilibrium value of around 78 percent. Also, the percentage of faculty who are forty-five or older rises from 40 to 52 percent during the decade. From these types of calculations we can see the advantages of a time-dependent model, since the path to

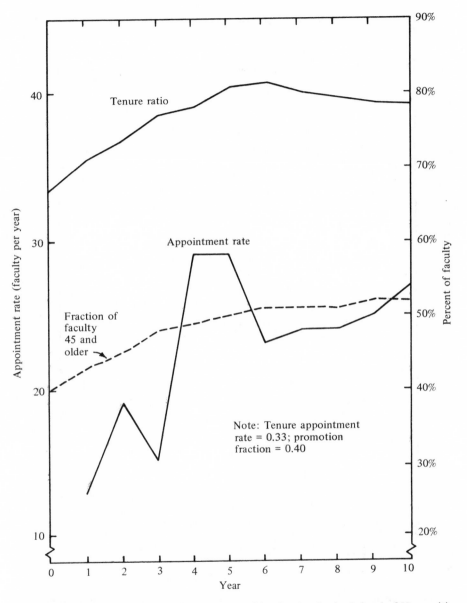

Figure 8.6. Ten-year faculty projections for a 10% reduction in the School of Humanities and Sciences faculty size: tenure attrition rate = 2.4%

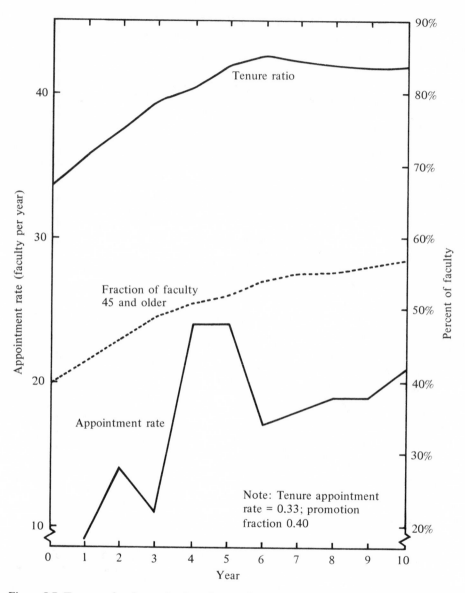

Figure 8.7. Ten-year faculty projections for a 10% reduction in the School of Humanities and Sciences faculty size: tenure attrition rate = 1.0%

equilibrium is often complex and cannot be predicted by an equilibrium model.

Next, we examine the implications of a reduction in attrition from tenure such as might be expected under the generally tighter job-market conditions of the 1970s. Suppose the combined resignation and death rate from each tenure state were to fall to 1 percent per year. Making the appropriate adjustments in the data for our model leads to the results depicted in figure 8.7. This seemingly minor change makes a significant difference in the ten-year projections. The appointment rate drops to an average of 11.3 new faculty members during the first three years, instead of 15.7, and to an average of 20.3, instead of 22.8, thereafter. The tenure ratio rises to 83 percent during the decade, while the fraction of faculty who are forty-five or older rises to 57 percent. These results suggest we would have to reduce the promotion fraction, or the tenure appointment fraction, or more likely both, in order to provide for sufficient flexibility during this difficult period. Of course, we can easily vary these parameters in the model to arrive at a reasonable combination of values, and this is exactly what we did.

Our second example concerns the probable effects of an incentive program for early retirement. For this example we hold the faculty size fixed, set the promotion variable q at 0.30 and the appointment variable r at 0.15, and manipulate the transition fractions $p_{13,14}$ and $p_{14,14}$ so that they will reflect the resulting change in faculty behavior. We assume that this behavior will be as follows: (a) 20 percent of the faculty members reaching age 55 will retire before age 60; (b) of those who do not, 50 percent will retire before reaching age 65 (the former mandatory retirement age at Stanford); (c) on the average, these early retirements will take place midway between the lower and upper age limits of each age group. Note that we are not concerned here with the form of the early retirement scheme, its incentives, and so forth; rather we aim to approximate the effects that any fairly attractive scheme might have.

The results of this analysis are presented in table 8.2. It is apparent that, when appointment and promotion policies are held fixed, early retirement programs can lead to an increase not only in appointments through turnover but in the fraction serving in nontenure. We note that the long-run impact is rather modest; for instance, in equilibrium the new-appointment rate increases by only 6 percent. In the short run, however, the institutional gains can be significant. Thus a 9 percent increase in the hiring rate of new faculty is achieved during the first five years of our simulated early retirement program; moreover, the number of nontenured faculty rises by 7 percent, an increase that is offset entirely by a decrease in the number of older faculty.

Over the next few years, as mandatory retirement is phased out, we expect to see such analyses being conducted more and more frequently. Models of the type just described can be extremely useful in examining an institution's options for dealing with these changes. This completes our discussion of faculty flow models. Next we turn our attention to procedures for making student enrollment projections.

Table 8.2. Steady-State and Transient Effects of Early Retirement

Results	No Early Retirement	Early Retirement	% Change
Steady-state results			
Appointment rate	35	37	+6%
Faculty levels			
Nontenure	148	154	+4%
Tenure: age 30 to 49	139	146	+5%
Tenure: age 50 to 64	128	115	−10%
Short-run results			
1972–77 appointments	164	179	+9%
1977 faculty levels			
Nontenure	135	145	+7%
Tenure: age 30 to 49	152	153	+1%
Tenure: age 50 to 64	128	117	−9%

SOURCE: Hopkins 1974a, table 3, p. 411.

Enrollment Projections of Undergraduate Students

A university needs accurate forecasts of student enrollment for at least three major purposes: (a) for predicting income from tuition; (b) for planning courses and curriculum; (c) for allocating marginal resources to academic departments. We shall focus here on (a) only, and shall assume that macro-level enrollment projections are sufficient for this purpose. The same techniques as we develop here can be used to serve (b) and (c) as well, although the models involved will need to be more detailed. And it is worth bearing in mind that, as a general rule, the more detail that is included in the model—that is, in the current context, the greater the number of possible student states—the more expensive, subject to error, and intellectually unmanageable it will tend to become.

In mathematical terms, the problem to be addressed in this section reduces to the following. Given the enrollment figures for all past time periods, $N(t-1)$, $N(t-2)$, $N(t-3)$, ..., and $f(t)$, or the number of students enrolling for the first time in period t, find a function $\mathscr{F}(\cdot)$ of the past enrollments such that

$$N(t) = \mathscr{F}[N(t-1), f(t-1), N(t-2), f(t-2), \ldots] + f(t). \quad (8.15)$$

The time periods generally correspond to quarters or semesters in the academic year, while the enrollment typically is measured a few weeks into each period. Two necessary properties of $\mathscr{F}(\cdot)$ are that its parameters should be estimable from available data and that it should be capable of giving statistically accurate projections of future enrollments. The challenge to the model builder is to find the simplest form for $\mathscr{F}(\cdot)$ that has these properties.

In modeling the enrollment behavior of students one typically will want to deal with them in certain discrete categories—by class, for instance, or major field of study. We shall use the notation $N_j(t)$ and $f_j(t)$ when referring to a particular category of students. For simplicity of exposition, we assume from now on that j stands for the class level (i.e., freshman, sophomore, junior, or senior) of an undergraduate, and that new students enter as freshmen only. It is relatively straightforward to adapt the models so that they give finer break-downs, or allow for upper-class transfers, or represent graduate student enroll-ments instead of undergraduate.

Our chief purpose in making these simplifying assumptions is to facilitate comparison of the flow models that are most applicable to enrollment planning. These are of three general types: (a) the *grade progression ratio method*; (b) *Markov chain models*; (c) *cohort flow models*. They range from very simple to mathematically complex, and their requirements for data are directly related to the level of complexity, as is the accuracy of the results. As we shall see, these alternative formulations have much to teach us about building models in general, and enrollment prediction models in particular.

Grade Progression Ratio Method

Often used by public higher education systems and their state funding agencies, this method employs so-called grade progression ratios (GPRs) of the form $a_{j-1,j} = N_j(t)/N_{j-1}(t-1)$, which represent the ratio of students in one class level (say j) at time t to students in the next-lower class level at time $t-1$. Given a set of such ratios for $j = 1, 2$, etc., and a set of starting enroll-ments by class level $\{N_j(0)\}$, one predicts enrollments in future years, t, by means of the equations

$$\begin{cases} N_1(t) = f(t) \\ N_j(t) = a_{j-1,j} N_{j-1}(t-1) \quad j = 2, 3, 4. \end{cases} \tag{8.16}$$

Since this type of model assumes that all students in each state move on between one time period and the next, it obviously is suitable only for making year-to-year (rather than quarter-to-quarter or semester-to-semester) pre-dictions of enrollment. It is predicated on the assumption that students follow an orderly progression from one year to the next: either they advance to the next-higher level or they leave the system for good. Such a pattern of flows is depicted in figure 8.8.

The chief advantages of the grade progression ratio method are the ease of doing calculations and the ready availability of data. State education agencies use it almost exclusively for enrollment planning at the primary and secondary levels and often at the postsecondary level as well. Unfortunately, its major assumption clearly is violated at many postsecondary institutions, both public and private, with which we are familiar. The difficulty is that many students at these institutions remain at the same class level for longer than one year and many others drop out (or, as is often said today, "stop out") temporarily and return in a later year. Since neither type of behavior is represented properly in this model, projections made with a fixed set of $a_{j-1,j}$'s may include large errors.

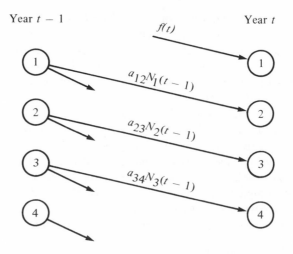

Figure 8.8. The grade progression ratio method

Although the GPR method certainly is more economical than the other two, its chief raison d'être seems to be its use of the most readily available input data. Most analysts find it too crude for enrollment planning at institutions where many students follow the complex flow patterns of the sort we have just described.[4]

Markov Chain Models

Some of the difficulties just mentioned can be overcome by using a Markov chain formulation, such as we employed for faculty planning in the previous section. The notation is exactly the same, although, for present purposes, the transition fraction p_{ij} would refer to the fraction of students in class i in one period that can be found in class j in the subsequent one. Projections are made with the system of equations

$$
\begin{cases}
N_1(t) = p_{11}N_1(t-1) & + f(t) \\
N_2(t) = p_{12}N_1(t-1) + p_{22}N_2(t-1) \\
N_3(t) = \qquad\qquad p_{23}N_2(t-1) + p_{33}N_3(t-1) \\
N_4(t) = \qquad\qquad\qquad\qquad p_{34}N_3(t-1) + p_{44}N_4(t-1)
\end{cases}
\tag{8.17}
$$

This system corresponds to the flow pattern shown in figure 8.9.

In contrast to the grade progression method, the Markov chain model explicitly incorporates the flows of students who remain in the same class level in consecutive time periods. It does so by means of the fractions p_{jj} as distinct from the $p_{j-1,j}$. Once these parameters have been estimated, the model also can handle quite easily the flows of new transfer students at each upper-class level, if that is required.

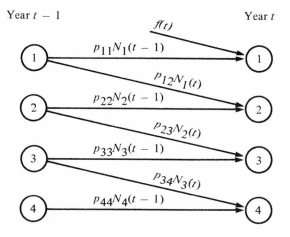

Figure 8.9. The Markov chain model

This finer and more reasonable representation of student flows is gained only at the expense of more extensive requirements for data. Whereas before there were only three GPRs to be estimated, using a Markov chain model to make predictions at yearly intervals requires one to estimate as many as $7 \times 3 = 21$ parameters when the academic year is divided into three regular quarters. This assumes that the model will actually be used to track enrollments quarter by quarter, in which case we would need to have three sets of p_{ij}'s (one for transitions between each pair of consecutive quarters). The advantages of constructing the model in this way are, first, that it can then provide estimates of attrition between quarters; and, second, that its estimates of enrollment for the autumn quarter presumably will be more accurate because they have been based on enrollments in the preceding spring. We have excluded the summer quarter from this discussion because at most institutions it attracts a relatively small proportion of the regular undergraduate population. Where this is the case, one expects the enrollment levels in the previous spring to be much better predictors of autumn quarter enrollments than are the summer quarter enrollments.[5]

Not only does the Markov chain model require more data but the data needed are less readily available at most institutions. GPRs are easily calculated from gross enrollment figures of the type collected almost anywhere; for example, to obtain the most recent value for the ratio a_{12} we need only observe the number of sophomores this year (minus sophomore transfers, if any) and compare it with the number of freshmen last year. Now consider a typical Markov transition fraction, say p_{12}. Its value should be calculated by dividing the number of last period's freshmen who advanced to sophomore standing by the total number of freshmen enrolled last period. Now, while university enrollment statistics usually distinguish between new students and old students, they rarely distinguish between old students according to their previous class level. Thus, the reported figure on old students in sophomore status would refer to the sum $p_{12}N_1(t-1) + p_{22}N_2(t-1)$. In order to separate the sum into its proper components, one would need either to reprocess the raw data contained in individual student records or to use a statistical estimation procedure. Either way the setup cost for the model would probably be considerable.

To get a better idea of how the second alternative might work, suppose we have historical data available on old students by class level, for a sequence of $T+1$ spring and autumn quarters. Let $\mathbf{N}^A(t)$ and $\mathbf{N}^S(t)$ denote the actual (observed) enrollment levels of old students for autumn and spring, respectively, in year t, and let $\hat{\mathbf{N}}^A(t)$ denote the model-derived estimate of autumn enrollment. The least-squares estimates of p_{12} and p_{22} for transitions from spring to autumn quarter would be obtained by solving:

Minimize

$$\sum_{t=1}^{T} [\hat{\mathbf{N}}^A_2(t) - \mathbf{N}^A_2(t)]^2$$

subject to the constraints

$$\hat{\mathbf{N}}^A_2(t) = p_{12}\mathbf{N}^S_1(t-1) + p_{22}\mathbf{N}^S_2(t-1) \quad t = 1, 2, \ldots, T$$

$$0 \le p_{12}, p_{22}$$

$$p_{12} + p_{22} \le 1.$$

This would call for application of the ordinary least-squares regression procedure were it not for the side constraints on the unknown parameters, constraints that require them to be nonnegative fractions whose sum is no more than one. To solve the problem one can try first setting aside these constraints and using ordinary regression. If the unconstrained results turn out to satisfy the constraints, then they are the best fit to the model. If not, one must use a special algorithm such as the one proposed by Henri Theil and Guido Rey (1966).

How much better can the four-state Markov chain model predict future enrollments than the GPR method? In an effort to answer this question experimentally, Robert M. Oliver (1968) estimated parameters for both models from historical student records at the Berkeley campus of the University of California. He used parameter estimates based on data prior to 1961, actual enrollments in fall 1961, and actual numbers of students entering in 1961/62 in order to predict enrollments for the fall semester of 1962/63. His results are compared with actual enrollments in table 8.3; they hardly seem to favor one model over the other for the one-year prediction period. However, the theoretical section of this paper points to certain statistical properties of the GPR method that make it less desirable than the Markov chain model. In any case, the Markov chain model is the more structurally pleasing of the two. Since, moreover, the Markov transition fractions at least distinguish properly between flows of continuing and advancing students, we do have a priori reason to expect that they will be more stable in a statistical sense. One major difficulty still remaining with the four-state version of this model, however, is that it,

Table 8.3.   A Comparison of the GPR and Markov Chain Models: Autumn 1962
Enrollments, University of California at Berkeley

Class Level	Actual	GPR Model		Markov Chain Model	
		Predictions	% Error	Predictions	% Error
Freshman	3,972	3,902	(-2%)	3,903	(-2%)
Sophomore	3,649	3,709	$(+2\%)$	3,746	$(+3\%)$
Junior	4,762	4,728	(-1%)	4,765	$(\ldots)$
Senior	4,210	4,341	$(+3\%)$	4,274	$(+2\%)$
TOTAL	16,593	16,680	$(+1\%)$	16,688	$(+1\%)$

SOURCE: Oliver 1968. Reproduced by permission.

too, fails to take account of the two-way flow of undergraduate "stopouts." Thus if we apply the model to a campus where so-called stopping out is common behavior, some of the old students counted in any given quarter will be returning from stopout status—i.e., from one or more periods away from the campus— rather than continuing directly from the just-preceding term. Unless explicit account is taken of this behavior where it exists, predictions of enrollments several years into the future still may be significantly in error.

In theory, at least, the Markov model can easily be adapted to represent stopouts by means of one or more *vacation states*. Adding a single vacation state would give a five-state model with additional parameters p_{i5} and p_{5i} ($i = 1, 2, 3, 4$) corresponding, respectively, to the fractions of students stopping out from and returning to active status. As a further refinement it might be better still to have a vacation state corresponding to each class level, in which case the model would need to have 8 states and $3 \times 15 = 45$ parameters altogether. Of course, we would expect to encounter the same problems of data estimation as before, only now we would require information on flows between active and stopout states as well. This type of information is practically never available from the standard statistical reports prepared by a university registrar, so extra data-processing effort would almost certainly be required.

The statistical properties and predictive capabilities of four-, five-, and eight-state Markov models have been examined, with data from Berkeley (Marshall, Oliver, and Suslow 1970). Each model incorporated data based on actual student flows that occurred at Berkeley between the autumn of 1960 and the autumn of 1961. These models were used to make enrollment predictions for the subsequent five years, with the results shown in table 8.4. Using two kinds of error statistics, the authors compared these results with actual enrollments and concluded:

> In terms of absolute error, the five-state model appears to be superior to the four- and eight-state models over short prediction periods. Our results show that for longer periods the four-state model gives better results.
>
> In terms of mean square error, the five-state model seems to be consistently better than the other two, although there is little difference in them at five years. If enrollment predictions are required over one or two years in the future, it seems that the five-state model is the most desirable one.

Table 8.4.   A Comparison of Markov Chain Models: Percent Absolute Error Between
Enrollment Forecasts and Actual Enrollments, University of California at
Berkeley, Academic Years 1962 to 1966

	Percent Error for Academic Year:				
Model	1962	1963	1964	1965	1966
Freshmen					
4-state model	**1.1%**	**1.6%**	**7.7%**	9.7%	6.7%
5-state model	1.5%	1.8%	7.8%	**9.4%**	**5.6%**
8-state model	2.9%	2.6%	8.5%	10.3%	6.8%
Sophomores					
4-state model	3.9%	1.4%	11.7%	3.9%	3.8%
5-state model	2.7%	**0.5%**	11.2%	3.9%	5.2%
8-state model	**0.5%**	1.4%	**9.7%**	**2.4%**	**3.4%**
Juniors					
4-state model	1.0%	5.1%	**7.4%**	**13.0%**	**16.6%**
5-state model	**0.4%**	2.5%	9.2%	14.7%	17.1%
8-state model	4.4%	**0.5%**	9.7%	14.7%	16.9%
Seniors					
4-state model	2.4%	1.5%	10.2%	13.9%	16.4%
5-state model	**1.9%**	**0.4%**	6.8%	10.9%	13.4%
8-state model	4.6%	6.0%	**3.1%**	**9.0%**	**12.9%**
TOTAL					
4-state model	1.5%	1.7%	0.9%	**1.5%**	**2.1%**
5-state model	**0.6%**	**0.3%**	**0.7%**	2.8%	2.5%
8-state model	3.2%	2.4%	2.3%	3.8%	3.2%

SOURCE: Computed from Marshall, Oliver, and Suslow 1970, table 14, p. 36.

Table 8.4 shows some rather large prediction errors for enrollments several
years into the future. One source of these errors, according to the authors, was
the models' use of transition fractions that were undifferentiated as to the origin
of the students they were tracking. There is good reason to believe that students
who transfer into a university at the junior level, say, will have different enrollment patterns at the junior and senior level than those who entered as freshmen.
Yet the aggregate models described thus far make no distinction between these
two types of students in tracking enrollments between the junior and senior
years. Whenever the mix of entering students is shifting between freshmen and
transfers, predictions made by such models may therefore be subject to
considerable error.

We should add that errors also are introduced through the somewhat
unrealistic assumption that the likelihood of a student currently enrolled as
(e.g.) a sophomore remaining a sophomore in the next time period does not
depend on how long he or she has been a sophomore already. To see that this is
indeed being assumed, notice that the single variable $N_2(t)$ represents all
sophomores enrolled in period t. Presumably this number includes students
who have been sophomores for zero, one, two, three, etc., periods, but none of
the models discussed in this section makes that distinction. When we go to
apply a fraction p_{22} to this aggregate variable, then, we are averaging across

all such students to represent their behavior in the aggregate. Whenever the mix changes, so will the behavior—but not the predictions made by these models. In the next section we present a third type of model that is designed to take these different patterns of enrollment into account.

Cohort Flow Models

The chief difference between cohort flow models and the Markov chain models just described is that the former take account of students' origins as freshmen, sophomore transfers, etc., and of the accumulated duration of their stay at the university, while the latter do not.* As a matter of common sense, one would expect to get better predictions from a model that makes these distinctions than from one that does not.

For this type of formulation we need to think once again of students grouped into cohorts at the time they enter the university, just as we did in constructing the network flow model of chapter 5. That is, we adopt a *longitudinal* outlook toward student flows—i.e., one that tracks each cohort throughout the students' period of attendance—rather than a *cross-sectional* one, which projects solely on the basis of the student enrollment profile in the immediately preceding time period. For the purposes of enrollment planning, cohorts are identified by the period in which they entered, their level at entry (freshman, sophomore, etc.), and perhaps other characteristics as well, such as their sex or ethnic identification, if these are considered relevant.

Suppose we have identified K types of cohorts that enter in each time period and have labelled them $k = 1, 2, \ldots, K$. The parameters of this model are the *survivor fractions*, defined as follows.

Let $P_j^k(s)$ = the fraction of students in cohorts of type k who are enrolled in class j, s periods after entry

We shall also need to separate the new student flows, $f(t)$, into cohorts and designate these by $f^k(t)$. We wish to predict the total enrollment of students in class j, say, at a particular point in time, say t. This enrollment may consist of students from any cohort that entered at any time up to t. The contribution from all past cohorts of type k is given by

$$N_j^k(t) = P_j^k(0)f^k(t) + P_j^k(1)f^k(t-1) + P_j^k(2)f^k(t-2) + \cdots$$

$$= \sum_{s=0}^{T} P_j^k(s)f^k(t-s)$$

(8.18)

where T = the practical maximum number of periods after entry that a student could still be enrolled.

---

*Actually, the cohort model may be viewed as a special case of the Markov chain model, a case in which the description of states has been expanded to include the origin of students and their length of stay. As we shall see, however, for tracking flows with a cohort model it is more convenient to develop a notation that differs from the one used in representing a Markov chain.

Summing these numbers over cohort types gives the total enrollment at level j, that is,

$$N_j(t) = \sum_{k=1}^{K} N_j^k(t). \tag{8.19}$$

Figure 8.10 gives a diagrammatic representation of the cohort flow model. For the sake of illustration, we have omitted both the designation of cohorts by types and enrollments by class levels. We have also made the assumption that no students remain beyond four time periods after entry. The sole purpose of this figure is to aid the reader in visualizing how the total enrollment in any class level at time t arises as the sum of contributions from cohorts arriving at times $t, t - 1, t - 2$, etc. Thus a convenient way to think of the enrollment in any one class level is as a cumulation of the survivors from all previous cohorts. It is in this sense that the parameters $P_j^k(s)$ may be thought of as survivor fractions.

Of course, the term "survivor" is being used loosely here, since students who stop out in the sth period after entering are not included in the fractions $P_j^k(s)$. When, in subsequent time periods, they return to active status, they will once again become part of the survivor fractions. With this interpretation it is also easy to see why some of these fractions might still be positive several periods beyond the normal point of graduation, since students who take one or more regular quarters off from their studies will usually require some additional time to earn their degrees.

The reader will readily appreciate the fact that this type of model has the most demanding data requirements. Suppose, for instance, that there are four cohort types, k (e.g., freshmen and transfers, men and women); four class levels, j; three regular quarters per academic year; and a maximum elapsed time for enrollment of six years.* To forecast enrollments in future quarters, then, would require us to estimate $4 \times 4 \times 3 \times 6 = 288$ distinct $P_j^k(s)$ values. (It is often surprising to see just how quickly such models get blown up in size!) We must further recognize that data on cohort attendance patterns are practically never included in routine enrollment reports, nor can they be inferred from other available information. To obtain these estimates, then, there is little alternative but to process raw data from individual student files.

What ought one to expect in return for this added burden and expense? Greater precision, for one thing; unlike the other types of models commonly used to forecast enrollments, the cohort model is formulated specifically to incorporate the differences in enrollment behavior that we know exist between various cohort types.

Oliver and his colleagues at Berkeley studied the enrollment patterns of certain cohort types and found them to be remarkably stable over time. For example, figure 8.11 shows actual $P(s)$ values for cohorts of freshmen who

---

*A period of six years would allow for some stopping out and also for the repeating of academic terms by students who fail to pass their courses.

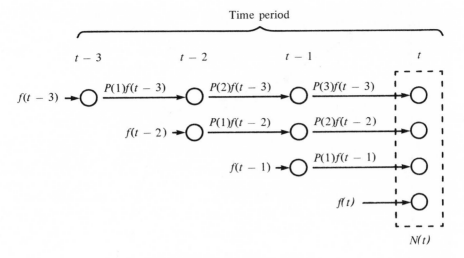

Figure 8.10. The cohort flow model

entered in 1955 and 1960. Despite the five-year separation of entry times, one is struck by the great similarity in attendance patterns between the two groups studied.

A stable pattern of cohort flows has also been evident at Stanford. A model involving four cohort types—male and female freshmen, male and female transfers—was constructed with survivor fractions based on the attendance records of all students who first came as undergraduates to Stanford in the autumn of 1967. Since the model was not implemented until 1972/73, five complete years of attendance data were available on these cohorts. As one sort of validity check on the model and the data, we specified the actual quarterly numbers of new students in each cohort for the years 1967/68 through 1973/74 and used the model to calculate undergraduate enrollments in each quarter of 1973/74. The results were as follows:

	Model Prediction	Actual	Error
Autumn 1973	6,510	6,466	+44 (0.7%)
Winter 1974	6,236	6,238	−2 (0.03%)
Spring 1974	5,855	5,830	+25 (0.4%)

Since 1972/73 the Stanford model has been used to predict the number of continuing and returning undergraduates in the autumn quarter of each year. The predictions have been made in the previous spring to establish targets for new student admissions in the fall. The track record so far has been extremely good, with errors usually well under 1 percent. Since we do not believe any model of human behavior with fixed data can be expected to make predictions with that degree of accuracy, these results must be partly fortuitous. Never-

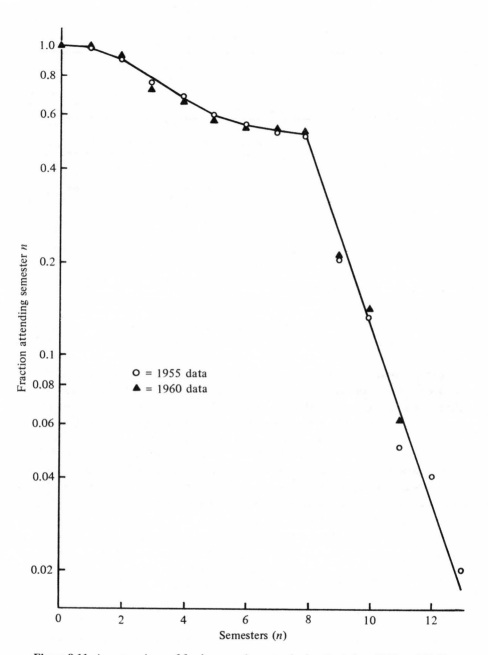

Figure 8.11. A comparison of freshman cohort survival at Berkeley, 1955 and 1960

theless, the finer structure of the cohort model is more consistent with observed behavior patterns, so we can reasonably expect it to give better predictions than models of the other two types.[6]

Summary of Enrollment Projection Techniques

We have considered three different approaches to meeting the needs for projected enrollment estimates at a college or university. To recapitulate, these are:

1. *Grade progression ratio method.* The method predicts autumn enrollments from ratios of (a) the number enrolled in a given class level at the beginning of a given year to (b) the number enrolled in the next-lower class level one year earlier. The parameters number less than ten and the statistical properties are not very good, particularly when the mix of new students is changing.

2. *Markov chain model.* The model uses fractional flow rates that represent the single-period transitions of students from one class level in one time period to the same level or the next-higher level in the next period. The model's parameters usually number between ten and fifty; its statistical properties are better than the first's but not as good as the third's.

3. *Cohort flow model.* The model adopts a longitudinal view of student flows: enrollment in any class level at any particular time is made up of survivors from cohorts that entered at various points in the past. The parameters may number as many as several hundred; once estimated, they have tended to remain rather stable, which means that one generally can rely on the model's estimates even when the new student mix is changing.

As we have seen, these models vary widely in complexity and data-processing costs. The choice of model should depend on the particular needs of the institution. For a rough-and-ready set of estimates of beginning of the year enrollments, the grade progression ratio method usually will do. If, on the other hand, one needs a quarterly estimate of tuition income that is accurate to within 1 or 2 percent, a cohort model is probably the best bet.

We have noted that cohort survivor fractions tend to be stable over quite long periods of time, an observation that we based on studies of actual student attendance data from Berkeley and Stanford. It follows that once these parameters have been estimated the same values can be used repeatedly for a period of several years before they will need to be updated. Thus the setup cost for a cohort model may be spread over several years, whereas the reestimation of parameters for less stable models will have to be done and paid for more often.

Finally, we should point out that calculations of cohort survivor fractions may have a value that is independent of the projection model itself. They may be used to study a variety of issues having to do, for example, with the relative persistence at the institution of different cohorts—male and female, minority and nonminority, etc.—or with the relative popularity of the various major fields of study with certain cohorts during their period of attendance.[7]

Models for Predicting Freshman Yield

We have assumed throughout our discussion of enrollment projections that the number of new students who will show up in each future time period is known. This assumption is more likely to hold for selective than nonselective institutions. In the short run, at least, selective ones need concern themselves only with techniques for predicting the yield of admitted freshman applicants, while nonselective ones need also to consider the demand for admission itself.

Our object in this section is to examine briefly some techniques for predicting freshman yield, given the number and composition of admitted applicants. *Yield rates* representing the proportion of admitted students who choose to attend the institution have long been used by college and university admissions offices. For their purposes it is often sufficient to use a single, overall yield rate in deciding upon the number of freshmen to admit. Finer structure may be called for, however, whenever the yield rates are known to vary with one or more background characteristics of the applicants—and the mix of applicants, in terms of these characteristics, is in fact changing. Then, too, it is often worthwhile to consider how yield rates vary with certain variables under the institution's control, such as the tuition rate and financial aid policy. Efforts to develop analytical models of freshman yield have been reported by Stanford, Bucknell, and Carnegie-Mellon universities, to name a few.

Suppose we denote the set of relevant student background characteristics by $\{X_1, X_2, \ldots, X_I\}$ and the set of institutional variables by $\{Y_1, Y_2, \ldots, Y_J\}$. Let $p(\mathbf{X}, \mathbf{Y})$ denote the yield rate for applicants with characteristics $\mathbf{X}$ when the institution's policy is $\mathbf{Y}$. The problem before us, then, reduces to finding a suitable form for the function $p(\cdot, \cdot)$, and then estimating its parameters.

One widely used approach is to specify a linear model of the form

$$p = p_0 + \sum_{i=1}^{I} \alpha_i X_i + \sum_{j=1}^{J} \beta_j Y_j \qquad (8.20)$$

and then, from historical data on admitted freshman applicants, to estimate its parameters by ordinary least-squares regression. There are at least three difficulties associated with this approach, however: (a) there may in fact be significant nonlinearities in the enrollment behavior of admitted freshmen; (b) two or more of the X_i's and Y_j's may interact with one another in influencing this behavior, so that the effect on yield of changes in these variables is not the same as the sum of the effects associated with each of them separately; (c) ordinary least-squares regression is an inappropriate estimation technique to apply when the dependent variable (i.e., p) can take on only two possible values in the data (i.e., individual students are either "coming" or "not coming" to the institution in question).

The first two difficulties may be countered by a judicious selection of independent variables. For example, if yield is thought to be a nonlinear function of the amount of scholarship provided in the financial aid offer one should probably represent that amount in nonlinear form in the set of policy variables. A common device is to replace the single variable by a set of dummy variables that take on values 0 or 1 depending on which interval the variable falls in. This preserves the linear form of the model in equation (8.20) while allowing the estimated coefficients to reveal the extent of actual nonlinearities.

To take the particular case of scholarship aid (call it S) at a reasonably high-priced institution, we might use a dummy variable scheme like the following.

Let $Y_1 = 1$ if $0 < S \leq \$1,000$, and 0 otherwise

    $Y_2 = 1$ if $\$1,000 < S \leq \$2,000$, and 0 otherwise

    $Y_3 = 1$ if $\$2,000 < S \leq \$3,000$, and 0 otherwise

    $Y_3 = 1$ if $\$3,000 < S$, and 0 otherwise.

The data for any particular student who was offered a scholarship would show one of these Y_j's to be 1 and all the others 0. If the student was offered no scholarship at all, all these Y's would be zero. The coefficients β_j would have the interpretation of the differential impact on yield of a scholarship at level j, when all other variables are held constant. If $\beta_1 < \beta_2 < \beta_3 < \beta_4$, we would conclude that scholarships have an increasing differential impact as the amount goes up; while a graph of these coefficients as compared with the scholarship amount would suggest whether the relationship is in fact significantly nonlinear.

This dummy variable technique extends also to the case where two or more of the independent variables are thought to be interacting. To take another example: suppose we believe the amount of scholarship interacts with the total amount of financial aid, the difference being made up by aid in the form of a job, a loan, or both. In this case, we would use dummy variables to represent various scholarship and total aid pairs (e.g., scholarship between $1,000 and $2,000 and total aid between $2,000 and $3,000).

The third difficulty with the linear regression approach is methodological: the ordinary least-squares technique never was intended for making estimates in situations involving a binary dependent variable. Fortunately, there is a variation of the technique, known as *generalized least squares*, that surmounts much of this difficulty (Goldberger 1964, pp. 231–36). Packages of statistical programs for the computer that include it are rare but not unobtainable.

To illustrate the use of this technique consider the set of coefficients shown in table 8.5. These were obtained by using the generalized least-squares method to fit a model that involved eleven student background and institutional policy variables to data on freshmen aid applicants admitted to Stanford for the academic years 1972/73 and 1973/74. The variables labeled "academic rating" and "nonacademic rating" refer to two five-point scales used by the Stanford Admissions Office to summarize an applicant's qualifications—the lower the rating figure, the more highly regarded the student. "Self-help" refers to the loan and job components of financial aid. The analysis is limited to aid appli-

Table 8.5.   Generalized Least-Squares Fits for Two Consecutive Years of Freshmen Admitted to Stanford University

Variable Class	Variable Value	Estimated Coefficients	
		1972/73 Cohort	1973/74 Cohort
Constant (p_0)		0.548	0.759
Academic rating	1 (highest)	−0.360	−0.360
	2	−0.180	−0.180
	3	−0.099	−0.108
	4	−0.066	−0.072
	5 (lowest)	−0.033	−0.036
Nonacademic rating	1 (highest)	0.074	−0.256
	2	0.037	−0.128
	3	0.090	−0.150
	4	0.060	−0.100
	5 (lowest)	0.030	−0.050
Sex	Female	0.123	0.029
Race	Minority	−0.140	−0.083
Region of residence	California	−0.017	0.007
	Far Western US	−0.034	0.014
	Middle US	−0.051	0.021
	Southern US	−0.068	0.028
	Northeastern US	−0.085	0.035
Parents' college	Stanford (mother or father)	−0.045	0.023
Parents' income[a]	$10,000–$14,999	−0.012	−0.052
	$15,000–$20,999	−0.060	−0.042
	$21,000+	0.036	0.005
Parents' assets[a] ($0,000)		0.003	0.011
Scholarships (outside and university)[a]	$1–$1,000	0.241	0.097
	$1,001–$2,000	0.295	0.257
	$2,001–$3,000	0.408	0.348
	$3,001+	0.468	0.373
Self-help ($000)[a]		−0.105	−0.054
Aid quality (fraction of Stanford's aid offer that is scholarship)		−0.157	−0.211

SOURCE: Delores A. Conway and Joseph S. Verducci, unpublished data (Stanford, Calif.: Department of Statistics, Stanford University).

[a] Financial variables for both years are expressed as 1972 dollars.

cants because we lacked financial data for students admitted to Stanford who did not apply for financial aid (slightly more than half the admitted freshmen in these two years were aid applicants). Also, we were primarily concerned with the influence of financial aid variables on the likelihood that these same students would enroll at Stanford.

By looking at the coefficients of this model—coefficients that were estimated from data on each of two consecutive freshman classes—we can learn something about the stability of its estimates. Viewed in this light, the results are rather disturbing: with the single exception of the coefficients associated with the academic rating variable, every value changes considerably between the two years. In several cases, a coefficient even changes its sign, thus leading one seriously to question whether it is in fact significantly different from zero.

What can explain the unstable nature of these results? A large part of the problem, presumably, is that the model was not well specified. One clue that supports this presumption is the negative sign on the coefficients associated with *aid quality*—that is, with the proportion of aid given in the form of a ·scholarship—in each of the two years. Surely, aid of higher quality would tend to attract more, not fewer, students to Stanford, when all other variables were held constant. The problem with relying on this variable is that major consideration is given to the so-called competitiveness of a student when the packaging of an aid offer is being decided. Aid quality, then, turns out to be more of a proxy for competition than a measure of Stanford's attractiveness to the student —hence, in all likelihood, the unexpected sign.

The point to bear in mind is that it is commonplace in applications of these linear regression techniques to find that one has not specified the proper model. One should therefore expect to spend a fair amount of effort seeking the right combinations of the right variables; indeed, there is no assurance of ever obtaining a very good fit.

In many ways, it would seem more promising to exploit other kinds of techniques in analyzing freshman enrollment behavior. Particularly appealing are the methods that have been developed for fitting a model to data set out in the form of a *contingency table*, as opposed to data on individual students such as one uses in regression analysis. A contingency table is a device for arraying individuals into cells according to two or more selected criterion variables. For example, we might arrange the total population of admitted freshmen into cells classified by (a) academic rating, (b) parents' income groupings, and (c) whether or not the student chose to enroll. This would give us a three-dimensional contingency table in which the entry corresponding to, say, high academic rating, parents' income between $15,000 and $21,000, and "enrolled" would specify the number of admitted freshmen with this set of characteristics. For our purposes, it is convenient to collapse the three-dimensional table into one with only two dimensions by replacing the numbers enrolling and not enrolling by the yield rate. Yield rates then become the entries in the cells of a table whose rows correspond to parents' income groups and whose columns correspond to academic rating groups. Table 8.6 gives such an array of data from four consecutive freshman classes at Stanford.

When the data are treated in contingency-table form, our problem becomes one of estimating the yield rate for each of a small number of discrete categories of students, rather than one of predicting individual behavior. As we can see from the entries in table 8.6 the yield rates for these fairly large groups of students are considerably more stable over time than are the regression coefficients of table 8.5. Thus, by employing contingency-table analysis to examine the behavior of students in groups, we stand a much better chance of finding models with stable parameters.

Table 8.6.   Actual Yield Rates at Stanford for Various Combinations of Academic
Rating and Parents' Income, 1973/74 Through 1976/77

Adjusted Parents' Income[a] and Yield Rate for Academic Year	Academic Rating	
	Low (3, 4, 5)	High (1 or 2)
Under $15,000		
1973/74	0.735	0.561
1974/75	0.753	0.601
1975/76	0.768	0.658
1976/77	0.730	0.599
$15,000–$25,000		
1973/74	0.674	0.508
1974/75	0.644	0.483
1975/76	0.720	0.546
1976/77	0.663	0.575
Over $25,000		
1973/74	0.675	0.523
1974/75	0.643	0.565
1975/76	0.651	0.472
1976/77	0.684	0.519

[a] To maintain comparability between years, figures on parents' income were adjusted for inflation in the raw data. The categories above refer to income in terms of 1972 dollars.

A form of model often used to describe a fractional variable, such as the yield rate, in terms of a set of discrete predictor variables is the *log-odds model*, which in our application would take the form

$$\log \frac{p(\mathbf{w})}{1 - p(\mathbf{w})} = p_0 + \sum_{i=1}^{3} p_i^I T_i^I(w_1) + \sum_{j=1}^{2} p_j^R T_j^R(w_2) \qquad (8.21)$$

where $\mathbf{w}$ = a pair of index values representing a particular combination of income and academic rating categories

$p(\mathbf{w})$ = the estimated yield rate for students with this attribute combination

p_0 = the "mean effect," or constant term

p_i^I = the difference in yield rate associated with the ith income level

p_j^R = the difference in yield rate associated with the jth rating level

$T_i^I(w_1)$ = a dummy variable that equals 1 if $w_1 = i$, and 0 otherwise

$T_j^R(w_2)$ = an indicator variable that equals 1 if $w_2 = j$, and 0 otherwise.

For example, the index values for the group with the low academic rating and parental income in the $15,000–$21,000 range would be $\mathbf{w} = (2, 1)$. By (8.21) the log-odds of the yield rate for this particular attribute combination would be estimated to be

$$p_0 + p_2^I + p_1^R.$$

It is worth pointing out that any order of interaction effects can be handled in a model of this form. If, for instance, one thought a better fit could be obtained by considering the joint interaction effect of parental income and academic rating, one would merely add another term to (8.21) of the form

$$\sum_{(i,\,j)} p_{ij}^{IR}\, T_{ij}^{IR}(\mathbf{w}).$$

Numerical techniques for fitting parameters to a log-odds model of a contingency table have been discussed by Yvonne M. M. Bishop and her colleagues (1975, chapter 5). Fortunately, there already exist computer routines that are tailor-made for this purpose. An example is the CONTAB program, obtainable from the Statistical Engineering Laboratory at George Washington University, in Washington, D.C. This procedure was used to fit a model to the data in table 8.6, above.[8] The results, when data for all four years were first pooled to generate a single contingency table, are given in table 8.7. As we can see, the procedure produces smoothed estimates of the coefficients of the model, in which much of the "noise" has been filtered out. These estimates should be better predictors, therefore, than the means that have been taken from the raw, noisy data, and that appear in table 8.6. A further advantage of employing this statistical estimation procedure is that it provides tests of statistical significance.

Table 8.7.   CONTAB-Predicted Yield Rates at Stanford, Based on Pooled Data for Years 1973/74 Through 1976/77

Parents' Income	Academic Rating	
	Low	High
Under $15,000	0.744	0.609
$15,000–$25,000	0.676	0.528
Over $25,000	0.665	0.515

For statistical stability and ease of explanation we prefer contingency tables to multivariate regression. In particular, contingency tables are fundamentally less foreign to most university decision makers than are equations of the form (8.20). The model can be made very simple (small numbers of dimensions with no interaction effects) or very complicated (large numbers of dimensions with many interaction effects)—it all depends on what one wants—yet the results can always be represented in a form that is fairly easy for most persons to understand.

Models for Affirmative Action Planning

In recent years considerable emphasis has been placed on so-called affirmative action in the recruiting of women and members of ethnic minority groups to faculty and professional staff positions in which they are underrepresented.

Most colleges and universities have established formal programs whose goal is to bring the representation of these groups up to something like their proportions in the pool of eligible outside candidates for the jobs in question. They have been hampered in their efforts, however, by a lack of analytical tools for assessing how rapidly this goal can be met, or for establishing goals that realistically can be met in the shorter run.

We suggest that the speed with which full representation can be accomplished will depend on these four factors:

1. The extent of underrepresentation of the relevant subpopulations on the current staff;
2. The rate of natural attrition from positions of the type being considered;
3. The rate at which incremental new positions are being added;
4. The degree to which the minority group is represented among eligible new hires.

In the case of faculty, service lifetimes tend to be long and attrition rates correspondingly low. Unless the faculty is expanding, full representation can take a very long time. In staff areas, the somewhat greater turnover gives affirmative action programs a better chance of succeeding in the short run.

The model to be described in the next subsection has been used in staff affirmative action planning at Stanford, that is, it has served as an aid to setting realistic numerical goals for the employment of women and minority persons in staff positions, and to evaluating progress in meeting such goals. By modeling personnel flows in terms of hiring and persistence rates for various job categories, we develop a mathematically consistent structure that enables us to predict likely future employment patterns within each job category as a function of hiring goals. These hiring goals are themselves made to depend on both the growth rate of staff size and the relative availability of women and ethnic minorities in the potential pool of job applicants. Thus the model provides an inexpensive tool for evaluating the effect on the employment patterns of women and minority-group staff members of alternative assumptions about (a) future staffing needs and (b) the availability of qualified job applicants. These projections can be made for each year over a period of ten or more years.

Also of concern is the statistical variance associated with the goals of affirmative action. By studying the statistical properties of a fixed-size personnel system, with employees categorized by population group, one can obtain the probability distribution of the number of persons in each group after the system has evolved for a given number of time periods. Such information is particularly useful for evaluating the progress of affirmative action in small administrative units, such as the faculty of a single academic department. In the last subsection of this chapter we will show how this can be done.

An Affirmative Action Planning Model for Staff

Let us suppose that we have identified a set of discrete job categories representing the level of aggregation to be used for making predictions. The model will treat each of these categories separately from the others. Several factors will govern the job categorization scheme; among these are: (a) the level of aggregation to be used for setting goals; (b) the availability of data on the pool of job applicants; (c) the extent of significant flows between job categories. Another criterion is the desired level of stability and accuracy in prediction, for this tends to depend on the number of staff positions covered by each category; generally speaking, the model should not be expected to deal with any categories that contain fewer than, say, 100 positions.

For convenience in formulating the model, we shall assume that either no flows ever occur between job categories or, if they do, they are insignificant and thus can be ignored. Should this assumption be invalid, it would not be difficult to introduce somewhat more complex notation and then to reformulate the model to have it incorporate such flows. The development below refers to the model for a single job category, which, by assumption, can be viewed independently of all other job categories.

In establishing a notation for hiring rates, it is important to distinguish between members of the different groups in question. Thus we let $f_i(t)$ denote the number of hires from *population group i* (e.g., minority males, nonminority females, etc.) during year t. To denote staffing levels, we introduce a further variable that is critical to the attrition process, namely, current *length of service* (LOS); thus $N_i(t, s)$ stands for the number of employees from population group i serving at the *end* of year t, where LOS $= s$. (By convention, any fractional portion of a year of service will not be counted in s; e.g., if an employee count was taken on December 31, 1975, an individual hired on April 15, 1972 would be counted in the group that has $s = 3$ years.)

Finally, the relationship between hiring rates and staffing levels involves a sequence of *persistence rates*, $\{p(s)\}_{s=1}^M$, where $p(s)$ is the fraction of personnel with $s - 1$ years of service at the end of one year who remain in service at the end of the next year. This notation assumes these fractions are not subject to significant change over time. While it would be easy enough to make them time-dependent in the theoretical development, such a move would have little utility in practical forecasting unless one were confident that one could predict how these numbers would change. For present purposes it will be assumed that the single set of values of $p(s)$ to be used in making predictions represents the best judgment of policy planners regarding average persistence rates for the short-to-medium-run future. Presumably, these values will depend much on recent historical data (see below s.v. "data for the personnel flow model"), but may be modified by informed judgment concerning current and future trends in staff attrition. Note also that the persistence rates are not indexed by population category; therefore, model projections will be based on the assumption that the attrition process is fundamentally the same for all population groups. Here again, if there is reason to believe otherwise, the model may be modified accordingly.

Having thus described the model's ingredients, we are in a position to write down the equations representing the dynamics of the flow process. Clearly, the number of staff serving at time t depends on (a) the number serving at $t - 1$ and (b) the number of new hires. With our notation we can now write

$$N_i(t, 0) = f_i(t)$$
$$N_i(t, s) = p(s) N_i(t - 1, s - 1) \quad \text{for } s = 1, 2, 3, \ldots, M.$$

(8.22)

The second equation states that the number of staff at time t with s years of service is equal to the number of staff at time $t - 1$ with $s - 1$ years of service, times the persistence fraction.

Suppose the total staffing requirement for time t is known and equals $\bar{N}(t)$. Since this represents the total over all LOS values and all population groups, we must have

$$\sum_{i=1}^{I} \sum_{s=0}^{M} N_i(t, s) = \bar{N}(t).$$

(8.23)

Notice that M represents the maximum possible LOS, which may be as long as thirty or forty years for some individuals. In practice, it may be reasonable to assume that once a staff member has served for some reasonably long period, say ten years, the annual persistence rate will be the same for all subsequent years. In terms of our model, this would be the same thing as assuming that $p(s) = p(11)$ for $s > 10$. In this event, the model can be kept small by setting $M = 10$ and lumping all employees with ten or more years of service into the LOS category labeled $s = 10$.

It is instructive to compare the structure of this model of personnel flows with the cohort model of enrollment projection in the previous section. Both models rest on the same footing, namely a longitudinal outlook on personnel flows. In the current context, we have taken advantage of the natural grouping of staff into LOS categories and hence have avoided the need for keeping track of them as cohorts that entered at various times in the past. For student enrollment the number of survivors at time t from the cohort that entered s periods earlier was given by the quantity $P(s)f(t - s)$; here it is given by $p(s) N(t - 1, s - 1)$. In the current situation we could have represented staff flows just as easily in true cohort form, in which case we would have calculated

$$P(s) = p(0)p(1) \cdots p(s) \quad \text{for } s = 1, 2, \ldots, M.$$

(8.24)

We use the special formulation in (8.22) because it is "cleaner" and less cumbersome for this application than the cohort model used earlier.

Next, it is useful to represent the hiring rate by population group in terms of a total hiring rate, $f(t)$, times an *availability fraction*, $a_i(t)$; thus we have

$$f_i(t) = a_i(t) f(t)$$

with

$$\sum_{i=1}^{N} a_i(t) = 1.$$

(8.25)

The values for $a_i(t)$ are presumably taken from current statistics on the various pools of job applicants, statistics modified by future expectations as to shifts in the mix of applicants over the prediction period. These data also may be modified according to whether one plans to follow a "fair" hiring policy (i.e., a policy based on representation) or a compensatory one.

Finally it may be useful to represent total staffing requirements in terms of a growth rate, θ, to be applied to the current level of staff; in this case, we would have

$$\bar{N}(t) = (1 + \theta)^t \bar{N}(0). \tag{8.26}$$

Of course, planned reductions in the working force can be represented simply by assigning a negative value to θ.

SOLUTION PROCEDURE 8.2. Manipulation of equations (8.22)–(8.26) leads to the following recursive procedure for predicting the hiring rate and employment mix of staff for a given set of values for θ, $p(s)$, and $a_i(t)$.

(1) Initialize with the known values of staffing levels at time 0, $N_i(0, s)$, for $i = 1, 2, \ldots, I$, and $s = 1, 2, \ldots, M$.

(2) Starting with time 1, for consecutive values of t calculate for each i

$$f_i(t) = a_i(t)\left[(1 + \theta)^t \bar{N}(0) - \sum_{i=1}^{I} \sum_{s=1}^{M+1} p(s) N_i(t - 1, s - 1)\right]$$

$$N_i(t, 0) = f_i(t)$$

$$N_i(t, s) = p(s) N_i(t - 1, s - 1) \quad \text{for } s = 1, 2, \ldots, M - 1$$

$$N_i(t, M) = p(M) N_i(t - 1, M - 1) + p(M + 1) N_i(t - 1, M)$$

where the last term allows for continuation in LOS category M beyond a single year.

The total hiring rate for this job category in year t will be given by

$$\sum_{i=1}^{I} f_i(t).$$

The fraction of personnel serving at t who are from population group i will be

$$\frac{\sum_{s=0}^{M} N_i(t, s)}{(1 + \theta)^t \bar{N}(0)}.$$

Data for the personnel flow model. The data requirements for this model are relatively modest. Data on the pool of job applicants provided by federal, state, and local agencies would be the primary source for the values of $a_i(t)$. The growth-rate factor, θ, is an institutional parameter reflecting future staffing needs as best as these can be determined. Thus only the persistence fractions should require a major investment in data processing.

Ideally, historical values for $\{p(s)\}$ should be based on the behavior of cohorts of employees who began their service a considerable time ago. That is, we would need to identify all persons hired in the given job category during a given period some ten or fifteen years ago and then track through how many remained after each successive year. The state of personnel records at most institutions is such as to make such an undertaking quite impractical.

An alternative is to adopt a *synthetic cohort* approach, that is, one in which all parameters are obtained from a single year's data on personnel flows. Provided that attrition behavior is not changing over time, we can obtain reliable data on the values of $p(s)$ by the following means. Suppose we observe $N(t, s)$ persons with LOS $= s$ employed at time t, and there were $N(t - 1, s - 1)$ persons with LOS $= s - 1$ one year earlier. Our estimate for the corresponding persistence rate then would be

$$p(s) = \frac{N(t, s)}{N(t - 1, s - 1)}. \tag{8.27}$$

Proceeding likewise for all LOS values between 0 and M will yield a full set of $p(s)$ values. In this way, one can use any consecutive pair of annual employee counts to construct the cohort persistence rates needed for the model.

Comparison of actual data on the persistence of staff at Stanford, as shown in figure 8.12, gives us a chance to observe how good an approximation to the behavior of real cohorts we can get by following the synthetic cohort approach. The graph shows the cumulative survival fractions, $P(s)$, as a function of the number of years in employment for all staff at Stanford. The curves labeled "actual" represent data obtained by tracking the cohorts of staff who were hired in each year between 1971 and 1976. The curve labeled "postulated from 1976 turnover" is the result of applying the synthetic cohort method to personnel flow data from the single most recent year. The fit of the synthetic cohort fractions to the actual ones is quite remarkable. There is yet another reason for comfort: these results support our assumption that the survival fractions for staff cohorts are stable over time.

An illustrative example. Consider a hypothetical job category with a current employment level of 2,000 people. Their distribution by sex and LOS is given as follows:

	$N_i(0, s)$	
s	$i = 1$(Male)	$i = 2$(Female)
0 (new hires)	500	300
1 year	350	100
2 years	200	50
3 or more years	400	100
	1,450 (72%)	550 (28%)

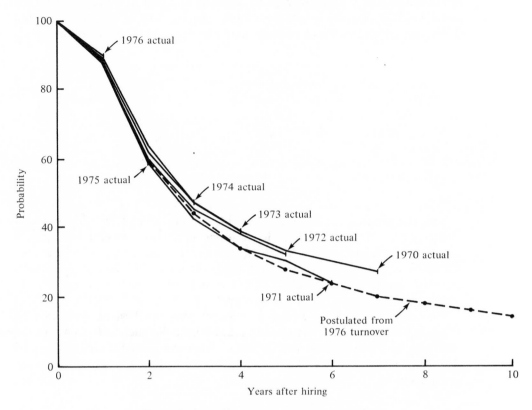

Figure 8.12. Staff cohort persistence at Stanford

A review of staffing needs for personnel in this category reveals that the current staffing level will be maintained for the foreseeable future. Thus, in terms of the model, we should set $\theta = 0$.

Data on persistence rates indicate that the following values should be used for projection purposes:

s	$p(s)$
1	0.7
2	0.6
3	0.8
>3	0.9

Finally, according to the latest statistics on the pool of job applicants for this category of employment, 40 percent of all qualified applicants will be women. This percentage is expected to remain constant over the foreseeable future; thus, if a fair hiring practice is followed, $a_2(t) = 0.4$ and $a_1(t) = 0.6$. The model is to be used to predict hiring rates and staffing levels for the next five years.

The calculations are performed by stepping one year at a time through the equations that describe the staff evolution process. The results of performing a five-year projection based on these data can be summarized as follows:

Year	Staffing Mix (% Female)	New Hires Male	Female
0	28%		
1	30%	312	208
2	32%	299	200
3	33%	266	177
4	33%	249	167
5	34%	238	159

Note the pronounced reduction in hiring rates resulting from the constraint on staff size, and the restricting effect this has on the system's ability to achieve a staffing mix in line with the hiring mix (assumed, let us recall, to be 40 percent female) over a five-year period. Presumably the jobs in this category had until recently experienced substantial growth in numbers, which explains why the initial conditions were out of equilibrium.

The utility of having a model such as this one can best be illustrated by showing what happens when we vary a key parameter such as θ. Consider the following two possibilities: $\theta = +0.05$ (5.0 percent growth); and $\theta = -0.05$ (5.0 percent retrenchment). The solutions for these alternative growth rates are given below:

	Solution for $\theta = +0.05$				Solution for $\theta = -0.05$		
Year	Staffing Mix (% Female)	New Hires Male	Female	Year	Staffing Mix (% Female)	New Hires Male	Female
0	28%			0	28%		
1	31%	372	248	1	30%	252	168
2	33%	380	254	2	31%	224	150
3	34%	373	249	3	31%	172	115
4	35%	379	252	4	32%	144	96
5	35%	389	259	5	32%	123	82

The contrast between the two solutions shows how dramatic an effect relatively modest growth or contraction can have on the overall hiring rate: when the system is contracting, the number of persons hired during the five-year period is expected to be less than one-half the number hired under a 5 percent expansion! Since there are proportionately more females in each group of new hires than there were on the staff to begin with, the contrast also has implications for the final staff distribution. The advantages of having a simple model available to make these sorts of calculations quickly and inexpensively should now be apparent. A sample printout from the planning model used for staff affirmative action at Stanford is shown in appendix 9.

In concluding this illustration, we should point out that sometimes policy-makers will want to run the model backwards. That is, they might be interested to know what male and female hiring rates would be called for if there were to be a fair representation of women on the staff after, say, five years. To answer this, one would treat the hiring fraction, a_2, as a dependent (policy) variable and would then iterate the model with successively higher values of a_2 until the desired final distribution of women in the workforce were obtained. The final value of a_2, then, would give the necessary hiring policy. The model quite often has been run in this mode; in our experience, it generally requires only a few iterations before the answer is obtained.

A Model for Evaluating Progress in Meeting Affirmative Action Goals

To conclude this chapter, we shall present a statistical model designed to measure progress in meeting the goals of affirmative action programs once they have been established. Here the focus will be quite different from that of the large staff-group models discussed so far. Rather than making aggregate projections of expected minority-group representation on the staff in future time periods, we shall be interested in checking the current mix of employees in a small unit (say, the faculty in a single academic department) against goals that were set some time ago. Accordingly, we shall develop a Markov chain model that can be used to obtain means, standard deviations, and even probability distributions of the number of minority group members employed in the unit after a specified period of elapsed time. Although our analysis applies to a unit of any size, it does assume that the size remains constant over the period of interest.

The practical advantages of such a model will be immediately obvious. One of the more difficult tasks faced by persons who monitor the progress of affirmative action programs is to develop criteria in terms of which an academic department or a school can be said to be "not doing a good enough job" of recruiting minority faculty members. The difficulties are particularly apparent at the departmental level, for one can hardly expect a department of 10 faculty members to have, say, exactly 2.5 women professors.

Some range of variation about the mean value, a statistician would emphasize, is inevitable; indeed, the observed number of minority faculty members may well result from chance as often as, say, two out of three times, even when there is no discrimination at all.

Theoretical development. Suppose the department under consideration has n faculty slots. Define a *state* in the Markov chain to be the number of positions out of n that are filled by persons representing the given minority class. A transition occurs whenever someone vacates a position, whether through termination, resignation, death, or retirement, in which case it is immediately filled by a new recruit. (Note the contrast with the Markov chain models defined earlier, in which transitions occurred annually.) Let $a(t)$ represent the *availability fraction*, i.e., the proportion of minority persons in the eligible pool at the time of the tth transition; and define $p_i(t) = \text{Prob }\{i \text{ out of } n \text{ positions are filled with minority persons at time } t\}$. Finally, define $p_{ij}(t) = \text{Prob }\{\text{there are } j \text{ minority faculty after the } t\text{th transition, given there were } i \text{ just before}\}$.

The *transition probability matrix* can now be described as follows (we assume that minority faculty leave in proportion to their relative number):

$$p_{0,1}(t) = a(t), \quad p_{0,0}(t) = 1 - a(t), \quad \text{all other } p_{0,j}(t) = 0$$

$$p_{i,i-1}(t) = \frac{i}{n}(1 - a(t)) \qquad \text{for } i = 1, 2, \ldots, n - 1$$

$$p_{i,i+1}(t) = \left(1 - \frac{i}{n}\right)a(t) \qquad \text{for } i = 1, 2, \ldots, n - 1$$

$$p_{i,i}(t) = \frac{i}{n}a(t) \qquad \text{for } i = 1, 2, \ldots, n - 1$$

$$+ \left(1 - \frac{i}{n}\right)(1 - a(t))$$

$$\text{all other } p_{i,j}(t) = 0$$

$$p_{n,n-1}(t) = 1 - a(t), \quad p_{n,n} = a(t), \quad \text{all other } p_{n,j}(t) = 0.$$

Call the resulting matrix of probabilities $P(t)$. If $\mathbf{p}(0)$ represents the starting probability distribution, one obtains the distribution after t transitions by means of the following equation:

$$\mathbf{p}(t) = \mathbf{p}(0) \prod_{\tau=1}^{t} P(\tau). \tag{8.28}$$

(Here, the symbol Π indicates sequential multiplication, i.e., $\Pi_{\tau=1}^{t} P(\tau) = P(1)P(2) \ldots P(t)$.) In the case where $a(\cdot)$ is constant, the transition probability matrix no longer depends on time, and (8.28) simplifies to

$$\mathbf{p}(t) = \mathbf{p}(0)P^t. \tag{8.29}$$

Steady-state results. Suppose the Markov chain process described above has been going on for a long time. One then can compute the steady-state distribution of minority faculty, $\boldsymbol{\pi}$, by means of:

$$\boldsymbol{\pi} = \boldsymbol{\pi}P$$

$$\sum_{i=0}^{n} \pi_i = 1 \tag{8.30}$$

This limiting, or stationary, distribution will in some sense represent an upper bound on the expected proportion of minority faculty members that is expected at the present time.

Actually, one need not even solve (8.30) to obtain the stationary distribution π; it can be deduced instead as follows. By assumption, inputs of new minority faculty follow a binomial distribution with probability of "success" $= a$. Since, also by assumption, the system is completely "fair" (i.e., people leave exactly in proportion to their relative numbers represented on the faculty), the number in service also must follow a binomial distribution with parameters a and n. Thus, we have

$$\pi_i = \binom{n}{i} a^i (1 - a)^{n-i}. \tag{8.31}$$

The mean and standard deviation of this distribution are given by na and $\sqrt{na(1-a)}$, respectively. Representative values of these statistics for several different department sizes are given in table 8.8. A "likely range," representing the mean plus or minus one standard deviation is also shown there, as is the probability of one's finding no minority faculty in the department even when a fair hiring practice has been followed. This probability is given by the quantity $(1 - a)^n$, and its value depends significantly on the department size, n.

Transient case. If an affirmative action hiring program has been in existence only a relatively short time, what one really needs to evaluate its progress is a set of *transient probability distributions*. If one is interested in monitoring the evolution of the faculty's minority component one, five, or ten years, say, since the adoption of such a program, it is first necessary to determine how many transitions have occurred in the specified interval of time. This can be done either by looking at the exact hiring figures in the past for the department or departments of interest, or, less precisely, by using the estimated average annual attrition rate for all faculty in the school.

For purposes of illustration, suppose that we have estimated this rate to be 7.5 percent per year. Under the assumption of no change in department size, it follows that the expected number of appointments per year to a department of size n would be $.075n$. Thus one would expect transitions to occur once every two to three years for a department of size 5, and once every year or two for one of size 10. When there are 15, 25, and 35 faculty members, we would estimate an average of 1.13, 1.88, and 2.63 appointments per year, respectively.

These mean values were used to calculate the number of transitions that would be likely to occur in departments of various sizes during various intervals of time.* The Markov chain model then was used to predict transient distributions of minority faculty under the assumption that there were no minority faculty at time $t = 0$. The results are summarized in table 8.9.

To read the table, proceed as follows. First, find the line that corresponds

---

*Of course, in practice whenever the model is used one knows the beginning state and exactly how many transitions have taken place since that time, so no such assumptions or estimation procedures are needed.

Table 8.8.   Means and Standard Deviations of Steady-State Number of Minority Faculty

Size of Department (n)	Minority Fraction in Eligible Pool[a] (a)	Mean	Standard Deviation	Likely Range	Probability (# of Minority Faculty = 0)[b]
5	0.01	0.05	0.22	0	0.95
	0.05	0.25	0.49	0–1	0.77
	0.10	0.50	0.67	0–1	0.59
	0.15	0.75	0.80	0–2	0.44
	0.25	1.25	0.97	0–2	0.24
10	0.01	0.10	0.31	0	0.90
	0.05	0.50	0.69	0–1	0.60
	0.10	1.00	0.95	0–2	0.35
	0.15	1.50	1.13	0–3	0.20
	0.25	2.50	1.37	1–4	0.056
15	0.01	0.15	0.39	0	0.86
	0.05	0.75	0.84	0–2	0.46
	0.10	1.50	1.16	0–3	0.21
	0.15	2.25	1.38	1–4	0.087
	0.25	3.75	1.68	2–5	0.013
25	0.01	0.25	0.50	0–1	0.78
	0.05	1.25	1.09	0–2	0.28
	0.10	2.50	1.50	1–4	0.072
	0.15	3.75	1.79	2–6	0.017
	0.25	6.25	2.17	4–8	0.000753
35	0.01	0.35	0.59	0–1	0.70
	0.05	1.75	1.29	0–3	0.17
	0.10	3.50	1.77	2–5	0.025
	0.15	5.25	2.11	3–7	0.0034
	0.25	8.75	2.56	6–11	0.000042

[a] I.e., the fraction of eligible job applicants that are from one or more minority groups (the so-called availability fraction).

[b] I.e., the probability of the event that one will find no members of minorities in the faculty group being studied.

to the desired combination of department size, availability fraction, and elapsed time. Suppose this combination is 15, .15, 10. Following this line across, one then reads off, first, the probability, 0.28, that there would be absolutely no minority faculty members after the specified period of time; second, the mean number, 1.197, of minority faculty expected to be in service; and third, the standard deviation, 1.022, of this number. To the extent that the assumptions behind our calculations are valid, these figures illustrate the great difficulty a moderate-sized department can have in exhibiting tangible results from an affirmative action plan, even after a considerable period of time.

It would be unfortunate if one were to blame the model for these unwelcome results. Our whole premise has been that personnel modeling can offer significant benefits to a university and its faculty, staff, and students. Surely, each of these major factions has an interest in knowing what is likely to happen to

Table 8.9. Means and Standard Deviations of Number of Minority Faculty
After t Years

Size of Department	Minority Fraction in Eligible Pool[a]	Elapsed Time (Years)	Probability (# of Minority Faculty = 0)[b]	Mean	Standard Deviation
5	0.01	1	. . . .	. . . .	. . . .
		5	0.98	0.018	0.134
		10	0.97	0.030	0.171
	0.05	1	. . . .	. . . .	. . . .
		5	0.91	0.090	0.293
		10	0.86	0.148	0.376
	0.15	1	. . . .	. . . .	. . . .
		5	0.75	0.270	0.483
		10	0.62	0.443	0.622
15	0.01	1	0.99	0.010	0.099
		5	0.95	0.051	0.224
		10	0.92	0.080	0.281
	0.05	1	0.95	0.050	0.218
		5	0.77	0.254	0.493
		10	0.66	0.399	0.618
	0.15	1	0.85	0.150	0.357
		5	0.44	0.763	0.813
		10	0.28	1.197	1.022
30	0.01	1	0.98	0.020	0.140
		5	0.91	0.093	0.304
		10	0.85	0.162	0.401
	0.05	1	0.90	0.098	0.306
		5	0.62	0.467	0.668
		10	0.44	0.812	0.882
	0.15	1	0.73	0.295	0.501
		5	0.22	1.401	1.102
		10	0.07	2.437	1.459

[a] I.e., the fraction of eligible job applicants that are from one or more minority groups (the so-called availability fraction).
[b] I.e., the probability of the event that one will find no members of minorities in the faculty group being studied.

student admissions, faculty appointments and promotions, staff hiring, and other measures of personnel flow. The models presented in this chapter can help to analyze such matters, and thereby to increase the capacity of the institution to do personnel planning of a serious kind.

Summary

Human resources planning involves predicting numbers of faculty, students, or staff, differentiated according to such attributes as (in the case of faculty) age and tenure. Flow models of various types can be employed to test the effects on these predictions of variables that are under an institution's control.

Many useful insights on how to affect a faculty's evolution are gleaned from a simple two-state equilibrium model of faculty flows. A more detailed time-dependent model of the Markov chain variety is also developed to handle situations in which the emphasis is more on shorter-run consequences than on those of the longer run. Examples are provided to demonstrate the sorts of policy analyses in which these models can be applied.

The second major section deals with projection models for student enrollments. Initially, we assume that the number of new students that will show up in any future time period is known; instead, we concentrate on how to estimate the enrollment of continuing students. Several techniques are presented, some conceptually simple and some more complex, with varying data requirements.

This section is followed by one on models for predicting the "yield" of students from a group newly admitted to the institution. Different approaches are again discussed, including the use of multivariate regression and contingency table analysis, and comparative results are given with actual data from Stanford.

Finally, we describe personnel models for affirmative action planning. These are intended to meet two separate kinds of needs: (a) the development of realistic goals for the future employment of women and ethnic minorities; and (b) the after-the-fact monitoring of progress towards meeting such goals. A model is formulated for goal-setting purposes that can project the future hiring and employment mix by population group in a staff unit of significant size. These projections are made to depend on such crucial variables as the anticipated growth rate of staff size and the hiring policy to be used vis-à-vis the composition of the job applicant pool. A second model is formulated to assist managers of smaller, fixed-size units in evaluating their degree of compliance with the goals of an affirmative action program. This model produces probability estimates of the observed composition of the staff—that is, estimates relative to what would have been expected given the actual amount of turnover and the empirical statistics on the composition of the applicant pool.

Notes to Chapter 8

Works cited here in abbreviated form are more fully described in the bibliography at the end of this book.

1. The initial formulation of this model and its application to Stanford were reported in Hopkins 1974a.

2. We are indebted to Donald Gallagher, who was a research assistant in Stanford's Academic Planning Office, for compiling these data on faculty flows.

3. These examples are taken directly from Hopkins and Bienenstock 1975.

4. The interested reader will find more details on the GPR method and its statistical properties in Oliver 1968.

5. An analysis of the summer quarter in the context of proposals for operating universities the year round is given in Hopkins 1973.

6. For additional mathematical details on cohort flow models and their application to personnel systems see Grinold and Marshall 1977, chaps. 3 and 4. An interesting analysis of such models' prediction errors may be found in Marshall and Oliver 1978, which also shows how one can obtain statistical confidence intervals for use in forecasts of student enrollment.

7. For an interesting discussion of some uses to which these data have been put at the Berkeley campus the reader may wish to consult Suslow 1977.

8. We are indebted to two Ph.D candidates in statistics, Delores Conway and Joe Verducci, for their extensive work in fitting yield models to Stanford admissions data for the academic years 1972/73 through 1977/78. A full account of this research is available in Conway and Verducci 1979.

9

Constrained Value Optimization

We return in this chapter to the value optimization problem introduced in chapter 3, a problem that lies at the very heart of our budget planning paradigm. While we have stressed financial relationships in the intervening chapters, we do not want to forget the prominent role played by value measures in financial decision making. However, we must caution the reader that this topic brings us to the very frontiers of management science as now practiced. While there are elegant theories to explain human decision making in terms of value optimization, relatively little is known about how to apply them. In particular, it is hard to quantify a person's values in the form of a mathematical value function that can adequately reflect his or her real attitudes and judgments. We have tried direct means of estimating such functions for administrators at Stanford, but we have had better success with indirect means that do not require direct estimation. We shall present research findings on approaches of both types.

The Value Optimization Problem in General Form

The basic problem to be addressed in this chapter can be formulated as follows. Let $\mathbf{x}$ be a vector of primary planning variables (PPVs), i.e., $\mathbf{x} = (x_1, x_2, \ldots, x_n)$. This set may include outputs, inputs, prices, stocks, and rates of change in any of these. Let $V(\mathbf{x})$ be an administrator's preference (i.e., value) function defined on these variables. For each set of possible values of $\mathbf{x}$—we shall refer to this as a *university configuration*—the function $V(\mathbf{x})$ will assign a numerical value representing the degree of relative desirability of that configuration. One would like it to have the property that, for all possible pairs of alternatives, $\mathbf{x}^1$ and $\mathbf{x}^2$, $V(\mathbf{x}^2) > V(\mathbf{x}^1)$ if, and only if, $\mathbf{x}^2$ is preferred to $\mathbf{x}^1$. (In this context, 2 and 1 are superscripts and not exponents. We shall follow this notation consistently in this chapter.)

A solution $\mathbf{x}$ will be said to be "feasible" if it satisfies all of the following conditions: (a) the budget is balanced in some base year; (b) the growth rates of income and expense also are equal; (c) each x_j lies within its prespecified upper and lower permissible limits; (d) certain demand-and-supply conditions are met. Conditions (a) and (b) ensure that $\mathbf{x}$ is a first-order dynamic equilibrium solution. Define the difference between budgeted income and expense to be the function $b(\mathbf{x})$, and the difference between the growth rates of income and expense to be $g(\mathbf{x})$. Lower and upper bounds on each x_j are given by ℓ_j and u_j, respectively. The value optimization problem then has the following compact representation.

Find $\mathbf{x}$ to maximize $V(\mathbf{x})$

subject to the constraints

1. $b(\mathbf{x}) \geq 0$

2. $g(\mathbf{x}) \geq 0$

3. $\ell \leq \mathbf{x} \leq \mathbf{u}$

4. demand/supply constraints.

The demand-and-supply constraints, listed fourth, often will be subsumed under the preference function, as we pointed out in chapter 3. We will assume this to be so for the moment and drop all further specific references to these constraints until a later section of this chapter.

ILLUSTRATION 9.1. To see how the constraint functions $b(\mathbf{x})$ and $g(\mathbf{x})$ can be constructed, suppose the PPV set consists of only four variables.

Let x_1 = faculty size

x_2 = undergraduate enrollment

x_3 = graduate student enrollment

x_4 = tuition rate.

We can express the budget expense as the sum of six separate terms that depend on one or more of the x_j's: a fixed term (c_0); plus faculty salaries and other expenses directly related to faculty ($c_1 x_1$); plus financial aid for undergraduates ($c_{24} x_2 x_4$); plus other expenses related to undergraduates ($c_2 x_2$); plus financial aid and other expenses related to graduate students ($c_{34} x_3 x_4 + c_4 x_4$). On the income side, we would have fixed income (i_0); plus income varying with faculty ($i_1 x_1$); plus tuition from undergraduates ($i_{24} x_2 x_4$); plus tuition from graduate students ($i_{34} x_3 x_4$). The budget balance constraint then would take the form

$$(i_1 - c_1)x_1 - c_2 x_2 - c_3 x_3 + (i_{24} - c_{24})x_2 x_4$$
$$+ (i_{34} - c_{34})x_3 x_4 + i_0 - c_0 \geq 0$$

with the entire expression to the left of $\geq$ representing the function $b(\mathbf{x})$.

The growth-rate function is constructed as follows:

Let r_j = the growth rate of expenditure coefficient j and

q_k = the growth rate of income coefficient k.

In a one-year period, each component of expense will grow from $c_j x_j$ to $(1 + r_j)c_j x_j$, which is an increase of $r_j c_j x_j$, while each income component will increase by $q_k i_k x_k$. The growth-rate constraint is formed by taking the difference between the one-year increases in income and expense and requiring these quantities to sum at least to zero:

$$(q_1 i_1 - r_1 c_1)x_1 - r_2 c_2 x_2 - r_3 c_3 x_3 + (q_{24} i_{24} - r_{24} c_{24})x_2 x_4$$

$$+ (q_{34} i_{34} - r_{34} c_{34})x_3 x_4 + q_0 i_0 - r_0 c_0 \geq 0.$$

The function $g(\mathbf{x})$ is represented by the expression appearing to the left of $\geq$.

Some Practical Considerations

Mathematically, our problem of devising a formula for value optimization at a university is a classic one in nonlinear programming. To operationalize a scheme for solving it, we must be able to do three things. First, we need to specify the relevant set of PPVs. While this task may seem straightforward enough, a clear conception of which variables are both controllable and relevant often evolves only after substantial experience with financial models of the types discussed in chapters 4 and 6. Such was definitely the case at Stanford.

It also should be noted that the relevant set of PPVs may and indeed probably will vary from time to time. Its composition depends partly on which items have the particular attention of the budget officers at any given time, and partly on what changes occur in the degree to which certain variables can be controlled. For example, the tuition rate may be controllable, in an upward-moving sense when its current value is well behind the market; that is, as long as it lags the market, one may raise it a little or a lot. Once it has caught up, however, it is probably going to be market-limited. This is not to suggest that the tuition rate necessarily should be dropped from consideration as a PPV; it may still belong to the primary set simply because of its dominant role in determining the income available to support the institution's operating budget. Even though the limits of variability may not be great, one might want to give PPV status to such a variable just to keep it visible.

The second requirement for attacking the problem is that the form and parameters of the constraints be known. Having first identified the PPVs we then must be explicit about how they affect the university's costs and revenue. The procedures laid out in chapter 4 can help us in this respect. Far more difficult, however, is the task of constructing the proper demand functions for university services. It is for this reason that most formulations of the value optimization problem we have worked with have not incorporated the demand-and-supply constraints in explicit form, but instead have subsumed them under the value function.

The third requirement is for a solid conceptualization of the administrator's value function, $V(\mathbf{x})$. This can be handled in one of two ways. The first option is to try to solve the problem in *closed form*, which would involve separately eliciting preference information and performing a numerical estimation of $V(\mathbf{x})$. This function then would be plugged into a computer programmed to do the optimization at a later stage. Usually, since one does not know beforehand where the decision maker's optimal solution will turn out to be, preference information must be obtained with reference to a large number of solution points—so large, in fact, that they virtually span the space of feasible university configurations. The instrument most commonly used for this purpose is a pencil-and-paper questionnaire; however, the gathering of preference data can (and probably should) take place at an interactive computer terminal instead. This option obviously requires the full attention and cooperation of the decision maker (DM) while the value function is being estimated, but it does not require any further participation on his or her part while the optimization is actually taking place.

Optional Approaches

The alternative to closed-form value optimization is to develop algorithms for solving the decision problem interactively. By this we mean that the solution process takes place during a session at a computer terminal in which the DM is directly involved throughout. A closed-form expression for the mathematical value function is never needed; instead, the computer is programmed to engage the DM in an iterative process that begins with the current operating point and leads him or her through a succession of improved solutions. One advantage of such a scheme is that it needs to elicit only local preference information at each step along the way. That is, the DM needs to respond only to questions concerning the direction and magnitude of preferred changes with reference to the most recent solution vector. The response occurs in "real time," so that the DM receives feedback instantaneously.

Ideally, we would still like to have a free-standing value function for the DM that we could use in combination with any formulation of the constraints to solve the problem in closed form. It is a most stringent condition, however, to require the availability of a well-defined and fully parameterized mathematical function that can properly represent, in the absence of the DM, the choices that he or she would make. Currently available techniques for eliciting and processing preference information to yield estimates of value function parameters are limited and fraught with practical difficulties. Indeed, our efforts to apply this approach at Stanford have not yet succeeded. Nevertheless, the reported success of certain of these techniques when applied in other organizational settings gives us reason to believe that they still might work in a university context.

A further difficulty with trying to solve the problem in closed form is that nonlinear optimization algorithms are notoriously costly and inefficient to run on the computer. Practically speaking, one cannot expect to solve nonlinear problems that involve more than a small number of variables and constraints. Thus it is necessary to give up some realism in the formulation stage by reducing the size of the problem.

In view of the practical difficulties just cited, the analyst must decide initially which one of two basic tacks to take. The first option is to devote one's attention to a careful and detailed representation of the institutional constraints and to include a diverse set of possible PPVs. Flexible computer routines, such as TRADES, can be developed to assist an administrator in searching through the feasible space. More structured procedures can be added to make use of elicited preference information in guiding the search. Such programs provide great flexibility to interested administrators who want to examine a number of feasible options and arrive at the solution they most prefer. If they are too busy or otherwise unwilling to interact with the computer, however, this technique obviously cannot be made to work. Also, of course there is no way for them to be confident that they have arrived at (or even close to) the solution that really would be optimal.

The other option is to tackle the optimization problem head-on, with most of the effort going into the estimation of the value function and the optimization algorithm rather than the formulation of constraints. As we noted above, much flexibility will be lost by taking this approach. If one wants to do sensitivity analyses that examine how optimal solutions differ when financial parameters are changed, however, there is no choice but to deal with the problem in closed form.

We have experimented with both types of approaches at Stanford. The remainder of this chapter will describe what was done and some of our results.

Exploring the Feasible Region with TRADES

TRADES is Stanford's primary tool for doing financial forecasting and tradeoff analysis. The model was designed to make it easy for an administrator to "fish around" for a favored solution in the space of all feasible university configurations. The computer program allows for detailed representation of the university's financial structure in terms of a large number of variables and parameters, and for an arbitrary number of (possibly nonlinear) constraints. No explicit recognition is made of the value function, but the user is given complete control over the process of searching for progressively "better" solutions. In essence, the computer is there to perform what might be called the bookkeeping functions of making financial calculations and checking for feasibility. Users are thereby freed to pursue their own value preferences.

Functionally, the model consists of a set of financial subroutines embedded in a program offering various interactive search options. These subroutines are specific to the institution, but the search options are quite universal in their application. For this reason, we tend to think of TRADES as a generic class of models rather than as a single model specific only to Stanford.

The financial subroutines in Stanford's TRADES model have come to in-

```
LIST PPV'S=1, SKIP=0
=>1

      1 FAC       790.0000      2 AFAC       80.0000
      3 UG       6500.0000      4 GR      4600.0000
      5 TENR        0.6500      6 STFR       0.5000
      7 P           0.0480      8 TR         0.0500
      9 F           0.0030     10 DT         0.0250
     11 DFS         0.0150     12 DSS        0.0200
     13 SBSL        0.2000     14 DCVL       0.0800
THIS CONFIGURATION IS INFEASIBLE
FINANCIAL SUMMARY=1, SKIP=0
=>1

BUDGET SUMMARY
YEAR                  78/79          79/80
EXPENSES           92890.00      100897.62
INCOME             93127.94      100949.31
DEFICIT(-)           237.94          51.69
ENDOW PO RATE         0.0480         0.0480
TUITION/BUDGET        0.5652         0.5646
PO/BUDGET             0.1193         0.1205
GROWTH TO                            79/80
EXPENSES                            8007.62
INCOME                              7821.37
DEFICIT(-)                          -186.25
ENDOW PO RATE                          0.0
TUITION/BUDGET                      -0.0006
PO/BUDGET                            0.0012
CONSTRAINT SUMMARY=1, SKIP=0
=>1
```

NAME OF CONSTRAINT	MIN	VALUE	MAX	OUTMIN(-)	OUTMAX(-)
NO DEFICIT--YEAR 0					
	0.0	237.9375**********		237.9375**********	
NO DEFICIT GROWTH FOR ONE YEAR					
	0.0	-186.2500**********		-186.2500**********	

Figure 9.1. Example of a TRADES working configuration

corporate a rich and detailed representation of the university's particular budget configuration, tailored to its policies and planning formats. However, a generalized version of the model has been designed and programmed by EDUCOM, Inc., to help other institutions in adopting and developing the same approach. We shall have more to say about the EDUCOM Financial Planning Model in the final chapter.*

We shall now review the building blocks of TRADES, with specific reference to the version currently being run at Stanford. The model is best described in terms of the following four basic constructs: primary planning variables (PPVs), background variables and parameters, financial routines (including submodels), and constraints.

Throughout this discussion we shall refer to the model's basic display, an example of which is shown in figure 9.1. This is labeled a *working configuration* because it represents the status of the model at some point during a user session. Users can obtain such a display at any time if they become disoriented or wish to document the output. The current values of the primary planning variables are

---

*EDUCOM is a nonprofit consortium of more than 250 colleges and universities founded in 1964 to promote computer resource sharing and the application of computer technology in higher education. It is located in Princeton, New Jersey.

given at the top of the table, followed by a financial summary of income, expenses, and key ratios for the base year and the following year. At the bottom of the table is a summary of currently active constraints.

Variables and Parameters

The version of TRADES that is implemented at Stanford involves several hundred variables and parameters. From this set can be selected a small number of quantities, usually ranging from five to fifteen, to be designated primary planning variables; all the rest remain background items. This selection can be changed at will from the user's terminal. The PPVs are treated like any other

Table 9.1.   Primary Planning Variables Used in Stanford TRADES

Variable Number	Label	Name and Definition	Variable Type[a]
(1)	FAC	"Regular faculty FTE." This category includes all professorial (i.e., tenure-line) faculty in schools other than business or medicine.	L
(2)	AFAC	"Auxiliary faculty FTE." Included here are all other teaching personnel, such as lecturers, instructors, and visiting faculty, but not teaching assistants.	L
(3)	UG	"Undergraduate student enrollment." Head-count of undergraduate students registered for autumn quarter.	L
(4)	GR	"Graduate student enrollment." Head-count of graduate students registered for autumn quarter in all schools other than business and medicine.	L
(5)	TENR	"Tenure ratio." The ratio of FTE tenured faculty to total FTE regular faculty.	R
(6)	STFR	"Staff/faculty ratio." The ratio of FTE academic support staff (i.e. administrators and staff personnel located in the schools) to FTE regular faculty. The FTEs are based on the operating budget portion of salaries only, i.e., they do not include the amounts charged to grants and contracts.	R
(7)	P	"Endowment payout rate." The dollar amount of investment return used for current expenditures, as a fraction of the market value of endowment at the beginning of the year.	R
(8)	TR	"Endowment total return." Expressed in *real* terms, i.e., net of inflation.	G
(9)	F	"Budget enrichment factor." The amount of money made available for new programs and program enhancements of all types, expressed as a fraction of the previous year's budget.	R
(10)	DT	"Tuition growth rate." Annual rate of growth of tuition price, in *real* fractional increase terms.	G
(11)	DFS	"Annual *real* rate of growth of faculty salaries."	G
(12)	DSS	"Annual *real* rate of growth of staff salaries."	G
(13)	SBSL	"Fringe benefits rate for faculty and staff." Fringe benefits costs per dollar of personnel salary costs.	R
(14)	DCVL	"Annual *real* rate of growth of library acquisitions." Technically, this is only the cost rise, net of inflation, on a per volume basis. However, it is used in the sample runs to represent the combined effect of cost rise and growth in volumes acquired.	G

[a] Variable types as follows: L = level-type variable; R = ratio-type variable; G = growth-rate-type variable.

independent variables in the program, except for their mode of display and their special role in tradeoff analyses. For the most part they should be true decision variables, such as the number of faculty and the size of the under-graduate student body, although some variables may be admitted that are not, strictly speaking, within the decision arena.

We have found it useful to consider the PPVs—and, for that matter, all the variables and parameters of TRADES—as classifiable into three general cate-gories: (a) *levels* or *stocks*, such as numbers of faculty or numbers of students; (b) *ratios* or *coefficients*, such as the fraction of faculty who are tenured or the annual budget enrichment fraction; (c) *growth rates*, such as the rate of increase in the tuition price or in faculty and staff salaries. The full definitions of the Stanford PPVs shown in figure 9.1 are given in table 9.1, along with their classification into these categories.

Another advantage of having the model spotlight a small set of PPVs in contrast to a much larger set of background quantities is to relieve the user of unnecessary cognitive strain. It has been observed many times that when models such as this have been put into practice, users tend to concentrate their thoughts on just a few of the quantities available for analysis. TRADES allows the user full choice of the variables to be placed in or out of the spotlight, and facilitates changing the set whenever that is appropriate.

A final point to stress about the PPVs is that they must be treated by the program as independent variables. That is, once a variable has been brought into the PPV set, its value is determined only by the user and not by some internal equation. To appreciate the significance of this point, consider the changes brought about by an increase in student enrollments when student numbers and faculty size both belong to the PPV set. The financial submodels of TRADES will automatically take account of changes in the budget due to such directly associated factors as increased financial aid, student support services, and tuition. They will not, however, make any change in the faculty size: as long as faculty remains in the decision set along with students, it will stay under user control.

Financial Routines

The function of the financial routines is to represent the income-and-expense components of the operating budget, with any other quantities used in the financial constraints, in terms of the PPVs. For level-type PPVs, the model contains the appropriate fixed and variable cost-and-revenue coefficients to perform these calculations as we described in chapter 4. Coefficients and growth rates in the PPV set are employed in computing present and future budgets. Thus the financial calculations of TRADES essentially are driven by the PPVs.

The figures displayed in the "budget summary" of figure 9.1 give the aggregate results of these calculations. The first column shows total expenses, total income, calculated surplus or deficit, the endowment payout rate, the ratio of tuition income to the total operating budget ("BUDGET"), and the ratio of budgeted endowment income ("PO") to the same quantity—all with reference to a particular base year (in this case, 1978/79). Since the model also contains the machinery for projecting the budget any number of years ahead, there is also a section to take care of updating the variables and parameters. Thus the second column in the budget summary display gives the same aggregate results as the first column, but for one year further into the future. Figures indicating the one-year change in each item are shown directly underneath. By scanning these figures the user can quickly gauge the first-order effects of the current (i.e., working) growth-rate configuration.

Current and future budget estimates are built from financial submodels of varying complexity. The simplest form of projection, in which a particular line item is grown at specified rates, is used, for example, when we project equipment expense. Such a projection is easily modified by adding or subtracting a specified dollar amount in any particular future year. This feature has helped us to build in current estimates of the operating expense anticipated for new buildings known to be coming on stream during the next several years. At a further level of complexity, some items are projected by means of a growth rate derived from other quantities in the budget. For example, the central administration at Stanford has targeted certain gift flows (namely, those under the control of deans of schools) to increase at the same rate as faculty compensation. In order to project this gift income, TRADES must first derive the rate at which faculty salaries and benefits will increase.

Most budget items, such as faculty salaries, library acquisitions, and tuition income are expressed inside the model as products of an underlying physical variable and its unit cost or price (e.g., tuition income = FTE enrollment × unit tuition price). Each item may have its own growth rate associated with it. More complex submodels involve specific relationships that we know to exist among certain budget variables in any given year. For example, according to the model developed in the second section of chapter 4, TRADES computes indirect cost recovery as a function of indirect cost-pool levels, research allocation parameters, and the research fraction of total direct cost. (It does not, however, make any adjustment for the price elasticity of research demand.) Other special submodels are used to compute staff benefits and undergraduate financial aid costs, and the income from tuition. These also were formulated in chapter 4.

In making forward projections, the model will calculate the level of endowment by combining the forecasted effects of gifts, total return from investments, and payout. Two options exist in TRADES for projecting endowment payout. In the first, one can stipulate a fixed payout rate (percentage of beginning market value). Budget surpluses and deficits are then calculated by the model, and added to or subtracted from endowment market value at the end of the year. Or one can let the model determine what payout is needed to balance the budget in each future year.

One of the model's chief advantages in operating with a fair degree of detail is its ability to keep track of multiple interactions among budget variables. Consider what happens when one goes to increase the faculty size. The direct effect, obviously, is to increase expenses due to salary costs. Also, more faculty require more staff support (e.g., secretaries), travel, supplies, etc., which add further to the budget expense. Some of the expense associated with the administrative work done by these new faculty is recoverable from the federal government as indirect cost on grants and contracts. This will increase income. Under the variable payout rate option, the excess of new expense over the new income will siphon more funds from the endowment, thus leading to an increase in the payout rate needed to balance the budget. However, since the payout rate on endowment restricted for student aid is pegged at the same university-wide rate, more of the student aid expense will be covered by restricted endowment, thus decreasing operating budget expenses somewhat. A larger payout rate also will reduce the growth of the endowment, thus lowering payout in future years. Finally, if faculty salaries are growing more slowly than the budget average, adding new faculty will push down the growth rate of expenses in future years. (The same could be said for a change in the amount of any item whose growth rate differs materially from the average growth rate of the budget as a whole.) Once these calculations are well enough understood, the benefits from automating such a string of them should be quite evident.

Switches are used in TRADES whenever a user desires to change a variable from PPV status to internal calculation mode. ("Switch" here simply means a variable that takes on the value zero, for "off," or one, for "on.") The switch that puts the user in control of the endowment payout rate is a good example. With this switch on, the payout rate is regarded as a decision variable; when the switch is off, however, it becomes a dependent variable used by a financial submodel to produce a balanced budget. Of course, the need for such switches must be anticipated at an early stage of implementation so that they can be incorporated in the model design.

Constraints

The constraint summary at the bottom of figure 9.1 reports the status of the working configuration with respect to various constraints that have been specified by the user. The report consists of the lower and upper bounds ("MIN" and "MAX"), the current value ("VALUE"), and the amount of slack ("OUT-MIN" and "OUT-MAX"). Negative slack in either direction indicates infeasibility. In the TRADES projection mode there is nothing to stop the user from specifying infeasible scenarios. However, he or she can be informed of the amount of slack each time the working configuration for any year is displayed. The constraints are binding in the tradeoff mode, as will be described later.

In this example there are two constraints:

1. *There must not be a budget deficit in the base year ("NO DEFICIT—YEAR 0").* This corresponds to the "zero-order" condition for financial equilibrium. The sample display in figure 9.1 shows a budget surplus of nearly $238,000, which translates into a positive slack. An inequality constraint with no finite upper bound is used in order to provide some degree of freedom in seeking tradeoffs; with most university value functions, however, the optimum will be at the point of budget balance rather than budget surplus.

2. *The deficit cannot grow during the year following the base year ("NO DEFICIT GROWTH FOR ONE YEAR").* This injects a dynamic element into the analysis, as it essentially requires balance in terms of budget growth rates. If long-run growth rates are used, this constraint when combined with the first one corresponds to first-order long-run financial equilibrium as defined and discussed in chapter 6. Generally speaking, these two constraints imply that subsequent years will be close to balance if long-run growth rates are used throughout. Budget balance in years subsequent to the base year plus one can also be added to the set of constraints. If long-run growth rates are used for the last such constraint and short-run factors are used in the intervening years, we have an analogue to the transition-to-equilibrium model discussed in chapter 6. Notice that in this sample run the constraint on deficit growth is being violated, since expenses are growing faster than income.

Provided an institution has an endowment of significant size, the endowment payout rate can play a key role in tradeoffs linking the base-level and growth-rate variables. Regardless of whether a fixed or a variable payout rate is used, the result is to determine the rate of growth of the endowment's market value. This, in turn, will affect the amount of income available in the base year plus one, and thus condition the permissible values of the growth-rate variables via the base-year-plus-one constraint. The user who wants to can first employ the option that calculates the dollar amount of payout needed to balance the budget, and then specify lower and upper bounds on the resulting payout rate.

Notice that the aforementioned constraints are purely financial in nature. However, operational constraints can also be included if desired; for instance,

Table 9.2. Optional Constraints in TRADES

(1) Base year payout rate limited to between 0.04 and 0.05.
(2) No payout rate growth allowed to year 1.
(3) No deficit growth allowed to year 1.
(4) Fourth-order tuition/budget equilibrium (no growth in the ratio of tuition income to budget from year 0 to year 4).
(5) Fourth-order payout/budget equilibrium (no growth in the ratio of endowment payout income to budget from year 0 to year 4).
(6) No deficit in year 0.
(7) No deficit in year 1.
(8) No deficit in year 2.
(9) No deficit in year 3.
(10) No deficit in year 5.
(11) Limit operating reserve in year 1.
(12) Limit operating reserve in year 2.
(13) Limit operating reserve in year 3.
(14) No deficit growth to year 2.
(15) No deficit growth to year 3.
(16) No deficit growth to year 5.
(17) No increase in deficit from year 1 to year 2.

one might specify lower and upper limits on the ratio of students to faculty, as was proposed in our theory of university optimization (see chapter 3, especially the discussion following equation [3.21]).

The TRADES program allows for flexible constraint design. We are able to specify up to fifth-order dynamic budget equilibrium (defined in chapter 6) when we wish. Other constraints permit interesting variations of the balanced growth condition discussed in chapter 6. For example, we can restrict the fraction of the budget that is supported by tuition to its present level. Another variation freezes the fraction of the budget supported by endowment. Stanford's current version of the model has a set of seventeen predefined constraints, any number of which can be called up from the terminal to be employed in making tradeoffs. These are listed in table 9.2.

Operation in Forecast Mode

TRADES may be operated in either of two different modes: *forecast* or *tradeoff*. The objective in the forecast mode is to project budget quantities forward over time, according to growth rates specified by the user. The results can be useful in their own right, or they may be used as the basis for tradeoff analyses. Operated in forecast mode, the model is capable of displaying some fifty income, expense, and asset categories for up to twenty-five years in the future, in the same format as the Medium-Range Financial Forecast (see chapter 4). Less detailed printouts also may be selected at the user's option.

The forecasting procedure makes use of a Forecast Data File that contains year-by-year growth rates for the base-level and coefficient-type variables. Each level or coefficient variable in the master list has up to five growth variables associated with it, one for each year of the planning period, except that the fifth value of a growth-rate variable is taken to be its *long-run* estimate. These growth variables may be in the form of rates or dollar (i.e., so-called add-on) changes and they may differ year by year. When the forecast option is called, the program projects the income-and-expense data ahead for the number of years specified by the user. It uses the short-run growth-rates from the Forecast Data File for the first five years following the initial year, and the long-run values for every subsequent year.

An example of the output from the forecast routine is shown in figure 9.2. (We have selected a more aggregate form of display than Stanford's MRFF for this illustration.) Note that the row headings are in terms of object-of-expense (i.e., line-item) categories. This is because the growth through time of income and expense items is best understood in line-item terms. If a functional breakdown were desired the model could be programmed to allocate the object-category expenditures to function classes. Breakdowns by organizational unit (e.g., by school) could be obtained similarly, since the whole of TRADES could be applied separately school by school or a hybrid program—i.e., one that incorporated separate budgets for all the schools—could be developed.*

---

*Stanford's TRADES does not deal with functional expense categories or disaggregate along organizational lines. In chapter 10 we shall propose a scheme for building a hierarchical version of the model to accommodate organizational subunits.

```
HOW MANY YEARS FORWARD SHOULD WE PROJECT?
=>3
DISPLAY OPTION? (25 GIVES LIST)
=>1
SHORT FORM=1, LONG FORM=2, LRF=3
=>2
```

YEAR ENDING	1979.	1980.	1981.	1982.
FACULTY SALARIES	18895.	20426.	22225.	24178.
OTHER SALARIES	31560.	34172.	37077.	40229.
STAFF BENEFITS	10091.	10919.	11860.	12881.
STAFF BEN. RATE	20.	20.	20.	20.
OTHER EXPENSES	20775.	22411.	24103.	25952.
LIBRARY ACQ.	3125.	3573.	4057.	4647.
UTILITIES	6140.	6915.	7563.	8306.
STUDENT AID	6608.	7146.	7665.	8199.
TOTAL EXPENSES	92890.	100897.	109496.	118911.
NEXT YEAR'S FUNDED I	278.	504.	547.	594.
TUITION/FEES	53211.	57734.	62411.	67466.
UNR. END. PO	6688.	7304.	8016.	8732.
RES. END. PO	4390.	4854.	5351.	5883.
GIFTS	2436.	2652.	2889.	3149.
SPECIAL FUNDS	2204.	2370.	2559.	2764.
OTHER INCOME	5329.	5677.	6049.	6451.
IND. COST RECOV.	20120.	21743.	23513.	25467.
TRF TO PLANT	-1684.	-1819.	-1965.	-2122.
ABF SCHOOLS	431.	431.	431.	431.
TOTAL INCOME	93127.	100949.	109256.	118222.
TRANSFER TO OP. RES.	237.	51.	-240.	-688.
OPERATING RESERVE	2759.	2997.	3049.	2808.
PAYOUT RATE	4.80	4.80	4.80	4.80
TUITION PRICE	5130.	5566.	6016.	6504.
ENROLLMENT	11700.	11700.	11700.	11700.
ENDOWMENT MKT. VAL.	231602.	253976.	278133.	303929.

Figure 9.2. TRADES forecast mode display for a three-year planning horizon

In addition to object categories for expense and income, certain key ratios and rates are presented. These include the amount of budget enrichment—i.e., the f of chapters 4 and 6—to be funded (this is labeled "next year's funded I"), the tuition rate, the endowment payout rate, and the market value of endowment. The value of f and the growth rate of tuition are specified by the user as PPVs, while the rate of inflation, which translates everything from constant to current dollars, appears in the Forecast Data File. (A 6 percent annual value for inflation was used in the runs exhibited here.)

The Move-Ahead Option

At times, a user preparing to perform tradeoff analyses may want to project the entire budget several years ahead. The *move-ahead option* of TRADES was designed for this purpose. At the completion of such a move, all base-level, coefficient, and growth-rate variables have been updated to the new base year and can be viewed via the basic display options. In addition to the standard

```
HOW MANY YEARS FORWARD SHOULD THE BASE BE MOVED?
=>3

YEAR 78/79 PAYOUT RATE 0.0480 DEFICIT (-)      237.94
YEAR 79/80 PAYOUT RATE 0.0480 DEFICIT (-)       51.69
YEAR 80/81 PAYOUT RATE 0.0480 DEFICIT (-)     -240.44
OPTION?  (TYPE 11 TO VIEW THE LIST.)
=>1

LIST PPV'S=1, SKIP=0
=>0

THIS CONFIGURATION IS INFEASIBLE
FINANCIAL SUMMARY=1, SKIP=0
=>1

BUDGET SUMMARY
YEAR                    81/82           82/83
EXPENSES              118911.50       128988.37
INCOME               118222.87       127784.37
DEFICIT(-)             -688.62        -1204.00
ENDOW PO RATE           0.0480          0.0480
TUITION/BUDGET          0.5598          0.5579
PO/BUDGET               0.1229          0.1232
GROWTH TO                               82/83
EXPENSES                             10076.87
INCOME                                9561.50
DEFICIT(-)                            -515.37
ENDOW PO RATE                            0.0
TUITION/BUDGET                       -0.0019
PO/BUDGET                             0.0003
CONSTRAINT SUMMARY=1, SKIP=0
=>1


NAME OF CONSTRAINT       MIN        VALUE        MAX      OUTMIN(-)     OUTMAX(-)
NO DEFICIT--YEAR 0
                         0.0     -688.6250**********  -688.6250**********
NO DEFICIT GROWTH FOR ONE YEAR
                         0.0     -515.3750**********  -515.3750**********
```

Figure 9.3. Illustration of a TRADES move-ahead option

display, it is possible through a special option to get a complete listing at the terminal of the master data file. The latter contains the underlying values of all variables and parameters for the current base year.

The move-ahead option is particularly useful if, as is usually the case, one does not want to let one's tradeoff analyses be greatly influenced by budget anomalies that are not expected to last long (e.g., major fund-raising campaigns). The point is that an analysis of levels of the budget variables and their growth rates can provide a good measure of the institution's financial health only if long-run trends are used, and that the move-ahead option, illustrated in figure 9.3, supplies such an analysis. At the same time, accurate short-run projections are indispensable.

Operation in Tradeoff Mode

So far we have shown how TRADES can be used to: (a) calculate total costs and revenues for a given configuration of primary planning variables; (b) project the costs and revenues ahead in time; (c) inform the user about the status of the given configuration, or a projection of it, with respect to certain financial and operating constraints. There remains the problem of maximizing the institution's implicit value function subject to such constraints.

The question for the planner is: What feasible configuration of primary planning variables will maximize that value function? Suppose, however, that a feasible working configuration has been found. The question then becomes: Is any feasible change in the working configuration to be preferred to the current one? Alternatively, one might ask: If we start at an infeasible point what is the best feasible one that can be identified?

The tradeoff features of TRADES provide a powerful tool for exploring the space of feasible PPV configurations. True, the model does not attempt to determine the value function either locally or globally. The advantage of this approach lies in its simplicity and in the flexibility it gives the user in specifying new configurations, determining whether they are feasible, and ascertaining what changes will destroy feasibility or restore it if it has been lost.

A word of caution should be injected at this point, however, lest the reader be given the impression that just because the model can search the entire feasible space it is valid for any move, however large, from the current operating point. In fact, every model has some finite range of validity associated with it, and TRADES is no exception. Among the limiting factors in this instance are the variable cost and revenue coefficients, estimates of which have been based on rather modest moves away from the current operating point. While it is not possible to pin down this range very precisely, it should be evident that the financial calculations in TRADES no longer could be trusted if, for example, the value of *UG* were changed from 6,475 to 2,000.

A number of *search options* exist in TRADES for determining the feasibility of departing from the working configuration:

1. *Direct changes.* The user may specify a *direct change* in one or more variables. Here the user simply substitutes his or her new value of a PPV for the one used previously. The computer responds with a message as to whether the proposed working configuration is feasible. Then the user decides whether to confirm the proposal—in which case it enters the new working configuration —or to cancel it.

2. *Single-variable feasibility searches.* Here the computer takes a more active role: each variable is moved in turn, while the others are held constant, until a *feasibility boundary* is reached. The procedure differs slightly depending on whether the starting configuration is feasible or infeasible. If it is feasible, each variable is moved first upward and then downward until a constraint is reached. This is illustrated in figure 9.4, where FAC is at 790 in the working configuration. The figure shows that it can be moved up to 797 or down to zero without violating any constraints—provided all other variables are held at their current values. The upward move uses up the approximately $238 thousand of slack in the current year's budget constraint.

If the starting configuration is infeasible, the variables are moved one at a

```
NAME        LIMIT OF DECREASE    CURRENT   LIMIT OF INCREASE

 1 FAC  *************          790.0000        797.1099
 2 AFAC*************           80.0000          92.1600
 3 UG         6422.0000      6500.0000*************
 4 GR         4526.3984      4600.0000*************
 5 TENR*************            0.6500           0.6805
 6 STFR*************            0.5000           0.5190
 7 P             0.0471          0.0480*************
 8 TR            0.0474          0.0500*************
 9 F      *************          0.0000           0.0005
10 DT            0.0241          0.0250*************
11 DFS  *************            0.0150           0.0167
12 DSS  *************            0.0200           0.0213
13 SBSL*************             0.2000           0.2062
14 DCVL*************             0.0800           0.0949
```
+++ INDICATES A VARIABLE THAT HAS REACHED ITS UPPER OR LOWER BOUND.
*** INDICATES THAT NO LIMIT EXISTS.

Figure 9.4. TRADES single-variable feasibility moves starting from a feasible configuration

time to a point where feasibility is just restored. This is illustrated in figure 9.5. This time, *FAC* is at 820 in the working configuration, a value that, as we have seen, violates a financial constraint. Feasibility could be restored by moving *FAC* back to 797 (as in figure 9.4); by leaving *FAC* at 820 and dropping *AFAC* to 40; and so on. The point to note is that the program could not find any change in the tuition growth rate that would restore feasibility. The same is true for the other growth-rate variables, as is indicated in figure 9.5 by the asterisks on either side of the current values. The reason is that, in this example, it is the current-year budget constraint that is being violated most severely; obviously, the growth rates begin to affect the budget only in year 2.

3. *Two-way feasibility graphs.* The effect of moves of pairs of variables can be explored by means of a *two-way feasibility graph* as shown in figure 9.6. The user specifies the two variables and the ranges for each. Then the computer displays a graph that shades in the feasible combinations. In this example the no-growth-in-deficit constraint limits feasible combinations of the growth-rate variables *DFS* and *DT*. A rough slope calculation is also performed: it indicates, beneath the graph, the approximate terms of trade (shown in this example to be about 1.80 percentage points increase in *DFS* to one percentage point increase in *DT*).

4. *Multivariable boundary probes.* The user with growing sophistication may want to consider a number of variables in combination. Starting from the working configuration, such a user can set reference numbers and increments or decrements for as many primary planning variables as desired in order to define the direction of a *boundary probe*, that is, a test of where the bounds of feasibility are reached. The program searches along the vector specified by these increments and decrements until it reaches the boundary. If the starting point is feasible, the result of the search is to remove slack. If the starting point is infeasible, the search will find the nearest feasible point in the direction specified.

```
NAME       LIMIT OF DECREASE   CURRENT  LIMIT OF INCREASE

    1 FAC       797.8599         820.0000*************
    2 AFAC       40.7200          80.0000*************
    3 UG    *************       6500.0000   6753.4961
    4 GR    *************       4600.0000   4848.3984
    5 TENR        0.5538           0.6500*************
    6 STFR        0.4405           0.5000*************
    7 P     *************          0.0480      0.0518
    8 TR    *************          0.0500*************
    9 F     *************          0.0000*************
   10 DT    *************          0.0250*************
   11 DFS   *************          0.0150*************
   12 DSS   *************          0.0200*************
   13 SBSL        0.1802           0.2000*************
   14 DCVL*************            0.0800*************
 +++ INDICATES A VARIABLE THAT HAS REACHED ITS UPPER OR LOWER BOUND.
 *** INDICATES THAT NO LIMIT EXISTS.
```

Figure 9.5. TRADES single-variable feasibility moves starting from
an infeasible configuration

```
OPTION? (TYPE 11 TO VIEW THE LIST.)
?5


      TWO-WAY FEASIBILITY GRAPH

 REF# FOR VAR.   1
?10
 GIVE THE MINIMUM FOR DT
?0
 GIVE THE MAXIMUM FOR DT
?.04
 REF# FOR VAR.   2
?11
 GIVE THE MINIMUM FOR DFS
?0
 GIVE THE MAXIMUM FOR DFS
?.04
     0.0400 *                                           ++
DFS         *
     0.0350 *                                     ++    ++
DFS         *
     0.0300 *                                     ++    ++
DFS         *
     0.0250 *                               ++    ++    ++
DFS         *
     0.0200 *                         ++    ++    ++    ++
DFS         *
     0.0150 *                         ++    ++    ++    ++
DFS         *
     0.0100 *                   ++    ++    ++    ++    ++
DFS         *
     0.0050 *                   ++    ++    ++    ++    ++
DFS         *
     0.0000 *             ++    ++    ++    ++    ++    ++
DFS         *
        *****I*****I*****I*****I*****I*****I*****I*****I*****I*****
          0.0        0.0100     0.0200     0.0300     0.0400
             0.0050     0.0150     0.0250     0.0350
          DT      ++  MEANS POINT IS FEASIBLE (APPROX LINEAR SLOPE  1.80)
 OPTION? (TYPE 11 TO VIEW THE LIST.)
?15
 FINAL FEASIBLE CONFIGURATION
```

Figure 9.6. TRADES: A two-way feasibility graph

```
TARGET VARIABLE (REF#,0=NONE)
=>0
THE ALTERED CONFIGURATION IS    FEASIBLE.
PLEASE INPUT A VECTOR OF VARIABLE INCREMENTS
TO SEARCH FOR THE FEASIBILITY BOUNDARY.
(USE REF#=0 TO END)
REF# FOR VAR.    1
=>1
FAC   NOW:         650.0000 INCREMENT:
=>1.
REF# FOR VAR.    2
=>3
UG    NOW:        6500.0000 INCREMENT:
=>5.
REF# FOR VAR.    3
=>4
GR    NOW:        4600.0000 INCREMENT:
=>3.
REF# FOR VAR.    4
=>


BOUNDARY REACHED.
     LIMITS:          CHANGE:
FAC       685.0977        35.0977
UG       6675.4492       175.4492
GR       4705.2617       105.2617
BACK TO OPTIONS=0, SAVE CONFIG.=1
=>
```

Figure 9.7. TRADES three-variable boundary probe starting from a feasible configuration

A three-variable boundary probe starting from an interior feasible point (i.e., one in which there is slack) is illustrated in figure 9.7. It is desired to increase *FAC*, and the user will accept additions to *UG* and *GR* in the ratio of 5 and 3 students, respectively, per faculty member. The computer responds that, with a move in this direction, the boundary will be reached at $FAC = 685$, which is an increment of 35 over its starting value. Note that the accompanying increases in *UG* and *GR* are in the ratios that the user specified.

The Use of TRADES

Repeated application of the TRADES options will enable a user to explore the decision space and determine which portions of it are feasible in terms of the desired financial and operational constraints. But feasibility is only a necessary condition for a good plan, not a sufficient one. Every change of configuration has implications for the intangible variables, and thus works both obvious and subtle effects on value. One must therefore consider value tradeoffs among the primary planning variables as well as tradeoffs in terms of the constraints.

Who should be using TRADES? The reasoning just given suggests that people responsible for top-level planning decisions should be the ones to search the feasible space, since it is their representation of the institution's value function that is to be maximized. Our experience is that where top officers help specify the primary planning variables and the operational constraints, and are familiar with and confident of the financial constraints, they will in fact become involved in the searching and evaluation process, either directly or through their staff. This involvement is the sine qua non of the approach to planning models for colleges and universities espoused in this book.

The on-line interactive format of TRADES permits rapid exploration of the feasible planning space. Questions can be asked and answered rapidly that would be difficult or impossible to deal with by hand or with conventional projection or forecasting models. The degree to which TRADES has been accepted by planners at Stanford and elsewhere suggests that this mode of operation is comfortable for them. This, in turn, lends support to our basic theory of university choice.

The TRADES model is a practical representation of many aspects of the abstract theory presented in chapter 3. At the same time, we must emphasize that TRADES is incomplete. TRADES provides for (a) modeling the financial functions in as much detail as may be desired by the user; (b) specifying financial constraints of a static or dynamic type; (c) specifying operating constraints on the activity variables, whether singly or in combination; (d) discovering, by means of a flexible mechanism, the effects of shifts in the working configuration of primary planning variables upon feasibility, as represented by the combined set of constraints. Still, the process of value assessment itself must take place entirely inside the decision maker's head; there is no help in this from the TRADES model.

Interactive Preference Optimization

At this point, we return to the macrodecision problem defined at the beginning of this chapter. We recall that there is a value function to be optimized and that this optimization involves the entire set of PPVs. How might TRADES be enhanced to aid us better in finding the overall optimal—i.e., most preferred —configuration that we are after?

To describe the general methodology, we refer to the graphic representation of the problem shown in figure 9.8. Here we are looking at the feasible set of alternatives for a particular pair of variables, say faculty (x_1) and undergraduate students (x_2); the bounded region in the figure is an ideal representation of that set.

Suppose our current feasible solution is at the point labeled $\mathbf{x}^0$ in figure 9.8. Any explicit optimization algorithm will move from the current point, $\mathbf{x}^0$, to a more preferred one, say $\mathbf{x}^1$, in two steps. First, it finds a good *direction*, $\mathbf{d}$, in which to move; second, it determines the optimal distance, or *step size, t*, for moving in the chosen direction. These steps are handled separately, and in each case the decision maker's value function, V, is taken directly into account. We will now explore the entire process in more detail.

The Direction-Finding Problem

It is a mathematically verified fact that the direction of locally fastest increase in the function $V(\mathbf{x})$ evaluated at a particular point $\mathbf{x}^0$ is given by the *gradient*

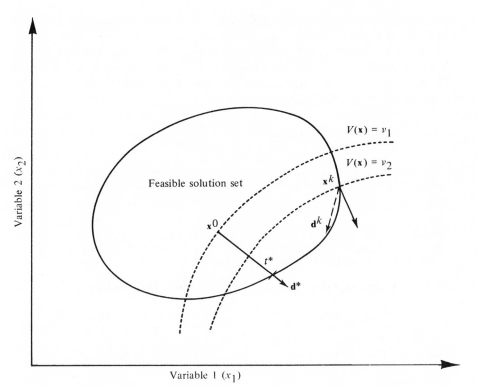

Figure 9.8. Finding the optimal direction and step size: An illustrative example

of V evaluated at $\mathbf{x}^0$. This is a vector of numbers, labeled $\nabla V(\mathbf{x})$, consisting of the first partial derivatives of V with respect to each x_j, evaluated at $\mathbf{x} = \mathbf{x}^0$. That is, in the two-dimensional case,

$$\nabla V(\mathbf{x}^0) = \left(\frac{\partial V}{\partial x_1}(\mathbf{x}^0), \frac{\partial V}{\partial x_2}(\mathbf{x}^0) \right)$$

We note further that the partial derivative $\partial V / \partial x_j$ may be interpreted as the marginal utility of additional units of x_j.

In view of the result stated above, we know that, if there are better nearby solutions than $\mathbf{x} = \mathbf{x}^0$, we will find one of them by moving in the direction of the gradient. Thus if we knew the first partial derivatives of the function V at $\mathbf{x} = \mathbf{x}^0$, we would choose

$$\mathbf{d} = \nabla V(\mathbf{x}^0).$$

This is the direction indicated as $\mathbf{d}\,*$ in figure 9.8, where we suppose the broken curves, labeled $V(\mathbf{x}) = v_1$ and $V(\mathbf{x}) = v_2$, are indifference (or isopreference) curves with $v_2 > v_1$. (By drawing these curves in the shape shown, we are assuming the decision maker thinks that, other things being equal, more faculty is "good" and more students is "bad.") The gradient vector is just normal (i.e., perpendicular) to the indifference curve that passes through the point $\mathbf{x}^0$, and it points in the direction of increasing preference.

As a practical matter, the decision maker (hereafter abbreviated as "DM") cannot be expected to know the marginal utility of more x_1 or x_2, but may still intuitively grasp a *marginal rate of substitution* (MRS) of x_1 for x_2. In formal terms, such a rate may be defined as

$$\mathrm{MRS}_{12}(\mathbf{x}^0) = \frac{\partial V(\mathbf{x}^0)/\partial x_2}{\partial V(\mathbf{x}^0)/\partial x_1}$$

or the ratio of the marginal utility for x_2 to the marginal utility for x_1. Less formally, the same ratio is approximated by the answer to the following sort of question, which can be addressed to the DM from the computer terminal:

```
WHAT VALUE OF   UG IN THE SECOND ALTERNATIVE DE-
SCRIBED BELOW WOULD MAKE YOU INDIFFERENT BETWEEN
THE TWO ALTERNATIVE CHARACTERIZATIONS OF STANFORD?

FIRST ALTERNATIVE            SECOND ALTERNATIVE

   FAC  =    600.               FAC  =    610.   *****
    UG  =   6000.                UG  =            *****
    GR  =   5000.                GR  =   5000.
  TUIT  =   4000.              TUIT  =   4000.

? 6200.
```

In other words, a DM who is assumed to remain indifferent between the two alternatives is being asked to fill in the level of undergraduates that would have to go along with an increase of ten faculty. Although their values remain constant, the other decision variables are included in the question to make sure that the DM expresses a preference with regard to a specific (that is, the most current) configuration. It is quite likely that the DM's answer to the tradeoff question involving FAC and UG would be different if GR were 3,000 instead of 5,000, for example.

Note, incidentally, that the tradeoff the DM is being asked to make depends on intangible factors and intrinsic values, and that financial considerations are not meant to enter the picture at this point.

Suppose the DM answers with 6,200. We then would calculate

$$\mathrm{MRS}_{12} \cong \frac{-\Delta x_1}{\Delta x_2} = \frac{-(610 - 600)}{(6{,}200 - 6{,}000)} = -0.05.$$

Thus, for every additional undergraduate student, the DM would require an additional 0.05 faculty FTE. (The leading minus sign indicates in each case that students and faculty do not substitute for each other; when students are added, the DM requires more, not fewer, faculty to stay indifferent.) To see why this is a proper (approximate) calculation of the MRS, note that the ratio $\Delta x_1/\Delta x_2$ is approximately equal to the first partial derivative, $\partial x_1/\partial x_2$, taken along an indifference curve, whose equation can be written

$$V(x_1, x_2) = v \quad \text{(a constant)}.$$

By implicit differentiation of this equation, we obtain

$$\frac{\partial V}{\partial x_1} \frac{\partial x_1}{\partial x_2} + \frac{\partial V}{\partial x_2} = 0$$

which rearranges to

$$\frac{-\partial x_1}{\partial x_2} = \frac{\partial V}{\partial x_2} \bigg/ \frac{\partial V}{\partial x_1} = \text{MRS}_{12}.$$

We emphasize that this information, with the inferences drawn from it, is valid only for small deviations from the current solution. That is, the preference information we obtain is of only local significance, and we shall employ it only in deciding the direction in which to move a small distance from the current point.

Note that MRS_{12} is just $\partial V(\mathbf{x}^0)/\partial x_2$ divided by $\partial V(\mathbf{x}^0)/\partial x_1$. The direction we want to move in is $\mathbf{d} = (\partial V(\mathbf{x}^0)/\partial x_1, \partial V(\mathbf{x}^0)/\partial x_2)$, but we can obtain the same direction by normalizing each component of $\mathbf{d}$ by any positive constant. Suppose we take as the normalizing factor the marginal utility of x_1, $\partial V(\mathbf{x}^0)/\partial x_1$. In effect, this establishes the first variable (i.e., *FAC*) as the numeraire against which all other variables are to be measured in utility space. Dividing both components of the gradient vector by $\partial V(\mathbf{x}^0)/\partial x_1$ we obtain

$$\mathbf{d} = (1, \text{MRS}_{12}).$$

Hence we do not need to worry about "absolute" measures of utility. Indeed, ordinal measures of utility are sufficient for determining marginal rates of substitution.[1]

We have assumed, of course, that the variable selected to be the numeraire is a "good," that is, that its marginal utility is positive. If, instead, $\partial V(\mathbf{x}^0)/\partial x_1$ is negative, we would take $\mathbf{d} = \nabla V(\mathbf{x}^0)/(-\partial V(\mathbf{x}^0)/\partial x_1)$, or

$$\mathbf{d} = (-1, -\text{MRS}_{12}).$$

The proper sign of $\partial V(x^0)/\partial x_1$ is easily determined by asking the DM

```
GIVEN THE FIRST ALTERNATIVE PRESENTED ABOVE, DO YOU
PREFER A HIGHER OR LOWER VALUE OF  FAC?  IF YOU PREFER
A HIGHER VALUE, TYPE 1.   IF YOU PREFER A LOWER VALUE,
TYPE 2.

? 1.
```

In order to generalize the procedure to higher dimensions, we would ask the indifference question with *FAC* compared to each of the other variables taken one at a time. Suppose, in the four-dimensional decision space used in

Table 9.3.   Examples of Indifference Points for the Four-Variable Case

Variable	Current Solution	Alternative 1	Alternative 2	Alternative 3
FAC	600	**610**	**610**	**610**
UG	6,000	**6,200**	6,000	6,000
GR	5,000	5,000	**5,100**	5,000
TUIT	$4,000	$4,000	$4,000	**$4,150**

our earlier example, this process were to yield the results shown in table 9.3. We then would have the computer calculate

$$\text{MRS}_{1j} = -\Delta x_1/\Delta x_j \quad (j = 2, 3, 4)$$

and it would display

```
YOUR MARGINAL RATES OF SUBSTITUTION FOLLOW:

MRS  OF  FAC  FOR   FAC  =   1.000
MRS  OF  FAC  FOR    UG  =  -0.050
MRS  OF  FAC  FOR    GR  =  -0.100
MRS  OF  FAC  FOR  TUIT  =  -0.067
```

This vector of MRS values defines the "best" direction in which to move (i.e., the steepest direction with respect to the value function).

We should point out here that most people find it difficult to locate their indifference points even when the two variables are obviously related, as are faculty and students. Empirically it has been found that decision makers are not very confident in their ability to make judgments of this kind. The difficulty is magnified considerably when the two variables involved in a tradeoff are not even directly related. Consider the indifference question that must be posed when an increase in faculty is paired off against a change in the tuition rate. Most people would place a positive value on an additional ten faculty members. In our case, however, they must ask themselves first, whether they would prefer a higher or a lower tuition rate; and second, how much higher or lower. The only way to answer the second part of the question is by making the connection not only between the variables *FAC* and *TUIT* but also with some overarching criterion or criteria relating directly to one's value function —for instance, the long-run effects on academic quality. (Recall that purely financial considerations are eschewed for this purpose.) Quantifying their preferences is not a step that most decision makers can take. Their inability to do so is a major obstacle to the use of this type of algorithm.

Finally, we must consider how to modify the direction-finding algorithm when (as it often will) the current solution already lies on the boundary of the feasible solution set. In the case of the point labeled $\mathbf{x}^k$ in figure 9.8 it is not possible to move in the most-preferred (i.e., gradient) direction without violating one or more of the constraints. (Given the preference structure indicated in the figure, it is easy to see why the preference search should take place mainly on the boundary of the constraint space. We do not ordinarily expect to find slack in a university's financial constraints.)

Now, it can be shown mathematically that any direction making an acute angle with the gradient vector will increase the function $V(\mathbf{x})$ in the vicinity of the point $\mathbf{x} = \mathbf{x}^k$—provided, of course, that this point is not already a local maximum of V. The best choice when the gradient itself is infeasible is the direction closest to the gradient that is (approximately) tangent to the constraint set; in figure 9.8 this direction is indicated by the vector labelled $\mathbf{d}^k$. Thus the algorithm is modified to choose the appropriate tangent vector whenever it finds it cannot move in the gradient direction. Analytic procedures for doing this are described in textbooks on nonlinear programming, and we do not need to go into the details here.[2] Alternatively, one can set up the computer code to find the tangent by numerical (i.e., iterative) means, much as we have done in programming the vector-probing options employed in TRADES.

Finding the Optimal Step Size

We have now identified the best feasible direction, say $\mathbf{d}^k$, in which to move from the current solution, say $\mathbf{x}^k$. We must next determine the optimal size of a step in that direction, i.e., the step size that will maximize the DM's value function over all feasible configurations lying in the indicated direction.

The reader may wonder, after looking at figure 9.8, why we are concerned with the step-size question at all. Given the picture of constraints and indifference curves shown there, it seems obvious that we ought to take the step needed to reach the constraint boundary—whatever that step might happen to be. This picture is a simplification of how things really are, however: the constraint set need not be convex, and the DM's preferences may lead to something other than a smooth, concave curve of indifference points. In the general case, the gradient still gives the *locally* best direction, but it certainly is possible to reach a less-preferred region as one moves far enough away from the current point. This is also a good point at which to recall that when the value and constraint functions are irregular, all that can be expected of any algorithm is to find a locally optimal solution. Unless the nonlinear model is completely well-behaved, no assurance can be given that the final solution will represent the global optimum.

The choice of step size must of course be presented in such a way that the DM can understand it. For the sake of illustration, suppose that, given the MRS values provided above, the best feasible direction at $\mathbf{x}^k = (600, 6000, 5000, 4000)$ turns out to be $\mathbf{d}^k = (1, 5, -2, 2.5)$. Suppose further that the program has determined (say, by using the trial-and-error probing options of TRADES) that $\mathbf{d}^k$ is feasible for any change in *FAC* from 0 to $+50$. The DM might be presented at the computer terminal with a preference question phrased in the following way:

```
CONSIDER THE POTENTIAL CHANGES IN THE CHARACTERIZATION OF
STANFORD UNIVERSITY PRESENTED BELOW.   EACH   10.000 UNIT
CHANGE IN  FAC IS ACCOMPANIED BY THE FOLLOWING CHANGES IN
THE REMAINING VARIABLES:

                                      POTENTIAL CHANGES IN THE
CHARACTERIZATION OF                   CHARACTERIZATION OF
STANFORD UNIVERSITY                   STANFORD UNIVERSITY

     FAC  =    600.                   CHANGE IN  FAC =   10.00
      UG  =   6000.                   CHANGE IN   UG =   50.00
      GR  =   5000.                   CHANGE IN   GR =  -20.00
    TUIT  =   4000.                   CHANGE IN TUIT =   25.00


YOU MAY CONSIDER ANY CHANGE IN  FAC BETWEEN ZERO AND 50.00.
ENTER THE CHANGE IN  FAC YOU WOULD LIKE TO CONSIDER.

? 20.
```

(For easier readability, the change vector is shown here as a tenfold multiple of the $\mathbf{d}^k$ just described.)

The answer to this question produces a value of the scalar quantity t that specifies the distance the DM desires to travel from the current solution. Thus if the current solution at the kth iteration of the algorithm is labelled $\mathbf{x}^k$ and the steepest feasible direction vector and step size are labelled $\mathbf{d}^k$ and t^k, respectively, then the next solution will be given by

$$\mathbf{x}^{k+1} = \mathbf{x}^k + t^k\mathbf{d}^k.$$

In our numerical example, where the DM specified a desired step-size value of 20, we would have

$$\begin{bmatrix} \text{FAC} \\ \text{UG} \\ \text{GR} \\ \text{TUIT} \end{bmatrix}^{k+1} = \begin{bmatrix} 600 \\ 6{,}000 \\ 5{,}000 \\ 4{,}000 \end{bmatrix} + 20 \begin{bmatrix} 1 \\ 5 \\ -2 \\ 2.5 \end{bmatrix} = \begin{bmatrix} 620 \\ 6{,}100 \\ 4{,}960 \\ 4{,}050 \end{bmatrix}$$

Having thus determined the next current solution, the program will continue to cycle through the same process until the user decides to terminate the session. (Note the absence of any built-in "stopping rule": the DMs terminate the program when they judge that it has gone through enough iterations. We must hope that they do so because they feel they have reached an optimal solution, not because they have become too tired to go on!)

As we mentioned before, questions of the type just presented are not easily answered by most university administrators. At the step-finding stage, the DM is being asked to make a precise choice among a continuous set of alternatives in which all n planning variables are changed simultaneously. Presumably, most people could pick out a "better" solution from this set. Finding the "best" one is a good deal harder, but we are interested in trying to get as much improvement as possible at each step.

To maximize the efficiency of the algorithm, we would suggest including some decision aids in the computer program. For example, the first answer to the step-size question might be taken as a trial value, and the computer instructed to present the user with the following binary choice:

```
WHICH OF THE TWO ALTERNATIVE CHARACTERIZATIONS OF
STANFORD UNIVERSITY PRESENTED BELOW DO YOU PREFER?
THE FIRST? - TYPE 1.   THE SECOND? - TYPE 2.
INDIFFERENT - TYPE 3.


      FIRST ALTERNATIVE              SECOND ALTERNATIVE

     FAC   =    600.                FAC   =    620.
      UG   =   6000.                 UG   =   6100.
      GR   =   5000.                 GR   =   4960.
    TUIT   =   4000.               TUIT   =   4050.

    ? 2.
```

Following this question, the computer might ask

```
DO YOU WISH TO CONSIDER OTHER VALUES ALONG THE LINE?
IF YES, TYPE 1.   IF NO, TYPE 2.

    ? 2.
```

The affirmative answer would lead the computer to cycle back through the step-size routine another time.

The iterative process we have just finished describing is an efficient means of solving the constrained value optimization problem interactively, when DMs are clear enough about their preferences to be able to give the information that is required. They must be able not only to express their MRSs in precise quantitative terms, but also to identify the optimal step size to be taken in a specified direction. These requirements may well be too strict for uninitiated DMs to handle. If so, we would recommend sacrificing some efficiency in the algorithm for the sake of being able to present easier choices. In particular, it is possible (although it may well take considerably more steps) to do the job with questions that offer only two choices. The next subsection describes such an algorithm, designed for use in conjunction with TRADES.

Preference Optimization with TRADES

The optimization routine that was added to TRADES is of a simple form.[3] The computer selects one variable at a time and quickly determines whether more or less of that variable is desired when all other variables are held at their current values. Having done this, the program then steps the selected variable up or down (whichever is better), in increments of increasing size. The first step is fixed at a small number, say around 0.1 percent of the initial value of x_j; call it Δ_j^1. Each subsequent step is a constant multiple, $t > 1$, of the previous step-size, i.e.,

$$\delta_j^{k+1} = t\delta_j^k.$$

Each time a step is taken, TRADES first determines whether the new solution

$$x_i^{k+1} = \begin{cases} x_i & i \neq j \\ x_j + \delta_j^{k+1} & i = j \end{cases}$$

is feasible. If not, it sets

$$x_j = x_j + \delta_j^k$$

and moves on to the next variable. Otherwise, DMs are asked if they prefer $\mathbf{x}^{k+1}$ to $\mathbf{x}^k$. An affirmative answer leads to a new step being tried out on x_j; if the former solution is preferred, on the other hand, x_j is fixed at the former value and the program moves on to the next variable.

An illustration of how the procedure works in two dimensions is given in figure 9.9. Starting at the point labeled $\mathbf{x}^0$, two steps involving increments in just the first variable are required to get to $\mathbf{x}^1$. The next step in that direction would lead to a point that is more preferred but infeasible. Since the first (small) increment in x_2 leads to a solution preferred less than $\mathbf{x}^1$, it must be that less of this variable is preferred to more. Thus x_2 is stepped down until, in the case illustrated, a further step becomes infeasible. The algorithm then returns to x_1 with its initial step size to find more-preferred solutions lying in the horizontal direction, and so on.

Notice a key feature of the algorithm: by employing a geometric progression of increasing step sizes it quickly oversteps the boundary, leaving the user at an interior solution that preserves some slack. As long as we begin the procedure at a point well inside the constraint set, we will not get too near the boundary until we have cycled through the entire set of variables several times. This feature ensures that there will be enough slack in the system to allow for significant changes in each of the PPVs during the procedure's early stages. Thus as long as the DM's value function is reasonably well-behaved, the algorithm should lead eventually to the most-preferred solution.

While there is little more to the procedure than that, several features have been added to streamline its use:

1. *Removing an irrelevant variable.* A simple instruction is available to freeze any variable in the PPV set at its current value, either temporarily or for all iterations of the value-optimization procedure. This feature permits one easily to narrow the focus to a pivotal set of planning variables.

2. *Changing bounds on any PPV.* Among the constraints employed in this procedure are lower and upper bounds on every decision variable. DMs are free to set their own limits whenever they wish further to restrict the range of search along any particular dimension.

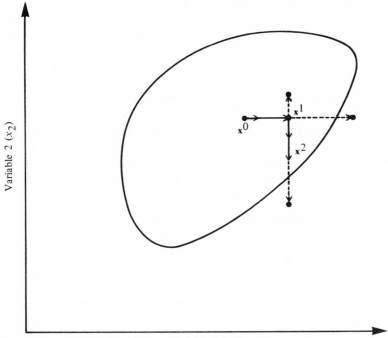

Figure 9.9. Illustration of a TRADES structured search option

3. *Automatic minimization/maximization.* Any variable of which a DM knows that either more or less will always be preferred can be so designated, in which case the program will automatically take the appropriate steps. This option can be selected to operate on either a permanent basis (i.e., every time the variable comes up) or a temporary one (i.e., for a particular cycle).

4. *Moving back to and forth from TRADES.* The program makes it easy to reenter TRADES from the structured search procedure any time the DM thinks it will be more advantageous to work directly with TRADES. Having gained further tradeoff information and perhaps altered the current configuration, the DM can return to the structured search option with a new starting point, or continue from the previous best point. This option can also be used to get away from a locally "optimal" solution.

The second and third options listed above are especially useful whenever the user can identify an ideal value for a particular PPV independently from all the other PPVs. Suppose, for example, that the ideal value for *UG* is seen as 6,000 and the procedure begins with *UG* = 6,500. By fixing the lower bound on UG at 6,000 and instructing the computer to "always min" this variable, one can speed up the optimization process considerably. For other variables, one may wish to move up or down, depending on where one is in the solution space. In such cases, one would want to retain control of the search procedure, and so would use the ordinary "see-and-search" option instead.

A sample session with the TRADES structured search option is shown in appendix 11, where we have included the instruction section. It is worth remarking that more effective search procedures are available than the one used in this implementation of TRADES.[4] This algorithm, however, is good enough for our purpose of directing DMs through the space of feasible solutions in such a way that they will follow their value preferences. We should also mention that the capability exists in an experimental version of TRADES to perform *group* value optimization through the use of Merrill M. Flood's procedure for dynamic value voting.[5]

Summary of Interactive Preference Optimization

This section has described in some detail alternative techniques for solving the value optimization problem interactively, that is, through interaction between the computer and the decision maker seated at the computer terminal. Two major alternatives were presented, one employing an efficient algorithm but demanding value statements in hard, quantitative terms, and the other probably requiring more decisions but asking only for binary choices along the way. Either type of interactive procedure has two chief advantages: (a) only local preference information, i.e., information in the vicinity of a current feasible configuration, need be elicited; (b) the procedure tends to maintain a certain level of interest on the user's part since it provides instantaneous feedback.

The chief drawback of the interactive approach is that it can only be used when the DM is available and willing to put in time at the terminal. It may be particularly troublesome for the DM to redo this work every time an important financial parameter or constraint is changed. For this reason, we and a few others have launched efforts to gather sufficient preference data off line (i.e., away from the computer that is going to be used to solve the problem) to define an explicit value function that properly represents a DM's preferences. Such a function then can be optimized at a later stage, subject to financial and operational constraints, by using some form of a nonlinear programming code. One set of such experiments actually performed at Stanford in 1974/75 will be described in the next section.

Closed-Form Value Optimization

Here, we are concerned with the problem of how actually to specify the function $V(\mathbf{x})$ that purports to represent the value that the DM attaches to a feasible configuration, $\mathbf{x}$. Of course, the very existence of such a function is open to question. Some researchers have argued that this type of problem is best solved by encouraging DMs to change their values as they learn more about the constraints and terms of trade.[6] If so, the interactive involvement of DMs is indispensable. Nevertheless, it may be worth acting on the assumption that the value function exists in isolation from the constraints, is well defined, and can be estimated. Some successes with the closed-form approach have been noted in other fields of application.[7] This has encouraged us to attempt the same thing in the context of university planning, despite the evident problems.

In estimating the value function, $V(\mathbf{x})$, two separate issues must be addressed: (a) the *form* of the function (e.g., linear additive, quadratic, etc.); (b) the *values* to be assigned to its parameters. The two alternative procedures to be presented below differ both in the assumed functional form, and in the type of preference information that must be elicted for the purpose of parameter estimation.[8]

Double-Tradeoff Method

The first procedure is known as the *double-tradeoff method*. To apply this method, we must assume that the value function is additive in the variables, x_j; that is, that it can be written as a sum of separate functions of each of the variables taken one at a time:

$$V(\mathbf{x}) = \sum_{j=1}^{n} v_j(x_j).$$

Thus interactions in preference between any two or more variables are ruled out at the outset. We do not need, however, to make any particular assumption about the functional form of the $v_j(x_j)$; these will be approximated by piecewise linear functions derived from the data.

Several techniques exist for constructing an additive value function.[9] The double-tradeoff method asks essentially the same questions as the search procedure described in the previous section. Here, again, we choose one of the decision variables to play the role of numeraire. The questions can be presented in a written questionnaire that solicits enough indifference points for each variable paired with the numeraire to span the relevant range of the decision space.

ILLUSTRATION 9.2. To see more precisely how this can work, suppose the variable FAC is selected as numeraire, and that only solutions with FAC varying from -100 to $+100$ from the current operating point (assumed to be 600) would ever be considered. The functions $v_1(x_1)$ and $v_2(x_2)$ would then be fitted to the answers to the following collection of pairwise tradeoffs. Here the person filling out the questionnaire has been instructed to specify the value for UG in the second alternative, viz, the one that would provide "just as favorable (*not* more favorable) an environment for academic activities (instruction and research) as the first." (Again, financial implications are not to be considered at this stage of the analysis.)

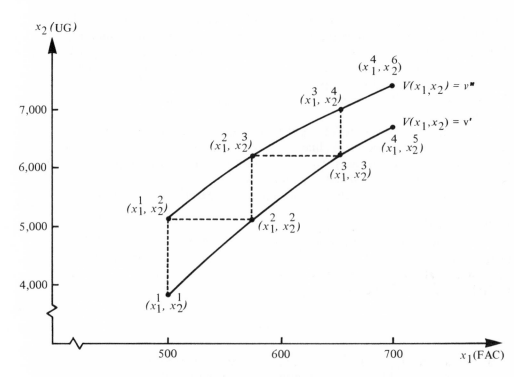

Figure 9.10. Construction of indifference curves

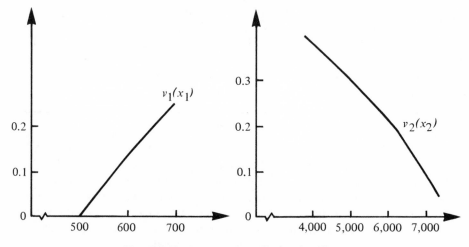

Figure 9.11. Construction of value functions

Alternative 1		Alternative 2	
FAC	UG	FAC	UG
600	5,500	500	3,800
600	5,500	550	4,700
600	5,500	650	6,200
600	5,500	700	6,700
600	6,500	500	5,100
600	6,500	550	5,900
600	6,500	650	7,000
600	6,500	700	7,400

NOTE: Each line in the above represents a separate question for the DM.

Suppose the DM has responded with the numbers shown underscored above. The process of estimating the value functions from these data follows the scheme portrayed in figures 9.10 and 9.11. In figure 9.10, the given data are used to plot the two indifference curves, $V(\mathbf{x}) = v'$ and $V(\mathbf{x}) = v''$, where, presumably, $v' > v''$. Notice the straight line segments drawn between each consecutive pair of points on a curve: these denote that we have assumed constant rates of substitution of x_2 for x_1 in these intervals.

Next, one draws a "staircase" between the two curves, beginning at the left end of the lower curve and proceeding alternately in a vertical and horizontal direction. Observe the distinguishing feature of the points where the staircase intersects either of the indifference curves: each one differs from the one just preceding it in only a single coordinate. In figure 9.10 we have labeled these points (x_1^j, x_2^k).

Now, in constructing the value functions $v_1(x_1)$ and $v_2(x_2)$, we are at liberty to choose any origin and scale we desire. (This is because any value function is unique only up to a monotonic transformation.) Suppose we pick as origins $v_1(x_1^1) = 0$ and $v_2(x_2^1) = 0.4$ (recall that value *decreases* as x_2 increases), and scale the function $V(x_1, x_2) = v_1(x_1) + v_2(x_2)$ so that $v' - v'' = 0.1$. This means that, as we move up the staircase, we are changing the value of one of the functions $v_j(k_j)$ by 0.1.

For example, the first move takes us from the point (x_1^1, x_2^1) to (x_1^1, x_2^2). The difference in V values is simply $v_2(x_2^1) - v_2(x_2^2) = 0.1$; since $v_2(x_2^1) = 0.4$, we now know that $v_2(x_2^2) = 0.3$. The next step is from (x_1^1, x_2^2) to (x_1^2, x_2^2), which tells us that $v_1(x_1^2) = v_1(x_1^1) + 0.1$, and so $v_1(x_1^2) = 0.1$. Proceeding up the staircase in this manner generates values for $v_1(x_1^j), j = 1, 2, 3$, and for $v_2(x_2^k)$, $k = 1, 2, 3, 4$, which points have been plotted in figure 9.5, and straight lines drawn in between (we assume a constant marginal utility between any two adjacent points). Finally, it can be shown by geometry that the right end points of the indifference curves lie a half-step away from the nearest staircase points; thus, we have

$$v_1(x_1^4) = v_1(x_1^3) + 0.05 = 0.25$$

and

$$v_2(x_2^6) = v_2(x_2^4) - 0.05 = 0.05.$$

Adding these points to the curves in figure 9.11 completes the construction of the value functions for the variables *FAC* and *UG*. Pairwise tradeoff data involving the other primary planning variables would be obtained and processed similarly, and would then be combined to generate a value function defined on the entire decision-variable space.

Notice that the value functions constructed from our example data turned out to be piecewise linear and concave. Such functions are quite suitable to employ in a nonlinear programming algorithm for solving the constrained optimization problem. Although the fitted functions will always be piecewise linear, there is nothing in the procedure that guarantees they will be concave. Concavity will result only when the DM's responses exhibit diminishing marginal utilities along each dimension. Otherwise, the result will be a nonconcave function that will be difficult, if not impossible, to optimize, given the current state of the art in nonlinear programming.

We have not had much success in employing this particular technique of data fitting with administrators at Stanford. Most persons filling out the written questionnaire were unable to grasp the concept of indifference as it needs to be grasped if the exercise is to be performed properly. This was in spite of our detailed instructions on the questionnaire and the briefing sessions we held before it was distributed. Probably, what is needed is an interactive computer program that can ask the tradeoff questions, process the responses instantaneously, and use various checking routines to determine whether the responses (a) are consistent and (b) exhibit diminishing marginal utility. If not, the program would so inform the DM and cycle back to request new responses. We have not tried to use the double-tradeoff method interactively, choosing instead to try out the alternative method (again based on a paper-and-pencil questionnaire) that is described in the next subsection.

Estimation from Pairwise Comparison Data

From a human engineering standpoint, methods that rely on ordinal rankings of alternative configurations have a major advantage over numerical tradeoffs. It is very much easier for a DM to provide data of the former type than of the latter. In this subsection, we discuss how to apply a method designed especially to estimate a closed-form value function from data on ranked comparisons. This method, dubbed LINMAP, was developed by Venkatarama Srinivasan and Allan D. Shocker (1973), and has seen several applications in the field of marketing.

In contrast with the double-tradeoff method, no assumption of additivity or separability of the value function $V(\mathbf{x})$ need be made at the data-gathering stage. The data are obtained as responses to questions like the following (usually presented in a written questionnaire):

Each line below describes the university in terms of four planning variables. For each set of alternatives, please write a "1" by the alternative corresponding to the situation that in your opinion would provide the *most* favorable environment for desired academic (instructional and research) activities. Please write a "2" by the next most favorable alternative, and a "3" by the least favorable alternative. Be certain to make your choices purely on the basis of the highest "academic quality" and *not* on the basis of financial considerations of any kind.

	FAC	UG	GR	TUIT
———	550	6000	4800	4000
———	600	6500	5000	4100
———	650	6200	5500	4500

Notice that all four PPVs are varied and that the ranking of three configurations will generate three paired comparisons. We found in pretesting the technique with a small group of Stanford's administrative staff that it was difficult for them to deal with more than four variables and three comparisons at a time. When we had more than four variables in the PPV set (actually, we used a total of eight), we held all but four of them constant in each set of comparisons.

When preference data are collected in this form, DMs are free to maintain a holistic view towards the set of PPVs. That is, if their preferences for alternative configurations of faculty and undergraduates should depend on the graduate enrollment and tuition rate, our questions will enable them to assess their preferences properly. By contrast, it was necessary in the double-tradeoff approach to assume preferential independence of the PPVs from the outset. (Our questions there concerning points of indifference between alternative *FAC* and *UG* pairs made no mention of the other variables.)

Unfortunately, structural assumptions about the form of the value function still must be made at the data-processing stage. In the case of LINMAP, the assumption is that V is additive in the variables, x_j, or at least in some transformation of those variables—say, $y_k = y_k(\mathbf{x})$. What is meant by the latter designation is that y_k is some function of one or more of the x_j's. For example, if the DMs' preferences for student-body size depend on the number of faculty but their preferences for a student-faculty ratio are independent of the level of faculty, this would suggest taking $y_1 = x_1$ and $y_2 = (x_2 + x_3)/x_1$, where the variables x_1, x_2, and x_3 represent faculty, undergraduates, and graduates, respectively. The assumption is that, for a suitable set of y_k's, V can be written in the form

$$V(\mathbf{x}) = \sum_{k=1}^{K} v_k[y_k(\mathbf{x})].$$

To reiterate: preference information can be obtained in terms of the x's (if that is the most natural way for a DM to think about things), with the transformation to the y variables being introduced later, at the data-processing stage.

For the purposes of parameter estimation with LINMAP, the functional form of the v_k is limited as well. It must be either *linear*, i.e., $v_k(y_k) = w_k y_k$, or *quadratic*, i.e., $v_k(y_k) = -w_k(y_k - y_k^*)^2$. In the quadratic, or so-called weighted ideal-point model, the parameter w_k stands for the relative importance weight and y_k^* is the ideal value of y_k. Strictly speaking, the quadratic form is required by the LINMAP estimation algorithm and not by any theoretical considerations. A weighted ideal-point model could, in principle, be specified with an exponent other than 2, for instance. This form of preference representation seems eminently reasonable, however, in the context of university decision making. It says, essentially, that each (possibly transformed) variable has an ideal value for the DM, and that it exhibits decreasing marginal utility throughout its relevant range. A sketch of such a function is shown in figure 9.12.

The LINMAP routine uses linear programming to estimate the parameters of the value function (w_k in the linear form or w_k and y_k^* in the quadratic form) that best fits the DM's stated preferences for alternative university configurations.[10] The criterion used to measure the goodness of fit may be described as follows. Suppose, for a given set of estimated parameters, $\hat{w}_k$ and $\hat{y}_k^*$, we separate the paired comparison data according to whether the DM's stated preference order is preserved or violated by the fitted function. Let the set of pairs whose preference ordering is (strictly) preserved by the function be designated by $\mathscr{S}$ and its complement by $\mathscr{T}$. The goodness-of-fit measure, G, is calculated by summing up the absolute differences in function values for pairs that are correctly ordered, while the poorness-of-fit measure, B, is calculated by summing over incorrectly ordered pairs. More precisely, one computes

$$G = \sum_{(\mathbf{y}^i, \mathbf{y}^j) \varepsilon \mathscr{S}} |V(\mathbf{y}^i) - V(\mathbf{y}^j)|$$

and

$$B = \sum_{(\mathbf{y}^i, \mathbf{y}^j) \varepsilon \mathscr{T}} |V(\mathbf{y}^i) - V(\mathbf{y}^j)|.$$

The linear program used in LINMAP finds the set of parameters $\{w_k, y_k^*\}$ that minimize the ratio of B to G (the so-called index of fit) subject to the w_k being nonnegative and summing to one. (The latter requirement is a scaling condition that does not affect the generalizability of the results.)

We should emphasize that the measures B and G, and hence the penalty function B/G, contain terms that arise only when the function V assigns *different* values to two members of a pair. No penalty is assessed for predicting indifference when a preference actually was expressed in the data. Consequently, the algorithm is somewhat prone to assigning zero weights to terms that involve variables for which the weighted ideal-point model does not fit the data particularly well. Since zero-importance weights do not seem to make sense for any primary planning variable in our university decision problem, one should be on the lookout for such occurrences and be prepared to take appropriate action. The action might be either helping DMs clarify their preferences (which would include having them redo the questionnaire); or, for DMs who remain confident that their original questionnaire responses are the right ones, helping them to fit some other model (perhaps the linear form).

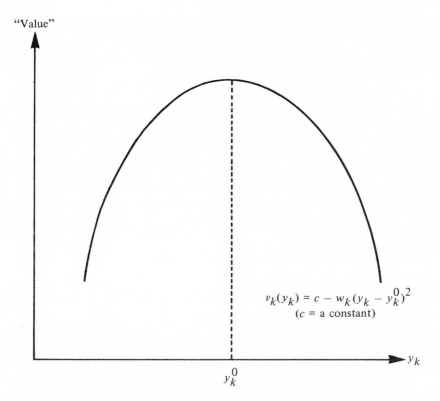

"Value"

$$v_k(y_k) = c - w_k(y_k - y_k^0)^2$$
$$(c = \text{a constant})$$

y_k^0

y_k

Figure 9.12. Illustration of the weighted ideal-point preference model

The Pilot Experiment at Stanford

In the summer of 1974 a group of twenty-two administrators and administrative staff personnel who were associated with budget planning at Stanford agreed to take part in an experimental study of value function estimation.[11] A case study was specially prepared to introduce the participants to the experiment, and various questionnaires were designed to elicit preference information.[12] (As we have already indicated, efforts to obtain indifference points for double-tradeoff analysis were unsuccessful.) Data on configuration rankings were obtained from two separate questionnaires, each one requiring the participant to make 180 paired comparisons (i.e., there were 60 triplets of configurations to be ranked).

We had thought originally that 180 paired comparisons would be sufficient data from which to estimate each participant's value function on the eight PPVs selected for this study (see table 9.4). It turned out, however, that something like double that number of data points were needed before the estimated functions would exhibit the stable properties necessary to justify their use in the optimization problem. This difficulty probably is associated with the technique. It suggests a fundamental tradeoff for anyone who is

Table 9.4.   Primary Planning Variables Used in Stanford Study

Variable Name	Symbol	1973/74 Value
(1) Regular faculty[a]	*FAC*	650
(2) Auxilary faculty[a]	*AFAC*	271
(3) Undergraduate enrollment[b]	*UG*	6,419
(4) Graduate student enrollment[b]	*GR*	4,518
(5) Percent of graduate enrollment in "professional" programs	*P*	33%
(6) Tuition rate	*T*	$3,135
(7) Ratio of academic support staff to faculty	*S/F*	0.695
(8) Faculty leverage[c]	*L*	0.136

SOURCE: Hopkins, Larréché, and Massy 1977, table 1, p. 366. Reprinted by permission of *Management Science*.
[a] Full-time equivalent.
[b] Autumn quarter head count.
[c] Fraction of faculty salaries paid from outside sources (e.g., research grants and contracts).

engaged in value function estimation: either one can work with the technique of indifference point approximation, which requires the DM to answer fewer questions, and be subject to its pitfalls; or one can take on a data-gathering and processing task of considerably greater magnitude. We do not mean to overemphasize this point, however, as most members of our experimental group were able to complete the two questionnaires in less than three hours.

Table 9.5 shows the goodness-of-fit measures obtained after LINMAP was used to fit a weighted ideal-point model to the data from the 360 paired comparisons made by the Stanford participants. With the exception of five out of the nineteen individuals (three members of the original group of twenty-two dropped out before completing the survey), the model was observed to fit the data extremely well. Those five cases, labeled "incomplete," were ones in which the "best-fitting" model gave zero weight to several of the PPVs.

We were able to use our data to test the validity of the fully fitted value functions in two ways. First, we checked for internal consistency by estimating separate value functions with different subsets of the data. Three such functions were compared in terms of their implicit marginal rates of substitution evaluated at the current operating point, with generally mixed results. On a scale ranging from -1 (totally inconsistent) to $+1$ (perfectly consistent), most values of our consistency index ranged between 0.4 and 1.0; a number of them were close to $+1$, but some were strongly negative. With these results we were unable to draw any firm conclusions regarding the consistency of the technique.

Far more conclusive results were obtained from a check on the predictive power of a function that we estimated from some of the data and then used to rank points in the remainder. Our procedure was to select 270 of the 360 data points for a given individual at random, fit an ideal-point model to those data, and then use the function to evaluate the remaining 90 alternatives. The estimated functions matched the choices actually made by the participants

Table 9.5. Goodness-of-Fit Results for the Weighted Ideal-Point Model

Subject No.[a]	Index of Fit[b]	% Pairs Violated[c]	Subject No.[a]	Index of Fit[b]	% Pairs Violated[c]
1	0.11	20	16	0.03	11
2	0.04	10	17	0.03	....[d]
4	0.04	15	18	0.04	....[d]
5	0.11	18	19	0.06	16
6	0.08	15	20	0.02	....[d]
7	0.11	21	21	0.09	16
8	0.03	10	22	0.03	10
10	0.10	20			
11	0.06	....[d]	AVERAGE FOR		
12	0.04	12	COMPLETELY		
13	0.10	18	DETERMINED		
15	0.05	....[d]	FUNCTIONS	0.07	15

SOURCE: Adapted from Hopkins, Larréché, and Massy 1977, table 2, page 370, by permission of *Management Science.*

[a] Subjects number 3, 9, and 14 did not complete the survey.

[b] Defined as the sum of absolute differences in function values for the pairs of stimuli whose preference order is violated, divided by the sum of absolute differences for pairs of stimuli whose preference order is preserved. Thus, values close to zero represent a good fit.

[c] Refers to the number of stimulus pairs ranked incorrectly by the estimated function as a percent of the 360 pairs used in the estimation.

[d] Incomplete, i.e., one or more of the estimated preference weights turned out to be zero.

in 66 to 77 of the 90 paired comparisons, the exact number depending on the individual in question. The odds *against* obtaining 66 or more correct predictions out of 90 independent trials merely by chance are better than 100,000 to 1.

The estimated value functions were then applied to the constrained optimization problem defined at the beginning of this chapter.* A special mathematical programming algorithm was developed in order to exploit the model's structure efficiently, and the problem was solved separately for each individual's value function.[13] A summary of the results for those participants with completely defined value functions is presented in table 9.6.

The entries in table 9.6 show, for example, that the optimal solutions for the remaining fourteen individuals were evenly divided between recommending a smaller or a larger faculty at Stanford than the one there in 1973/74, which numbered 650 FTE. There was considerably more agreement regarding student-body size: nine of the fourteen favored a smaller student population while only five chose a larger one.

We also noted from this exercise that in more than half the cases an individual's optimal solution occurred on the boundary of the constraint set, i.e., with one or more of the PPVs at its prespecified lower or upper limit. This was disturbing to us because the PPV limits represented our own subjective

---

*Actually, we omitted the growth-rate constraint from the mathematical programming setup after we found that it introduced serious numerical sensitivities into the solutions. Instead, we calculated the growth rate of tuition postoptimally to achieve the required balance in growth rates. The tuition growth rates calculated in this manner were all within the range of acceptability for Stanford.

Table 9.6.   Comparison of Optimal Configurations with Current Operating Point for
a Group of Fourteen Stanford Administrators

	Proportion Favoring:		Probability Level[a]
	Decrease	Increase	
Total faculty ($FAC + AFAC$)	0.50	0.50	n.a.
Ratio of FAC to $AFAC$	0.50	0.50	n.a.
Total students ($UG + GR$)	0.64	0.36	0.21
Ratio of UG to GR	0.71	0.29	0.09
Tuition	0.21	0.79	0.03
Ratio of S to FAC	0.64	0.36	0.21
Leverage	0.71	0.29	0.09

SOURCE: Hopkins, Larréché, and Massy 1977, table 3, p. 372. Reprinted by permission of *Management Science*.
   [a] Probability of getting at least this difference, if the true proportion is 50 percent; computed from the binomial distribution.

estimates of how far one could realistically change the university's current configuration in any particular dimension. In a sense, then, the limits were intended to summarize the effects of the large number of ill-defined constraints that restrict the institution's ability to undergo a major transformation within any reasonable planning horizon. Given the obvious degree of arbitrariness in selecting particular values for these limits, it was regrettable to find so many of the solutions pressing these bounds.

We observed that in many cases our participants had used certain key ratios—most commonly the student-faculty ratio—to aid them in making their choices. We therefore decided to try a transformed-variable model that replaced the original PPVs by these ratios at the estimation stage. Accordingly, we repeated the analysis for a sample of six of the original nineteen participants, replacing the variables $AFAC$, UG, and GR in the value function by the ratios $AFAC/FAC$, $(UG + GR)/FAC$, and $GR/(UG + GR)$, while leaving all other variables the same. It was not necessary to readminister the questionnaire for this new analysis; rather, we translated the original data into the new terms and then processed it using LINMAP. The new estimated functions exhibited improved internal consistency in every case.

The final step in the experiment was to compare, for the six members of our subsample, the solutions to the constrained optimization problem that had been obtained by using alternative value functions. Not surprisingly, what we found was that the solutions were similar when both value functions were characterized by a positive consistency index *and* a high prediction proportion. In the cases of individuals for whom either of these conditions failed to hold, there was a markedly different solution when the transformed variable function was used in place of the original one.

Summary of results. Our experiment was a mixed success. Although we were able to develop and operationalize a complete procedure for nonlinear value function estimation and optimization, in the process we uncovered two major pitfalls: (a) the questionable validity of some individuals' estimated value functions; (b) the presence of optimal solutions on the boundary of the feasibility domain. For some individuals the preference functions obtained were highly consistent internally, had a strong predictive power, and were stable after transformation of the variables. For others, the results were not as satisfactory. We can only speculate about the possible reasons; whatever they were, it is clear that individual preference functions must be determined in a rigorous and individualized fashion. A number of steps should be taken to check the internal and external validity of the results; the methods used here will do very well. When appropriate, a limited set of valid preference functions may be selected from a sample of individuals by means of these procedures. When, on the contrary, it is critical to determine the preference function for a particular individual, special measures may need to be taken to improve the quality of the preference information being collected.

The presence of optimal solutions at the boundary of the feasibility domain illustrates the type of problem that may arise from having two independent procedures, one for determining the preference function and the other for carrying out the optimization. The limits for each variable were set at the beginning of the research project to represent what we called reasonable ranges of variation. It is, however, only at the optimization stage that one may find that some of these constraints are critical. To investigate the behavior of the optimum solution beyond the limits of the current constraints would require gathering additional data in the appropriate range of variable values. This may be a difficult and time-consuming process.

The difficulties we have encountered in applying any of the constrained value optimization techniques discussed in this chapter strongly suggest that addressing the optimization problem in explicit form is just too large a chunk for most university administrators to bite off all at one time. Similar findings have occurred in other settings. For example, Jyrki Wallenius (1975) has reported on a set of laboratory experiments he conducted with business school students and managers from industry. The decision makers in these experiments far preferred (and had more confidence in their ability to master) an unstructured search procedure than either of two interactive optimization programs.

An interesting question is whether a DM would not be in a better postion to explicate his or her preferences *after* "muddling around" with an iterative unstructured search procedure. Perhaps, after using the TRADES model to train DMs, one could then succeed in eliciting from them preference information of suitable quality and quantity for use in one of the interactive or closed-form estimation procedures we have been discussing. Some experiments have been performed along these lines at Stanford.[14]

A Decision Calculus Approach

We close this discussion—most appropriately, we think—with a consideration of whether formal decision aids (i.e., models) can be used to advantage in dealing with the full-blown value optimization problem, including demand constraints. The argument in favor of including some demand-and-supply relationships in the optimization model is obvious.

Certain pricing decisions that have a major impact on university budgets (e.g., setting the tuition rate) are coming more and more to depend on outside markets. To recall the point made by John D. C. Little (1970; see our chapter 1, above), models should be complete on important issues if they are to be effective managerial tools. The critical market relationships, then, may have to be included in the formulation, even when no one really "knows" what the correct parameter values are.

The practical difficulties, of course, are formidable. Not only must the decision maker's value function be estimated, but some way must also be found of coping with the uncertainties about the form and parameters of the market relationships. Universities, however, are not the only decision-making institutions that suffer from such ambiguity. Little has described decision making in the field of industrial marketing, for example, in the following way.

> Marketing has high managerial content in the sense that decisions are often nonroutine and usually require a bringing together of people, ideas, data, and judgments from diverse sources. Although something is known about underlying processes, much uncertainty remains to confront the manager. Data is prolific but usually poorly digested, often irrelevant, and some key issues entirely lack the illumination of measurement.[15]

What university administrator would deny that this just as aptly describes the way things are in his or her own arena of decision making?

Yet some practical successes have been claimed with quantitative models in marketing, as Little reports.[16] The type of tool that he recommends for dealing with a situation in which many parameters are uncertain is a rapid, flexible, on-line computer model that makes these parameters easy for DMs to see and play with. The chief idea is to give them the opportunity to test their judgment on the few parameters that quantify the most critical relationships underlying the process in question. In the course of making such runs they will come to identify the quantities that really make a difference. Having done so, they will then consider mobilizing further resources—analytical and otherwise—to reduce the range of uncertainty about these items.

To take a relevant example, one might want to know whether or not the actual value of the tuition-price elasticity really makes much difference to the university. This could be tested by asking the question, How might you do things differently if you learned that the tuition price elasticity was y instead x? where x and y represent the best judgments about practical lower and upper limits of this parameter for the institution in question. By invoking the model to answer this question one is assured that the answer will be developed within an agreed-upon and internally consistent structure.

Little's name for the kind of tool needed to address a complex decision problem that has many uncertain parameters is *decision calculus*. He coined the term in the context of model-building to aid managers in dealing with pricing, advertising and sales force appropriations, and similar important but "soft" decision areas in business firms. These models were designed expressly to help managers make better decisions on the basis of imperfect information about key marketing parameters. We think the same approach is called for in dealing with the university's value optimization problem, and so we shall apply the same term here.

The ingredients of our decision calculus are of four primary types:

1. A (relatively small) set of decision variables;
2. The DM's value function defined on these (and possibly some other, auxiliary) variables;
3. One or more financial constraints;
4. A set of market-derived relationships.

These components of the problem need to be incorporated in a flexible, on-line procedure that provides easy access to the subjective parameters.

In the same spirit of compromise between completeness and simplicity that Little has argued for, we shall propose as a prototype version of the university's model one that contains six primary decision variables, three financial constraints, and four market equations. This level of detail leads to a fairly rich structure that can be exploited for important new information without loss of intellectual control. It thus serves as a good starting point in developing the decision calculus approach, and it certainly is sufficient for our expository purposes.[17]

The Prototype Model

The key variables in the model are defined as follows.

Let $x_1 = FAC$ = regular faculty (FTE)

$\quad x_2 = UG$ = undergraduate enrollment (autumn head count)

$\quad x_3 = GR$ = graduate student enrollment (autumn head count)

$\quad x_4 = T$ $\quad$ = tuition rate

$\quad x_5 = R$ $\quad$ = indirect cost rate on sponsored research

$\quad x_6 = M$ $\quad$ = expenditures for fund raising

$\quad x_7 = SR$ = direct expenditures for sponsored research

$\quad x_8 = TG$ = total gifts (expendable and endowment) raised from private sources.

Note that the first three of these variables describe the physical configuration of students and faculty, while the next three single out the variables that play a predominant role in determining university revenues (and an important one in demand relationships). The variable SR is a surrogate for activities in the research sphere, while TG denotes gifts that are used in support of academic programs. Given values for T, R, M, and certain of the other variables, the variables UG, GR, SR, and TG are assumed to be determined by outside markets.

The financial constraints are the conditions for first-order budget equilibrium; they are further restricted to balanced growth of endowment payout, on the one hand, income from all other sources, on the other. Before the constraints can be expressed, however, we must show how budget expense, B, and income, I, depend on the decision variables.

FORMULATION 9.1. For reasons that soon will become clear, we first separate the budget into its direct and indirect components:

$$B = IN + AID + M + IC \tag{9.1}$$

where IN = instructional budget

AID = student financial aid budget

M = fund-raising budget (a decision variable)

IC = budget for indirect costs (i.e., overhead activities).

Now each of the budgets in this equation can be constructed from the decision variables by use of the appropriate financial parameters, which are not viewed as belonging to the subjective set; rather, they are assumed to be known or at least derivable from actual accounting data.

$$
\begin{aligned}
IN &= a_{10} + a_{11}FAC + a_{12}UG + a_{13}GR \\
AID &= -a_{20} + (a_{224}UG + a_{234}GR)T \\
IC &= a_{30} + a_{37}SR + a_{39}IN.
\end{aligned}
\tag{9.2}
$$

Here, a_{20} is the contribution from restricted aid sources, entered with a minus sign because it offsets a portion of the need. Obviously, we have made some simplifying assumptions in writing (9.2); for instance, if a significant portion of indirect costs were found to depend on student enrollments independently of instructional costs, additional terms would need to be added to the third equation.

On the income side, we include separate terms for tuition revenue, TUR, indirect cost recovery, ICR, gifts, and other income, OI:

$$I = TUR + ICR + \eta TG + OI. \tag{9.3}$$

The parameter η signifies the fraction of gifts that is "expendable," i.e., that can (and presumably will) be spent in the operating budget soon after the gifts have been received. Separate equations are used to relate the first two income components to the primary variables. In the case of tuition revenue, we have

$$TUR = b_{124}T \times UG + b_{134}T \times GR \tag{9.4}$$

where b_{124} and b_{134} are the appropriate FTE factors. Budgeted indirect cost recovery is the product of the indirect cost rate, R, with the research volume, *SR*, less a contingency reserve, *ICRES*:

$$ICR = R \times SR - ICRES. \tag{9.5}$$

To develop the standard first-order equilibrium constraints, we (or rather the model) calculate the equilibrium endowment payout rate, given a base endowment value E and the long-run total return and budget inflation factors, from equation (6.12) (note that in the current application $h = 0$ and $\zeta = (1 - \eta)TG/E$):

$$p = \rho + (1 - \eta)TG/E - r - f. \tag{9.6}$$

This p-value is then placed in the single-year budget constraint,

$$B \leq I + pE \tag{9.7}$$

which, of course, needs to be expressed in terms of the primary variables through the use of (9.1)–(9.5).

We come next to the demand functions to be used in the model. Four are needed: one for each type of student, plus one each for sponsored research and gifts. We recognize that here one is working with uncertain, and hence judgmental, parameters. We therefore propose to use the constant-elasticity form, the chief advantage of which is that it reduces the number of parameters to a bare minimum, one for each variable associated with a given demand item. In logarithms this form is linear. Accordingly, after making assumptions about which variable should enter each demand equation, we write:

$$\log UG = k_2 + \varepsilon_{21}\log FAC + \varepsilon_{24}\log T$$

$$\log GR = k_3 + \varepsilon_{31}\log FAC + \varepsilon_{34}\log T + \varepsilon_{37}\log SR$$

$$\log SR = k_7 + \varepsilon_{71}\log FAC + \varepsilon_{75}\log(1 + R) \tag{9.8}$$

$$\log TR = k_8 + \varepsilon_{81}\log FAC + \varepsilon_{86}\log M.$$

The ε_{ij} appearing in these equations represent the elasticity of demand for x_i with respect to x_j, while the k_i are normalizing constants calculated to balance each equation when initial values are used for all the variables. Thus the ε_{ij} are viewed as subjective estimates, while the k_i can be calculated from actual data.*

In addition to the financial and demand constraints, we must recognize that the indirect cost rate cannot exceed the amount allowable under government reimbursement policies. (It might, however, be less if the university decided

---

* Note that the effective "price" of a dollar's worth of direct expenditure for sponsored research is $1 + R$.

to forego some of the recovery for which it was eligible.) Following the scheme laid out in chapter 4, we assume that the recoverable portion of indirect costs can be approximated by a fraction consisting of a fixed term plus a second term that is proportional to the research/instruction mix of direct costs. Under this assumption, we can write the constraint as

$$R \times SR \leq \left[\delta_0 + \delta_1 \frac{SR}{SR + IN} \right] (IC + DEPR) \tag{9.9}$$

where the parameters δ_0 and δ_1 should be derivable from accounting data. Notice the appearance of a term for depreciation, $DEPR$, in the indirect cost sum above; this non-cash-flow item must be added to the cash expenditures to yield the total pool of indirect costs.

This completes our development of the constraints. For an objective function, we assume a weighted-ideal-point model for which the DM must specify (a) ideal values and (b) substitution rates for whatever variables are to be included. Only the first four of the variables we have defined are included in the value function; the others have primarily financial implications rather than academic ones. (Of course, if one wished to attach intrinsic values in the objective to such financial quantities as IN and SR, this certainly could be done.) Thus, we assume

$$V(FAC, UG, GR, T) = w_1(FAC - FAC^*)^2 + w_2(UG - UG^*)^2 \\ + w_3(GR - GR^*)^2 + w_4(T - T^*)^2. \tag{9.10}$$

The ideal values FAC^*, UG^*, etc., and marginal rates of substitution, MRS, between FAC and the other variables, belong to the set of subjective parameters for which the DM must specify values at the time the computer run is made. Given ideal values for two variables, x_1^* and x_2^*, and the MRS of x_2 for x_1 at the current point (x_1^0, x_2^0), the program will calculate the objective weight

$$w_2 = (\mathrm{MRS}_{21})^{-1} [(x_1^0 - x_1^*)/(x_2^0 - x_2^*)].$$

Of course, the option must be provided in the computer program whereby the DM can easily change any ideal point or MRS value and discover its effect on the optimal solution.

The Interactive Program

The logic of our computer implementation for this decision calculus is illustrated in figure 9.13. When the user logs on, the program automatically initializes the model with data stored on two separate disk files. One file, which should be viewed as being relatively permanent, contains all the relevant financial data, while the other contains the subjective parameters. Once the initialization has taken place, the user is prompted for any changes that he or she may care to make in the subjective data set. (To preserve the integrity of the financial data, one would probably want to arrange them so that items

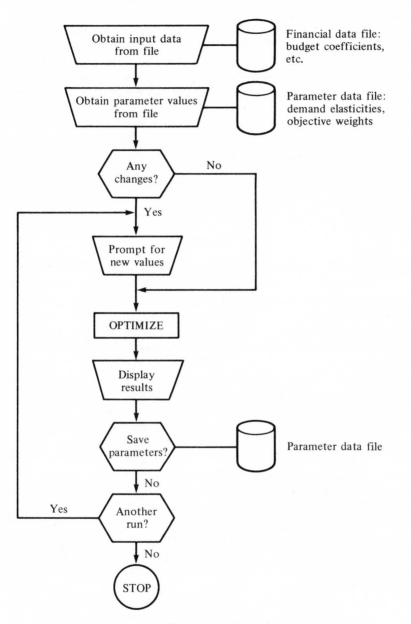

Figure 9.13. Flow chart for the decision calculus program

in that set could only be changed by running another computer program separate from the model and with more limited access.)

Each time a parameter or group of parameters is varied, the program reoptimizes according to the new data and displays the results. At this point, the user is asked whether the new parameter values should replace the previous ones in the disk file; following this he or she is given the option of quitting or making another run. Whenever the latter option is selected, the program recycles through the input prompting, optimizing, and display routines.[18] Of course, it goes without saying that the program should be set up to "speak the user's own language" when it requests information on line. For example, the parameters to which the user is given access must be described in the way in which that person is likely to think about them. The reader who is interested in following an analysis actually performed with this model should consult appendix 10.

Conclusion

In this chapter we hope to have convinced the reader of two things about the use of planning models in universities. First, various technical and operational complexities make the value optimization problem very difficult to deal with in explicit form. Second, because of the complex nature of this problem, no single model or approach is likely to do. Several approaches need to be tried out, refined, and developed to the point where the decision makers involved can really come to grips with at least one of them. Without the involvement and support of key administrators in this exercise, there is little hope of getting the institution to face its overarching planning problem.

Given the essential role to be played by decision makers in carrying out this exercise, great thought and care should go into the computer software that is developed to house whatever models are used. At the outset, considerations of human engineering should dominate concerns over the formulation of constraints. We say this because, unless the program is designed to overcome a decision maker's natural resistance to a systematic and comprehensive handling of the optimization problem, it will never get used. As Wallenius has remarked, in connection with the experiment we referred to earlier, it may be that "the man-machine cooperation in the interactive methods tested is not ideal. A logical direction for future research would be to attempt to better adjust the methods to match the characteristics of a human decision maker and vice versa" (1975, p. 1395).

We agree emphatically with Wallenius that more effort is required in designing the appropriate interface between the user and the computer program. The answer to whether or not design features can ever be invented that will overcome the difficulties of formulating and solving the macrodecision problems of universities will have to await further developments in the field. We remain optimistic, and are hopeful that some readers of this volume will be motivated to do research on this fundamentally important problem.

Summary

In this chapter the value optimization problem that we introduced in chapter 3 is covered in much greater detail. Here the emphasis is on practical approaches to solving that problem. After describing it in general mathematical terms, we discuss the requirements for obtaining a direct solution. Often these are too stringent to be met in practice, in which case the university planner must settle for one or another indirect means.

The TRADES model was developed at Stanford to facilitate making plans that do not violate the conditions of long-run financial equilibrium. It is a flexible and inexpensive tool for searching the set of feasible primary planning variable (PPV) configurations in a number of ways. The various options it provides for making budget projections and revealing financial tradeoffs are described and illustrated here.

This is followed by a discussion of methods for solving the macro-decision problem in an interactive environment (i.e., one in which the decision maker [DM] actually converses with the computer). After dealing with the general features of all such methods we go on to particularize them in two forms: a general algorithm, and a special routine that is part of TRADES. The TRADES implementation uses a less direct approach and therefore takes considerably longer to work through; it does, however, contain other features that are more attractive from a DM's point of view.

Next, we take up the topic of value optimization in closed form. Here the DM's value function is first estimated from data that he or she must provide. The function is then inserted in a computer program that automatically finds the solution without any further participation on the DM's part. Alternative estimation procedures are compared, including the so-called double-tradeoff method and a method that was designed to do the job with data only on the preference ranking of a set of PPV configurations. Results are presented from a pilot experiment conducted at Stanford that tried to apply both of these procedures to the university decision problem.

The final model presented in this chapter takes demand-and-supply relationships into account as well as financial and operational constraints. Solving the complete problem is a very ambitious undertaking and, given the current state of knowledge about the demand for university services, it requires one to make certain compromises along the way. A solution technique is offered in the form of a "decision calculus," which allows for easy experimentation with any of a number of uncertain-demand and other parameters.

We conclude the chapter by summing up what we have learned from considering various ways of dealing with the value optimization problem. The current state of the art is found to be lacking in a number of ways. In particular, more attention needs to be paid to making the computer programs that are employed in such endeavors more hospitable to their users.

Notes to Chapter 9

Works cited here in abbreviated form are more fully described in the bibliography at the end of this book.

1. See Samuelson 1974, or most intermediate texts in microeconomics; see also the discussion in chap. 3, above.

2. See Hadley 1964, chap. 9.

3. We are indebted to Merrill M. Flood for formulating and programming this algorithm for us. Earlier research at Stanford, based on a different interactive optimization scheme, is reported in Wehrung, Hopkins, and Massy 1978. While it was far more elegant mathematically, the algorithm employed in that work imposed too much structure on the decision maker to be of much practical use.

4. See, for example, Flood and Leon 1964, 1966.

5. For further details see Flood 1978.

6. Zeleny 1976 is a good reference for the theory behind this approach.

7. See, for instance, Srinivasan, Shocker, and Weinstein 1973.

8. An excellent reference source for the reader who seeks deeper understanding of value theory and its application to multidimensional preference problems is Keeney and Raiffa 1976.

9. See Keeney and Raiffa 1976, chap. 3; Fishburn 1976.

10. Documentation and running decks for the LINMAP computer program may be obtained from Allan D. Shocker at the School of Management, University of Rochester, Rochester, New York.

11. A complete account of this experiment will be found in Hopkins, Larréché, and Massy 1977. For the data estimation procedures see Larréché, Hopkins, and Massy 1977.

12. The case study was prepared by Jean-Claude Larréché, a doctoral student in business at Stanford; it is included in this book as appendix 12.

13. How to maximize the efficiency of a computer solution procedure is a constant concern in nonlinear programming. Further details on the procedure used in this instance may be found in Massy and Hopkins 1975b.

14. See Dickmeyer 1979.

15. Little 1970, p. B-466.

16. Ibid., pp. B-471–B-482.

17. A more complete formulation was proposed in Massy and Hopkins 1975a. It was never fully implemented on the computer, however.

18. We are indebted to Professor Leon Lasdon for formulating and to Eric Rosenberg for writing the computer program that enabled us to run this model on Stanford's IBM 370/158. This program made use of the GRG code developed by Lasdon, Jain, and Rattner (1976) to perform the nonlinear optimization.

10

Applying the Planning Models at

Other Schools

We have now come full circle in our rather complete tour of the planning models currently in use at Stanford and some other universities. Along the way we have tried to show how these models have aided top-level decision making at Stanford. Yet we recognize that many factors, such as its relatively large volume of sponsored research and degree of reliance on an endowment, distinguish Stanford from most other schools. Thus we would not be surprised if, at this point, the reader is wondering about the applicability of these techniques to other kinds of institutions. What about the case of a smaller college with hardly any endowment and a budget supported almost entirely by tuition? Or of a public university that is almost totally dependent for its funding on the highly unpredictable outcome of a political process?

By reviewing several examples of similar models implemented elsewhere, we hope to demonstrate that many of the planning tools discussed in this book can be applied directly at many colleges and universities besides Stanford and, in some cases, at other kinds of nonprofit organizations as well. Still others are based on concepts that certainly apply to different types of schools, even though the specific form of the model may have been tailored to fit the situation of a major privately endowed research university. As we shall see, it is nearly always the case that a model designed to "fit" one institution's budget format, say, cannot be expected to fit another's in its original form. Nevertheless, while institutions may apply somewhat idiosyncratic labels to their budget items, there is a similarity in their underlying financial structure that provides a common thread for modeling purposes.

For example, it is well known that faculty and staff salaries and fringe benefits constitute the lion's share of expenditures in all college and university budgets. It should make sense in any budget forecasting model, therefore, to separate the faculty and staff into whatever categories are relevant and then to deal with FTEs, salaries, and benefits as separate planning variables. Such a model would have the cost structure we described in chapter 4, even though the number and labeling of personnel categories might well be different. A similar point obviously can be made regarding calculations of tuition income for a private institution. Thus, if we are to consider the question of whether a model can be used elsewhere, we must be sure that we are talking about its structure (the concept) rather than its categories and their labels (the form).

On the Transferability of University Modeling Concepts

At this point, it would be well to reconsider our modeling concepts in the light of the transferability issue. Let us begin at the most general level, with the paradigm for budget planning that was developed in chapter 3. There, we formulated the problem as one of finding values for a set of primary planning variables that would maximize the institution's value function subject to a budget constraint. Due to its generality, we can safely assert that this paradigm is equally applicable to private universities, public universities, smaller colleges, and, for that matter, just about any other institution that is organized on a not-for-profit basis.

In later chapters these concepts became more operational. Chapter 4 laid out the specifications for a medium-range financial forecasting, or budget projection, model. There, we developed the basic building blocks for representing a university budget in such a way that rapid revenue and expense projections could be produced under a variety of planning assumptions. We know that such financial simulation models are in use throughout higher education, and we would venture to guess that in this age of tight resources few institutions would not have some use for them.

The budget projection model can be simple or complex, depending on the amount of detail it incorporates and the extent to which financial submodels are used. By and large, most institutions have the same types of expenses; thus one would not expect there to be a great difference in the way the models adopted by different institutions would represent the expense side of the budget. Most differences are likely to lie on the income side, where the relative emphasis given to such items as tuition, gifts, indirect cost recovery, state appropriations, and endowment payout will depend on a given institution's degree of reliance on each. Indeed, we know of one campus of a major public university with a budget projection model in which expenses have been worked out in careful detail, by object within functional categories, but in which income is missing entirely. This is because the state appropriation forms the only source of revenue for the operating budget (tuition money paid by its students goes directly back to the state), and the campus planners lack confidence in their (or anyone else's) ability to predict future appropriations. This model is used, therefore, to determine what level of appropriation is needed to attain certain goals, such as maintaining the current set of programs in the face of anticipated inflation.

Generalizing TRADES

The basic projection model can be embedded in a structure that facilitates tradeoff analyses (as discussed in chapter 9) among an institution's primary planning variables. The Stanford TRADES model was developed as we were learning to live within the constraints of long-run financial equilibrium and had begun to need better financial tradeoff information, i.e., information more rapidly obtained, and on a more consistent basis. TRADES has proved to be an invaluable budget planning tool. Moreover, by looking after the financial details, it has enabled the university's top officers to concentrate more thought on optimizing their subjective values.

As we write this, several other schools are experimenting with their own versions of TRADES. Among them are another major private research university (Harvard) and a smaller private university (Lehigh). In addition, EDUCOM, which is a nonprofit membership organization of colleges and universities, has developed a generalized version of the model in the hope of making it more widely available (Updegrove 1978). As one of its more convenient features, this EDUCOM Financial Planning Model incorporates a special computer language for expressing the institution's financial structure and constraints as defined by the user. This language enables the user to define variables or structural relationships and input them as data, rather than having to write his or her own computer subroutines.

We believe, then, that there are excellent prospects for the application of TRADES to other kinds of institutions. Of all the models with which we have worked, this one appears to be the most directly exportable. Not that we believe there exists a single set of financial routines adequate to describe the budget relationships at any institution in sufficient detail. The budget structures and accounting policies of colleges and universities are far too idiosyncratic for this to be true. The key to seeing where it can be used is to separate in one's mind the institution's financial constraints from the search options provided by TRADES. The latter most certainly can be useful to any serious effort at forecasting and tradeoff analysis; planners everywhere should benefit from not having to reinvent these subroutines when they want them.

The chief idea of a generalized TRADES model, then, is to provide an umbrella-like structure of convenient forecasting and tradeoff options within which any institution can insert its own set of definitions of variables, report formats, and financial routines. The TRADES package might even include a very general budget formulation into which the institution could fit its data to get the model running. The formulation should be so simple that it becomes obvious to the managers involved that they need to develop a better financial model, yet it needs to be realistic enough to capture their interest from the start.[1]

Production and Cost Models

Next, we turn our attention to the production and cost models discussed in chapter 5. The large-scale, disaggregate cost-simulation models described there have been tried out in many different kinds of institutions and, in some cases, are still being used. When successful they have been limited chiefly to community colleges and rather specialized kinds of institutions (e.g., medical schools), for, as we indicated, such models are not really designed for costing or resource allocation at a general college or university campus. Also, it takes a great deal of work (chiefly data gathering) to get them running.

What about the more aggregate formulations, in which cost and revenue coefficients were constructed from a network representation of student flows? We would argue that models of this type can be useful to any institution that is interested in studying the likely financial consequences of a change in admissions or degree programs. Here, the distinction between public and private institutions is of very little consequence. In fact, the same model has been applied at Stanford, the University of California's Berkeley campus, and the University of Colorado.[2] It is more important, if this type of modeling is to be worthwhile, that there be a sufficient number of different cohort types, with significant interactions, so as to give richness to the structure. For this reason, we would expect the model to be more applicable to a university than to a smaller college. Also, the planners at the institution in question must be willing to consider new ways of configuring student inputs and outputs. If the institution is viewed as indissolubly wedded to its current mix of undergraduate and graduate degree programs, and the inputs are stable, it makes little sense to construct a model for testing changes in these variables. There still may be some value, however, in working through the construction of the production and cost functions in terms of enrollments, so that the budgetary consequences of changing some basic parameters, such as average class sizes or faculty course loads, can be examined.

The Financial Equilibrium Concept

In chapter 6 we went to some lengths to study the dynamic interrelationships between budget variables in different time periods. This ultimately led us to the notion of long-run financial equilibrium and (for institutions that find themselves some distance away from a stable budget growth path) to a particular kind of model for planning the transition to equilibrium. These concepts, and hence the models derived from them, are of course most applicable to institutions with a fair degree of control over their budgets. The critical role played by endowment in these calculations is evident from even a quick review of the equilibrium concept. The endowment is a primary link between budgets in consecutive years, and the tradeoffs between payout and endowment growth provide a richness of structure not otherwise obtainable. The size or complexity of the budget seems not to be particularly important, however. Thus, we view the equilibrium concept and the models that embody it as being definitely applicable to endowed institutions of any size, but with much less to offer a college or university that has little or no endowment.

This is not to suggest that any institution, whether public or private, could fail to benefit from learning more about the conditions for its own long-run financial viability. In the absence of an endowment, this amounts (just as it did in our calculations of financial equilibrium) to matching up the longer-term expected growth rates of income and expense, for when the institution does not have much of an endowment, all tradeoffs must be viewed primarily in terms of growth rates. Once the growth rates have been determined, a change in the budget at time t will have little effect at times $t + 1$, $t + 2$, etc., other than to perpetuate whatever surplus or deficit is introduced by that change. Contrast this with the situation where extra endowment payout can be used to plug a financial gap in any given year, but only at the cost of progressively lesser amounts of endowment payout being available in future years. Our conclusion is that, if income from endowment is not a significant component of the budget, it probably makes more sense to concentrate one's efforts directly on an automated projection and tradeoffs model, like TRADES, rather than first trying to develop an independent equilibrium model.

As for the transition-to-equilibrium model, its transferability should be judged in the same way. The greatest potential for its use is at an endowed institution that finds, as a result of carrying out its own calculations of financial equilibrium, that its endowment payout rate currently is too high. This model obviously has been a great help at Stanford in planning for an orderly transition from a budget that had grown out of proportion to the endowment to one that represents a more stable posture. A similar story can be told of Oberlin College in Ohio, whose provost used our model to determine a transition sequence requiring budget cuts that amounted to slightly under 10 percent of the original base. The model helped him convince the Oberlin faculty of the need for such measures and thereby made it possible for them to get on with the job. Incidentally, Stanford's transition model, formulated as it was in very aggregate terms and without budget submodels, turned out to be completely transferable to Oberlin in its original form. No variables or equations were changed; only new data had to be entered to make the model valid.

Budgeting Under Uncertainty

Sooner or later, any institution engaged in serious budget forecasting will become concerned with prediction errors. Given the uncertainty inherent in all forecast estimates, budget planners will want to know, for example, what the chances are of running a deficit even when the "best-guess" prediction is for a balanced budget. Calculation of such chances, performed well in advance, can help to avert unfortunate surprises that have sometimes been sprung upon unsuspecting administrators and trustees at the time when financial results have been reviewed.

As we saw in chapter 7, the probability of deficit is inversely related to the size of the conditional budget, while the seriousness of actually running a deficit depends on the operating reserve. These concepts, and the stochastic control models derived from them, are applicable to any institution able to quantify the uncertainties in its income and expense predictions. Given the vagaries inherent in the political process, this probably rules out most schools that are publicly funded.

Notice that the applicability of the probability models discussed in chapter 7 really does not depend on the existence of an endowment. True, the endowment did enter into some of our calculations, but its role was chiefly as a major source of budget uncertainty. There are plenty of other uncertainties that plague virtually all educational institutions (consider, for example, tuition income when enrollment is driven by demand), and so the need for such models, in the private sector at least, is quite common. When endowment is not a factor, it and the smoothing rule for payout obviously would not be used; most likely, endowment would be replaced in the models by some other major income variable, such as tuition. Parenthetically, we should note that endowment is distinctive in that one must of course save some total return in order to retain equilibrium. In contrast, all tuition revenue can safely be spent in any given year.

We have found the conditional budget to be a particularly rich and meaningful concept when we come to consider the probable errors in our future budget plans. Interestingly enough, few schools acknowledge the presence of such an entity, let alone deal with it in a formal and systematic way. Rather, the tendency is to be somewhat conservative in estimating income, so as to "tuck away" some money that otherwise would be used in support of ongoing expenses. Only by formalizing these practices in a statement of conditional income which is allocated only as the year actually progresses do we gain the capability to discuss what the amount withheld means in relation to the institution's regular operating budget and long-run goals. It requires only one further step of logic to bring the conditional budget, the operating budget, and the operating reserve together in a single stochastic control model, which then enables one to do a complete job of budget planning under uncertainty.

Human Resource Modeling

Finally, we come to the techniques for modeling human resource flows that were developed in chapter 8. In this area, more than any other, we see opportunities for application in all segments of higher education, regardless of an institution's size or source of funding. As long as (a) there is a need for accurate enrollment projections, (b) the faculty tenure system prevails, and (c) concern over the employment of women and minorities is widespread, there will continue to be many uses for the different types of flow models that we discussed.

There is no question that enrollment projection models of some type are in use nearly everywhere; they range from very simple to very complicated. One of the purposes of our review has been to acquaint the reader with this variety of choice. Probably, most institutions still use returning enrollment or grade progression ratios to predict enrollments of continuing and returning undergraduates. Some Markov chain models are in use, but no cohort models, as far as we know, except at Stanford and Berkeley.

Models for predicting freshman yield are becoming more and more familiar in private higher education. This is hardly surprising given the current serious concern over an aging national population and resistance to the ever-increasing cost of attending a private school. We know of efforts parallel to our own that have taken place at Bucknell and Carnegie-Mellon universities. No doubt countless other schools are conducting similar kinds of analyses with respect to their own freshmen populations.

As for faculty tenure planning, there is a universal need for this sort of analysis whenever an institution either has reached a stable size or is in process of cutting back. Markov-type models have been used to study faculty flows not only at Stanford but at Berkeley, Oregon State, and undoubtedly many other schools as well. Like TRADES, these models are structurally transferable from one kind of institution to another. Since, however, they are straightforward to program, most institutions have found it just as easy to write their own as to adapt one developed elsewhere.

As an aside, we cannot resist pointing out that the same modeling techniques that we have used in faculty tenure planning are just as applicable to service organizations in the profit-making sector. For example, law, accounting, and consulting firms all operate under a de facto tenure system in which a person initially joins for some probationary period and later becomes eligible for life-long partnership. The future pattern of professional employment in these firms, and the frequency with which they will be able to bring in new blood, obviously depend on the promotion fraction, just as they do for a college or university.

Our models for affirmative action planning could also be widely applied. Just about any organization that chooses systematically to examine its future employment opportunities for women and minorities will find it worthwhile to engage in flow modeling of this sort. While the categories of personnel being studied may be quite different, the basic concepts to be used are those presented at the end of chapter 8.

A Pilot Experiment in Modeling and Technology Transfer

In fall 1976 a group of four institutions joined with us in an experiment to test the transferability of the modeling concepts developed at Stanford to other schools. The project was directed by Joe B. Wyatt, formerly president of EDUCOM and now vice-president for administration at Harvard University, and was funded by a grant from the Lilly Endowment. The other schools involved were Harvard, Lehigh University, the State University of New York at Albany (SUNY–Albany), and the University of Pennsylvania (Penn). While admittedly it was a small group, these four schools provided a diversity of organizational structures, styles for decision making, and degrees of support from public revenues.

Initially, we exposed the group to the following set of financial models: budget projection, long-run financial equilibrium, transition to equilibrium, and TRADES. Each institution then went off to try out one or more of the models on its own data. Periodic meetings were held during the ensuing fourteen months to check on each school's progress and to provide a forum for members of the group to share their experiences. Not surprisingly, the experiences of the four schools were quite varied. A brief summary follows.[3]

Harvard. In contrast to Stanford, which traditionally maintains a high degree of central authority over the budgets of all but two of its schools, Harvard operates in a highly decentralized mode, with each school having practically complete autonomy. Initially, a budget projection model was constructed for the largest school, known as the Faculty of Arts and Sciences (FAS). The model was run with a number of different sets of planning assumptions, and these runs were the subject of much fruitful discussion both within FAS and between FAS and the central administration. Perhaps their greatest value was in pinpointing areas of excessively high growth within the FAS budget. Such areas could then be probed more deeply by creating new, more refined submodels or, as actually happened, by developing separate, more detailed financial models, each of which was restricted to the particular subunit being examined.

The group at Harvard decided to take a closer look at Buildings and Grounds (B & G) and at the undergraduate library, using in the former case a budget projection model and in the latter a version of TRADES. These particular choices were guided partly by a concern over excessive future cost rise and partly by administrative considerations. In the case of B & G, the head of the operation was reporting directly to the vice-president for administration, who also was in charge of the modeling activity; this was in contrast with the original FAS situation in which the analysts worked with a dean who had the ultimate authority over the budget, but who was basically skeptical about whether the model could be of much help. Another factor that contributed to the success of the B & G model was that the deans and faculties of each school were themselves concerned about the potential for runaway costs because the B & G budget was getting charged out to the various units for which they were responsible. Since their own autonomy was not threatened by the model, they could much more easily accept its potential as a decision tool for use by the central administration.

The decision to model the library budget was based on a somewhat different set of circumstances. In this instance, the budget responsibility resided in the dean of FAS; however, initially he was quite concerned about library inflation, and had had the matter under study for some time. This situation made it easier for him to appreciate the value of a model incorporating library income and expense data in a way that would facilitate tradeoff analyses. Of course, the model was not greeted so kindly by some library staff, who no doubt felt threatened by the dean's easy access to a vehicle for examining tradeoffs in their own activities. This sort of tension arises when models are viewed at the lower echelons as powerful tools in the hands of a higher authority. Administrators at other institutions who are considering implementing their own models of subunits would be well advised to keep this in mind.

The choice of models used by the Harvard group in their examination of the B & G and library budgets was guided by two considerations: the complexity of the operation, and the purpose being served. The B & G budget was relatively easy to understand and, since the primary emphasis here was on trying to gain cost control over line items, a simple projection model sufficed.

The library, on the other hand, represented a very intricate system with many interlocking parts. Since the decision makers involved were keen to separate the fixed from the variable costs of the library operation, and since they were anxious to take a hard look at various financial tradeoffs within the operation, TRADES seemed to be the appropriate vehicle.

What did these ventures into modeling actually do for Harvard? Regrettably, the final story cannot be told here: at the time of this writing, these exercises still were being actively pursued. At a minimum, however, the models had served to illuminate financial relationships that previously had been ill understood; to focus discussions on the variables that had been found to exert the most leverage; and, ultimately, to educate the administrators and others involved about their future options. Of course, the difficulty of abandoning traditional styles of management should not be minimized. Indeed, the progress made at Harvard was quite remarkable when one considers the psychological and organizational hurdles that initially had to be overcome.

Lehigh. As at Stanford, budget parameters at Lehigh—a medium-sized private university located in eastern Pennsylvania—are set centrally, but unlike Stanford, Lehigh derives no less than 80 percent of its operating budget income from tuition.

Before the project began, the administration already had acquired some sophistication in financial forecasting. A simple off-line (i.e., noninteractive) budget projection model was in place and had revealed some future growth-rate problems that would need to be brought under control. At the same time, the budget planners at Lehigh had begun to feel they had outgrown their basic projection model and were in need of a more advanced means of analysis. The deficiencies of the existing model were observed to be that: (a) it was not understood very well by most constituencies and was viewed as a furtive and even conspiratorial operation; (b) it lacked sufficient structure for dependable calculation in certain areas, particularly in the modeling of financial aid and utilities costs; (c) the search for configurations of planning variables that would satisfy the conditions of financial equilibrium could be conducted only by trial and error. In the hope of overcoming these difficulties the planners decided to apply TRADES.

Initially, the Lehigh group took the TRADES computer program developed at Stanford and inserted their own financial routines, including the appropriate submodels. (Some of these were suggested by earlier models at Lehigh, and some by the work at Stanford.) They also chose to overhaul the tradeoff options so that the model would conform to the way in which financial tradeoffs were generally viewed. Specifically, this involved identifying a set of "feasibility pivot variables" (really, these were their primary planning variables), and then setting up the model so that any one of these variables could be selected to gauge the distance from feasibility when everything else was fixed. In other words, a feasibility pivot variable was one that might have been used to plug the gap when the assumed values for all other variables failed to meet the necessary equilibrium conditions. The set consisted of (a) the growth rates (in real terms) of tuition price, salaries, and other expenses, and (b) the endowment payout rate. For whichever item was chosen, the model would report the value that would be necessary for financial equilibrium.

As of this writing, the Lehigh TRADES model had been operating for about one year. The budget planners had found TRADES beneficial. In particular, —and unlike the earlier, trial-and-error technique—it had greatly facilitated their search for feasible budget configurations. Also, they had found it easier to involve representatives of their various constituencies in actually running the model, and thereby had succeeded in removing some of the mystery that had shrouded financial planning activities in the past. The model was undergoing further refinements, including reincorporation of the original Stanford tradeoff options, and probably had become a fixture.

At the same time, it should be noted that the Lehigh group was forced to devote a very considerable effort to reprogramming the Stanford TRADES model once they had decided to implement it. This was necessary because the structure of the Stanford model already had become too closely adapted to our institution's way of looking at things to be directly applicable elsewhere. It was in recognition of this problem that development of the far more flexible EDUCOM Financial Planning Model was undertaken.

SUNY–Albany. As a medium-sized public university campus with very strict state control over most of its operating budget, the State University of New York at Albany provided a pure public-sector test bed for models that had achieved some success in the private sector. The state of New York controls SUNY's expenditure budget at the line-item level within each major function; moreover, tuition receipts are passed directly along to the State, as are dormitory charges, so neither represents a source of revenue at the campus level. Finally, it was evident to the campus planners that too little attention had been paid to longer-range considerations in reaching agreement with the state funding authorities about one-year budget allocations.

Under the circumstances just described, it was logical for the modeling strategy at SUNY–Albany to begin with the development of a computerized tool for projecting expenditures several years into the future. These projections were made by line item within function category, and hence were dependent upon growth-rate estimates made at that same level of detail. Much of the effort was expended on the methodology for developing systematic estimates of these growth rates.

The SUNY model was designed to operate interactively. Its chief function was to generate a sequence of future cost indices for discussion with authorities at the state level. These indices could be displayed at various levels of aggregation. They could also be translated into dollar budget projections that when coupled with the assumed growth rates for state appropriations, enabled the model to project a sequence of "deficits" for each major function.

In evaluating their experience, the SUNY–Albany group reported two advantages gained with the model. First, while the nature of the campus's fiscal problems already was well known, the model had helped to gauge their magnitude. Second, it had assisted them in their efforts to engage the state in more serious discussions about the longer-run financial future of the university. In recent years, decisions had been handed down from the state that the funding for a particular functional area would be increased by only 2 percent, say, and that it was up to the campus authorities to find a way to live within that sum. Since the campus already had endured a sequence of real budget reductions, the model strengthened SUNY's position as it began to point out the consequences if this trend were to continue.

Of course, these consequences could be portrayed only in financial terms, since the model lacked a representation of the budget in terms of physical variables. We would imagine that SUNY's case might be made even more persuasively if the projected budget deficits could be described numerically in terms of fewer faculty, fewer students, higher work loads, lower salaries (and presumably lower-quality faculty and staff), etc. Ultimately, such tradeoffs would need to be made simultaneously along several dimensions, in which case a TRADES approach would recommend itself. Still to be assessed, however, are the political dynamics of revealing one's internal tradeoffs to the major external funding source, and so it is impossible for us to say whether such an approach would recommend itself to a public institution.

Penn. Like Harvard, the University of Pennsylvania is an Ivy League institution with a major commitment to research and graduate instruction. The primary responsibility for budgeting at Penn (again as at Harvard) resides with the schools, although the university moved away from a more centralized operation only as recently as 1973. By 1976 the university administration had devised a rather elaborate system of overhead charges, tuition taxes, and subventions for use in determining each school's budgeted share of the general funds. Within this overall budget constraint, decisions were to be made locally about the appropriate mix of items to be supported by a given school's allocation.

Previous modeling efforts at Penn had been in direct support of this new system. For example, projections had been made of each school's operating budget two years in the future, under what were called "default" planning assumptions, and these had then been used to engage the school in discussions that would lead to corrective action. A simple model also had been devised to assist in longer-range planning. This model made estimates of each school's so-called durable resources under the new budgeting formula, and then, by assuming that the fraction of the budget used to support regular faculty would remain fixed at its current or some other level, converted these dollar figures into the equivalent numbers of tenured faculty slots. The last-named figures could be compared with current faculty levels, both tenured and nontenured, to see what the limitations on hiring and promotion might be over the near-term future. While ostensibly the model was designed to produce faculty tenure plans, in fact it had served the much wider purpose of getting the deans to focus more effectively on the issue of balancing needs with resources over the five-year planning period. Because the model made it easy to change assumptions about future amounts and mixes of income and expenses, it provided a convenient vehicle for examining various kinds of options available to the school for keeping its budget out of deficit.

As it happened, the planners at Penn had real difficulty in seeing how they could introduce the more aggregate, centralized planning models developed at Stanford into their particular environment. With many of the important tradeoffs and budget decisions being made at the school level, a model of the entire university's operating budget did not seem to make much sense. At the same time, a self-sufficient model of a school's budget would need to deal with the administration's inputs as coming from outside, and would therefore fail to show how they linked one school with another.

It may seem strange that having the model deal explicitly with the linkage between schools was deemed essential at Penn but not at Harvard. Indeed, Harvard's FAS projection model had entries for the overhead charges levied by the central administration, but had no difficulty in treating these as exogenous variables. The explanation lies in the degree of decentralization represented by the budget-making styles of these two universities. At Harvard, each tub truly does sit on its own bottom; each school keeps all its earned income and there is no central fund for the awarding of subventions. By contrast, a fair degree of centralized budget authority still is maintained through Penn's system of taxes on tuition income and centrally determined subventions. With its built-in mechanism for reallocating income among schools, the new system at Penn was (and probably still is) highly controversial. Under these circumstances, one can easily understand why the administration would hesitate to introduce a budget planning model for a school when the model neglected the financial interplay with other schools.

Although the Penn group would have liked a model such as TRADES for performing interactive tradeoff analyses at both the central and school levels, it would have had to have taken the form of an interacting collection of models of the individual schools—a collection that also incorporated the relevant university-wide decision variables, such as the endowment payout rate. The model should have been capable of displaying outputs for any particular school, but it also should have had a feature for aggregating and displaying them for the university as a whole. We offer the outlines of such a "hierarchical TRADES model" in the next section of this chapter.

Guidelines for Modelers

The lessons of this pilot project have been summarized by J. Wyatt.[4] His five major recommendations, we believe, are worthy of any potential model user's serious consideration.

1. *"Decision makers who use models must be involved in their development."* Modeler and decision maker, Wyatt emphasizes, should work closely together. The decision maker needs to know what the model is for and how it works. Likewise the modeler needs to know exactly what kinds of decisions involving what variables will have to be made by the decision maker. For all these reasons, effective communication between modeler and decision maker is essential.

The modeler, in particular, should be a skilled interpreter not only of the model's technical requirements but of its user's needs and values.

2. *"Data must be representative and reliable."* The data requirements of the four institutions that took part in the project had nothing in common that could be specified as a standard component of all university planning models. There can be no universally transferable set of data elements, Wyatt concludes; moreover, the temptation to incorporate ever finer levels of detail in the model should, in his opinion, be resisted.

3. *"Models must have an executive godfather."* The project suggests that a planning model is far more likely to be accepted if it is backed by an "executive godfather," that is, a key executive (preferably the university president) who "makes it happen." Almost as effective in this role, according to Wyatt, is an executive who reports directly to the president and who is trusted by the rest of the executive staff.

4. *"Models must be comfortable to their users."* The key to acceptability is simplicity, not only in the model's analytical formulas but in its inputs and, above all, its outputs. Once the model's usefulness has been established, there may well be a period of general enthusiasm for models and modeling. Modelers should beware lest, during this period, they raise unjustifiable hopes of what their models can do. Wyatt suggests that, in general, no major changes should be made to the model "unless they contribute specifically and directly to the desired output that is understood by both the decision maker and the modeler."

5. *"Results must be communicated with care."* Model outputs may be controversial just because they come from a computer (for the same reason, they are often misinterpreted). At least two ways of coping with this problem were found among the schools that took part in the project. At Harvard, every effort was made to downplay the role of planning models in decision making. Policy alternatives were explored quietly among small groups of executives; policy decisions were announced with little reference to the computer at all. Stanford, Penn, and Lehigh, on the other hand, chose to publicize their use of computer-based models. These schools seem to have overcome what Wyatt calls the "computer mystique" that is, the fear that "computers rather than people are doing the planning."

Application of Modeling Concepts to Administrative Subunits

Nearly all the models presented in this book were devised for use by a central university administration, and thus are represented in terms of highly aggregated variables. Does it make sense to apply them at the level of an academic subunit, or, for that matter, to a multicampus university system?

In large part, the answer to this question must depend on what the model is being expected to do. If it is built around a set of independent planning (or decision) variables that exist at either the subunit or the system-wide level, there should be no particular problem in using it to examine tradeoffs in terms of those variables. Harvard's budget projection models for the Faculty of

Arts and Sciences and for the Buildings and Grounds operation, as well as their TRADES model of the undergraduate library, are examples of such applications. Each of these areas at Harvard is administratively self-contained and thus amenable to modeling at the subunit level.

If, on the other hand, the individual subunit cannot be studied in isolation from other subunits or, perhaps, from the central administration either, a different model setup will be required. (A situation like this was encountered in our pilot project at the University of Pennsylvania.) A proper modeling strategy will tie the various subunits with the central administration in a unified framework that embodies the decisions made at various levels within the institution. This is the hierarchical TRADES concept that we referred to earlier and about which we shall have more to say in a moment.

One general caveat in applying models to smaller subunits must be stated. Most of our models are deterministic (or certainty-equivalent) representations of what in reality are stochastic (i.e., random) processes. In many cases, even the so-called decision variables may be subject to random fluctuations. Consider, for example, the tenure promotion fraction used to compute flows in our faculty appointment, promotion, and retirement models in chapter 8. Certainly, the institution is free to set the standards governing the promotion of faculty to tenure, and these standards, in turn, will be reflected in the promotion parameters of the model. Given any particular group of junior faculty, however, it will not be possible to predict the exact proportion of them who will make it to tenure.

The significance of this observation in the current context is that the smaller the unit, the less reliable will be the prediction. In more formal terms, whenever the variables or parameters of a model are subject to random fluctuation, the smaller the absolute size of these quantities the greater, in proportional terms, will be the statistical variance inherent in the predictions made by a deterministic model. At some point the predictions become practically meaningless, as when, for example, the unit holds a total of 10 faculty positions and the model predicts a promotion flow of 0.2 faculty members per year.

With this caution in mind, one should be careful not to subdivide the units of prediction to the point of meaninglessness. How does one know when such a point has been reached? There are no hard-and-fast rules for determining an answer. Rather, it is part of the art of model building to judge when a particular problem no longer is amenable to a deterministic form of analysis. One's judgment will be tempered by whatever estimates are available of the statistical variances in the relevant parameters. Fundamentally, however, the decision about whether to construct a deterministic model of a particular subunit must be based on the purposes for which the model is to be used.

Hierarchical TRADES

We envision a model that lends itself easily to examining tradeoffs among PPVs at the subunit level, while retaining the budget constraints of the university as a whole. The subunit might be a single campus within a multicampus university system; or a school, an academic or administrative support operation; or even, possibly, an academic department within a single college or university campus. To accomplish this, such PPVs as faculty and graduate students, and their coefficients in the budget equations, will need to be represented internally in disaggregate terms, although the model should be able to aggregate for display purposes. Of course there are some PPVs that do not need disaggregate representation because they are typically determined at the central level; examples are undergraduate enrollment and the undergraduate tuition rate. A DM from the central administration should be provided with easy access to all PPVs belonging to any subunit as well as to any PPVs aggregated across subunits. The model might even be set up so that the administrator of a subunit has access to any variable or coefficient that belongs there but not to any others. This probably would be the best setup for budget planning and value optimization in a decentralized organization.

A schematic representation of hierarchical TRADES is shown in figure 10.1. At the lower levels, we assume that there are m planning variables, labeled $X_1, X_2, \ldots, X_m$, somewhat under local control. Presumably, this is the same set of variables for each subunit, and we use a superscript k, as in X_i^k, to denote the value for the ith PPV in the kth subunit. In addition, there is a set of n planning variables under direct central control, which we label $X_{m+1}, X_{m+2}, \ldots, X_{m+n}$. Budget functions also exist for the individual subunits; we let $B^k(\mathbf{X}^k)$ stand for the (net) budget of the kth subunit as a function of that unit's PPVs. This may also be a function of one or more central PPVs, such as the undergraduate tuition rate, in which case the notation would need to be expanded. The figure shows that planning takes place at the subunit level in terms of the subunit PPVs, X_i^k, $i = 1, 2, \ldots, m$; and with reference to the budget function B^k. For central university planning, the resulting X_i^k and B^k values must be aggregated so that plans can be made in terms of the overall configuration of university PPVs, X_i, $i = 1, 2, \ldots, m + n$.

To convey the general notion, let us suppose there is a single overall budget constraint of the form

$$B(\mathbf{X}) = 0$$

(e.g., total expense minus total income equals zero). This would be represented inside the model as

$$B^0(\mathbf{X}) + \sum_{k=1}^{K} B^k(\mathbf{X}^k) = 0$$

where $B^0(\mathbf{X})$ is the part of the budget that is controlled centrally. Whenever the model was used to examine tradeoffs for subunit j, say, the central budget, $B^0(\mathbf{X})$, and all other subunit budgets, $B^k(\mathbf{X}^k)$ for $k \neq j$, would be fixed, and only the net budget (local expenditures less local income) for that subunit would be affected. (Note the similarity of this approach to the hierarchical value maximization model described in chapter 3.)

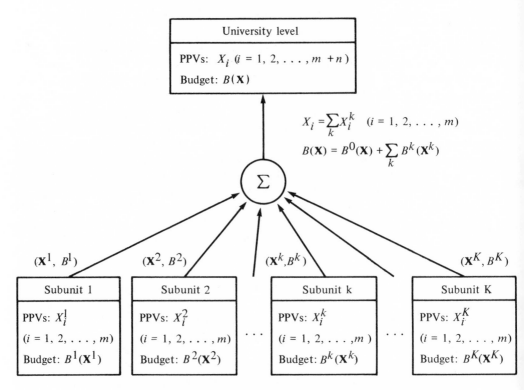

Figure 10.1. Schematic diagram for hierarchical TRADES

To facilitate analyses conducted at either the local or central level, the user options of TRADES should be adapted as follows.

1. *Changes in aggregate variables.* Suppose that a central administration user wishes to examine changes in a PPV belonging to the subunit set. To facilitate such analyses, it might be advisable to build into the model a rule governing the apportionment of aggregate changes in such a PPV among the subunits. For example, if the user desires to change the value of one of the composite X_i's, say X_j, across all the subunits, the model might be programmed to make the same proportional change in each X_j^k, unless instructed otherwise. This would be the default option in manipulations at the central level of any composite PPV. Of course, the program should allow for this option to be easily overridden, thus enabling the user to change each X_j^k individually.

2. *Display options.* The model should be capable of displaying PPVs and financial summaries for any individual subunit, as well as for the institution as a whole.

3. *Single-variable feasibility searches.* These should be capable of operating in three modes. In the first, each PPV would be taken in the aggregate and, for PPVs relating to subunits, manipulated as above. In the second mode, one would specify a particular variable and obtain feasibility information by

subunit. For example, the resulting display for the variable representing faculty might look like this:

	Regular Faculty		
	Min Value	Last Value	Max Value
Subunit 1			
Subunit 2			
Subunit ·			
Subunit ·			
Subunit ·			
Subunit K			

The third mode would reverse this scheme so that the feasibility search would take place over all PPVs relating to a particular subunit. In this mode of operation, the display for the subunit representing the engineering school, for instance, might take the form

	Engineering School		
	Min Value	Last Value	Max Value
Regular faculty			
Auxiliary faculty			
Staff personnel			
. . . etc.			

4. *Feasibility searches in multiple dimensions.* Finally, we come to the TRADES options for eliciting feasibility information on two or more variables at a time. (This would include the two-way feasibility graph discussed in chapter 9.) The most flexible procedure would be to have the user specify a pair of numbers, the first to identify the PPV and the second to identify the subunit, for each variable to be used in the tradeoffs. If the second number were zero, the variable would represent the aggregate value of the PPV across all subunits. Setting the options up in this fashion would make it particularly easy to examine tradeoffs in any of the following ways: between two or more variables in the same subunit; with the same variable between two or more subunits; or between two or more PPVs aggregated to the central level (in which case changes in each of the PPVs would be assumed to occur proportionately in each subunit).

Having thus laid out the basic specifications for a hierarchical TRADES program, we must emphasize that several practical difficulties will have to be surmounted before it can become a reality. First, adding further layers of disaggregation to a model that already contains a large number of variables, parameters, and equations is bound to multiply several times over the number of calculations involved in making a single feasibility check. Unless strenuous efforts are made to increase the efficiency of the program, it will become too slow and too costly to run. It would be wise to start with a basic budget model that omits much of the fine detail of the original TRADES. By making reasonable approximations (e.g., in place of financial submodels), it should be possible to reduce the number of calculations for an aggregate budget run by a factor of three or four. In addition, since all boundary searches are performed numerically, it certainly would be worthwhile to install in the program the most efficient search algorithm one can find. Finally, if the hierarchical model will be used heavily for central budget planning, some thought should be given to building in routines for approximating the overall effect on income and expense of a proportional PPV change in all subunits. If, for example, a single coefficient can be calculated to approximate the aggregate effect of changing the numbers of faculty in each subunit by the same proportional amount, this can be used in making university-wide feasibility checks. This should suffice for preliminary planning purposes. Only when a new aggregate value is incorporated in the working configuration will the refined budget calculations need to be made, at which time a new aggregate approximation can be obtained as well.

Such are the technical obstacles that currently stand in the way of producing a live, running version of hierarchical TRADES. Given the current state of computer technology, we do not regard any of these obstacles to be insurmountable.

Getting Started with Planning Models

The process of developing planning models is very much an open-ended one. A good deal can be accomplished with just a little effort: a week's work or less may be all that is needed to get started with a simple version of TRADES, and the same can be said of the long-run financial equilibrium models presented in chapter 6. But we must confess that the right kind of modeling, once it has been experienced, usually whets an institution's appetite for more of the same. More accuracy, more flexibility, more power, more detail—the vistas are endless as long as modeling is viewed as being useful. We believe such appetites are healthy and have found that satisfying them is well worth the costs if the work is done right. We suggest, then, that not only should institutions consider getting a taste of modeling but that they should be prepared to make a long-term commitment to it.

We are often asked whether planning models have anything to offer the small institution. Can the small institution even afford modeling? Our answer to both questions is, unequivocally, yes. Once again, TRADES provides a good case in point. The expense of getting started is modest and the program costs very little to run, yet the benefits from the thinking that goes into using TRADES can be significant. Having tried out TRADES, the institutions can henceforth make decisions about longer-term commitments on a cost-effectiveness basis.

But what of such practical matters as the number of technical staff to hire or the type of computer to lease? Where should the effort be lodged administratively, and how should it be supported by the chief administrators? What is a logical sequence for model development? We shall have some suggestions to make in answer to these and related questions presently. First, however, we must recognize that the most basic decision any institution is liable to face is whether to develop its own computer models or to try to import them from outside. Our recommendations on this matter are given below.

The "Make-or-Buy" Decision

As a general rule, we would strongly recommend that each institution be prepared to develop and program its own set of aggregate planning models rather than procure them ready-made from some outside source. We say this for at least two major reasons: (a) the differences in styles of record keeping and decision making among institutions undoubtedly will influence the form their respective models will take; (b) the very process of model building almost always yields valuable insights about the system that is under study.

With regard to (b), we cannot emphasize too strongly the value to be gained from engaging in this process of introspection and modeling at the local level. Indeed, an institution often can expect to gain as much from going through the model-building process as from making actual runs with the model when it is finished. Certainly, technical assistance should be solicited from the outside if it has to be. But only if the budget planners at the institution in question play a leading role in developing the model will they come to feel that it is really theirs. And, in conformity with a general rule of human nature, it is only when they have this personal investment in the model that they are likely to take its outputs seriously.

Of course, there may well be an opportunity to purchase a well-documented computer program from outside that is versatile enough to accommodate a specific institution's modeling needs. An example is the EDUCOM Financial Planning Model, discussed above. Ideally, one should look for programs that can provide the superstructure for the models being developed locally. In this way, one can take advantage of the expertise and development costs already invested in a general-purpose computer program, while preserving the opportunity to inject the institution's own characteristics into the model's actual structure. Whenever such a program cannot be found, the development of the model and the program should be undertaken locally; it is simply a waste of time and money to import some other program that is neither adequate nor versatile enough to do the job. Novice users need to be particularly cautious about importing large, detailed models that have not been fully tested in environments similar to their own. Several unfortunate stories can be related about the experiences of certain institutions that failed to observe such caution in the late 1960s and early 1970s.

For the most part, the actual programming of the small, aggregate planning models we have discussed in this book is a relatively minor task. Most of the models we used earlier on at Stanford—and they included the long-run financial equilibrium and transition-to-equilibrium models, as well as all the personnel-flow models discussed in chapter 8—were programmed by one of us or by one of our research assistants in a few lines of APL code. The more time-consuming tasks have to do with defining the proper variables, building the equations, and obtaining the necessary data. Whether or not one is able to find a good model on the outside, these tasks still need to be performed locally. Indeed there is no sense in trying to apply models at all unless the institution itself is prepared to do the essential groundwork.

Staff and the Organizational Environment

On the personnel front, we feel there are two necessary preconditions for a successful venture into modeling. One is the hiring of a well-trained operations research analyst who is competent to work out technical details and write programs when necessary. This person should have a good quantitative background, including graduate-level coursework in statistics and modeling techniques, plus a basic understanding of the nature of a university. If the analyst is properly positioned in the organization and has the attention of the top administrators, he or she can serve as the keystone for a successful modeling effort. A single full-time analyst hired at a fairly senior level may be enough to do the job. If extra analytical support is needed, very often this can be provided at minimal cost by drawing upon the institution's own graduate student population.

The hiring of a staff analyst is necessary but not sufficient to get the effort under way, for many modeling ventures have failed for lack of support by top management. It is essential, therefore, that the staff analyst have the full attention and support of high-level administrators, particularly the academic ones. Usually, there needs to be at least one well-placed administrator who is an enthusiast from the first and can act as the model's "executive godfather," in Wyatt's phrase.

Once the analyst is on board, it is vital that provision be made for him or her to take part in the central planning process. There can be no more certain way to failure than to set the model builder to work in isolation from the problems. To be effective, this person needs to be a party to most of the important planning discussions. The best way to ensure this is to make the analyst a member of the regularly constituted budget planning groups so that he or she can translate the groups' ideas into modeling terms.

Staff and organization at Stanford. The modeling work at Stanford was conducted principally by DSPH and WFM, the first of whom (the "analyst") was located on the staff of the vice-provost for budget and planning and the second (the "advocate" and also a model builder) was serving as vice-provost for research, only two levels removed from the president.* Probably it was significant that at the outset both of us were located on the academic rather than the business side of the central administration.

Two groups had been established for budget planning within the adminis-

---

*As a vice-provost he reported to the vice-president/provost who, in turn, reported to the president. The provost also served as an advocate at crucial points in the process.

tration. The senior Budget Group was chaired by the provost; it included the president, the vice-president for business and finance, and their staffs. This group monitored key budget parameters as they were being developed. In addition, a Budget Staff, chaired jointly by the vice-provost for budget and planning and a deputy of the vice-president for business and finance, provided the necessary staff support. As we noted in chapter 2, DSPH was a member of both groups, while WFM belonged to the Budget Group only.

Further support of the modeling effort was provided by the Office of Management and Financial Planning, a separate agency within Business and Finance. The director and his staff were constructive critics, and helped also to provide much of the requisite data. In order to cope with the exigencies of budgetary retrenchment, a close alliance was developed between the Office of the Provost, Management and Financial Planning, and the Office of the Controller. This alliance also proved invaluable in furthering the modeling activities.

Finally, we were able to call on graduate students from the Ph.D programs in the Graduate School of Business, the Department of Operations Research, and the Department of Statistics. For most of the project, one or two research assistants were employed half-time during the academic year and full-time in the summers. They helped to develop some of the models and wrote many of the computer programs. Since they lacked detailed knowledge about the university, however, they could not help much with the data. Student interns from the School of Education, who were assigned to the Academic Planning Office, also provided invaluable assistance.

In summary, our experience suggests that a lot can be done with a small nucleus of professional staff that is permitted firsthand experience of the major problems and given wide latitude in deciding upon the proper analytical approach. The minimum complement is one centrally placed professional model builder working with a higher-level "advocate"; not many more may be needed. If more analytical manpower is required it can usually be found on the existing staff of the business office and among the population of graduate students in management science, operations research, statistics, and related programs.

How to Maintain Intellectual Control

Having described staffing requirements, we will now offer some advice on how the client-administrator can keep the process of model building under intellectual control. Unfortunately, it is all too easy for an effort at model building to get out of hand if the technicians and decision makers drift out of communication. When only the technicians know why the models do what they do, then this is undoubtedly happening. We discussed the problem in chapter 1 and have also quoted Wyatt's guidelines for preventing its occurrence. Here are a few additional guidelines of our own.

1. *Decision makers should know their models.* Members of the top-level budget and planning groups should be encouraged to have practical experience of models and modeling. It is important for the decision makers to know how much control they have over their models. It is equally important that the model builders listen and try to make changes to overcome the shortcomings that are perceived in the models.

2. *Model builders should share their assumptions.* The technical staff should always write up and circulate the assumptions that underlie any forecast or model. Sometimes a model builder is dissatisfied with the way in which some item has been modeled. By sharing the full set of assumptions with the decision makers and various other staff members he or she can often obtain good suggestions as to how else to proceed.

3. *The computer can be challenged.* The analysts must be ready to explicate in simple terms and perhaps calculate by hand any number that a model produces, should any decision maker question it. Results often are counterintuitive (at least initially) when there are a number of feedback loops. We have found it very helpful to stop a session and show how the questioned numbers were derived. Even if no error is found (and it rarely is, in our experience), the decision maker becomes better able to deal with the model.

4. *Model builders don't know everything.* Specialists in relevant subject areas should be involved in developing the model whenever appropriate. We could not have built our indirect-cost recovery submodel, for example, without the aid of those who negotiate the recovery rate. Although we found our views of the process to be somewhat different from theirs, every session with them improved our understanding.

It is not easy to maintain intellectual control when there is practically no end to the ways in which the model can be enhanced and extended to cover ever more budget situations. In the long run, however, intellectual control is essential for validity and credibility. Accordingly, one must proceed cautiously with enhancements while broadening participation. Sometimes it is better to eschew expansion into complex areas, especially when the returns from doing so are small. From time to time it is even a good idea to retreat to less sophisticated techniques until greater understanding can be achieved and shared. Always the objective must be to develop models that are credible and helpful rather than merely interesting or technically sophisticated.

Computers and Data Resources

It is clear that a serious modeling effort will require computing facilities beyond the capabilities of an electronic calculator. Ready access to an interactive programming language such as BASIC or (our own preference) APL is essential. Many computer installations offer interactive FORTRAN or dialects of ALGOL, all of which can also be used to advantage. Most medium-to-large institutions already own or lease large computers that have such capabilities. Two alternatives available to smaller colleges currently lacking computers of their own are to purchase a minicomputer to support both the modeling and basic accounting needs of the campus or to lease time on a large computer located at some other institution. In recent years, computer networks such as TELENET and TYMNET have been established; they can link a user located on one college or university campus to the computer at any of a large number of others.* Through a local telephone connection, then, the network provides a means for gaining remote access to almost any kind of computing resources one might need.

It should also be clear that the models cannot be run in the absence of actual historical data on the variables and parameters of interest. This does not mean it is necessary to launch an intense effort to design and implement a formal management information system before the models can be effective. Most of the models presented in this book are not at all hungry for data. Generally they involve a small number (tens, not hundreds or thousands) of variables and parameters, most of which should be available from any institution's basic budget, registrar, and personnel records. Whenever we lacked one or more pieces of necessary data, we would either sit down with the specialists to work out an approximate value or else launch a small-scale effort to investigate the appropriate historical files.

Institutions that follow a strategy of starting small, instead of getting bogged down with large-scale, more detailed sorts of models that consume many hours of data processing and computing, will find that a lot can be done on a relatively small computer budget and with data that are more-or-less readily available. In our opinion a good model for planning purposes is one that has few variables or parameters—and just the right ones. Usually, the numbers that need to be fed into the model, and those that are produced as output, will fit on just a few pages.

Perhaps an anecdote will help to make the point about how much can be done even without staff, major computer support, or a formalized management information system. We have already mentioned the application of the transition-to-equilibrium model (discussed in chapter 6) at Oberlin College. The provost of that school read about the model in one of our early reports. Working just from our paper, he was able to program his own version and test it out with the Stanford data in a weekend (although a phone call was required to verify some of our numbers), compile his own data for Oberlin in the next few days, and finish the process of applying the model—including consultation with faculty and other constituencies—during a single academic term.

This experience stands out as an example that we hope many other institutions will be able to follow. Those that keep their models small and directed towards answering questions of major importance should find that a well-focused effort more than pays for itself over rather a short period of time.

*TELENET and TYMNET are communications networks for linking geographically dispersed computer resources. At this writing a new network, EDUNET, was being launched with the aim of providing services beyond communications to facilitate the sharing of computer resources among colleges and universities. EDUNET is an activity of the Planning Council for Computing in Higher Education and Research and also of EDUCOM, Inc. The EDUCOM Financial Planning Model, to which we have referred, is available on EDUNET.

Moving Ahead

A development strategy for financial modeling at a college or university is presented in table 10.1. This is a crowded chart, but we do not want to give an impression of overwhelming complexity; each part, in fact, can be rather simple.

Phase 1: Primary Planning Variables

We have reviewed many examples of PPVs in earlier chapters. We believe that they should be couched in terms of activities (X), prices (P), and stocks (S). However, an institution may, like SUNY–Albany, prefer to start with purely financial PPVs such as dollar figures for object-of-expenditure categories. Such a strategy avoids any need to determine the breakdown between fixed and variable costs, since projections and tradeoffs are made directly in dollar terms. However, the use of X, P, and S comes closer to the real decision problem of the university, and makes the planning model richer and far more powerful than if it lacked the capacity to separate activities from costs.

Often, too little attention is paid to the selection of PPVs. For instance, a projection model based on aggregate financial figures may identify problems but offer little guidance to administrators who must find ways of solving them. Some PPVs, at least, must be controllable by decision makers. All should be important, understandable, and so defined that data can be made available or subjective judgments brought to bear. That is, the selection of PPVs should take account of how planners and decision makers actually look at problems. Finally, the controllable PPVs (i.e., the decision variables) should be acceptable, in the sense that they can be talked about openly within the institution's organizational and political environment.[5] PPVs should be chosen carefully since they limit the choice of questions and hence of plans.

Phase 2: Financial Structure Models

Since we have said so much about financial structure already, little needs to be added here. Aside from the problem of variable cost determination, the main issue is how various revenue and cost items are linked and how they depend on institutional policies. Examples are the effect of tuition growth on financial aid expenditures and of changes in support costs upon indirect cost recovery from research contracts and grants. These and similar questions were considered in chapter 4.

Phase 3: Production and Demand Submodels

We have argued that not enough is known about production and demand relations to warrant a comprehensive modeling effort, and that any submodels must include ways to take account of the intangible variables. However, the decision maker must come to grips with such relations somehow. For TRADES, production and demand considerations may enter via operational constraints, the value maximization process, or both. In any case, as much understanding

Table 10.1. A Development Strategy for Financial Planning Models

Phase	Tasks	Issues	Learning Objectives
(1) Primary planning variables (PPVs)	Identify variables on which institutional planning will be focused.	Should PPVs be purely financial or should they be activities (X), prices (P), and stocks (S)? What intangibles should be studied?	Evaluation of variables in terms of (a) understandability, (b) data availability, (c) controllability, (d) importance, and (e) acceptability.
(2) Financial structure models	Develop and quantify relationships between PPVs and revenues and costs: e.g., specify $R(X, P, S)$ and $C(X, P, S)$.	Estimation of variable and fixed costs. Determination of linkages between specific revenue and cost items.	Better understanding of financial structure, including relations between policies and linkages among variables.
(3) Production- and-demand models	Develop models for demand-and-production relations where possible. Specify operational constraints among PPVs.	What is truly important for the institution? To what extent can data and/or judgments be used to specify bounds on the tangible variables in terms of the intangibles?	Better understanding of "production" and "demand" functions, including relations between tangible and intangible variables.
(4) Forecasts and long-run financial equilibrium	Develop internal price or cost-rise indices. Work out mechanisms, for three- to five-year forecasting, for estimating these trends, and doing the computing needed to process these estimates.	How should estimates be made and by whom? How should policy parameters like budget enrichment, tuition growth, and endowment payout be determined? What kind of equilibrium is desired?	Becoming focused on short- and long-run growth rates as well as levels of the PPVs. Use of the long-run financial equilibrium concept, and an ability to make value tradeoffs among rates as well as levels.
(5) Preferred feasible configu- rations	Search the decision space and determine feasibility with respect to financial and operational con- straints. Make value tradeoffs among feasible points.	What effects do feasible changes in PPVs have on intangible variables and institutional value? Who should decide, and how?	Ideally, insight into values, effects of the intangibles, and how these interact with financial realities. An optimum plan.
(6) Forecast errors and smoothing	Develop models describing the deviation between forecasts and actual outcomes in probability terms. Find good ways of compensating for forecast errors and/or absorbing their impact.	What kinds of errors will occur and how big are they likely to be? Will one error be correlated with another? How fast should corrections be taken, and how big should be reserves and other uncertainty- absorbing devices?	Ideally, better under- standing of the uncertainty factors in planning. A better definition of when to be "surprised" by an unplanned outcome. An optimal strategy for dealing with uncertainty.

as possible is needed and certain kinds of submodeling can help. Demand models were covered in chapter 4 and also in chapter 9. Production-function models for institutions, and their implications for the costing of aggregate degree programs, comprised the main subject matter of chapter 5. Some other kinds of operational constraints, such as the ones arising from faculty tenure policies, were dealt with in chapter 8.

Phase 4: Forecasts and Long-Run Financial Equilibrium

A great deal can be learned from close consideration of institutional cost-rise indices, price trends, and dynamic decision variables such as the real rate of budget enrichment. The concept of long-run financial equilibrium, discussed at length in chapter 6, is needed to determine the conditions necessary for continued financial viability.

Phase 5: Preferred Feasible Configurations

In this phase we are concerned with maximizing an institutional value function subject to constraints. There will be financial constraints, and there may be operational ones as well. Whenever possible (it will not be often, given the present state of the art), demand relations should be made explicit and included in the optimization models. Also, more than one time period will be involved if long-run financial equilibrium is to be sought. We said a good deal about these matters in chapter 3. Our research on procedures for finding the most preferred feasible configuration was described in more depth in chapter 9.

Phase 6: Forecast Errors and Smoothing

The last phase of our paradigm for model development deals with uncertainty. One thing *is* known: nothing will come out exactly as forecast or planned. The probability structure of these deviations needs to be modeled and procedures developed for coping with them. We speak of "smoothing" because the procedures amount to softening the effects of unanticipated events, often by spreading them out over time. Our study of planning under uncertainty builds directly upon the certainty-equivalent plans developed by the use of TRADES. As we showed in chapter 7, the outputs of TRADES can be used as inputs to models for optimal smoothing. Ideally, the smoothing rules and random variables could even be incorporated directly into TRADES.

A Program—and a Warning

The six phases of table 10.1 do not necessarily have to be approached chronologically, though there is opportunity for a steady increase in sophistication and complexity as one moves down the list. Many institutions including Stanford have started with computer models for financial projection (part of phase 4). This leads to detailed consideration of alternative PPVs (phase 1), more detailed financial structure models (phase 2), and so on. At Stanford, at the time this was written, we had only recently gotten around to a systematic consideration of uncertainty (phase 6).

The core TRADES program provides a mechanism for doing projections and value tradeoffs (phases 4 and 5) based on a set of PPVs (phase 1) and financial and operational constraints (phases 2 and 3). A basic, generalized version of TRADES might provide a rudimentary set of PPVs and financial structure equations; it might also give the user a language in which to specify constraints. Once some experience has been gained and momentum established, the program can (and should) be modified better to represent the unique circumstances of one's own institution.

Quite possibly, some institutions will develop such financial planning models at the same time that they are trying to model personnel flows using techniques from chapter 8. In any case, most institutions that have not engaged even in rudimentary modeling of student enrollment and faculty tenure planning should find immediate uses for these models, which do not depend in any way on prior developments in the financial area.

We close this section with some strongly felt words of warning. In chapter 3, when discussing theoretical foundations, we repeatedly stressed the importance of the intangible attributes of a university; in chapter 9 we presented a modus operandi for dealing with them within the context of value maximization subject to constraints. By means of this approach we were able to specify all our models in terms of tangible variables only, with the understanding that the intangibles would be handled implicitly by means of the "hooks" provided by the explication and maximization of value.* Unfortunately, the provision of "hooks" does not guarantee that they will be used, and it is possible that the process of focusing on tangibles in this new and more powerful way will downgrade the intangibles. In our view that would be tragic, and would twist the message of this book inside out. We hope and trust that this will not happen.

An Agenda for Future Research

It would be misleading to conclude this book as if all the important general problems have been resolved and there is no room for future developments in modeling for universities. In fact, we can think of several important areas in need of further research.

Financial Projection and Tradeoff Models

In this area, three needs stand out as particularly worth pursuing. First, further research and development is badly needed on variable costing and revenue techniques. We have argued that, to be fully effective, a financial planning model must incorporate information about the full incremental costs

---

*Providing for intangibles in this way should not be confused with the approach, often used in benefit-cost analysis, that assigns imputed dollar values to the intangibles (as when economists speak of the "value" of a human life). We tend to agree with Eric Ashby (1978, p. 52) that such an exercise represents an unfortunate oversimplification. Our approach is to separate clearly the modes of considering the tangibles and intangibles, and to deal with each in their own terms rather than trying to redefine the latter in terms of the former.

and revenues associated with each of an institution's PPVs. Unfortunately, the state of the art allows only for crude estimates of these important quantities. When we wrote this, there were hopeful signs that a serious job of developing appropriate costing procedures soon might be undertaken by a task force of the National Association of College and University Business Officers (NACUBO). Certainly, the current state of ignorance about university cost and revenue behavior was unfortunate, and a national effort on this front was badly needed.

Second and third, there are two logical extensions of TRADES that would greatly enhance its utility as a financial planning tool. One of these, already mentioned, would be having it incorporate a hierarchical structure that would allow for integrated planning at the subunit level. The other would be to introduce the stochastic modeling concepts of chapter 7 into the TRADES formulation. This would be done by specifying variances and covariances, as well as mean values, of the important growth-rate quantities along with the appropriate smoothing rules. A new forecast option would be programmed to perform Monte Carlo simulations or even, perhaps, closed-form estimation of the important measures of uncertainty. The probabilities of running a deficit, exceeding a permissible payout rate, and making sizable budget adjustments are ones that immediately come to mind. Marginal or joint probability distributions of such random variables as effective payout rate, dollar payout flow, and "effective f" (i.e., budget enrichment plus budget adjustment, divided by the previous year's budget) would be particularly valuable outputs to have.

By thus embedding a stochastic structure in TRADES, we would gain ready capability to examine tradeoffs as a function of the parameters of the smoothing formulas and other key quantities. Of course, our comments regarding the necessity for a highly efficient computer code in hierarchical TRADES apply equally well to stochastic TRADES. Since it would take many runs through the model to produce a single simulation run, having an efficient main program would be crucial to the practical success of this new option.

Value Optimization Models

We have used the value optimization framework throughout this book to represent the process of integrating (a) the important financial constraints and (b) a decision maker's preferences with respect to both tangible and intangible variables. We remain committed to the view that a complete practical decision paradigm, based on our theory of university choice, would materially improve the state of the art in university decision making, since it would help administrators to sort out and articulate their values. While progress has been made in this area, development of a unified practical procedure for university choice remains an open challenge.

In chapter 9 we commented at length about the apparent lack of reliable methodologies for preference estimation. More needs to be done to improve the state of the art in this critical area. We would recommend further exploration of interactive techniques for obtaining the kind of preference data used in constructing a decision maker's value function. We continue to believe that, for certain purposes, closed-form estimation and optimization can offer significant advantages over interactive optimization. However, closed-form optimization will not be practical until such a time as an individual's value function can be estimated to reproduce more faithfully the decisions he or she would make.

To the extent that certain supply constraints (e.g., gifts) and demand constraints (e.g., enrollments) are binding on the institution—a situation that is becoming more and more frequent nowadays—such constraints should be included explicitly in the formulation of its value optimization problem. Yet so little is known at this time about the demand-and-supply relations affecting a college or university that working with the proper formulation is precluded. Further research on the manner in which certain institutional decision variables affect these relations is therefore highly desirable.

Our final suggestion relating to the problem of value-optimization is that it really ought to be addressed in the context of group decision making. It is truer of a university than of most other organizations that solutions to problems are arrived at through consensus. This means that our models, which incorporate the values of a single decision maker, do not adequately represent the true decision process. To deal with this problem, one can either attempt to estimate a *group value function* or else find a way to represent the process by which compromises are made between two or more parties whose values may differ. We suspect the latter approach will prove to be more fruitful, since there is good reason to believe that different decision makers have somewhat different values (at least in terms of how they weight the various factors).

Fortunately, there are some promising new developments in the field of group decision models. One technique for resolving intragroup differences that has worked in other settings is the Delphi method (for which see Dalkey 1969). This takes the form of successive iterations in the course of which information is provided about the distribution of the solutions preferred by group members, along with their stated reasons. Each round attempts to narrow the range of disagreement by influencing each individual to move closer to the center of the group. After a few rounds the process usually converges on a single solution that represents, in some sense, the best compromise. Of course, this technique is valid only when each party has equal weight as far as the final decision is concerned.

More recently, Merrill M. Flood (1978) has proposed a dynamic "value voting" procedure that seems especially applicable in a university setting. The essence of this scheme is a rational and objective method for assigning weights to each individual's preferences according to the depth of his of her feeling (also possibly adjusted for the person's level of importance as a member of the group). Through a process of sequential voting, the algorithm will arrive at a group compromise that best meets these desirable criteria. We feel that this technique comes closest to fitting the actual decision-making style of universities, and would therefore encourage its application where group decisions are important.

Yet another promising approach is the one developed by Thomas Saaty and others at the University of Pennsylvania (Saaty 1977). This research is directed at building an institutional value function from values held by decision makers who are situated at various levels in the organizational hierarchy. As such, it should be particularly applicable to the same type of situation that gave rise to the proposal for a hierarchical version of TRADES. In fact, an example already exists of a trial application of this technique to a budget allocation problem in a multicampus community college system (Sinuany 1978). We look forward to its further use in other college and university decision situations where a hierarchical approach is appropriate.

Personnel Models

Much more needs to be known about prediction errors in the processes of enrollments, faculty tenure, and staff attrition. We have presented (in chapter 8) a variety of models for making expected value calculations of future stocks and flows of personnel. With one exception (the Markov chain model for monitoring compliance with affirmative action goals), these models do not, however, provide any information about the range of uncertainty surrounding the calculations. Such information can come only from a careful examination of the system's statistical properties, either through closed-form analysis or through Monte Carlo simulation.[6]

Moreover, the value-optimization approach should also be brought to bear on the problems of personnel systems. This area is more riddled with conflicting goals than practically any other: consider, for instance, the need, in deciding on a tenure promotion policy, to balance the junior faculty's morale against institutional flexibility. It therefore requires a more rigorous and systematic optimization approach than has been used before. We envision an amalgamation of the personnel flow models of chapter 8 with the preference optimization techniques of chapter 9. In this way the full power of the analysis would be brought to bear on these difficult and controversial institutional problems.

This suggestion, like all the others we have made, is in keeping with a persistent theme of this book, namely, that it should be the values we hold, not merely the numbers representing the variables and parameters of a model, that influence the outcome of our analysis. The surest way of reconciling the objective calculations with one's subjective values is to incorporate the calculations directly into a value-optimization framework.

By allotting the values a prominent place in the models, we can hope to avert the tragedy of decisions being made purely "by the numbers" in institutions with such cherished ideals as colleges and universities. In so doing, we aim to quiet the fears of administrators who are rightfully skeptical about the potential of computers to replace human judgment. What we *would* like to see computers do is to relieve decision makers from routine numerical calculations in favor of the qualitative, intangible aspects of educational planning.

Summary

This final chapter attempts in several ways to wrap up the discussion of planning models for colleges and universities. First, we discuss the applicability of our models to different kinds of educational institutions—large and small, public and private. Our thesis is that, in concept at least, the models are broadly applicable. We suggest, in particular, a method for applying the TRADES model to subunits within a hierarchical administrative structure.

Second, we offer some guidelines to modelers and decision makers, guidelines aimed at achieving the best integration of their mutual efforts. Suggestions are made as to how other institutions might begin developing and using planning models, and a recommended plan is presented for sequencing the tasks of model development. Precursors of successful modeling ventures—especially in terms of staff and computer support—are also discussed.

Finally, we present a brief agenda for future research. This agenda is grouped into three general categories of models: financial projection and tradeoff, value optimization, and personnel planning.

Notes to Chapter 10

Works cited here in abbreviated form are more fully described in the bibliography at the end of this book.

1. As a postscript we note that, by mid-1980, EFPM was being used by 92 postsecondary educational institutions throughout the U.S. Of this number, 23 were under public control and 28 represented small colleges and religious seminaries. In addition, a French-language version had been implemented at the University of Louvain in Belgium.

2. For Berkeley see Oliver and Hopkins 1976; see also "A Planning and Budgeting Model for the University of Colorado" (term paper prepared under the supervision of Robert M. Oliver by students enrolled in Engineering Design and Economic Evaluation 595, University of Colorado, spring 1971).

3. Wyatt et al. 1979 gives the results of the project in casebook form.

4. Ibid., pp. 6–10.

5. Sometimes variables that decision makers are initially unwilling to change can be turned into decision variables by putting them into the PPV set (see Dickmeyer 1977), but as a practical matter they must be basically acceptable at the outset.

6. For a prototype analysis of the prediction errors in enrollment forecasts see Marshall and Oliver 1978.

Appendixes

Other Modeling Projects at Stanford

A number of other modeling projects were going forward at Stanford, mostly with support of the Lilly Endowment grant mentioned in chapter 2, during the period from 1972 to 1978. While not directly related to the quest for long-run financial equilibrium that has formed the core of our narrative, they are important in their own right. All of them contributed in some way to the LRFF, to actual policy judgments, or to useful avenues of follow-on research.

Preference Modeling

We have already mentioned the work on preference optimization that motivated the development of the TRADES model. Our first attempt at building such a model was to experiment with ways of eliciting preference information from university administrators by means of a paper-and-pencil test and then fit a mathematical value function to these data. Twenty-two friends and colleagues agreed to participate in a pilot test of our methods during the spring and summer of 1974. Working with Professor Jean-Claude Larréché of INSEAD, Fontainebleau, France (who was then a doctoral student in the Stanford Graduate School of Business), we succeeded in obtaining estimates of each individual's value function and, later, optimizing these functions subject to the constraints of LRFE. The results, though interesting, suffered from a number of drawbacks (described in chapter 9), and we did not attempt to put them to practical use. This work spanned the period from the spring of 1974 to late 1976, when the final paper was prepared.

A second experiment in preference optimization was undertaken during the fall of 1974. It was initiated and led by Professor Donald A. Wehrung of the University of British Columbia. The idea of this experiment was to combine the two processes, preference function elicitation and optimization, much as had been done earlier by Arthur M. Geoffrion, James S. Dyer, and Abraham Feinberg (1972) for academic department planning at UCLA. Eight primary planning variables were identified, and piecewise linear approximations to our long-run equilibrium constraints were developed. Optimization was performed interactively: preference questions were asked on line and the answers used in a linear programming procedure (as in Wehrung, Hopkins, and Massy 1978). The project achieved some success technically but did not result in anything of immediate operational usefulness. The problem seemed to be that the LP algorithm imposed too much structure on the decision maker; it kept coming up with counterintuitive results that soon caused subjects to lose interest. (The results from the model may have been helpful to some extent, but that is beside the point.) DSPH worked with Mr. David Clark and Professor Peter Keen to evaluate the model during the spring of 1976. As a result, we decided to abandon the preference optimization experiment and work instead on options for searching the feasible space directly, which in turn led to Dickmeyer's development of the TRADES model.

Student and Faculty Models

Work on modeling the flow of students from year to year in the undergraduate program had been undertaken in 1972 by DSPH and William Witscher, of the Office of Management and Financial Planning. The object here was to predict accurately the fraction of the previous quarter's enrollees who would return the following quarter. A cohort flow model of student enrollments (for which see chapter 8) was developed, and a report was submitted for comment to the dean of students and the registrar in late 1972. The model was used during the winter of 1973 to predict enrollments during 1973/74. The results were good and it is still in use today; indeed, the model has a direct link to policy. The process is as follows. Each year returning enrollments are estimated and added to the number of freshman applicants who accept Stanford's invitation to enroll. The resulting figure is then subtracted from the target enrollment and the difference made up by admitting transfer applicants during the late spring and summer. As a result of this uncertainty-absorbing device and the accuracy of the cohort flow model on which it rests, there is very little variance in Stanford's undergraduate tuition income account.

The other critical student variable, for the undergraduate population at least, is the freshman "matriculant to admit" ratio (i.e., the ratio of those who actually enter the university to those who are offered admission but do not enter). Obviously, not all students who are admitted show up the following autumn. Although the admission of transfer applicants, as we have said, prevents the variance in this figure from affecting the budget, it still is important to understand the underlying forces involved. Since the early 1970s Stanford has collected data on the characteristics of students who do or do not accept its offer of admission and the reasons for their choice. In early 1973 we began to study these data by means of econometric modeling and went on to produce a number of model variations, ending in late 1975 with a generalized least-squares approach. In the latter stages we were assisted by Delores Conway and

Joseph Verducci, doctoral students in the Department of Statistics. The four of us discussed results periodically in a graduate statistics seminar conducted by Professors Ingram Olkin and Rosedith Sitgreaves Bowker. This kind of interaction with faculty and graduate students is invaluable, and represents an immense resource for a college or university that is committed to working with planning models.

The statistics seminar led to a whole new model of enrollment decisions, namely, an advanced contingency-table approach. It was begun by Conway and Verducci in 1975; they finished it in 1978.[1] The method is described and some results are presented for both this and the least-squares model in chapter 8. The principal findings concerned the effect of financial aid policies and family income upon enrollment decisions. The models, together with the findings of a Financial Aid Study Task Force set up during the summer of 1975 by Vice-Provost Bacchetti, added significantly to our knowledge of student choice.

Another kind of human resources model concerns itself with faculty flows. A faculty-flow model tracks appointments and promotions through time, usually for the entire university or some other fairly high level of aggregation, thus enabling forecasts to be made and the effects of policy changes or outside events to be ascertained. This type of model was considered in detail in chapter 8. The chronology of the development of faculty-flow models at Stanford was as follows.

Fall/Winter, 1971/72

DSPH (newly arrived in APO) was engaged by the dean of humanities and sciences to study the prospects for continued appointment and promotion of junior faculty in that school. The dean, concerned about sagging morale due to junior faculty apprehension about their chances at Stanford, was searching for some general quantitative guidelines. DSPH developed a simple two-state Markov chain model, programmed it in BASIC, and made a number of runs for the dean. He, in turn, used the results to reassure the junior faculty that they would continue to have a reasonable chance (i.e., something like one in three) for promotion.[2]

Winter/Spring, 1972

DSPH was engaged by the provost (through Bacchetti) to design and cost out a financial incentive scheme for faculty early retirement. This was perceived to be a natural device for freeing up a few more tenured faculty positions for incremental appointments or promotions now that the "steady-state" had set in. Traditional schemes were discarded in favor of one that would tend to attract the less productive members of the older tenured faculty, while offering less incentive to those whose services continued to be more highly valued. The initial report and recommendations were issued in spring 1972. The proposed early retirement plan was refined and deliberated on campus during the following year, and the plan was officially adopted in April 1973.[3]

(The same early retirement plan was subjected to renewed scrutiny in fall 1978 when the Stanford administration was searching for an appropriate response to federal and state legislation nullifying mandatory retirement. Specifically, the Advisory Panel on Retirement Alternatives, appointed by President Lyman early in 1978, examined the plan and compared it to other, more commonplace schemes for encouraging early retirement. The panel recommended retaining the plan with one minor modification, stating in its final report that the plan, when combined with "more liberal part-time service options" for those who wished to retire gradually, seemed to provide "about the best set of options Stanford [could] offer its faculty in response to the changing legal status of mandatory retirement.")

Spring/Summer, 1975

Task Force IV, directed by the Commission on Budget Priorities to look into "professorial rank and faculty development," was concerned with the feasibility and advisability of budget cuts affecting faculty positions. DSPH collaborated with Arthur I. Bienenstock, the vice-provost for faculty affairs, on faculty-flow analyses of impending cuts; the models used were ones developed by DSPH earlier.[4] These analyses led directly to Task Force IV recommendations for a general target of 20 percent new appointments to tenure and a 20 percent tenure promotion fraction, as contrasted with historical values of 33 percent and 40 percent, respectively, in the School of Humanities and Sciences. In recognition of the high quality of Stanford's junior faculty, the administration later adopted a 30 percent promotion rate guideline instead of the more stringent 20 percent recommended by Task Force IV. It is clear from this chronology that faculty-flow models played an important role in policy determination at Stanford, partly in connection with the implementation of the Budget Equilibrium Program and partly on more general questions of faculty manning and development.

Models of Indirect Cost Recovery

Indirect cost recovery on grants and contracts amounts to nearly $30 million annually at Stanford. Despite its importance, it is in many ways one of the most difficult of all quantities to understand and predict. It was also a prime area of concern for WFM, for as vice-provost for research he was heavily involved in making decisions about the indirect cost rate, predicting research volume and overhead recovery as part of the LRFF and budget processes, and explaining and justifying the university's overhead structures and policies to interested faculty. This led to a series of modeling efforts, beginning in 1972.

The first such effort was to build an "indirect cost budgeting model" (ICBM), which was an interactive computer program "designed to predict changes in indirect cost [recovery] as a result of changes in the university's budget."[5] The basic input was a matrix of costs arranged by functional category (e.g., instruction, sponsored research, libraries, administration) and object of expenditure (whether faculty salaries, staff salaries, benefits, supplies, or expenses), where the instruction and research functions were further broken down by school and broad field (e.g., humanities, physical sciences, and "other"). The program would then allocate indirect costs to the final cost objectives, and calculate predicted on-campus and off-campus indirect cost rates for sponsored research and instruction. Allocation of these costs was based on the allocation co-efficients developed by the Controller's Office as part of the last government rate study. We were assisted in this work by Professor David A. Butler, who was then a doctoral student in operations research.

Unfortunately, this early modeling effort was not successful inasmuch as the program was never used for policy purposes. There were two reasons for this. First, people in the Controller's Office had not been very much involved in the model's development. Second, the fact that the model operated from fixed historical allocation coefficients severely limited its accuracy, and hence its usefulness. This problem could have been circumvented had the Controller's Office been actively involved from the start. The ICBM model was allowed to lapse after about a year.

However, the need for more refined predictions in this area persisted and indeed became more acute. The associate controller, Frank Riddle, had been predicting overhead recovery for LRFF and budget purposes for some years. He was (and is) extremely knowledgeable about overhead factors and calcula-tions, and though he worked closely with us his estimates were, in the end, intuitive and personalistic. Janet Sweet of Riddle's staff worked closely with him, and also was a big help in our efforts at overhead recovery modeling. Their predictions were fairly accurate for the most part, but we still saw a need to build a cost allocation model that could be incorporated into TRANS or at any rate could be used to perform sensitivity analyses. For instance, the dean of engineering, William Kays, had expressed concern that certain BEP measures proposed for his school might prove to be unwise because of their effect upon indirect cost allocations and recovery. Questions about the "demand function" for sponsored research and the effect of Stanford's "price" (i.e., the indirect cost rate) upon sponsored research volume also were being raised by the Task Force on Models and Assumptions of the Budget Priorities Commission.

A renewed effort at modeling overhead recovery was launched in April 1975 by WFM. This time the model was at a very high level of aggregation: it dealt only with (a) the total size of the indirect cost pools (before allocation) and (b) the gross direct expenditures for instruction and departmental research, spon-sored research, and sponsored instruction. It predicted the indirect cost alloca-tions and the resulting overhead rates and carryforwards. After a certain amount of refinement, this model was incorporated into TRANS II and used from autumn 1975 onwards.[6] This, by the way, was the model that led to the two errors of data manipulation that were mentioned earlier. Despite these difficul-ties, however, the model was successful in linking budget reductions and overhead recovery estimates, albeit roughly.

A major effort at modeling the overhead subsystem properly was launched in December 1975, when WFM took a two-week leave of absence from his administrative duties for that purpose. He did the programming in APL, initially on an IBM 5100 minicomputer; later the model was transferred to Stanford's IBM 370/168. This model combined the disaggregative approach of the original ICBM with certain of the characteristics of the overhead submodel in TRANS II. Importantly, it also included procedures for predicting all the cost allocation coefficients as functions of budget variables and volume of research. John R. Curry, a doctoral student in the School of Education and an administrative intern in APO during 1975/76, refined the model and completed preparation of a handbook (in manuscript) to go with it.

The new model, which is described in chapter 4, has a considerable appetite for data. Partly for this reason we did not try hard to get it fully operational during the concluding months of BEP. Since then other priorities and assignments have intervened, while the need for sensitivity analysis that led to its development has not reoccurred. Also, the major uncertainty clouding the government rules for overhead recovery has made suspect any such analysis based on the rules as of 1977/78. However, we consider the model to be available in our inventory and are prepared to update and use it when the need arises. A simplified version of the structural relations of the model has been incorporated in TRADES, and is being used there.

Modeling Uncertainty

Nearly all the models discussed so far are "certainty equivalent," that is, they ignore all the various manifestations of uncertainty, such as forecast error, that interpenetrate the budget process. However, the need for modeling these manifestations and trying to understand the implications of uncertainty for budget planning was discussed early on, in our proposal to the Lilly Endowment. Work was started on this set of tasks in the summer of 1974 and is continuing at this writing.

Rodney Adams, Stanford's director of finance, suggested and helped to implement the first serious model of uncertainty to be employed in Stanford's budget processes. In cooperation with two finance professors in the Graduate School of Business, William Sharpe and John McDonald, and a number of outside consultants, Adams had for several years been working to apply modern investment principles to the Stanford endowment portfolio. In the spring of 1974 he approached us with the idea that a simulator should be constructed, one that could be used to evaluate alternative investment strategies. We agreed, and during the following summer Professor Sharpe constructed the simulator with support from the Lilly Endowment grant.[7] The simulator helped greatly in determining targets for investment return and yield, as well as new guidelines for the payout of capital appreciation. In early 1975/76 Adams and Vice President Robert Augsburger began to discuss these policy changes with the Budget Group and the Council of Deans; the changes were approved by the trustees later that year. The issues centered around the two opposing goals of maximizing long-run investment return and meeting the university's current income needs in a stable and predictable fashion. The results, in terms of actions taken, were: (a) a slight tilt toward yield in the common stock portfolio; (b) the determination of payout on the basis of a five-year moving average of market values (by this time the payout rate was itself being determined in the budget process, on the basis of the LRFE calculations); (c) a decision to reinvest yield if it exceeded the current payout target, or to pay out up to one percent in capital appreciation if yield plus reinvestment reserves were insufficient to meet the payout target. It is fair to say that such a comprehensive set of policies could not have been weighed effectively without the help of a formal model that incorporated the uncertainty attending return on investment. The model also provided estimates of important parameters used in subsequent models.

We have already described our abortive attempt to include uncertainty in the TRANS II model during the spring and summer of 1975. It was not until 1976 that serious progress on this front began to be made. The breakthrough came as a result of collaboration with Professor Richard C. Grinold, a management scientist at the University of California at Berkeley. Grinold was (and is) interested in the application to real-life decision problems of models for dynamic programming under conditions of uncertainty. While such models are simple in conception, solving them is mathematically complex; indeed, they represent a frontier in management science. Working from our certainty-equivalent models and from previous experience of uncertainty in university budget planning, we formulated and solved a dynamic programming model for making expenditure and investment decisions (see Grinold, Hopkins, and Massy, 1978). The planner's objective was assumed to be to minimize a weighted sum of the discounted future values of squared deviations of certain budget quantities (e.g., the funded improvement fraction, the endowment payout rate, and the tuition growth rate) from their long-run target values, which are based on equilibrium theory. The result was a decision rule, linear in the variables describing the current status and past history of the university's financial situation, that could be used to calculate the optimal values of the decision variables.

The dynamic programming model is very elegant and very powerful, but we do not feel comfortable in trying to apply the decision rules as actual budget-making criteria at Stanford. It is very doubtful if our colleagues in the administration, let alone the trustees, would accept such a strategy even if we were to propose it—and they would have good reason not to make such a leap of faith, in our judgment. The problem lies in the counterintuitive character of using a linear combination, or weighted sum, of *all* the financial variables, historical and contemporaneous, for determining each decision variable. Likewise, the weights themselves are not easily interpretable. Though the decision rules, within the context of the model's assumptions can be proved to be optimal, they may appear "mindless" and in any case are vulnerable to specification errors and problems of validation. In addition to its value as basic research, however, the dynamic programming model has both motivated and helped us to structure a simplified approach that is proving itself in use. This new approach is based on the idea of formulating a limited number of smoothing rules, for key budget quantities like the payout rate and funded improvement, that can make sense to decision makers without stirring up arcane mathematical arguments. The rules in question are not unlike the linear decision rules determined by the dynamic programming model, but they are based on a limited number of variables and are defined in terms of readily interpretable parameters. An example of such a rule is the five-year moving average of market values for smoothing endowment payout; though this particular formulation has its faults and is not included in our model, it does demonstrate the idea of common-sense appeal. The model itself includes a comprehensive representation of the uncertainties facing the decision maker and provides a way to test alternative smoothing rules. A way was devised to optimize the parameters of the smoothing rules (an analogue is the number of years in the moving average mentioned above) in terms of an objective function that represents the users' relative aversion to risk with respect to different budget and financial quantities.

The smoothing rule model was designed by WFM in April 1977, at the beginning of a six-month sabbatical leave, and was refined in consultation with DSPH and Richard Grinold. Programming and testing was done over the summer by Alejandro Gerson, then a graduate student in operations research and business and later a staff member in the Office of Management and Financial Planning, who also made significant contributions to the formulation and solution procedures. The original model and results have been described by the authors (Massy, Grinold, Hopkins, and Gerson, 1977). A slightly simplified version of it provides the core of the ideas presented in chapter 7. It is also the basis for the evaluation of policy decisions now going forward at Stanford.[8]

Notes to Appendix 1

Works cited here in abbreviated form are more fully described in the bibliography at the end of this book.

1. See Conway and Verducci 1978.

2. See Hopkins 1974*a*, 1974*b*.

3. The faculty-flow model used to cost out the early retirement program was reported in Hopkins, ibid. It was based on the earlier model for the School of Humanities and Sciences and led, ultimately, to the fourteen-state formulation discussed in chapter 8.

4. See Hopkins and Bienenstock 1975.

5. David A. Butler, "Indirect cost budgeting model program documentation" (Stanford University, Academic Planning Office, April 27, 1973).

6. The TRANS II program was written in APL by Peter Orkenyi and Philip Heidelberger, who at that time were Ph.D students in operations.

7. The work was reported in Sharpe 1974; a summary description is included in Adams 1977.

8. For an additional account of the evolution of planning models at Stanford see Hopkins 1979.

APPENDIX 2

Value Maximization Subject to Constraints

The static optimization problem facing nonprofit enterprises, including colleges and universities, was represented in the text as

$$\text{maximize } V(\mathbf{X})$$

$$\text{with respect to } \mathbf{X}$$

$$\text{subject to}$$

$$F(\mathbf{X}) = 0$$

$$G(\mathbf{X}) = 0 \qquad\qquad (2.A.1)$$

$$\mathbf{X} \geq 0$$

where $\mathbf{X} = $ a vector of n activities.*

The value function $V(\mathbf{X})$ is assumed to be strictly concave, the production function $F(\mathbf{X})$ convex, and the financial function $G(\mathbf{X})$ concave.

The necessary conditions for the optimum are obtained by forming the Lagrangian, as in equation (3.5), and setting the partial derivatives to zero:

$$V_i - \lambda F_i + \mu G_i = 0 \qquad i = 1, 2, \ldots, \text{n}$$

$$F(\cdot) = 0 \qquad\qquad (2.A.2)$$

$$G(\cdot) = 0$$

where λ and μ are the shadow prices for the production and financial constraints. The assumptions about the form of the functions, given in the previous paragraph, are sufficient to guarantee that λ and μ are nonnegative.

---

*In the text we referred to "lists" of variables to keep the discussion as simple as possible. Vector notation will be used in this appendix.

Displacement of the Optimum

We turn first to the problem of deducing some properties of the effect on the optimum of making changes in the parameters of the value, production, and/or financial functions. An example of this problem was introduced in connection with figure 3.3, viz, in the question "What is the effect on output of increasing the marginal value of that output?" Other such questions concern changes in technology, market prices and/or factor costs, or the characteristics of the demand functions.

Let α be a shift parameter that may affect $F(\mathbf{X})$ and/or $G(\mathbf{X})$—as, for instance, in the examples given above. We differentiate the necessary conditions for optimality, given by (2.A.2), with respect to α:

$$V_{i\alpha} + \sum_j V_{ij}X^j_\alpha - \lambda_\alpha F_i$$

$$- \lambda(F_{i\alpha} + \sum_j F_{ij}X^j_\alpha) + \mu_\alpha G_i$$

$$+ \mu(G_{i\alpha} + \sum_j G_{ij}X^j_\alpha) = 0 \qquad i = 1, \ldots, n \qquad (2.A.3)$$

$$F_\alpha + \sum_j F_j X^j_\alpha = 0$$

$$G_\alpha + \sum_j G_j X^j_\alpha = 0$$

where X^j_α = the displacement of the optimal value of the jth element of $\mathbf{X}$ with respect to α

$\lambda_\alpha, \mu_\alpha$ = the displacements of the shadow prices.

The above result can be written compactly in partitioned matrix and vector form. After multiplying the last two equations of (2.A.3) through by λ and μ respectively, and changing variables to λ_α/λ and μ_α/μ, we have

$$
\begin{bmatrix}
V_{ij} - \lambda F_{ij} + \mu G_{ij} & -\lambda F_i & \mu G_i \\
\hline
- \lambda F'_j & 0 & 0 \\
\hline
\mu G'_j & 0 & 0
\end{bmatrix}
\begin{bmatrix}
X^j_\alpha \\
\hline
\dfrac{\lambda_\alpha}{\lambda} \\
\hline
\dfrac{\mu_\alpha}{\mu}
\end{bmatrix} \qquad (2.A.4)
$$

$$
= -
\begin{bmatrix}
V_{i\alpha} - \lambda F_{i\alpha} + \mu G_{i\alpha} \\
\hline
- \lambda F_\alpha \\
\hline
\mu G_\alpha
\end{bmatrix}
$$

The left-hand expression is a symmetric matrix of order $n + 2$. It consists of the $n \times n$ submatrix of elements $V_{ij} - \lambda F_{ij} + \mu G_{ij}$, bordered by $n \times 1$ (or $1 \times n$) vectors with elements λF_i and μG_i. We shall denote this matrix by **M**. The other two expressions in (2.A.4) are column vectors of order $n + 2$.

The general solution to (2.A.4) is readily obtained through Cramer's rule, which states that the solution for any X_j is the ratio of (a) the determinant of the matrix formed by substituting the right-hand side in place of the jth column and (b) the determinant of the original matrix (cf. Allen 1963, p. 457). Let M_{ij} be the $(i,j)^{\text{th}}$ cofactor of **M**, M_{iF} be the $n + 1^{\text{st}}$ cofactor, M_{iG} be the $n + 2^{\text{th}}$ cofactor, and M be the determinant. Employing Cramer's rule and expanding in terms of cofactors down the jth column, we have:

$$\frac{dX_j}{d\alpha} \equiv X_\alpha^j = - \sum_i (V_{i\alpha} - \lambda F_{i\alpha} + \mu G_{i\alpha}) \frac{M_{ij}}{M}$$

$$+ \lambda F_\alpha \frac{M_{iF}}{M} - \mu G_\alpha \frac{M_{iG}}{M} \qquad j = 1, \ldots, n. \tag{2.A.5}$$

Similar equations hold for λ_α / λ and μ_α / μ.

Invariance to Transformations of the Value Function

It is much easier for decision makers to explicate their preferences in ordinal or rank-order terms than it is for them to do so in terms of a utility function where scale as well as rank must be defined. Usually an ordinal function is sufficient for the desired analysis; if mistakes are to be avoided, however, it is important to know when this is not so. The analyst must be alert: it is easy to fit mathematical functions to rank-order data and once this has been done the functions look natural in every respect. But they cannot be used as the basis for operations like time discounting or the taking of expected values. (See chapter 3, subsections on optimization over time and on optimization under uncertainty; the process of fitting a function to ordinal data is illustrated in chapter 9.) The purpose of this section is to determine what operations relating to static optimization under certainty are valid when based on rank-order data.

Let V be our original value function, as fitted to rank-order data. Now consider a new value function V^*, which is related to V by a monotonic function, ϕ, so that

$$V^* = \phi(V), \text{ where } \phi'(V) = \frac{d\phi}{dV} > 0 \text{ always.}$$

The monotonicity condition implies that the transformed function V^* will be consistent with the underlying rank-order data, and indeed V and V^* are completely equivalent so far as the decision maker's preferences are concerned.

PROCEDURE 2.A.1. The necessary conditions for the optimum in terms of the original value function were given by equation (2.A.2). The conditions in terms of the transformed value function are changed to $V_i^* - \lambda^* F_i + \mu^* G_i = 0$. We now show that this is identical to (2.A.2).[1]

$$V_i^* \equiv \frac{\partial \phi(V)}{\partial X_i} = \phi'(V) V_i$$

Suppose $\lambda^* = \phi'(V)\lambda$ and $\mu^* = \phi'(V)\mu$. Then the necessary conditions in terms of V^* are

$$\phi'(V) V_i - \phi'(V)\lambda F_i + \phi'(V)\mu G_i = 0$$

$$\Rightarrow V_i - \lambda F_i + \mu G_i = 0$$

which is the same as (2.A.2).

Hence we are free to optimize a mathematical function $V(\mathbf{X})$ that has been fit to rank-order preference data.

PROCEDURE 2.A.2. Now we turn to the invariance of displacements from the optimum, i.e. of X_α^j as given by equation (2.A.5).

It is shown by Allen (1963, p. 656) that

$$\frac{M_{i\cdot}^*}{M^*} = \frac{1}{\phi'(V)} \frac{M_{i\cdot}}{M}.$$

(His proof does not depend on the number of constraints, so it applies here.) Once again let $\lambda^* = \phi'(V)\lambda$ and $\mu^* = \phi'(V)\mu$. This leads immediately to the conclusion that all products of $M_{i\cdot}/M$ with λ or μ are invariant to monotonic transformations of the value function.

Now consider the terms $V_{i\alpha} M_{ij}/M$. Differentiating V_i^* with respect to α yields

$$V_{i\alpha}^* = \phi'(V) V_{i\alpha} + \phi''(V) V_\alpha V_i.$$

If α does not pertain to $V(\mathbf{X})$, then V_α and $V_{i\alpha}$ are zero and the result is both null and invariant. If α does pertain to $V(\mathbf{X})$, then invariance of the product $V_{i\alpha} M_{ij}/M$ will occur if and only if $\phi''(V) = 0$, i.e. if the transformation is linear.

Our conclusion is that equation (2.A.5) is invariant to all monotonic transformations if α pertains to $F(\mathbf{X})$ and/or $G(\mathbf{X})$ but not $V(\mathbf{X})$. If α does pertain to $V(\mathbf{X})$, then invariance exists only up to a linear transformation. In other words, measuring the effect of a change in preferences upon the optimum joins time discounting and taking expected values on the list of cases in which a utility function rather than a value function is required. However, a value function is sufficient if we want to consider the effects of changes in the production and financial functions.

Substitution, Productivity, and Financial Effects

The ratios of determinants in (2.A.5) have natural interpretations, two of which are familiar from the theory of consumer demand.[2]

Let $\mathscr{S}_{ij} = \dfrac{M_{ij}}{M}$, the kernel of the *substitution effect* between i and j

$\mathscr{P}_i = \dfrac{M_{iF}}{M}$, the kernel of the *productivity effect* for i, and

$\mathscr{F}_i = \dfrac{-M_{iG}}{M}$, the kernel of the *financial effect* for i

With the new notation equation (2.A.5) can be written more simply:

$$X_\alpha^j = -\sum [(\mathscr{S}_{ij} V_{i\alpha}) - (\lambda \mathscr{S}_{ij})\mathscr{F}_{i\alpha} + (\mu \mathscr{S}_{ij}) G_{i\alpha}]$$
$$+ (\lambda \mathscr{P}_j) F_\alpha + (\mu \mathscr{F}_j) G_\alpha. \tag{2.A.6}$$

The definitions of $\mathscr{S}_{ij}$, $\mathscr{P}_i$, and $\mathscr{F}_i$ were of the kernels of the effects. In equation (2.A.6) the effects themselves now are seen to be the product of each kernel with the appropriate scaling factor: μ, λ, or $V_{i\alpha}$. For shifts affecting the value function the scaling is included in $V_{i\alpha}$; for those affecting the production or financial functions the shadow price is the scaling factor.

From the results of the previous section it follows that $\lambda \mathscr{S}_{ij}$, $\mu \mathscr{S}_{ij}$, $\lambda \mathscr{P}_j$, and $\mu \mathscr{F}_j$ are invariant to monotonic transformations of the value function. Also, $V_{i\alpha} = 0$ if the shift α does not affect $V(\mathbf{X})$, so in that case X_α^j is invariant, as we showed earlier. If α does affect the value function, then the substitution effect $\mathscr{S}_{ij} V_{ij}$ is invariant to linear transformations of $V(\mathbf{X})$, but not to more general monotonic transformations.

Further insight into the substitution, productivity, and financial effects can be obtained from some simple examples. First, let us assume that α represents the constant term in $G(\mathbf{X})$. This is what, in connection with figure 3.2, we called *net fixed revenue*, that is, the difference between fixed revenue and fixed cost. Then

$$G_\alpha = +1, \text{ and } G_{j\alpha} = F_\alpha = F_{j\alpha} = V_{j\alpha} = 0 \quad \text{for all } j.$$

Equation (2.A.6) becomes

$$X_\alpha^j = \mu \mathscr{F}_j. \tag{2.A.7}$$

Hence the result of a shift in net fixed revenue is simply the financial effect. This is analogous to what is called the "income effect" in the theory of consumer demand.

Now assume that $G(\mathbf{X})$ is linear and that α is the price coefficient of X_j, which we shall further assume is an input. In this case

$$G_\alpha = -X_j \qquad G_{j\alpha} = -1$$

and all the other partials are zero. Then equation (2.A.6) becomes

$$X^j_{P_j} = \mu \mathscr{S}_{jj} - (\mu \mathscr{F}_j) X_j. \tag{2.A.8}$$

This equation is familiar from consumer demand theory (see Allen 1963, p. 662). The first term is the own-price substitution effect; the second term reflects the fact that an increase in the price of the jth commodity represents a reduction of effective income proportional to the amount of the commodity being consumed.

A similar line of reasoning holds for the production function. If α is a constant added to the function F, then X^j_α is analogous to the income effect in equation (2.A.7). This addition means that there has been a shift in technology that can be applied at the discretion of the decision maker to increase any outputs or decrease any inputs—all the while maintaining $F(\mathbf{X}) = 0$. If α refers to a technological change that affects the marginal physical product of a single input with respect to a single output, or the marginal rate of substitution between a single pair of inputs or outputs, the result will be analogous to (2.A.8).

The sign of the "own-parameter" substitution effect ($\mathscr{S}_{jj}$) can be deduced from the second-order conditions for the optimum. That it is negative, just as in the theory of consumer demand, is demonstrated by the following (heuristic) procedure.

PROCEDURE 2.A.3. The kernel of any substitution effect, $\mathscr{S}_{ij}$, can be interpreted as

$$\mathscr{S}_{ij} = \left. \frac{\partial X_j}{\partial m_i} \right|_{H \,=\, H^0}$$

where $m_i = $ the slope of the tangency between the value function and constraints at the optimum point, measured along the ith axis.

The condition $H = H^0$ requires that the movement be along the surface

$$V - \lambda F + \mu G = H^0$$

where $H_0 = $ the value of H achieved at the optimum with the original parameters.

In other words, $\mathscr{S}_{ij}$ implies movement along a *given* indifference surface. (Note that $V_{i\alpha} - \lambda F_{i\alpha} + \mu G_{i\alpha}$, in equation [2.A.6], represents the change due to α in the tangency slope m_i.) Since H is strictly concave for positive λ and μ, it follows immediately that $\partial X_j / \partial m_j < 0$ for $H = H^0$.

While the "own-parameter" substitution effect $\mathscr{S}_{jj}$ is always negative, the sign of $\mathscr{S}_{ij}$ for $i \neq j$ cannot be predicted. Pairs of commodities are defined as *substitutes* when $\mathscr{S}_{ij} > 0$ and as *complements* when $\mathscr{S}_{ij} < 0$. These properties depend not only on the value function (as in the consumer demand case), but also on any nonlinearities in the production function and/or financial functions.

In contrast, $\mathscr{P}_j$ and $\mathscr{F}_j$ represent the expansion path induced by additive changes in the production and financial functions. Nothing can be deduced regarding the signs of $\mathscr{P}_j$ and $\mathscr{F}_j$, although—analogously to consumer demand theory—it can be said that j is an "inferior" good with respect to marginal income if $\mathscr{F}_j < 0$ and "inferior" with respect to marginal productivity if $\mathscr{P}_j < 0$. Whether the commodity is an output or an input, "inferiority" means that it is used as something of a stopgap, when the decision maker is lacking in degrees of freedom. As the situation becomes less tight (financially or in terms of productivity), substitution will be away from the inferior good even though its own marginal value may have increased.

The sign of $X^j_{P_j}$ in (2.A.7) is not determinable a priori, since $\mathscr{F}_j$ may be positive or negative. However, we would expect $\mathscr{F}_j > 0$ for most (though by no means all) the elements of **X**. This would imply $X^j_{P_j} < 0$, just as for the theory of consumer demand. The same comments apply to $\mathscr{P}_j$ and to the effect of changes in the production function. However, the result of increasing V_j due to $d\alpha$ always will be to increase X_j, as stated in connection with figure 3.3.

Differences Between Nonprofit and Profit-Maximizing Enterprises

The results of the foregoing section can be used to make some predictions about the differences between nonprofit and profit-maximizing enterprises. First, the adjustment of the quantity of any variable to a parameter change for that same variable (e.g., change in factor cost or output price change) by a nonprofit enterprise will always be less than or equal to the adjustment of a profit maximizer. That is,

$$\left.\frac{dX^i}{d\alpha_i}\right|\text{Nonprofit} \leq \left.\frac{dX^i}{d\alpha_i}\right|\text{Profit maximizer}$$

PROCEDURE 2.A.4. This difference can be demonstrated in terms of the Le Chatelier–Samuelson principle, which states that the effect upon a variable of changing its own parameter will be greatest when no constraints are binding and will decline as more constraints are brought into play.[3] To apply the principle, write the dual of equation (2.A.1) for the nonprofit enterprise:

$$\text{maximize } G - \frac{\lambda}{\mu}F + \frac{1}{\mu}(V - V^0)$$

$$\text{with respect to } X$$

$$\text{subject to}$$

$$F(\mathbf{X}) = 0$$

$$V(\mathbf{X}) = V^0$$

where V^0 = the maximizing value of (2.A.1).

The dual leads to the same necessary conditions as the original problem, given in (2.A.2).

For the profit maximizer the optimization problem is

$$\text{maximize } G - \frac{\lambda}{\mu}F$$

with respect to X

subject to

$$F(\mathbf{X}) = 0$$

which is identical to the above except for the value constraint.

Thus the two optimization problems are the same except for the addition of the value constraint in the nonprofit case, so the Le Chatelier–Samuelson principle applies.

Among other things, procedure 2.A.4 implies that nonprofit institutions will tend to pay less attention to price in setting output and be less cost-sensitive with respect to their input mix than similarly situated profit maximizers. This generalization seems to ring true with respect to, for example, the behavior of nonprofit as compared to proprietary schools and hospitals.

What about the "cross-parameter" effects $dX^i/d\alpha_j$ where $i \neq j$? The *generalized* Le Chatelier–Samuelson principle, as used here, suggests that there may be a tendency as additional constraints are applied, for some commodities that are complements to switch to being substitutes.* In other words, there can be qualitative changes (i.e., changes of sign) in the substitution effects. While it is impossible to predict how many variables might be affected, the above suggests that nonprofit institutions may be affected by more substitution among inputs and outputs than profit-maximizing ones.

Another possible difference between the two types of institution pertains to a particular set of substitution-complementarity relations, viz., between outputs and inputs. The situation for the profit maximizer has been summed up by Allen (1963, p. 616):

> As Hicks has shown, it can be taken generally that substitution dominates in product-factor [i.e., output-input] relations; an increase in a factor price reduces supplies of products and an increase in a product price raises usages of factors. Against this there may be considerable relations of complementarity within a group of products (a price increase raising supplies), and within a group of factors (a price increase reducing their use).

*See Kusumoto 1976. The conditions of his theorem 2 would seem to apply in our case since, if $\mathbf{A}$ is the matrix on the left-hand side of (2.A.4) and $\mathbf{B}$ is its inverse, and $\mathbf{A}_{11}$ is the upper left-hand submatrix of $\mathbf{A}$ shown there and $\mathbf{B}_{11}$ is the corresponding submatrix of $\mathbf{B}$, it would be very fortuitous, given V, F, and G all nonlinear, for $\mathbf{B}_{11}$ to equal $\mathbf{A}_{11}^{-1}$.

The view quoted depends entirely upon the curvature of the production function, since the profit function for the business firm is taken to be linear. For the nonprofit enterprise, however, the curvature of the linear combination $V - \lambda F + \mu G$ is the important thing, and the value function will exert an influence along with the production function even if the financial function is linear. We have not stated any general limitations on V: indeed, we have argued that, for colleges and universities, it is possible to value inputs as legitimately as outputs. If this is the case, it may well be that for the nonprofit institution many input-output pairs will be complements rather than substitutes.

Decentralized Optimization

Equation (3.16) poses the following problem of decentralized optimization for the nonprofit institution. We postulate a central administration that wishes to set a transfer price vector, $\mathbf{p}^s$, such that the independent value-maximizing decisions of organizational subunits (schools, for instance) will maximize the central administration's value function.

The problem is:

$$\text{maximize } \bar{V}(\mathbf{X}^s) \quad (s = 1, \ldots, n)$$

$$\text{with respect to } \mathbf{P}^s$$

$$\text{subject to}$$

$$\sum_s \sum_j \bar{\bar{P}}_j^s X_j^s + \bar{\bar{P}}_0 - \sum_s \sum_j P_j^s X_j^s - \sum_s P_0^s = 0.$$

The solution proceeds as follows.

PROCEDURE 2.A.5. Form the central administration's Lagrangian, with ϕ as the shadow price on the financial constraint.

$$\text{maximize } H = \bar{V}(\mathbf{X}) + \phi \left[\sum_s \sum_j (\bar{\bar{P}}_j^s - P_j^s) X_j^s + P_0 - \sum_s P_0^s \right]. \quad (2.A.9)$$

Then differentiate with respect to $\mathbf{P}^s$, for $s = 1, \ldots, n$.

$$\frac{\partial H}{\partial P_k^s} = \sum_j \bar{V}_j^s \frac{\partial X_j^s}{\partial P_k^s} + \phi \sum_j (\bar{\bar{P}}_j^s - P_j^s) \frac{\partial X_j^s}{\partial P_k^s} - \phi X_k^s = 0$$

$$\frac{\partial H}{\partial P_0^s} = \sum_j \bar{V}_j^s \frac{\partial X_j^s}{\partial P_0^s} + \phi \sum_j (\bar{\bar{P}}_j^s - P_j^s) \frac{\partial X_j^s}{\partial P_0^s} - \phi = 0$$

$$(2.A.10)$$

where $\bar{V}_j^s = $ the partial of $\bar{V}$ with respect to X_j in school s.

It is assumed that each school will maximize its own value function subject to its own financial constraint.

That is,

$$\text{maximize } V^s(\mathbf{X}^s) \quad (s = 1, \ldots, n)$$

$$\text{with respect to } (\mathbf{X}^s)$$

$$\text{subject to}$$

$$\sum_j P_j^s X_j^s + P_0^s = 0$$

(2.A.11)

for schools. (For purposes of simplification, because the emphasis here is on financial incentives, the production function constraint has been left out of [2.A.11.] In chapter 3 we showed how, for practical purposes, production function information can be subsumed in the value function, which is what we assume is happening here.)

Now we need a means for determining the partial derivatives X_j^s in (2.A.10). Application of equation (2.A.5) yields

$$\frac{\partial X_j^s}{\partial P_0^s} = -\mu^s \frac{M_{jG}^s}{M^s} = F_j^s$$

$$\frac{\partial X_j^s}{\partial P_k^s} = -\mu^s X_k^s \frac{M_{jg}^s}{M^s} - \mu^s \frac{M_{jk}^s}{M^s} = X_k^s \mathscr{F}_j^s - \mathscr{S}_{jk}^s$$

where $\mathscr{F}_j^s$ = the "financial" effects within school s

$\mathscr{S}_{jk}^s$ = the "substitution" effects within school s.

Substitute (2.A.11) into (2.A.10) and collect terms. Then multiply the equation for $\partial H/\partial P_0^s$ through by X_k^s and substitute it into the one for $\partial H/\partial P_k^s$. This yields

$$\sum_j [\bar{V}_j^s + \phi(\bar{\bar{P}}_j^s - P_j^s)]\mathscr{S}_{jk}^s = 0$$

$$\sum_j [\bar{V}_j^s + \phi(\bar{\bar{P}}_j^s - P_j^s)]\mathscr{F}_j^s = 0.$$

(2.A.12)

Differentiation yields the necessary conditions for each school's optimum (given $\mathbf{P}^s$); i.e., $V_j^s = -\mu^s P_j^s$. Hence $\sum_j V_j^s \mathscr{S}_{jk}^s = 0$ through expansion by alien cofactors in equation (2.A.4), and $\sum_j V_j^s \mathscr{F}_j^s = \mu^s$ through expansion by own cofactors. Now add the first expression, which is equal to zero, to the first equation in (2.A.12) and subtract the second expression, μ^s, from both sides of the second equation. The necessary conditions for the central administration's optimum are, therefore,

$$\sum_j [(\bar{V}_j^s - V_j^s) + \phi(\bar{\bar{P}}_j^s - P_j^s)]\mathscr{S}_{jk}^s = 0 \quad (\text{over } k, s)$$

$$\sum_j [(\bar{V}_j^s - V_j^s) + \phi(\bar{\bar{P}}_j^s - P_j^s)]\mathscr{F}_j^s = \phi - \mu^s \quad (\text{over } s)$$

$$\sum_s \sum_j (\bar{\bar{P}}_j^s - P_j^s)X_j^s = \sum_s P_0^s - \bar{\bar{P}}_0.$$

(2.A.13)

In other words, various weighted averages of marginal value and price deviations for each variable are set to zero, with the schools' substitution and financial effects being taken as weights.

It is assumed that the value functions for all the schools and the central administration are comparable up to the same monotonic transformation. That is, a monotonic transformation will affect $\bar{V}_j^s$, V_j^s, μ^s, and ϕ proportionately and thus cancel out of (2.A.13). This assumption is necessary in order for marginal values to be compared. Note that invariance up to the same *linear* transformation is not required, although this may be the best practical strategy for achieving comparability.

Notes to Appendix 2

Works cited here in abbreviated form are more fully described in the bibliography at the end of this book.

1. The proof follows Samuelson 1974, p. 98, and Allen 1963, p. 656.

2. The theory can be found in Samuelson 1974, Allen 1963, and most microeconomic texts.

3. See Samuelson 1974, p. 38. The principle is very broad in its application, and applies to nonlinear as well as linear constraints (Kusumoto 1976, p. 512).

A Budget Model for Need-Based
Financial Aid Programs

The purpose of this model is to show how the financial aid budget depends on the number of students enrolled, the price of attendance, and the distribution of financial need in the student population.

Let X = student enrollment (in FTE terms)

P = price of attendance (tuition, plus room and board, plus incidental expenses)

$f(C)$ = the frequency distribution of "family contribution" (including student "self-help") for the student population.

Since we shall treat $f(C)$ as a continuous distribution, we can say that, roughly speaking, $f(C)$ times a small increment in C is the fraction of all students who can contribute approximately $\$C$ towards the total cost, P. The fraction of students who need some aid at a given price P (i.e., whose contribution is less than P) is given by

$$F(P) \equiv \int_0^P f(C)dC$$

while $1 - F(P)$ have no need.

We recognize three sources of scholarship aid for students who are needy. First, there are outside scholarship programs for which only a fraction of students (call this fraction η) are eligible. We assume that such programs provide the full amount of aid needed, up to some stipulated ceiling that we designate by s^*. (This is characteristic of most state scholarship programs for students going to private institutions.)

Let $OS(P, C)$ = the outside scholarship amount provided to a student whose family contribution is C when the price of attendance is P.

We can now write

$$OS(P, C) = \begin{cases} 0 & \text{for } P \le C \\ P - C & \text{for } (P - C) \le s^* \\ s^* & \text{otherwise.} \end{cases} \tag{3.A.1}$$

Other sources of scholarships are university funds that are specifically restricted for student aid and university funds that are unrestricted.

Let RA = the amount of restricted funds available for expenditure on financial aid

$A(P)$ = the unrestricted university financial aid budget when the price is P.

We seek an expression for $A(P)$ in terms of the other quantities just defined. First, we write

$$A(P) = PX - PX \int_P^\infty f(C)dC \\ - X \int_0^P [C + \eta OS(P, C)]f(C)dC - RA \tag{3.A.2}$$

$$\begin{array}{c} \text{Total unrestricted} \\ \text{scholarship aid} \end{array} = \begin{array}{c} \text{Total cost for} \\ \text{all students} \end{array} - \begin{array}{c} \text{Costs paid by students} \\ \text{who pay the full bill} \end{array}$$

$$- \begin{array}{c} \text{Partial costs paid} \\ \text{by those on aid, from} \\ \text{family resources and} \\ \text{outside scholarships} \end{array} - \begin{array}{c} \text{Restricted} \\ \text{aid.} \end{array}$$

This simplifies to

$$A(P) = \left\{ PF(P) - \int_0^P [C + \eta OS(P, C)]f(C)dC \right\} X - RA. \tag{3.A.3}$$

Next, we substitute for $OS(P, C)$ under the integral in (3.A.3), using (3.A.1), and rearrange terms. After a good deal of algebra, the following expression results:

$$A(P) = \left\{ - \int_0^{P - s^*} Cf(C)dC - (1 - \eta) \int_{P - s^*}^P Cf(C)dC \\ - \eta F(P - s^*)s^* + [(1 - \eta)F(P) + \eta F(P - s^*)]P \right\} X - RA. \tag{3.A.4}$$

Contributions from
families up to the
− level subsidized by
outside scholarships
(*OS*)

Contributions from
families for those
− *not* on *OS* and with
$(P - s^*) \leq C \leq P$

Full subsidies
from *OS* for
− those on *OS* and
with $C \leq (P - s^*)$

+

Full aid (before sub-
sidy) for students
who are *not* on *OS*
and require some aid

Full aid for students
+ on *OS* who require
university aid as well

Note that (3.A.4) can be arranged to yield the desired form

$$A(P) = [-\beta_0(P) + P]\beta_1(P)X - RA$$

where $\beta_1(P)$ is the fraction of students requiring aid at price P and $\beta_0(P)$ is the average contribution from all outside sources for students who receive aid.

Matrix Calculation of Final
Allocation Coefficients

Our purpose here is to give a direct algebraic representation of the coefficients α_i resulting from the stepping-down process used in the allocation of indirect costs (refer at this point to the stepdown schedule in table 4.11).

Let x_j = preallocation total for indirect cost type j

x'_j = postallocation total for indirect cost type j

y_i = preallocation total for direct cost type i

y'_i = postallocation total for direct cost type i

a_{ij} = the fraction of indirect cost type j that is allocated to (indirect or direct) cost category i (note that $\sum_i a_{ij} = 1$).

The allocation of indirect costs is carried out in two steps. In the first, a portion of each indirect cost is allocated to the other indirect costs:

$$
\begin{aligned}
x'_1 &= x_1 \\
x'_2 &= a_{21}x'_1 + x_2 \\
x'_3 &= a_{31}x'_1 + a_{32}x'_2 + x_3 \\
&\ \ \cdots\cdots \\
x'_6 &= a_{61}x'_1 + a_{62}x'_2 + \ldots + a_{65}x'_5 + x_6.
\end{aligned}
\tag{4.A.1}
$$

Indirect costs are then allocated to direct costs as follows:

$$
\begin{aligned}
y'_1 &= y_1 + a_{71}x'_1 + a_{72}x'_2 + \ldots + a_{76}x'_6 \\
y'_2 &= y_2 + a_{81}x'_1 + a_{82}x'_2 + \ldots + a_{86}x'_6 \\
&\ \ \cdots\cdots \\
y'_4 &= y_4 + a_{10,1}x'_1 + a_{10,2}x'_2 + \ldots + a_{10,6}x'_6.
\end{aligned}
\tag{4.A.2}
$$

Table A4.1.   Initial Allocation Fractions, A_1 and A_2

	Pool					
	Depreciation	O & M	G & A	IDA	Student Services	Library
Indirect costs (A_1)						
Depreciation	....	....	....	....	....	....
Operation & Maintenance	0.0326	....	....	....	....	....
General & Admin.	0.0617	0.0760	....	....	....	....
Departmental Admin.	0.2660	0.2618	0.1303	....	....	....
Student Services	0.0277	0.0239	0.0422	....	....	....
Library	0.1468	0.1903	0.0513	....	....	....
Direct costs (A_2)						
Instruction & Departmental Research	0.1190	0.1080	0.2685	0.4732	0.8539	0.6835
Sponsored Research	0.3085	0.3038	0.3533	0.4568	0.1306	0.2535
Sponsored Instruction	0.0307	0.0278	0.0549	0.0699	0.0138	0.0316
Other	0.0071	0.0086	0.0996	0.0000	0.0017	0.0315
	1.0000	1.0000	1.0000	1.0000	1.0000	1.0000

Table A4.2.   Final Allocation Fractions, $A_2(I - A_1)^{-1}$

	Pool					
	Depreciation	O & M	G & A	IDA	Student Services	Library
Instruction & Departmental Research	0.4070	0.4128	0.4012	0.4732	0.8539	0.6835
Sponsored Research	0.5140	0.5075	0.4313	0.4568	0.1306	0.2535
Sponsored Instruction	0.0602	0.0575	0.0662	0.0699	0.0138	0.0316
Other	0.0187	0.0223	0.1012	0.0000	0.0017	0.0315

The analysis can be simplified by the use of vector-matrix notation. Let $A = [a_{ij}]$ be the matrix of initial allocation coefficients, and partition A as follows:

$$A = \left[\frac{A_1}{A_2} \right]$$ The first six rows correspond to indirect costs.
   The last four rows correspond to direct costs.

The first set of equations is written compactly as

$$\mathbf{x}' = \mathbf{x} + A_1\mathbf{x}'$$

or

$$(I - A_1)\mathbf{x}' = \mathbf{x}.$$

Now, since the matrix $(I - A_1)$ has strictly positive diagonal elements, non-positive off-diagonals, and column sums strictly less than one, it is nonsingular and has a nonnegative inverse. Thus, we may write

$$\mathbf{x}' = (I - A_1)^{-1}\mathbf{x}. \tag{4.A.3}$$

Equations in the second set are represented by

$$\mathbf{y}' = \mathbf{y} + A_2\mathbf{x}'. \tag{4.A.4}$$

Combining this result with the previous one, we obtain the final equations for postallocation direct costs in terms of preallocation directs and indirects:

$$\mathbf{y}' = \mathbf{y} + A_2(I - A_1)^{-1}\mathbf{x}. \tag{4.A.5}$$

It is further evident from (4.A.5) that the matrix $A_2(I - A_1)^{-1}$ contains the final allocation coefficients we are after. Specifically, the final allocations to sponsored research are given by the second row of this matrix.

For the sake of illustration we have carried through these calculations using the data in table 4.11. The results are shown in tables A4.1 and A4.2.

A Brief Technical Description of the Stanford Investment Simulator

The model is described in terms of the following notation.*

Let r_t = the one-year (risk-free) interest rate applicable to year t

r_t^f = the "forward-interest rate" for year t

R_{Bt} = the total return on the bond portion of the endowment portfolio

R_{St} = the total return on the stock portion of the endowment

α_C = the fraction of the portfolio invested in short-term cash equivalents

α_B = the fraction of the portfolio invested in bonds

α_S = the fraction of the portfolio invested in stocks.

It is desired to examine the statistical properties (the mean, the variance, etc.) of the total return on the endowment portfolio in year t, which we shall denote by ρ_t. This return is expressed in terms of the policy variables α_i and the random variables r_t, R_{Bt}, and R_{St} by means of

$$\rho_t = \alpha_C r_t + \alpha_B R_{Bt} + \alpha_S R_{St}. \tag{5.A.1}$$

Submodels for each of the three classes of investments are built separately and then combined in the simulator to yield the probability distribution of total return on endowment.

* This model was developed by Professor William F. Sharpe of the Stanford Graduate School of Business (see Sharpe 1974).

Short-Term Cash Equivalents

The model postulates a mean reversion process for the short-term interest rate in which the next year's rate is the expected long-term rate (denoted r_∞), adjusted by some fraction of the difference between this year's rate and the long-term value, plus a random error term (denoted ε_1). To express this relationship, we write

$$r_t = r_\infty + b(r_{t-1} - r_\infty) + \varepsilon_1 \qquad (5.A.2)$$

where b = the mean reversion coefficient.

We assume that ε_1 is normally distributed with mean zero and standard deviation $\sigma(\varepsilon_1)$. Fitting this model with real data on interest rates during the period of forty-seven years beginning with the year 1926 yielded values of 0.94 for b and 0.3 percent per year for $\sigma(\varepsilon_1)$. The adjusted coefficient of determination, R^2, was 0.79.

To simulate short-term interest rates, then, we begin with a known initial value, r_0. Equation (5.A.2) is used in iterative fashion to step ahead from one year's rate to the next, each time including an error term drawn randomly from the distribution $N(0, .3^2)$. (It should be noted, however, that the model of short-term rates used in the simulator actually is somewhat more complicated than this: it employs a multiplicative, rather than an additive error term, and also includes a fixed barrier through which the simulated interest rate is not permitted to fall.)

Long-Term Bond Returns

The one-year total return on long-term bonds is derived from the changes in the set of forward interest rates (r^f) from one year to the next. Sharpe found that the forward interest rate for year t could reasonably be expressed as the sum of the expected short-term rate in year t and a so-called liquidity premium, L_t:

$$r_t^f = E[r_t] + L_t \qquad (5.A.3)$$

where $E[r_t]$ is calculated with (5.A.2) and the liquidity premium is determined by

$$L_t = (1 - b_L^t)L_\infty \qquad (5.A.4)$$

with parameters b_L and L_∞. If one sets the value of b_L at 0.94, one obtains from the historical time series of bond market returns a value of 1.5 percent per year for the very long-term liquidity premium, L_∞.

Consider a newly issued twenty-year bond selling at par. Let V_t denote the bond's value t years after issuance. At the time of issue, we know that $V_0 = 100$, and this must also equal the sum of future coupons (plus the repayment of $100 at the end of year 20), all discounted with the forward interest rates. Thus letting C stand for the amount of coupon attached to the bond, we can write

$$100 = \frac{C}{1 + r_1^f} + \frac{C}{(1 + r_1^f)(1 + r_2^f)} + \cdots$$
$$+ \frac{C + 100}{(1 + r_1^f)(1 + r_2^f) \cdots (1 + r_{20}^f)}. \tag{5.A.5}$$

This equation is used to solve for C.

After one year, we will have a new set of forward interest rates, say $\{r_t^{f'}\}$, since the introduction of a random error will have caused the short-term rate in that year to be different from its expected value. The updated forward rates are then used to determine the value of the bond at that time via

$$V_1 = \frac{C}{1 + r_1^{f'}} + \frac{C}{(1 + r_1^{f'})(1 + r_2^{f'})}$$
$$+ \cdots + \frac{C + 100}{(1 + r_1^{f'})(1 + r_2^{f'}) \cdots (1 + r_{19}^{f'})}. \tag{5.A.6}$$

The total return for such a bond is equal to the sum of the coupon plus price appreciation; thus we have

$$R_B = (C + V_1 - V_0)/V_0. \tag{5.A.7}$$

Of course, a bond portfolio will consist of bonds with many different maturity dates. The above logic can be applied to each maturity date, and the return on the complete portfolio can then be obtained as the return on the corresponding mix of maturities.

Total Return on Stocks

The model assumes that the random variable that is one plus the excess return (i.e., above the risk-free interest rate) on the stock market as a whole is (approximately) lognormally distributed with parameters μ_S and σ_S. The long-run values for these parameters were estimated to be 7.3 percent and 21.5 percent, respectively, but the simulator has the capability of generating returns according to a mean-reverting process in which the standard deviation, σ_S, starts out with a value different from its long-run expectation, and the mean value, μ_S, is adjusted accordingly.

Let R_{St}^M be the total return on the stock market as a whole. The total return on a particular stock portfolio (say the one held by Stanford) is characterized by a parameter, β, which signifies the degree of systematic risk in the portfolio relative to the market, and an additional error term that indicates a lack of perfect diversification. Thus, the total return on the stock portion of the endowment portfolio, denoted R_{St}, is simulated by drawing at random from the distributions of R_{St}^M and ε_2 in the equation

$$R_{St} = \beta R_{St}^M + \varepsilon_2 \tag{5.A.8}$$

where ε_2 is presumed to be normally distributed with mean zero and standard deviation $\sigma(\varepsilon_2)$. Values found for β and $\sigma(\varepsilon_2)$ that characterize the stock holdings in Stanford's endowment over the past several years were 1.0 and 4.35 percent per year, respectively.

Operation of the Simulator

It should be evident from the formulation of these investment submodels that the return on the university's endowment portfolio is a complicated function of several random variables. Note especially that the bond- and stock-market returns are both correlated with the short-term interest rate, and hence with each other. For this reason it is nearly impossible to specify the probability distributions of endowment total return in closed form. Sharpe's model avoids this difficulty by simulating a large number of such returns and displaying a frequency distribution of the results. As one increases the number of simulations performed, the distribution of observed outcomes becomes (in theory) a closer and closer approximation to the actual distribution one is after—provided, of course, that the models are sound.

Each simulation involves drawing values for the random variables ε_1, ε_2, and $(R_{St}^M - r_t)$ from the appropriate probability distributions, and then using the logic described in previous sections to obtain values for r_t, R_{Bt}, and R_{St} for a sequence of years t. These values are combined with the policy fractions α_i as weights to obtain the total return on the university's endowment as in (5.A.1). This process is repeated a number of times, resulting in a frequency distribution of endowment total return for each future year. The program also contains a stochastic model of the one-year inflation rate so that the results can be displayed in real as well as nominal terms.

A Compact Representation of the Production, Cost, and Revenue Models in Vector-Matrix Form

---

PRIMARY VARIABLES

Let $\mathbf{h}$ = vector of student cohort flows

$\mathbf{y}$ = vector of student enrollments

$\mathbf{z}^F$ = vector of faculty FTEs

$\mathbf{z}^S$ = vector of staff FTEs

z^O = scalar representing the dollar cost of other resources

r^O = scalar representing the dollar income that is not associated with either students or faculty.

PARAMETERS

Let V = matrix of student lifetimes, v_{jk}, where j corresponds to student type and k is the cohort number

A = matrix of faculty-student ratios, a_{ij}, for determining FTE staffing levels, in which the rows correspond to faculty types and the columns to student types

Λ = diagonal matrix containing the fractions of FTE faculty of each type that are associated with classroom teaching

D = matrix of faculty-student ratios for determining instructional FTE associated with activities other than classroom teaching

B^{SS} = matrix of incremental *staff-student* ratios

B^{SF} = matrix of incremental *staff-faculty* ratios

$\mathbf{b}^{OS}$ = vector of incremental *other* expense-*student* ratios

$\mathbf{b}^{OF}$ = vector of incremental *other* expense-*faculty* ratios

$\mathbf{s}^F$ = vector of salary-plus-benefits costs per FTE faculty

$\mathbf{r}^F$ = vector of unit revenues per FTE faculty

$\mathbf{s}^S$ = vector of salary-plus-benefits costs per FTE staff

$\mathbf{r}^S$ = vector of unit revenues per FTE staff.

We assume there is given a system of linear constraints on the cohort flows that is of full rank. We represent the system as

$$\mathbf{Mh} = \mathbf{d}. \tag{6.A.1}$$

Solving for h yields

$$\mathbf{h} = \mathbf{M}^{-1}\mathbf{d} \tag{6.A.2}$$

and the cohort flows are converted to enrollments by means of the lifetimes matrix, $\mathbf{V}$:

$$\mathbf{y} = \mathbf{Vh}. \tag{6.A.3}$$

Note that it certainly is possible for some of the flows in (6.A.2) to turn out negative. This would imply that the system of constraints is infeasible.

Next, we solve for faculty staffing levels by means of

$$\mathbf{z}^F = A\mathbf{y} = A\mathbf{Vh}. \tag{6.A.4}$$

By assumption, staff FTEs and other expenses can be expressed as linear functions of students and faculty:

$$\begin{aligned}\mathbf{z}^S &= \mathbf{z}_0^S + B^{SS}\mathbf{y} + B^{SF}\mathbf{z}^F \\ z^O &= z_0^O + \mathbf{b}^{OS} \cdot \mathbf{y} + \mathbf{b}^{OF} \cdot \mathbf{z}^F. \end{aligned} \tag{6.A.5}$$

To develop formulas for total expense, C, and total income, R, we make use of the "price" vectors $(\mathbf{s}^F, \mathbf{s}^S)$ and $(\mathbf{r}^y, \mathbf{r}^F, \mathbf{r}^S)$ to write:

$$\begin{aligned}C &= \mathbf{s}^F \cdot \mathbf{z}^F + \mathbf{s}^S \cdot \mathbf{z}^S + z^O \\ R &= \mathbf{r}^y \cdot \mathbf{y} + \mathbf{r}^F \cdot \mathbf{z}^F + \mathbf{r}^S \cdot \mathbf{z}^S + r^O \end{aligned} \tag{6.A.6}$$

where the "other income" term, r^O, does not depend on students, faculty, or staff. Note that the price vector $\mathbf{r}^y$ includes the unit tuition paid by students. Combining (6.A.6) with (6.A.4) and (6.A.5) leads to the following compact expressions for the total cost and income in terms of students (or cohort flows) alone:

$$C(\mathbf{y}) = c_0 + \mathbf{c} \cdot \mathbf{y} = c_0 + (\mathbf{c}V)\mathbf{h}$$
$$R(\mathbf{y}) = r_0 + \mathbf{r} \cdot \mathbf{y} = r_0 + (\mathbf{r}V)\mathbf{h} \tag{6.A.7}$$

where
$$c_0 = z_0^O + \mathbf{s}^S \cdot \mathbf{z}_0^S$$
$$r_0 = r^O + \mathbf{r}^S \cdot \mathbf{z}_0^S$$
$$\mathbf{c} = \mathbf{s}^S B^{SS} + \mathbf{b}^{OS} + (\mathbf{s}^F + \mathbf{s}^S B^{SF} + \mathbf{b}^{OF})A$$
$$\mathbf{r} = \mathbf{r}^y + \mathbf{r}^S B^{SS} + \mathbf{r}^{OS} + (\mathbf{r}^F + \mathbf{r}^S B^{SF} + \mathbf{r}^{OF})A.$$

Because we have not yet taken into account the joint activities of the faculty, only some of which are considered to be related to instruction, it would be a mistake to interpret the unit cost and revenue vectors, $\mathbf{c}$ and $\mathbf{r}$, as the instructional cost and revenue per student. We need to make use here of the matrix Λ, whose i^{th} diagonal element gives the proportion of total effort for faculty category i that is associated with classroom teaching; and the matrix D, whose $(i,j)^{\text{th}}$ element signifies the per student FTE of faculty type i associated with student type j in activities other than classroom teaching. For the numerical example used in chapter 5 (see figure 5.6 and table 5.5), we would have $\lambda_1 = 0.35$; $\lambda_2 = \lambda_3 = 1.0$; $d_{11} = 0.0041$; $d_{12} = 0.0234$; $d_{13} = 0.0198$; and all other $d_{ij} = 0$.

The instructional FTE of faculty is expressed with the aid of these matrices as

$$\mathbf{z}^{FI} = (\Lambda A + D)\mathbf{y}. \tag{6.A.8}$$

If the same linear functions that were used in (6.A.5) seem reasonably appropriate for estimating the staff and other expenses associated with *instructional* faculty, we may then follow the derivation of the unit cost and revenue vectors. In order to obtain the vectors of unit costs, $\mathbf{c}^I$, and revenues, $\mathbf{r}^I$, per student for instruction, we replace the matrix A by the matrix $\lambda A + D$:

$$\mathbf{c}^I = \mathbf{s}^S B^{SS} + \mathbf{b}^{OS} + (\mathbf{s}^F + \mathbf{s}^S B^{SF} + \mathbf{b}^{OF})(\lambda A + D)$$
$$\mathbf{r}^I = \mathbf{r}^y + \mathbf{r}^S B^{SS} + \mathbf{r}^{OS} + (\mathbf{r}^F + \mathbf{r}^S B^{SF} + \mathbf{r}^{OF})(\lambda A + D).$$

Finally, calculating the instructional costs and revenues per unit of output is simply a matter of postmultiplying these vectors of costs and revenues per student by the lifetimes matrix, $\mathbf{V}$.

APPENDIX 7

Computer Printout from a Sample Session with the University Planning Model

```
      INPUT
TYPE: 1 TO SKIP CONSTRAINT INPUT ROUTINE
[]:
      0
SPECIFY STUDENT LIFETIMES MATRIX
[]:
      3.75 2.8 2.5 1.5 0    0    0    0
[]:
      0    0    0    0   2.5 1.5 3.5 2.5
[]:
      0    0    0    0    0    0   1.0 1.0
SPECIFY COHORT DROPOUT RATES
[]:
      .13 .10 .25 .45
ADMISSIONS RATES:INPUT [PROGRAM NO.] (SPACE) [ADMISSION RATE]
INPUT: 0 0 WHEN FINISHED
[]:
      0 0
PROGRAM GRADUATES: INPUT [PROGRAM NO.] (SPACE) [GRADUATES]
INPUT: 0 0 WHEN FINISHED
[]:
      0 0
PROGRAM ENROLLMENT: INPUT [PROGRAM NO.] (SPACE) [ENROLLMENT]
INPUT: 0 0 WHEN FINISHED
[]:
      1 6500
[]:
      0 0
LINEAR EQUALITIES IN ENROLLMENT
INPUT A VECTOR AND R.H.S
INPUT: 0 0 WHEN FINISHED
[]:
      0 1 0 4000
[]:
      1 0 ⁻13 0
[]:
      0 0
LINEAR CONSTRAINTS ON COHORT FLOWS
INPUT Q VECTOR AND R.H.S.
INPUT: 0 0 WHEN FINISHED
[]:
      0 0 1 1 0 0 0 0 400
ALL CONSTRAINTS HAVE BEEN SPECIFIED...MOVING RIGHT ALONG...
```

UNIVERSITY   PLANNING   MODEL

FLOWS/STOCKS	COST TOTAL	UNIT	REVENUE TOTAL	UNIT
COHORT FLOWS				
1.00 1329.05	11933.00	8.98	20123.46	15.14
2.00 198.59	1331.38	6.70	2245.19	11.31
3.00 360.00	2154.86	5.99	3633.90	10.09
4.00 40.00	143.66	3.59	242.26	6.06
5.00 825.00	8055.70	9.76	7924.27	9.61
6.00 275.00	1611.14	5.86	1584.85	5.76
7.00 275.00	4304.70	15.65	4248.75	15.45
8.00 225.00	2643.22	11.75	2611.78	11.61
NEW STUDENTS				
1.00 1927.64	15562.90	8.07	26244.81	13.61
2.00 1600.00	16614.76	10.38	16369.66	10.23
3.00 .00	.00	.00	.00	.00
DEGREES				
1.00 1689.05	14087.86	8.34	23757.36	14.07
2.00 825.00	8055.70	9.76	7924.27	9.61
3.00 275.00	4304.70	15.65	4248.75	15.45
ENROLLMENTS				
1.00 6500.00	15562.90	2.39	26244.81	4.04
2.00 4000.00	15623.18	3.91	15368.29	3.84
3.00 500.00	991.58	1.98	1001.38	2.00

FACULTY

INSTRUCTIONAL:				
REGULAR	357.92	14531.75	40.60	2165.45	6.05
AUXILIARY	143.60	3230.91	22.50	89.03	.62
T. ASST.	500.00	1725.00	3.45	.00	.00
OTHER:					
REGULAR	292.85	11889.62	40.60	1771.73	6.05
AUXILIARY	.00	.00	22.50	.00	.62
T. ASST.	.00	.00	3.45	.00	.00

BUDGET SUMMARY

	COST	REVENUE
FACULTY SALARIES	22386	3902
STAFF SALARIES	29234	4555
FINANCIAL AID/TUITION	9200	39840
OTHER EXPENSES/INCOME	13368	17109
TOTAL OPER. EXPENSE/INCOME	74187	65406
ENDOWMENT PAYOUT		8781
ENDOWMENT PAYOUT RATE		.044

```
      BUILDM
      FAC
ENTER STUDENT F.T.E. FACTORS
□:
      .97 .86 .43
ENTER VECTOR OF FINANCIAL AID FACTORS BETA0 AND BETA1
□:
      0 0 0 .20 .25 0
ENTER TUITION VECTOR (IN THOUSANDS)
□:
      4 4 4
ENTER UNIVERSITY ENDOWMENT (IN THOUSANDS)
□:
      200000
SPECIFY AVE. COURSELOAD FOR REG. FACULTY
□:
      4.53
SPECIFY REGULAR FACULTY EFFORT FRACTIONS
□:
      .35 .1 .2 .35
SPECIFY OUTSIDE TEACHING FTE DIVISION AMONG STUDENTS
□:
      1 2 3
SPECIFY (TEACHING WT.,RESEARCH WT.) FOR JOINT TEACH/RES FTE
□:
      .5 .5
SPECIFY TEACHING WTS. FOR JOINT TEACH/RES FTE
□:
      0 1 .5


      COST

      OUTPUT
```

The computer program was written in APL by Eric Rosenberg, a Ph.D student in operations research who provided valuable assistance in several of our research projects at Stanford.

Mathematical Expressions for Deterministic

Dynamic Equilibrium

The theory of deterministic dynamic equilibrium is presented in compact mathematical form in this appendix. A compact representation of LRFE can be obtained by writing the laws of motion (equation [6.2]) in detached coefficient form.

$$
\begin{bmatrix} B_t \\ I_t \\ E_t \\ G_t \end{bmatrix} = \begin{bmatrix} (1+r+f) & 0 & 0 & hp \\ 0 & (1+i) & 0 & 0 \\ 0 & 0 & (1+\rho-p) & 1 \\ 0 & 0 & 0 & (1+g) \end{bmatrix} \begin{bmatrix} B_{t-1} \\ I_{t-1} \\ E_{t-1} \\ G_{t-1} \end{bmatrix}
$$

Let $\mathbf{x}_t$ = vector of state variables

$\mathbf{M}$ = coefficient matrix.

The above now can be written as

$$\mathbf{x}_t = \mathbf{M}\mathbf{x}_{t-1}. \tag{8.A.1}$$

Budget balance requires that

$$B_t - I_t - pE_t = 0.$$

Let $\mathbf{b}' = \{-1, 1, p, 0\}$, a row vector. Then $b'x_t = 0$ implies budget balance at time t.

The conditions for first-order equilibrium are, from equation (6.4),

$$\mathbf{b}'\mathbf{x}_0 = 0 \qquad \mathbf{b}'(\mathbf{x}_1 - \mathbf{x}_0) = \mathbf{b}'\mathbf{x}_1 = 0.$$

Using (8.A.1) we have

$$\mathbf{b}'\mathbf{x}_0 = 0$$
$$\mathbf{b}'\mathbf{M}\mathbf{x}_0 = 0 \tag{8.A.2}$$

which is to be solved for first-order equilibrium. Let the coefficient matrix for first-order equilibrium be denoted by

$$\mathbf{F}^{(1)} = \begin{bmatrix} \mathbf{b}' \\ \mathbf{b}'\mathbf{M} \end{bmatrix}.$$

(Note that in the case of zero-order equilibrium we have $\mathbf{F}^{(0)} = \mathbf{b}'$.) Then the set of conditions for first-order equilibrium is

$$\mathbf{F}^{(1)}\mathbf{x}_0 = \mathbf{0}.$$

This system is linear in the initial conditions but there are nonlinear interactions between the elements of $\mathbf{F}^{(1)}$ and $\mathbf{x}_0$.

Second-order equilibrium is obtained by adding a third row to $\mathbf{F}$. The second-order condition is $\mathbf{b}'(\mathbf{x}_2 - \mathbf{x}_0) = \mathbf{b}'\mathbf{x}_2 = 0$, and $\mathbf{x}_2 = \mathbf{M} \cdot \mathbf{M}\mathbf{x}_0 = \mathbf{M}^2\mathbf{x}_0$. Thus

$$\mathbf{F}^{(2)} = \begin{bmatrix} \mathbf{b}' \\ \mathbf{b}'\mathbf{M} \\ \mathbf{b}'\mathbf{M}^2 \end{bmatrix} \tag{8.A.3}$$

$$= \begin{bmatrix} -1 & 1 & p & 0 \\ -(r+f) & i & p(\rho - p) & p(1 - h) \\ -(r+f)^2 & i^2 & p(\rho - p)^2 & p[\rho + g - p - h(r + f + g)] \end{bmatrix}.$$

Now the nonlinearities among the coefficients for both first- and second-order equilibrium can be seen clearly. Here are the numerical magnitudes for $\mathbf{F}^{(2)}$, obtained for the basic numerical data used for examples in the text:

$$\mathbf{F}^{(2)} = \begin{bmatrix} -1.000 & 1.000 & 4.500 \times 10^{-2} & 0.000 \\ -2.397 \times 10^{-2} & 2.300 \times 10^{-2} & 4.500 \times 10^{-4} & 4.275 \times 10^{-2} \\ -5.744 \times 10^{-4} & 5.290 \times 10^{-4} & 4.500 \times 10^{-6} & 1.679 \times 10^{-3} \end{bmatrix}.$$

From these the reader can verify that the results presented in the text are indeed equilibrium solutions of the order specified.

SOLUTION PROCEDURE 8.A.1. Solutions involving only the initial conditions for equilibria of orders 0, 1, or 2 are easily obtained from the foregoing.

The approach will be illustrated for second-order equilibria. Since there are four initial conditions and only three equations, one value of x must be predetermined. Let this be x_i, and let $\mathbf{F}_i^{(2)}$ be the ith column of $\mathbf{F}^{(2)}$ and $\mathbf{F}_{\bar{i}}^{(2)}$ be the 3×3 matrix with $\mathbf{F}_i^{(2)}$ removed. Then

$$\mathbf{x} = [\mathbf{F}_{\bar{i}}^{(2)}]^{-1} \mathbf{F}_i^{(2)}$$

if $\mathbf{F}_{\bar{i}}^{(2)}$ is nonsingular.

Singularity for $\mathbf{F}_{\bar{i}}^{(2)}$ occurs in certain cases of balanced growth. For instance, if $r + f = i$ then $\mathbf{F}_{\bar{3}}^{(2)}$ and $\mathbf{F}_{\bar{4}}^{(2)}$ are singular. If in addition $h = 0$ and $g = i$, then every combination is singular. (The same holds for $\mathbf{F}^{(1)}$.) Singularity of $\mathbf{F}$ implies that there is no unique solution for the initial conditions. This is consistent with the discussion of equation (6.12), where we noted that in perfectly balanced growth with $h = 0$ the growth-rate constraint for first-order equilibrium is independent of the initial conditions.

SOLUTION PROCEDURE 8.A.2. For n^{th}-order equilibrium, where $2 < n < \infty$, the coefficient matrix is extended to $\mathbf{F}^{(n)}$ with final row $\mathbf{b}'\mathbf{M}^n$. Though the order of $\mathbf{F}^{(n)}$ is $n \times 4$, the rank cannot exceed four. Indeed, the rank of $\mathbf{F}$ cannot exceed three if a nontrivial solution in $\mathbf{x}_0$ is to be achieved, since with rank 4 we would write the equilibrium conditions as

$$\mathbf{F}^{(n)'} \mathbf{F}^{(n)} \mathbf{x}_0 = 0$$
$$\Rightarrow \mathbf{x}_0 = (\mathbf{F}^{(n)'} \mathbf{F}^{(n)})^{-1} \cdot 0$$

which means that $\mathbf{x}_0$ vanishes. Hence, there are conditions on the coefficients that must be met if a nontrivial solution for fourth- or higher-order equilibrium is to be achieved. Note that these restrictions are not necessary for lower-order solutions. The reason is that, as t exceeds the order of the equilibrium, the system is allowed to drift away from perfectly balanced growth. If x is to be positive, however, certain combinations of parameters are eschewed for equilibria of any order.

SOLUTION PROCEDURE 8.A.3. We turn now to the case of *infinite-order equilibria*, which requires perfectly balanced growth from an initial condition of budget balance.*

By perfectly balanced growth we mean that all the elements of $\mathbf{x}_t$ grow at the same rate. That is,

$$\mathbf{x}_t = \lambda \mathbf{x}_{t-1}$$

*Professor Arie P. Schinnar brought this idea to our attention in his unpublished manuscript, "Note on balanced budget growth solutions of Massy's university budget planning model" (University of Pennsylvania, January 1977). For the published version, see Schinnar 1978.

where λ (a scalar) is the common growth rate. But equation (8.A.1) must also be true by virtue of the postulated laws of motion. Hence

$$\lambda \mathbf{x} = \mathbf{M}\mathbf{x}$$

which holds for all t. The above can be rewritten as

$$(\mathbf{M} - \lambda\mathbf{I})\mathbf{x} = \mathbf{0}$$

so we see that λ is an eigenvalue and $\mathbf{x}$ an eigenvector of $\mathbf{M}$. Note that if $\mathbf{x}$ is an eigenvector of $\mathbf{M}$, then $\mathbf{M}^n\mathbf{x} = \lambda^n\mathbf{x}$, so if $\mathbf{b}'\mathbf{x} = 0$, then $\mathbf{b}'\mathbf{M}^n\mathbf{x} = 0$, too.

The triangularity of $\mathbf{M}$ and the condition $\mathbf{x} \geq \mathbf{0}$ makes the solution straightforward. The system is

$$(\mathbf{M} - \lambda\mathbf{I})\mathbf{x} = \mathbf{0}$$

$$= \begin{bmatrix} 1 + r + f - \lambda & 0 & 0 & hp \\ 0 & 1 + i - \lambda & 0 & 0 \\ 0 & 0 & 1 + \rho - p - \lambda & 1 \\ 0 & 0 & 0 & 1 + g - \lambda \end{bmatrix} \begin{bmatrix} B_0 \\ I_0 \\ E_0 \\ G_0 \end{bmatrix}$$

By inspection we see that the only eigenvalue for which $\mathbf{x} > \mathbf{0}$ is $\lambda = 1 + i = 1 + g$. This implies

$$(r + f - i)B_0 + hpG_0 = 0$$
$$(\rho - p - i)E_0 + G_0 = 0$$
$$i = g \qquad i > \rho - p \tag{8.A.4}$$

and

$$i > r + f \quad \text{if} \quad h > 0 \quad \text{or} \quad i = r + f \quad \text{if} \quad h = 0.$$

The budget balance constraint $B_0 = I_0 + pE_0$ is required also for infinite-order equilibrium.

The absence of a unique solution for B and I if $r + f = i$ and $h = 0$ is easily seen. If $r + f = i$ and $h > 0$, then G must equal zero. Also, $\rho - p - i$ must vanish in order for E_0 to be positive. As noted in the text, the simplicity of the conditions for perfectly balanced growth may aid in understanding long-run financial equilibrium and also be useful in special situations. These conditions do not, however, represent practical criteria for financial health.

A Sample Session with the Staff Affirmative

Action Planning Model

The computer printout from a sample session with Stanford's affirmative action planning model is given below. The program operates interactively, that is, with the user sitting at a remote teletype or video (CRT) terminal connected to a central computer (which in Stanford's case was an IBM 370/158). After logging on and loading the proper workspace, the user begins the run by typing the function (i.e., program) name "AFF." The computer responds by listing the allowable job categories and asking the user which one he or she wishes to work with. The user selects job type 3, "professional research."

Next, the user is asked to choose the population group for which the staffing projections are to be made, and responds with a "1," denoting the ethnic minority group. Values then are given in response to queries about the growth rate ($\theta = 0$) and the minority availability fraction ($a = 0.15$). This ends the input phase of the program, and it begins to make the calculations described in the main body of chapter 8. Once the iterations are complete for a five-year projection period, the model displays the results in tabular form.

The rows of the output table are the "L.O.S." groups, while its columns are the years being projected. The first column gives the actual figures for the base year, in this case 1976. Proceeding down the third column, for example, we see that, at the end of the year 1978, there are projected to be 20.4 FTE new minority professional research staff, 17.3 FTE with L.O.S. = 1, 9.3 FTE with L.O.S. = 2, etc., for a total of 77.0 FTE minority professional research staff. According to the figure at the bottom of the table, this would correspond to 12.0 percent of the total FTE in this job category projected for that year.

This sample run took less than five minutes of the user's time at the terminal, and cost well under $1.00 in billed computer resources. Obviously it is practical to make a great many such runs, and thereby to explore many possible options with the aid of this simple yet timesaving tool.

This program was written in APL by Eric Rosenberg.

```
        AFF
SELECT JOB TYPE BY IDENTIFICATION NUMBER:
[1]ADMINISTRATIVE ASSISTANTS
[2]PROFESSIONAL NON-RESEARCH
[3]PROFESSIONAL RESEARCH
[4]OFFICE AND CLERICAL
[5]CRAFTS
[6]OFFICIALS AND MANAGERS
[7]MANAG./ADMIN./OFFICIALS
▢:
        3


SELECT GROUP BY IDENTIFICATION NUMBER:
[1]MIN.
[2]NON-MIN.
[3]FEMALE
[4]MALE
[5]TOTAL
▢:
        1


SPECIFY GROWTH RATE:
▢:
        0


SPECIFY AVAILABILITY FRACTION(SINGLE NUMBER):
▢:
        .15
```

PROFESSIONAL RESEARCH   :MIN.

YEAR

L.O.S.	1976	1977	1978	1979	1980	1981
NEW	18.0	19.7	20.4	19.3	19.0	18.7
1	14.0	15.8	17.3	17.9	17.0	16.8
2	5.0	8.2	9.3	10.1	10.5	9.9
3	5.0	3.2	5.3	6.0	6.5	6.8
4	6.0	4.2	2.7	4.4	5.0	5.4
5	8.0	4.9	3.4	2.2	3.6	4.0
6	3.0	6.3	3.8	2.6	1.7	2.8
7	4.0	2.7	5.6	3.4	2.4	1.5
8	1.0	3.6	2.4	5.1	3.1	2.2
9+	3.0	3.7	6.8	8.6	12.8	14.8
TOTAL:	67.0	72.3	77.0	79.7	81.5	82.9

FRACTION OF TOTAL STAFFING LEVEL:

	.104	.113	.120	.124	.127	.129

An Illustrative Use of the Decision

Calculus Model

The purpose of this appendix is to illustrate the use of the decision calculus model described in chapter 9. By exercising the model with some representative data, we get some idea of the sort of insights it can provide. Table A10.1 contains a set of initial values and financial data that roughly correspond to Stanford's position in the year 1973/74. In table A10.2 we have indicated our own suggested values for the subjective parameters (this particular set of numbers has no significance beyond that of providing some trial values for our sample runs). The variables and parameters shown in these tables are all defined in chapter 9.

If we plug the data from tables A10.1 and A10.2 into our program and solve for the optimal configuration of planning variables, we obtain the results shown in the third column of table A10.3.* As one readily can see, with these data the optimal solution is not very different from the current operating point (shown in the second column of the same table). No variable changes by more than 7.6 percent, which indicates that we have obtained a good "fit" of the model to the Stanford data.

As a demonstration of the model's capabilities, let us employ it to check the sensitivity of the solution to some of the uncertain demand-elasticity coefficients. Suppose, in particular, that we take each of the parameters ε_{24}, ε_{75}, and ε_{86} in (9.8) and double them in absolute magnitude from the base-case values in table A10.2. Making just these changes in the data, one at a time, and then reoptimizing leads to the results shown in the "sensitivity" columns of

---

*Stanford's current running version of this program uses the Generalized Reduced Gradient (GRG) algorithm, as coded by Lasdon, Jain, and Rattner 1976, to perform the nonlinear optimization. This step must be run in the batch mode. The interactive program sets up the data for the batch run, sees that it is executed, and then fetches the results. Further details are given in Rosenberg 1978. The program operates quite efficiently on this small problem, with each run costing somewhere around $1.00.

Table A10.1. Illustrative Data for the Decision Calculus Model

I. Initial Values

$FAC =$	650	$R =$	0.5
$UG =$	6,400	$M =$	\$ 1.6 million
$GR =$	4,500	$SR =$	\$25.0 million
$T =$	\$3,100	$TG =$	\$ 6.25 million

II. Budget Coefficients (in \$ Millions)

Equation	Constant	Variable							
		FAC	UG	GR	$T \times UG$	$T \times GR$	SR	TG	IN
IN	5.73	0.0365	0.00021	....	....	....	....	....	....
AID	−7.00	....	....	....	0.217	0.430	....	....	....
IC	9.70	....	....	....	....	....	0.3	....	0.3
TUR	....	....	....	....	1.05	0.80	....	....	....

III. Other Constants and Financial Parameters

$OI =$	\$ 6.9 million		
$DEPR =$	\$ 5.0 million	$\eta = 0.40$	
$ICRES =$	\$ 1.2 million	$\delta_0 = 0.33$	
$E =$	\$160.0 million	$\delta_1 = 0.20$	
		$\rho = 0.055$	
		$r = 0.0234$	
		$f = 0.005$	

Table A10.2. Subjective Parameters for the Decision Calculus Model

I. Demand Elasticities

Demand Equation	Variable				
	FAC	T	$1 + R$	M	SR
UG	0.8	−0.1	....	....	....
GR	1.0	−0.1	....	....	0.50
SR	0.6	....	−0.25	....	....
TG	0.1	....	....	0.25	....

II. Objective Weights

	Variable			
	FAC	UG	GR	T
Initial values	650	6,400	4,500	\$3,100
Ideal values	900	6,000	5,000	\$2,500
$MRS_{x,FAC}$	−1.0	8.0	−3.0	4.0

table A10.3. (Only one elasticity is displaced in each run.) For example, the figures in the "sensitivity to $\varepsilon_{UG,T}$" column were obtained by changing the value of ε_{24} from −0.1 to −0.2 and rerunning the program. The first column under this heading shows the actual solution obtained, while its deviations from the base-run optimal values are shown in the second. The other two sensitivity runs changed ε_{75} from −0.25 to −0.5, and ε_{86} from 0.25 to 0.5, respectively.

Table A10.3.   Sample Runs with the Decision Calculus Model

		Base Run		Sensitivity to $\varepsilon_{UG\,T}$		Sensitivity to $\varepsilon_{SR.R}$		Sensitivity to $\varepsilon_{TG.M}$	
Variable	Initial Values	Opt. Values	Change from Initial Values	Opt. Values	% Change	Opt. Values	% Change	Opt. Values	% Change
FAC	650	689	6.0%	690	0.1%	689	0.0%	687	(0.3%)
UG	6,400	6,687	4.5%	6,678	(0.1%)	6,688	0.0%	6,724	0.6%
GR	4,500	4,842	7.6%	4,855	0.3%	4,846	0.1%	4,863	0.4%
T	$3,100	$3,174	2.4%	$3,185	0.3%	$3,175	0.0%	$2,948	(7.1%)
R	0.500	0.494	(1.2%)	0.494	0.0%	0.494	0.0%	0.494	0.0%
M^a	$1.60	$1.56	(2.5%)	$1.56	0.0%	$1.56	0.0%	$6.17	296.0%
B^a	$60.60	$63.59	4.9%	$63.71	0.2%	$63.61	0.0%	$67.37	5.9%
SR^a	$25.00	$25.91	3.6%	$25.94	0.1%	$25.94	0.1%	$25.87	(0.2%)
TG^a	$6.25	$6.25	0.0%	$6.25	0.0%	$6.25	0.0%	$12.34	97.4%

[a] Dollar figures in millions.

These three runs reveal something about the response of each class of "demand" variable (i.e., students, research, and gifts) to the elasticity with respect to its major "price" (i.e., tuition, indirect cost rate, and fund-raising budget). Apparently student enrollment and research volume are almost totally insensitive to quite large changes in the magnitude of the elasticities within the range we tested. This is evident from the fact that no variable's optimal value changes by more than a few tenths of one percent from the base case. In the case of gifts, on the other hand, an increase in its elasticity coefficient leads to a large increase in the fund-raising budget. This, in turn, is seen to result in considerably higher gift receipts, which are used mainly to reduce tuition. Finally, as a second-order effect, the reduced tuition leads to small increases in the enrollments of both undergraduate and graduate students, in accordance with their own associated demand constraints.

If these data were meant to be taken seriously, we would conclude from this analysis that errors in estimating the first two types of elasticity coefficients hardly matter at all, while the value of the third is an important consideration in setting the approximate level for the fund-raising budget. This would suggest that little payoff can be expected from refining the values of ε_{24} and ε_{75} as long as we know they are close to zero, but that efforts to pin down better estimates of the elasticity coefficient for TG would be worthwhile.*

It should be obvious that the model is quite rich in parameters that one might wish to experiment with in the manner shown above. This example has sufficed for our purpose, however, which was to demonstrate the potential for such a tool in dealing with the value optimization problem in its most complete form.

*The reader should not lose sight of the highly nonlinear character of this model. Had the base case started out with much larger elasticities for enrollments and/or research, even the qualitative results might have been quite different.

A Sample Run of the TRADES
Structured Search Option

This appendix illustrates the use of the structured search option of TRADES, developed by Merrill M. Flood, that was discussed in chapter 9. The instructions and initial information pertaining to a set of fourteen primary planning variables (PPVs) are as given below. (The full definitions of these variables were given in the text—see table 9.2.)

```
       YOU WILL NOW CHOOSE ON EACH OF A SEQUENCE
OF TRIALS BETWEEN A NEW CONFIGURATION AND THE ONE
YOU HAVE PREVIOUSLY PREFERRED.  WHEN YOU SEE THE
RESPONSE "BETTER?" TYPE "1" IF YOU PREFER THE CURRENT
CONFIGURATION TO THE ONE YOU PREFERRED MOST RECENTLY --
OTHERWISE TYPE "0".  ALSO TYPE "0" IF YOU ARE INDIFFERENT
BETWEEN THE TWO MOST RECENT CONFIGURATIONS.
       WHENEVER YOU SEE "ANY CHANGES" YOU HAVE SEVERAL OPTIONS:
TYPE "0" TO SEARCH WITH NO FURTHER CHANGES.
TYPE "1" TO SKIP THIS VARIABLE THIS STEP.
TYPE "2" TO SKIP THIS VARIABLE EVERY STEP.
TYPE "3" TO SECURE STEPSIZE CHANGE OPTIONS.
TYPE "4" TO SECURE LOWER BOUND CHANGE OPTIONS.
TYPE "5" TO SECURE UPPER BOUND CHANGE OPTIONS.
TYPE "6" TO STOP SEARCHING AND RETURN TO TRADE2.
       WHEN YOU ELECT TO MAKE CHANGES IN BOUNDS OR IN STEPSIZES,
YOU DO SO BY TYPING THE REFERENCE NUMBER FOR THE VARIABLE
FOLLOWED BY THE VALUE FOR ITS NEW BOUND OR NEW STEPSIZE IN
FORMAT(I2,F15.5). TYPE "0" TO RETURN AGAIN TO THE
"ANY CHANGES" STATUS.
```

LABEL	#	VALUE	BMIN	BMAX	DELT
FAC	1	700.00000	500.00000	1500.00000	1.00000
AFAC	2	80.00000	0.0	250.00000	0.25000
UG	3	6500.00000	5000.00000	8000.00000	3.00000
GR	4	4600.00000	3000.00000	7000.00000	4.00000
TENR	5	0.65000	0.50000	0.90000	0.00040
STFR	6	0.50000	0.20000	0.80000	0.00060
P	7	0.04800	0.04000	0.06000	0.00002
TR	8	0.05000	0.0	0.08000	0.00008
F	9	0.0	0.0	0.03000	0.00003
DT	10	0.03000	0.0	0.04000	0.00004
DFS	11	0.01000	0.0	0.04000	0.00004
DSS	12	0.01000	0.0	0.04000	0.00004
SBSL	13	0.20000	0.0	0.05000	0.00005
DCVL	14	0.08000	0.0	0.10000	0.00010

In the first cycle through the algorithm, the user selects out the variables with which he or she does not wish to work and designates others that are always to be minimized or maximized. In the example below, the user has dropped the variables *TENR*, *STFR*, *P*, *TR*, *SBSL*, and *DCVL* from further consideration—so they will remain frozen at their current values—and has indicated that *FAC* and *F* are to be always maximized, subject to no effective upper bounds. On the other hand, the bounds on *UG* and *GR* have been set at their finite ideal values and the program has been told to "always min"—in the case of *UG*—or "always max"—in the case of *GR*—these variables subject to their new bounds.

```
THIS IS VAR #  1  FAC          700.00000   ANY CHANGES?
->0
TYPE "0" TO SEE AND SEARCH, TYPE "1" TO MAX OR MIN.
->1
ENTER 1 TO ALWAYS MAX THIS VAR, 2 TO ALWAYS MIN IT
3 TO TEMPMAX IT, AND 4 TO TEMPMIN IT.
->1
CONFIG #   0  FAC   1      700.00000
CONFIG #   1  FAC   1      700.99976
CONFIG #   2  FAC   1      704.99951
CONFIG #   3  FAC   1      720.99927
CONFIG #   4  FAC   1      784.99902
CONFIG #   5  FAC   1     1040.99878
THIS CONFIGURATION IS INFEASIBLE
THIS IS VAR #  2  AFAC          80.00000   ANY CHANGES?
->1
THIS IS VAR #  3  UG          6500.00000   ANY CHANGES?
->4
CHANGE LOWER BOUND
->03  6000.
NEW LOWER BOUND IS: 3       6000.00000
CHANGE LOWER BOUND
->0
THIS IS VAR #  3  UG          6500.00000   ANY CHANGES?
->0
TYPE "0" TO SEE AND SEARCH, TYPE "1" TO MAX OR MIN.
->1
ENTER 1 TO ALWAYS MAX THIS VAR, 2 TO ALWAYS MIN IT
3 TO TEMPMAX IT, AND 4 TO TEMPMIN IT.
->2
CONFIG #   5  UG   3      6502.99609
CONFIG #   6  UG   3      6497.00000
CONFIG #   7  UG   3      6485.00000
CONFIG #   8  UG   3      6437.00000
CONFIG #   9  UG   3      6245.00000
THIS CONFIGURATION IS INFEASIBLE
THIS IS VAR #  4  GR          4600.00000   ANY CHANGES?
->5
CHANGE UPPER BOUND
->04  5000.
NEW UPPER BOUND IS: 4       5000.00000
CHANGE UPPER BOUND
```

```
->0
  THIS IS VAR #  4  GR         4600.00000  ANY CHANGES?
->0
  TYPE "0" TO SEE AND SEARCH, TYPE "1" TO MAX OR MIN.
->1
  ENTER 1 TO ALWAYS MAX THIS VAR, 2 TO ALWAYS MIN IT
  3 TO TEMPMAX IT, AND 4 TO TEMPMIN IT.
->1
  CONFIG #   9  GR    4      4603.99609
  CONFIG #  10  GR    4      4619.99219
  CONFIG #  11  GR    4      4683.98828
  CONFIG #  12  GR    4      4939.98437
  CONFIG #  13  GR    4      5963.98047
  OUT OF YOUR BOUNDS
  THIS IS VAR #  5  TENR        0.65000  ANY CHANGES?
->2
  THIS IS VAR #  6  STFR        0.50000  ANY CHANGES?
->2
  THIS IS VAR #  7  P           0.04800  ANY CHANGES?
->2
  THIS IS VAR #  8  TR          0.05000  ANY CHANGES?
->2
  THIS IS VAR #  9  F           0.0      ANY CHANGES?
->0
  TYPE "0" TO SEE AND SEARCH, TYPE "1" TO MAX OR MIN.
->1
  ENTER 1 TO ALWAYS MAX THIS VAR, 2 TO ALWAYS MIN IT
  3 TO TEMPMAX IT, AND 4 TO TEMPMIN IT.
->1
  CONFIG #  13  F    9        0.00003
  CONFIG #  14  F    9        0.00015
  CONFIG #  15  F    9        0.00063
  CONFIG #  16  F    9        0.00255
  CONFIG #  17  F    9        0.01023
  THIS CONFIGURATION IS INFEASIBLE
  THIS IS VAR # 10  DT          0.03000  ANY CHANGES?
->1
  THIS IS VAR # 11  DFS         0.01000  ANY CHANGES?
->1
  THIS IS VAR # 12  DSS         0.01000  ANY CHANGES?
->1
  THIS IS VAR # 13  SSSL        0.20000  ANY CHANGES?
->2
  THIS IS VAR # 14  DCVL        0.08000  ANY CHANGES?
->2
```

The second cycle begins to improve on each of the remaining free decision variables, taken in PPV order. First, *FAC* is automatically stepped up to the point just before it reaches infeasibility:

```
CONFIG #  17  FAC   1        785.99878
CONFIG #  18  FAC   1        789.99854
CONFIG #  19  FAC   1        805.99829
CONFIG #  20  FAC   1        869.99805
THIS CONFIGURATION IS INFEASIBLE
THIS IS VAR #  2  AFAC        80.00000  ANY CHANGES?
```

Next, the user-directed "search-and-see" option is used to improve the value of the second variable, *AFAC*:

```
->0
   TYPE "0" TO SEE AND SEARCH, TYPE "1" TO MAX OR MIN.
 ->0
CONFIG # 20  AFAC  2        80.24998
LIST PPV'S=1, SKIP=0
->
FINANCIAL SUMMARY=1,SKIP=0
->
CONSTRAINT SUMMARY=1,SKIP=0
->
 BETTER?
->1
 CONFIG # 21  AFAC  2        81.24997
 LIST PPV'S=1, SKIP=0
->
FINANCIAL SUMMARY=1,SKIP=0
->
CONSTRAINT SUMMARY=1,SKIP=0
->
 BETTER?
->1
 CONFIG # 22  AFAC  2.       85.24995
 LIST PPV'S=1, SKIP=0
->
FINANCIAL SUMMARY=1,SKIP=0
->
CONSTRAINT SUMMARY=1,SKIP=0
->
 BETTER?
->1
 CONFIG # 23  AFAC  2       101.24994
 LIST PPV'S=1, SKIP=0
->
FINANCIAL SUMMARY=1,SKIP=0
->
CONSTRAINT SUMMARY=1,SKIP=0
->
 BETTER?
->0
```

The first step of the "search-and-see" with *AFAC* determines whether (for this cycle) more or less of the variable is preferred. At each subsequent step, the user is provided with the new value for *AFAC* and prompted to choose between the new configuration and the one just before. (Note that such binary choices are all that are called for in operating the algorithm.) In the example at hand, three steps were taken before the user indicated that the next increase would lead to a less-preferred configuration.

At this point, the algorithm moves on to the third variable, *UG*, which the user already chose to minimize subject to the aforementioned lower bound:

```
CONFIG # 24  UG  3     6439.99609
CONFIG # 25  UG  3     6434.00000
CONFIG # 26  UG  3     6422.00000
CONFIG # 27  UG  3     6374.00000
CONFIG # 28  UG  3     6182.00000
THIS CONFIGURATION IS INFEASIBLE
```

It proceeds with the remaining variables, either performing an automatic optimization, or eliciting choices from the user along a single dimension at a time:

```
CONFIG #  28   GR    4      4943.98047
CONFIG #  29   GR    4      4959.97656
CONFIG #  30   GR    4      5023.97266
OUT OF YOUR BOUNDS
CONFIG #  30   F     9        0.00258
CONFIG #  31   F     9        0.00270
CONFIG #  32   F     9        0.00318
CONFIG #  33   F     9        0.00510
CONFIG #  34   F     9        0.01278
THIS CONFIGURATION IS INFEASIBLE
THIS. IS VAR # 10   DT          0.03000   ANY CHANGES?
->0
    TYPE "0" TO SEE AND SEARCH, TYPE "1" TO MAX OR MIN.
    ->1
    ENTER 1 TO ALWAYS MAX THIS VAR, 2 TO ALWAYS MIN IT
    3 TO TEMPMAX IT, AND 4 TO TEMPMIN IT.
    ->4
    CONFIG #  34   DT   10       0.03004
    CONFIG #  35   DT   10       0.02996
    CONFIG #  36   DT   10       0.02980
    CONFIG #  37   DT   10       0.02916
    CONFIG #  38   DT   10       0.02660
    CONFIG #  39   DT   10       0.01636
    THIS CONFIGURATION IS INFEASIBLE
    THIS IS VAR # 11   DFS         0.01000   ANY CHANGES?
    ->1
    THIS IS VAR # 12   DSS         0.01000   ANY CHANGES?
    ->0
    TYPE "0" TO SEE AND SEARCH, TYPE "1" TO MAX OR MIN.
    ->1
    ENTER 1 TO ALWAYS MAX THIS VAR, 2 TO ALWAYS MIN IT
    3 TO TEMPMAX IT, AND 4 TO TEMPMIN IT.
    ->3
    CONFIG #  39   DSS  12       0.01004
    CONFIG #  40   DSS  12       0.01020
    CONFIG #  41   DSS  12       0.01084
    CONFIG #  42   DSS  12       0.01340
    CONFIG #  43   DSS  12       0.02364
    THIS CONFIGURATION IS INFEASIBLE

CONFIG #  43   FAC   1        806.99805
CONFIG #  44   FAC   1        810.99780
THIS CONFIGURATION IS INFEASIBLE
THIS IS VAR #  2   AFAC       85.24995   ANY CHANGES?
=>6
```

Here, the variables *DT* and *DSS* are used to illustrate, respectively, the "TEMP-MIN" and "TEMPMAX" options of the program.

Upon completion of the second cycle, we have the configuration shown below:

```
OPTION? (TYPE 11 TO VIEW THE LIST.)
=>1


LIST PPV'S=1, SKIP=0
=>1
    1 FAC          806.9980      2 AFAC       85.2500
    3 UG          6374.0000      4 GR       4959.9766
    5 TENR           0.6500      6 STFR        0.5000
    7 P              0.0480      8 TR          0.0500
    9 F              0.0051     10 DT          0.0266
   11 DFS            0.0100     12 DSS         0.0134
   13 SBSL           0.2000     14 DCVL        0.0800
FINANCIAL SUMMARY=1,SKIP=0
=>1
BUDGET SUMMARY
YEAR                   78/79     79/80
EXPENSES            93844.56  101792.31
INCOME              94146.25  102097.06
DEFICIT(-)            301.69    304.75
ENDOW PO RATE         0.0480    0.0480
TUITION/BUDGET        0.5683    0.5693
PO/BUDGET             0.1181    0.1194
GROWTH TO                    79/80
EXPENSES                    7947.75
INCOME                      7950.81
DEFICIT(--)                    3.06
ENDOW PO RATE                  0.0
TUITION/BUDGET              0.0010
PO/BUDGET                  0.0014
CONSTRAINT SUMMARY=1,SKIP=0
=>1
NAME OF CONSTRAINT  MIN        VALUE        MAX       OUTMIN(-)   OUTMAX(
NO DEFICIT---YEAR 0
                   0.0     301.6875**********    301.6875********
NO DEFICIT GROWTH FOR ONE YEAR
                   0.0       3.0625**********      3.0625********
```

According to the financial summary, there still remains considerable slack in the budget balance constraint for the first year, since there is a surplus of nearly $302 thousand, but the deficit growth constraint has become fairly tight. This base-period slack would be removed during subsequent iterations.

A Case Study: The University of

Northern California (UNC)

The University of Northern California (UNC) is a well-known private western university located in San Miguel in Northern California. It was founded in 1885 by a group of businessmen to provide on the West Coast an educational environment for undergraduate and graduate studies comparable to those then existing at the better schools on the East Coast. Over the years, UNC acquired a national reputation for high standards in nearly all its instructional and research activities. In 1975, UNC was recognized as one of the top American universities, and, due to the high quality of the faculty's academic scholarship and research, many of its departments rightfully claimed leadership in their respective fields.

The president of UNC was Dr. James Colley. He had been at the university since 1950, holding first a teaching position in the School of Education, then being named provost of the university in 1960 and president in July of 1964. Since assuming the presidency he had been successful in constituting a very competent and unified administrative team, including Provost John Clarke. Under their direction, UNC followed a program of expansion, the main objectives of which were to maintain and where possible enhance the academic qualities of the institution as well as to upgrade its physical plant.

In the years just prior to 1975 the increasing stringency of academic budgets led President Colley, Provost Clarke, and their staffs to question some of their basic premises about the size and structure of UNC. As long as opportunities for government support and private fund-raising had continued to advance during the 1960s, decisions about departmental academic and research programs could be made largely on their individual merits. (There were instances

The situation, institution, and individuals described in this case are fictitious. The case was prepared as a basis for group discussion rather than to illustrate either effective or ineffective handling of an administrative situation. It was developed by Jean-Claude Larréché under the authors' direction.

where one program impacted another, but the effects were often mutually reinforcing rather than the other way around.) Given a "steady state" or perhaps even a declining level of constant-dollar support, however, individual program evaluations were no longer adequate by themselves. Some basic decisions about the overall size and structure of the institution were needed to provide a context in which separate programmatic tradeoffs could be made.

It was agreed that the "size and structure" of UNC should be a function of its objectives as a university with its particular values and history, as well as the realities of the current budget squeeze. The list of "objectives" was headed by "academic quality," which was defined to include excellence in both teaching and research. There was no particular desire to enlarge the university just for the sake of expansion; and the same was true with respect to contraction. However, there was a good deal of discussion about the proper mix of undergraduate and graduate teaching and research, and many other factors related to "academic quality."

The first problem was that of isolating what main variables affect the academic quality of the university. Any decision that would bring about a change in the present status of the university would eventually have an effect on its academic quality. However, it was recognized that for long-range planning purposes it would be impractical to consider all the factors which affect academic quality most strongly. The number of graduate and undergraduate students and the number of faculty members should certainly be among these variables. Beyond this, there was considerable debate about how many and which other variables were needed to represent the structure of UNC adequately without becoming impractical.

It was agreed that once these variables were isolated, a second problem would be to investigate exactly how they relate to academic quality. As there was no generally acceptable measure of "quality," these relationships were not well defined. Thus, each person would have to use his or her own best judgment to see how changes in the planning variables would be likely to affect the academic quality of the university. For instance, most of the staff thought that, at least within certain limits, increasing the number of faculty members with the same number of students would add to the quality of academic programs. So also would decreasing the number of undergraduate students with the same number of faculty members. (They were not so sure about the effect of reducing the number of doctoral students, however.) If the numbers of both students and faculty members were to be changed at the same time the problem would become more complicated although still relatively simple. However, when one tries to change a larger number of variables, the complexity of the problem increases rapidly and it becomes a great deal more difficult to evaluate the impact of these simultaneous changes on the academic quality of the university. More importantly, since the effects of these changes on the university's budget are better understood than their more subtle effects on academic quality, Dr. Colley and Provost Clarke felt there was a danger that budgetary considerations would tend to dominate in the evaluations.

It is probably with all these thoughts in mind that Drs. Colley and Clarke encouraged the development of an interdisciplinary research program on university management. While this program had a strong "basic" component, it was also addressed directly to the problems of the UNC administration. Dr. Kingsley Roberts served as manager of the program; his experience included research and teaching in operations research, management, and academic planning and analysis.

A key assignment for Dr. Roberts was to assist the president's planning and budgeting group in studying the impact of strategic decisions on academic quality at UNC by:

1. Isolating a limited set of variables which affect most strongly the quality of academic programs;
2. Studying the relationships between this set of variables and academic quality.

This project was a team effort involving the president and provost as well as Donald Ross (vice-president for planning), Peggy Wilson (vice-president for finance), and Edgar Herrmann (vice-president for research).

Dr. Roberts considered his role as one of coordinator and facilitator for this activity. He knew the president and his team had many preoccupations and that their time was precious. He had to decide on a research strategy, to prepare meetings of the administrative officers on the project, and to analyze and present results so that the team sessions would be most efficient.

From November 1974 to April 1975, the group's task was to isolate a limited set of variables which affected most the academic quality of UNC. After a number of sessions the group agreed on the set of eight variables listed in exhibit A12.1. Also shown in exhibit A12.1 are the current values of these variables at UNC.

The next task for the group was to determine the relationship between these variables and academic quality. Dr. Roberts knew that a major problem would be to direct the team towards considering aspects of quality without being biased by budgeting considerations. He believed this would be difficult as each person was used to dealing with budgeting or financial problems and would naturally tend to focus on those aspects of a situation with which he or she was most familiar.

As a preliminary investigation of the impact of the variables on academic quality free of budgeting considerations, Dr. Roberts had decided to present each member of the team with two alternative configurations for UNC, both of which could be supported budgetarily. These two configurations are presented in exhibit A12.2. Each member of the team would be asked to consider carefully each alternative and to select the one which in their opinion would provide the highest level of academic quality at UNC. In so doing, they would have to analyze how each of the variables affects the academic quality of the institution; however, budgetary considerations were to be discounted entirely for purposes of this exercise. The detailed instructions provided for the team are presented in exhibit A12.3.

Dr. Roberts presented the exercise to the group during its meeting on

Exhibit A12.1.   Primary Planning Variables

Variable Name	Description	Current UNC Value
(1) Regular faculty (F)	"Full-time equivalent (FTE) regular faculty members involved in teaching." Includes only professors and senior lecturers.	1,000
(2) Auxiliary faculty (AF)	"FTE other teaching personnel." Includes instructors, lecturers, visitors, etc., but not teaching assistants.	200
(3) Undergraduate student enrollment (UG)	"Head count of undergraduate students registered for autumn quarter."	8,000
(4) Graduate student enrollment (G)	"Head count of graduate students registered for autumn quarter."	7,000
(5) Non-Ph.D graduate enrollment (P)	"The percentage of graduate students included in variable 4 who are enrolled in a master's or 'first professional' degree program (such as MS in computer science, MFA, Ed.D, or JD)."	25%
(6) Base tuition level (T)	"Tuition rate expressed in 1973/74 constant dollars."	$2,500
(7) Staff/faculty ratio (S/F)	"Ratio of FTE academic support staff to regular faculty." Includes all "other personnel appointments" in the academic budget as well as faculty administrators.	1.0
(8) Faculty leverage (L)	Fraction of salaries paid to regular faculty that are not included in the operating budget, i.e., that are funded by government of foundation grants or contracts, corporate affiliation funds, gift funds, or similar term-support sources rather than by endowments or unrestricted income.	0.10

Exhibit A12.2.   Alternatives for UNC

	Alternative 1	Alternative 2
Regular faculty	900	1,000
Auxiliary faculty	250	200
Undergraduate student enrollment	7,000	9,000
Graduate student enrollment	7,000	6,000
Non-Ph.D graduate enrollment	30%	20%
Base tuition level	$2,300	$2,700
Staff/faculty ratio	1.25	0.75
Faculty leverage	0.15	0.05

Wednesday, May 15. The group decided that the exercise would be valuable and that each member should do it individually and discuss it in a meeting on the next Monday, May 20, at 10:00 A.M.

President Colley was looking forward to his weekend. The spring quarter had been particularly busy and it was the first weekend over the last two months during which he would have a chance to relax. On Sunday afternoon, he was comfortably installed by the side of his swimming pool—sometimes intervening in a discussion between his wife and daughter, sometimes going through the exercise he had received from Dr. Roberts. After an hour of talk and reflection, and two strawberry milkshakes, he was feeling quite pleased about the exercise. First, he realized that it was perhaps the first time he had felt free to think about the quality and overall objectives of UNC in fairly operational terms and in the absence of budgetary constraints. Second, although he had previously thought about some of the relations between the variables and academic quality, other relations were now appearing which he had never had a chance to consider before. Deciding that the exercise deserved better concentration, the president put it aside and joined the discussion between his wife and daughter.

After dinner, the president isolated himself in his study to complete the exercise. After two hours of concentrated thought, he decided he had a sufficiently good grasp of the situation. He was aware that some of the relations were ill defined and that he may have overlooked some other ones. However, he was confident that the alternative he had selected would provide a higher level of quality and that he could make a good case for it. As he was leaving his study, he was looking forward to a lively and challenging discussion with the members of his staff the next morning.

You are Donald Ross, vice-president for planning, and you have to prepare the exercise for the Monday meeting of the group. You know that the implications of this meeting will be significant for the project, and, more importantly, for the future of strategic planning at the university. You will have to present which of the two alternatives in your opinion would better meet the objectives of UNC and to explain why. Other members of the group will certainly challenge your recommendation and you must be prepared to defend it.

Exhibit A12.3.   Instructions for Assessment of Alternative Size and Structure on the Academic Quality and Other Objectives of UNC

In recent years the budgetary stringencies adopted in the face of declining income growth have received a great deal of attention at this and many other universities. Too often, in making decisions about adjustments in our income and expenditure budgets from one year to the next, we have not had the opportunity to make a systematic evaluation of the university's posture with respect to enrollments, faculty size, tuition level, academic support staff, etc. Accordingly, we have decided at this time to ask a selected group of administrative officers to evaluate the desirability of different future alternatives for UNC.

You will be presented with limited information of alternative university postures and asked to choose, other things being equal, which in your opinion would provide the highest-quality academic environment. Since we wish to obtain your judgments based solely on issues of quality, *financial considerations should not enter into your decisions.** That is, in judging among the alternatives

*Financial considerations are being dealt with in another part of our study; they will be combined with the results of this survey later.

presented to you we would like you to concentrate on the quality of education and other academic and research issues, *not* on the limitations imposed by any budgetary constraints. (For example, the number of students should be viewed as affecting the university's environment for learning, and tuition as possibly influencing the student body mix, but resultant changes in revenue should be ignored.) We are also abstracting from the details of specific programs. You are free to imagine where in the university students or faculty might be added or subtracted. Finally, any specific problems of actually implementing the change (e.g., departmental politics) should not be taken into account. General problems like the effect of reducing the faculty upon the ability to attract new blood in key disciplines should of course be considered.

Obviously, a great number of factors affect the academic environment of a university and most of these cannot be quantified. Thus, it is not possible to provide you with complete descriptions of university postures from which to judge. Rather, we shall be dealing here with only a few critical (and quantifiable) planning variables. A set of eight "primary planning variables" was selected in consultation with administrative officers at UNC as capturing the most significant information that is relevant for budget planning at the top levels of the administration. These are described in exhibit A12.1, which includes their current values at UNC for your reference information.

Two of the variables on this list deserve special comment, for it might seem that tuition and leverage are more related to university finances than to academic quality. Regarding tuition, you should assume that, no matter what the base tuition level is, UNC will remain committed to the principle of meeting each student's "demonstrated need" with financial aid. Thus, the chief effect to be considered is the more subtle impact tuition may have on the quality of the academic environment, for instance on the socioeconomic mix of students choosing to come to UNC. Regarding faculty leverage, this variable has implications for both the freedom of faculty to do scholarly research on topics of their own choosing and the exposure of the university to the risk of future funding uncertainties. While you should weigh these effects in your analyses, you should not be concerned with the effect of leverage on finances in the short run. Also assume that it would be possible, in the short run at least, to increase leverage to the levels contemplated in the questionnaire through a combination of appeals to government agencies, foundations, corporations, and private sources of term support.

One final caveat before proceeding to the questionnaire itself: be sure not to let the current physical constraints (e.g., dormitory, classroom, and office facilities) of the UNC campus weigh in your decisions. For example, suppose you are asked to consider an increase in the size of the undergraduate population from 6,400 to 7,000. If you know that undergraduate dormitory space is very scarce at the present time you might be tempted to rule out the proposed increase on the grounds that UNC has already reached the limits of its capacity for undergraduates. However, our perspective here is much more that of the long run in which, were it to be deemed educationally sound, presumably we could find ways of adding to the capacity, such as through the construction of additional dormitory space. The crucial issue is whether you think the proposed increase in undergraduates would impact the quality of the education offered by UNC to both its undergraduates and graduate students. You should also think about whether increasing undergraduate admissions will alter the composition of the student body in the foreseeable future.

As a general rule, you should ignore a problem or effect if applications of money and effort would solve it in a reasonable time. Consider only the more fundamental aspects of changes in the primary planning variables on the quality of the educational process and other basic UNC objectives.

Bibliography

Adams, Rodney H. 1977. Endowment funds are a distinct case. *Journal of Portfolio Management* 3, no. 2 (winter), pp. 37–45.

Allen, R. D. G. 1963. *Mathematical Economics*. 2d ed. London: Macmillan.

Alpert, Paul. 1968. A critical appraisal of the application of systems analysis to educational planning models. *Institute of Electrical and Electronics Engineers Transactions on Education* E-11: 94–98.

Ashby, Eric. 1978. *Reconciling Man with the Environment*. Stanford, Calif.: Stanford University Press.

Bacchetti, Raymond F. 1977. Using cost analysis in internal management in higher education. *NACUBO Professional File* 1, no. 9 (January).

Balachandran, K. R., and Donald Gerwin. 1973. Variable-work models for predicting course enrollments. *Operations Research* 21: 823–34.

Balderston, Frederick E. 1974. *Managing Today's University*. San Francisco: Jossey-Bass.

Balderston, Frederick E., and Roy Radner. 1971. *Academic Demand for New Ph.D.s 1970–90: Its Sensitivity to Alternative Policies*. Ford Foundation Project on University Administration. University of California, Berkeley: Office of the Vice-President for Planning and Analysis.

Baumol, William J. 1961. *Economic Theory and Operation Analysis*. Englewood Cliffs, NJ: Prentice-Hall.

Baumol, William J., and Tibor Fabian. 1964. Decomposition, pricing for decentralization, and external economies. *Management Science* 11: 1–32.

Bellman, Richard E., and Stuart E. Dreyfus. 1962. *Applied Dynamic Programming*. Princeton, NJ: Princeton University Press.

Bierman, Harold, and Thomas R. Hofstedt. 1973. University accounting (alternative measures of Ivy League deficits). Unpublished paper, Graduate School of Business and Public Administration, Cornell University, Ithaca, NY.

Bishop, Yvonne M. M., Stephen E. Fienberg, and Paul W. Holland. 1975. *Discrete Multivariate Analysis: Theory and Practice*. Cambridge, Mass.: MIT Press.

Bloomfield, Stefan. 1977. Comprehensive faculty flow analysis. In *Applying Analytic Methods to Planning and Management*, ed. David S. P. Hopkins and Roger G. Schroeder, pp. 1–18. San Francisco: Jossey-Bass.

Blume, Marshall E. 1973. An analysis of spending rules for the University's endowment. Unpublished paper, Wharton School of Finance and Commerce, University of Pennsylvania, Philadelphia, Pa.

Boskin, Michael J. 1976. Estate taxation and charitable bequests. *Journal of Public Economics* 5: 27–56.

Bowen, Howard R. 1977. Systems theory, excellence, and values: will they mix? *NACUBO Professional File* 9, no. 2 (February).

Bowen, William G. 1968. *The Economics of the Major Private Universities*. Berkeley, Calif.: Carnegie Commission on Higher Education.

Brown, Eric, and Paul F. Maeder. 1973. A fiscal fitness exercise. In *Strategies for Budgeting*, ed. George Kaludis, pp. 51–62. Issue no. 2 (summer) of *New Directions for Higher Education*, ed. J. B. Lon Hefferlin, a quarterly sourcebook. San Francisco: Jossey-Bass.

Carnegie Commission on Higher Education. 1971. *Less Time, More Options*. New York: McGraw-Hill.

———. 1972. *The More Effective Use of Resources*. New York: McGraw-Hill.

Cartter, Allan M. 1970. After effects of blind eye to telescope. *Educational Record* 51: 333–38.

Cheit, Earl F. 1971. *The New Depression in Higher Education*. New York: McGraw-Hill.

———. 1973. *The New Depression in Higher Education—Two Years Later*. New York: McGraw-Hill.

Churchill, Neil C., and John K. Shank. 1976. Affirmative action and guilt-edged goals. *Harvard Business Review* 54: 111–16.

Coelho, Philip R. P. 1976. Rules, authorities, and the design of not-for-profit firms. *Journal of Economic Issues* 10: 416–28.

Conway, Delores A., and Joseph S. Verducci. The influence of financial aid factors on freshmen enrollment decisions at Stanford University. Unpublished manuscript, Department of Statistics, Stanford University, Stanford, Calif.

Cootner, Paul H. 1974. Economic organization and inefficiency in the modern university. In *Efficiency in Universities: The La Paz Papers*, ed. Keith G. Lumsden, pp. 217–40. Amsterdam: Elsevier Scientific.

Cyert, Richard M. 1973. *Private and Public Higher Education*. Annual Report of the President, Carnegie-Mellon University, Pittsburgh, Pa.

Cyert, Richard M., and Charles L. Hedrick. 1972. Theory of the firm: past, present, and future: an interpretation. *Journal of Economic Literature* 10: 398–412.

Dalkey, N. C. 1969. *The Delphi Method: An Experimental Study of Group Opinion*. RAND Report No. RM-5888-PR. Santa Monica, Calif.: The RAND Corporation.

Dalkey, N. C., B. Brown, and S. Cochran. 1969. *The Delphi Method III: Use of Self Ratings to Improve Group Estimates*. RAND Report No. RM-6115-PR. Santa Monica, Calif.: The RAND Corporation.

Dalkey, N. C., and O. Helmen. 1963. An experimental application of the Delphi method to the use of experts. *Management Science* 9: 458–67.

Dickmeyer, Nathan C. 1977. *The Use of an Unstructured Preference-Search Model in University Decision Making*. Academic Planning Office Report 77–6. Stanford, Calif.: Academic Planning Office.

———. 1979. Computer-aided university budget policy making. Ph.D dissertation, School of Education, Stanford University.

Dickmeyer, Nathan C., David S. P. Hopkins, and William F. Massy. 1978. TRADES— a model for interactive financial planning. *National Association of College and University Business Officers* 11, no. 9 (March).

Doermann, Humphrey. 1968. *Crosscurrents in College Admissions.* New York: Teachers College Press, Columbia University.

Dresch, Stephen P. 1972*a. Intergenerational Equity and the Optimal Endowment Policy.* New York: National Bureau of Economic Research.

———. 1972*b.* Toward a normative theory of endowment policy. Unpublished paper, Institute for Social and Policy Studies, Yale University, New Haven, Conn.

Dyer, James S. 1973. A time-shared computer program for the solution of the multiple criteria problem. *Management Science* 19: 1379–83.

Ennis, Richard M., and J. Peter Williamson. 1976. *Spending Policy for Educational Endowments.* Money Market Reports: a research and public project of The Common Fund.

Feldstein, Martin S., and Charles Clotfelter. 1974. *Tax Incentives and Charitable Contributions in the US: A Micro-Econometric Analysis.* Discussion Paper 381, Harvard Institute of Economic Research. Cambridge, Mass.: the Institute.

Fishburn, Peter C. 1976. Methods of estimating additive utilities. *Management Science* 13: 435–53.

Flood, Merrill M. 1978. Let's redesign democracy. *Behavioral Science* 23: 429–40.

Flood, Merrill M., and A. Leon. 1964. *A Generalized Direct Search Code for Optimization.* Reprint 128, Mental Health Research Institute, University of Michigan. Ann Arbor, Mich.: the Institute.

———. 1966. A Universal Adaptive Code for Optimization (GROPE). In *Recent Advances in Optimization Techniques,* ed. A. Larr and T. Vogl, pp. 101–30. New York: Wiley.

Forrester, Jay W. 1961. *Industrial Dynamics.* Cambridge, Mass.: The MIT Press.

Furniss, W. Todd. 1971. Is there a perfect faculty mix? *Educational Record* 52: 244–50.

Furniss, W. Todd. 1973. Steady-state staffing in tenure-granting institutions. Unpublished paper bound with related papers, American Council on Education, Washington, DC.

Gani, Joseph. 1963. Formulae for projecting enrollments and degrees awarded in universities. *Journal of the Royal Statistical Society* Series A (General), 126: 400–409.

Geoffrion, Arthur M., James S. Dyer, and Abraham Feinberg. 1972. An interactive approach for multi-criterion optimization. *Management Science* 19: 357–70.

Goldberger, Arthur S. 1964. *Econometric Theory.* New York: Wiley.

Gray, Paul. 1976. College and university planning models. Paper read at the Conference on Academic Planning for the Eighties and Nineties, sponsored by University of Southern California Office of Institutional Studies, and held on 22–23 January 1976 at the University of Southern California, University Park, Los Angeles.

Greenberger, Martin, Matthew A. Crenson, and Brian L. Crissey. 1976. *Models in the Policy Process.* New York: Russell Sage Foundation.

Grinold, Richard C., David S. P. Hopkins, and William F. Massy. 1978. A model for long-range university budget planning under uncertainty. *Bell Journal of Economics* 9: 396–420.

Grinold, Richard C., and Kneale T. Marshall. 1977. *Manpower Planning Models.* New York: American Elsevier.

Gulko, Warren W. 1971. *The Resource Requirements Prediction Model 1 (RRPM-1): An Overview.* Technical Report No. 17, National Center for Higher Education Management Systems, Western Interstate Commission on Higher Education. Boulder, Colo.: the Center.

Gulko, Warren W., and Khateeb M. Hussain. 1971. *A Resource Requirements Prediction Model (RRPM-1).* Technical Report 19, National Center for Higher Education Management Systems, Western Interstate Commission on Higher Education. Boulder, Colo.: the Center.

Hadley, George. 1964. *Nonlinear and Dynamic Programming*. Reading, Mass.: Addison-Wesley.

Haggerty, Patrick E. 1973. Research and development, educational productivity and the American economy. *Educational Researcher* 2, no. 9 (September), pp. 4–10.

Halstead, D. Kent. 1975. *Higher Education Prices and Price Indexes*. Publication No. (OE) 75–17005, US Department of Health, Education, and Welfare. Washington, DC: US Government Printing Office.

———. 1977. *Higher Education Prices and Price Indices—1977 Supplement*. Washington, DC: US Government Printing Office.

Harrison, M. Diane. 1976. *A Report on Freshman Admissions, Financial Aid, and Enrollment, 1976–77*. Stanford, Calif.: Academic Planning Office, Stanford University.

Hartman, William T., and David P. Bell. 1978. The predictive value of the Stanford University admissions rating system. *College and University* 53: 280–90.

Hoenack, Stephen A., P. Meagher, William Weiler, and Ronald Zillgitt. 1974. University planning, decentralization, and resource allocation. *Socio-Economic Planning Sciences* 8: 257–72.

Hopkins, David S. P. 1971. On the use of large-scale simulation models for university planning. *Review of Educational Research* 41: 467–78.

———. 1973. An analysis of university year-round operation. *Socio-Economic Planning Sciences* 7: 177–87.

———. 1974a. Analysis of faculty appointment, promotion, and retirement policies. *Higher Education* 3: 397–418.

———. 1974b. Making early retirement feasible. *Change* 6, no. 5 (June), pp. 46–47, 64.

———. 1974c. Faculty early retirement programs. *Operations Research* 22: 455–67.

———. 1979. Computer models employed in university administration: the Stanford experience. *Interfaces* 9, no. 2 (February), pp. 13–23.

Hopkins, David S. P., and A. Bienenstock. 1975. Numerical models for faculty planning. In Allan M. Cartter, ed., *Assuring Academic Progress Without Growth*, pp. 23–47. San Francisco: Jossey-Bass.

Hopkins, David S. P., Jean-Claude Larréché, and William F. Massy. 1977. Constrained optimization of a university administrator's preference function. *Management Science* 24: 365–77.

Hopkins, David S. P., and William F. Massy. 1977. A model for planning the transition to equilibrium of a university budget. *Management Science* 23: 1161–68.

Hopkins, David S. P., and William F. Massy. 1977. Long-range budget planning in private colleges and universities. In *Applying Analytic Methods to Planning and Management*, ed. David S. P. Hopkins and Roger G. Schroeder, pp. 43–66. No. 17 in New Directions for Institutional Research Series. San Francisco: Jossey-Bass.

Ibbotson, Roger G., and Rex A. Sinquefield. 1976. Stocks, bonds, bills, and inflation: year-by-year historical returns (1926–1974). *Journal of Business* 49: 11–47.

Janis, Irving L. 1972. *Victims of Groupthink*. Boston: Houghton Mifflin.

Jellema, William W. 1973. *From Red to Black?* San Francisco: Jossey-Bass.

Jenny, Hans, with the assistance of Mary Ann Acton. 1974. *Early Retirement: A New Issue in Higher Education*. Essay prepared for Teachers Insurance and Annuity Association, New York, NY. New York: the Association.

Judy, Richard W. 1969. Systems analysis for efficient resource allocation in higher education. In *Management Information Systems: Their Development and Use in the Administration of Higher Education*, ed. John Mintner and Ben Lawrence, pp. 41–58. Boulder, Colo.: Western Interstate Commission on Higher Education.

Keeney, Ralph L., and Howard Raiffa. 1976. *Decisions with Multiple Objectives: Preferences and Value Tradeoffs.* New York: Wiley.

Kemeny, John G. 1972. What every college president should know about mathematics. Paper read at 53rd Summer Meeting of the Mathematical Association of America, 28–30 August 1972, held at Dartmouth College, Hanover, NH.

Koch, James V. 1973. A linear programming model of resource allocation in a university. *Decision Sciences* 4: 494–504.

Kusumoto, Sho-Ichiro. 1976. Extensions to the Le Chatelier–Samuelson principle and their application to analytical economics—constraints and their analysis. *Econometrica* 44: 509–36.

Larréché, Jean-Claude, David S. P. Hopkins, and William F. Massy. 1975. Multi-attribute functions for university top management. In *Seminaire de recherche en marketing, Abbaye de Senanque, 20–23 mai 1975*, pp. 171–94. Université de Droit, d'Economie, et des Sciences d'Aix-Marseille, France: Institut d'Administration des Entreprises.

———. 1977. *Multi-Attribute Preference Functions of University Administrators.* Academic Planning Office Report 77–2. Stanford, Calif.: Academic Planning Office, Stanford University.

LaSalle, J. 1972. Appointment, promotion, and tenure under steady-state staffing. *Notices of the American Mathematical Society* 19: 69–73.

Lasdon, Leon S., A. Warren Jain, and M. Rattner. 1976. *Design and Testing of a Generalized Reduced Gradient Code for Nonlinear Programming.* Technical Report SOL 76–3, Department of Operations Research, Stanford University.

Little, John D. C. 1961. A proof for the queueing formula: $L = \lambda W$. *Operations Research* 9: 383–87.

———. 1970. Models and managers: the concept of a decision calculus. *Management Science* 16: 466–85.

Litvack, J., Burton G. Malkiel, and Richard E. Quandt. 1973. A plan for the definition of endowment income. Unpublished paper, Department of Economics, Princeton University, Princeton, NJ.

Malkiel, Burton G., and Paul B. Firstenberg. 1976. *Managing Risk in an Uncertain Era: An Analysis for Endowed Institutions.* Princeton, NJ: Princeton University Press.

Marshall, Kneale T. 1973. A comparison of two personnel prediction models. *Operations Research* 21: 810–22.

Marshall, Kneale T., and Robert M. Oliver. 1970. A constant-work model for student attendance and enrollment. *Operations Research* 18: 193–206.

———. 1979. Estimating errors in student enrollment forecasting. *Research in Higher Education*, in press.

Marshall, Kneale T., Robert M. Oliver, and Sidney S. Suslow. 1970. Undergraduate enrollments and attendance patterns. In *Statistical Models for Education and Training*, ed. David Bartholomew. Proceedings of the NATO Sunningdale Conference, Sunningdale, England.

Massy, William F. 1973. *The Economics of Endowed Universities.* Academic Planning Office Report 73–3. Stanford, Calif.: Academic Planning Office, Stanford University.

———. 1974. Planning for Stanford's long-range financial stability: a time for hard choices. In *Stanford University Annual Financial Report*, pp. 5–19. Stanford, Calif.

———. 1975. Resource management and financial equilibrium. *NACUBO Professional File* 7, no. 7 (October).

———. 1976. A dynamic equilibrium model for university budget planning. *Management Science* 23: 248–56.

————. 1978. Reflections on the application of a decision science model to higher education. *Decision Sciences* 9: 362–69.

Massy, William F., Richard C. Grinold, David S. P. Hopkins, and Alejandro Gerson. 1977. *Optimal Smoothing Rules for University Budget Planning*. Academic Planning Office Report 77–3. Stanford, Calif.: Academic Planning Office, Stanford University.

Massy, William F., and David S. P. Hopkins. 1975a. A decision calculus model for university budget planning. Unpublished paper, Academic Planning Office, Stanford University, Stanford, Calif.

————. 1975b. *Constrained Maximization of a University Preference Function*. Academic Planning Office Report 75–1. Stanford, Calif.: Academic Planning Office, Stanford University.

Massy, William F., David S. P. Hopkins, and J. Curry. 1976. *Indirect Cost Recovery: A Model and a Protocol*. Academic Planning Office Report 76–2. Stanford, Calif.: Academic Planning Office, Stanford University.

McDonald, John G. 1974. Faculty tenure as a put option: an economic interpretation. *Social Science Quarterly* 55: 362–71.

————. 1974. The wealth effect on gifts to universities. Unpublished paper, Graduate School of Business, Stanford University, Stanford, Calif.

Meckling, William H., and Michael C. Jensen. 1970. University endowments and spending policies. Unpublished paper, Graduate School of Management, University of Rochester, Rochester, NY.

Miller, Leonard. 1974. College admissions and financial aid policies as revealed by institutional practices. Unpublished paper, School of Social Welfare, University of California, Berkeley, Calif.

Miller, William F. 1978. How Stanford plans. *Association of Governing Boards of Universities and Colleges Reports* 20, no. 5 (September/October), pp. 26–31.

National Association of College and University Business Officers. 1974. *College and University Business Administration*. 3d ed. Washington DC: the Association.

Newhouse, Joseph P. 1970. Toward a theory of nonprofit institutions: an economic model of a hospital. *American Economic Review* 60: 64–74.

Newton, R., J. Griffiths, and C. Mottley. 1970. *Models for University Systems Planning*. University Park, Pa.: Office of the Vice-President for Planning, Pennsylvania State University.

Oliver, Robert M. 1968. *Models for Predicting Gross Enrollments at the University of California*. Ford Foundation Project on University Administration. University of California, Berkeley: Office of the Vice-President for Planning and Analysis.

————. 1969. *An Equilibrium Model of Faculty Appointments, Promotions, and Quota Restrictions*. Ford Foundation Project Research Report 69–10. Berkeley, Calif.: President's Office, University of California.

————. 1972. Operations research in university planning. In *Analysis of Public Systems*, ed. A. Drake, Ralph L. Keeney, and P. M. Morse, pp. 468–96. Cambridge, Mass.: The MIT Press.

Oliver, Robert M., and David S. P. Hopkins. 1976. Instructional costs of university outputs. In *Education as an Industry*, ed. Joseph N. Froomkin, Dean T. Jamison, and Roy Radner pp. 371–404. National Bureau of Economic Research University Conference Series 28. Cambridge, Mass.: Ballinger.

Oliver, Robert M., David S. P. Hopkins, and Robert Armacost. 1972. An equilibrium flow model of a university campus. *Operations Research* 20: 249–64.

Patton, Carl. 1974. Effectiveness of incentive-based early faculty retirement plans. Unpublished paper, Graduate School of Public Policy, University of California, Berkeley, Calif.

Pauly, Mark V., and Michael Redisch. 1973. The not-for-profit hospital as a physicians' cooperative. *American Economic Review* 63: 87–89.

Pindyck, Robert S., and Daniel L. Rubenfeld. 1976. *Econometric Models and Economic Forecasts.* New York: McGraw-Hill.

Praether, J., and G. Smith. 1974. Salary prediction technique—a tool for affirmative action. In *Public Policy: Issues and Analysis,* ed. R. Cope, pp. 72–76. University, Tallahassee, Fla.: Association for Institutional Research, Florida State University.

Raiffa, Howard. 1968. *Decision Analysis: Introductory Lectures on Choices Under Uncertainty.* Reading, Mass.: Addison-Wesley.

Robinson, D., H. Ray, and F. Turk. 1977. Cost behavior analysis for planning in higher education. *NACUBO Professional File* 9, no. 5 (May).

Rogers, Frederick A., and Richard L. Van Horn. 1976. *Goal Oriented Resource Allocation for University Management.* Carnegie-Mellon University Administration Paper. Pittsburgh, Pa.: Office of the Vice-President for Management, Carnegie-Mellon University.

Rosenberg, Eric. 1978. *Decision Calculus Model: Program Documentation.* Stanford, Calif.: Academic Planning Office, Stanford University.

Saaty, Thomas L. 1977. A scaling method for priorities in hierarchical structures. *Journal of Mathematical Psychology* 15: 234–81.

Samuelson, Paul A. 1974. *Foundations of Economic Analysis.* New York: Atheneum.

Schinnar, Arie P. 1978. Sufficient conditions for maintaining a balanced university budget. *Management Science* 14: 1538–41.

Schipper, Katherine. 1977. Financial distress in private colleges. *Journal of Accounting Research* 15, supplement, pp. 46–51.

Schroeder, Roger G. 1972. *Resource Planning in University Management by Goal Programming.* University of Minnesota Working Paper 6. Rochester, Minn.: College of Business Administration, University of Minnesota.

———. 1973. A survey of management science in university operations. *Management Science* 19: 895–906.

Sharpe, William F. 1974. The Stanford Investment Simulator. Unpublished paper, Graduate School of Business, Stanford University, Stanford, Calif.

———. 1978. *Investments.* Englewood Cliffs, NJ: Prentice-Hall.

Shimada, T. 1972. Industrial dynamics model of a Japanese university. *Bulletin of Faculty of Commerce, Meiji University.* 55, no. 1 (May), pp. 89–149.

Shirley, Robert, and Wendell Lorang. 1979. Financial planning at SUNY–Albany: a case study. In *Financial Planning Models: Concepts and Case Studies in Colleges and Universities,* ed. Joe B. Wyatt et al., pp. 173–94. Princeton, NJ: EDUCOM.

Shocker, Allan D., and Venkatarma Srinivasan. 1974. A consumer-based methodology for the identification of new product ideas. *Management Science* 20: 921–37.

Sinuany, F. 1978. A network optimization model for multi-year budget allocation in a multi-campus institution using multiple goals. Unpublished paper, Department of Operations Research, Case Western Reserve University, Cleveland, Ohio.

Smith, R. Longworth. 1971. Accommodating student demand for courses by varying the classroom-size mix. *Operations Research* 19: 862–74.

Spies, Richard R. 1978. *The Effect of Rising Costs on College Choice.* New York: College Entrance Examination Board.

Srinivasan, Venkatarama, and Allan D. Shocker. 1973. Linear programming techniques for multidimensional analysis of preference. *Psychometrika* 38: 337–69.

Srinivasan, Venkatarama, Allan D. Shocker, and Alan G. Weinstein. 1973. Measurement of a composite criterion of managerial success. *Organizational Behavior and Human Performance* 9: 147–67.

Stanford University. 1974. *Long-Range Financial Forecast, 1975/76 to 1979/80.* Stanford, Calif.

Strauss, Jon C. 1976. *The Pennsylvania Responsibility Center Management System: Organization and Performance.* University of Pennsylvania Budget Office Report FY77-1. Philadelphia, Pa.: Budget Office, University of Pennsylvania.

Suslow, Sidney S. 1977. Benefits of a cohort survival projection model. In *Applying Analytic Methods to Planning and Management*, ed. David S. P. Hopkins and Roger G. Schroeder, pp. 1–18. San Francisco: Jossey-Bass.

Systems Research Group. 1969. CAMPUS: Comprehensive Analytical Methods for Planning in University Systems. Unpublished paper, Toronto, Canada.

Taylor, A., and H. Coolidge. 1974. Survey and analysis of early retirement policies. *Educational Record* 55: 183–87.

Theil, Henri, and Guido Rey. 1966. A quadratic programming approach to the estimation of transition probabilities. *Management Science* 12: 714–21.

Tintner, Gerhard, and Jati K. Sengupta. 1972. *Stochastic Economics.* New York: Academic Press.

Tou, Julius T. 1964. *Modern Control Theory.* New York: McGraw-Hill.

Updegrove, Daniel A. 1978. *EDUCOM Financial Planning Model—EDUCOM Financial Planning Model User's Manual.* Princeton, NJ: EDUCOM.

US Office of Management and Budget. 1979. Principles for determining costs applicable to grants, contracts and other agreements with educational institutions. Circular A-21. *Federal Register*, March 6, 1979.

Vroom, Victor H., and Kenneth R. MacCrimmon. 1968. Toward a stochastic model of managerial careers. *Administrative Science Quarterly* 13: 26–46.

Wallenius, Jyrki. 1975. Comparative evaluation of some interactive approaches to multi-criterion optimization. *Management Science* 21: 1387–96.

Wehrung, Donald A. 1975. Mathematical programming procedures for the interactive identification and optimization of preferences in a multi-attributed decision problem. Ph.D dissertation, Graduate School of Business, Stanford University.

Wehrung, Donald A., David S. P. Hopkins, and William F. Massy. 1978. Interactive preference optimization for university administrators. *Management Science* 24: 599–611.

Weisbrod, Burton A. 1976. Some collective-good-aspects of nongovernment activities: not-for-profit organizations. Yale University Institution for Social and Policy Studies Working Paper No. 777. New Haven, Conn.: the Institution.

———. 1977. The private nonprofit sector: what is it? Yale University Institution for Social and Policy Studies Working Paper No. 784. New Haven, Conn.: the Institution.

Whitcomb, David K. 1972. *Externalities and Welfare.* New York: Columbia University Press.

Williamson, J. Peter. 1974. Endowment funds: income, growth, and total return. *Journal of Portfolio Management* 1, no. 1 (fall), pp. 74–79.

Williamson, Oliver E. 1970. *Corporate Control and Business Behavior.* Englewood Cliffs, NJ: Prentice-Hall.

Wyatt, Joe B., James C. Emery, and Carolyn P. Landis, eds. 1979. *Financial Planning*

Models: Concepts and Case Studies in Colleges and Universities. Princeton, NJ: EDUCOM.

Young, A., and G. Almond. 1961. Predicting distributions of staff. *Computer Journal* 3:4 (January), pp. 246–50.

Zeleny, Milan, ed. 1976. *Multiple Criteria Decision-making: Kyoto 1975.* New York: Springer-Verlag.

Zeleny, Milan, and James L. Cochrane, eds. 1973. *Multiple Criteria Decision-making.* Columbia, SC: University of South Carolina Press.

Zeleny, Milan, and Martin K. Starr., eds. 1977. *Multiple Criteria Decision-making.* New York: North-Holland.

Zemach, Rita. 1968. A state-space model for resource allocation in higher education. *Institute of Electrical and Electronics Engineers Transactions of Systems Science and Cybernetics* 4, no. 2 (July), pp. 108–18.

Zionts, Stanley, and Jyrki Wallenius. 1976. Interactive programming for the multiple criteria problem. *Management Science* 22: 652–63.

Glossary-Index

Academic Planning Office (APO), 30, 31, 65
Academic rating, 365, 366, 368
Activity class, 53, 209, 211. *A set of activities (e.g., classroom teaching) in which regular faculty members are engaged.*
Activity variable, *see* Variables—activity
Adams, Rodney, 472
Adaptive control, 277–78
Ad Hoc Budget Committee of the Board of Trustees, 50, 51
Administration: accountability of, 11, 12; control by, 12–17, 20, 276; budget for, 27, 29, 32, 135; support work of, 210; subunits of, 445–46
Administrators, *see* Decision makers
Admissions, 27, 198, 199
Advisory Panel on Retirement Alternatives, 470
Affirmative action, 32, 332; models for planning, 371–81, 439
Aggregate demand, *see* Industry demand
Aggregate income/expense items, 280, 291–93, 436
Aggregate laws of motion, 284–85
Aggregate variables, 448
Aid quality. *The proportion of student aid given in the form of a scholarship. See also* Financial aid; Need-based financial aid policy; Scholarship aid; Self-help
Allocation, 21, 86, 103, 149, 279, 490
—coefficients, 165, 211–12
—tree, 214. *A graphic device for portraying the allocation and apportionment of faculty to instruction and research.*
American Council on Education (ACE), 5
American Institute for Decision Science (AIDS), 6
Annual planning, *see* Budget
Appointments, *see* Faculty—appointments
A Programming Language (APL), 48. *A computer language used in modeling that allows for compact algebraic representations of mathematical expressions.*
Augsburger, Robert R., 31
Automated projection and tradeoffs model, 437. *See also* TRADES
Availability fraction, 372, 378, 380, 381. *In modeling for affirmative action, the proportion of eligible persons available for a vacancy at the time it occurs who are from designated minority groups.*

Bacchetti, Raymond F., 30–31, 32
Bachelor's degree program, 217–19, 220–23
Baseline gap, 33, 34, 179. *An actual or potential deficit, as shown in a long-range financial forecast (q.v.).*
Behavioral stocks, 76. *Current stocks of university assets that are behavioral in nature, e.g., the quality of the human resource base.*
Berkeley, University of California at, 224, 356, 357, 358, 360–61, 362, 383
Bienenstock, Arthur I., 470
Bierman, Harold, Jr., 38
Bonds, long-term, 268, 493–94
Boundary probe, 399, 401, 402, 421–22
Bowen, Howard, 10–11, 13
Bowen, William G., 14, 43
Bowker, Rosedith Sitgreaves, 469
Budget, 25–26, 28, 32, 34, 53, 184, 253–54. *See also* Conditional budget; Long-range financial forecast; Medium-range financial forecast
—adjustments, 42, 47, 49; timing of, 48, 50, 53, 56; effect of risk on, 261–64, 272–74; smoothing rules for, 293–94, 303; disadvantages of, 298, 300; as variable, 311
—balanced, 40, 48, 384–85. *See also* Equilibrium